D0760881

OH WHAT A FEELING

A VITAL HISTORY OF
CANADIAN MUSIC
THE NEXT GENERATION

OH WHAT A FEELING

A VITAL HISTORY OF
CANADIAN MUSIC
The Next Generation

FOX
MUSIC
BOOKS

Foreword by Chris Taylor

Martin Melhuish

PUBLISHER'S TRIBUTE

The first edition of *Oh What a Feeling* was the genius
of Lee Silversides, then the President of the Canadian
Academy of Recording Arts and Sciences (CARAS), and
Martin Melhuish, who decided that the best way to celebrate
the 25th anniversary of the JUNO Awards in 1996 was in
words and song. The book *Oh What a Feeling* was launched
at the anniversary dinner and subsequently was spread far
and wide to libraries and secondary schools with the support
of the CARAS board of directors education committee
led by Sylvia Tyson. At the same time a box set of CDs
celebrating Canadian recording artists was compiled by Larry
LeBlanc. Like the book, the CD set enjoyed considerable
success. We thank our predecessors for laying the track taken
in the New Generation edition of *Oh What A Feeling* and we
hold in special regard the amazing effort Martin Melhuish
made to see this edition come alive, rockin' roll, and jive.

Oh What a Feeling, indeed.

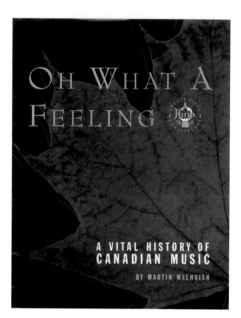

ISBN 978-1-894997-31-7

Edited by Bob Hilderley.
Designed by Susan Hannah.
Author photograph (jacket) by Susan Hannah.

Published by Fox Music Books, an imprint of Quarry Press Inc,
PO Box 1061, Kingston, Ontario Canada K7L 4Y5
www.quarrypress.com

OH WHAT A FEELING
Contents

CHRONICLE

BOOK OF LISTS

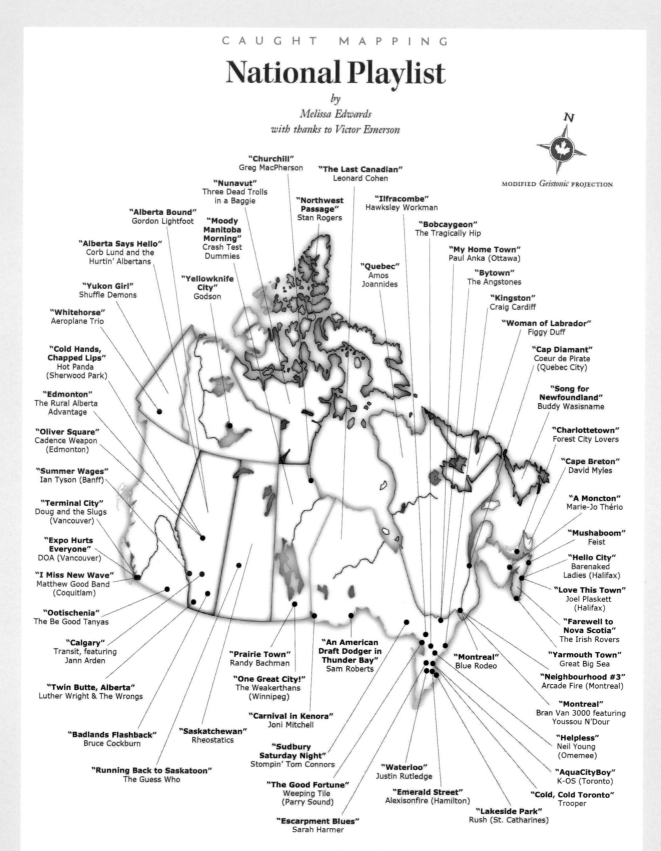

CAUGHT MAPPING

National Playlist

by

Melissa Edwards
with thanks to Victor Emerson

N

MODIFIED *Geistonic* PROJECTION

"Churchill"
Greg MacPherson

"The Last Canadian"
Leonard Cohen

"Nunavut"
Three Dead Trolls
in a Baggie

"Ilfracombe"
Hawksley Workman

"Northwest Passage"
Stan Rogers

"Bobcaygeon"
The Tragically Hip

"Alberta Bound"
Gordon Lightfoot

"Moody Manitoba Morning"
Crash Test Dummies

"My Home Town"
Paul Anka (Ottawa)

"Alberta Says Hello"
Corb Lund and the
Hurtin' Albertans

"Quebec"
Amos
Joannides

"Bytown"
The Angstones

"Yellowknife City"
Godson

"Kingston"
Craig Cardiff

"Yukon Girl"
Shuffle Demons

"Woman of Labrador"
Figgy Duff

"Whitehorse"
Aeroplane Trio

"Cap Diamant"
Coeur de Pirate
(Quebec City)

"Cold Hands, Chapped Lips"
Hot Panda
(Sherwood Park)

"Song for Newfoundland"
Buddy Wasisname

"Edmonton"
The Rural Alberta
Advantage

"Charlottetown"
Forest City Lovers

"Oliver Square"
Cadence Weapon
(Edmonton)

"Cape Breton"
David Myles

"Summer Wages"
Ian Tyson (Banff)

"A Moncton"
Marie-Jo Thério

"Terminal City"
Doug and the Slugs
(Vancouver)

"Mushaboom"
Feist

"Expo Hurts Everyone"
DOA (Vancouver)

"Hello City"
Barenaked
Ladies (Halifax)

"I Miss New Wave"
Matthew Good Band
(Coquitlam)

"Love This Town"
Joel Plaskett
(Halifax)

"Ootischenia"
The Be Good Tanyas

"Farewell to Nova Scotia"
The Irish Rovers

"Calgary"
Transit, featuring
Jann Arden

"An American Draft Dodger in Thunder Bay"
Sam Roberts

"Montreal"
Blue Rodeo

"Yarmouth Town"
Great Big Sea

"Prairie Town"
Randy Bachman

"Neighbourhood #3"
Arcade Fire (Montreal)

"Twin Butte, Alberta"
Luther Wright & The Wrongs

"One Great City!"
The Weakerthans
(Winnipeg)

"Montreal"
Bran Van 3000 featuring
Youssou N'Dour

"Carnival in Kenora"
Joni Mitchell

"Helpless"
Neil Young
(Omemee)

"Badlands Flashback"
Bruce Cockburn

"Saskatchewan"
Rheostatics

"Sudbury Saturday Night"
Stompin' Tom Connors

"Waterloo"
Justin Rutledge

"AquaCityBoy"
K-OS (Toronto)

"Running Back to Saskatoon"
The Guess Who

"The Good Fortune"
Weeping Tile
(Parry Sound)

"Emerald Street"
Alexisonfire (Hamilton)

"Cold, Cold Toronto"
Trooper

"Escarpment Blues"
Sarah Harmer

"Lakeside Park"
Rush (St. Catharines)

For more Geist maps and to purchase the *Geist Atlas of Canada*, visit geist.com.

OH WHAT A FEELING

*I got to see this country from the front seat
of a Ford Econoline that took us from Lee's Palace to
The Spectrum and on to the Commodore Ballroom. ...*

— Chris Taylor

»Foreword

»Foreword

From 1990 to 1996, I lived in a van with nine other guys trying to "make it" in the music business. Our live show brought the circus to town, one nightclub at a time — over 1000 shows with not a single cancellation — from Nanaimo, BC on the west coast to the northern reaches of Grande Prairie, AB to the east coast hospitality of Halifax, NS.

Like other touring groups of our era, despite being signed to the Canadian affiliate of a major record company (Virgin/EMI), we failed to make serious in-roads into the international marketplace. All around us, better Canadian acts were suffering the same fate: rocking our way across Highway 1, but finding our careers shipwrecked above the 49th parallel.

That experience played out in similar fashion by many Canadian artists over the years, inspired a great respect for those who went before and for those who struggle now to make an impact. But as you will see with the Canadian artists that populate the timeline and the appended lists of hit songs and Hall of Fame achievements in *Oh What A Feeling*, Canada is second to none in producing world-class songwriters, singers, musicians and producers, many of whom have changed the face of contemporary music, despite the country's relatively small population base.

When the band folded, I started a career as an entertainment lawyer and experienced the music business from both sides of the curtain as a performer and a manager. I started travelling regularly around the world in 1997 with artist demo recordings in my bag. Record company representatives would ask me if I had anything like Rush or Celine Dion to play them, as that was the extent of their apparent appreciation of Canadian music up to that point. It was also a dig; one of those comments to keep a Canadian in his place — a not so subtle reminder, that only a select few would/could be allowed into the vital international marketplace. I'd pull CDs out of my bag and play early recordings of Nelly Furtado, Metric, Three Days Grace, Sum 41 and Billy Talent for them to try and turn them on to the great music I heard coming out of Canada.

The barriers for Canadian music have always been significant. The Brits think they do it best and weren't overly interested in what non-British acts were trying to do. The Americans think they do it best and you might argue they do, based on historical evidence. Canadians: propped up by CanCon quotas and government funding agencies have their music forced upon them — no?

That myth is dispelled in *Oh What A Feeling* as Martin Melhuish traces Canada's place in the history of the music, recording and broadcasting industries from a time prior to the turn of the 20th century, when the first devices of recording and playback were being invented, through to today's easy availability of music in a digital universe. The significant role that Canada's artists and music executives have played in the music world over the years will no doubt come as a surprise and a revelation to many, at home and abroad.

As you will see, notwithstanding the biases, Canadian music, given the chance, succeeded. Nelly flew like a bird, Sum 41 sold over six million albums in the U.S. and Billy Talent became arena rock gods to millions of fans around the globe. We started a record label, Last Gang, for Metric, and blossomed alongside other indie kindred spirits, Dine Alone, Paper Bag, and Arts & Crafts. A golden era started to take shape......Us Against the World.

It feels like Canada always had Anne Murray, Gordon Lightfoot and Triumph to thump our chests about, but the door truly started to open when the Internet and the Napster platform allowed music to flow like water between borders and into the speakers of music lovers around the world. Music now had a direct line to music fans free of record label gatekeepers. Powerful online music blogs launched Canadian indie artists like Arcade Fire, Death From Above 1979, Broken Social Scene and Crystal Castles into the stratosphere and onto festival stages around the world.

Foreword

At the same time, Canada's more mainstream talent took center stage as four Canadian artists — Michael Bublé, Justin Bieber, Drake and Nickelback — had four of the top five best-selling albums in the U.S. all in the same week in November of 2009. Today, those artists are all considered titans of their respective genres. As Gary Trust of *Billboard* magazine's chart department commented at the time, "It shows the variety of music coming out of Canada — the balladeer, the teen pop star, a rapper from Canada? Who would have expected that, and a straight-ahead rock band. There's great music coming out of Canada and it's resonating in the U.S. and worldwide."

International music industry gatekeepers no longer make jokes about Canadians as our accomplishments over the past decade, most of them documented in *Oh What A Feeling*, have illustrated what we have always known to be true: Canadian music has always had something to say and when the world gets a chance to listen, it likes what it hears.

A lot.

— *Chris Taylor*

>> *Chris Taylor is the founder of the entertainment law firm, Taylor Klein Oballa LLP, representing Grammy Award-winning talent, such as Drake and Nelly Furtado. He is also the founder of Last Gang Entertainment, a company credited with launching the careers of Metric, Crystal Castles and Death From Above 1979. He first burst onto the music scene as lead vocalist in the JUNO-nominated reggae band, One.*

▲ Chris Taylor and Drake

OH WHAT A FEELING

Bop bada baa, Bop bada baa,
Bop bada baa, Bop bada baa,
Oh what a feelin', what a rush!
Oh what a feelin', what a rush!

— Lyrics & Music by Crowbar.

»Introduction

≫Introduction

Here's a tune and title with a tale to tell from the salad days of the Canadian music scene.

In January 1971, the song "Oh What A Feeling" hit the airwaves in Canada, a raucous and rollicking celebration of life with a fanfare chorus that not only heralded the arrival of the Canadian group Crowbar on the scene but also the dawning of a new day for Canadian music.

The song became a Top 10 hit in Canada for the rabble-rousing group, who had graduated from the Ronnie Hawkins school of hard rock knocks, the same fraternity of higher learning fellow Canadians The Band had attended. "Oh What A Feeling" was the first single released under the so-called "CanCon" legislation that the government of Pierre Elliott Trudeau had enacted following the groundwork laid by CRTC Chairman Pierre Juneau, whose name, in tribute, was subsequently attached to the JUNO Awards, Canada's equivalent to the Grammys.

When the time came to celebrate the 25th anniversary of the JUNOs, *Oh What A Feeling* was the title given to a special four album celebration of our greatest hits and to a companion book, with the subtitle "A Vital History of Canadian Music," released at the awards ceremonies at Copps Coliseum in Hamilton, Ontario, Crowbar's hometown. Things had come full circle

The celebrations that year marked the coming-of-age of the Canadian music industry and gave recognition to the international achievements of superstars like Celine Dion, Shania Twain, and Alanis Morissette. Things would never be the same. Few people at the time could have predicted how far those silver anniversary celebrations would extend into the future with the subsequent success of a new generation of Canadian artists like Avril Lavigne, Diana Krall, Nickelback, Michael Bublé, Drake and Justin Bieber. Oh what a feeling!

≫THE STORY BEHIND THE SONG

The story of the song "Oh What A Feeling" takes us back to the year 1969 and an around-the-world excursion undertaken by Toronto-based rockabilly legend Ronnie Hawkins and music journalist Ritchie Yorke as ambassadors for John Lennon and Yoko Ono's War Is Over peace initiative. A stop-over on that trip was London, England where Yorke introduced Hawkins to a young EMI record executive by the name of Frank Davies. At the time, they talked about the quality of musical artists in Canada, and the Hawk urged Davies to look into the possibility of crossing the Atlantic to set up a record label in Toronto. Davies decided to take their advice.

"I remember that Ronnie was really upset at the time that he had lost his previous group, who had become The Band and were working with Bob Dylan," recalls Davies, the founder of Love Productions and its associated label, Daffodil Records. "His new group, And Many Others, had just completed a tour with him doing dates at major venues, like the Fillmore East in New York (March 27–28, 1970), as part of the Joe Cocker Mad Dogs & Englishmen tour. When I later arrived in Canada on what was an exploratory trip, Ronnie asked me to take the group, known as Crowbar by that time, into the studio and lay down a couple of tracks. I got my papers and returned to Canada. Shortly after that, we just took what we had started at Terry Brown's studio, Toronto Sound, and kept going to create a whole album. We finished it in December of 1970."

▲ Ritchie Yorke and Ronnie Hawkins at the Chinese /Korean border, 1969

The album was called *Bad Manors*, an appropriate name, given the manor where they lived communally, a 120-year-old farm house in Ancaster, Ontario, near Hamilton.

The band had evolved from Kelly Jay and the Jamies, who became And Many Others before taking on the name Crowbar. The players included vocalist/keyboardist Kelly Jay (Blake Fordham), guitarist John "The Ghetto" Gibbard, bass player Roly Greenway, guitarist Rheal Lanthier, drummer Larry Atamniuk and keyboardist Rick Bell (Rick Belanger). After the group left Ronnie Hawkins in

May 1970, they cut the album *Official Music* with harp player/vocalist King Biscuit Boy (Richard Newell). During this period, Rick Bell left the group to become a member of Janis Joplin's Full Tilt Boogie Band, and Larry Atamniuk joined the American group, Seatrain.

"It was pretty crazy for Frank to be dropped in with these guys," Ritchie Yorke recalls. "The whole ethos around the band was somewhat removed from Chelsea in England. It was a huge culture shock for him, but he managed to keep control. Ronnie had dropped out of the picture when the group crossed the border with dope in their pockets and he figured he couldn't afford to be associated with a band that would do something like that. The official reason he gave for them parting company was that 'They could fuck up a crowbar in 15 seconds,' which is how they got their name. In the studio, we just got in there and caught the energy. They had left Ronnie and they were looking to make an impression themselves and they had this song... a pretty special song."

That song was "Oh What A Feeling," recorded during those *Bad Manors* album sessions.

Frank Davies adds: "Kelly Jay always tells the story that we didn't have enough money for horns so we had to do the horns ourselves vocally. I don't actually remember that, but it's certainly true there was not a lot of money around for this. We did the whole album for $6000. But let's not forget that at Toronto Sound, Terry Brown's partner was Doug Riley, so there was lots of access to great horn players from his band Dr. Music. What I do remember is the band getting around some mics and 'singing' the horn parts. It sounded okay, but not very big, so we created multiple tracks of them singing 'bah bah-bah-bah.' In the end, it sounded huge and became a real hook. The only other minor regret I have is that Kelly's little speaking part, which was so good, was a bit clearer on the finished record. At the time Kelly wanted it to sound like he was on a telephone or speaking in the background and with the listener happening to hear what he is saying: 'One is for the boogie and the life we love to live...' and so on. Kelly made such a big deal, as he still does whenever they play, of that speaking part. Those things stand out in my mind, but it was 42 years ago.

"The recording sessions were a combination of a party and a zoo. I remember the great reaction we received for the album. And then I managed to make a deal for the rest of the world with Paramount Records. It was their first big signing because they had just launched as a record label. When I delivered the record to Capitol in Canada, we decided to release the first single, 'Oh What A Feeling,' on the very first day of Canadian Content... January 18, 1971."

The group made its U.S. debut as Crowbar at the Whisky A Go Go in Los Angeles in the summer of 1971. On September 23, 1971, they returned to Toronto's Massey Hall, where on November 22 of the previous year, they had appeared on the same bill with Van Morrison, for a homecoming concert. It was recorded for the subsequent album,

Larger Than Life, the first "live-in-concert" record by a Canadian rock group. Broadcast live by Toronto radio station CHUM-FM, the concert featured more than 50 musicians — members of Canadian bands Lighthouse, Dr. Music, Everyday People and several others — who appeared with Crowbar on stage. Also on the bill were Christmas and King Biscuit Boy. The two-record set uniquely featured a list of every person who had attended the show.

Ritchie Yorke notes, "When I hear the phrase 'Oh what a feeling' now on a Toyota commercial that's everywhere these days, I lament the fact that the song never caught on in America because radio considered it a pro-drug song... 'oh what a feeling, oh what a rush!' The implication being that the 'feeling' was from smoking a joint, snorting a line of coke, or whatever, but that was as far from their minds at the time as could be. It had nothing to do with drugs at all. 'Oh what a feeling, what a rush!' — life, meeting a girl or boy, anything that makes you feel good. It was a naturally exuberant thing... like when spring comes to Canada. Pity it didn't become an international hit... and all because of ill-informed drug censorship."

≫THE TRUDEAU JUNEAU ERA

"Oh What A Feeling" was the first single released after the introduction of the Canadian Content regulations for AM radio. Government legislation committed Canadian AM radio stations to devote at least 30 percent of their playlists to Canadian artists and their music. The notion at the time was that if something were not done to stem the domination of foreign repertoire on Canadian radio airwaves, the domestic record industry would shrivel up and die from lack of exposure of homegrown music and artists.

"The problem was that Canada had plenty of great artists but they weren't given a chance in their own country," says Ritchie Yorke, who now resides in Brisbane, Australia but lived in Canada through the late-'60s and '70s when he made an inestimable contribution to the development of what he coined as the Maple Music Industry. "Because of Canada's cultural domination by America and the fact that Canadians grew up totally awash in American self-aggrandisement on TV, on radio, in magazines and in movies, Canadians were somewhat intimidated. I call this the quandary of closeness. Down here in Australia, artists have talked about the tyranny of distance being the big problem of trying to succeed in North America. Canadian radio program directors, just like all other Canadians, had this inferiority complex about their own stuff. It was almost self-loathing... 'Oh, this is Canadian, it can't be very good.' They just refused to accept that 'Canadian' can be good. Canadians were never going to get heard in their own country until there was some enforced legislation. That comes from my belief, and that of others like Walt Grealis and Stan Klees [of *RPM Weekly* magazine], that people who are granted the privilege and monopolistic position of having a radio station license should have the obligation to put something back. How better to put something back than to support local talent?"

It's no surprise then that for the Canadian recording industry, Pierre Juneau, the chairman of the CRTC, known today as the Canadian Radio-television and Telecommunications Commission, the government agency instrumental in the introduction of the so-called CanCon regulations, should be held in high esteem and that his name should be adopted to identify the awards presented annually for musical excellence in Canada. At those first JUNO Awards in 1971, Pierre Juneau was honoured as Music Industry Man of the Year. In 1989, with the benefit of retrospect and tangible evidence of a booming Canadian recording industry, Juneau was presented with the first Lifetime Achievement Award at the annual awards show by Peter Steinmetz, then the president of the Canadian Academy of Recording Arts & Sciences (CARAS), the industry organization which oversees the yearly gala.

▲ Prime Minister Trudeau rocking his Crowbar pendant

"When countries are young and their structure is still unformed, one person can, and often does, have an astounding influence over matters of public policy," Steinmetz told the gathering in Toronto. "In Canada, we always believe that one of the most important of those public pursuits is our culture: the music, words and images we give each other. There is, without a doubt, no Canadian who has had as pervasive an influence on how we see ourselves than Pierre Juneau. As the first chairman of the CRTC, Juneau was on hand for a media revolution. Over the previous decade, Canada had been forced to move quickly into the new information age. Canada had opened up, and Juneau was faced with the task of preserving a Canadian identity in a world whose borders were disappearing. He left his mark on policy almost immediately. Canadian radio and television stations are 80 percent owned by Canadians because Juneau's CRTC made it that way. And when the CRTC decided in 1970 that 30 percent of recorded music on radio must be Canadian, a Canadian recording industry was born almost overnight. The fact that tonight's awards are named after him is recognition of that one bold controversial decision."

In most areas of the world, government and the arts have an arms-length relationship at best. Over the years, but particularly during the Trudeau era in Canada, relations could be characterized as downright chummy. John Lennon and Yoko Ono dropped by for a chat on world peace. Then Crowbar popped up again, this time on the national political stage. Prime Minister Trudeau, and his wife Margaret, showed up at a Crowbar gig in Perth, Ontario. The Prime Minister, dressed in buckskin, and wearing a crowbar medallion, clutched a copy of Pop Magazine, one of the publications that Ritchie Yorke and I had co-founded back then. This was head-turning stuff for not only the music community in Canada but also around the world.

In 1972, the Canadian recording industry had the chance to get an outside perspective on things as an ambitious project called The Maple Music Junket was organized with Ritchie Yorke, once again, as one of the motivating forces and organizers. The idea was to expose the European market to the Canadian music scene by demonstrating its inherent differences from that of the U.S. The press junket saw many of Europe's most influential music journalists flown into Canada for three days of concerts in Toronto and Montréal by some of Canada's top English- and French-speaking artists courtesy of the Canadian government and music industry. Robin Denselow of the *Manchester Guardian*, for one, was incredulous at what he found. "I could hardly believe it; a government actually promoting rock music — it sounded incredible. I was impressed too that Prime Minister Trudeau should go out of his way to send us all a welcoming message."

In 1979, Prime Minister Trudeau was on hand at the JUNOs in Toronto to induct Nova Scotia-born country music legend Hank Snow into the Canadian Music Hall of Fame. As part of his *ex tempore* remarks at the time, he noted: "We're living in an industrial age, an industrial society and, thanks to technology, music can reach out and touch many people in our country and all countries across the world... The cultural activities are the ones in which Canadians engage themselves the most of any other activity. The cultural industries are bigger than steel in Canada. They are bigger than pulp and paper — some six billion dollars a year. It's a big industry, and we have to remember that, we the audiences, we the outsiders, we the government, we the onlooker.

"But if an artist creates and performs for himself or herself, he is also up against industrial competition in Hollywood, in New York, in Europe and other parts of the world and that's why it's not possible for any country to be without a cultural policy any more than it is to be without an industrial policy. I like to think that the people of Canada: those who listen and hear you and often adore you, those who buy your records, watch your programs, go to your shows, I like to think that they're aware of that and that the people they elect are aware of that too.

"As we gather together on this festive occasion, I can assure you that we are very often reminded of that. We realize that the performers are more than the contributors to an industry which is big business. We realize that they also express first, their own soul, their own feelings, their own interior strength, but they also sing the song of Canada. They sing from the heart of Canada. They sing of the feelings of Canada and for this reason they deserve our support."

❯❯INTERCONNECTIONS

The core of this book is a chronology of the artists, the music and the events that have defined Canadian popular music since Father Brébeuf composed the "Huron Carol" at the Jesuit mission in Midland, Ontario in the mid-17th century and Alexander Muir published the sheet music for "The Maple Leaf Forever" in October 1867, a few months after Confederation. By the turn of that first Canadian century, Henry Burr had recorded, thanks to Thomas Edison, the first of several score of chart topping songs as the original "King of Pop."

There is nothing like a chronology to put things into perspective. Chronologies reveal otherwise hidden relationships and connections, some of which happened by design, most through serendipity. To borrow the title of a song written by my friend Rosie Emery, "We Are All Interconnected." For years, I have adopted the routine of creating timelines when writing music biographies for publication or broadcast. They bring an invaluable clarity to the story-telling process.

In sorting names and dates for this chronology, it seemed like almost every town in the nation had a place in the history of Canadian music, whether it be Port Hope, Ontario, home of Joseph Scriven, who wrote the best-selling hymn, "What A Friend We Have in Jesus," or the small town of Tillsonburg, Ontario, deep in tobacco-growing country. Not far from Tillsonburg, in Vienna, Ontario, the family of phonograph inventor Thomas Edison settled before fleeing the country after taking a stand against the Family Compact with William Lyon MacKenzie in the Rebellion of 1837. More than a hundred years later, Stompin' Tom Connors worked as a migrant "primer" in the local tobacco harvest and found there the inspiration for his song, "Tillsonburg." In that same era, Tillsonburg-born trumpeter Johnny Cowell hit the top of the charts in the United Kingdom with his song "Walk Hand in Hand," while down the road at Green's Corners, Rick Danko of The Band grew up before heading to Toronto as a teenager to hook up with Ronnie Hawkins in the bars on the Yonge Street strip. There is no end to the interlaced stories of Canadian musicians who migrated to this rock 'n' roll Mecca in the 1950s and 1960s.

≫BOOK OF LISTS

Oh What A Feeling is more than a chronology of Canadian popular music. Increasing the cultural value of the book is a year-by-year chart of Canadian songs that hit the upper echelons of the charts on both sides of the 49th Parallel from 1900 to 2013.

Celebrating the artists behind these songs is a set of profiles of the 47 members of the Canadian Music Hall of Fame.

In addition, there is a complete alphabetical list of the artists who have been honoured with the more than 2700 JUNO Awards presented since 1971 when Crowbar, that roisterous band of brothers, spellbound by the boogie woogie, were first heard to sing ….

Oh what a feeling
What a rush ….

Martin Melhuish

OH WHAT A FEELING

'Twas in the moon of winter-time
When all the birds had fled,
That mighty Gitchi Manitou
Sent angel choirs instead...

— The Huron Carol
Lyrics by Jean de Brébeuf.

»Pre-1900

CHRISTMAS NOËL   JESOUS AHATONHIA

CANADA   10

>> **1642** "The Huron Carol," with lyrics by Patron Saint of Canada, Jean de Brébeuf, set to the melody of a 16th-century French carol, "Une jeune pucelle," is considered the first Christmas carol written in Canada. Brébeuf established the Sainte-Marie among the Hurons mission near Midland, Ontario, but was martyred on March 16, 1649.

>> **1769** French-Canadian fur trader Jacques-Timothe Boucher de Montbrun (anglicized as Demonbreau) becomes the first citizen of Nashville when he blazes a trail through the Tennessee wilderness to settle at the site of Music City. Today, Demonbreun Street runs by his homestead, behind the Bridgestone Arena, and on into the heart of Music Row. Fellow Canadians Hank Snow, Anne Murray, and Shania Twain, among others, would follow this trail to fame.

>> **April 22, 1778** Captain James Cook arrives at Nootka Sound to refit his ships the *Discovery* and the *Resolution* and describes in his journal the musical talents of the native Pacific Northwest inhabitants: "On advancing towards the ships, they all stood up in their canoes and began to sing. ... After entertaining us with this specimen of their music, which we listened to with admiration ... they came alongside the ships and bartered what they had to dispose of." They would not be the last aboriginal musicians in Canada to impress European critics.

>> **September 12, 1828** The parents of inventor Thomas Alva Edison — Samuel Ogden Edison Jr. of Marshalltown, Nova Scotia, and Nancy Matthews Elliott of Chenango County, New York — are married in Vienna, Ontario, just south of Tillsonburg. Ten years later they would flee Canada following the failed Rebellion of 1837 in Upper Canada, in which Thomas' father had participated. Four of the seven Edison children were born in Vienna, the other three, including Thomas, were born in Milan, Ohio. More than a century later, Stompin' Tom Connors would write his anthem to migrant tobacco-farm workers, "Tillsonburg."

>> **1842** Québecois college student/poet Antoine Gérin-Lajoie writes the song "Un Canadien errant (A Wandering Canadian)" in tribute to the French Canadian patriots who had been deported as political prisoners to Australia and Tasmania. In 1884, the song was adopted and adapted by the Acadians, who suffered a similar fate of banishment. In their song "Acadian Driftwood," The Band would commemorate this forced migration from Canada to Maine and Louisiana.

>> **1846** Born to wail: the saxophone is patented by Belgian musician and musical instrument designer, Adolphe Sax.

>> **April 9, 1860** French printer, bookseller and inventor Édouard-Léon Scott de Martinville, records the earliest recognizable reproduction of a human voice on a device he had patented three years earlier on March 25, 1857, called the phonautograph. In 2008, a group of researchers came across his old phonautograph papers and used a computer program to play a barely audible 20-second recording of a man, presumably Scott himself, singing part of the French folk song, "Au clair de la lune."

>> **January 10, 1861** An enamored Colonel Richard Moody, commander of the Corps of Royal Engineers on the Canadian West Coast, names Lulu Island, one of the islands that today make up the city of Richmond, British Columbia, in tribute to 16-year-old Miss Lulu Sweet, a singer and actress who was passing through with the Potter Theater Troupe from San Francisco. She was one of the area's first entertainment stars.

>> **1866** With music by English-born American composer J.A. Butterfield, school teacher George Washington Johnson of Hamilton, Ontario has the poem, "When You and I Were Young Maggie," written for his girlfriend and former pupil Maggie Clark became a major hit song. George and Maggie

would later marry and move to Cleveland, Ohio. The farm in Stoney Creek, Ontario, where Maggie once lived, now has a plaque commemorating the song, thanks to the late radio show host Ray Sonin of Down Memory Lane (CFRB Toronto).

>> **July 1, 1867** The British North America Act proclaims the founding of the Dominion of Canada, and several months later in October, Alexander Muir composes the patriotic song, "The Maple Leaf Forever," which serves as an unofficial Canadian anthem for the rest of the century.

>> **1870** In the events now known as the the Red River Resistance, Métis leader Louis Riel unsuccessfully attempts to establish a provisional government for the territory of Assiniboia (Manitoba). The classic song of the Old West, "Red River Valley," was written during this period.

>> **1875** Irish-born Canadian Joseph M. Scriven, with American-born composer Charles Crozat Converse, write the popular hymn, "What A Friend We Have In Jesus," which is included in the best-selling hymn collection, *Sankey's Gospel Hymns, Number One*. A monument in Scriven's honour was erected in Port Hope, Ontario, following his death in 1896.

▲ Joseph M. Scriven

>> **March 10, 1876** Having written the first patent specifications for the telephone at his family home in Brantford, Ontario, Alexander Graham Bell communicates with his assistant Thomas A. Watson who is in another room. As part of his personal correspondence on this day, Bell wrote: "I then shouted into M [microphone] the following sentence: 'Mr. Watson — Come here — I want to see you!' To my delight, he came and declared that he had heard and understood what I said."

>> **August 10, 1876** The first "intelligible" long distance telephone call is made from Brantford, Ontario to Alexander Graham Bell at Robert White's Boot and Shoe store and Telegraph office in Paris, Ontario, 11 kilometres away.

>> **April 18, 1877** French poet/inventor Charles Cros advises countryman Édouard-Léon Scott de Martinville, whose phonautograph had no playback function, that by photoengraving the scribed trace onto metal, it might be possible to retrace the wave pattern produced to enable reproduction of the sound.

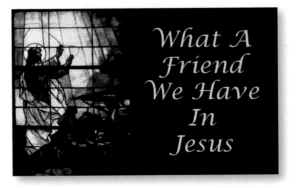

>> **June 4, 1877** Having invented a new and improved microphone, Emile Berliner patents his discovery. The following September, he sells the rights to the Bell Telephone Co. of Boston and is retained by the company as a consultant.

>> **December 24, 1877** Thomas Alva Edison, scion of a Canadian family, files a patent application for his "phonograph," a machine with a tin-foil cylinder with two diaphragm-and-stylus units, one for recording and the other for playback. Sound waves caused the stylus to indent the tin foil wrapped around the cylinder. Edison tested the machine by reciting the nursery rhyme "Mary Had A Little Lamb." As reported in the December 22, 1877 issue of the magazine *Scientific American*: "Mr. Thomas A. Edison recently came into this office, placed a little machine on our desk, turned a crank, and the machine inquired as to our health, asked how we liked the phonograph, informed us that it was very well, and bid us a cordial good night."

>> **January 24, 1878** Thomas Edison establishes the Edison Speaking Phonograph Company to exploit the interest his machine has created. At the time, the reproduction of music is only one of the ten possible future uses for the machine envisioned by Edison.

>> **February 19, 1878** The patent for Thomas Edison's phonograph, covering talking machines and sound writers, is issued.

>> **May 17, 1878** The first recordings in Canada are made on this date by Governor-General, Lord Dufferin and his guests at Rideau Hall in Ottawa. Lady Dufferin wrote in her diary: "This morning we had an exhibition of the phonograph. Two men brought this wonderful invention for us to see. It is quite a small thing, a cylinder which you turn with a handle, and which you place on a common table. We were so amazed when we first heard this bit of iron speak that it was hard to believe there was no trick! But we all tried it. Fred sang 'Old Obadiah,' D. made it talk Greek, the Colonel sang a French song, and all our vocal efforts were repeated. As long as the same piece of tinfoil is kept on the instrument, you can hear all you have said over and over again. The last performance

was for D. to say something which should be repeated by the machine to a public exhibition in Ottawa in the evening."

▲ Thomas Edison, Inventor of the Phonograph

» **1879** The Canadian National Exhibition in Toronto, known as the Toronto Industrial Exhibition until 1912, is held for the first time.

» **1880** The Bell Telephone Company of Canada is incorporated by a special act of Parliament.

» **May 4, 1886** Alexander Graham Bell's cousin Chichester Bell, a chemical engineer, and English scientist and instrument maker Charles Sumner Tainter, are awarded a patent on a wax cylinder player called the graphophone, which differs from Edison's phonograph in that it uses a solid wax cylinder rather than tin foil and has a floating sapphire-point stylus instead of a rigid needle. Bell and Tainter establish the American Graphophone Company in 1887.

» **1881** Emile Berliner takes a leave of absence from his job at Bell and, with his brother Joseph, sets up Telefabrik Berliner in Hanover, Germany to manufacture telephone equipment for the German market.

» **1884** Nipper, the terrier that would be immortalized in the painting "His Master's Voice," one of the most recognizable trademarks of the 20th Century, is born in Bristol, England.

» **1885** Tin Pan Alley, a community of songwriters and publishers, is established in New York City.

» **November 7, 1885** "The Last Spike" is driven to complete the Canadian Pacific transcontinental railway. That same year, the first cross-Canada telegraph line, which runs along the Canadian Pacific Railway line, is completed.

» **June 13, 1886** During the Great Fire of Vancouver, one of the few structures that survives is the Oppenheimer Bros. Wholesale Grocers brick building at Powell and Columbia, which now houses Bryan Adams' Warehouse Studio.

» **July 4, 1886** The first scheduled Canadian Pacific Railway transcontinental passenger train arrives on the West Coast at Port Moody, BC.

» **September 9, 1886** The Berne Convention for the Protection of Literary and Artistic Works, an international agreement on copyright protection, is initially adopted by eight countries and in December 5, 1987, The Berne Convention comes into force.

» **September 26, 1887** Emile Berliner files a patent for his gramophone, which utilizes zinc discs instead of wax-covered cylinders. At the time, he also invented a way of mass producing copies of an original recorded disc, which would have an enormous impact on the nascent music industry.

» **October 8, 1887** Thomas Edison forms the Edison Phonograph Company to market his new and improved phonograph, which operates on battery-powered electricity and uses cylinders coated in wax. The previous tin foil covered cylinders would only allow a single playback and limited duplication of the cylinders. You could only have a handful of tubes running from the master phonograph to the blank cylinders to make copies. An artist with a best-selling hit song would literally have to perform the song hundreds of times to refresh the master cylinder given its playback limitations.

▲ Lyrics by Lady Dufferin, wife of the Governor-General

» **February 1888** Whaley, Royce & Co., the music publishers and manufacturer of musical instruments, who once referred to themselves as "Canada's Greatest Music House," is founded in Toronto by Eri Whaley and George Royce.

» **May 16, 1888** Emile Berliner demonstrates his gramophone at the Franklin Institute of Philadelphia.

» **July 14, 1888** American businessman Jesse H. Lippincott looks to corner the market on "sound machines" as he sets up an association with the Edison Phonograph Company and becomes the sole licensee of the American Graphophone

Pre-1900

Co. He forms the North American Phonograph Company to market the machines, not for music and entertainment, but for office dictation, which, as you can imagine, was not a popular idea with thousands of stenographers.

>> **January 1889** Columbia Phonograph Company, named for the location of its headquarters in Washington, District of Columbia, opens as licensee for the North American Phonograph Company in that area.

>> **1898** Danish inventor Valdemar Poulson develops magnetic wire recording.

>> **1890** New York Phonograph Company opens the first recording studio.

>> **1890** Thomas Edison opens the Edison Phonograph Toy Manufacturing Co., which initially produces a line of talking dolls with tiny wax recording cylinders inside them. The Edison Phonograph Works, in competition with Columbia, also begins manufacturing commercial musical recordings on wax cylinders to service the "Phonograph Parlours," which featured coin-operated phonographs, the precursor to jukeboxes.

>> **February 9, 1891** The Canadian Pacific Railway opens the Vancouver Opera House adjacent to the first Hotel Vancouver.

>> **1892** As the companies begin producing cylinders for home entertainment use as well as for the coin-slot industry, even though the number of cylinders that could be made from the master had increased to 2000, the demand far outweighed production at this point.

>> **1892** "After the Ball," a song from the first major Broadway musical, *A Trip To Chinatown*, which debuted on November 9, 1891, becomes the first million-selling piece of sheet music. It ultimately sells over five million copies.

>> **1893** Emile Berliner establishes the United States Gramophone Company in Washington, DC.

>> **June 14, 1894** Toronto's Massey Hall opens with a performance of Handel's "Messiah."

>> **November 1894** Emile Berliner's United States Gramophone Co. markets the first 7-inch disc records on the Berliner Gramophone label.

>> **November 1894** *Billboard*, the American music-trade magazine, begins publication.

>> **1894** Columbia begins marketing their new spring-motored phonograph that retails for about $40. This marvelous new home entertainment option had now become affordable for most households.

>> **January 15, 1895** The 175-voice Toronto Mendelssohn Choir, formed by Augustus Stephen Vogt at the Jarvis Street Baptist Church in Toronto the previous year, makes its concert debut at Toronto's Massey Hall.

>> **Fall 1895** The Berliner Gramophone Company markets the first commercial flat disc recordings. The company also revolutionizes the recording industry as it introduces an electroplating process by which their wax-coated zinc discs can be mass-produced using a "stamper," which, when pressed into a ball of vulcanite (hard rubber), could produce the final recordings in large numbers.

>> **1895** Nipper, later to be immortalized as the "His Master's Voice" dog, dies and is buried in a small park surrounded by magnolia trees on Clarence Street in Kingston-upon-Thames, England. A branch of Lloyd's Bank later occupied the spot, but, on March 10, 2010, a road close to his resting place is renamed Nipper Alley.

>> **January 1896** Thomas Edison begins selling his Edison Spring Motor Phonograph for home entertainment use through his newly-formed manufacturing company, the National Phonograph Co. In competition with Columbia, he also begins selling cylinders, with a maximum length of two minutes, containing a variety of music selections.

>> **1896** Eldridge R. Johnson of Camden, New Jersey designs and manufactures a "clockwork" spring motor for use in the Berliner gramophones.

>> **1896** Composer, pianist and conductor John Stromberg from Milton, PEI, becomes music director for popular comedy team Weber and Fields (Joe Weber and Lew Fields) at their newly-opened Weber and Fields Music Hall in New York. Stromberg, who wrote the hit song "My Best Girl's A Corker" in 1895,

▲ Compo Company Ltd. Pressing Plant

later formed a music publishing company with Weber and Fields.

≫ **1897** The Vancouver Symphony Orchestra first forms in Vancouver, BC.

≫ **1897** Emile Berliner opens the United Kingdom branch of The Gramophone Co. in London (later EMI) with record executive William Barry Owen in charge.

≫ **1898** In part, due to the increasingly litigious environment in the U.S.A. among competitors Berliner, Edison and Columbia, Emile Berliner divests himself of his American patents in an arrangement with Eldridge Johnson and moves his operations to Montréal. Johnson would later found the Victor Talking Machine Company in the United States.

≫ **1898** Emile Berliner and his brother Joseph establish Deutsche Grammophon in Hanover, Germany, to produce disc records.

≫ **September 18, 1899** Scott Joplin, "The King of Ragtime," has his "Maple Leaf Rag" published, as Ragtime music gains popularity.

≫ **November 18, 1899** Hamilton-born ballad singer Harry Macdonough, second

only to New Brunswick-native Henry Burr as the most prolific recording artist during two decades at the turn of the century, has his first chart hit with the song "'Mid the Green Fields of Virginia."

≫ **February 11, 1899** English artist Francis Burraud registers the painting of his brother's dog (a terrier) as "Dog looking at and listening to a phonograph" (later retouched to make it a disc-playing gramophone). The picture is subsequently purchased by the Berliner-affiliated Gramophone Company (later EMI) in London, England. The trademark first appears in Montréal on the back of the record "Hello My Baby" by Frank Bata. It begins showing up in Gramophone Company advertising in January 1900. The image would subsequently be used by the Victor Talking Machine Co. It is the origin of the name of the HMV record store chain.

≫ **1899** The first jukebox is installed at the Palais Royal Hotel in San Francisco by the Pacific Phonograph Company.

CHART-TOPPING CANADIAN SONGS PRE-1900

1842 **Un Canadian errant (A Wandering Canadian)** VARIOUS ARTISTS

1867 **The Maple Leaf Forever** VARIOUS ARTISTS

1870 **Red River Valley** VARIOUS ARTISTS

1899 **Mid the Green Fields of Virginia** HARRY MACDONOUGH AND S.H. DUDLEY

1899 **Just As the Sun Went Down** HARRY MACDONOUGH AND JOHN BIELING

OH WHAT A FEELING

Walking down the streets of my hometown
I'm back again to end my roaming round
I'm looking for the girl I left behind
The one I love, an old sweetheart of mine...

— Sweetheart of Mine

Lyrics by Frank Tyler Daniels. Music by
Leo Friedman.

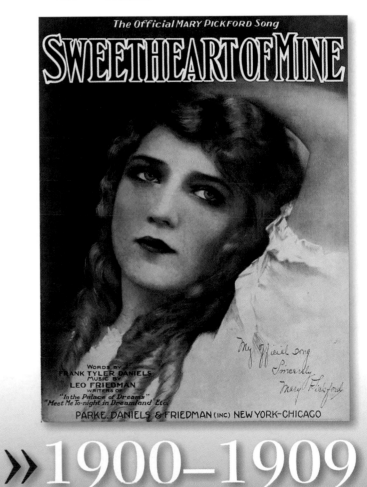

» 1900–1909

»1900–1909

▶ Henry Burr, the
"Original King of Pop"

» 1900

» **1900** Emile Berliner moves his company to Montréal. He had previously received a Canadian patent for the gramophone and rubber discs, but in order to meet the legal requirements, he was required to establish production in Canada. Berliner subsequently sets up manufacturing facilities in the Bell Telephone factory at 367-371 Aqueduct Street (now Lucien L'Allier) and a retail outlet at 2315-2316 Ste-Catherine Street. Reportedly, the company sold 2000 records during its first year of operation and over 2 million in the second year (1901).

» **December 22, 1900** The Berliner Gram-O-Phone Co. (this spelling now popularized) placed an ad in the French-language newspaper, *La Patrie*, in Québec informing readers that the company was producing French records.

» **December 23, 1900** Canadian Reginald A. Fessenden, a former Edison employee, makes what is considered to be

▲ Reginald A. Fessenden,
the Father of Radio

the first audio radio transmission over a distance of about 1.6 kilometers at Cobb Island, Maryland. He said: "Hello! One, two, three, four. Is it snowing where you are Mr. Thiessen? If it is, telegraph back and let me know." Thiessen replied immediately.

» 1901

» **December 12, 1901** Guglielmo Marconi receives the first transatlantic "morse-code" transmission from Poldhu, Cornwall, England at Signal Hill, St. John's, Newfoundland. The Canadian government subsequently gives Marconi, rather than native son Reginald Fessenden, the exclusive rights to build the first transmitting station in Canada at Glace Bay, Nova Scotia.

» **October 1901** In the United States, Eldridge Johnson's Consolidated Talking Machine Co. becomes the Victor Talking Machine Co. with Johnson holding 60% of the company and Emile Berliner, 40%. Victor markets "Improved Gram-o-Phone Records," claiming an improved sound quality. The company's recordings are pressed and distributed in Canada by Berliner.

» **1901** "Chant National," which will later evolve to the Canadian national anthem, "O Canada," is first heard in English-speaking Canada during the royal visit to Toronto by the Duke of York who would become King George V.

» 1902

» **May 20, 1902** Cuba gains independence from the United States.

>> **June 24, 1902** The Québec Symphony Orchestra/Orchestre symphonique de Québec debuts at Laval University on the occasion of the school's golden jubilee celebrations.

>> **July 1902** The Belleville Kilties Band becomes the first Canadian group or ensemble to record.

>> 1903

>> **June 13, 1903** New Brunswick-born tenor Henry Burr (Harry H. McClaskey), who will become the top ballad singer over four decades of the nascent recording industry (1890-1930), makes his first appearance on the charts with the single, "The Rosary."

>> **December 17, 1903** Orville and Wilbur Wright make four brief flights at Kitty Hawk, North Carolina with their first powered aircraft, thereby inventing the first successful airplane.

>> 1904

>> **April 19, 1904** The Great Toronto Fire.

>> **1904** Barbershop quartets are all the rage, defined mainly by male vocal groups like the Empire City Quartet and the American Quartet, which features Canadian tenor Harry Macdonough on a couple of their records, and the Peerless Quartet, which for most of its 20-year career features Canadian tenor Henry Burr. Burr will also enjoy a spectacularly successful solo career, as lead vocalist. In late 1904, "You're the Flower of My Heart Sweet Adeline," a staple in the barbershop quartet repertoire, becomes the first of seven #1 songs from among close to 100 Top 10 singles by the group.

>> **1904** Berliner installs a recording studio at 138A Peel Street in Montréal. The manufacturing plant moves to 201 Fortification Lane, while the shop and offices remain on Ste-Catherine St.

>> **1904** Columbia Phonograph establishes a Toronto branch.

>> 1905

>> **1905** *Variety*, the influential show business weekly, begins publication.

>> 1906

>> **April 7, 1906** On April 7, Naples, Italy is devastated by eruption of Mount Vesuvius, followed by the April 18 San Francisco Earthquake, one of the worst natural disasters in American history, killing more than 3000 people.

>> **December 24, 1906** Knowlton, Québec-native Reginald Aubrey Fessenden makes the first radio broadcast of entertainment and music as he transmits a short program to ships at sea from Brant Rock, Massachusetts using an alternator-transmitter. Fessenden, who would become known as "The Father of Radio," described the historic program: "... first a short speech by me saying what we were going to do, then some phonograph music... Then came a violin solo by me... which I sang one verse of, in addition to playing the violin, though the singing, of course, was not very good. Then came the Bible text, Glory to God in the highest and on earth peace to men of good will, and we finally wound up by wishing them a Merry Christmas and then saying that we proposed to broadcast again on New Year's Eve."

>> **1906** The Toronto Symphony first forms as the Toronto Conservatory Symphony Orchestra. It becomes the Toronto

▲ Harry Macdonough, Recording artist and music business executive

Symphony Orchestra in 1908, though there is a five-year hiatus prior to 1922 when the orchestra returned as The New Symphony Orchestra. It would later change its name back to The Toronto Symphony.

» **1906** Ragtime and jazz pianist, composer William Eckstein returns to Montréal following his time in the U.S., during which he worked the Vaudeville circuit and even played for President Theodore Roosevelt at the White House.

» **1906** The Victor Talking Machine Co. of New Jersey markets the first Victrola, a gramophone with a speaker in the cabinet. The machine's popularity helps standardize disc speed at 78 rpm. When Berliner significantly expanded its Montréal factory with a four-storey annex during this period, they put a large billboard on top of it with a picture of Nipper and the proclamation, "Home of the Victrola."

» 1907

» **1907** Italian tenor Enrico Caruso singing Ruggero Leoncavallo's "Vesti la giubba" on the Victor label becomes the first record to sell a million copies.

» 1908

» **October 1908** Columbia begins marketing two-sided discs.

» **December 3, 1908** The Regina Symphony Orchestra, founded by Frank Laubach, gives its inaugural concert.

» **1908** Judge Robert Stanley Weir writes English lyrics to "Chant National," which becomes the English version of the anthem when its name is changed to "O Canada."

» 1909

» **1909** Canadian-born Mary Pickford becomes a star of silent films and co-founder of United Artists with D.W. Griffith, Charlie Chaplin and Douglas Fairbanks. Known as "America's Sweetheart," her official song is "Sweetheart of Mine."

CHART-TOPPING CANADIAN SONGS 1900-1909

1901 Tell Me, Pretty Maiden HARRY MACDONOUGH & GRACE SPENCER
1901 The Tale of the Bumble Bee HARRY MACDONOUGH
1901 Absence Makes the Heart Grow Fonder HARRY MACDONOUGH
1902 The Mansion of Aching Hearts HARRY MACDONOUGH
1903 Come Down, Ma Ev'ning Star HENRY BURR
1903 In the Sweet Bye and Bye HARRY MACDONOUGH & JOHN BIELING
1903 Hiawatha HARRY MACDONOUGH

1905 In the Shade of the Old Apple Tree IRVING GILLETTE (AKA HENRY BURR)
1906 Love Me and the World Is Mine HENRY BURR
1907 Because You're You HARRY MACDONOUGH & ELISE STEVENSON
1909 To the End of the World With You HENRY BURR
1909 I Wonder Who's Kissing Her Now HENRY BURR
1909 Shine On, Harvest Moon HARRY MACDONOUGH WITH "MISS WALTON"

OH WHAT A FEELING

K-K-K-Katy, beautiful Katy,
You're the only g-g-g-girl that I adore;
When the m-m-m-moon shines, over the cowshed,
I'll be waiting at the k-k-k-kitchen door.
— K-K-K-Katy

Lyrics & Music by Geoffrey OHara.

»1910–1919

»1910–1919

▶ The lyrics for *O Canada* were translated from "Chant National."

O CANADA

O Canada!
Our home and native land!
True patriot love
in all thy sons command.
With glowing hearts
we see thee rise,
The True North
strong and free!
From far and wide,
O Canada,
We stand on guard
for thee.
God keep our land
glorious and free!
O Canada,
we stand on guard for thee.
O Canada,
we stand on guard for thee.

O Canada!
Terre de nos aïeux,
Ton front est ceint
de fleurons glorieux!
Car ton bras
sait porter l'épée,
Il sait porter
la croix!
Ton histoire
est une épopée
Des plus
brillants exploits.
Et ta valeur,
de foi trempée,
Protégera nos foyers
et nos droits,
Protégera nos foyers
et nos droits.

» 1910

» August 16, 1910 The Vancouver Exhibition, forerunner of the Pacific National Exhibition, opens.

» October 18, 1910 Brantford, Ontario-born lyricist Alfred Bryan co-writes the song "Come Josephine In My Flying Machine" with American composer Fred Fisher. It becomes the first major hit of many for the prolific writer. His other hits include "Peg O' My Heart" (1910), "When It's Night Time Down in Burgundy" (1914), "I Didn't Raise My Boy To Be A Soldier" (1915), "Sweet Little Buttercup" (1917), "Oui Oui Marie" (1918) and "When Alexander Takes His Ragtime Band To France" (1918).

» 1910 Singer Sophie Tucker introduces "Some of These Days," the song with which she will always be identified. She records the song, written by Canadian songwriter, Shelton Brooks, on an Edison cylinder about a year later.

» 1910 The saxophone gains popularity in contemporary music as the Brown Brothers Saxophone Quintet (later the Six Brown Brothers) form in Lindsay, Ontario and take their show on the road on the North American vaudeville circuit.

» 1911

» 1911 The spectacular popularity of sheet music is confirmed as sales hit two billion. This success is in part driven by two six million-selling songs in 1911 featuring Canadian vocalists: "Let Me Call You Sweetheart" by The Peerless Quartet featuring Henry Burr, which holds down the #1 position on the charts for seven weeks, and "Down by the Old Mill Stream" by Harry MacDonough, which is also a chart-topper for seven weeks.

» 1911 Guitarist Jimi Hendrix' grandparents Ross Hendrix and his wife Nora, a chorus girl in the vaudeville touring troupe, the Great Dixieland Spectacle, decide to move on to Vancouver after finding themselves jobless in Seattle. Subsequently, they become Canadian citizens and have a daughter Patricia and three sons, Leon, Al and Jimmy, Jimi Hendrix' father. Nora will become one of the most prominent citizens in the black community in Vancouver.

» 1912

» April 15, 1912 British passenger liner RMS *Titanic* sinks in the North Atlantic during its maiden voyage. The tragic event alerts the public to the value of wireless radio.

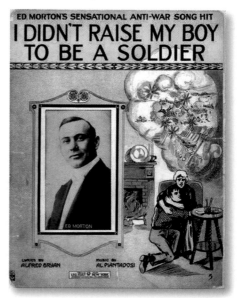

▲ Early Recording Studio

» 1913

» **1913** The song "Peg O' My Heart," co-written by Brantford, ON-born lyricist Alfred Bryan and American composer Fred Fisher, is published. It inspires a movie of the same name, first filmed in 1923 and then remade in 1933 with actress Marion Davies. The Harmonicats record a million-selling version in 1947. In 2000, the American Society of Composers, Authors and Publishers (ASCAP) would pay tribute to the song as one of the most-performed love songs of the 20th Century.

» **1913** The Canadian Vitaphone Co., Canadian manufacturers and distributors of the Vitaphone and importer of records on the Columbia label, is established.

» 1914

» **1914** Toronto-born singer/comedienne Beatrice Lillie makes her stage debut at the Chatham Music Hall in England.

» **1914** Guy Lombardo and brother Carmen first perform at a church lawn party in London, Ontario.

» **1914** The American Society of Composers, Authors & Publishers (ASCAP) is founded.

» 1916

» **1916** Herbert Berliner, through the subsidiary company His Master's Voice, introduces the HMV 216000 series devoted to Canadian recordings. He would subsequently designate the HMV 263000 series exclusively for French-Canadian recordings.

» 1917

» **May 30, 1917** "Darktown Strutters' Ball," a song written by Amherstburg, Ontario-born Shelton Brooks, which would sell more than three million copies in sheet music form, is recorded by, among many others, the Original Dixieland "Jass" Band, whose recording was inducted into the Grammy Hall of Fame in 2006. It is considered to be the first commercial jazz recording.

» **1917** The Starr Co. of Canada (formerly the Canadian Phonograph Supply Co.) is established in London, Ontario as an importer of records from its parent company, The Starr Piano Company, and the Gennett label.

» 1918

» **March 16, 1918** "K-K-K-Katy (The Stammering Song)," written by Geoffrey O'Hara in Kingston, Ontario, is published. It goes on to sell over a million copies in sheet music form. Jack Oakie revived the song in the movie musical *Tin Pan Alley* (1940).

» **1918** Another song of the World War I era, "Mademoiselles From Armentieres," is written by New Glasgow, Nova Scotia-native Lieutenant Gitz Rice.

» **1918** "Till We Meet Again," the wartime hit song written by Windsor, Ontario-born lyricist Raymond Egan and American writing partner, Richard A. Whiting, is published. A few years later, he collaborates with Whiting and Gus Kahn on the song, "Ain't We Got Fun" (1921). In 1926, he

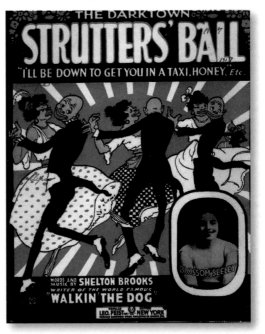

▲ Wilfrid Pelletier, conductor, pianist, composer

co-writes another chart-topper — "Sleepy Time Gal" with Whiting, Joseph R. Alden and Ange Lorenzo.

» **1918** The Compo Company Ltd. is established in Lachine, Québec by Emile Berliner's son, Herbert, to manufacture records for other recording labels.

» **1918** Tennessee-born Zenora "Nora" Hendrix, guitarist Jimi Hendrix' grandmother, co-founds the local chapter of the African Methodist Episcopal Church (AME) in the Fountain Chapel at 823 Jackson Avenue in the ethnically-diverse "Hogan's Alley" area of Strathcona in Vancouver's East End. Pre-'70s, it was the heart of African-Canadian culture in the city.

» 1919

» **September 24, 1919** Marconi station XWA in Montréal receives government authorization to send voice transmissions.

» **1919** "The World Is Waiting For the Sunrise," written by London, Ontario-born, Academy Award-nominated actor/lyricist Eugene Lockhart, who once played for the Toronto Argonaut football team, and concert pianist Ernest J. Seitz (aka Raymond Roberts), a member of the faculty of the Toronto Conservatory of Music, is first heard. Though more than 100 versions of the song have been recorded, a 1949 version by Les Paul and Mary Ford sells over a million copies.

CHART-TOPPING CANADIAN SONGS 1910-1919

1910 **Meet Me Tonight In Dreamland** HENRY BURR

1910 **Where the River Shannon Flows** HARRY MACDONOUGH

1910 **Every Little Movement** HARRY MACDONOUGH & LUCY ISABELLE MARSH

1910 **In the Valley of Yesterday** HARRY MACDONOUGH

1911 **Down By the Old Mill Stream** HARRY MACDONOUGH

1912 **When I Was Twenty-One And You Were Sweet Sixteen** HENRY BURR & ALBERT CAMPBELL

1913 **When I Lost You** HENRY BURR

1913 **Last Night Was the End of the World** HENRY BURR

1913 **The Trail of the Lonesome Pine** HENRY BURR & ALBERT CAMPBELL

1914 **The Song That Stole My Heart Away** HENRY BURR

1914 **I'm On My Way To Mandalay** HENRY BURR & ALBERT CAMPBELL AND WILL OAKLAND

1915 **Close To My Heart** HENRY BURR & ALBERT CAMPBELL

1915 **They Didn't Believe Me** HARRY MACDONOUGH & "ALICE GREEN" AKA OLIVE KLINE

1916 **M-O-T-H-E-R (A Word That Means the World To Me)** HENRY BURR

1916 **Good-Bye, Good Luck, God Bless You (Is All That I Can Say)** HENRY BURR

1916 **There's A Quaker Down In Quaker Town** HENRY BURR & ALBERT CAMPBELL

1916 **The Girl On the Magazine** HARRY MACDONOUGH

1917 **Lookout Mountain** HENRY BURR & ALBERT CAMPBELL

1918 **Just A Baby's Prayer At Twilight (For Her Daddy Over There)** HENRY BURR

1918 **I'm Sorry I Made You Cry** HENRY BURR

1919 **Beautiful Ohio** HENRY BURR

1919 **Oh! What A Pal Was Mary** HENRY BURR

1919 **Till We Meet Again** HENRY BURR & ALBERT CAMPBELL

1919 **I'm Forever Blowing Bubbles** HENRY BURR & ALBERT CAMPBELL

OH WHAT A FEELING

Two by two, they go marching through,
The sweethearts on parade
I can't help crying as they pass me by,
The sweethearts on parade...

— Sweethearts on Parade

Lyrics by Carmen Lombardo. Performed by Guy Lombardo and His Royal Canadians.

▲ Guy Lombardo

»1920–1929

▶ Guy Lombardo and His
Royal Canadians record at
Gennett Records.

>> 1920

>> **May 20, 1920** Marconi's Montréal
radio station XWA (later CFCF
"Canada's First, Canada's Finest," CIQC
and CINW) becomes the first on air in
a non-experimental mode. On this date,
the station broadcasts a performance
by Dorothy Lutton from the Marconi factory in Montréal
to a meeting of the Royal Society of Canada at the Chateau
Laurier hotel in Ottawa.

CFCF

>> **November 11, 1920** Two former Royal Air Force officers,
Lionel Guest, a former aide to a Canadian Governor
General, and Hamilton, Ontario-native Horace Owen
Merriman, who had been experimenting with electrical
recording by microphone, record the ceremony of the
burial of the Unknown Warrior in Westminster Abbey. The
electrical era of recording had dawned.

>> **November 15, 1920** The Edmonton Symphony Orchestra
debuts at the Pantages Theatre in Edmonton, Alberta.

>> 1921

>> **1921** The first Canadian Copyright Act is passed and
establishes performing rights as a constituent part of
copyright. The Act comes into effect in 1924.

>> 1922

>> **1922** The New Symphony Orchestra, forerunner to the
Toronto Symphony Orchestra, is founded by a group of
Toronto musicians and Vienna, Austria-born conductor,
Luigi von Kunits.

1922 Montréal French daily newspaper *La Presse*
launches CKAC, the first French-language radio station in
Canada.

>> 1923

>> **April 23, 1923** The New Symphony Orchestra, four years
later the Toronto Symphony Orchestra, debuts at Toronto's
Massey Hall.

>> **1923** Formed initially as The Lombardo Brother's
Orchestra and Concert Company in London, Ontario,
and featuring brothers, Guy, Carmen, Victor and Lebert
Lombardo, the group goes through a name change to Guy
Lombardo and His Royal Canadians during a two-year
residency at the Claremont Tent nightclub in Cleveland.

>> **1923** Percy Faith, who is working as a silent film
accompanist in Toronto movie houses, gives his first piano
recital at the Toronto Conservatory of Music and makes his
Massey Hall debut at age 15.

>> **1923** Canadian National Railway (CNR) Network begins broadcasting, the unofficial beginning of public radio. Newspapers see radio as a potential threat.

>> 1924

>> **March 10, 1924** Guy Lombardo and His Royal Canadians make their first recording in Richmond, Indiana for the Gennett label.

>> **November 29, 1924** The Montréal Forum opens.

>> **1924** Trumpeter Alfie Noakes travels to England with the New Princes' Toronto Band and ultimately becomes one of Britain's top dance-band musicians.

>> **1924** Beatrice Lillie makes her New York debut in the Andre Charlot Revue of 1924.

>> **1924** Victor purchases the Berliner Gram-o-Phone Co. and forms the Victor Talking Machine Co. of Canada with Edgar Berliner as President.

>> **1924** The Canadian National Railway, at the instigation of President Sir Henry Thornton, installs radio receivers on their transcontinental trains and builds their first transmitting studio in Ottawa with the call letters, CRNO.

>> **1924** The Canadian Copyright Act comes into effect which, in part, specifies that the royalty rate for recorded music is two cents per recorded surface. That initially applied to 78 rpm records, which traditionally had one song each side. Remarkably, this rate saw no change for 64 years until 1988. The 1924 act also adopted Life+50 as the basic term of copyright.

>> 1925

>> **November 28, 1925** The WSM Barn Dance goes on the air in Nashville. It is renamed *The Grand Ole Opry* in 1927.

>> **1925** Compo Company Ltd. issues the first electronically-recorded discs on its Apex label using a process initially developed by Lionel Guest and Horace Owen Merriman.

>> **1925** The Canadian Performing Rights Society (CPRS) is formed to administer royalties of composers, lyricists and music publishers when their works are performed in Canada. It becomes CAPAC in 1945 and evolves into SOCAN in 1990.

>> 1926

>> **January 28, 1926** The Canadian Association of Broadcasters (CAB) is incorporated.

>> **1926** A freak accident significantly alters the direction of Percy Faith's career. His sister's clothing had caught fire and, in dousing the flames with his bare hands, he damages them to the point that he is told by doctors that it will be a long time before he is able to play the piano again. He subsequently turns to composing, arranging and conducting.

>> **1926** 12-year-old Clarence Eugene Snow, later known as "Hank," runs away to sea as a cabin boy on the freighter Grace Boehner out of Lunenburg, Nova Scotia.

>> **1926** Battery-less radio is introduced as Edward (Ted) Samuels Rogers of Toronto invents the 110 volt AC vacuum tube. One year later, he founds Toronto radio station CFRB (Canada's First Rogers Batteryless).

>> 1927

>> **July 1, 1927** The first North American coast-to-coast radio network broadcast in the form of speeches by Prime Minister Mackenzie King and music from the Diamond Jubilee of Canadian Confederation celebrations in Ottawa.

>> **October 6, 1927** *The Jazz Singer*, starring Broadway sensation Al Jolson, is the first feature-length motion picture with synchronized dialog and singing sequences.

>> **November 7, 1927** The Orpheum Theatre in Vancouver opens. It is restored in the early '70s and reopens on April 2, 1977.

>> **1927** The Saskatoon Symphony Orchestra is founded.

>> 1928

>> **1928** While playing in Chicago at the Granada Cafe, the

» 1929

» **February 28, 1929** Having joined the Metropolitan Opera in New York as assistant conductor in 1922, Canadian-born Wilfrid Pelletier becomes conductor, a position he holds until 1950.

» **October 29, 1929** The Wall Street Crash, on what has come to be known as "Black Tuesday," marks the beginning of the Great Depression, which lasts for more than a decade.

» **December 3, 1929** Commodore Cabaret (later Commodore Ballroom) opens on Granville Street in Vancouver.

» **1929** Guy Lombardo and His Royal Canadians begin a 33-year residency at The Roosevelt Grill in New York and later at the Waldorf Astoria. CBS begins broadcasting the band's annual New Year's Eve performances that for millions becomes an indispensable part of the yearly transition from the old year to the new. The orchestra performs at the inaugural balls for every American President from F.D. Roosevelt to Dwight Eisenhower as well as at a number of World Series celebrations at New York's Yankee Stadium.

» **1929** Fiddler Don Messer begins his radio career on CFBO, Saint John, New Brunswick.

» **1929** Victor, including the Victor Talking Machine Company of Canada, is purchased by David Sarnoff's Radio Corporation of America (RCA) and the RCA Victor Co. Ltd. is formed.

» **1929** The Royal Commission on Broadcasting, also known as the Aird Commission, recommends the establishment of a publicly-owned broadcast system in Canada.

musical styling of Guy Lombardo and His Royal Canadians' is characterized as "The sweetest music this side of heaven" by Ashton Stevens of the *Chicago Tribune*. It's a description that remains with the band over the years.

» **1928** At only 15 years old, Newfoundlander Arthur Scammell writes the song that will forever be associated with his home province. Taking the fiddle air "Larry O'Gaff," Scammell gives it fresh life as "Squid Jiggin' Ground."

» **1928** Canada becomes signatory to the Berne Convention (Rome revision), an international copyright agreement. Requirement for registration of copyright was abandoned in favour of a regime that recognizes copyright in a work when it is fixed in some tangible form.

CHART-TOPPING CANADIAN SONGS 1920-1929

1922 **My Buddy** HENRY BURR
1927 **Charmaine** GUY LOMBARDO & HIS ROYAL CANADIANS

1928 **Sweethearts On Parade** GUY LOMBARDO & HIS ROYAL CANADIANS

OH WHAT A FEELING

Deep in my heart is a song

Out on the range I belong

Drifting along with the tumbling tumbleweeds...

— Tumbling Tumberweeds

*Lyrics by Bob Nolan and Recorded
by Sons of the Pioneers.*

>> 1930–1939

≫1930–1939

▲ Roy Rogers (centre) with Sons of the Pioneers

≫ 1930

≫ **1930** Hank Snow returns home to Lunenburg, Nova Scotia, where his mother and stepfather are living. His mother, who had already instilled a love of traditional music in the young Hank, had bought a copy of Jimmie Rodgers' *Moonlight and Skies* album. It was a defining moment in Snow's life as he became a devotee of Rodgers' music and was inspired to follow in "The Blue Yodeler's" footsteps.

≫ 1931

≫ **October 9, 1931** Canada's first television station, VE9EC, a joint venture of radio station CKAC and the newspaper, *La Presse*, goes on the air in Montréal in experimental mode.

≫ **October 18, 1931** Inventor Thomas Alva Edison dies in West Orange, New Jersey.

≫ **November 12, 1931** Toronto's Maple Leaf Gardens opens.

≫ **December 11, 1931** Statute of Westminster grants British dominions, including Canada, complete autonomy.

≫ **1931** Bert Niosi, later known as Canada's "King of Swing," forms a nine-piece band to play at the Embassy Club in Toronto.

≫ **1931** Mart Kenney and His Western Gentlemen form to play at the Alexandra Ballroom in Vancouver.

≫ 1932

≫ **May 26, 1932** Canadian Radio Broadcasting Commission (CRBC) established.

≫ **1932** The Wilf Carter single "My Swiss Moonlight Lullabye," recorded for the Canadian Victor label in Montréal by A. Hugh Joseph, becomes the first Canadian hit recorded domestically.

≫ **1932** Brunswick Records is signed to the Compo Co. for manufacturing and sales in Canada.

≫ **1932** The first trans-Canada telephone system is completed.

≫ 1933

≫ **December 5, 1933** The repeal of prohibition in the United States results in the opening of thousands of clubs and bars. It's a real boost for the slowly recovering music business as jukeboxes, which had become a fixture in most drinking establishments, grow in popularity over the next few years.

≫ **1933** Sons of the Pioneers form in Los Angeles around Roy Rogers, Winnipeg-born Bob Nolan and Tim Spencer.

≫ **1933** Canadian Music and Radio Trades, formerly the *Canadian Music Trades Journal*, publishes its last issue after a 33-year run.

≫ 1934

≫ **July 8, 1934** The Vancouver Symphony gives its first performance at the official opening of the Malkin Bowl in Vancouver.

≫ **1934** In Bridgewater, Nova Scotia, Hank Snow makes his first public appearance at a minstrel show. He is subsequently offered his own radio show on CHNS in Halifax, NS, where he is billed as Clarence Snow and His Guitar.

≫ **1934** Guy Lombardo and His Royal Canadians appear in the first of a number of movies as they are seen in the [George] Burns & [Gracie] Allen

musical comedy, *Many Happy Returns*. Though they appear on screen during Larry Adler's harmonica number, it is actually Duke Ellington who provides the music. Lombardo makes cameo appearances in a number of World War II era films, including *Stage Door Canteen* (1943) and *No Leave, No Love* (1946).

» **1934** Don Messer's band the New Brunswick Lumberjacks, featuring Charlie Chamberlain, begin broadcasting from CHSJ Saint John, New Brunswick.

» 1935

» **January 14, 1935** The Montréal Symphony Orchestra/L'orchestre symphonique de Montréal, then known as the Société des concerts symphoniques de Montréal, play their first concert at Montréal's Plateau Hall. Wilfrid Pelletier becomes the orchestra's first artistic director on April 11, 1935.

» **April 18, 1935** RCA Victor's A. Hugh Joseph invites Hank Snow, by letter, to come in and audition for the label if he is ever in Montréal.

» **May 1935** Canadian operatic tenor Edward Johnson appointed GM of the Metropolitan Opera in New York, a position he holds for 15 years.

» **August 1935** The first magnetic tape recorder, the Magnetophon, is put on display by AEG/Telefunken at the Berlin Funkausstellung in Germany.

» **1935** The Mutual Broadcasting Co. picks up the Percy Faith radio show, *Music by Faith*, for the U.S. market.

» **1935** Bob Nolan of Sons of the Pioneers is born in Winnipeg and spends some of his adolescence in Hatfield Point, New Brunswick. His song "Tumbling Tumbleweeds" is introduced to a wider audience by Gene Autry in the movie of the same name. Autry reprises the song in the film *Don't Fence Me In* (1945). Sons of the Pioneers member Roy Rogers performs it in the film *Silver Spurs* (1943) and the group reprises, what soon becomes their signature tune, in the movie *Hollywood Canteen* (1944). Bing Crosby tops the charts with the song in 1940.

» **1935** David Cullen Rockola of Virden, Manitoba, is instrumental in the development of the jukebox as he introduces his 12-record (78 rpm) Rock-Ola Multi-Selector phonograph. On May 27, 1936, one of the Multi-Selector jukeboxes is on board as the RMS *Queen Mary* makes her maiden voyage from Southampton to New York. A headline read: "The Queen Will Have Music Wherever She Goes."

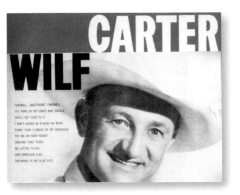

» **1935** Decca Records, one of the hottest labels in the world at the time, is picked up by The Compo Company for manufacturing and distribution in Canada.

» **1935** Music publisher Boosey & Hawkes (Canada) Ltd. opens in Toronto.

» **1935** Your Lucky Strike Hit Parade, which counts down the week's most popular songs according to sheet music sales and radio play, debuts on radio in the U.S.

» 1936

» **April 1936** During the Moose River mine disaster, all of Canada and the United States tune in to CRBC broadcasts as Frank Willis reports from Moose River for 69 hours. Two men were eventually rescued after being buried alive for 10 days.

» **September 1936** Kimberley, Saskatchewan-natives The Harmony Kids (initially Hahn and His Kids), featuring siblings Robert, Lloyd, Kay and Joyce Hahn, head eastward across Canada from frontier Saskatchewan to the bright lights of Broadway during the Great Depression. Joyce Hahn becomes one of Canada's first television stars in the early 1950s. The late Robert Hahn becomes a pioneer in the advertising jingle business as Canada's "Jingle King" before founding a number of record labels, including the Montréal-based Rising Records.

» **October 29, 1936** Hank Snow successfully auditions for A. Hugh Joseph at RCA Victor in Montréal. He records his own compositions "Lonesome Blue Yodel" and "The Prisoned Cowboy" and is signed to the label initially as Hank, The Yodeling Ranger.

» **1936** Canadian Radio Broadcasting Commission (CRBC) becomes the Canadian Broadcasting Corporation (CBC).

» **1936** Singer Phyllis Marshall debuts on radio station CRCT, a CBC affiliate in Toronto. She will later be heard on CBC Radio with Percy Faith.

» 1937

» **June 14, 1937** The Happy Gang, a troupe of musical entertainers, debut their popular radio show on CRCT (CBC Toronto). The show, which runs for 22 years, is organized by

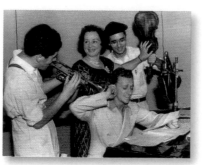

singer/pianist Bert Pearl. Members over the years included Eddie Allen, Lloyd Edwards, Robert Farnon, Les Foster, Bobby Gimby, Blain Mathé, Herb May, Cliff McKay, Jimmy Namaro, Bert Niosi, Joe Niosi, Lou Snider and Kathleen Stokes. One of the people responsible for bringing it to air is broadcast/advertising executive William Byles who, among other things, was an owner of Toronto's Celebrity Club and active in the early careers of Canadian comedy duo Shuster & Wayne. At his suggestion, they become Wayne & Shuster in 1945. His daughter is rock singer Alannah Myles, who dedicated her multi-million selling debut album to him.

» **November 6, 1937** Hank Snow records "The Blue Velvet Band," one of his biggest hits during this period. Over four days, Hank Snow records eight songs for RCA Victor in Montréal.

» **1937** The London Civic Symphony Orchestra, later renamed London Symphony Orchestra before adopting its current name Orchestra London Canada in 1981, is founded by conductor Bruce Sharpe.

» **1937** Renowned record retailer, the late Sam "the Record Man" Sniderman, first enters the world of records while working in the family business then known as Sniderman Radio Sales and Service on College Street in Toronto.

» **1937** The Cave Supper Club opens on Hornby Street in Vancouver.

» 1938

» **1938** Hank Snow makes his first cross-Canada tour.

» **1938** Mart Kenney and His Western Gentlemen record for RCA Victor in Montréal. The first record is the band's theme song, "The West, A Nest and You, Dear."

» **1938** Windsor, Ontario-born Dorothy Collins gets her first taste of show biz as she enters a hometown talent contest, wins a wristwatch and a chance to sing on a children's radio program in Detroit. She is such a hit that she is held over.

» **1938** While working at the CBC in Toronto, Percy Faith introduces his own show, *Music By Faith*, which will later also be heard in the U.S. on the Mutual Broadcasting System.

» **1938** Guitarist Jimi Hendrix' grandmother, Nora Hendrix, moves into a house at 827 East Georgia in Vancouver, where she will live until 1952. Jimi will often spend time with her there as he makes frequent visits from Seattle with his father Al. It is dubbed "The Hendrix House" and given heritage building status in 2006.

» 1939

» **May 24, 1939** The third Hotel Vancouver opens at West Georgia and Burrard Streets in Vancouver. Big band leader, Dal Richards, known as "The King of Swing," begins his lengthy career here in the Panorama Roof Ballroom.

» **1939** Don Messer and His Islanders form for performances on radio station CFCY Charlottetown, PEI, where Messer holds the position of music director. By 1944, the group is heard nationally on CBC Radio.

» **1939** The National Film Board/Office national du film du Canada, 12-time Academy Award-winning public film producer and distributor, is created.

» **1939** Sherbrooke Symphony Orchestra/Orchestre symphonique de Sherbrooke founded.

» **1939** Legendary Québécois singer/songwriter Félix Leclerc debuts in Montréal singing "Notre sentier."

CHART-TOPPING CANADIAN SONGS 1930-1939

1931 **By the River St. Marie** GUY LOMBARDO & HIS ROYAL CANADIANS
1931 **(There Ought To Be A) Moonlight Saving Time** GUY LOMBARDO & HIS ROYAL CANADIANS
1931 **Goodnight, Sweetheart** GUY LOMBARDO & HIS ROYAL CANADIANS
1932 **Too Many Tears** GUY LOMBARDO & HIS ROYAL CANADIANS
1932 **Paradise** GUY LOMBARDO & HIS ROYAL CANADIANS

1932 **We Just Couldn't Say Goodbye** GUY LOMBARDO & HIS ROYAL CANADIANS
1933 **The Last Round-Up** GUY LOMBARDO & HIS ROYAL CANADIANS
1934 **Stars Fell On Alabama** GUY LOMBARDO & HIS ROYAL CANADIANS
1935 **What's the Reason (I'm Not Pleasin' You)** GUY LOMBARDO & HIS ROYAL CANADIANS
1935 **Red Sails In the Sunset** GUY LOMBARDO & HIS ROYAL CANADIANS

OH WHAT A FEELING

That big eight-wheeler rollin' down the track
Means your true-lovin' daddy ain't comin' back
'Cause I'm movin' on, I'll soon be gone...
— Movin' On

Lyrics & Music by Hank Snow.

» 1940–1949

OH WHAT A FEELING
»1940–1949

» 1940

» April 15, 1940 Al Hendrix, Jimi Hendrix's father, is seen jitterbugging at The Forum with his sister Patricia in a picture that accompanies coverage in the *Vancouver Sun* of Duke Ellington's first Vancouver concert, which was billed as "The Biggest Dance in Vancouver's History!"

» May 1, 1940 Dal Richards and his 11-piece band, featuring 13-year-old Juliette, are booked into the Panorama Roof Room at the Hotel Vancouver to replace Mart Kenney and His Western Gentlemen. The contract was for an initial six weeks — Richards and his band stay for more than 25 years.

» July 27, 1940 *Billboard* introduces its first retail singles chart (National and Regional List of Best Selling Retail Records) and "I'll Never Smile Again," written by Ruth Lowe of Toronto is the first number one record. The song, recorded by the Tommy Dorsey Orchestra with Frank Sinatra and The Pied Pipers on vocals, tops the chart for 12 weeks. Lowe had written the song in the summer of 1939 following the loss of her first husband, publicist Harold Cohen. Percy Faith first introduces the song on CBC Radio and Glenn Miller first records it in the U.S. in a faster tempo, but it is Dorsey's version that becomes definitive. It is the band's biggest hit and, according to George T. Simon in his book *The Big Bands,* it is the song that established vocal groups forever. "Sinatra and The [Pied] Pipers wanted to create a more intimate version and, though they tried several times for just the right take, they could not seem to project a personal enough mood," writes Simon. "Dorsey, noting how hard they were trying, finally suggested that they sing it as though they'd just gathered around the piano at somebody's house. They followed his advice and a wonderfully personalized performance was the result." Sinatra later commissions Lowe to write his closing theme song, "Put Your Dreams Away for Another Day."

» 1940 CBC staff conductor Percy Faith lands a job in Chicago as music director of *The Carnation Contented Hour* on NBC Radio. In 1946, he takes on the musical directorship of Coca Cola's *The Pause That Refreshes.*

» 1940 An automobile accident causes Wilf Carter to retire from the music business for nine years.

▲ Frank Sinatra, Ruth Lowe and Tommy Dorsey

» 1940 The American Society of Composers, Authors and Publishers (ASCAP), the performance rights organization which represents its members' musical copyrights, and the National Association of Broadcasters (NAB) come to blows over the compensation for music played over the radio. The dispute results in a nine-month blackout of ASCAP songs on radio and the formation by the broadcasters of Broadcast Music Incorporated (BMI), which begins representing more regionally-significant artists and a more diverse catalogue of music genres.

» 1941

» January 1, 1941 Lorne Greene is the first announcer at the newly-launched English Network News Service at the CBC.

▲ Lorne Greene

>> **December 7, 1941** The Japanese bomb Pearl Harbour.

>> **1941** The Victoria Symphony Orchestra is founded by its first conductor, Melvin Knudson.

>> **1941** The Vogue Theatre opens at 918 Granville Street in Vancouver.

>> 1942

>> **April 1942** *Sweet and Low*, the CBC radio series featuring Mart Kenney and His Western Gentlemen, is broadcast on the full NBC network in the U.S.

>> **August 1, 1942** A dispute over how much musicians are compensated for recording results in a ban on all recording by the American Federation of Musicians (A F of M) led by its president James Petrillo. Vocalists and harmonica players — for some reason the harmonica was not considered an instrument in those days — were not affected by the ban. Suddenly, acappella music was ubiquitous. An agreement was finally made with most of the record labels on September 18, 1943 and with Columbia and Victor on November 11, 1944.

>> **December 13, 1942** *The Canadian Army Show*, a weekly music revue featuring artists like comedy team Wayne & Shuster, among others, is first broadcast on CBC radio. With trumpeter and musical director Robert Farnon and singers Roger Doucet and Denny Vaughan, among others, the show debuts at Toronto's Victoria Theatre and then tours Canada.

>> **December 1942** A Toronto Christmas tradition begins with the Toronto Mendelssohn Choir's first appearance under conductor Sir Ernest MacMillan in Handel's "Messiah."

>> **1942** At the age of 16, Dorothy Collins is introduced to band leader Raymond Scott whose quintet she subsequently joins. In 1949, when Scott leaves the orchestra for the radio show *Your Hit Parade*, Collins takes the group on the road herself. The following year, Scott is commissioned by the American Tobacco Company, sponsors of *Your Hit Parade*, to write some jingles for the company. Collins and Scott sing the jingles and the sponsors are so impressed with Collins' talent that when *Your Hit Parade* moves to television, she is chosen as the featured singer. Collins and Scott marry in 1952.

FOLKWAYS RECORDS FW 6821
FOLK SONGS OF THE CANADIAN NORTH WOODS
SUNG BY WADE HEMSWORTH

>> 1943

>> **December 1943** *The Canadian Army Show* (now known as *The Army Show*), which has been split into five units to entertain the troops overseas, arrives in England. Two members of the troupe, Robert Farnon and Denny Vaughan, remain in England. Robert Farnon becomes a renowned composer, arranger and conductor while recording under his own name and working with artists like Vera Lynn and Ted Heath's band as well as international singing stars like Tony Bennett, Frank Sinatra, Lena Horne and Sarah Vaughan. Denny Vaughan, once dubbed "the English Sinatra," moves to New York in 1951, where he works as an arranger for singers like Kate Smith, Eddie Fisher and Ezio Pinza.

>> **1943** Arthur Scammell records a version of his song, "Squid Jiggin' Ground," which becomes the first hit song by a local artist in Newfoundland as it sells more than 15,000 copies.

>> **1943** Lorne Greene founds the Toronto Academy of Radio Arts, a broadcasting school, which counts among its students Leslie Nielsen and James Doohan (later Engineer Montgomery Scott of the Star Trek Starship Enterprise).

>> 1944

>> **September 6, 1944** The Ottawa Philharmonic Orchestra debuts at the Capitol Theatre in Ottawa.

>> **December 20, 1944** At a recording session for RCA Victor in Montréal, Hank Snow records, among others, "You Played Love On the Strings of My Heart," one of his biggest songs in Canada.

▲ Johnny Wayne and Frank Shuster

>> **December 24, 1944** Hank Snow and family drive to Wheeling, West Virginia, where Snow auditions successfully for a job at radio station WWVA. In 1944, Snow had made his first U.S. appearance in Philadelphia, where he sings on local radio stations WCAU and WIP.

>> **1944** Music publisher Peer-Southern Organization (Canada), now peermusic Canada, opens in Toronto.

>> **1944** Mart Kenney and His Western Gentlemen continue to enjoy great success across Canada. Kenney would quip many years later: "I was the Bryan Adams of 1944!"

>> 1945

>> **February 16, 1945** Glenn Gould makes his first concert appearance on the organ at the Toronto Conservatory of Music.

>> **April 30, 1945** Adolf Hitler commits suicide in an underground bunker in Berlin.

>> **May 7, 1945** VE Day, the end of World War II in Europe.

>> **Summer 1945** Mart Kenney and His Western Gentlemen begin a long association with the Casa Loma in Toronto.

>> **June 26, 1945** The charter of the United Nations is signed by 50 countries.

>> **July 16, 1945** U.S. explodes first experimental atomic bomb in Alamogordo, New Mexico.

>> **August 6, 1945** U.S. drops atomic bomb on Hiroshima, Japan.

>> **August 14, 1945** World War II ends with the surrender of Japan.

>> **October 1, 1945** AM radio station CHUM Toronto begins its broadcasting life.

>> **October 5, 1945** Pianist, saxophonist, vocalist Art Hallman, a member of Mart Kenney and His Western Orchestra, forms his own 15-piece band and on this date he opens at the Casa Loma in Toronto with a weekly broadcast on the CBC radio network. The band will remain active for 45 years. First lead trumpet player in the band is Fred Davis, who later becomes a popular TV personality as the host of CBC-TV's *Front Page Challenge*.

>> **November 1, 1945** Mart Kenney and His Western Orchestra are booked for the winter season in the Imperial Room of the Royal York Hotel. Kenney had purchased a property at 125 Dupont Street in Toronto, where he sets up a booking office working with artists like the Art Hallman Orchestra, Bobby Gimby and Stan Patton.

▲ Guy Lombardo

>> **November 1945** *Ebony Magazine* launches in the U.S.

>> **1945** Jazz saxman Dizzy Gillespie popularizes Bop.

>> **1945** The Canadian Performing Rights Society (CPRS) becomes the Composers, Authors and Publishers Association of Canada/Association des compositeurs, auteurs and éditeurs du Canada Ltée (CAPAC).

>> **1945** CBC International Service, known as "the voice of Canada abroad," produces its first music recordings — five 78 rpm discs known as Canadian Album No. 1 — and later evolves into the CBC-SM and CBC-LM labels in 1966. In 1982, they come under the auspices of CBC Enterprises, formed to market CBC-produced discs.

>> 1946

>> **January 1, 1946** Kathleen Casey Wilkens is born in Philadelphia, America's first official "baby boomer."

>> **May 8, 1946** Glenn Gould debuts as a pianist with the Toronto Conservatory Symphony Orchestra at Toronto's Massey Hall.

>> **June 17, 1946** 7000 fans turn out for Mart Kenney and His Western Gentlemen's "homecoming" show at the Pacific National Exhibition Grounds in Vancouver.

>> **July 5, 1946** The bikini, named after the Atom Bomb test held at Bikini Atoll a few days earlier, debuts in Paris.

>> **1946** At age eight, Gordon Lightfoot begins singing in his hometown of Orillia, Ontario.

>> **1946** Musicana Records begins manufacturing and distributing

▲ Mart Kenney and His Western Gentlemen

records in Canada for newly-formed Capitol Records U.S.A.

>> **1946** Country trio The Rhythm Pals form in New Westminster, BC. They are destined to become the longest-lasting group in Canadian music history.

>> **1946** Aragon Recording Studios, one of Canada's first recording facilities, opens in Vancouver with the participation of musician, big band leader and broadcaster Al Reusch, one of the pioneers of the Canadian West Coast music scene.

>> **1946** Construction of Flamingo Hotel and Casino puts Las Vegas, Nevada on the map.

▲ The Rhythm Pals

>> **1946** First year of the Cannes Film Festival in France.

>> **1946** The late Canadian broadcast legend Max Ferguson found out first-hand just how much Hank Snow and Wilf Carter meant to the folks in the Canadian Maritimes when, early in his career, he moved from his hometown of London, Ontario to take a job as an announcer at CBC Radio's Halifax studios. Partial to artists like Sons Of the Pioneers that he considered legitimate, he was lukewarm to the point of petulance over most of the "cowboy music" he had to play during the course of his half-hour Rawhide radio show. On one occasion, instead of introducing Hank Snow as the Yodeling Ranger, he presented him as Hank Snow, the yodeling Mongolian idiot, an utterance he half-heartedly retracted when station manager Sid Kennedy warned him that he wasn't going to get out of the place alive if he didn't. A very delicate balance had to be maintained in the playing of Hank Snow and Wilf Carter records as well. Ferguson once played two of Wilf's records and only one of Hank's and he heard about it immediately from a brother and sister from Mahone Bay who brought it to the attention of their Member of Parliament. The matter made it all the way to the floor of the House of Commons.

"Wilf Carter's mother wrote me one time and almost made a little trouble," Ferguson recalls in the Bill MacNeil/Morris Wolfe-authored Signing On: The Birth Of Radio In Canada. "Wilf would always open his records with a little spoken monologue that went: 'Well, boys, kinda nice sittin' around the old campfire. Tex, throw another log on the fire and I'll tell you all about the Strawberry Roan.' Then he'd sing 'The Strawberry Roan'... Wilf had another song titled 'My Silvery Gray-Haired Mother in the West.' I'd say something like: 'Throw my silvery gray-haired mother on the fire, Tex, and I'll tell you the story about such and such.' I had no idea that Wilf's own mother was living in New Brunswick. She naturally was a little put out."

>> 1947

>> **January 14, 1947** Glenn Gould plays Beethoven's Concerto No. 4 with the Toronto Symphony Orchestra.

>> **April 11, 1947** Jackie Robinson plays with the Brooklyn Dodgers, the first black baseball player in the majors.

>> **August 15, 1947** As Great Britain ends its rule of India, the sovereign states of India and Pakistan are founded.

>> **October 20, 1947** Glenn Gould gives his recital debut as a pianist at the Eaton Auditorium in Toronto.

>> **November 16, 1947** The Windsor Symphony Orchestra, founded by Matti Holli, gives its first concert at Patterson Collegiate.

>> **December 31, 1947** American Federation of Musicians President James Petrillo announces that, come 1948, there will be no more phonograph records or radio transcriptions recorded by union musicians. His contention is that phonograph records, played continuously on radio and jukeboxes, compete with musicians that play live so their needs to be a royalty paid. United Press (UP) reported: "The big five recording companies are working on a hectic round-the-clock schedule and will have enough records to keep the country in tunes for three years when James C. Petrillo's edict against all new recordings goes into effect Dec. 31." The recording ban lasted close to a year, ending on December 14, 1948.

>> **1947** The Four Lads, alumni of St. Michael's Cathedral School, form in Toronto around Jimmy Arnold, Bernie Toorish, Frank Busseri and Connie Condarini.

>> **1947** Winchester, Ontario-born George Beverly Shea becomes a soloist with Billy Graham's evangelical crusade, a position he holds for more than 40 years. He has been called "the most widely recognized voice in Christian music."

>> **1947** Inspired by the reaction of one of her young patients at the sight of a sparrow outside his hospital room window, Winnipeg-born Elizabeth Clarke, a nurse at the Vancouver Hospital for Sick and Crippled Children, writes the poem "Bluebird On Your Windowsill," which she later sets to music. It subsequently becomes a hit song for artists like The Rhythm Pals, Bing Crosby and Doris Day. Clarke donates all royalties from the song to the hospital.

>> **1947** Vocalist Marg Osborne joins Don Messer and His Islanders.

>> **1947** Vocalist Phyllis Marshall tours the U.S. with the Cab Calloway Orchestra.

>> **1947** Capitol Records of Canada Ltd. is established, initially in London, Ontario.

>> **1947** A second performing rights society, BMI Canada (later known as PRO Canada and then PROCAN), is established in Canada.

>> **1947** The term "Cold War" is coined.

>> 1948

>> **January 28, 1948** The first Emmy Awards for television presented.

>> **March 17, 1948** The Hell's Angels form.

>> **April 1, 1948** The first production of the Toronto revue *Spring Thaw* opens at the Museum Theatre by Mavor Moore and produced by his mother, Dora Mavor Moore.

>> **May 14, 1948** The new nation of Israel is proclaimed.

>> **June 20, 1948** *The Ed Sullivan Show* first airs.

>> **June 21, 1948** Dr. Peter Goldmark of CBS/Columbia Records introduces the 33 1/3 RPM long-playing record.

>> **June 30, 1948** Bell Laboratories announces the development of the transistor.

>> **September 9, 1948** North Korea (Korean People's Democratic Republic) declared by Kim Il Sung.

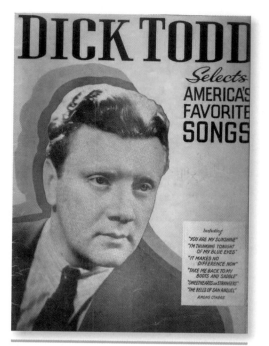

▲ 'Canada's Bing Crosby'

>> **September 20, 1948** Crooner Bing Crosby arrives in Vancouver to record his radio show but is first made a full-blooded Chief by members of the Squamish tribe who named him "Chief Thunder Voice."

>> **September 1948** Band leader Mart Kenney organizes a "talent quest" with a number of radio stations in western Canada. One of the winners is Ed Bickert, a young guitarist from Vernon, BC, who is destined to become one of the most influential jazz guitarists in Canada.

>> **December 16, 1948** Winnipeg Symphony Orchestra, conducted by Walter Kaufmann, debuts at the Winnipeg Auditorium.

>> **1948** Gordon Lightfoot, at age 10, is singled out in the junior choir as a soloist. Lightfoot later points to choir master Ray Williams as a major influence on his early career.

>> **1948** Singer/pianist Billy O'Connor begins his career on CBC Radio and becomes a regular headliner over the next decade on shows like *The Late Show*, *Club O'Connor* and *Saturday Date*, which were all early boosters of homegrown talent like Peter Appleyard, Juliette, Vonda King, Rhonda Silver and the Two Tones, featuring Gordon Lightfoot.

>> **1948** A collaboration between jazz trumpet player Miles Davis and Canadian composer and arranger Gil Evans is destined to usher in the Cool Jazz era.

>> **1948** Toronto Jazz musician Moe Koffman signs to the New York-based Mainstream Records after winning a poll as Best Flute Player in *Metronome* magazine.

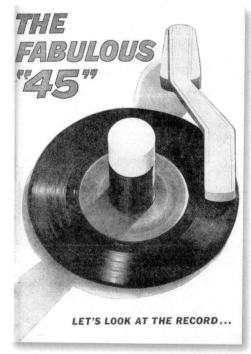

>> **1948** "What A Fool Was I?" written and recorded by Saskatchewan-native Stu Davis, a pioneer of Canadian country radio and television, becomes a major hit when covered by country star, Eddy Arnold.

>> **1948** Earl Heywood, known as "Canada's Number One Cowboy Singer," signs to RCA Victor and records a number of hits, including "Alberta Waltz" and "Tears of St. Anne."

>> **1948** The Rhythm Pals become one of the first Canadian groups to appear on television in the U.S.

>> **1948** The London Gramophone Corp. of Canada opens in Montréal.

>> **1948** McDonald's and Baskin-Robbins begin to franchise.

>> **1948** The Slinky is the toy sensation of the year.

>> 1949

>> **March 8, 1949** Hank Snow records for the first time in the U.S. with RCA's Steve Sholes in Chicago. It results in Snow's first U.S. release and first Top 10 single, "Marriage Vow."

>> **March 31, 1949** Newfoundland becomes Canada's 10th province.

>> **May 1949** Hank Snow and family relocate to New Westminster, BC, where he sings with the staff band at radio station CKNW. The Rhythm Pals are also regulars on the station. U.S. country star Ernest Tubb, who had previously met Hank Snow in Fort Worth, Texas, where they shared a concert bill, records Snow's "My Filipino Rose," which Tubb takes into the Top 10 of the U.S. country charts in September.

>> **Summer 1949** Winnipeg-born singer, trombonist Wally Koster, who later goes on to star in CBC-TV's *Cross Canada Hit Parade*, joins Mart Kenney and His Western Gentlemen.

>> **September 18, 1949** Having fielded and turned down offers at this point from band leaders like Count Basie and Jimmie Lunceford to join their outfits, one night in New York pianist Oscar Peterson does find an offer from American impresario Norman Granz intriguing. At one of his renowned "Jazz at the Philharmonic" presentations at Carnegie Hall, Grantz "plants" Peterson in the audience and

later brings him on stage as a surprise guest. The youthful Peterson brings the house down on a night that proves to be the catalyst for his career launch internationally.

>> **October 1, 1949** Mao Tse Tung declares China a Communist state.

>> **1949** "Far Away Places," a song co-written by Montréal-born composer Alex J. Kramer and his American wife Joan Whitney is taken to the upper echelon of the charts in the U.S. by Bing Crosby, Margaret Whiting, Perry Como and Dinah Shore. Kramer's other co-writes with Whitney had included "Ain't Nobody Here But Us Chickens" (1946) and "Love Somebody" (1947). With Whitney and Mack David he co-wrote "It's Love, Love, Love" (1943) and "Candy" (1944) and "My Sister and I" (1941) with Hy Zaret and Whitney.

>> **1949** The Four Lads debut on Elwood Glover's *Canadian Cavalcade* show on the CBC, tour Canada and subsequently get a regular paying gig at New York's Ruban Bleu, where they are booked for close to eight months.

>> **1949** In Seattle, Al Hendrix, the father of future guitar legend Jimi Hendrix, splits with his wife Lucille and sends his two children Jimmy (later to change the spelling of his first name to Jimi) and Leon to stay with his sister Patricia in Vancouver. The boys stay for about a year and six-year-old Jimmy attends Dawson Street Annex Elementary School on Burrard Street in the west end of Vancouver, the same school his father used to attend.

>> **1949** RCA issues the world's first 45 rpm record, which becomes the standard for pop music singles.

>> **1949** The Canadian Music Publishers Association (CMPA)/Association canadienne des éditeurs de musique is formed in Toronto.

>> **1949** Rodeo Records Ltd. is founded in Montréal by Don Johnson and George Taylor.

>> **1949** Wilf Carter returns to the North American circuit after a nine-year hiatus and tours Canada with the Canadian Ploughboy, Orval Prophet.

» **1949** Joan Anderson (Joni Mitchell) moves with her parents to North Battleford, Saskatchewan.

» **1949** Brantford, Ontario-native Wade Hemsworth writes "The Black Fly Song," about working in the backwoods of Northern Ontario, which becomes a standard in the pantheon of Canadian folk music. Among others, it was recorded by Kate and Anna McGarrigle, who also recorded Hemsworth's song

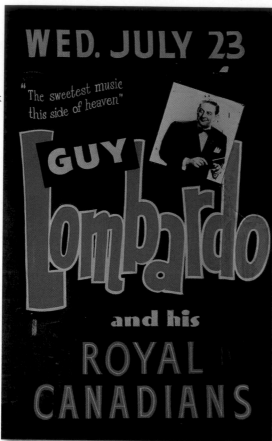

"The Log Driver's Waltz" with the Mountain City Four. It is the soundtrack for a 1979 animated short film by the National Film Board.

» **1949** The Latin Samba is the newest dance craze.

» **1949** Canada becomes a founding member of NATO.

» **1949** Construction of Toronto's Yonge Subway begins.

CHART-TOPPING CANADIAN SONGS 1940-1949

1941 **The Band Played On** GUY LOMBARDO & HIS ROYAL CANADIANS

1941 **Intermezzo (Souvenir de Vienne)** GUY LOMBARDO & HIS ROYAL CANADIANS

1944 **It's Love, Love, Love** GUY LOMBARDO & HIS ROYAL CANADIANS

1947 **"Mangua, Nicaragua,"** GUY LOMBARDO & HIS ROYAL CANADIANS

OH WHAT A FEELING

I'm so young and you're so old
This, my darling, I've been told...
Oh, please stay by me, Diana...

— Diana

Lyrics & Music by Paul Anka.

»1950–1959

»1950–1959

» 1950

» January 7, 1950 Hank Snow makes his first appearance on the *Grand Ole Opry* in Nashville, where he is introduced by old friend, Ernest Tubb. He is billed as Hank Snow, the Singing Ranger.

» January 1950 Jazz man Moe Koffman moves to New York to play with a number of well-known big bands and becomes friends with trumpeter Doc Severinson, who would become music director for NBC-TV's *Tonight Show* during Johnny Carson's reign.

» April 1950 Herbert "H.S." Berliner sells the Compo Company to Decca Records after undergoing surgery. Reportedly, he was convinced that he had a terminal disease like cancer and that convinced him to sell. He would live to regret the impetuous sale.

» August 19, 1950 The Hank Snow single "I'm Movin' On," recorded at the RCA Victor studios on Music Row in Nashville, tops the Billboard country chart for 21 weeks. It is one of only three songs to hold the number one spot for that number of weeks. It exceeds a million in sales and radio performances. It has been recorded by a number of artists over the years, including The Rolling Stones, Ray Charles, Elvis Presley, Emmylou Harris and Steppenwolf, among many others.

» September 29, 1950 The first telephone answering machine introduced.

» October 1950 Windsor, Ontario's Dorothy Collins becomes a featured singer on the popular American TV show *Your Hit Parade* as it begins its first season.

» December 24, 1950 Glenn Gould makes his CBC network broadcast debut. As he would recall in a later essay titled "Music and Technology," it proves to be one of the most significant and memorable events in Gould's career "not simply because it enabled me to communicate without the immediate presence of a gallery of witnesses... but rather because, later the same day, I was presented with a soft-cut 'acetate,' a disc which dimly reproduced the felicities of the broadcast in question and which, even today, a quarter-century after the fact, I still take down from

▲ Moe Koffman

the shelf on occasion in order to celebrate the moment in my life when I first caught a vague impression of the direction it would take... when my love affair with the microphone began."

» 1950 Wilf Carter plays to close to 70,000 fans during a one-week stand at the Canadian National Exhibition Bandshell in Toronto. The Rhythm Pals tour with Carter during this period.

» 1950 Quality Records, with its trademark red and yellow label that would become ubiquitous over the next three and a half decades, is established in Toronto. It closes in 1985 but reopens from 1990 to 1997.

» 1950 Canadian Music Sales, distributor of Columbia Records in Canada during the '30s, establishes the Dominion record label, which over the years records country and folk performers like Isidore Soucy, Stompin' Tom Connors and Earl Heywood.

» 1950 Percy Faith is hired by Mitch Miller as director of popular music for Columbia Records in New York.

» 1950 During his stint with Stan Kenton's band, Maynard Ferguson wins

▲ Percy Faith

the *Downbeat* Reader's Poll for best trumpet player three consecutive years from 1950 to 1952.

>> **1950** Robert Goulet becomes a radio announcer at CKUA Edmonton.

>> **1950** Maxwell House introduces the first instant coffee.

>> **1950** The first credit cards are marketed by Diner's Club.

>> **1950** Shopping malls, drive-in movies theatres, bowling alleys and chain supermarkets proliferate as part of the expanding suburban landscape.

>> 1951

>> **May 16, 1951** The first concerts of the newly-formed Canadian League of Composers are devoted to the music of one of its founders, John Weinzweig.

>> **May 27, 1951** Tibet becomes a Chinese province.

>> **June 14, 1951** Univac 1 becomes the first commercially built computer.

>> **1951** Crew cuts become the hair-styling fashion for men.

>> **1951** The Four Lads back up Johnny Ray on his hit song "Cry." Group member Bernard Toorish would later arrange their background vocals for Ray's "Little White Cloud That Cried" as well as Frankie Laine's 1954 single, "Rain, Rain, Rain."

>> **1951** The Royal Commission on the National Development of the Arts, Letters and Sciences (Massey Commission) tables its report in the House of Commons. It has a profound effect on the development of the arts in Canada. Among its recommendations is the creation of the Canada Council. It also suggests that the CBC go into television.

>> **1951** Leonard Cohen keeps it country as he plays in the group The Buckskin Boys while attending Montreal's McGill University.

>> **1951** Gisele MacKenzie moves to the U.S. with band leader/manager/husband Bob Shuttleworth after hosting her own CBC radio show in the late '40s. This same year, *Meet Gisele*, a National Film Board documentary on MacKenzie's life, is released.

>> **1951** Contralto Maureen Forrester makes her professional debut with the Montréal Elgar Choir in Elgar's *The Music Makers* at the Salvation Army Citadel.

1951 At the age of 13, Toronto-born operatic soprano Teresa Stratas (Anastasia Stratakis) makes her radio debut singing Greek pop songs.

>> 1952

>> **March 9, 1952** The Mart Kenney Show, originating at Mart Kenney's Ranch northwest of Toronto, debuts on CBC Radio.

>> **March 21, 1952** Deejay Alan Freed emcees the first rock concert (Moondog Coronation Ball) at the Cleveland Arena.

>> **November 4, 1952** Republican Dwight D. Eisenhower elected U.S. President.

>> **December 2, 1952** Toronto-born soprano Lois Marshall makes her New York debut at the Town Hall.

>> **December 2, 1952** The first recorded nuclear power plant accident occurs at Chalk River, Ontario.

>> **1952** The Four Lads' own recording career begins with the single "Mocking Bird."

>> **1952** Rudi Maugeri and John Perkins, former students at St. Michael's Cathedral Choir School in Toronto, quit the group The Jordonaires and put together The Four Tones, the group that would evolve into The Canadaires and then The Crew Cuts.

>> **1952** Canada becomes signatory to the Universal Copyright Convention, an international copyright agreement.

>> **1952** Singer/actress Gisele MacKenzie tours for a couple of years with her mentor, comedic actor Jack Benny, on whose TV show she became a frequent guest.

>> **1952** The first CBC Television broadcast season includes Canada's first country music TV show, *Holiday Ranch*.

>> **1952** A very youthful Gordon Lightfoot, in from Orillia, appears at Toronto's Massey Hall in a concert of Kiwanis Festival winners.

>> **1952** Bert Niosi and his band begin an 18-year residency at Toronto's Palais Royale dance hall.

>> **1952** Ronnie Hawkins enters the University of Arkansas to study arts and sciences and physical education.

>> **1952** *American Bandstand*, hosted by Dick Clark, debuts on ABC TV.

>> **1952** The first pocket-size transistor radios are introduced — made in Japan.

>> **1952** "No-cal" drinks first introduced.

>> **1952** The fascination with UFOs intensifies.

>> **1952** Groups formed this year include The Crew Cuts, Toronto.

>> 1953

>> **March 26, 1953** Dr. Jonas Salk announces discovery of a polio vaccine.

>> **March 29, 1953** Maureen Forrester makes her recital debut at the Montréal YMCA with John Newmark, who will become her regular accompanist and collaborator over the years.

>> **March 1953** During the Korean War, Hank Snow and the Rainbow Ranch Boys and Ernest Tubb and His Texas Troubadours volunteer to go to South Korea to entertain the troops.

>> **April 3, 1953** The first issue of *TV Guide* published.

June 2, 1953 Queen Elizabeth II's coronation at Westminster Abbey in London.

>> **Jul 17, 1953** Gisele MacKenzie begins a 29-week, non-consecutive run on the British chart with the single "Seven Lonely Days," which peaks at number six.

>> **Summer 1953** Folk group The Travellers, who will become well-known for their Canadian version of the Woody Guthrie song "This Land Is Our Land," forms around Jerry Gray, Sid Dolgay, Helen Gray, Jerry Goodis and Oscar Ross.

>> **November 1953** Joan Anderson (Joni Mitchell) contracts polio and spends several months away from school. She credits her seventh-grade English teacher at Queen Elizabeth School in North Battleford, Sasktachewan for piquing her interest in writing. She will dedicate her first album, *Songs To A Seagull*, to him with the simple inscription, "This album is dedicated to Mr. Kratzman who taught me to love words."

>> **December 8, 1953** Operatic contralto Maureen Forrester makes her debut with the Montréal Symphony in her hometown.

>> **Late 1953** An appearance on the *Gene Carroll* TV Show in Cleveland proves to be the turning point of the Crew Cuts' career. Known then as the Canadaires, they meet influential Cleveland deejay Bill Randle, who is not only responsible for the change of their name to The Crew Cuts (after the hairstyles they were sporting at the time), but also for the group's audition at Mercury Records in Chicago who signed them.

>> **1953** The first pre-recorded reel-to-reel (at 7½ ips) is offered for sale.

>> **1953** Actress Mitzi Gaynor portrays Canadian vaudeville star Eva Tanguay in the film *The I Don't Care Girl*, a fictionalized account of her life.

>> **1953** Percy Faith records the theme from the motion picture "The Song From Moulin Rouge (Where Is Your Heart?)" which becomes the top-selling single of the year.

>> **1953** While on vacation in Gloucester, Massachusetts with his parents Camelia and Andrew, Paul Anka wins a talent contest doing his best dramatic vocal impression of Johnny Ray. During his first year at Fisher Park High School in Ottawa, Anka forms a group called The Bobby Soxers with friends Jerry Barbeau and Ray Carrier.

>> **1953** After working on CBC-TV's *The Big Revue*, vocalist Shirley Harmer works in the U.S. over the next five years on Dave Garroway's NBC-TV show, with Paul Whiteman's

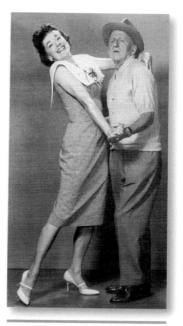

▲ Gisele MacKenzie and Jimmy Durante

Orchestra, on ABC Radio and in concert, and on NBC-TV's *The George Gobel Show*.

>> **1953** Dave Somerville, Ted Kowalski, Phil Levitt and Bill Reed, collectively known as The Diamonds, form at the University of Toronto.

>> **1953** Gisele MacKenzie begins a long association with Jack Benny and becomes a regular on the NBC-TV show *Your Hit Parade*. During her first four years on the show, she becomes the only resident vocalist ever to perform her own hit on the program. "Hard To Get," a song first heard on an episode of NBC-TV's *Justice* (1955), reaches number four on the *Billboard* chart as well as number seven on the *Your Hit Parade* chart.

>> **1953** Toronto-born trombonist Murray McEachern, working as a Hollywood studio musician, handles the trombone solos heard in the movies *The Glenn Miller Story* (1953), *The Benny Goodman Story* (1955) and *Paris Blues* (1961).

>> **1953** *Casino Royale*, the first of the James Bond novels by Ian Fleming, is published.

>> **1953** Movie theatres introduce Cinemascope.

>> **1953** The word board game *Scrabble* sees its popularity skyrocket.

>> **1953** Groups formed this year include The Diamonds, Toronto; and The Travellers, Norval, ON.

>> 1954

>> **March 1, 1954** The U.S. tests an H-Bomb in the Marshall Islands that is close to 700 times more powerful than the bomb that destroyed Hiroshima. The thermonuclear era begins.

>> **March 30, 1954** Toronto's Yonge Subway, the first in Canada, opens to the public from Union Station to Eglinton.

>> **April 12, 1954** Bill Haley and the Comets' "Rock Around the Clock" arguably becomes the first number one rock single. Some point to Haley's single, "Shake, Rattle and Roll" as the milestone recording.

>> **May 6, 1954** British runner Roger Bannister breaks the four-minute mile for the first time.

>> **May 22, 1954** Bob Dylan's bar mitzvah is celebrated in Hibbing, Minnesota.

>> **July 6, 1954** Elvis Presley records his first single, "That's Alright," at Sun Records in Memphis.

>> **July 28, 1954** The Crew Cuts' cover of The Chords R&B hit "Sh-Boom" hits number one on the *Billboard* chart, where it remains for seven weeks.

>> **September 27, 1954** *The Tonight Show* debuts on the NBC Network with Steve Allen as host.

>> **October 15, 1954** Hurricane Hazel devastates the Toronto area, resulting in the death of 81 people and over $135 million in damage.

>> **November 23, 1954** General Motors rolls out its 50 millionth car.

>> **1954** Columbia Records of Canada is founded with its head office in Toronto.

>> **1954** Lucille Starr begins her singing career in Vancouver.

>> **1954** Hank Snow has his second million-selling single with "I Don't Care Anymore," which tops the Billboard country chart for 20 weeks.

>> **1954** Trombonist Rob McConnell begins his musical career in Edmonton as a member of saxophonist Don Thompson's band.

>> **1954** The Travellers make their TV debut on CBC's *Haunted House*.

>> **1954** *The Denny Vaughan Show* debuts on CBC-TV.

>> **1954** Working as a deejay at Vancouver radio station CJOR and hosting the show *Theme For Teens* while still attending high school, 16-year-old Red Robinson, who is now in the Rock and Roll Hall of Fame, becomes the first broadcaster in Vancouver — and perhaps in all of Canada — to begin playing rock'n'roll and R&B records. The first spin? The pop/R&B crossover hit, "Marie" by The Four Tunes.

>> **1954** TV dinners become popular.

>> **1954** The mambo and the cha cha from Cuba are this year's hot dances.

>> 1955

>> **Jan. 1, 1955** Hank Snow's management contract with Colonel Tom Parker goes into effect.

>> **January 15, 1955** *Billboard* magazine cites the success of The Crew Cuts' cover of The Chords' "Sh-Boom" as a main factor in pop artists' interest in R&B covers.

>> **February 5, 1955** The Crew Cuts are winners of radio station WNEW New York's annual music popularity poll along with Perry Como, Patti Page and Ray Anthony.

>> **April 1, 1955** Priscilla Wright's single "Man In A Raincoat," which had been arranged by her father Don Wright, a noted Canadian choir conductor/broadcaster and recorded at London, Ontario radio station CFPL, becomes a number one song in Canada and a Top 10 record in the U.S., U.K., Australia and New Zealand, qualifying it as the first Canadian record by a female to become an international hit. *Cashbox* in the U.S. names her Most Promising Singer of the Year.

>> **April 15, 1955** "Earth Angel," The Crew Cuts' cover of the Penguins' number one R&B hit, begins a 20-week run on the British charts and hits number three in the U.S.

>> **June 15, 1955** John Lennon meets Paul McCartney at a church party in Woolton, Liverpool.

>> **June 1955** At the Columbia Studios in New York, Glenn Gould first records the "Goldberg Variations," originally a work for the harpsichord composed and published in 1741 by Johann Sebastian Bach.

>> **July 1, 1955** 15-year-old singer Priscilla Wright appears on the *Ed Sullivan Show* and then plays a series of concerts with Elvis Presley and Pat Boone.

>> **August 15, 1955** Hank Snow Enterprises-Jamboree Attractions, headed by Snow and his manager Colonel Tom Parker, sign 20-year-old Elvis Presley for management... or so Snow believes. Parker and Snow split later in the year when Snow finds that Elvis had, in fact, been secretly signed to a personal contract with Parker. Snow recalls his confrontation with Parker in his book *The Hank Snow Story*: "He twirled his big cigar back and forth in his mouth, pointed his finger at his chest, and said, 'You don't have any contract with Elvis Presley. Elvis is signed exclusively to the Colonel.'

With my experience from the beginning of our association and the haphazard way in which things had been handled, I was actually prepared for this. But it still cut me deep. I felt it was my influence with Elvis and his parents, and with Steve Sholes of RCA Victor, that brought about the signing of the recording contract, as well as signing him to what I thought was our agency. By then the pieces had fallen together in my mind, and I wondered how one human being could undermine, con and rob another in such a conniving scheme from the start."

>> **October 23, 1955** The Republic of South Vietnam is established.

>> **October 1955** Moe Koffman returns to Toronto from New York and records his debut album at the RCA Victor Studios on Mutual Street in 1957. One of the songs he records is "Blues A La Canadiana." The name is changed at the suggestion of the producer to "Swingin' Shepherd Blues," which becomes an international hit in 1958.

>> **1955** Singer/actress Gisele MacKenzie becomes a naturalized U.S. citizen following her move to Los Angeles in 1951.

>> **1955** "I's the B'y," a traditional song of Newfoundland, thought to be composed sometime in the 19th century, appears in the third edition of *Old-Time Songs and Poetry of Newfoundland: Songs of the People From the Days of Our Forefathers* compiled by Newfoundland-born businessman and folksong collector Gerald S. Doyle. It gets wide-distribution across the country and results in the popularity of featured songs like "I's the B'y."

>> **1955** Paul Anka heads for New York after winning a contest that had involved collecting labels from Campbell Soup cans.

>> **1955** The Diamonds are discovered by deejay Bill Randle while playing the Alpine Village Club in Cleveland. The group makes its TV debut on CBC's *Pick the Stars*.

>> **1955** Joyce Hahn and Wally Koster begin a six-year stint as co-stars on CBC-TV's popular *Cross Canada Hit Parade*.

>> **1955** At age 14, country singer Myrna Lorrie from Cloud Bay, Ontario (near Thunder Bay), has her biggest hit with "Are You Mine?"

>> **1955** Denny Doherty's singing career begins in his hometown of Halifax as vocalist for a dance band led by Peter Power.

▲ Elvis and Hank Snow

>> **1955** Maureen Forrester makes her European debut in Paris at the Salle Gaveau.

>> **1955** This year's dance craze is the meringue. Play-Doh is the kid's diversion of choice.

>> **1955** Estimates indicate that close to one billion comic books a year are sold in the U.S. at ten cents each.

>> 1956

>> **January 28, 1956** Elvis Presley makes his TV debut on the Dorsey Brothers' CBS *Stage Show*.

>> **Early 1956** Paul Anka travels to Hollywood to visit his uncle Maurice. He takes a job as an usher at the Civic Playhouse to support his songwriting. He gets a deal with Modern Records and records the single "I Confess" backed by The Cadets.

>> **April 1956** The Vancouver jazz club The Cellar opens. The original club closes in 1964.

>> **April 1956** The Rhythm Pals host a TV series originating in Vancouver for CBC-TV.

>> **May 9, 1956** The Happy Gang make their TV debut on CBC's *Cross-Canada Hit Parade*.

>> **June 27, 1956** The first rock'n'roll concert in Vancouver takes place at the Kerrisdale Arena featuring Bill Haley and the Comets with local group Les Vogt and the Prowlers opening. It was promoted by local radio personality Jack Cullen, who hosted the radio show *Owl Prowl* on CKNW — the program had actually inspired the name of the group The Prowlers — and hosted by popular local deejay, Red Robinson.

>> **Summer 1956** Gisele MacKenzie becomes one of Dinah Shore's summer replacements on NBC-TV's *The Chevy Show*.

>> **September 1956** Paul Anka, returning from a sojourn in

▲ The Diamonds

▲ Myrna Lorrie (right) and friend perform at a drive-in

Hollywood, appears on the CBC-TV shows *Pick the Stars* and *Cross Canada Hit Parade*. During this period he writes an ode to Diana Ayoub, the 18-year-old babysitter of his younger brother Andrew and sister Mariam.

>> **November 12, 1956** Operatic contralto Maureen Forrester makes her New York recital debut at Town Hall in New York with long-time accompanist, pianist John Newmark.

>> **1956** Toronto vocal group The Rover Boys sign with producer Don Costa at ABC/Paramount Records in New York, with whom they record their biggest hit, "Graduation Day."

>> **1956** Tillsonburg, Ontario-born trumpeter Johnny Cowell has his biggest hit with the self-penned single, "Walk Hand In Hand," which hits the top of the sheet music chart in the U.K., where fellow Canadian Denny Vaughan records a version.

>> **1956** Singer Norman Brooks portrays Al Jolson in the film, *The Best Things In Life Are Free*.

>> **1956** Ian Tyson, whose main interest in youth and beyond has been the rodeo, sings at the Heidelberg Cafe in Vancouver while attending the Vancouver Art School.

>> **1956** The popular CBC-TV program *Juliette* debuts and runs for 11 years, usually following *Hockey Night in Canada* on Saturday nights.

>> **1956** A compilation of some of Leonard Cohen's earliest poems is published in his first book, *Let Us Compare Mythologies*.

>> **1956** Doug Cole opens George's Jazz Room in George's Spaghetti House in downtown Toronto, which becomes the longest running jazz club in Canada prior to its closing

in 1984. Moe Koffman, who booked the club, was also the leader of the house band, which featured some of the area's top jazz musicians.

>> **1956** Phil Nimmons' jazz band, later to be known as Nimmons 'N' Nine, debuts at the Stratford Festival in Stratford, Ontario.

>> **1956** Walter Susskind succeeds Sir Ernest MacMillan as conductor of the Toronto Symphony Orchestra.

>> **1956** Grace Metalious' novel *Peyton Place* is the *50 Shades of Gray* of 1956.

>> **1956** Calypso has its day in the sun with the popularity of Harry Belafonte's album of the same name.

>> **1956** *My Fair Lady* is the Broadway and soundtrack hit of the year.

>> 1957

>> **January 10, 1957** The Crew Cuts appear live on CBS-TV's Dorsey Brothers Stage Show out of Cleveland, Ohio.

>> **January 1957** Prince Albert, Saskatchewan-born heldentenor (unique tenor voice) Jon Vickers debuts with the Royal Opera of Covent Garden, London while on tour.

>> **March 1957** In Ottawa, Paul Anka is thrown out of the backstage area of a Fats Domino concert by promoter Irvin Feld. As he leaves, Anka tells Feld that he better take down his name and phone number because he might need to use it one day. Paul Anka subsequently heads for New York, where he spends time with The Diamonds and The Rover Boys, who suggest he drop by the offices of ABC/Paramount. Within a month he is in the studio recording "Diana" and "Don't Gamble On Me."

>> **April 1957** Jimmy Morrison, known for fronting the Vancouver group The Sensational Stripes, which in one configuration included Ian Tyson, wins a contest organized by radio station CJOR to find a local Elvis Presley. As Jeff Bateman reports in *The Greater Vancouver Book*: "Later that year, Morrison and The Stripes recorded 'Singin' the Blues b/w 'Your Cheatin' Heart,' a 45 that's regarded as the city's first rock'n'roll recording."

>> **May 27, 1957** Toronto "hit parade" radio station CHUM publishes the first issue of the CHUM Chart, which lists the top songs of the week. It runs as a

pocket chart distributed through local retailers until the April 26, 1975 issue and thereafter is published weekly in local newspapers until it was discontinued in 1979.

August 5, 1957 American Bandstand, which has only aired in the Philadelphia area, goes national on the ABC-TV Network.

>> **August 7, 1957** Paul Anka performs "Diana" on American Bandstand.

>> **August 31, 1957** A riot during Elvis Presley's SRO concert at the Empire Stadium in Vancouver results in Elvis drastically reducing his show to a handful of songs.

>> **August 1957** Irvin Feld, the promoter who had only months before kicked Paul Anka from the backstage area of a Fats Domino concert in Ottawa, hears Paul Anka's single "Diana" while going through new releases at his record store in Washington, DC. Without recalling the incident or Anka's name, he books him on his next *Greatest Show of Stars* tour, which sets out on an 80-day excursion the following month. Feld, who is eventually reminded of the Ottawa incident becomes Anka's manager. "Diana," which hits the top of the Billboard singles chart on September 9, 1957, will become one of the biggest selling singles in music history. Reportedly, Chuck Berry wrote "Sweet Little Sixteen" after seeing film footage of Anka performing to a crowd of screaming girls during an Ottawa concert in 1957.

>> **September 28, 1957** *The Gisele MacKenzie Show* is first telecast on NBC-TV, showcasing MacKenzie's talents as a singer, violinist, dancer and actress.

>> **October 4, 1957** Sputnik, the first satellite, is launched by the U.S.S.R.

▲ Norman Brooks

>> **December 1957** Paul Anka sets out on a tour of Europe, including dates in the U.K., at the Trocadero Theatre in London and an appearance on the TV show *Saturday Night at the Palladium*.

>> **1957** Gordon Lightfoot plays drums in a number of jazz bands before moving from Toronto to Los Angeles for 14 months to take a course in contemporary jazz, orchestration and harmony at Westlake College.

>> **1957** Ronnie Hawkins is recruited into the U.S. Army.

>> **1957** *Music World*, a bi-weekly magazine billed by its publisher and managing editor Ray Sonin as

"Canada's Only Publication Devoted To Popular Music," is launched.

1957 Former gospel singer Tommy Ambrose makes his pop singing debut on the CBC-TV program *Cross Canada Hit Parade*. He is later responsible for the theme songs for Citytv in Toronto ("People City") and the Global Television Network ("A Point of View") as they sign on.

>> **1957** Windsor native Jack Scott signs with ABC/Paramount and has his first hit with "Two Timin' Woman."

>> **1957** Nimmons 'N' Nine begins an association with CBC Radio that lasts over two decades.

>> **1957** "Little Darlin'" by The Diamonds, a note-by-note copy of the song originally recorded by Maurice Williams and his group The Gladiolas, becomes one of the biggest hits of 1957. This same year, the group starts a dance craze after their single "The Stroll" becomes popular with the kids on Dick Clark's *American Bandstand*. The Stroll had originated in black communities with a record by Chuck "The King of the Stroll" Willis titled "C.C. Rider."

>> **1957** The beat movement, with poets like Allen Ginsberg in the vanguard, is given further momentum with the release of Jack Kerouac's book *On the Road*.

>> **1957** Groups formed this year include Little Caesar and the Consuls, Toronto; The Martels, Midland, ON; The Mercey Brothers, Hanover, ON; The Rebels/The Revols, Stratford, ON.

>> 1958

February 14, 1958 Iran bans rock'n'roll.

>> **March 1958** John Krauledat (aka John Kay) arrives in Toronto from Germany. He initially attends Humberside Collegiate but because of his poor eyesight, he is sent to special eye-saving classes at Deer Park Elementary School, sponsored by the Canadian National Institute for the Blind.

>> **March 23, 1958** Elvis is inducted into the U.S. Army.

>> **May 16, 1958** Jack Scott performs "Leroy" and "My True Love" on Dick Clark's *American Bandstand*.

>> **July 1958** Mercury Records produces two three-minute films for The Diamonds and The Platters performing their current releases and makes them available free to a list of 200 TV personalities with afternoon teenage programs. Film (and

later video) as a music marketing tool has arrived.

>> **August 29, 1958** Michael Jackson is born in Gary, Indiana.

>> **August 1958** Vancouver radio station CKWX begins issuing The Sensational Sixty, a weekly hit parade chart that reflects local tastes in pop music often influenced by local deejays like Red Robinson and Dave "Big Daddy" McCormick.

>> **September 1, 1958** Mart Kenney and His Western Gentlemen undertake a tour of 66 communities throughout British Columbia to celebrate the province's Centennial.

>> **September 1958** Paul Anka sets out on a tour of the Orient. Back in New York, Buddy Holly is recording Anka's "It Doesn't Matter Anymore" at the Pythian Temple Studios.

>> **October 4, 1958** BOAC inaugurates the first transatlantic passenger jet (as opposed to propeller) service between London and New York.

>> **1958** Harold Jenkins (aka Conway Twitty) writes his career-launching pop hit, "It's Only Make Believe," with his drummer Jack Nance while performing at the Flamingo Lounge (the site of Hamilton Place today) and staying at the Fischer Hotel in Hamilton, Ontario.

>> **1958** As part of Centennial celebrations in British Columbia, work begins on the construction of the Queen Elizabeth Theatre and the Vancouver International Festival premiers.

>> **1958** Springhill mining disaster in Nova Scotia.

>> **1958** Ronnie Hawkins forsakes the Memphis club circuit to make his first foray into Canada with his band The Hawks, which at this point consists of drummer Levon Helm, pianist Willard "Pop" Jones, bassist Jimmy "Lefty" Evans and guitarist Jimmy Ray Paulman. They play their first gig in Canada at the Golden Rail Tavern in Hamilton. During this period a version of Hawkins' group known as The Ron Hawkins Quartet records the single "Hey Bo Diddley" in a Hamilton garage studio.

>> **1958** Paul Anka tours Hawaii and Australia with Buddy Holly and Jerry Lee Lewis before making his movie debut in the film *Let's Rock* (also known as *Keep It Cool*).

>> **1958** Following a stint with country group The Sensational Stripes, Ian Tyson moves to Toronto from

1950-1959

Vancouver and gravitates towards the local folk scene.

>> **1958** Lucille Starr and Bob Regan form the group The Canadian Sweethearts in Vancouver.

>> **1958** Torontonian Fred Steiner moves west to Vancouver and opens the first of his A&B Sound record stores.

>> **1958** Raffi, who will become an internationally recognized kids entertainer, is a child himself as he moves to Toronto with his family from Cairo, Egypt.

▲ Little Caesar and the Consuls with Robbie Robertson

>> **1958** Following a stint as host of his own CBC TV variety show, Winnipeg-born songwriter, musician Jackie Rae, who spent the war years in England flying Spitfires subsequently earning the Distinguished Flying Cross, returns to old blighty where he becomes a music variety regular on British TV and records for the Philips/Fontana label. Such is his fame that in 1961 he gives a Royal Command Performance at London's Victoria Palace. He returns to Toronto in 1976 and in 1981 forms The Spitfire Band, a dance band with which he tours over the next few decades.

>> **1958** Dick Nolan, dubbed "The Johnny Cash of Newfoundland," moves to Toronto and begins playing at clubs like the Horseshoe Tavern with his group the Blue Valley Boys.

>> **1958** Arc Records is formed in Toronto by Phil Anderson and Bill Gilliland.

>> **1958** The Board of Broadcast Governors is created to regulate Canadian radio.

>> **1958** The hula hoop craze is brief but profitable as millions of the 30-inch hoops are sold.

>> **1958** Stereophonic long-playing discs and compatible stereos to play them on become the new state-of-the-art for music lovers.

>> **1958** Drive-in theatres continue to be hugely popular with the movie-going public.

>> **1958** Groups formed include The Beau-Marks, Montréal; The Canadian Sweethearts, Vancouver.

>> 1959

>> **January 1959** The Buddy Holly single "It Doesn't Matter Anymore," written by Paul Anka, is released.

>> **February 3, 1959** The Day the Music Died. Buddy Holly, Ritchie Valens and the Big Bopper are killed in a charter plane crash near Clear Lake, Iowa.

>> **February 6, 1959** Fidel Castro becomes the ruler of Cuba.

>> **Early 1959** Richard Manuel joins Stratford, Ontario-based group The Rebels (later The Revols), which also features guitarist John Till.

>> **March 1959** Paul Anka appears in the film *Girl's Town* — later retitled *The Innocent and the Damned* — with Mamie Van Doren, in which he sings "Ave Maria" and "Lonely Boy."

>> **April 13, 1959** Ronnie Hawkins records the songs "Forty Days" and "Ruby Baby" at the Bell Sound studios in New York.

>> **May 4, 1959** The first Grammy Awards are presented by the National Academy of Recording Arts and Sciences during a formal banquet in the Grand Ballroom of the Beverly Hilton Hotel in Hollywood.

>> **May 20, 1959** Glenn Gould makes his London, England debut with the London Symphony.

>> **May 1959** Jacques Blanchet, Hervé Brousseau, Clémence Desrochers, Jean-Pierre Ferland, Claude Léveillée, who is at the time working with Edith Piaf in Paris, and Raymond Lévesque, collectively known as The Bozos (from the Felix Leclerc song "Bozo"), herald the upcoming decade of the chansonnier in Québec as they join together to open a boite à chansons on Montréal's Crescent Street called Chez Bozo, where they regularly perform.

>> **June 5, 1959** The last regular broadcast of *The Happy Gang* on CBC Radio.

>> **June 8, 1959** Ronnie Hawkins' single "Forty Days" debuts on the U.S. chart. It peaks at number 45.

>> **Summer 1959** Paul Anka works with actress Mamie Van Doren on the film *The Private Lives of Adam and Eve*. His hectic touring schedule, which continues through the year, includes stops in Japan, North Africa, Sweden and the U.S. He also becomes the first North American pop singer to perform behind the Iron Curtain. During his European tour, he breaks the existing attendance record at the Olympia in Paris drawing 107,843 people over the course of his five-week stand.

>> **July 4, 1959** The Rhythm Pals move to Toronto where they become regular guests on the CBC TV series *Swing Time,* which debuts on this date. They will soon become regulars on *The Tommy Hunter Show* on both CBC-TV and radio. It is an association that lasts until 1977.

>> **July 5, 1959** The Queen Elizabeth Theatre opens in Vancouver.

>> **August 7, 1959** *The Don Messer Show* begins broadcasting on CBC-TV. It becomes *Don Messer's Jubilee* that fall and runs for a decade on the CBC and in syndication from CHCH-TV in Hamilton, Ontario until Messer's death in 1973.

>> **August 17, 1959** Ronnie Hawkins and the Hawks perform "Forty Days" and "Mary Lou" on *American Bandstand* and a couple of weeks later appear on Alan Freed's huge Labor Day show at the Brooklyn Fox Theater in New York. Morris Levy's Roulette Records releases his self-titled album in mid-September. On this date, his single "Mary Lou" debuts on the U.S. chart. It reaches number 26.

>> **August 21, 1959** Hawaii becomes the 50th state.

>> **August 1959** Paul Anka debuts at the Sahara Hotel in Las Vegas.

>> **September 12, 1959** *Bonanza*, the first Western series to be televised in colour, debuts on NBC-TV, where it runs for an unprecedented 14 seasons. It stars former CBC news reader Lorne Greene as patriarch Ben Cartwright.

>> **October 1959** Ronnie Hawkins & the Hawks, which now includes Fred Carter Jr. on guitar, spend most of the month in Toronto playing Le Coq d'Or and the Concord Tavern. Guitarist Robbie Robertson begins hanging out with the group. Robertson had been in groups like Little Caesar and the Consuls, The Rhythm Chords, Robbie & the Robots and Thumper & the Trambones, which included pianist Scott Cushnie; Peter Derimigis; Gene MacLellan, whose compositions "Snowbird" and "Put Your Hand In the Hand" would become major international hits for Anne Murray and Ocean, respectively; and Pete Traynor, who would later develop his own line of sound equipment. The group played dances hosted by Dave Johnson of Toronto radio station CHUM at Merton Hall. One of Ronnie Hawkins' roadies for a short time during this period is Peter Pocklington, later the owner of the Edmonton Oilers hockey franchise.

>> **October 26, 1959** Ronnie Hawkins cuts two of Robbie Robertson's songs, "Hey Baba Lou" and "Someone Like You" as part of his album session for *Mr. Dynamo.*

>> **October 1959** Operatic soprano Teresa Stratas debuts with New York's Metropolitan Opera.

>> **December 5, 1959** Isy and Richard "Ritchie" Walters, who had owned The Cave club in Vancouver from 1952 — 1959, build Isy's Supper Club in the same city.

>> **1959** Singer Norman Brooks begins a 44-week residency at The Sands Hotel, Las Vegas.

>> **1959** Young singer Bobby Curtola teams up with songwriters Dyer and Basil Hurdon in his hometown of Port Arthur (now Thunder Bay), Ontario and has his first single "Hand In Hand With You" released on the Hurdons' label, Tartan Records. They will continue to write his song material throughout his early-'60s career as a teen idol.

>> **1959** Gordon Lightfoot returns home from L.A. and initially works for his dad in Orillia before heading for Toronto to actively pursue his music career. To keep himself alive, he works as a music copyist, truck driver, drummer in a revue, an office worker, a member of the chorus, singing and dancing on the CBC-TV show *Country Hoedown*, and a vocalist with the Gino Silvi Singers.

>> **1959** In Toronto, Ian Tyson meets, and begins singing with, Sylvia Fricker, who had recently moved to Toronto from Chatham, Ontario and was performing in Yorkville Village.

>> **1959** Motown Records is founded in Detroit by Berry Gordy, Jr.

>> **1959** In Toronto, German immigrant Werner Graeber opens Yorkville Village's first coffee house, Club 71.

>> **1959** The St. Lawrence Seaway opens.

>> **1959** Groups formed this year include: Ian & Sylvia, Toronto.

CHART-TOPPING CANADIAN SONGS 1950-1959

1950 The Third Man Theme **GUY LOMBARDO & HIS ROYAL CANADIANS**
1950 I'm Movin' On **HANK SNOW & THE RAINBOW RANCH BOYS**
1954 I Don't Hurt Anymore **HANK SNOW & THE RAINBOW RANCH BOYS**

1957 Diana **PAUL ANKA**
1959 Lonely Boy **PAUL ANKA**

OH WHAT A FEELING

Four strong winds that blow lonely
Seven seas that run high,
All those things that don't change, come what may ...
but our good times are all gone
And I'm bound for moving on,
I'll look for you if I'm ever back this way...

— Four Strong Winds

Lyrics & Music by Ian Tyson.
Performed by Ian & Sylvia.

»1960–1969

》 1960

》 February 1960 During his high school days in Port Arthur (Thunder Bay), Ontario, Bobby Curtola meets local songwriters Dyer and Basil Hurdon. He subsequently records one of their songs, "Hand In Hand With You," at a local radio station and the Hurdons make the rounds of the major record companies in Toronto. When they receive rejections from all of them, they open their own Tartan Records label and release the single themselves this month. Within a year, Curtola becomes one of Canada's earliest teen idols. He tours exclusively across the country causing hysteria among his youthful audiences. The Hurdons write all of Curtola's subsequent hits, including "Fortune Teller" (1962), "Aladdin" (1962), "Hitchhiker" (1962) and "Three Rows Over" (1963). Early in his career, Curtola is involved promotionally with Coca-Cola and is one of the first artists to record a jingle that sounds more like a song than a product plug. He also pioneers playing shopping malls across the country, a career-boosting strategy that is also used successfully almost 30 years later by teen favourite, Tiffany.

》 February 1, 1960 The Four Lads sing with Toronto's St. Michael's Boys Choir on a national CBC-TV show.

》 February 22, 1960 Percy Faith tops the Billboard Top 100 chart with the Max Steiner composition "Theme From A Summer Place." The song, which becomes the most successful instrumental single of the rock era and is Billboard's number one single of 1960, holds down the penthouse position for nine weeks. It also wins a Grammy Award as Record of the Year. Through the '60s, Faith stays active in the movie business, scoring films like *Tammy Tell Me True* (1961), *I'd Rather Be Rich* (1964), *The Love Goddesses* (1964), *The Third Day* (1965) and *The Oscar* (1966). He wins another Grammy Award in 1969 in the category of Best Contemporary Performance By A Chorus for his record, "Love Theme From Romeo and Juliet."

▲ Bobby Curtola

》 March 2, 1960 Jack Scott performs "What In the World's Come Over You" and "Burning Bridges" on the *American Bandstand* TV show.

》 March 5, 1960 Elvis is discharged from the army.

》 June 26, 1960 "Shakin' All Over," the song that would later launch The Guess Who's career, enters the U.K. charts as a single for Johnny Kidd and the Pirates.

》 July 6, 1960 Paul Anka's performance at the Copacabana in New York, one of three sold-out shows, is recorded and later released as *Anka At the Copa*. He was the youngest star ever to appear at the venue.

》 October 1, 1960 Robert Goulet is warmly received in the role of Lancelot starring opposite Richard Burton and Julie Andrews as the Lerner and Lowe musical *Camelot* premieres at the newly-opened O'Keefe Centre for the Performing Arts in Toronto.

》 August 6, 1960 Vancouver's Les Vogt has his single "The Blamers" knock Elvis out of the top spot on the CFUN chart in his hometown.

》 December 1, 1960 *Camelot* has its New York premiere. It becomes the first of Robert Goulet's many Broadway appearances. He becomes a regular on the

▲ Robert Goulet

Ed Sullivan Show and the exposure to an international audience and his subsequent popularity led to a contract with Columbia Records.

>> **1960** Paul Anka writes the title songs for, and stars in, the film *Look In Any Window,* while his hit tune "Lonely Boy" becomes the basis of an award-winning documentary film on his life by Canada's National Film Board. He tours South America and makes his Broadway acting debut in *What Makes Sammy Run?* "Puppy Love,' the song documenting his crush on Disney star and Mouseketeer Annette Funicello, reaches the number two position on the charts. A collector's item from this period is the song "She's Our Pet, Annette," which Anka recorded with his brother and some kids in the neighbourhood.

>> **1960** Al Steiner opens Club Bluenote on Toronto's Yonge Street. It will become one of the major centres for R&B and soul music in the city and the jumping off point for a number of top Canadian artists of the day in the genre, including Shawn Jackson, Jay Jackson, Eddie Spencer, Shirley Matthews, Jackie Shane and The Mandala, among others.

>> **1960** Gordon Lightfoot becomes a folk music devotee after hearing *The Weavers At Carnegie Hall* album and is encouraged by Ian Tyson (Ian & Sylvia) to continue to pursue it as a singer and songwriter. Bob Gibson is also a major influence on Lightfoot at the time. A local music industry believer during this period is Art Snider, the owner of Toronto's Sound Canada studio and its affiliated Chateau record label.

>> **1960** Singer Norman Brooks plays himself in the Frank Sinatra/"Rat Pack" film, *Ocean's Eleven.* He is seen on stage with his sister, nightclub singer Annie Brooks, singing "I'm Gonna Live Til I Die." Brooks, who is the first Québec-born entertainer to play Las Vegas, sold out The Sands Hotel and Casino, where some of this movie was shot, for 44 weeks in 1959.

>> **1960** Singer/songwriter David Wiffen gets his first big career boost singing at Toronto's Village Corner Club with Ian & Sylvia.

>> **1960** Neil Young plays guitar in the Winnipeg group, The Jades.

>> **1960** Hamilton, Ontario-born guitarist Sonny Greenwich begins his jazz career in Toronto clubs like The Cellar, the First Floor Club and the Bohemian Embassy.

>> **1960** *The Tommy Hunter Show* debuts on CBC Radio.

>> **1960** Les Vogt and the Prowlers have the first number-one hit in Vancouver with "The Blamers," which spends 11 weeks at the top of the CFUN radio chart.

>> **1960** Anne Murray gets serious about her singing career as she makes regular trips to Tatamagouche, Nova Scotia from

▲ Oscar Peterson

her hometown of Springhill to take voice lessons with Karen Mills.

>> **1960** Oscar Peterson, Ray Brown, Ed Thigpen and Phil Nimmons open the Advanced School of Contemporary Music in Toronto.

>> **1960** Thunder Bay Symphony Orchestra is founded.

>> **1960** Groups formed this year include The Jades, Winnipeg.

>> 1961

>> **August 18, 1961** The annual Mariposa folk festival, founded by Ruth Jones, Dr. Crawford Jones and Pete McGarvey, is held for the first time at Oval Park in Orillia, Ontario, featuring Ian & Sylvia, The Travellers, Jean Carignan, O.J. Abbott, Alan Mills and Jacques Labrecque.

>> **Labour Day 1961** Record retailer Sam Sniderman opens the flagship Sam the Record Man store at 347 Yonge Street in the heart of downtown Toronto.

>> **October 1, 1961** The CTV Television Network is launched in Canada.

>> **October 2, 1961** The first *Tonight Show* with Johnny Carson is broadcast on NBC-TV. The jazzy theme music, which becomes synonymous with the show over the years, is written by Paul Anka.

>> **Winter 1961** Keyboardist Garth Hudson joins Ronnie Hawkins' group The Hawks, completing the new lineup that now includes Robbie Robertson, Levon Helm, Rick Danko and Richard Manuel.

>> **1961** Medicare is introduced in Canada.

>> **1961** Toronto folk singer/songwriter Bonnie Dobson writes "(Walk Me Out to the) Morning Dew" in Los Angeles while on tour. The song, though initially recorded in the mid-'60s by folksingers Fred Neil and Tim Rose, who adds his own verse, becomes a rock and pop staple recorded by Jeff Beck Group with Rod Stewart, the Grateful Dead, Nazareth,

Long John Baldry, Devo, Dave Edmunds, the Chieftains and Lulu, whose version hits the pop charts in 1968.

>> **1961** The Two Tones, an act formed by Gordon Lightfoot and Terry Whelan, begin playing the coffee house circuit. Over the next three years, they record three albums together, including their *Two Tones: Live at the Village Corner* (1962).

>> **1961** John Kay lands a part-time job selling peanuts and popcorn at Toronto's Maple Leaf Garden.

▲ Richie Knight and the Mid-Knights

>> **1961** In Toronto, Ian Tyson and Sylvia Fricker form the folk duo Ian & Sylvia and subsequently sign to the prestigious Vanguard Records label in the U.S. While working in New York, Ian Tyson writes his folk classic "Four Strong Winds" at the office of his manager Albert Grossman after hearing Bob Dylan's "Blowing In the Wind" and joking that anything Dylan could do, he could do better. Ian & Sylvia record the song as the title track of their second album, while Bobby Bare makes it a hit in 1964. Neil Young covers the song in 1979.

>> **1961** Singer/TV personality Dorothy Collins joins the cast of popular TV show, *Candid Camera* in the U.S.

>> **1961** *Singalong Jubilee* debuts locally on CBC-TV Halifax.

>> **1961** Soprano Teresa Stratas makes her Covent Garden, London debut.

>> **1961** Yugoslavian-born Boris Zerafa, who, along with fellow countryman Richard Wookey and the Dreyfuss family of Paris, will own close to a quarter of Yorkville Village in Toronto, first becomes involved in the area which will briefly become the centre of the folk and rock music scene in Canada before becoming the "Rodeo Drive of Canada."

>> **April 6, 1962** Prior to a Glenn Gould performance of Brahms' "D Minor Concerto" with the New York Philharmonic, conductor Leonard Bernstein disassociates himself with the "unorthodox performance" of the work.

>> 1962

>> **May 18, 1962** American jazz and blues man Clarence "Big" Miller makes his first Canadian appearance in Toronto with Don Thompson at Club Kingsway. In the '70s, Miller moves to Edmonton, Alberta where he would live for the rest of his life.

>> **June 20, 1962** Bobby Curtola performs "Fortune Teller" on *American Bandstand.*

>> **August 4, 1962** Armstrong, British Columbia native Shirley Field, once known as Canada's top female yodeler, appears on the *Grand Ole Opry* in Nashville.

>> **August 8, 1962** *Arnold Schonberg: The Man and His Music,* a CBC radio documentary on Schonberg's life and works, written and narrated by Glenn Gould, marks the Toronto pianist's debut as a producer of radio documentaries.

>> **August 21, 1962** Robert Goulet performs "What Kind of Fool Am I?" on *American Bandstand.*

>> **September 29, 1962** "Alouette," the first Canadian satellite is launched into orbit.

>> **October 31, 1962** Joni Mitchell's first paying gig as a singer is at the Louis Riel folk club in Saskatoon, Saskatchewan, where she also worked and first came into contact with artists like Bonnie Dobson and Joe and Eddie, who often appeared there.

>> **1962** Marshall McLuhan's *The Medium is the Message* is published.

>> **1962** Paul Anka has a small acting role in the Daryl Zanuck film, *The Longest Day,* for which he has written the soundtrack.

>> **1962** Andy Kim makes the trip from Montreal to New York with his brother Joe to make the rounds of record companies without any demo tapes or even the ability to play guitar. He ends up quitting school and moving there spending the next four and a half years selling lawn mowers and flogging candy floss at amusement parks to survive. During a brief trip back to Montreal, he even works at the Eaton department store in the hardware department selling hammers and nails.

>> **1962** Vancouver's Little Daddy and the Bachelors, featuring guitarist Tommy Chong, release the single "Too Much Monkey Business." The group later changes its name to Four Niggers and a Chink and then Bobby Taylor and the Vancouvers. Chong will become one half of the comedy duo Cheech & Chong.

» 1962 Gordon Lightfoot's first single "Remember Me (I'm the One Who Loves You)," which was recorded in Nashville, is released. Lightfoot actually made his first record for a social function while in grade four in his hometown of Orillia, Ontario. The record is broadcast to the school.

» 1962 Pierre Lalonde becomes a mainstay on TV in Québec as he hosts a number of variety shows, including the popular teen program, *Jeunesse d'Aujourd'hui* (later *Jeunesse*). He begins recording in the mid-'60s and in 1967, under the name Peter Martin, and he hosts a one-hour TV variety show in New York.

» 1962 Neil Young becomes the guitarist in the Winnipeg group, The Squires.

» 1962 Lucille Starr is heard on the popular TV series *The Beverly Hillbillies* yodelling for the character Cousin Pearl Bodine (Bea Benaderet).

» 1962 The Travellers live up to their name as they make an excursion to the U.S.S.R. with their show A Musical Tour of Canada.

» 1962 Robert Goulet receives a Grammy Award as Best New Artist in the wake of his first major hit, "What Kind Of Fool Am I?"

» 1962 Soprano Teresa Stratas debuts at La Scala in Milan, Italy.

» 1962 The Montréal Symphony Orchestra embarks on a European tour, the first by a Canadian orchestra.

» 1962 The Canadian Talent Library (CTL) is founded by broadcast executive J. Lyman Potts and the Standard Broadcasting Corporation-owned radio stations CFRB Toronto and CJAD Montréal.

» 1962 A&M Records is formed in Los Angeles by trumpet player Herb Alpert and producer Jerry Moss.

» 1962 Groups formed this year include The Esquires, Ottawa; The Night Train Revue, Vancouver.

» 1963

» February 16, 1963 Paul Anka marries former model Marie-Ann DeZogheb in Paris. They will have four daughters together — Alexandra, Amanda, Alicia and Anthea.

» February 18, 1963 The Beatles' single "Love Me Do" is released in Canada and sells a mere 171 copies according to Capitol Canada label executive, Paul White, who was an early champion of the group.

» April 1, 1963 Folk duo Malka and Joso debut at Toronto's Lord Simcoe Hotel. Joso Spralja had arrived in Canada in 1961 and begun performing at Club 71 in Toronto's Yorkville Village. It is here that he meets Malka Himel. They subsequently form a duo and begin appearing at the Inn On the Parking Lot coffee house as well as at clubs in Yorkville.

» April 1963 The Canadian Record Manufacturer's Association (CRMA), the forerunner to the Canadian Recording Industry Association (CRIA) and current-day Music Canada, is founded by ten participating companies.

» June 1963 John Kay graduates from Humberside Collegiate in Toronto.

» July 1963 "Charlena," recorded by Toronto group Ritchie Knight and the Mid-Knights, becomes the first single recorded in Canada to reach number one on the influential chart published by radio station CHUM in Toronto. Band alumni include record executive (A&M, Virgin, Mercury/Polydor) Doug Chappell and respected producer/recording engineer George Semkiw.

» Summer 1963 Gordon Lightfoot, now married, moves to England and hosts the BBC-TV summer replacement program, the *Country and Western Show.*

▲ Gordon Lightfoot

» **November 22, 1963** U.S. President John F. Kennedy is assassinated in Dallas, Texas.

» **Late 1963** Ronnie Hawkins' backing group The Hawks jump ship and set out on their own, first as the Levon Helm Sextet and then as Levon and the Hawks.

» **Late 1963** Singer/songwriter Les Emmerson joins the Staccatos at a time when the group is a regular fixture at La Chaudière Club in Hull, Québec across the river from Ottawa.

» **December 1963** The Toronto Symphony Orchestra, under the baton of Walter Susskind, makes its first appearance at New York's Carnegie Hall.

» **August 1963** Robert Goulet marries actress, singer Carol Lawrence and moves to Los Angeles from New York.

» **August 1963** Philips introduces a prototype of the Compact Cassette and cassette player at the Berlin Radio Show.

» **September 21, 1963** Wilfrid Pelletier and Zubin Mehta share the conducting duties with the Montréal Symphony Orchestra in the inaugural concert at the newly-opened Place des Arts in Montréal. The MSO subsequently moves from the Plateau Hall Auditorium to the Grande Salle of the Place des Arts, which is renamed Salle Wilfrid Pelletier in 1966.

» **Fall 1963** Joan Anderson (later Joni Mitchell) enrols in an art course at the Southern Alberta Institute of Technology in Calgary. Though she excels as an artist, music is still a powerful force in her life and she regularly plays The Depression folk club in that city, singing and playing ukulele.

» **Fall 1963** *Let's Sing Out*, a half-hour folk music series, is launched on CTV with Winnipeg-native Oscar Brand as host. The show originates from Canadian university and college campuses, featuring top folk acts from Canada and the U.S. One of the first guests is Gordon Lightfoot just returned from his sabbatical in England.

» **Labour Day Weekend 1963** J.B. and the Playboys formed in Montréal by Allan Nicholls and Bill Hill.

» **October 3, 1963** Gisele MacKenzie plays the part of comedian Sid Caesar's wife in the ABC-TV comedy/variety series, *The Sid Caesar Show*.

» **December 31, 1963** One of Gordon Lightfoot's earliest live performance breaks comes with a New Year's Eve appearance with actor/singer Brock Peters at the Purple Onion in Toronto. He is subsequently brought back as headliner and is soon playing the club circuit in Canada and the U.S. that includes venues like Toronto's Fifth Peg, The Village Corner, New Gates of Cleve, Steele's Tavern and The Riverboat, Ottawa's L'Hibou and the Livin' End in Detroit. He performs solo and with artists like Ian & Sylvia, Bonnie Dobson and The Halifax Three.

» **1963** The Halifax Three, featuring Denny Doherty and Zal Yanovsky, record the album *San Francisco Bay Blues*. After leaving the group, Doherty ends up in New York where he works with a group called The Big Three, which also features Cass Elliot and Tim Rose.

» **1963** Drummer Skip Prokop is a winner at the 1963-64 National Individual Rudimental Drumming Championship.

» **1963** Ian & Sylvia appear at the Newport Folk Festival for the first time.

» **1963** Singer, songwriter Stan Rogers first begins performing at the Ebony Knight coffee house in Hamilton, Ontario.

» **1963** *After Four*, CTV's national teen program hosted by Carol Goss and Johnny Bassett (later featuring a house band, The Big Town Boys), airs for the first time with the object of finding, promoting and showcasing new Canadian talent.

>> **1963** Montréal musician, composer Galt MacDermot heads for New York to try his luck as a studio musician. He subsequently becomes a member of various local R&B groups.

>> **1963** Kate and Anna McGarrigle begin playing Montreal coffee houses as members of the Mountain City Four.

>> **1963** Actor/singer Don Francks releases his album, *Jackie Gleason Says No One In This World Is Like Don Francks.*

>> **1963** Oscar Peterson's "Canadian Suite" has its debut.

>> **1963** Vancouver's Tom Northcott, who had previously sung for guests at a British Columbia ranch where he worked in the summer, plays his first professional gig at the Inquisition Coffee House in his home town.

>> **1963** Country singer, songwriter Gary Buck hits the international charts with the song "Happy To Be Unhappy." That same year, the American music trade magazine *Cashbox* hails him as Newcomer of the Year.

>> **1963** Scopatones are introduced with about a thousand made for jukeboxes in pre-video days.

>> **1963** Groups formed this year include Bobby Kris and the Imperials, Toronto; Bobby Taylor and the Vancouvers, Vancouver; Carlton Showband, Brampton, ON; Mountain City Four, Montréal; The Irish Rovers, Toronto/Calgary; J.B. and the Playboys, Montréal; The Squires, Winnipeg; The Staccatos, Ottawa.

>> 1964

>> **February 9, 1964** The Beatles appear for the first time on the *Ed Sullivan Show.* That evening at Cass Elliot's house, John Sebastian meets Zal Yanovsky for the first time. They watch the show and then play some music together for a few hours. At Elliot's urging, both Sebastian and Yanovsky become members of the Mugwumps, a group which also features Elliot, James Hendricks and Denny Doherty. The group is short-lived, and Yanovsky and Sebastian head for New York, where they form The Lovin' Spoonful. Doherty becomes Marshall Brickman's replacement in John and Michelle Phillips' group, The New Journeymen.

>> **February 24, 1964** The first issue of the Canadian trade magazine *RPM Weekly* is published by former RCMP officer/Toronto cop Walt Grealis with associate Stan Klees.

▲ Stan Rogers

>> **April 10, 1964** Glenn Gould plays his last concert date in Los Angeles. He subsequently ends his career as a concert artist.

>> **May 18, 1964** *RPM Weekly* announces the establishment of a music awards program in Canada like the Grammy Awards in the U.S.

>> **June 15, 1964** Joey Dee (Joseph DiNicola), who had a number one hit in January of 1962 with "Peppermint Twist – Part 1," opens his own club in New York called The Starliter. His band at the time consists of Ottawa-born guitarist Gene Cornish, Felix Cavaliere and Eddie Brigati, who would later become The Young Rascals. Levon and the Hawks begin a two-week engagement at the Peppermint Lounge on this date. They soon get the boot for playing electric blues in a twist club. The gig is memorable in that they are reunited with old friend John Hammond Jr., with whom they later tour and record *So Many Roads* (1965).

>> **Summer 1964** John Kay and friend Klaus Schultz drive to Los Angeles from Buffalo. By the end of the year, Kay and his family had moved to Santa Monica. Kay initially begins working at a West Los Angeles folk club called The New Balladeer and at The Troubadour as a dishwasher. It is here that he hears Hoyt Axton perform "The Pusher" for the first time, a song that would become a show-stopper for Kay's group, Steppenwolf.

>> **Summer 1964** With the success of her single "The French Song (Quand le soleil dit bonjours aux montagnes)," St. Boniface, Manitoba-native Lucille Starr becomes the first Canadian female vocalist to have a million seller. Herb Alpert and the Tijuana Brass back her on both the single and the subsequent album.

>> **July 17, 1964** The CBC-TV national music show *Music Hop*, one of the most influential shows of the era for the exposure of up-and-coming Canadian artists, debuts. A year later it expands to five times a week, originating from five different Canadian cities. On Mondays, the show broadcasts from Vancouver with hosts Fred Latremouille and Red Robinson with Randi Conlin, who presents teen fashion. Susan Jacks is a regular on the show. Tuesday, the spotlight moves to Montréal, where the show, known there as *Jeunesse Oblige* and hosted by Jean-Pierre Ferland, features many of the city's French and English-speaking vocalists. On Wednesday, the show travels to Winnipeg, where initially Ray St. Germain is host with music supplied

by an instrumental trio with Lenny Breau on guitar and a seven-piece vocal group. The show spotlights the folks songs and histories of each Canadian province. In Winnipeg, the program would later become the TV home of local group, The Guess Who. Thursdays, *Music Hop* moves east to Toronto where regulars include Alex Trebek (later the host of the game show *Jeopardy*), The Girlfriends (Rhonda Silver, Stephanie Taylor and Diane Miller), Shawne Jackson and Norm Amadio and His Rhythm Rockers. On Fridays, Halifax hosts a dance party (*Frank's Bandstand*), featuring vocalists Patricia MacKinnon, Karen Oxley and D.J. Jefferson. Anne Murray would later make frequent guest appearances on the show.

>> **August 22, 1964** The Beatles appear at Vancouver's Empire Stadium.

>> **September 7, 1964** The Beatles appear at Toronto's Maple Leaf Gardens.

>> **October 1964** The Riverboat club is opened at 134 Yorkville Avenue by former coffee salesman Bernie Fiedler.

>> **Late 1964** "So Many Other Boys" becomes the biggest hit for Ottawa band The Esquires, one of Canada's first noteworthy pop groups of the early '60s. Through numerous personnel changes, the one bridging member is drummer Richard Patterson, who even after the band's dissolution around 1967, becomes a fixture on the music scene in the nation's capital.

>> **November 1964** The boite à chansons La Patriote is opened in Montréal by Yves Blais and Percival Broomfield. The club, which features local singers/songwriters seven days a week, is responsible for discovering and introducing a number of major Québecois artists.

>> **December 1964** Quality Records releases the single "Shakin' All Over" by a group from Winnipeg which had previously been known as Chad Allan and the Expressions. But as the record emerges, the label is white and there's a question mark where the artist's name should have been. As a promotion, and in part an attempt to circumvent negative reaction from the Canadian radio programmers of the day given the fact that the group was Canadian, the record company asks people in the industry to guess who the artist actually is. It isn't long before the group is being referred to as The Guess Who... and the name stuck. By the early spring of 1965, "Shakin' All Over" had topped the charts in Canada and eventually peaked at number 22 in the U.S.

>> **December 5, 1964** Lorne Greene, the former CBC newscaster who went on to find TV immortality in the role of Ben Cartwright in the NBC series *Bonanza*, hits number one on the Billboard Top 100 chart with the single, "Ringo." At the height of *Bonanza*'s popularity on TV, RCA Records released a Christmas album featuring the cast of the show. It was successful enough to sign Greene to

a recording contract. When a second *Bonanza* cast album, *Welcome to the Ponderosa*, was recorded, Greene was asked to read a six-verse poem about the story of a sheriff who saved the life of Johnny Ringo. When the album was released, a radio deejay in Lubbock Texas played the track titled "Ringo." The phones lit up and RCA eventually released it as a single. Greene first heard of this development when he was in Prince Edward Island acting as emcee for a ceremony attended by Queen Elizabeth II. Following the success of "Ringo," Greene recorded seven albums for RCA over the next three years.

>> **1964** Irish/Canadian group The Carlton Showband form in Toronto and later have success with their 1966 record "The Merry Ploughboy" aka "The Green On the Green." They subsequently became the home band for a decade (1967-1977) for CTV Toronto's *Pig and Whistle* TV variety show.

>> **1964** Will Millar puts together the Irish/Canadian group The Irish Rovers while singing at tables at Phil's Pancake House in Calgary, Alberta.

>> **1964** Singer Norman Brooks plays Brand in the Tony Orlando film, *The Block*.

>> **1964** Stompin' Tom Connors makes his professional debut in Timmins, Ontario, where he is a regular at the Maple Leaf Hotel and on local radio station CKGB. He gets the "Stompin'" moniker from the way he kept rhythm on a piece of well-worn plywood with his cowboy boot.

>> **1964** Anne Murray meets her future husband Bill Langstroth as she auditions for *Singalong Jubilee*, a CBC-TV summer show on which he is associate producer and co-host. She accompanies herself on a baritone ukulele and leads the others in singing "Mary Don't You Weep." She wasn't hired initially because they already had enough alto singers in the chorus. Brian Ahern, musical director for the TV show, also meets Murray for the first time during the audition. He would produce her first ten albums.

>> **1964** Joan Anderson (aka Joni Mitchell) visits Toronto for the first time to see the Mariposa Folk Festival, which features an appearance by Buffy Sainte-Marie. Though intending to return to college in Calgary, she stays when she finds work in Toronto at a Yorkville club called The Penny Farthing, an early showcase venue for artists like Neil Young,

RIVERBOAT
COFFEE HOUSE
EVERY NIGHT
134 YORKVILLE AVE. 922-6216
8 p.m - 3 a.m.

The Riverboat re-opens Jan. 6 with an important new composer and folksinger that everyone is talking about...

Maurey Haydn

JAN. 14-26 **BUDDY GUY**
CHICAGO BLUES BAND
Brilliant guitarist, outstanding blues vocalist

JAN. 28-FEB. 2 **MIKE SEEGER**

FEB. 4-9 **NEIL YOUNG**
former lead guitarist, singer, composer with
THE BUFFALO SPRINGFIELD

FEB. 11-16 **DOC WATSON**

FEB. 18-23 **JOHN HAMMOND**
His voice is a supple multi-coloured instrument capturing the tension, rhythmic drive and emotional anguish of the deep blues...
Robert Shelton, New York Times

SPIDER JOHN KOERNER
FEB. 25 — MARCH 2

JERRY JEFF WALKER
MARCH 4-9
His single and album Mr. BOJANGLES

Lenny Breau
master guitarist jams the Riverboat every time.

The Irish Rovers and Jose Feliciano.

>> **1964** Ian (Tyson) & Sylvia (Fricker) make the partnership official as they take the marital plunge.

>> **1964** Ian & Sylvia become the first act to record a Gordon Lightfoot song. "Early Morning Rain" becomes the title track of their third album the following year. After seeing him perform at Steele's Tavern in Toronto, Ian & Sylva are also the catalyst for Lightfoot's signing with influential manager Albert Grossman and his subsequent association with producer John Court. Grossman places his songs "For Lovin' Me" and "Early Morning Rain" with Peter, Paul & Mary. Lightfoot makes his Mariposa Folk Festival debut this year.

>> **1964** Bruce Cockburn enrols in a two-year music course at the Berklee School of Music in Boston.

>> **1964** David Clayton-Thomas and the Shays tour with Dave Clark Five in Canada.

>> **1964** Vancouver native Terry Black, one of Canada's first pop stars, has some chart success with "Unless You Care," which has a "British Invasion" sound. This year, he plays Elvis Presley's brother in the film *Outside Sunshine* that is never released, signs to be in a movie with Jan & Dean that is never made and plays one of the Hardy Boys in a TV pilot. Glen Campbell plays on his early recording sessions and tours with Black in California.

>> **1964** At age 16, singer/songwriter Ann Mortifee performs publicly for the first time at Vancouver's Bunkhouse. She subsequently tours with Josh White Jr.

>> **1964** Catherine McKinnon records the song "Farewell To Nova Scotia," the official song of Nova Scotia, as the theme song for the long-running CBC-TV Halifax series, *Singalong Jubilee*. It brings contemporary popularity to a song, adapted from "The Soldier's Adieu," by Scottish poet Robert Tannahill and thought to have been written around the time of the First World War.

>> **1964** Winfield, Alberta-native Ray Griff, whose songs have already been recorded by a number of major country artists, including Jim Reeves and Johnny Horton, moves to Nashville, where he becomes a respected member of the songwriting community.

>> **1964** Bobby Curtola has the lead role in the CBC-TV play, *Charlie Love From Liverpool,* by David French.

Stompin' Tom Connors

>> **1964** Liona Boyd takes up classical guitar at age 14.

>> **1964** Vancouver-based instrumental group The Chessmen, featuring Terry Jacks on guitar, have their first single "Meadowlands/Mustang" released. Producer is Vancouver radio personality, Red Robinson.

>> **1964** Gilles Vigneault writes "Mon pays," a song which will become inextricably linked with nationalist sentiment in the province of Québec, for Arthur Lemothe`s National Film Board film *La neige a fondu sur Manicouagan*.

>> **1964** A consortium that includes Bill Lear of the Lear Jet Corporation, Ampex, Ford Motor Company, General Motors, Motorola and RCA Victor creates the 8-track stereo tape cartridge for car use.

>> **1964** Groups formed in this year include Billy ThunderKloud and the Chieftones, Edmonton; Jack London & the Sparrows, Toronto; Jon and Lee & the Checkmates, Toronto; Luke & the Apostles, Toronto; The Carlton Showband, Toronto; The Irish Rovers, Calgary; The Mynah Birds, Toronto; The Stampeders, Calgary.

>> 1965

>> **February 15, 1965** The "Canadian Ensign Flag" is officially replaced by the red maple leaf flag.

>> **February 27, 1965** Ian & Sylvia play their first Town Hall concert in New York.

>> **March 12, 1965** Joan Anderson meets her future husband Chuck Mitchell while performing at the Penny Farthing in Toronto's Yorkville Village. She becomes Joni Mitchell as they marry in Detroit a couple of days after they meet. They

become a duo and eventually head for New York, where they appear at the Gaslight Cafe in Greenwich Village. They also play the folk club circuit on the east coast of the U.S. and Canada during this period.

>> **April 13, 1965** Yorkville residents in Toronto, alarmed by the number of young people now flocking to the area, threaten a march on a downtown police station.

>> **April 23, 1965** The Rolling Stones open their third North American tour at the Maurice Richard Arena in Montréal. Canadian dates are opened by popular Montréal group J.B. and the Playboys and Toronto's Jon and Lee and the Checkmates.

>> **April 30, 1965** Bob Dylan's British tour, filmed by D.A. Pennebaker for what will become the documentary film *Don't Look Back*, begins in Sheffield.

>> **Spring 1965** Peter, Paul & Mary have a Top 30 U.S. hit with the Gordon Lightfoot song "For Lovin' Me."

>> **June 7, 1965** Sony Corporation introduces the first commercial home video tape recorder.

>> **June 1965** John Kay returns to Toronto from Los Angeles and meets a group called The Sparrows playing at the nearby Devil's Den club. He subsequently joins the group with former Mynah Birds keyboardist Goldy McJohn.

>> **Summer 1965** The Guess Who, following the release of the single "Shakin' All Over," which finds success in the U.S. and Canada, embark on a U.S. package tour with The Turtles, Eddie Hodges and The Crystals.

>> **July 3, 1965** Terry Black performs "Unless You Care" on Dick Clark's American Bandstand TV show.

>> **July 1965** Bob Dylan plays the Newport Folk Festival with Al Kooper and members of Paul Butterfield's band, including Michael Bloomfield. It is his first move into electric folk and the purists hate it.

>> **July 20, 1965** Kama Sutra records releases "Do You Believe In Magic," the debut single by The Lovin' Spoonful, formed by John Sebastian and Toronto native Zal Yanovsky.

▲ Bob Dylan and Ronnie Hawkins

>> **August 7, 1965** We Five perform the Sylvia Tyson-penned "You Were On My Mind" on Dick Clark's *American Bandstand* show.

>> **August 11, 1965** The Orford String Quartet give their first concert at their temporary home, the Jeunesse musicales of Canada Orford Art Centre in Mount Orford Provinical Park near Magog, Québec. The Quartet moves to Toronto a few months later.

>> **August 18, 1965** The Beatles play a second concert at Toronto's Maple Leaf Gardens.

>> **August 28, 1965** Mary Martin, an old friend of The Hawks from Toronto and now the assistant to Bob Dylan's manager Albert Grossman, has been trying to get the group and Dylan together as he goes electric. Her persistence pays off as, on this date, Dylan performs at the Forest Hills Tennis Stadium in Queens, New York and later at the Hollywood Bowl with a band that includes The Hawks' Robbie Robertson and Levon Helm.

>> **September 1965** The Sparrows play their first gig with their new line-up of John Kay, Goldy McJohn, Jerry and Dennis Edmonton (aka Mars Bonfire) and Nick St. Nicholas at Waterloo Lutheran University in Waterloo, Ontario.

>> **September 13, 1965** Jon and Lee and the Checkmates are among the local acts to play for 65,000 people at the opening of Toronto's new City Hall.

>> **September 16, 1965** Bob Dylan flies into Toronto for a couple of days to see Levon and the Hawks at Friars Tavern and to spend after hours rehearsing with them.

>> **September 17, 1965** *A Go Go 66*, CTV Television's half hour, Friday night pop music show debuts replacing its

▲ Lovin' Spoonful

former pop music program, *After Four*. Robbie Lane and the Disciples are the resident house band, while CHUM Toronto radio announcer Mike Darrow is the host. The show, which later changes its name to *It's Happening*, runs for four years.

>> **September 25, 1965** "You Were On My Mind," written by Sylvia Tyson of Ian & Sylvia and recorded by We Five, peaks at number three on the Billboard chart.

>> **October 1, 1965** Bob Dylan with Levon and the Hawks play New York's Carnegie Hall.

>> **November 9, 1965** The east coast of North America is in the dark after a massive power failure.

>> **November 14, 1965** Bob Dylan and Levon and the Hawks play the first of two nights at Toronto's Massey Hall.

>> **Winter 1965** Buffy Sainte-Marie's song "Universal Soldier" becomes an international hit for Donovan.

>> **December 31, 1965** Ronnie King (Kees Van Sprang), formerly of the Calgary group The Paint Brushes, joins The Stampeders.

>> **December 1965** Burton Cummings is recruited from the Winnipeg group The Devrons to replace the departing Chad Allan on vocals in The Guess Who.

>> **December 1965** Johnny Bower, the renowned goaltender for the Toronto Maple Leafs hockey team, records the single, "Honky the Christmas Goose."

>> **1965** John and Michelle Phillips, Denny Doherty and Cass Elliot form The Mamas and the Papas.

>> **1965** Richard Newell (aka King Biscuit Boy) plays U.S. army bases in Germany with his group Son Richard and the Gooduns.

▲ The Mamas and the Papas

>> **1965** 17-year-old folk singer Murray McLauchlan works odd jobs and plays folk clubs as he travels around North America. He eventually settles in Toronto and becomes part of the burgeoning folk scene in Yorkville Village.

>> **1965** 3's A Crowd, formerly The Bill Schwartz Quartet, which had an alumni that includes Brent Titcomb, Bruce Cockburn and Colleen Peterson, move to Toronto from Vancouver by way of Edmonton and add members Ken Koblun, David Wiffen and Richard Patterson. When the original three members leave, Colleen Peterson, Bruce Cockburn and Dennis Pendrith join Wiffen and Patterson in the second configuration of the group. The ensemble records an album for Dunhill in 1967 with the help of Denny Doherty and Cass Elliot of The Mamas and the Papas titled *Christopher's Movie Matinee*.

>> **1965** Tom Northcott forms his own New Syndrome record label in Vancouver when Capitol Records turns down one of his recordings. He subsequently travels to England and works with producer Tony Hatch, who cuts some Petula Clark songs with him.

>> **1965** Brooklyn, New York-born singer, actress, Nanette Workman, who had been working on Broadway in the lead role of the hit musical *How To Succeed In Business Without Really Trying*, moves to Montréal at the suggestion of local singing star and music biz entrepreneur Tony Roman and becomes an instant hit with the single "Et maintenant." She becomes a regular presence on the charts there before moving to England for five years in 1968.

>> **1965** Neil Young moves from Winnipeg to Toronto, where he initially gets a job as a stock boy at a downtown Coles book store to make ends meet. Before the end of the year, he joins the group The Mynah Birds, which also features Rick James and Bruce Palmer.

>> **1965** Ken and Chris Whiteley form the Original Sloth Band in Toronto.

>> **1965** *The Tommy Hunter Show*, hosted by "Canada's Country Gentleman," succeeds the weekly *Country Hoedown* show on CBC-TV.

>> **1965** Folk singer/songwriter Bonnie Dobson returns to Toronto and becomes a regular on the CBC Radio show *1967 and All That*.

>> **1965** *Rolling Stone* magazine calls Robert Charlebois "The Dylan of Québec."

>> **1965** Groups formed this year include Copperpenny, Kitchener, ON; Full Tilt Boogie Band; Mandala, Toronto; The Bells, Montréal; The Guess Who, Winnipeg, MB; The Haunted, Montréal; The Mamas and the Papas, New York; The Original Sloth Band, Toronto; The Paupers, Toronto; The Ugly Ducklings, Toronto.

>> 1966

>> **March 1966** Leonard Cohen sings a couple of his poems, including "Suzanne" and "Stranger," during a reading at the YMCA in New York. It becomes an increasingly popular part of his readings, which soon become concerts as Cohen's evolution to singer of songs begins.

>> **March 2, 1966** Stephen Stills and Richie Furay, caught in a Los Angeles traffic jam on Sunset Boulevard in the Bentley of producer Barry Friedman (aka Frazier Mohawk), spot a hearse with Ontario license plates. Stills had been looking for Neil Young, whom he had met during a tour through Canada with the Au Go Go Singers. Young was known to favour a hearse as the most practical vehicle of choice for lugging and loading band equipment. "I was in the left hand lane driving down the street and I looked over to the right and there was this hearse pulling up next to us," Friedman recalled. "I had never met Neil Young but I'd heard about the hearse and I turned to Stephen and said, 'This is your friend here...!' and it was. It was really telepathic and quite bizarre. Actually it was Neil and Bruce Palmer." They all end up living at Freidman's house on Fountain Avenue in West Hollywood and, with the addition of Chesterville, Ontario-born drummer, Dewey Martin, a group is born. "As far as the eventual name for the group... we pulled up in front of the house one day when they were repaving Fountain," Friedman explained. "There was a steam roller there and on the back it said 'Buffalo Springfield.' I said, 'Hey, that's the name!' I pried the sign off, took it into the house and nailed it on the wall." Buffalo Springfield, one of the most influential groups of the '60s, was born.

Neil Young recalled that period in the book *Neil and Me* written by his late father, Scott Young. "Barry Friedman put us in a house on Fountain and told us to start working. The whole thing was great, a tremendous relief. We had a place to sleep and could take a shower. We had a house and weren't on the street. Barry gave us a dollar a day each for food. All we had to do was keep practicing. Barry did it all, you know. He basically put it together and kept it together."

Scott Young continues: "Barry Friedman, their hard-bitten angel, had talked to his friend, the road manager for The Byrds. The Byrds had a concert tour scheduled at sites within driving distance, the first at Pasadena, and were looking for a group to be the opening act. Buffalo Springfield couldn't have started under better auspices. The Byrds were the hottest group in the United States right then. Their 1965 recording of Bob Dylan's 'Mr. Tambourine Man' had made them nationally famous. The crowds that came to hear them

▲ Tommy Commons, Gordie Tapp and Tommy Hunter

went away talking also about Buffalo Springfield. The Byrds themselves started showing up early to listen." Barry Friedman would later tour with The Byrds through the U.S. and Canada and did the sound mix for the group during their Monterey Pop Festival appearance in 1967. (As an aside, the late Barry Friedman/Frazier Mohawk, who worked at Elektra Records as a producer with artists like the Paul Butterfield Blues Band, Rhinoceros, Jackson Browne, among others, later moved to Canada and settled near Schomberg, Ontario as the owner of Puck's Farm, a working farm open to the public, which also has a recording studio on the premises.)

>> **April 11, 1966** Paul Anka hosts the last episode of the TV pop music show, *Hullabaloo*.

>> **April 28, 1966** The Sparrows — they shortly drop the "s" to become The Sparrow — record the tracks "Goin' To California," "Twisted" and "Square-Headed People" at the Allegro Sound Studios in New York. Following the signing of a record deal with Columbia, the group travels back to New York from Toronto in June for more sessions with David Kaprilik and an extended engagement at Arthur, the club owned by Richard Burton's ex-wife, Sybil.

>> **May 7, 1966** The Mamas and the Papas hit the top of the Billboard Top 100 singles chart with "Monday, Monday."

>> **May 14, 1966** After touring Australia and Scandinavia, Bob Dylan and The Hawks — minus Levon Helm who can't take the negative reaction from audiences to Dylan's new electric sound and has been replaced by Mickey Jones of The First Edition — head for the

U.K. where on this date, they play a concert in Liverpool, England. The live recording of "Just Like Tom Thumb's Blues" from this concert will later be released as the B-side of Dylan's single, "I Want You."

>> **May 21, 1966** The Mamas and the Papas top the album charts in the U.S. with *If You Can Believe Your Eyes and Ears*.

>> **May 26, 1966** Bob Dylan and the Hawks world tour culminates with a concert at the Royal Albert Hall in London. In attendance are the Rolling Stones and members of The Beatles.

>> **July 1, 1966** Luke and the Apostles debut at the Purple Onion coffee house in Toronto's Yorkville Village.

>> **July 1, 1966** Rooming houses in the Yorkville area are referred to in a Toronto City council meeting as "a breeding ground for immorality and corruption" by a parent and "filthy and unspeakable" by Alderwoman Helen Johnston.

>> **July 8, 1966** A by-law, preventing new clubs from opening in the Yorkville area, is voted down.

>> **July 25, 1966** Buffalo Springfield play a concert at the Hollywood Bowl even before they have a record released.

>> **July 29, 1966** Bob Dylan breaks his neck in a motorcycle accident in Woodstock, New York, and is forced to take a lengthy hiatus from touring. Dylan spends nine months recuperating, and during this period, Levon and the Hawks, who have made the move themselves to Woodstock, begin working on songs that are destined to become part of their own debut album. The group, originally calling themselves The Crackers changed the name to The Band — that's what everyone in town called them — are living in a house nicknamed "Big Pink" at 2188 Stoll Road in nearby West Saugerties, New York.

>> **July 1966** Calgary pop group The Stampeders head east to Toronto from Calgary with manager Mel Shaw bringing a little cowboy culture with them, if not in their music, at least in their stage garb, which consists of matching cowboy outfits complete with hats and boots.

» August 13, 1966 The Lovin Spoonful's "Summer In the City" hits number one on the Billboard Hot 100 singles chart.

» Fall 1966 Anne Murray joins the faculty of Athena Regional High School in Summerside, Prince Edward Island as a physical education teacher. During this period, Murray also becomes a member of the chorus on CBC Halifax's *Singalong Jubilee*.

» September 1966 18-year-old Shawne Jackson, formerly with The Tiaras and a regular attraction at Toronto's Club *Bluenote*, joins her brother Jay in fronting the R&B/soul group, The Majestics.

» September 10, 1966 The Five Rogues, soon to become The Mandala, make their last Canadian appearance at the Whitby Arena in Whitby, Ontario with the Associates and Shawne and Jay Jackson and the Majestics.

» September 24, 1966 The 14-hour Toronto Sound show at Toronto's Maple Leaf Gardens attracts 16,400 fans at two dollars a ticket to see a line-up of 14 of the hottest groups in the city, including R.K. & the Associates, Bobby Kris & the Imperials, The Spasstiks, The Tripp, Stitch 'n Tyme, The Last Words, Five Rising Sons, The Paupers, Luke & the Apostles, The Secrets, Little Caesar & the Consuls, Susan Taylor & the Peytons, Big Town Boys and The Ugly Ducklings. The groups all play twice. One of the show's aims was to showcase Toronto artists for record executives, especially those from the U.S. Among the American VIPs to attend are Billy Sherrill (Epic Records), John Simon (Columbia) and Jerry Ragavoy (Warner Bros.).

» October 14, 1966 The Mamas and the Papas play New York's Carnegie Hall.

» October 1966 The Sparrow leave New York for Los Angeles.

» November 26, 1966 Folk duo Malka and Joso, who in Canada are the hosts of the CBC-TV series *A World of Music*, appear at Carnegie Hall in New York.

» December 9, 1966 The Flick opens at 90 Yorkville Avenue with the Stitch 'n Tyme.

» December 1966 The Sparrow head for San Francisco and

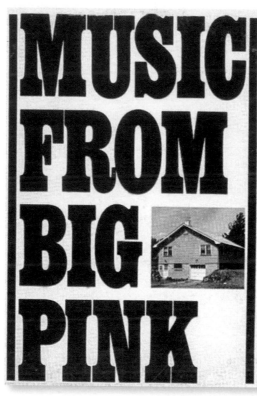

a booking at the The Ark. They remain in the city by the Bay playing venues like Matrix, the Avalon and the Fillmore until June 1967. A gig recorded by the club manager at Matrix in May 1967 is later released by ABC/Dunhll as *Early Steppenwolf*.

» 1966 Chad Allan departs The Guess Who, opting to return to university. In less than a year, he's back in the music business as host of the Winnipeg version of *Music Hop*, an afternoon teen TV program on the CBC that frequently features his former band mates.

» 1966 Singer Norman Brooks hosts CTV's *Musical Showcase*.

» 1966 Mandala, formerly The Rogues and the house band at Toronto's Club Bluenote, record the single "Opportunity" at the Chess Records studios in Chicago with vocal group The Dells singing backup.

» 1966 Terry Jacks, a once-promising architecture student from Winnipeg, meets Susan Pesklevits in Vancouver. They initially form the group Powerline and play for skiers up on Whistler Mountain. They are later married and begin touring as The Poppy Family.

» 1966 Teenage Hull, Québec-native Daniel Lanois moves with his family to Ancaster, Ontario, where, in due course, he builds a recording studio in the basement of the family home with brother Bob. Later, with the co-signature of his mother on a $100,000 loan, he opens the Grant Avenue Studio, a 24-track studio.

» 1966 Ian & Sylvia and Gordon Lightfoot tour England.

» 1966 Leonard Cohen writes the song "Suzanne" in Montreal.

» 1966 Joni Mitchell moves to New York and becomes part of the Greenwich Village coffee house scene.

» 1966 Men of the Deeps, a choir of Cape Breton coal miners, forms.

» 1966 Murray McLauchlan makes his first major concert appearance at the Mariposa Folk Festival.

» 1966 Bruce Cockburn joins local Ottawa group The Children as an organ player. He will become a member of a number of Ottawa-based groups, including 3's A Crowd, The

Esquires, Olivus and Flying Circus, before he sets out on a solo career in 1969 with former Kensington Market member Gene Martynec as producer and noted manager Bernie Finkelstein (Kensington Market, The Paupers, Luke and the Apostles). When Finkelstein sets up his True North record label, Cockburn is his first signing. He has been with Finkelstein ever since, which may constitute some kind of record for a management/record label/artist relationship. Martynec was the producer of 13 of Cockburn's 14 albums to 1983.

>> **1966** Adam Mitchell replaces Bill Misener in The Paupers.

>> **1966** Oscar Brand begins hosting a Saturday morning radio series for NBC in the U.S. titled *First Look* and his own TV show in Canada called *Brand New Scene*.

>> **1966** Mother Tucker's Yellow Duck form in Vancouver and record their debut album, *Home Grown Stuff*, on their own Duck label, later picked up by Capitol Records.

>> **1966** Toronto group The Bossmen, inspired by the piano virtuosity of child prodigy Tony Collacott, who had played with Sarah Vaughan at the age of 14, becomes David Clayton-Thomas' first experiment in the fusion of jazz and rock three years before his involvement with Blood, Sweat & Tears. The groups' single "Brainwashed," a scathing commentary on the Vietnam War, which had the word "damn" bleeped out of the recording because of a threatened ban in the U.S., becomes a number one record in Canada.

>> **1966** Bob Segarini forms The Family Tree who become regulars at Bill Graham's Fillmore Auditorium in San Francisco. Their concept album *Miss Butters* (1968) becomes a favourite of up-and-coming songwriters Bernie Taupin and Reg Dwight (Elton John).

>> **1966** Leonard Cohen hits the book best-seller list with *Beautiful Losers,* which he had written living on the Greek Island of Hydra in 1964. One of the poems from Cohen's book *Parasites From Heaven* that Cohen had set to basic musical accompaniment as "Suzanne" catches the ear of folk singer Judy Collins, who records it, as well as his "Dress Rehearsal Rag," on her *In My Life* (1966) album, giving Cohen invaluable exposure to her significant audience. The Stormy Clovers, who were the first to perform some of Cohen's songs in concert, provided a soundtrack of Cohen material for the National Film Board short film, *Angel.*

▲ Mandala

>> **1966** Colleen Peterson begins playing with 3's A Crowd at the Mariposa Folk Festival.

>> **1966** Operatic contralto Maureen Forrester makes her New York City Opera debut on opening night in Handel's *Giulio Cesare* singing Cornelia to Beverly Sills' Cleopatra.

>> **1966** "(Clear the Track) Here Comes Shack," a tribute song to rough-and-ready Toronto Maple Leaf hockey player Eddie Shack and co-written by CBC-TV Hockey Night In Canada commentator Brian McFarlane, is released by the Toronto group, The Secrets.

>> **1966** Bruce Allen opens booking agency Bruce Allen Talent in Vancouver.

>> **1966** Record company Polydor Ltd. is established in Canada.

>> **1966** Colour TV broadcasts begin in Canada.

>> **1966** Groups formed in this year include A Passing Fancy, Toronto; Buffalo Springfield, Los Angeles; David Clayton-Thomas and The Bossmen, Toronto; Edward Bear, Toronto; Gary & Dave, London, ON; Grant Smith & the Power, Toronto; Leigh Ashford, Toronto; Luke and the Apostles, Toronto; Men of the Deeps, Cape Breton, NS; Mother Tucker's Yellow Duck, Vancouver; The Collectors, Vancouver.

>> 1967

>> **January 1967** "Opportunity," a single by Toronto band Mandala, which makes the most definitive comment yet about the lot of Canadian musicians or songwriters living in the shadow of the U.S. music industry, is released.

>> **January 1, 1967** Gordon Lightfoot's *Canadian Railroad Trilogy*, commissioned by the CBC for the Canadian centennial show *100 Years Young*, is first heard during the airing of the program. Lightfoot sells out the month of January at the Riverboat Coffee House in Toronto's Yorkville Village.

>> **January 21, 1967** Buffalo Springfield perform "For What It's Worth" on Dick Clark's *American Bandstand* show.

>> **February 24, 1967** John Kay marries Jutta Maue, a former Toronto model, in Los Angeles.

>> **February 1967** Joni Mitchell is featured on CBC-TV show *Take 30* with Adrienne Clarkson and Paul Soles. The show was broadcast on May 1, 1967.

» **February 27, 1967** Toronto group The Paupers open for Jefferson Airplane at the Cafe Au Go Go in New York to great critical acclaim. Richard Goldstein of the Village Voice writes: "There is this incredible group from Toronto called The Paupers, who descended on the New York scene like electronic thunder. Their music makes the average combo sound like a string quartet doing Wagner. They have a power and discipline I've never seen before in performance. The miracle is The Pauper's ability to reproduce live all the structured atonality it takes other groups months in the studio to create. They swooped down out of nowhere, from a scene nobody knew about and suddenly they were playing real electronic music with a teenage audience screaming allegiance in the background."

» **March 31, 1967** Gordon Lightfoot gives the first of what will become a regular concert at Toronto's Massey Hall. It is held annually until 1984 and then every 18 months. It's a sell-out, even though he played a month at The Riverboat in the same city two months before.

» **Spring 1967** Drummer Skip Prokop of The Paupers records with Peter, Paul & Mary and is heard on their subsequent hit single, "I Dig Rock and Roll Music."

» **Spring 1967** The Stampeders make a trip to New York, where they cut some song demos, including "Morning Magic."

» **Spring 1967** Toronto group Mandala, managed by TV clown Randy Dandy (aka Randy Markowitz or Randy Martin), are featured on Murray the K's annual Easter show in New York. A Variety review calls the group, "not only insipid, but tasteless." Not everyone is a devotee of the Soul Crusade.

» **Spring 1967** The Guess Who sign a long-term contract with CBC-TV to host 65 segments over a two-year period of a national teen music series called *Let's Go*, which originates from five cities across Canada each weekday afternoon. The Guess Who host the Winnipeg segment. A direct result of their appearances on the series is their subsequent association with advertising executive turned producer, the late Jack Richardson, who sees them on the show. As an executive at McCann-Erickson advertising agency in Toronto, Richardson had produced a radio show for them called *The Hi-Fi Club*, sponsored by Coca-Cola. Moving into commercial production, he came up with the concept of having top recording artists like Bobby Curtola, Boots Randolph, Chet Atkins, Petula Clark and David Clayton-Thomas record commercials for Coke and then took it one step further by offering specially-recorded albums by pop artists as sales incentives for Coke. The first promotional LPs recorded by Bobby Curtola and Michel Louvain/Margot Lefebvre, both sold over 100,000 copies. In 1968, Richardson convinced Coke to record both The Guess Who and Ottawa group The Staccatos for a promotional album called *A Wild Pair*, which goes on to sell over 85,000 copies.

» **April 28, 1967** Expo '67 — Man and His World — opens in Montréal.

» **April 29, 1967** André Prevost's "Terre des Hommes" premieres at the Salle Wilfrid-Pelletier of Montréal's Place des Arts during the inauguration of Expo 67.

» **April 30, 1967** Ian & Sylvia appear at Carnegie Hall in New York for the first time.

» **May 1967** Newly-formed Toronto group The Kensington Market provide the soundtrack for the National Film Board's *The Ernie Game*, which airs on CBC-TV on Nov. 2, 1967.

▲ The Paupers, from *Teenset*, December, 1967

» **May 1967** Singer Renée Claude from Québec appears on NBC-TV's *Johnny Carson Show*.

» **May 5, 1967** The first issue of *Georgia Straight* is published in Vancouver.

» **May 17, 1967** *Don't Look Back*, D.A. Pennebaker's film documentary of Bob Dylan's 1965 British tour with The Band, premiers in San Francisco. Dylan doesn't like the film and attempts to stop it being shown.

» **May 27, 1967** Trips Festival featuring Jefferson Airplane, The Collectors, The Painted Ships and Magic Fern at the Richmond Arena, Richmond, BC.

» **June 1, 1967** The first McDonald's restaurant opens in Canada in Richmond, BC.

» **June 3, 1967** The Beatles' album *Sgt. Pepper's Lonely Hearts Club Band* is released in America.

» **June 10, 1967** In Woodstock, New York, The Band and Bob Dylan begin recording what they call *The Basement Tapes*, a session that is widely bootlegged under the name *Great White Wonder* before it is officially released by CBS under the name *The Basement Tapes* in 1975.

» **June 16, 1967** The Monterey Pop Festival begins its three-day run in Monterey, California, featuring a wide variety of acts, including Janis Joplin, The Mamas and the Papas, Buffalo Springfield, The Who, Jimi Hendrix, The Grateful Dead, The Byrds and Otis Redding.

» **June 24, 1967** Zal Yanovsky leaves the Lovin' Spoonful following a concert at the Forest Hills Music Festival in New York. He is replaced by Jerry Yester, brother of Jim Yester of The Association. By the end of the '60s, Yanovsky forms his own record production company, Hairshirt Productions, and works with artists like Pat Boone, Tim Buckley and Judy Henske.

» **June 1967** A disagreement over musical direction sees Dennis Edmonton and Nick St. Nicholas leave The Sparrow, who have relocated to Los Angeles. Edmonton changes his name to Mars Bonfire and makes solo records, while St. Nicholas joins Los Angeles group, TIME. Michael Monarch and Ruston Moreve subsequently join the group on guitar and bass, respectively.

» **July 1, 1967** Canada's 100th birthday.

» **July 1967** Joni Mitchell appears at the Ottawa Summer Music Festival. Portions of her two shows are recorded by CBC Radio for broadcast on its *Showcase* program.

» **July 1967** Montréal group The Jaybees, formerly J.B. and the Playboys, make their New York debut at the Rolling Stone club.

▲ Steppenwolf

» **August 21, 1967** Newspaper reports estimate that from 5000 to 10,000 "hippies" jammed the streets of Yorkville, staging a sit-in to protest the traffic on the streets. 50 people are arrested and there are charges of police brutality.

» **August 31, 1967** David DePoe, the leader of the federally-supported Company of Young Canadians and the Yorkville Diggers Inc., takes over the Toronto city council with a group of followers. They want, among other things, the closing of Yorkville Avenue or another street in the area to traffic, the establishment of a social centre in the area and permission for a second love-in at Queen's Park. The requests were greeted with a collective yawn from the councillors and for all intents and purposes, it was the end of Yorkville as an arts centre in Toronto before the developers moved in.

» **August 1967** The Sparrow, who shortly change their name to Steppenwolf (after the Herman Hesse novel) at the suggestion of producer Gabriel Meckler, begin rehearsals in Los Angeles. Subsequent demo recordings bring them a new record deal with ABC/Dunhill.

» **September 23, 1967** The opera *Louis Riel* premieres at Toronto's O'Keefe Centre.

» **September 1967** The Stampeders record their first single, "Morning Magic," in Montréal. It leads to the group being signed with MGM Records in New York.

» **September 1967** Vancouver club Dante's Inferno at 1024 Davie St. becomes the Retinal Circus, one of the major showcase venues on the West Coast during this period for local artists like The Collectors, United Empire Loyalists, Seeds of Time, Painted Ship, Papa Bear's Medicine Show, 3's A Crowd, Hydro Electric Streetcar, My Indole Ring, Mock Duck, Mother Tucker's Yellow Duck, Tomorrow's Eyes, Yellow Brique Road, Winters Green, Black Snake Blues Band and Tom Northcott.

» **Fall 1967** While playing at the Cafe Au Go in New York's Greenwich Village as opening act for Richie Havens, influential agent/manager Elliot Roberts, on the urging of one of his clients, Buffy Sainte-Marie, drops by to see Joni

Mitchell. He subsequently signs her for management.

» **Fall 1967** Warner Brothers Records of Canada, with head office in Montréal, is established.

» **October 21, 1967** "To Sir With Love," the title song from the movie of the same name co-written by Montréaler Mark London and lyricist Don Black, becomes a number one single on the *Billboard* chart for Lulu, who also co-starred in the film with Sidney Poitier. London had recorded for Chateau Records in 1962, which released the single, "How Much Longer Must I Wait?"

» **October 29, 1967** *Hair*, with the musical score written by Montréal composer Galt MacDermot and advertised as "The American Tribal Love-Rock Musical," opens off-Broadway at the Public Theater in New York's East Village.

» **November 9, 1967** *Rolling Stone Magazine* is launched in San Francisco — a free roach holder is distributed with the first issue.

» **November 11, 1967** The Lords of London from Toronto appear on *Upbeat*, the syndicated American pop music TV show out of Cleveland.

» **November 22, 1967** The Orford String Quartet make their Carnegie Recital Hall debut in New York.

» **December 1967** In a pop poll held by the Toronto Telegram's *After Four* teen section, Gordon Lightfoot is named Top Canadian Male Singer, Susan Taylor takes the honours as Top Canadian Female Singer and The Big Town Boys are named Top Canadian Group.

» **December 1967** Steppenwolf begin the recording of their debut album at the American Recording Company in Los Angeles.

» **December 10, 1967** Otis Redding passes away.

» **December 21, 1967** Andy Kim's brother Joe had been teaching him to play guitar during this period and young Andy writes the song "How'd We Ever Get This Way?" with the only two chords he knows — C and F. In New York, Kim had met producer/songwriter Jeff Barry, whom he would keep pestering to take him into the studio to record. On this date, Barry relents and Kim records his new

song. It is released in March of 1968 and goes on to sell close to a million copies.

» **Late 1967** Leonard Cohen's debut album, *Songs of Leonard Cohen*, is released.

» **1967** Expo 67 in Montréal gives a real boost to pride in a Canadian national identity.

» **1967** "C-A-N-A-D-A," the song written for Canada's centennial by trumpet player Bobby Gimby and performed by Gimby and the Young Canada Singers, is the top single of 1967.

» **1967** Singer, songwriter, producer Stéphane Venne's "Un jour, un jour/Hey Friend, Say Friend" becomes the theme song for Expo 67. It is premiered by singer Donald Lautrec.

» **1967** French President Charles de Gaulle visits Quebec and declares "Vive le Quebec libre!"

» **1967** Folk group The Travellers undertake a Centennial tour of Canada playing more than 100 concert dates.

» **1967** Gordon Lightfoot undertakes his first Canadian tour.

» **1967** Bruce Cockburn makes his first appearance at the Mariposa Festival.

» **1967** The Collectors, comprising Claire Lawrence, Ross Turney, Bill Henderson, Glenn Miller and Howie Vickers, form at a Vancouver cabaret called The Torch.

» **1967** Clubs like the Retinal Circus, the Sound Gallery, the Light House, the Afterthought and the Big Mother, spring up in Vancouver, giving rise to a vibrant West Coast music scene.

» **1967** Ann Mortifee and Willie Dunn compose the score for George Ryga's stage play *The Ecstasy of Rita Joe,* in which Mortifee appears as The Balladeer.

» **1967** Bossier City, Louisiana-born and Memphis-raised singer, songwriter Jesse Winchester moves to Montréal to evade the draft and initially joins the group Les Astronauts before going solo. It's here in 1970 that Winchester records his self-titled debut album co-produced by Robbie Robertson and Todd Rundgren.

» **1967** Michel Pagliaro, formerly with the ye-ye group Les Chanceliers, embarks on a solo career.

>> **1967** Montréal-born guitarist Walter Rossi, after playing with his first professional group the Soul Mates in 1965, heads out on tour with Wilson Pickett. Over the next decade, he becomes the instrumental mainstay of a number of groups and solo artists, including Influence, Buddy Miles Express ("Changes"), Luke and the Apostles, Charlee, Michel Pagliaro and Nanette Workman.

>> **1967** Toronto's Ugly Ducklings have their biggest hit with "Gaslight," a song written by a New York cab driver. Only vocalist Dave Byngham of the group is featured on the session, which makes use of studio musicians.

>> **1967** Anne Murray begins appearing on the CBC Halifax pop music TV show *Let's Go*, later known as *Frank's Bandstand*.

>> **1967** With the break-up of the group The Bossmen, singer, songwriter David Clayton-Thomas takes a gig with bluesman John Lee Hooker as his guitarist and chauffeur and ends up in New York for a club date with Hooker at the Cafe Au Go Go. When Hooker goes AWOL in pursuit of a girlfriend who has absconded with his GTO, Clayton-Thomas is left holding the bag. To save the booking, he puts together a makeshift group called The Charlie Musslewhite South Side Blues Band with bass player Harvey Brooks, guitarist Michael Bloomfield, drummer Sam Lay and harp player Charlie Musslewhite. The date is ultimately extended to five weeks and during this period, Clayton-Thomas meets Bobby Colomby, who's talking about putting together a rock group that would incorporate some of New York's top jazz musicians. Harvey Brooks, Michael Bloomfield and new associate Buddy Miles eventually leave for San Francisco where they put together Electric Flag. Clayton-Thomas stays in New York, where he is the house band at Steve Paul's Scene on 47th Street that includes organist Mike Fonfara and guitarist Larry Leishman from the recently disbanded Jon and Lee and the Checkmates.

>> **1967** Leonard Cohen performs at the Newport Folk Festival, signs a long-term contract with Columbia Records and sings the song "Stranger" in the movie *The Ernie Game* for the National Film Board, which would later put the spotlight on his life in the documentary, *Ladies and Gentlemen...*

▼ David Clayton-Thomas

A Bearsville Record Production produced by Robbie Robertson for Ampex Records & Tapes

"...his songs transcend all barriers with the exception of one: art"

(ED WARD)
ROLLING STONE

▲ Jesse Winchester

Mr. Leonard Cohen. It is the first of three films on Cohen's life during this period. Tony Palmer's *Bird On the Wire* (1971) focuses on his European success while in Canada, Harry Rasky produces a film biography on his life as an artist. His debut album *Songs of Leonard Cohen* is released in late 1967.

>> **1967** A decade before he returns to the U.S. to form the Stone City Band and introduce "funk'n'roll" to the music world, Buffalo, New York-native Rick James (James A. Johnson, Jr.) decides he'd rather pursue a musical career in Canada than to complete his tour of duty in the U.S. Navy. He becomes a landed immigrant during his stay in Toronto and forms a group called The Mynah Birds with roommate Neil Young (likely named after the Yorkville Village club owned by Colin Kerr and featuring his mynah bird, Rajah). The group signs to Motown Records, where James is producing artists like Bobby Taylor, The Spinners and The Marvelettes, but no material is ever released. By 1970, group members, which include James, Young, Goldy McJohn (later with Steppenwolf), Bruce Palmer (later with Young in Buffalo Springfield), Rick Mason and John Taylor, have gone their separate ways. James moves to London, Ontario and for the next seven years commutes between Canada and the U.S. before he takes his permanent leave of Canada in 1977.

>> **1967** Singer Denny Vaughan moves to Hollywood where he works as chorale director on TV shows like *The Smothers Brothers* and *The Glen Campbell Hour*.

>> **1967** Pianist André Gagnon begins his solo career by renting a hall in Montréal's Place des Arts for a Mozart recital.

>> **1967** Soprano Riki Turofsky makes her debut in a touring production of *Hansel and Gretel*.

>> **1967** London Records of Canada (1967) Ltd. evolves from the London Gramophone Co. of Canada.

>> **1967** Groups formed this year include Barry Allen and the Lords, Edmonton; Influence, Montréal; Kensington Market, Toronto; Leigh Ashford, Toronto; Rhinoceros, Los Angeles; Steppenwolf, Toronto/Los Angeles; The Collectors, Vancouver; The Family Brown, Ottawa.

» 1968

» **January 20, 1968** Bob Dylan and the Band play a Woody Guthrie memorial tribute concert at Carnegie Hall in New York.

» **February 22, 1968** *The Toronto Telegram* newspaper names The Lords of London, The Ugly Ducklings, The Stitch 'n Tyme, Grant Smith and the Power and Little Caesar and the Consuls as Toronto's top five groups.

» **April 4, 1968** Martin Luther King is shot and killed on the balcony of Memphis' Lorraine Motel, which is now encompassed by the National Civil Rights Museum.

» **April 28, 1968** After six months at the off-Broadway New York Shakespeare Festival Theater, the "American Tribal Love-Rock Musical" *Hair* opens at New York's Biltmore Theatre. It is the first "rock musical" to play on the Great White Way. Cast includes Diane Keaton, Melba Moore, Paul Jabara, Ronald Dyson and creators James Rado and Gerome Ragni. Musical score is by Montréal composer Galt McDermot, who is also the show's music director.

» **April 31, 1968** Founder Al Kooper and saxophonist Randy Brecker leave Blood, Sweat & Tears after recording the group's first album, *Child Is Father To the Man*. Toronto-native David Clayton-Thomas is recruited as the group's vocalist and front man as the second configuration of Blood, Sweat and Tears is born.

» **April 1968** The Paupers return to Toronto after a gig at the Kinetic Circus in Chicago to begin work on their sophomore album, *Ellis Island*.

» **May 4, 1968** Steppenwolf make their national TV debut as they perform "Born To Be Wild," written by former group member Dennis Edmonton (aka Mars Bonfire), on Dick Clark's *American Bandstand*.

» **May 5, 1968** Buffalo Springfield play their final concert in Long Beach, California.

» **Summer 1968** McKenna Mendelson Mainline is formed by Mike McKenna and Joe Mendelson (now Mendelson Joe) in Toronto. They leave for England in December, where they live for six months and record their debut album, *Stink*.

» **June 1, 1968** The Irish Rovers perform "The Unicorn" and "Whiskey On Sunday" on *American Bandstand*.

» **June 5, 1968** U.S. Senator Robert F. Kennedy is assassinated in the Ambassador Hotel in Los Angeles.

» **July 5, 1968** Steppenwolf play the Hollywood Bowl in

The Essential LEONARD COHEN

Los Angeles with The Doors and the Chamber Brothers the week before their single "Born To Be Wild" enters the Billboard chart.

» **August 10, 1968** *Music From Big Pink*, the debut album by The Band, enters the American charts.

» **September 19, 1968** Steppenwolf earn their first gold record in the U.S. with the single "Born To Be Wild," a song later featured in the soundtrack of the film, *Easy Rider*. A phrase from the song, "heavy metal thunder," is believed by some to be the source of the term "heavy metal" as it refers to loud and bombastic music, although the term previously appeared in *Naked Lunch*, a novel by William Burroughs.

» **September 19, 1968** The Guess Who enter A&R Studios in New York to start recording their debut album, *Wheatfield Soul*.

» **September 23, 1968** Drummer Skip Prokop (The Paupers) flies into San Francisco to be part of a live jam session at Bill Graham's Fillmore Auditorium (Sept. 26, 27 & 28) with Al Kooper, Mike Bloomfield, Elvin Bishop, Carlos Santana and Steve Miller, among others. The proceedings are recorded for a double-sided album titled *The Live Adventures of Mike Bloomfield and Al Kooper*. Prokop is an active session musician during this period, working with the Pozo Seco Singers, Richie Havens and Cass Elliot. He is heard on Peter, Paul and Mary's Top 10 single, "I Dig Rock and Roll Music," from the summer of 1967.

» **Fall 1968** The Stampeders, now based full-time in Toronto, are reduced from a sextet to a trio as three of the group's members head back to Calgary. Remaining group members include Rich Dodson, Ronnie King and Kim Berly.

» **November 2, 1968** The newly-refurbished Montreal Forum is open again.

» **November 9, 1968** Andy Kim performs "Shoot 'Em Up Baby" and "Rainbow Ride" on *American Bandstand*.

» **November 14, 1968** Ian & Sylvia play the Cafe Au Go Go in New York prior to a nationwide tour of college campuses. At this point, the duo has integrated an electric steel guitar in the group, giving it a distinct country flavour as their group, the Great Speckled Bird (after a Wilf Carter song), begins to take shape.

» **November 27, 1968** Steppenwolf's eponymous debut album is certified gold. Almost simultaneously, the group's single "Magic Carpet Ride" heads into the top five of the Billboard chart.

>> **December 28, 1968** Buffy Sainte-Marie, Steppenwolf, Joni Mitchell and Ian & Sylvia are among those appearing at the three-day Miami Pop Festival.

>> **1968** Liberal Pierre Trudeau becomes Prime Minister of Canada.

>> **1968** Parti Québecois (PQ) is formed to push for complete independence for Québec.

>> **1968** *The Tommy Banks Show* debuts on CBC-TV. It runs initially from 1968 to 1974 and then from 1980 to 1983.

>> **1968** Judy Collins records the Joni Mitchell composition "Both Sides Now." It helps to launch Mitchell's career internationally and is in part responsible for the Grammy Award she wins in the category of Best Folk Performance for her album *Clouds*.

>> **1968** The musical review *L'Osstidcho*, featuring Robert Charlebois, Louise Forestier, Yvon Deschamps and Mouffe (Claudine Monfette), considered one of the landmark moments in Québec music history, is produced by impresario Guy Latraverse at Théâtre de Quat'Sous in Montréal.

>> **1968** Robert Charlebois, representing Québec at the fifth International Festival of French Song at Spa, Belgium, wins the Grand Prize for the song "Lindberg." The recording of the song with Louise Forestier wins the Prix Félix-Leclerc at the 1969 Festival du disque.

>> **1968** Québec singing star Nannette Workman moves to England where she lands spots on a number of major variety shows, including Peter Cook and Dudley Moore's top-rated show, *Not Only, But Also*. While working at the Olympic Studios in London, she becomes one of the most sought after backing vocalists of the day working with artists like The Rolling Stones ("Honky Tonk Women"), John Lennon, George Harrison, Ringo Starr and Reg Dwight (aka Elton John), who wrote her first U.K. single, "Rebecca." Visa problems cause Workman to move to France, where she embarks on a world tour with France's top star Johnny Hallyday as an opening act and back-up vocalist. During this period, Hallyday produces an album with her that features Peter Frampton, Gary Wright and Mike Kelli of Spooky Tooth, among others.

>> **1968** Joni Mitchell moves west to California from Toronto to take up residence in a Laurel Canyon cottage.

>> **1968** Carole Pope and Kevan Staples form the songwriting partnership that will evolve to the group, Rough Trade.

>> **1968** Harmonica player Richard Newell, who had previously been playing with The Mid-Knights, joins Ronnie Hawkins' group The Hawks in Toronto. During this period, Hawkins dubs Newell, "King Biscuit Boy." Early in his career, Hawkins had rehearsed at radio station KFFA in Helena, Arkansas, which has a regular music show, *King Biscuit Time*, sponsored by the King Biscuit Flour Company. Harmonica legend Sonny Boy Williamson was a regular on the show.

>> **1968** Paul Anka had been playing a club date in Miami in 1966 when Frank Sinatra, who was in town filming *Tony Rome*, tells Anka that he is looking for a song that will sum up his career. This stays in Anka's head, and while on a visit to France this year, he hears the Claude Francois hit "Comme d'habitude" and purchases the worldwide rights. In a fit of inspiration one night in New York, Anka rewrites the lyrics, changing the title to "My Way," and sends it to Sinatra as his potential swan song. He got a call from Sinatra from the studio as he was recording it. "My Way" becomes one of the most covered songs in the history of pop music. In 1969, Sinatra's version of the song enters the British charts where it remains for 127 weeks. Even the late punk rocker Sid Vicious records a version in 1978 for the Sex Pistols' film and album *The Great Rock 'N' Roll Swindle*.

>> **1968** Three Dog Night form in Los Angeles with three lead vocalists, Danny Hutton, Cory Wells and Chuck Negron, along with four musicians including Calgary, Alberta-native Floyd Sneed on drums.

>> **1968** Vocalist Jon Finley and keyboardist Michael Fonfara, former members of the Toronto group Jon and Lee and the Checkmates, are recruited by Elektra Records producer Paul Rothchild for a "supergroup" he is putting together. The band known as Rhinoceros also features guitarist Doug Hastings (Buffalo Springfield), drummer Billy Mundi (Frank Zappa's Mothers of Invention), guitarist Danny Weis and bassist Jerry Penrod (Iron Butterfly) and pianist, vocalist Alan Gerber.

>> **1968** Anne Murray begins her recording career with Arc Records, initially as a member of the cast of the CBC-TV show, *Singalong Jubilee*.

>> **1968** Edward Bear, formerly the Edward Bear Revue, sign to Capitol Records and have almost immediate success with their debut single, "You, Me and Mexico." Though it is the group's pop songs that bring them most of their chart success, the Bear also has a heavy rock and blues side.

>> **1968** The new Broadcasting Act establishes the Canadian Radio-Television Commission (CRTC) as the regulating and licensing authority for broadcasters.

▲ The Stampeders

>> **1968** Groups formed in this year include Fraser & DeBolt, Toronto/Hamilton; Lighthouse, Toronto; McKenna Mendelson Mainline, Toronto; Merryweather, Toronto; Rob McConnell and the Boss Brass, Toronto; Rush, Toronto; The Band, Woodstock, NY; The Minglewood Band; The Modern Rock Quartet (MRQ), Ottawa; The Poppy Family, Vancouver.

>> 1969

>> **January 18, 1969** Blood, Sweat & Tears' self-titled sophomore album, featuring vocalist David Clayton-Thomas, is released. It includes the Clayton-Thomas song "Spinning Wheel."

>> **January 18, 1969** In the wake of the enormous success of their Shel Silverstein-penned single "The Unicorn," which sells over eight million copies worldwide, The Irish Rovers launch an Australian tour before returning to the U.S. for a full schedule of TV and college engagements.

>> **January 23, 1969** Toronto's Electric Circus rock club opens.

>> **January 1969** Rob McConnell and the Boss Brass make their first live appearance at the Savarin in Toronto.

>> **February 1, 1969** Joni Mitchell plays Carnegie Hall in New York.

>> **February 16, 1969** Janis Joplin plays two shows at Toronto's O'Keefe Centre.

>> **February 1969** Neil Young returns to Toronto for a week-long solo engagement at the Riverboat Coffee House in Yorkville Village.

>> **February 1969** Mashmakhan, formerly known as The Triangle, the backing group for Trevor Payne, debut at the Laugh In club in Montréal.

>> **March 1969** Canadian Conservative MP Lloyd Cruce calls on Liberal Justice Minister John Turner and Postmaster General Eric Kierans to ban John Lennon and Yoko Ono's *Two Virgins* album, describing the jacket as "foreign-made pornographic material."

Robert Charlebois

▲ The Collectors, 1968: From front to back: Howie Vickers, Glenn Miller, Claire Lawrence, Ross Turney and Bill Henderson. Later known as Chilliwack

>> **March 7, 1969** Buffy Sainte-Marie and Ian & Sylvia plays the Fillmore East in New York.

>> **March 13, 1969** Former Buffalo Springfield member Neil Young plays solo at the Bitter End in New York.

>> **March 29, 1969** Blood, Sweat & Tears' self-titled album reaches number one on the Billboard chart. It holds the position, non-consecutively, over seven weeks by the end of the summer.

>> **March 1969** 3's A Crowd, with Sandy Crawley replacing Bruce Cockburn, debut their own TV variety show, *One More Time*, which originates from the CBC in Montreal.

>> **April 12, 1969** Toronto group Motherlode make their first hometown appearance at The Rock Pile.

>> **April 17, 1969** The Band perform their first concert as an independent group (without Bob Dylan) at Winterland, San Francisco opening a U.S. tour to promote their debut album, *Music From Big Pink*. Robbie Robertson fell ill prior to the show but was able to perform with the help of a hypnotist.

>> **April 17, 1969** Steppenwolf appear on *The Ed Sullivan Show*.

>> **April 26, 1969** The original cast album of the Broadway hit show *Hair* reaches number one on the Billboard chart where it resides for 13 weeks.

>> **May 1969** Vocalist Howie Vickers leaves Vancouver group The Collectors. By 1970, the group is known as Chilliwack.

>> **May 1969** Colleen Peterson joins New York band TCB, who appear at Toronto's Electric Circus.

>> **May 3, 1969** Jimi Hendrix is arrested at the Toronto airport for possession of narcotics and is subsequently released on $10,000 bail. He plays Maple Leaf Gardens that same evening.

>> **May 4, 1969** Ian & Sylvia and the Great Speckled Bird, John Lee Hooker, Hagood Hardy, Salome Bey and Stan Thomas, among others, play a benefit concert for New Orleans-born, pioneering jazz and blues guitarist Lonnie Johnson at Toronto's Ryerson Theatre. Johnson, who had been

living in Toronto for the past four years, was in critical condition after being struck by a car while walking home on Webster Avenue (near Avenue Road) in Yorkville in March of 1969. He partially recovered but passed away on June 16, 1970 and is buried in Toronto's Mount Hope Cemetery.

>> **May 14, 1969** Rock orchestra Lighthouse, formed by rock drummer Skip Prokop and jazz pianist Paul Hoffert, debuts in Toronto at the Rock Pile. Duke Ellington introduces the group. Opening act is Tony Kosinec. They make their U.S. debut the following day at the Boston Pop Festival.

▲ Joni Mitchell, self-portrait

>> **May 24, 1969** The Guess Who perform "These Eyes" and "Laughing" on *American Bandstand.*

>> **May 26, 1969** John Lennon and Yoko Ono begin their bed-in at Montreal's Queen Elizabeth Hotel (Suite 1742). Among the visitors during the week are Timothy Leary, cartoonist Al Capp, Tom Smothers, Petula Clark and Patrick Watson.

>> **June 1, 1969** Toronto-group Mandala hold their last "soul crusade."

>> **June 2, 1969** John Lennon and Yoko Ono (Plastic Ono Band) record the single "Give Peace A Chance" during their bed-in at Montréal's Queen Elizabeth Hotel. Joining in were guests Tommy Smothers on guitar, Timothy Leary, Beatles' press officer Derek Taylor, Capitol Records Canada A&R rep Pierre Dubord, Rabbi Abraham Feinberg, disc jockey Murray the K, Alan Ginsberg, Dick Gregory, Petula Clark and a host of others including local journalists and a TV camera crew. The song — as well as the B side "Remember Love," recorded in the room later with Yoko — is recorded on a four-track recorder rented from RCA by Montréal studio owner/producer/engineer André Perry (Les Studios André Perry), who also mixed the track.

>> **June 10, 1969** Tenor Jon Vickers, soprano Régine Crespin and the Montréal Symphony Orchestra perform at the opening of the National Arts Centre in Ottawa.

>> **June 20, 1969** CBC-TV's youth/ rock show *Where It's At* (formerly known as *Music Hop*), airs for the final time.

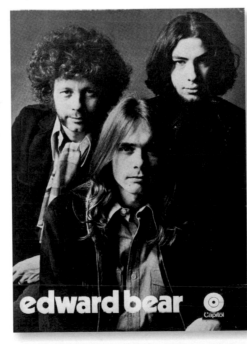

edward bear

>> **June 21, 1969** Toronto's first major rock festival, the two-day Toronto Pop Festival, is held at Varsity Stadium and Varsity Arena featuring Steppenwolf, The Band, Procol Harum, Chuck Berry, Blood, Sweat & Tears, The Byrds, Jose Feliciano, Al Kooper, Tiny Tim, Slim Harpo, Robert Charlebois, Kensington Market and Tobi Lark, among others. For Steppenwolf, it marks the first ever appearance of the current band in their hometown.

>> **June 25, 1969** Lighthouse play Carnegie Hall in New York for the first time. Radio personality Murray the K hosts what is a free concert organized by the group's label RCA. Everyone at the concert received a free Lighthouse album.

>> **Summer 1969** Toronto group Motherlode has a number one hit in Canada and Top 20 hit in the U.S. with the single "When I Die" from their debut album of the same name.

>> **Summer 1969** After the demise of the spectacular, blue-eyed soul group Mandala, band members Domenic Troiano, Roy Kenner and Whitey Glan spend the summer on a Phoenix ranch putting together the group that would emerge as Bush with the addition of Toronto bass player, Prakash John.

>> **July 1969** Anne Murray signs to Capitol Records in Canada.

>> **July 6, 1969** The Sugar Shoppe appear on the *Ed Sullivan Show.*

>> **July 14, 1969** Bob Dylan makes a surprise appearance with The Band at the Mississippi River Rock Festival in Edwardsville, Missouri.

>> **July 19, 1969** Andy Kim performs "Baby I Love You" on *American Bandstand.*

>> **July 20, 1969** Neil Armstrong becomes the first man on the moon at 4:18 p.m. EDT during the Apollo II mission.

>> **July 25, 1969** Joni Mitchell, Ian & Sylvia and Neil Young appear at the three-day, ninth annual Mariposa Folk Festival in Toronto, hosted by Oscar Brand.

>> **July 25, 1969** Neil Young makes his first in-concert appearance with Crosby, Stills and Nash.

» **August 15, 1969** The three-day Woodstock Music and Arts Fair begins on Mike Yasgur's farm in Bethel, New York.

» **August 16, 1969** The Guess Who perform "Undun" on *American Bandstand.* They are also presented with a gold record for their Top 10 hit, "These Eyes."

» **August 18, 1969** Led Zeppelin become the last major rock act to play at The Rock Pile in Toronto.

» **August 18, 1969** Instead of appearing at Woodstock, Joni Mitchell honours a commitment to appear on the Dick Cavett TV talk show. She writes the song "Woodstock" from media reports of the event.

» **August 23, 1969** The Rolling Stones' "Honky Tonk Women," featuring backing vocals by Québec star Nanette Workman, hits number one. She is also heard on the tracks "Country Honk" and "You Can't Always Get What You Want" on the band's *Let It Bleed* album.

» **August 24, 1969** Toronto's Rock Pile venue closes, a victim of the exorbitant fees now being charged by U.S. and U.K. groups.

» **August 24-29, 1969** Vancouver Pop Festival is held at the Paradise Valley Resort in Squamish, BC, featuring the Grateful Dead, Chicago, Love, Alice Cooper, Little Richard, Poco, Canned Heat, The Guess Who, Motherlode, Chamber Brothers, the Rascals, Sonny Terry & Brownie McGhee, Strawberry Alarm Clock, Taj Mahal, Flying Burrito Brothers, Grass Roots, Merryweather, Merrilee Rush and Crome Circus.

» **August 31, 1969** Bob Dylan, backed by The Band, appears at the Isle of Wight Festival in the U.K.

» **September 1969** The Band's eponymous sophomore album is released.

▲ Ronnie Hawkins, Wanda Hawkins, John Lennon, Yoko Ono

» **September 13, 1969** The Rock 'N' Revival, held at Toronto's Varsity Stadium, could well be the concert bargain of all time. For $6, punters are treated to the debut of John Lennon and Yoko Ono's Plastic Ono Band, which also features guitarist Eric Clapton, Klaus Voormann and Alan White, as well as performances by Chuck Berry, Alice Cooper, Tony Joe White, Little Richard, Bo Diddley, Chicago Transit Authority, Jerry Lee Lewis, Cat Mother and the All-Night News Boys, Doug Kershaw, Milkwood and Screaming Lord Sutch backed by local band, Whiskey Howl.

» **September 20, 1969** The Archie's "Sugar Sugar," co-written by Montreal-native Andy Kim and Jeff Barry and arguably the definitive bubble gum song, hits the number one position on the Billboard chart.

» **October 7, 1969** The National Arts Centre Orchestra/ Orchestre du Centre National des Arts, with conductor Mario Bernardi, gives it's first concert at Ottawa`s National Arts Centre.

» **October 29 – November 2, 1969** The Collectors play the Whisky A Go Go in West Hollywood with the Velvet Underground.

» **October 1969** The rumour of Paul McCartney's death causes a sudden jump in sales of all Beatles' albums, especially *Sgt. Pepper's Lonely Hearts Club Band* and *Magical Mystery Tour*, which were said to contain clues of Macca's demise in November of 1966. There had been a rumour that his replacement in the Beatles was from Ontario (Canada). The Ontario Provincial Police (OPP) crest on the jacket that Paul is wearing in the picture on the inside of the Sgt. Pepper's album sleeve did nothing to dampen that theory.

» **November 1969** As her debut album is released, Anne Murray plays her first major solo concert at Saint Mary's University in Halifax. It is organized by Leonard Rambeau, a student placement officer on campus, who will later become her manager, a position he holds for close to 25 years until his passing in April 1995.

» **November 1, 1969** Andy Kim performs "So Good Together" on *American Bandstand.* The same day, The Archies' "Sugar Sugar," co-written by Kim, hits the top of the singles chart in the U.K.

» **November 2, 1969** Led Zeppelin and local trio Edward Bear play Toronto's traditionally staid O'Keefe Centre.

» **November 2, 1969** The Band appears on the *Ed Sullivan Show.*

» **November 3, 1969** Bonnie Dobson makes her London, England debut at the Queen Elizabeth Music Hall. She

moves there the following year and becomes a regular performer on TV, radio and in concert in the U.K. and Europe.

>> **December 1969** John and Yoko spend five days at Ronnie Hawkins farm near Toronto. John signs 3000 erotic lithographs titled Bag One.

>> **December 6, 1969** The Rolling Stones play a free "thank you" concert for 300,000 fans at Altamont Speedway in Livermore, California. The disastrous event is documented in the film, *Gimme Shelter*.

>> **December 6, 1969** Steppenwolf play New York's Carnegie Hall.

>> **December 8, 1969** In Toronto for his trial for possession of hashish and heroin — he was arrested at the Toronto International Airport on May 3, 1969 — Jimi Hendrix tells the jury that he has outgrown drugs. After eight hours of deliberation, they find him not guilty.

>> **December 15, 1969** On the day that the Plastic Ono Band debut their War Is Over concert in the U.K., billboards go up in 12 major cities around the world, including New York, London and Hollywood, proclaiming: "War is Over/If You Want It."

>> **December 21, 1969** A recording of the Plastic Ono Band's debut at the Toronto Rock 'N' Roll Revival is released as Live Peace in Toronto.

>> **December 22, 1969** John Lennon and Yoko Ono arrive in Ottawa, where they meet with Canadian Prime Minister Pierre Trudeau. Earlier in the day, they chat with Canadian Minister of Health John Munro about drug abuse.

>> **December 29, 1969** The Toronto production of *Hair* opens at the Royal Alexandra Theatre with a cast that includes Terry Black, Gale Garnett, Tobi Lark, Mary Ann MacDonald and Colleen Peterson. It closes January 3, 1971.

>> **1969** *Singalong Jubilee*, the popular TV variety show from Canada's East Coast, goes national on the CBC-TV network, giving viewers across the country the chance to experience show-regular Anne Murray in performance.

>> **1969** Gordon Lightfoot records one of his three concerts at Toronto's Massey Hall. The

resulting recording is released as *Sunday Concert* (1969).

>> **1969** The Downchild Blues Band, named after the Sonny Boy Williamson song "Mr. Downchild" forms in Toronto with guitarist/harmonica player Don "Mr. Downchild" Walsh and alternating singers Rick "The Hock" Walsh and Tony Flaim. The group are regulars at Toronto's Grossman Tavern.

>> **1969** King Biscuit Boy joins the newly-formed Crowbar with whom he records the album *Official Music*. In the mid-'70s he works with the Electric Flag and The Meters on tour.

>> **1969** Hamilton, Ontario-native Harrison Kennedy joins Detroit-based group Chairmen of the Board, who have their biggest hit, "Give Me Just A Little More Time," the following year.

>> **1969** Drummer Corky Laing from Montréal, a former member of groups like Bartholomew Plus Three and Energy, joins the band Mountain, featuring Leslie West and Felix Pappalardi.

>> **1969** Tom Northcott returns to Canada following a three-year hiatus in England, and within a year he appears in concert with the Vancouver Symphony Orchestra performing the original composition, "And God Created Woman."

>> **1969** The inclusion of Steppenwolf's "Born To Be Wild" and "The Pusher" on the soundtrack of the Dennis Hopper/Peter Fonda film *Easy Rider* establishes the group's reputation internationally. "Born To Be Wild" becomes the unofficial anthem for the biker lifestyle.

>> **1969** A prolific songwriter, Jackie Rae has his biggest chart successes this year as "Please Don't Go" becomes an international hit for Eddy Arnold and is named Country Song of the Year by ASCAP. Later this year, "Happy Heart," co-written with German bandleader James Last, is a million-seller for Andy Williams, one of the many artists who cover the song.

>> **1969** The 16-member Dr. Music formed in Toronto by producer/musician Doug Riley as a group and chorus for the *Ray Stevens Show* being taped at CFTO-TV in Toronto, but turns into a full-blown recording project as the group signs to GRT Records in 1972.

▲ Anne Murray

>> **1969** Harry Hibbs, "Newfoundland's Favourite Son," becomes a popular TV star through his appearances on CHCH Hamilton's *At the Caribou* and the *Harry Hibbs Show* (1969-75).

>> **1969** Joni Mitchell tours North America with Crosby, Stills, Nash & Young

>> **1969** Salome Bey makes her stage debut in Robert Swerdlow's *Blue S.A.* in Toronto. She subsequently wins an Obie Award for her work in the New York production of *Justine* (re-titled *Love Me, Love My Children*) and takes the lead role in Galt MacDermot's New York production of *Dude* in 1972.

>> **1969** Ann Mortifee and David Wiffen co-host the TV program *Both Sides Now* at CJOH-TV in Ottawa.

>> **1969** Pianist/songwriter Jackie Mittoo moves to Toronto from Jamaica.

>> **1969** Ottawa group The Staccatos, who had a Canadian hit record in 1967 with "Half Past Midnight," change their name to Five Man Electrical Band. During the next five years, the group has a string of hit records before Les Emmerson leaves to pursue a solo career in 1974.

>> **1969** Vancouver-based band Chilliwack is commissioned by the Canadian government to compose and record the music for the Canadian pavilion at the 1970 World's Fair in Osaka, Japan. They also appear there in concert.

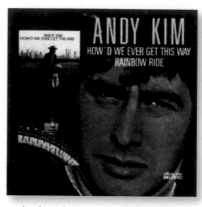

>> **1969** GRT of Canada Ltd., the Canadian subsidiary of General Recorded Tape of California, opens initially in London, Ontario, but moves to Toronto later in the year.

>> **1969** A group of 12 key Canadian Top 40 radio stations form the Maple Leaf System (MLS) to give exposure to Canadian talent by programming a minimum of three local records each week.

>> **1969** Groups formed this year include April Wine, Waverley, NS; Brutus, Toronto; Bush, Toronto; Chimo! Toronto; Crowbar, Toronto; Dionysos, Salaberry-de-Valleyfield, QC; Downchild Blues Band, Toronto; Dr. Music, Toronto; Five Man Electrical Band, Ottawa; Great Speckled Bird, Toronto; Kate & Anna McGarrigle, Saint-Sauveur des Monts, QC; Mashmakhan, Montréal; Milkwood, Toronto; Motherlode, London, ON; Myles & Lenny, Toronto; Neil Young & Crazy Horse, Los Angeles; Offenbach, Montréal; Perth County Conspiracy, Stratford, ON; Ryan's Fancy, St. John's, NF; Simon Caine, Toronto; Steel River, Toronto; Stonebolt, Vancouver.

▲ Anna and Kate McGarrigle

CHART-TOPPING CANADIAN SONGS 1960-1969

1960 **The Theme From A Summer Place** PERCY FAITH AND HIS ORCHESTRA
1960 **Clap Your Hands** THE BEAU MARKS
1960 **The Blamers** LES VOGT
1963 **Charlena** RITCHIE KNIGHT AND THE MID-KNIGHTS
1964 **Ringo** LORNE GREENE
1965 **Shakin' All Over** THE GUESS WHO

1965 **You Really Got A Hold On Me** LITTLE CAESAR AND THE CONSULS
1967 **Canada** YOUNG CANADA SINGERS
1968 **Born To Be Wild** STEPPENWOLF
1968 **Magic Carpet Ride** STEPPENWOLF
1969 **Laughing** THE GUESS WHO
1969 **When I Die** MOTHERLODE

OH WHAT A FEELING

Beneath its snowy mantle cold and clean

The unborn grass lies waiting for its coat to turn to green.

The snowbird sings the song he always sings ...

— Snowbird

Lyrics & Music by Gene MacLellan and performed by Anne Murray.

» 1970–1979

»1970-1979

»1970

» **January 1970** Ginette Reno plays a two-week engagement at London's Savoy Hotel, appears on a BBC-TV special *Young Generation* and guests on the Tom Jones TV show. The globe-trotting Reno becomes the first singer from Québec to appear on Johnny Carson's *Tonight Show*.

» **January 2, 1970** Lighthouse plays the Fillmore East in New York with the Grateful Dead.

» **January 12, 1970** The Band makes the cover of *Time* magazine. The group's Garth Hudson is referred to as "beyond question, the most brilliant organist in the rock world."

» **January 15, 1970** Ronnie Hawkins and rock journalist Ritchie Yorke set out on an around-the-world trip as peace emissaries for John Lennon, risking their lives at one point to hold up posters in both Chinese and English at the Hong Kong/China border that read "War Is Over (If You Want It)."

» **January 17, 1970** The Band plays Toronto's Massey Hall with Jesse Winchester.

» **January 31, 1970** The Ronnie Hawkins single "Down In the Alley" debuts on the Billboard chart in the U.S.

» **February 1970** The first RPM Weekly Gold Leaf Awards, precursor to the JUNO Awards, are presented at a ceremony at St. Lawrence Hall in Toronto.

» **February 5, 1970** The Irish Rovers appear at the Bitter End in New York.

» **February 17, 1970** Joni Mitchell announces she will retire from live performances after her show at London's Royal Albert Hall. The retirement is short-lived, though, as she's back on the road within a year.

» **February 26, 1970** Ronnie Hawkins appears on Britain's *Top of the Pops* TV Show.

» **March 3, 1970** Canadian folk duo Fraser & DeBolt play the Fillmore East in New York.

» **March 11, 1970** The sophomore Blood, Sweat & Tears album, featuring

▲ The Irish Rovers

David Clayton-Thomas as vocalist/co-songwriter, wins three Grammy awards, unprecedented to that point.

» **March 14, 1970** Ronnie Hawkins introduces his new group, And Many Others (later Crowbar), at a press gathering at the Hawk's Nest on Yonge Street in Toronto before appearing at the Fillmore East in New York with Joe Cocker and Mad Dogs and Englishmen and Stone the Crows. Bob Dylon was in the audience. Crowbar leave Hawkins in May 1971 to record the album *Official Music* with King Biscuit Boy.

» **March 16-18, 1970** Having departed The Guess Who, Randy Bachman records a solo album (*Axe*) at RCA's Mid-America Recording Center in Chicago.

» **April 1, 1970** April Wine drives into Montréal from the Maritimes believing that a kindly-worded rejection of a demo tape they had sent to Terry Flood, who, in partnership with concert promoter Donald Tarlton, ran the Laugh-In Club and Aquarius Records, was in fact a couched invitation to come west to La Belle Province. Flood and Tarlton take pity on them and put the band up in a ski chalet in the rustic setting of The Laurentians, just north of Montréal, where they rehearse songs for what they hope will be their debut album.

» **April 3, 1970** Tobi Lark from the Toronto cast of Hair, backed by 600

singers at Toronto's St. Paul's Church and 15 musicians, records a "gospel/rock message of peace" titled "We're All In This Together" written by Mike McQueen of the group, Cat. The ambitious recording project, which also spawns a half hour TV special, is packaged under the name *Toronto Together*.

>> **April 4, 1970** Lighthouse plays in concert with The Toronto Symphony.

>> **April 21, 1970** Drummer Skip Prokop (Lighthouse, The Paupers) becomes the first Canadian musician to address the Canadian Parliament. He was invited by Prime Minster Pierre Elliott Trudeau to speak about the lot of musicians and songwriters in Canada as part of hearings that led to the formation of the Canadian Radio and Television Commission (CRTC).

>> **May 1970** The Canadian group Full Tilt Boogie Band makes its debut as Janis Joplin's backing band at a Hell's Angel benefit in San Rafael, California. Members include ex-Pauper Brad Campbell, Stratford, Ontario-raised guitarist John Till, pianist Richard Bell, Woodstock, Ontario-raised organist Ken Pearson, and drummer Clark Pierson.

>> **May 4, 1970** The killing of four students by National Guard troops at a campus demonstration at Kent State University protesting the escalation of the Vietnam War inspires Neil Young to compose "Ohio," an angry diatribe against the dehumanization of American society. The incident itself gives rise to the May 4th Movement (M4M), a continent-wide movement. In Canada, they would disrupt the Festival Express tour in Canada by urging people to crash the concert as they believed music should be free.

>> **May 9, 1970** The Guess Who hit the top of the Billboard charts for three weeks with the single, "American Woman." They are the first Canadian group to have a number one record on the Billboard chart in the U.S. and the first to have a Top 10 album (*American Woman*).

>> **May 16, 1970** Crosby, Stills, Nash & Young's studio LP, Déjà Vu, the first of only three, hits the number one position on Billboard's album chart. The album includes the Joni Mitchell-penned hit, "Woodstock" and "Helpless," a staple of Neil Young's repertoire.

>> **May 16, 1970** When The Guess Who appear at The White House with Prince Charles and Princess Anne in attendance, they are politely asked by First Lady Pat Nixon

not to perform "American Woman." Founding member Randy Bachman decides to leave the group shortly after a concert at New York's Fillmore East. He is replaced by former members of the Winnipeg group Gettysburg Address, guitarists Greg Leskiw and Kurt "The Walrus" Winter.

>> **May 30, 1970** John Kay, whose group Steppenwolf is on the Cheap Thrills 2 bill at Toronto's Maple Leaf Gardens with James Gang, Buddy Miles Express and Taj Mahal, doesn't get the chance to return in triumph to the venue where he once sold popcorn and peanuts due to a case of strep throat.

>> **May 30, 1970** Toronto's "total environment" multi-room rock club, The Electric Circus at 99 Queen Street East, closes. It had contained adult play-rooms like The Womb Room, where you could crawl into a hole in the wall, and The Meditation Room, with a computerized sound and light show. It later becomes the first home of the Canadian video network, *MuchMusic*, and its local sister station, Citytv.

>> **June 1970** Crowbar move into a 120-year old farmhouse/mansion in Ancaster, Ontario and name it "Bad Manors."

>> **June 12, 1970** The Full Tilt Boogie Band debut in concert with Janis Joplin at Freedom Hall in Louisville, Kentucky.

>> **June 13, 1970** The Poppy Family, featuring the husband

and wife team of Terry and Susan Jacks, hit the number two position on the Billboard chart with the single "Which Way You Goin', Billy?" Susan Jacks becomes only the second Canadian female vocalist to earn a gold record (Lucille Starr was the first in the mid-'60s) as the single sells over 50,000 copies.

» **June 14, 1970** Blood, Sweat & Tears embark on a tour of Yugoslavia, Romania and Poland. It is one of the first tours by a Western rock band of Soviet-bloc countries and they face a backlash from some quarters upon their return to the U.S.

» **June 24, 1970** The Canadian Radio and Television Commission (CRTC) declares that 30% of AM radio music content must be Canadian.

» **June 28, 1970** The Festival Express Toronto-Calgary train/concert excursion sets out from Toronto. On board are The Band, Janis Joplin and the Full Tilt Boogie Band, Delaney & Bonnie and Friends, Buddy Guy's Band, Ian & Sylvia and the Great Speckled Bird, Eric Andersen, Tom Rush, James and the Good Brothers, The New Riders of the Purple Sage, Robert Charlebois, Mashmakhan, and Bob Weir of the Grateful Dead.

» **July 10, 1970** The Band appear at the Hollywood Bowl in Los Angeles with Miles Davis as opening artist.

» **July 24-26, 1970** Joni Mitchell appears at the Mariposa Folk Festival on the Toronto Islands, her first public engagement in 6 months.

» **July 1970** *A Ballet High*, a collaboration of Lighthouse and the Royal Winnipeg Ballet, opens at Ottawa's National Arts Centre before moving on to Toronto's St. Lawrence Centre.

» **August 1970** Montréal band Mashmakhan make an immediate impact at home and abroad with the single "As the Years Go By" from their self-titled debut album. Never intended as a single until a Montréal deejay, the late Roger Scott, begins playing it to good response on his show on radio station CFOX. It tops the charts in Canada and, in the fall, is a Top 40 hit in the U.S., but it is in Japan where the group makes its biggest mark. The success of the single, which reportedly sells close to 800,000 copies there, leads to major concert dates in Osaka and Tokyo in July 1971, the latter of which draws 40,000 people.

» **August 6, 1970** Janis Joplin and the Full Tilt Boogie Band make their last New York appearance at the Festival for Peace at Shea Stadium.

» **August 7-10, 1970** The Strawberry Fields Rock Festival, organized to take advantage of the publicity surrounding John Lennon's aborted peace festival, was planned for July in Moncton, New Brunswick but was run out of

town by local officials. Toronto-based promoter John Brower moves the whole operation to the Mosport Race Track near Bowmanville, Ontario. The festival, which is only advertised in the U.S. to get around legal problems surrounding the event in Canada, gets off to a shaky start when organizers have trouble getting motorcycles to make at least one revolution of the track through the huge crowds to qualify the event as a race with music rather than just a rock festival, which had been the basis of getting a permit. Thousands of Americans are refused entry to Canada on the grounds that they "failed to produce adequate monies to support themselves." Over 8000 Americans make it to the event anyway to join the estimated 75,000 to 100,000 strong crowd in seeing an impressive line-up of talent, including Alice Cooper, James Ambrose, Cactus, Crowbar (featuring King Biscuit Boy), Delaney and Bonnie & Friends, Fat Chance, Jose Feliciano, Freedom Express, Grand Funk Railroad, Hog Heaven, Jethro Tull, Leigh Ashford, Lighthouse, Luke and the Apostles, Melanie, Mountain, Procol Harum, Sly and the Family Stone, Syrinx, Ten Years After, and The Youngbloods. Led Zeppelin and Leonard Cohen were also on the bill, but both were no-shows.

» **August 8, 1970** Having recently entered the concert promotion business with his company Cymba Presents, Michael Cohl, who over the years would establish himself as one of the pre-eminent concert promoters of his time working with artists like The Rolling Stones, Pink Floyd, David Bowie, and U2, among many others, produces his first multi-artist concert at the long-departed Stanley Park Stadium on King Street West (south side) near Bathurst Street in Toronto. Billed as Beggar's Banquet, the festival includes a free health food meal and performances by Procol

Harum, Poco, Melanie, Sha Na Na and local group Icarus, which Cohl is managing with Bob Ezrin, who is today one of the music world's top record producers. The concert struggles mightily at the box office when it is announced that the Strawberry Fields Festival had moved from Moncton to Mosport.

>> **August 12, 1970** Janis Joplin and the Full Tilt Boogie Band play their final concert together at Harvard Stadium, Cambridge, Massachusetts in front of 40,000 fans.

>> **August 26, 1970** An appearance at the Isle of Wight Pop Festival in England, which features Jimi Hendrix, Bob Dylan, Joan Baez, Lighthouse, Leonard Cohen and Ritchie Havens, among others, comes to a tearful end for Joni Mitchell as a man jumps onto the stage during her set, grabs the mic and shouts: "This is just a hippie concentration camp!"

>> **August 26-30, 1970** By the early '70s, Leonard Cohen is touring extensively in the U.S. and in Europe with backing group The Army, which includes producer and long-time friend, Bob Johnston. He appears at the Isle of Wight Festival in England, on the same bill as Jimi Hendrix, who is making one of his last concert appearances.

>> **August 29, 1970** Toronto-born songwriter, producer, and recording artist R. Dean Taylor performs "Indiana Wants Me" on Dick Clark's *American Bandstand* TV show.

>> **August 29, 1970** The Man-Pop Festival, which was originally to be held at the outdoor Winnipeg Stadium but was shifted to the Winnipeg Arena because of a violent rain storm, features Led Zeppelin, Iron Butterfly, Chilliwack, The Ides of March and The Youngbloods, among others. The change of site had caused issues with capacity and some ticket holders were left outside causing a near riot. The delays meant that headliners Led Zeppelin weren't scheduled until the wee hours of the morning. Local lore has it that it was the late Dianne Heatherington (Dianne Heatherington and the Merry-Go-Round), one of the local artists on the bill, who saved the show when she "shamed" the members of Led Zeppelin into taking to the stage instead of bailing on the date, even though they had already been paid their reported $50,000 fee given the rain clause in their contract.

>> **September 11, 1970** Jimi Hendrix dies.

>> **September 22, 1970** A French adaptation of *Hair* opens in Montréal at the Comédie-Canadienne starring Marie-Louis Dion, Francois Guy and Sebastian.

>> **Fall 1970** R. Dean Taylor hits the Top 5 of the Billboard Singles chart with "Indiana Wants Me." At the time, Taylor is working at Motown Records in Detroit as a contract producer and songwriter. He co-wrote a number of chart-toppers for The Four Tops ("I'll Turn To Stone"), The Temptations ("You Keep Turning Away") and The Supremes ("I'm Living In Shame" and "Love Child," a number one song).

>> **Fall 1970** Janis Joplin and the Full Tilt Boogie Band enter the studio in Los Angeles to begin recording her *Pearl* album.

>> **Fall 1970** Ian Tyson and the Great Speckled Bird star in the new CTV series, *Nashville North*.

>> **October 1970** Randy Bachman begins work on a recording project for singer Chad Allan, which will soon be joined by Robbie Bachman, his brother, on drums.

>> **October 1970** Terry and Susan Jacks (The Poppy Family) perform "Which Way You Goin' Billy?" during the taping in Toronto of Bobby Darin's syndicated Canadian television variety special, *The Darin Invasion*, which also features George Burns, Pat Carroll and Linda Ronstadt.

>> **October 1970** The War Measures Act is invoked at the height of the October Crisis. Members of a radical Québec separatist group, the Front de Liberation du Québec (FLQ), kidnap British trade official James Cross and murder Québec minister, Pierre Laporte. During this period, singer Pauline Julien is detained.

>> **October 4, 1970** Janis Joplin passes away in Hollywood.

>> **October 4, 1970** Anne Murray makes her first appearance on CBS-TV's *The Glen Campbell Goodtime Hour*. During the next two years, she becomes a regular guest.

>> **October 12, 1970** The original hand-written lyrics to Joni Mitchell's first album, *Song To A Seagull*, are among the items on offer at a Bill Graham-organized auction at the Fillmore East in New York with the proceeds benefitting the political campaigns of candidates committed to peace and the end of the Vietnam War.

◀ Jimi Hendrix, with his father, "Al," a Vancouver resident

>> **October 23, 1970** Anne Murray has the first of many CBC-TV specials.

>> **November 1970** Lighthouse appear in concert with the Edmonton Symphony Orchestra at the Jubilee Auditorium in Edmonton, Alberta.

>> **November 7, 1970** Following a short Japanese tour, Chilliwack appear in concert with the Toronto Symphony at Toronto's O'Keefe Centre.

>> **November 7, 1970** Matthew's Southern Comfort hits number one on the U.K. singles chart with the Joni Mitchell song, "Woodstock."

>> **November 10, 1970** Anne Murray receives a gold record for "Snowbird" on the *Merv Griffin Show*. It is the first record by a Canadian female singer to exceed a million sales in the U.S.

>> **November 22, 1970** Crowbar appear with Van Morrison at Toronto's Massey Hall shortly before the release of their

album, *Bad Manors*, and the single "Oh What A Feeling," the biggest hit of their career and the first Canadian single released after the inception of the CRTC Canadian Content rulings.

>> **Winter 1970** The Guess Who's producer Jack Richardson wins a Trendsetter Award from *Billboard* for his part in the international success of the group in 1970, the year they sold more singles internationally than any other act in the world.

>> **Winter 1970** Having just made a guest appearance on the Johnny Cash Show in Nashville, Anne Murray drops into a little Irish pub during a stop-over in New York for a bite to eat. It is about seven o'clock in the evening and somebody in the restaurant put her single "Snowbird" on the jukebox. "I freaked," Murray recalled. "The song had already been up

and down the charts but it was the first time that it struck me that 'Snowbird' was, in fact, a hit record. It was just hearing it out of the blue, in the middle of New York, being played by someone I didn't know, that really hit home."

>> **December 23, 1970** Joni Mitchell, who has to this point gained international recognition as a songwriter through Judy Collins' rendition of "Both Sides Now" and Matthews Southern Comfort and Crosby, Stills, Nash & Young's versions of "Woodstock," earns her first gold record in the U.S. for her third album, *Ladies of the Canyon*.

>> **December 31, 1970** Cymba Presents the Winter Pop concert at Toronto's Maple Leaf Gardens featuring James Gang, Johnny Winter, Sha Na Na, Rare Earth, Chilliwack and Steel River.

>> **1970** Having discovered improv comedy at numerous clubs and through various comedy troupes like Chicago's Second City and San Francisco's The Committee (which he would visit while on tour with Bobby Taylor & the Vancouvers), Tommy Chong decides to form his own company called The City Works at his brother's club, the Shanghai Junk, in Vancouver. Among the comics who perform there during this period is Richard "Cheech" Marin. Chong found that he played well off Cheech and, when he eventually disbanded his City Works troupe, the duo hit the road together doing the comedy club circuit.

>> **1970** Singers Terry Black and Laurel Ward join Dr. Music, the Toronto-based group fronted by acclaimed keyboardist/arranger Doug "Doc" Riley.

>> **1970** The MAPL Logo, which designates the Canadian Content in a record (M=music composer and songwriter; A=artist; P= production; and L=lyricist), is designed by Stan Klees of the Canadian music trade magazine, *RPM Weekly*.

>> **1970** Bruce Cockburn provides the soundtrack for the critically-acclaimed Canadian feature film, *Goin' Down the Road*.

>> **1970** Bob McBride joins Lighthouse as lead vocalist.

>> **1970** With Jimi Hendrix as his major inspiration, Frank Marino forms the heavy rock trio, Mahogany Rush in Montréal.

>> **1970** Murray McLauchlan signs a management agreement with Toronto-based Bernie Finkelstein (joining The Paupers and Bruce Cockburn) following performances in New York's Greenwich Village.

>> **1970** The Poppy Family turn down an appearance on *The Ed Sullivan Show* to play at Expo '70 in Osaka Japan.

>> **1970** Composer/Moog synthesizer player John Mill-Cockell, a former member of the Toronto group Kensington

Market and a pioneer in electronic music in Canada, is seen weekly with his group Syrinx on the CBC-TV program, *Here Come the Seventies*, playing the theme, "Tillicum," that he had written for the show.

» **1970** Nine-year-old Rene Simard is discovered by currently disgraced Québec impresario, Guy Cloutier.

» **1970** When a back injury forces Gary Fjellgaard to retire from his work as a lumberjack , he turns to music full time.

» **1970** James and the Good Brothers record their first album in San Francisco.

» **1970** Robert Goulet wins a Tony Award for his role in the Broadway production of *The Happy Time*. Through the '60s, Goulet had been a regular on TV and appeared in a number of stage-to-TV productions, including *Brigadoon* (1966), *Carousel* (1967) and *Kiss Me Kate* (1968).

» **1970** Myrna Lorrie and Don Tremaine co-host *Countrytime*, a CBC-TV program originating from Halifax.

» **1970** Jazzman Clarence "Big" Miller moves to Edmonton and becomes a staple of the local jazz scene.

» **1970** Montréal group The Five Bells, formed around the husband and wife team of Cliff and Anne Edwards, change their name to The Bells following the departure of Anne Edwards and the arrival of her sister Jackie Ralph.

» **1970** Crosby, Stills, Nash & Young's *Déjà Vu* is the year's best-selling album in the U.S.

» **1970** Anne Murray signs the first ever exclusive contract with CBC-TV as she begins another series of *Singalong Jubilee* and makes a number of appearances on the *Tommy Hunter Show*.

» **1970** Daniel Lanois and his brother Bob build a studio at their mother's home in Ancaster, Ontario. In 1980, the brothers build the popular Grant Avenue Studio in Hamilton. Daniel Lanois' collaboration there with Brian Eno in the early '80s led to an international reputation, which saw Lanois work with artists like U2 (*The Unforgettable Fire*, *The Joshua Tree*), Peter Gabriel (*So*), Robbie Robertson (*Robbie Robertson*), The Neville Brothers (*Yellow Moon*) and Bob Dylan (*Oh Mercy*).

» **1970** A&M Records of Canada Ltd., the Canadian subsidiary of A&M Records based in Los Angeles, is established in Canada.

» **1970** MCA Records Canada, which evolved from Herbert S. Berliner's The Compo Company, is established in Toronto.

» **1970** Aquarius Records Ltd. is founded in Montréal by Terry Flood, Donald Tarlton, Bob Lemm and Jack and Dan Lazare.

» **1970** Public broadcaster TV Ontario (TVO) signs on.

» **1970** Groups formed this year include A Foot In Coldwater, Toronto; Bush, Toronto/Phoenix; Canadian Brass, Toronto; Chilliwack, Vancouver; Crowbar, Hamilton; Mahogany Rush, Montréal; Ocean, Toronto; Painter, Calgary; The Bells, Montréal; and Wednesday, Oshawa.

» 1971

» **January 1971** Anne Murray moves to Toronto from Springhill, Nova Scotia

» **January 6, 1971** Neil Young plays Vancouver's Queen Elizabeth Theatre, his first Canadian concert since his pre-stardom coffee house days.

» **January 18, 1971** The Canadian Content Regulations for AM radio go into effect requiring that 30% of all musical compositions played between 6:00 a.m. and midnight be Canadian. The Crowbar song "Oh What A Feeling" is the first Canadian single release of the CanCon era.

» **February 1971** April Wine, who have become a regular attraction at the Laugh-In club in Montreal, record their first album for Aquarius Records

» **February 22, 1971** The first annual JUNO Awards ceremony is held at the St. Lawrence Hall in Toronto hosted by George Wilson of Toronto radio station CFRB. Spear-headed by Anne Murray's "Snowbird," the Maritimers are already movin' in. Anne Murray means business 'cause she's wearing shoes now, not barefoot like on *Singalong Jubilee* and *Frank's Bandstand*. The "Snowbird" single does emerge as the story from these first JUNOs, responsible for five of the 16 trophies presented this year including Murray's first ever JUNO, which she picks up for Top Female Vocalist, and the Composer of Year JUNO, which is taken home by the late Gene MacLellan, the song's writer. Almost 40% of the JUNOs are presented to industry organizations, and award presenters are all Canadian music industry executives. Just over a month after the Canadian Content regulations for radio had taken effect, Pierre Juneau, the chairman of the Canadian Radio and Television Commission (CRTC), who had been the person most responsible for their introduction, picks up a JUNO as Music Industry Man of the Year.

» **March 20, 1971** The late Janis Joplin, backed by Canadian group The Full Tilt Boogie Band, tops the Billboard Hot 100 singles chart with "Me and Bobby McGee" from the album *Pearl*, which was left unfinished at the time of her death in October of 1970.

» **March 27, 1971** Meredith Davies conducts Vancouver group Spring and the Vancouver Symphony Orchestra in a Bob Buckley rock/symphony composition, "Son of Zonk."

>> **April 1971** The group Brave Belt, which had evolved from a recording project for singer Chad Allan overseen by Randy Bachman, signs to Reprise Records. The touring group consists of Randy and Robbie Bachman, Chad Allan and bassist Fred Turner. The *Brave Belt I* album is released the following month. Allan departs shortly after the release of the album and is replaced on vocals by Turner as the material takes a significantly heavier turn. The *Brave Belt II* album is released the following year, during which time, Randy and Robbie Bachman's brother Tim is added to the group on guitar.

>> **April 5, 1971** Lighthouse appear with the Vancouver Symphony Orchestra with Paul Hoffert of the group conducting.

>> **May 3, 1971** Gordon Lightfoot is the first non-classical act booked to play New York's Philharmonic Hall at Lincoln Centre.

>> **May 15, 1971** The Crosby, Stills, Nash & Young album *Four Way Street* hits the number one position on the Billboard albums chart. It is the group's second consecutive number one album. Déjà Vu topped the chart in 1970.

>> **June 3, 1971** The Band complete their first European tour with a concert at London's Royal Albert Hall.

>> **June 26, 1971** The first of three "Cymba Presents" Beggars Banquet (Dance) Festivals held at the Borough of York Stadium in Toronto this summer, featuring Alice Cooper, Bread, The Beach Boys, Chilliwack, Steppenwolf, Blood Rock, Lighthouse and Old Rationals.

>> **July 1971** Bim (Roy Forbes), one of the most distinctive voices and songwriters in Canadian music, arrives in Vancouver from Dawson Creek, BC, and hits the club circuit. He plays the Queen Elizabeth Theatre in the city by the end of the year.

>> **July 18, 1971** The next Beggars Banquet (Dance) Festival held at Toronto's Borough of York Stadium this summer features Black Sabbath, The Guess Who, Humble Pie, Grease Band and Three Dog Night.

>> **Summer 1971** Crowbar make their U.S. debut at the Whisky A Go Go in Los Angeles.

▲ Gary Brooker (left) and Keith Reid (right) of Procol Harum with Ritchie Yorke (centre)

>> **August 6, 1971** The Edmonton Symphony Orchestra, with conductor Lawrence Leonard and the 24-member Da Camera Singers, record a live album with British group Procol Harum for A&M Records during the course of a concert at the Jubilee Auditorium in Edmonton. (Procol Harum had previously appeared in concert with the Stratford Festival Orchestra in Stratford, Ontario.) The resulting album, *Procol Harum with the Edmonton Symphony Orchestra*, becomes the group's most successful album in the wake of the hit single, "Conquistador."

>> **August 21, 1971** The third Beggars Banquet (Dance) Festival held at Toronto's Borough of York Stadium features The Band, Edgar Winter's White Trash, Lee Michaels, Sea Train, Sundance and Sha Na Na.

>> **September 11, 1971** The Stampeders' single "Sweet City Woman" follows up a chart-topping summer in Canada by climbing into the Top 10 of the Billboard chart in the U.S. It peaks, on this day, at number eight.

>> **September 23, 1971** Crowbar return from a U.S. tour and play a homecoming concert at Toronto's Massey Hall on this date.

>> **December 31, 1971** Bob Dylan joins The Band onstage for their encore at a New Year's concert at the New York Academy of Music. The Band's set is later released as the live album, *Rock of Ages*.

>> **December 31, 1971** David Clayton-Thomas makes his last appearance (for the moment) with Blood, Sweat & Tears at the Anaheim Convention Center. It also marks the last gig for The Poppy Family, who are on the same bill.

>> **1971** Canadian Independent Record Production Association (CIRPA) is founded.

>> **1971** Daffodil Records is co-founded in Toronto by English expatriate record executive and producer Frank Davies.

>> **1971** Boot Records is founded in Toronto by recording artist Stompin' Tom Connors and his manager, Jury Krytiuk.

>> **1971** Quadraphonic (four channel) records make a brief appearance on the market.

>> **1971** Jackie Ralph's unique vocal style is showcased at its sensual best

as Montreal group The Bells have their biggest hit, "Stay Awhile," written by Ken Tobias.

» **1971** Leonard Cohen provides the soundtrack for the Warren Beatty film *McCabe and Mrs. Miller.*

» **1971** Ten-year-old René Simard makes his performance debut at Montréal's Place des Arts and is an instant hit.

» **1971** Windsor, Ontario-born singer Dorothy Collins is given a starring role in the Stephen Sondheim musical, *Follies.* She receives a Tony nomination for her performance.

» **1971** Blue Rodeo's Jim Cuddy and Greg Keelor are "first down and 110 yards to go" with their music career at this point as members of the North Toronto Collegiate football team.

» **1971** *The Ian Tyson Show*, formerly known as *Nashville North*, debuts on the CTV Network.

» **1971** The Irish Rovers begin a five-year run with their own CBC-TV series out of Vancouver.

» **1971** Sixteen-year-old singer/songwriter Shirley Eikhard, who has already appeared on CBC-TV's *Singalong Jubilee* and at the Mariposa Folk Festival, gets the big career break as her song "It Takes Time" is recorded by Anne Murray. She signs with Capitol Records the same year.

» **1971** Rita MacNeil leaves Big Pond, Cape Breton and moves to Toronto, where she takes odd jobs and records her self-titled debut album.

» **1971** Record executive Lou Adler sees the comedy duo Cheech & Chong at The Troubadour in Los Angeles and signs them to his Ode Records label.

» **1971** Guitarist Danny Marks leaves Edward Bear and joins Rick James' Stone City Band, while Edward Bear, led by drummer, vocalist, songwriter Larry Evoy, go on in a poppier vein and hit the top of the charts with the singles "Last Song" (1972) and "Close Your Eyes" (1973).

» **1971** Vancouver group Brahman forms around its primary songwriters, Robbie King and Duris Maxwell.

» **1971** Winnipeg-born singer Dianne Heatherington hosts the national CBC-TV series, *Dianne.*

» **1971** Popular Vancouver radio personality Red Robinson becomes the host of the morning show at radio station CKWX, a position he will hold for the next 12 years.

» **1971** Trumpeter Maynard Ferguson, having previously moved to the U.K., makes his North American debut with his 17-piece English band.

» **1971** Wilf Carter (aka Montana Slim) is inducted into the Nashville Songwriters Association Hall of Fame.

▲ Dorothy Collins in Stephen Sondheim's *Follies*

» **1971** Groups formed this year include Brave Belt, Winnipeg; Fludd, Toronto; Skylark, Vancouver; and Stringband, Toronto.

» 1972

» **February 1972** Terry Black and Laurel Ward, who began their singing collaboration when they both appeared in the Toronto production of *Hair*, have a hit internationally with their single, "Goin' Down (On the Road to L.A.)."

» **February 14, 1972** Los Angeles Mayor Sam Yorty declares this "Steppenwolf Day" on the occasion of the group's announced "retirement." It actually turns into a sabbatical and the group returns after a few years.

» **February 28, 1972** At the second annual JUNO Awards, held at the Centennial Ballroom of the Inn On the Park hotel in Toronto and hosted by George Wilson of CFRB, the Stampeders round up three JUNOs on the strength of "Sweet City Woman." The short-lived Outstanding Performance categories for male, female and group are introduced. Nashville-based George Hamilton IV becomes the first foreign performer to win a JUNO. Hamilton, to this point, has recorded three albums of all-Canadian material. CRTC Chairman Pierre Juneau presents Anne Murray with her second consecutive JUNO as Female Vocalist of the Year. Writes Marci McDonald of the *Toronto Star*: "From an industry that has barely begun to burgeon — scarcely a year since the institution of radio's 30 percent Canadian content quotas — it was a ceremony that lasted not quite an hour, lagged not a second and was carried off with such simple panache and dispatch that it made all those interminable glory shows, the Grammys and the Oscars and even the Canadian film awards, look like amateur night at the high school gym."

» **March 11, 1972** Neil Young's *Harvest* album reaches number one on the Billboard album chart.

» **March 18, 1972** Neil Young tops the Billboard singles chart with "Heart of Gold," which had been recorded in

Nashville with Linda Ronstadt and James Taylor on back-up vocals.

» **April 1972** Tim Bachman is added to the line-up of Brave Belt on guitar following the release of the band's sophomore album. He is the brother of group members Robbie and Randy Bachman.

» **June 2, 1972** The Maple Music Junket, a project designed to develop markets in Europe for Canadian pop records, is launched by Canada's recording industry with financial support from the federal government. On this day, a party of more than 100 leading writers, editors, broadcasters, producers and filmmakers from more than a dozen European countries arrive in Canada for seven days of hospitality and concerts in Montréal (Place des Arts), Val David (La Butte a Mathieu) and Toronto (Massey Hall).

» **June 3, 1972** Québec Chaud 1, Butte a Mathieu, Val David, QC: Edith Butler, France Castel, Gabriel Charbonneau, Richard Huet, Les Contretemps, Martin Peltier, Isabelle Pierre, Richard et Marie-Claire Séguin.

» **June 4, 1972** Québec Chaud 2, Place des Arts, Montréal, QC: Julie Arel, Luc et Lise Cousineau, Joel Denis, Marc Hamilton, Karo, Shirley Théroux, Guy Trépanier, Vos Voisins.

» **June 5, 1972** Maple Music Spectacular 1, Place des Arts, Montréal, QC: André Gagnon, Moe Koffman, Frank Mills, Anne Murray, The Poppy Family, The Stampeders, Tapestry.

» **June 6, 1972** Maple Music Spectacular 2, Massey Hall, Toronto, ON: Gary Buck, Bruce Cockburn, Fergus, Christopher Kearney, Murray McLauchlan, Perth County Conspiracy, The Mercey Brothers.

» **June 7, 1972** Maple Music Spectacular 3, Massey Hall, Toronto, ON: April Wine, Crowbar, Edward Bear, Fludd, Lighthouse, Mashmakhan, Noah.

» **July 1, 1972** The "Tribal Love-Rock Musical" *Hair* closes on Broadway after 1729 performances.

» **July 1972** Northern Lights/Festival Boréal, Canada's oldest continuously running folk festival, is first held in Bell Park, including the Grace Hartman Amphitheatre, on the shore of Sudbury, Ontario's Lake Ramsey. The festival presents an annual Jackie Washington Award "for distinguished contribution to Northern Ontario's cultural life." Past recipients have included musician and politician Charlie Angus, Robert Paquette, Ken Whiteley and Paul Dunn.

» **August 19, 1972** Heart forms in Seattle/Vancouver around Ann Wilson, Roger Fisher and Steve Fossen of the Seattle band Hocus Pocus. The line-up was completed with the later addition of Howard Leese and Nancy Wilson.

» **August 28, 1972** The album, *Procol Harum Live in Concert with the Edmonton Symphony Orchestra* is certified gold in the U.S. for sales of over 500,000 copies. The record includes the Top 20 U.S. hit, "Conquistador."

» **September 28, 1972** Paul Henderson scores the winning goal with 34 seconds left in the game as Team Canada defeats the Soviet National Team 6-5 in the final game of the Canada-Soviet Hockey series.

» **November 18, 1972** Danny Whitten, former member of the group Crazy Horse, dies in Los Angeles of a heroin overdose. Bruce Berry, a former roadie for Crosby, Stills, Nash & Young, died of the same drug during this period. They are both memorialized in Neil Young's *Tonight's the Night* album (1975).

» **1972** Journeyman musician David Foster, at this point a member of the Vancouver group Skylark, heads for Los Angeles in a Volkswagen van packed with the band members' worldly belongings. The group is about to record for Capitol Records, but while they attended a meeting at the Capitol Tower, the van is broken into and everything is stolen. They don't leave L.A. empty-handed though. The subsequent album produces the hit single, "Wildflower."

» **1972** MusicFest Canada is founded, initially as the Canadian Stage Band Festival, by Robert Richmond, Gary Wadsworth and Paul Milner. This competition festival is credited with the development of student interest in big-band jazz in Canadian high school and universities.

» **1972** Guitarist Domenic Troiano and vocalist Roy Kenner join The James Gang.

» **1972** Larry Good replaces James Ackroyd in James and the Good Brothers, and the three Good Brothers debut at The Riverboat in Toronto's Yorkville Village.

» **1972** While touring Europe in *Catch My Soul*, a stage musical version of Shakespeare's *Othello*, Claudja Barry catches the ear of German producer Jorgen Korduletsch, who signs her to his Lollipop label in Munich. She subsequently moves to Munich and her singing career, marked by a number of international hits in the disco field including the biggest, "Boogie Woogie Dancin' Shoes" (1978), begins in earnest. Barry is

▲ Heart

also a founding member of the European supergroup, Boney M.

>> **1972** Toronto band A Foot In Coldwater — British slang for "bad luck" — which features former members of the Lords of London and Nucleus, have their self-titled debut album released on the Daffodil Records label. It features the classic single, "(Make Me Do) Anything You Want."

>> **1972** April Wine's cover of the song "You Could Have Been A Lady," which had been a British hit for Hot Chocolate, marks the group's earliest visit to the U.S. Top 40 chart.

>> **1972** Sam Feldman, a former night club doorman in Vancouver, establishes S.L. Feldman & Associates, which will ultimately become the biggest booking agency in Canada.

>> **1972** RCA moves its Canadian head office from Montréal to Toronto.

>> **1972** United Artists opens a Canadian subsidiary of the record label founded in the U.S. in 1958.

>> **1972** Groups formed this year include The Good Brothers, Richmond Hill, ON; Harmonium, Montréal; Heart, Seattle/Vancouver; Southcote, Toronto; The DeFranco Family, Port Colborne, ON.

>> 1973

>> **January 5, 1973** Neil Young sets out on a 65-city North American tour with the band Stray Gators.

>> **January 16, 1973** *Bonanza*, starring Lorne Greene, completes an unprecedented 14 season run on NBC-TV.

>> **January 23, 1973** Neil Young interrupts his New York concert to tell a joyous audience that "peace has come." The Vietnam War is over.

>> **March 1973** Rush begin recording their debut album in Toronto with producer Terry Brown.

>> **March 1973** Construction begins in Toronto on the CN Tower, at that time, the world's tallest free-standing structure.

>> **March 12, 1973** The third annual JUNO Awards, hosted by George Wilson of CFRB, are held again at the Centennial Ballroom of the Inn On the Park Hotel in Toronto. The spirit of

share the wealth prevails as Gordon Lightfoot, Anne Murray, Edward Bear and Lighthouse all have their recording projects recognized with two trophies each. Valdy picks up the first JUNO in the newly-introduced category of Outstanding Performance of the Year, Folk. Toronto native David Clayton-Thomas of Blood, Sweat & Tears is honoured with a special JUNO for his contribution to the Canadian music scene. Gordon Lightfoot is feeling particularly patriotic on this night: "I've been accepted in my native country on a scale I never dreamed possible. I'm going to sing the praises of Canada far and wide for as long as I can."

>> **March 13, 1973** The National Film Board documentary *Rock-A-Bye*, which profiles the Canadian pop music business, has its premiere as part of the JUNO celebrations.

>> **April 8, 1973** Neil Young's documentary film *Journey Through the Past*, based on events in his own life, premieres at the U.S. Film Festival in Dallas.

>> **April 10, 1973** Vancouver group Skylark, featuring keyboardist David Foster and vocalist Donny Gerrard, begin a five-night stand at The Troubadour in Los Angeles with Link Wray. The group has just had their single "Wildflower" reach the Top 10 on the Billboard chart.

>> **April 27, 1973** The Diamonds reunite for the first time in 14 years for a *Midnight Special* show that features other golden oldie artists and is hosted by Jerry Lee Lewis.

>> **May 1, 1973** Bachman-Turner Overdrive release their self-titled, debut album.

>> **June 5, 1973** On his show *Let's Be Personal* on radio station CFRB in Toronto, the late Canadian commentator and author Gordon Sinclair delivers an emotional editorial on the lack of support the American Red Cross is receiving outside of the U.S. as it verges on bankruptcy. A number of American border radio stations pick up the editorial and listener reaction is immediate. Byron MacGregor, the 25-year-old News Director at powerhouse radio station CKLW Windsor/Detroit, reads it on the air with "America the Beautiful" in the background. So overwhelming is the reaction from CKLW's Detroit/Philadelphia audience that Detroit's Westbound Records takes MacGregor into the studio with the Detroit

▲ April Wine

▲ Anne Murray with John Lennon, Harry Nilsson, Alice Cooper and Mickey Dolenz

Symphony Orchestra to record it for release as "Americans." It takes only five days for orders of a million copies of the disc to come rolling in and eventually it reaches number four on the Billboard singles chart early the following year (1974). Sinclair records a version for Avco/Embassy, backing his narration with "Battle Hymn of the Republic." Sinclair's version under the title "The Americans (A Canadian's Opinion)" only reaches number 24 on the Billboard chart. The late Tex Ritter records a version in Nashville for Capitol Records on Dec. 20, 1973, the same day a news crew is interviewing Sinclair for John Chancellor's NBC-TV program. Ritter's version ultimately hits number 90 on the Billboard chart.

» **June 8, 1973** Bachman-Turner Overdrive play their first major U.S. concert at the Fairgrounds in Nashville.

» **July 1973** The Home County Folk Festival is first held in Victoria Park in downtown London, ON.

» **September 1973** At their annual free concert at Toronto's Nathan Phillips Square in front of the City Hall, which this year draws close to 50,000 people, Lighthouse are presented with a platinum record by Toronto Mayor David Crombie for their album *Lighthouse Live!* They are the first Canadian group to reach the sales plateau of 100,000 records in Canada.

» **September 20, 1973** Neil Young and Crazy Horse play the first of four nights to open The Roxy, Los Angeles' newest rock'n'roll nightclub.

» **October 1973** Beau Dommage debut at the University of Québec at Montréal.

» **October 15, 1973** The Vancouver East Cultural Centre, which will become affectionately known as "The Cultch," opens at 1895 Venables in the east end of Vancouver.

» **Thanksgiving 1973** Anne Murray appears at the Troubadour in Los Angeles. Among the audience members are John Lennon, Harry Nilsson, Mickey Dolenz of The Monkees and Alice Cooper.

» **Winter 1973** With girlfriend Daphne, Bob Geldof flees the "rat trap" of his life in Dublin and flies to Montréal to begin a cross-Canada bus trip by Greyhound to

▲ Randy Bachman

Vancouver. On the West Coast, he works for a while as a building site labourer before noticing an ad in local alternative newspaper, *Georgia Straight*, which is looking for an assistant in their bookstore. Geldof applies and publisher Dan McLeod hires him. It's not long before the voluble Irishman moves into the editorial department and ultimately becomes Music Editor.

» **1973** Anik satellite launched.

» **1973** The Toronto franchise of Chicago's famed comedy institution Second City is opened by Andrew Alexander. Alumni over the years include Dan Aykroyd, the late John Candy, Martin Short, Dave Thomas, Eugene Levy, Catherine O'Hara and Andrea Martin.

» **1973** Vancouver-based agent Bruce Allen becomes the manager of Bachman-Turner Overdrive, who under his direction in tandem with Randy Bachman, sell 10 million albums from 1973-1978.

» **1973** Bryan Adams, now in his early teens, settles in North Vancouver with his family and attends Sutherland Secondary School.

» **1973** In one of his earliest acting roles, Victor Garber, former vocalist of the Canadian group Sugar Shoppe, takes the lead role of Jesus in the movie adaptation of Stephen Schwartz's stage musical *Godspell*.

» **1973** Harmonium debuts at Montréal's Le Patriote club.

» **1973** Rush opens for the New York Dolls in Toronto.

» **1973** By the time of the release of April Wine's sophomore album *Electric Jewels*, David and Ritchie Henman had left the group to be replaced by Jim Clench, Jerry Mercer and Gary Moffet. With the new line-up, April Wine becomes one of the first bands to headline in arenas across Canada, playing in 80 towns and cities across the country on their Electric Adventure Tour. The excursion results in a live album, recorded in Halifax, Nova Scotia and produced by fellow Canadian Gene Cornish and Dino Danelli, members of The Young Rascals.

» **1973** Groups formed this year include Bachman-Turner Overdrive, Winnipeg; Klaatu, Toronto; Pied Pumkin, Vancouver; Simply Saucer, Hamilton.

» 1974

» **January 1974** Anne Murray's "Send A Little Love My Way" from the movie *Oklahoma Crude* is nominated for an Academy Award, Grammy and a Golden Globe Award.

» **January 3, 1974** Bob Dylan and the Band open a six-week North American tour at the Chicago Stadium. During the subsequent excursion, they play two concerts at Toronto's Maple Leaf Gardens (January 9 & 10). On the second night, they drop by to see Ronnie Hawkins, who is playing at The Nickelodeon on Yonge Street and celebrating his 39th birthday. Dylan will later cast Hawkins as "Bob Dylan" in the Rolling Thunder film *Renaldo and Clara*. On February 14, after 39 shows in 21 cities, the Bob Dylan/Band tour comes to an end in Los Angeles at The Forum in front of a star-studded audience, which includes Jack Nicholson, Neil Young, Carole King and Ringo Starr. Many of the tracks on Dylan's *Before the Flood* album are recorded during this concert.

» **March 2, 1974** Terry Jacks hits the top of the Billboard singles chart with "Seasons In the Sun," an English adaptation (lyrics by Rod McKuen) of the Jacques Brel song "Le Moribond." Besides becoming an international hit with sales of more than 10 million copies, it is one of the biggest selling singles of all time in Canada. In February, "Seasons In the Sun" becomes the first Canadian platinum single with sales of more than 100,000 copies.

» **March 25, 1974** The fourth annual JUNO Awards are held at the Centennial Ballroom at Toronto's Inn On the Park Hotel and hosted by George Wilson of CFRB. Terry Jacks and Murray McLauchlan are the year's big winners as both take home three JUNOs each. Jacks takes bows for the enormous worldwide success of his single "Seasons In the Sun," while bemused folkie McLauchlan finds that the success of his "Farmer's Song" single has now truly made him a man outstanding in the country field as well. This is the first year in which the award winners are not known prior to the awards ceremony. In the early years, original awards organizers *RPM Weekly* magazine would publish the winners in advance of the presentations. The musical theme for the evening, "Stars In the North," performed by the 23-piece orchestra, was composed by Stan Klees, one of the event's organizers. Though not televised, the 1974 JUNO Awards are taped as a trial run for future presentations.

This inadvertently causes a last-minute problem with the Musicians Association, which threatens to pull the orchestra from the show. After hours of negotiations with JUNO organizers, Walt Grealis and Stan Klees, the show finally does go on.

» **March 1974** Blair Thornton, formerly with Vancouver group Crosstown Bus, replaces Tim Bachman in Bachman-Turner Overdrive. Thornton has the nerve-wracking experience of playing his first show with the band on ABC-TV's *In Concert*, the internationally-televised music series.

» **April 1974** Rush release their self-titled debut album on their own Moon Records label. In August, the album is released by Mercury Records in the U.S. After the departure of original drummer John Rutsey for health reasons, St. Catharines, Ontario-native Neil Peart joins the group in July before they head out on August 19 on their first U.S. tour opening for artists like Uriah Heep, Rory Gallagher and Kiss.

» **May 4, 1974** Ian Thomas performs with the Hamilton Philharmonic in the wake of his hit "Painted Ladies."

» **June 29, 1974** Gordon Lightfoot becomes one of the few artists in rock history to have a single and album hit the top of the Billboard charts in the U.S. at the same time. On this date, Lightfoot achieves the double honor with the album *Sundown* and the single of the same name. "I've been writing for deadlines for the last three years and 'Sundown' was one of a string of songs that I wrote when I lived on a farm out in King Township, just outside of Toronto, last summer," he tells *Billboard Magazine*. "I was getting off a tune every day out there. It certainly turned out to be a royal flush."

» **July 9, 1974** Neil Young is back with David Crosby, Stephen Stills and Graham Nash as the reunion tour begins in Seattle. On November 2, the group's *So Far* album hits number one on the Billboard album chart.

» **August 24, 1974** The Paul Anka single "You're Having My Baby," a duet with Odia Coates, causes a furor with feminist groups who denounce the song for what they consider sexist lyrics. Notwithstanding, the record becomes Anka's first number one single since 1959. On this date, he sets a record for the longest gap between number one singles to that point. It had been a full 15 years and two weeks since his chart-topping "Lonely Boy" in 1959.

1970-1979

» **September 28, 1974** Though he has previously topped the charts as co-writer and singer with Ron Dante of The Archies' single, "Sugar Sugar," Andy Kim has his first number one record with the single, "Rock Me Gently."

» **October 1, 1974** CBC Radio Roots music series *Touch the Earth*, hosted by Sylvia Tyson, debuts.

» **October 19, 1974** Bachman-Turner Overdrive's *Not Fragile* hits the number one position on the Billboard album chart in the U.S. The following month both the *Not Fragile* and *Bachman-Turner Overdrive II* albums are certified platinum in Canada for sales of more than 100,000 copies each, a first for a Canadian group. They round out the year nicely in November with a concert date at New York's Fillmore East (Nov. 7) and a number one single. Two days later, on November 9, "You Ain't Seen Nothin' Yet," the song Randy Bachman of the band originally didn't want to see released, hits the top of the Billboard singles chart.

» **December 7, 1974** Bachman-Turner Overdrive wrap up an eventful year in style as they become the first group to play the New Fillmore East in New York, a short-lived attempt to re-open Bill Graham's legendary Fillmore East, which Bachman had played four years earlier with The Guess Who.

» **December 16, 1974** Having appeared on the cover of Canada's *Maclean's* magazine in June with an interview by her close friend, Malka Himel, Joni Mitchell appears on the cover of *Time* magazine as "Rock 'N' Roll's Leading Lady." About a week later, she is spotted with James Taylor, Carly Simon and Linda Ronstadt singing Christmas carols around the streets of Los Angeles.

» **1974** Randy Bachman of Bachman-Turner Overdrive signs the band Applejack, which he had booked into a Mormon church dance, to his newly-founded Legend Records, at which point the group, featuring Ra McGuire and Brian "Smitty" Smith, becomes Trooper.

» **1974** The inaugural Winnipeg Folk Festival is held, initially as a one-time celebration to mark Winnipeg's 100th anniversary. Founded by Mitch Podolak, Colin Gorrie and Ava Kobrinsky, it is held annually over the second week of July in Birds Hill Provincial Park near Winnipeg.

▲ Paul Anka

» **1974** Tom Cochrane makes his recording debut with the album, *Hang On To Your Resistance*.

» **1974** Tommy Hunter receives a citation from the Country Music Hall of Fame in Nashville for "continuous and outstanding contribution to country music."

» **1974** Having taken up the guitar at age 10, Kathy Dawn Lang (aka k.d. lang) begins writing songs in her hometown of Consort, Alberta.

» **1974** At the age of 60, Hank Snow has his seventh number one hit in the U.S. with "Hello Love."

» **1974** Domenic Troiano joins The Guess Who.

» **1974** In Montréal, Robert Charlebois collaborates with Frank Zappa on a song titled "Petroleum." Zappa also guests on guitar on Charlebois' 1977 album, *Swing Charlebois Swing*.

» **1974** Attic Records (Canada) is established in Toronto by Alexander Mair and Tom Williams.

» **1974** Groups formed this year include Beau Dommage, Montréal; Deliverance, Lorach, Germany/Calgary; Helix, Kitchener, ON; Jackson Hawke, Toronto; Moxy, Toronto.

» 1975

» **January 11, 1975** Gino Vannelli appears on the long-running U.S. TV show *Soul Train*, one of the few white artists to do so to that point.

» **January 1975** CRTC issues proposed new policy for FM radio programing.

» **March 22, 1975** Guitarist Liona Boyd makes her New York debut at the Carnegie Recital Hall.

» **March 25, 1975** The 5th annual JUNO Awards ceremony, the first to be televised (CBC), is held at the Queen Elizabeth Theatre on the grounds of the Canadian National Exhibition in Toronto hosted by Paul Anka. Vancouver-based band Bachman-Turner Overdrive make their first major impression at the JUNOs as they pick up three awards. Anne Murray and Gordon Lightfoot continue their winning ways with two each. As the non-profit industry organization the Canadian Music Awards

Association (CMAA) takes over the awards presentation from the Canadian music trade publication *RPM Weekly*, the categories are completely overhauled with sales playing a larger part in the nominations procedure. The actual JUNO Award is redesigned for television by its original designer, Stan Klees. CHIN Radio (Toronto) pulls its McGowan Award from the JUNOs when they learn it will not be presented as part of the one-hour TV show. The JUNO for Best Album Graphics is first presented and goes to Bart Schoales for his work on Bruce Cockburn's *Night Vision* album. Ian Thomas, looking at the silver, foil-like stage set, quips: "We owe this occasion to the CBC and I'm sure they'd like to thank Alcan for the set."

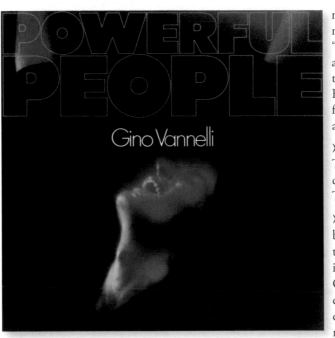

>> **April 2, 1975** The CN Tower in Toronto is completed.

>> **April 28, 1975** Bachman-Turner Overdrive open a three-week tour of Europe.

>> **May 1975** Ian & Sylvia make their last appearance as a duo at Toronto's Horseshoe Tavern.

>> **July 28, 1975** Bachman-Turner Overdrive kick off their first Canadian tour with a press conference and concert as part of Buffalo Days at the Regina Exhibition Fairgrounds in Regina, Saskatchewan.

>> **July 1975** Sylvia Tyson's first solo album, *Woman's World*, is released. It is produced by husband, Ian Tyson.

>> **August 28, 1975** Musician/agent Billy O'Connor reunites The Happy Gang for one last hoorah at the Canadian National Exhibition in Toronto. Their two concerts, broadcast by the CBC, draw more than 30,000 people.

>> **September 13, 1975** Burton Cummings plays his last gig with The Guess Who at the Montréal Forum before embarking on a solo career. Since that time, the group with various refreshed line-ups, but with original bass player Jim Kale and drummer Garry Peterson as the constants, has continued to tour. There was a short-lived reunion of the original group for a tour in the summer of 1983.

>> **October 11, 1975** *Saturday Night Live*, a creation of former CBC producer Lorne Michaels, is broadcast for the first time on NBC. George Carlin is guest host. The show's

music director is a former member of the Toronto-based "rock orchestra" Lighthouse and current superstar in the world of movie scoring, Howard Shore, who hired fellow Canadian Paul Shaffer as keyboardist in the band.

>> **November 12, 1975** Toronto rock trio Triumph debut at the Knob Hill Tavern in Toronto.

>> **1975** Céline Dion's career begins at the age of 7 singing the songs of Ginette Reno in her parent's restaurant in Charlemagne, Québec. A demo of the song "Ce n'était qu'un reve," written by Dion's mother, is sent to Reno's manager, René Angélil, who is impressed. He commissions French lyricist Eddy Marnay to write "La voix du bon Dieu" for her and supervises Dion's recording of the song.

>> **1975** "The Homecoming," originally recorded as a Salada Tea jingle in 1972, is released as a single by its composer Hagood Hardy to great acclaim and chart success at home and abroad.

>> **1975** Toronto-band Moxy release their debut, self-titled album. The band features vocalist Buzz Shearman, who is replaced in 1977 by Mike Rynoski (aka Mike Reno), co-founder of Loverboy in the early '80s.

▲ Burton Cummings

>> **1975** Walter Ostanek, who will win a number of Grammy Awards over the years, earns his title as Canada's Polka King as host of *Polka Time* seen on CKCO-TV in Kitchener, ON. The show runs until 1989.

>> **1975** Eclectic music group Pied Pumkin come together in Vancouver around former Lotus Eaters member and San Antonio, Texas native Rick Scott, Regina, Saskatchewan native Joe Mock of Mock Duck and singer, multi-instrumentalist, Shari Ulrich.

>> **1975** Kids entertainer Raffi forms his own label, Troubadour Records, and releases his debut album, *Good Luck Boy.*

>> **1975** Singer Wendy Matthews, at the age of 15, leaves Montréal and busks her way across America to Los Angeles. Here she meets and becomes friends with Glenn Shorrock of the Little River Band, who invites her to tour with him in Australia (1982). She accepts the invitation and ends up staying in Australia, where she initially finds herself in-demand as a session singer (The Models, Jimmy Barnes, Tim Finn) before becoming one of the top female artists in that country, who has been honoured with seven Australian Recording Industry Association (ARIA) Awards.

>> **1975** The self-titled debut album by Vancouver-based group Trooper is released as they tour the U.S. opening for bands like Aerosmith, ZZ Top, Fleetwood Mac, AC/DC and Bachman-Turner Overdrive.

>> **1975** René Simard makes his first appearance at the Olympia in Paris.

>> **1975** Kate and Anna McGarrigle record their self-titled debut album for Warner Bros.

>> **1975** The Big Country Awards and the Canadian Academy for Country Music Advancement are founded by the Canadian music trade magazine, *RPM Weekly.*

>> **1975** Ronnie Prophet takes on the hosting duties of CTV's Grand Old Country program.

>> **1975** Operatic contralto Maureen Forrester makes her debut with New York's Metropolitan Opera singing Wagner's Erda in *Das Rheingold.*

▲ Walter Ostanek

She gave 14 performances at the Metropolitan Opera, all of them in 1975.

>> **1975** Singer Norman Brooks appears in the Broadway production of *The Magic of Jolson.*

>> **1975** Charlie Galbraith is inspirational in the formation of the not-for-profit British Columbia Country Music Association (BCCMA).

>> **1975** Groups formed this year include CANO, Sudbury; Garolou, Québec; Goddo, Scarborough, ON; Hammersmith, Calgary; Harlequin, Winnipeg; Hometown Band, Vancouver; Sweeney Todd, Vancouver; The Raes, U.K./St. Thomas, ON; Triumph, Toronto.

>> 1976

>> **February 14, 1976** Heart's debut album *Dreamboat Annie* is released on Shelley Siegel's Vancouver-based Mushroom Records, produced by Mike Flicker at Can-Base Studios.

>> **March 15, 1976** Bachman-Turner Overdrive and Hagood Hardy are the big winners at the 6th annual JUNO Awards held at the Ryerson Theatre in Toronto and hosted by John Allen Cameron. BTO picks up three JUNOs for their *Four Wheel Drive* album project and number one single, "You Ain't Seen Nothin' Yet." Pianist/composer Hagood Hardy also picks up three awards. Though she doesn't win an award on the night, Carroll Baker sets her career alight with a memorable rendition of "I've Never Been This Far Before," a performance that, in part, led to her subsequent signing to RCA. The newly-formed Canadian Academy of Arts & Sciences (CARAS) takes over the annual organization and presentation of the JUNOs. With the transition, JUNO founder Walt Grealis is presented with a "People Award" by Randy Bachman of BTO inscribed, "You were always there when we needed you," signed The Musicians of Canada. Instrumental Artist of the Year and Recording of the Year categories are added. First winners are Hagood Hardy and Don Geppert, respectively. All categories are now voted on by the CARAS membership, except for the international awards, which are based on sales.

>> **April 4, 1976** The Stampeders have their last major hit with "Hit the Road Jack," a song that features a staged phone conversation between Wolfman Jack and group member Ronnie King. King's Dutch heritage — his birth name is Cornelis Van Sprang — had helped to make the group popular in The Netherlands. With "Hit the Road Jack," the group have a number one hit there and earn a coveted Edison Award.

>> **May 8, 1976** Nick Gilder and Jim McCulloch, formerly with the Vancouver group Sweeney Todd, sign to Chrysalis Records in the U.S. Gilder is initially replaced as vocalist in Sweeney Todd by Clark Perry. Perry records a version of the group's Canadian hit "Roxy Roller" for release in the U.S., but it is scrapped in August as Vancouver singer Bryan Guy Adams replaces Perry and re-records the single, which is released on August 27. Gilder's version with the group peaks at number 90 after 2 weeks on the Billboard singles chart while Adams' version makes a 1 week visit at number 99.

>> **June 11, 1976** Rush plays the first of three nights at Toronto's Massey Hall.

>> **July 4, 1976** Neil Diamond's *Beautiful Noise* album, produced by Robbie Robertson, peaks at number four on the Billboard album chart in the U.S.

>> **July 17-August 1, 1976** The 21st Summer Olympics are held in Montréal. Trumpet player and hometown boy Maynard Ferguson is the featured soloist at the opening of the Games.

>> **September 8, 1976** Heart's *Dreamboat Annie* is certified gold for sales of over 50,000 albums in Canada.

>> **September 1976** The Academy of Country Music Entertainment (ACME) is founded to organize, promote and develop a Canadian country music industry, which includes the founding of Country Music Week. The first awards presented were the RPM Big Country Awards. ACME is the forerunner to the Canadian Country Music Association (CCMA) formed in 1987.

>> **October 1, 1976** The CN Tower in Toronto has its official opening.

>> **October 29, 1976** Bachman-Turner Overdrive embark on a Japanese tour.

>> **October 30, 1976** The Band performs "Georgia On My Mind" on *Saturday Night Live* in honor of presidential candidate Jimmy Carter, who is elected a few days later.

>> **November 8, 1976** Burton Cummings, the former vocalist for The Guess Who, plays his first concert as a solo

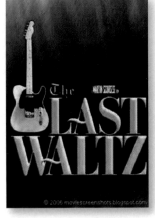

artist at the Manitoba Centennial Concert Hall in his hometown of Winnipeg.

>> **November 25, 1976** The Last Waltz, The Band's swansong performance at Winterland in San Francisco, takes place on Thanksgiving night before the cameras of director Martin Scorsese. Promoter Bill Graham convinces the group to turn the event into a grand affair complete with buffet supper, chandeliers, an orchestra for dancing and a $25 ticket price. Musicians and friends on hand to say goodbye include Bob Dylan, Ronnie Hawkins, Joni Mitchell, Van Morrison, Neil Young, Paul Butterfield, Bobby Charles, Neil Diamond, Dr. John, Muddy Waters, Eric Clapton, Stephen Stills, Ron Wood and Ringo Starr. The event is later released as the film *The Last Waltz* (November 4, 1977) and as a triple album set (1978).

>> **1976** Canadian Music Hall of Fame established.

>> **1976** Parti Québecois, with an agenda to separate Québec from the rest of Canada, wins the provincial election.

>> **1976** Rough Trade Live! produced by Jack Richardson, becomes the first direct-to-disc album recorded in Canada.

>> **1976** Prism is organized in Vancouver by producer/horn player Bruce Fairbairn, featuring Lindsay Mitchell and vocalist Ron Tabak and various session players, including Rodney Higgs (Jim Vallance), Tom Lavin and Tom Keenlyside.

>> **1976** Anthem Records (previously Moon Records) is established in Toronto by members of the band Rush and their manager, Ray Danniels, with Tom Berry as Managing Director.

>> **1976** The T.H.P. Orchestra (Three Hats Productions Orchestra), a studio project masterminded by producers Willi Morrison and Ian Guenther, has a number one hit in Canada with "Theme from S.W.A.T."

>> **1976** The Good Brothers appear at the Troubadour in Los Angeles

>> **1976** Fourteen-year-old Corey Hart, with the help of Paul Anka's organization, records the single "Ooh Baby!" for United Artists records.

>> **1976** Montréal singer Patsy Gallant has an international hit with "From New York To L.A.," an English disco version of Gilles Vigneault's "Mon pays," the unofficial anthem of Québec.

>> **1976** Classical guitar makes some new friends as Liona Boyd embarks on a North American tour as opening act for Gordon Lightfoot.

▲ Valdy

» **1976** Shari Ulrich departs Vancouver group Pied Pumkin to become a member of Valdy's Hometown Band, leaving Joe Mock and Rick Scott as Pied Pear.

» **1976** Such is April Wine's fan base in Canada that the album *The Whole World's Going Crazy* becomes the first Canadian album to ship platinum (100,000 copies). An extensive Canadian tour follows, which grosses more than one million dollars.

» **1976** Rush's *All the World's A Stage* becomes the first live album to be certified gold for sales over 50,000.

» **1976** Festival for the Folks, the forerunner of the Ottawa Folk Festival, premieres in Ottawa, Ontario. It runs until 1979.

» **1976** The CRTC is renamed the Canadian Radio-television and Telecommunications Commission.

» **1976** Groups formed this year include FM, Toronto; Figgy Duff, Newfoundland; Fosterchild, Calgary; Kick Axe, Regina; La Bottine Souriante, Québec; Lavender Hill Mob, Montréal; Prism, Vancouver; Queen City Kids, Regina; The Diodes, Toronto.

» 1977

» **January 10, 1977** At presentation ceremonies at the Roxy Theater in Los Angeles, Hagood Hardy receives the Billboard award as Number One Instrumentalist For Singles in 1976 for "The Homecoming."

» **February 13, 1977** Klaatu's first album had been released with very little fanfare in the late summer of 1976. In fact, the identity of the members of this Toronto-based group was shrouded in mystery because they had asked Frank Davies, President of their record label/production company, Daffodil Records, not to reveal their names... to just let the music speak for itself. And then came an article on this date in the *Providence Journal* (Rhode Island) by Steve Smith, who compared Klaatu to The Beatles and put forward the persuasive argument that members of the Fab Four were indeed involved in the recording project. This led to the extraordinary rumor, far and wide, that this was in fact The Beatles reunion the music world had been clamoring for. (The group was on Capitol Records in the U.S., the same label as The Beatles.) "Think about it — this band of anonymous, unknown musicians from Canada suddenly had half the music world believing their album was, in fact, The Beatles reunited!," says British expatriate Frank Davies. "Germans, Australians, Scandinavians, Japanese and Brits proclaiming that this album was without question the production work of George Martin, the penmanship of Lennon/McCartney, recorded by four lads from Liverpool, with some English industry colleagues, in [producer] Terry [Brown] and myself, fronting for them all!" Before it was revealed that Klaatu were John Woloschuk, Terry Draper and Dee Long, three Toronto studio musicians, Klaatu's self-titled debut album had hit number 32 on the Billboard album chart that summer. Later that year, The Carpenters had a Top 40 hit in the U.S. with the group's "Calling Occupants of Interplanetary Craft," a song that became the anthem of World Contact Day. The group's name was inspired by the 1951 film *The Day the Earth Stood Still* in which Klaatu, an alien peace emissary played by Michael Rennie, travels to earth to warn of the dangers of nuclear power. Klaatu barada nikto!

» **February 1977** Triumph play their first U.S. concert with The Runaways at the Municipal Auditorium in San Antonio, Texas as a replacement for Sammy Hagar.

» **March 4, 1977** The Rolling Stones, with April Wine as opening act, play the first of two nights at Toronto's El Mocambo club. While most of the attention at the time focuses on Keith Richards' recent arrest by Canadian authorities and the presence in the small audience of Margaret Trudeau, the wife of Canadian Prime Minister Pierre Trudeau, the real significance of the club concerts becomes apparent in September when the album *Love You Live* is released with one side comprising the vintage R&B the band had performed over the two nights in Toronto.

▲ Klaatu

>> **March 16, 1977** The 7th annual JUNO Awards are held in the Canadian Room of Toronto's Royal York Hotel and hosted by comedian David Steinberg with a number of broadcasters from across Canada, including Roy Hennessy (CKLG Vancouver), Jay Nelson (CHUM Toronto), Ralph Lockwood (CKGM Montréal), Bob Burns (CKY Winnipeg) and Len Theusen (CHED Edmonton). The Folk category, which had been dropped earlier but was later reinstated due to negative public and industry reaction, helps Gordon Lightfoot share the spotlight with Burton Cummings as top award winner. Lightfoot picks up two JUNOs, as does Cummings. Cummings was prompted to say: "Don't let anyone tell you that things don't happen fast in Canada. In just 75 minutes, I went from Best New Male Vocalist to the Best Male Vocalist of the Year." Controversy swirls around Heart's win as Group of the Year as the band's Ann Wilson tells a U.S. magazine that they have always been an American act. Bryan Adams, who has replaced Nick Gilder as vocalist in the group Sweeney Todd, is on hand to pick up the band's award as Top New Group. The Good Brothers begin their run of an unprecedented seven consecutive JUNO Awards as Country Group of the Year.

>> **April 2, 1977** The newly-renovated Orpheum Theater becomes the new home of the Vancouver Symphony Orchestra.

>> **June 1977** The Diodes open the Crash and Burn punk club on Duncan Street in Toronto

>> **June 2, 1977** Rush open their first U.K. tour in Manchester.

>> **July 4, 1977** April Wine open for The Rolling Stones at Rich Stadium in Buffalo, New York.

>> **Summer 1977** Montreal's Harmonium tour Europe with British group Supertramp.

>> **August 13, 1977** Bachman-Turner Overdrive disband after the departure of Randy Bachman. Fred Turner moves to guitar and former April Wine member Jim Clench is brought in on bass and the band shortens the name to BTO.

>> **Fall 1977** The Blues Brothers are initially formed by comedic actors Dan Aykroyd and the late John Belushi to get the crowd in a party mood before the tapings of NBC-TV's *Saturday Night Live*, of which they are two of the marquee stars. The act eventually moves into the body of the show and Jake and Elwood Bluesmania ensues. The premise of the group was light-hearted but the music was serious business. Aykroyd plays a fair blues harp and they surround themselves with the best musicians in the genre, including guitarist Steve Cropper and bassist Donald "Duck" Dunn, who had actually played on some of the original versions of the songs they are covering, including Sam & Dave's "Hold On I'm Coming" and "Soul Man." Their first album, *Briefcase Full of Blues*, is

▲ Margaret Trudeau

recorded live in September of 1978 during an opening set for comedian Steve Martin in Los Angeles. The album contains two songs by Toronto's Downchild Blues Band: "(I Got Everything I Need) Almost" and "Shot Gun Blues." The record goes on to sell more than a million copies in North America and leads to their appearance in the biographical film, *The Blue Brothers*, directed by John Landis and co-starring Aretha Franklin, James Brown, Ray Charles and Cab Calloway. It premieres in New York on June 18, 1980. The group's music director is Thunder Bay, Ontario-native, Paul Shaffer from the *Saturday Night Live* Band.

>> **Fall 1977** Tom Cochrane joins Toronto group Red Rider (later Tom Cochrane and Red Rider).

>> **November 1977** Maynard Collins' musical revue, Hank Williams: The Show He Never Gave, premieres at the Beacon Arms Hotel in Ottawa with Sneezy Waters (Peter Hodgson) in the lead role.

>> **1977** Bryan Adams meets drummer Rodney Higgs (aka Jim Vallance) in a Vancouver music store. Higgs is writing material for a new local group, Prism. Shortly after their first meeting, they began a writing collaboration destined to launch both of their careers.

>> **1977** The Raes' single "Que Sera Sera" sells over 65,000 copies, one of A&M Records' biggest Canadian singles in history.

>> **1977** Rough Trade co-star with U.S, transvestite Divine in the revue *Restless Underwear* at Toronto's Massey Hall and in New York.

>> **1977** Bruce Cockburn and Murray McLauchlan tour Japan.

>> **1977** The 100th anniversary of recorded sound is celebrated with the elaborate and well-funded 100 Years of Recorded Sound show at the Canadian National Exhibition in Toronto. In the Pavilion, there is a record manufacturing display, a recording studio and exhibitors from all segments of the music industry in Canada. It spotlights Canada's significant role in the development of recorded sound as it features the contributions of visionaries like Emile and Herbert Berliner, who for many years made Montréal the cradle of the recording industry.

▲ The Blues Brothers: Dan Aykroyd and John Belushi

>> **1977** Leonard Cohen collaborates with legendary pop music producer Phil Spector on the album *Death of a Ladies Man*, which features a guest appearance by Bob Dylan.

>> **1977** Paul Shaffer takes a break from *Saturday Night Live* to star in the summer comedy series *A Year At the Top*, a '70s version of The Monkees' TV shows. He later returns to *Saturday Night Live* and collaborates with Gilda Radner on her Broadway show.

>> **1977** Groups formed this year include Doug and the Slugs, Vancouver; Martha and the Muffins, Toronto; Prism, Vancouver; Streetheart, Winnipeg/Regina; The Battered Wives, Toronto; The Kings, Vancouver.

>> 1978

>> **March 29, 1978** The 8th annual JUNO Awards are held at the Harbour Castle Convention Centre in Toronto, hosted by comedian David Steinberg. The success of Dan Hill's "Sometimes When We Touch" single from the album *Longer Fuse* puts the Toronto-based singer/songwriter in the winner's circle as the project picks up five JUNOs, three for Hill as an artist and two for producers Matt McCauley and Fred Mollin. It's not a bad year for Montréal's Patsy Gallant either as she picks up her second consecutive Female Vocalist award and takes Single of the Year honors for "Sugar Daddy." Oscar Peterson and Guy Lombardo become the first Canadian Music

Hall of Fame members. The JUNOs have their first tie as Terry Brown and David Greene cross the finish line together in the category of Recording Engineer of the Year. Alex Lifeson of Rush: "We'd like to thank Dan Hill for not being a group."

>> June 25, 1978 The legendary Riverboat coffee house at 134 Yorkville Ave. in Toronto's Yorkville Village, established by Bernie Fiedler in October of 1964, closes with a performance by Murray McLauchlan.

>> **June 30, 1978** The Raes' (Cherrill and Robbie Rae) summer special TV series debuts.

>> **July 29, 1978** Tafelmusik give their first concert in Toronto.

>> **Summer 1978** Martha and the Muffins have a Top Five single in Canada with the single "Echo Beach," which sells over 75,000 copies. It also becomes a number one hit in Australia, Portugal, Spain and The Netherlands and goes Top 10 on the U.K. charts.

>> **August 11, 1978** The Vancouver Folk Music Festival debuts in Stanley Park before moving to Jericho Beach Park on the west side of Vancouver in subsequent years. It is initially conceptualized and developed by Winnipeg Folk Festival Artistic Director Mitch Podolak with help from Ernie Fladell, Cultural Planner for the city of Vancouver at the time. Others on the team include Gary Cristall, Frances Fitzgibbon and Lorenz von Fersen.

>> **August 26, 1978** Canada Jam, which draws 110,000 fans, is held at Mosport Park near Bowmanville, Ontario featuring Triumph, The Commodores, Kansas, Prism, Wha-Koo, Dave Mason, The Village People, Atlanta Rhythm Section, The Doobie Brothers, Ozark Mountain Daredevils and Fun Zone. The concert is promoted by Sandy Feldman and Lenny Stogel, who produced California Jam and California Jam II in the U.S., with logistical help by Toronto-based promoter, John Brower.

>> **Fall 1978** Harmonium perform in Los Angeles and at the University of Southern California at Berkeley.

>> **October 1978** Keith Richards of The Rolling Stones goes on trial in

▲ Murray McLauchlan and Bruce Cockburn

Toronto after his bust at the Harbour Castle Hilton hotel for cocaine and heroin possession. He is let off on probation on the promise that he performs a special benefit concert in the area with proceeds going to the Canadian National Institute for the Blind (CNIB).

>> **October 1978** Rush embark on their Hemispheres tour of Canada, U.S., U.K. and Europe.

>> **October 28, 1978** Nick Gilder, former lead singer of the Vancouver-based group Sweeney Todd, who was briefly replaced by Bryan Adams following his departure, hits the top of the Billboard Hot 100 chart with the single, "Hot Child In the City."

>> **November 1978** Raffi's album *Singable Songs* is certified gold in Canada for sales over 50,000 copies, the first Canadian children's record to achieve this milestone.

>> **November 4, 1978** Anne Murray has the biggest single of her career as "You Needed Me" from her album *Let's Keep It That Way* hits the top of the Billboard Hot 100 chart.

>> **December 1, 1978** The Last Pogo at Toronto's Horseshoe Tavern as the venerable Queen St. W. Venue reverts back to a policy of booking country music after a brief fling with punk/new wave music. The law closes the party early as, in typical punk fashion, it gets well out of hand.

>> **1978** Tommy Banks' big band, which features, among others, Clarence "Big" Miller and P.J. Perry, perform at the Montreux Jazz Festival in Switzerland. A subsequent double live album of the performance will later win a JUNO Award as Best Jazz Recording.

>> **1978** Sharon, Lois and Bram, who become one of the most popular children/family acts in North America, record their debut album *One Elephant, Deux Elephants* on their own Elephant record label.

>> **1978** Melissa Manchester has an international hit with the Lisa Dalbello song, "Pretty Girls."

>> **1978** Elvis Presley's version of Paul Anka's "My Way" hits the 500,000 sales mark after The King's death. Meanwhile, Sid Vicious of the Sex Pistols films his rendition of the song for the movie *The Great Rock 'n' Roll Swindle.*

>> **1978** Denny Doherty, formerly with the Mamas and the Papas, becomes the host of the CBC-TV musical variety program, *The Denny Sho**.

>> **1978** Neil Osborne and Brad Merritt, who will become the core members of the band 54-40, meet while both are attending South Delta High School in Tsawwassen, BC.

>> **1978** Bruce Cockburn, one of the few English-Canadian artists to have success in the French-speaking province of Québec, has his first hit there with "Prenons le mer."

>> **1978** Salome Bey writes and stars in *Indigo: A History of the Blues* that plays for close to a year at Toronto's Basin Street Club (180 Queen St. W.) before being produced for television.

>> **1978** Hank Snow is inducted into the Songwriters Association Hall of Fame in Nashville.

>> **1978** After spending time in Los Angeles and New York, British blues legend Long John Baldry settles in Vancouver.

>> **1978** Ginette Reno's exposure in the U.S. is greatly increased by appearances on the *Johnny Carson, Merv Griffin* and *Dinah Shore TV* shows.

>> **1978** The Toronto Symphony Orchestra, conducted by Andrew Davis, tours China and Japan with soloists Maureen Forrester and pianist Louis Lortie.

>> **1978** Lausanne, Switzerland-born conductor Charles Dutoit becomes artistic director of the Montréal Symphony Orchestra.

>> **1978** First announcement of the Compact Disc (CD) from Phillips Industries.

>> **1978** Groups formed this year include Anvil, Toronto; Blue Peter, Toronto; Bowser and Blue, Montréal; D.O.A., Vancouver; Exciter, Ottawa; Ironhorse, Vancouver; The Nylons, Toronto; Red Rider, Toronto.

>> 1979

>> **January 5, 1979** The Blues Brothers' album *Briefcase Full of Blues* is certified platinum on this date for over a million sales in the U.S.

» **January 8, 1979** Rush are named the country's official "Ambassadors of Music" by the Canadian government.

» **January 17, 1979** Shelley Siegel, who launched Heart's career on the Vancouver-based Mushroom Records label but later fell out with the group who moved to Portrait Records, dies of a brain aneurysm in Los Angeles.

» **February 6, 1979** Canadian Brass make their New York debut at the Lincoln Center.

» **February 15, 1979** David Foster wins his first Grammy Award during the 21st annual Grammy Award gala at the Shrine Auditorium in Los Angeles for his work on Earth, Wind & Fire's "After the Love Is Gone," which is named Best Rhythm & Blues Song. It is written by Foster, Bill Champlin and Jay Graydon. By 2010, Foster will have 16 Grammys on his mantelpiece.

» **March 21, 1979** The 9th annual JUNO Awards are held at the Harbour Castle Convention Centre in Toronto, hosted by Burton Cummings. On a night when Anne Murray, Gino Vannelli and Nick Gilder are multiple award winners, the emotional high point of the evening comes with the induction of country legend Hank Snow into the Hall of Fame by Prime Minister Pierre Elliott Trudeau. In the audience, and introduced by Snow, is A. Hugh Joseph, the RCA Victor record executive who first recorded Snow in an old church in Montréal in October of 1936. Comedy and Children's Album categories are introduced. First winners are The Royal Canadian Air Farce and Anne Murray, respectively. Prime Minister Trudeau notes: "We're living in an industrial age, an industrial society and, thanks to this technology, music can reach out and touch many people in our country and all countries across the world. Because it has been taken up by the industrial arts, because it has become a very real and big industry in Canada, it's important that the country deal with that fact. The cultural activities are the one in which Canadians engage themselves the most of any other activity. The cultural industries are bigger than steel in Canada. They

are bigger than pulp and paper — some six billion dollars a year. It's a big industry and we have to remember that, we the audiences, we the outsiders, we the government, we the onlookers."

» **Spring 1979** Frank Mills, former member of the Montréal group The Bells ("Stay Awhile"), makes his solo return to the U.S. single charts in a big way — his number one Canadian single "Love Me Love Me Love" (1972) peaked at number 46 — as his piano instrumental "Music Box Dancer" reaches number three on the Billboard Hot 100 chart. Sheet music sales of the song exceed two million copies, the single sells over three million and the album of the same name closes in on two million copies sold. Over 50 artists have covered the song.

» **April 10, 1979** Luc Plamondon and the late Michel Berger's *Starmania* premieres at the 4000-seat Palais de Congres in Paris. It is the first French language rock opera and the first major rock collaboration between Québec and France.

» **April 22, 1979** As part of the sentence handed down by the judge to Keith Richards for his 1977 drug bust in Toronto, the Rolling Stones' guitarist performs a concert to benefit the Canadian National Institute for the Blind (CNIB) at the Oshawa Civic Auditorium with his newly-formed band, The New Barbarians.

» **June 4, 1979** Rush's Tour of the Hemispheres comes to a close at the Pink Pop Festival in The Netherlands after eight months of dates in Canada, the U.S., the U.K. and western Europe

» **June 15, 1979** Joni Mitchell appears at the Charlie Mingus tribute during the Playboy Jazz Festival at the Hollywood Bowl.

» **July 1, 1979** Filming wraps on the movie *Carny*, a film produced and co-written by Robbie Robertson, formerly of The Band. He also stars in the film alongside Jodie Foster and Gary Busey.

» **July 11, 1979** The Neil Young concert film *Rust Never Sleeps* premieres at the Bruin Theater in Westwood,

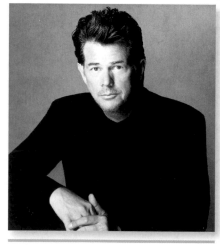

▲ David Foster

California. The movie documents his previous U.S. tour.

>> **September 19, 1979** Anne Murray plays to an SRO audience at New York's Carnegie Hall.

>> **September 23, 1979** The first annual Félix Awards, named in honor of Québec songwriter Félix Leclerc, are presented by the Association du disque, de l'industrie du spectacle québécois (ADISQ) as part of a gala at Montréal's Expo Theatre. Leclerc makes a brief appearance.

>> **September 27, 1979** *Glenn Gould's Toronto*, a TV film that forms part of the CBC Cities series, airs.

>> **October 1979** 16-year-old Montréal-based disco diva France Joli hits the Top 15 of the Billboard singles chart with "Come To Me."

>> **November 1979** Raffi's *Singable Songs* album is certified platinum in Canada, the first Canadian produced children's record to do so.

>> **November 1979** Loverboy debuts in concert at Vancouver's Pacific Coliseum as opening act for Kiss.

>> **December 1979** *The Village Voice* newspaper in New York names Neil Young Artist of the Decade.

>> **1979** Singer Norman Brooks plays a homecoming concert at Montréal's Place des Arts.

>> **1979** Toronto-born operatic soprano Teresa Stratas' recording of Alban Berg's Lulu is a milestone in her career, earning a Gramophone Award and two Grammys.

>> **1979** The Nylons debut at a Toronto cabaret across from the Art Gallery of Ontario (AGO).

>> **1979** Brian Eno comes to Canada to record at Daniel Lanois' Grant Avenue Studio in Hamilton, Ontario. A close working relationship develops between the two, and in 1984 they begin working with the young Irish group U2 for whom they co-produce the albums *The Unforgettable Fire* (1984) and the *Joshua Tree* (1987).

>> **1979** Paul Hyde and Bob Rock, who had first met in high school, form The Payola$ at Vancouver's Little Mountain Sound, where Rock is working as a recording engineer. They initially record the independent "China Boys" single before signing to A&M Records.

>> **1979** Bruce Allen, who had managed Bachman-Turner Overdrive, takes on management of a promising young newcomer on the Vancouver music scene, Bryan Adams.

▲ Frank Mills

>> **1979** Bumstead Records is founded in Edmonton, Alberta by Larry Wanagas, who will launch k.d. lang's career.

>> **1979** Trooper's *Hot Shots* greatest hits album becomes the first by a Canadian to be certified quadruple platinum for sales of over 400,000 copies. It goes on to sell over a half million copies.

>> **1979** Roch Voisine moves to Québec City to join Les Remparts de Québec junior hockey team. An injury will later end his aspirations to become a professional hockey player. He subsequently moves to Ottawa to study kinanthropology and physiotherapy and, through his university years, he continues to develop his songwriting talents, which had already become apparent.

>> **1979** Hank Snow is inducted into the Country Music Hall of Fame in Nashville during the Country Music Association's (CMA) nationally-televised awards show on CBS.

>> **1979** Anne Murray is given a star on the Country Music Hall of Fame's Walkway of Stars.

>> **1979** Colleen Peterson works as back-up singer for Charlie Daniels on tour.

▲ Daniel Lanois

1970-1979

▲ Trooper

>> **1979** Sony introduces the Walkman cassette player.

>> **1979** Groups formed this year include Alta Moda, Toronto; Brandon Wolf, Vancouver; Bundock, Grand-Mère, QC; Dayglo Abortions, Victoria, BC; Headpins, Vancouver; Loverboy, Calgary; Sheriff, Toronto; Spoons, Burlington, ON; The Lincolns, Toronto; The Payola$, Vancouver; Voggue, Montréal.

CHART-TOPPING CANADIAN SONGS 1970-1979

1970 **No Time** THE GUESS WHO
1970 **American Woman** THE GUESS WHO
1970 **Snowbird** ANNE MURRAY
1970 **As Years Go By** MASHMAKHAN
1971 **If You Could Read My Mind** GORDON LIGHTFOOT
1971 **Put Your Hand In the Hand** OCEAN
1971 **Sweet City Woman** STAMPEDERS
1972 **Heart of Gold**, NEIL YOUNG
1972 **Love Me Love Me Love** FRANK MILLS
1972 **Cotton Jenny** ANNE MURRAY
1973 **Danny's Song** ANNE MURRAY
1973 **Last Song** EDWARD BEAR
1973 **Could You Ever Love Me Again** GARY & DAVE
1973 **The First Cut Is the Deepest** KEITH HAMPSHIRE
1974 **(You're) Having My Baby** PAUL ANKA WITH ODIA COATES

1974 **You Ain't Seen Nothing Yet** BACHMAN-TURNER OVERDRIVE
1974 **Seasons In the Sun** TERRY JACKS
1974 **Rock Me Gently** ANDY KIM
1974 **Sundown** GORDON LIGHTFOOT
1974 **Help Me** JONI MITCHELL
1974 **You Won't See Me** ANNE MURRAY
1974 **Love Song**, ANNE MURRAY
1976 **The Wreck of the Edmund Fitzgerald** GORDON LIGHTFOOT
1976 **Roxy Roller** SWEENEY TODD
1978 **Hot Child In the City** NICK GILDER
1978 **You Needed Me** ANNE MURRAY
1978 **I Just Wanna Stop** GINO VANNELLI
1979 **I Just Fall In Love Again** ANNE MURRAY
1979 **Shadows In the Moonlight** ANNE MURRAY
1979 **Broken Hearted Me** ANNE MURRAY

OH WHAT A FEELING

Everywhere I go the kids wanna rock
Around the world or around the block
Everywhere I go the kids wanna rock

— Kids Wanna Rock

Lyrics & Music by Bryan Adams
& Jim Vallance.

»1980–1989

» 1980–1989

» 1980

» January 1980 The original John Kay and Steppenwolf hit the road again motivated by the appearance of a competing group calling itself Steppenwolf, fronted by former group members Nick St. Nicholas and Goldy McJohn.

» February 27, 1980 Musician, producer, songwriter David Foster wins his first Grammy Award.

» April 2, 1980 The 10th annual JUNO Awards are held at the Harbour Castle Convention Centre in Toronto, hosted by Burton Cummings. Anne Murray, who isn't in attendance due to the recent death of her father in Nova Scotia, adds another four JUNOs to her already crowded mantelpiece as she gets the nod in the categories of Album, Single, Female Vocalist and Country Female Vocalist of the Year. Bryan Adams, who is in attendance, is a nominee for Most Promising Male Vocalist for his disco-oriented single "Let Me Take You Dancing," which features Adams with his voice speeded up to an octave below The Chipmunks. The eventual winner in the category is Montréal-based guitarist Walter Rossi. Ken Taylor, Canada's former Ambassador to Iran, who became an American and Canadian hero when he assisted the escape of a number of American citizens from Iran during the hostage crisis, was on hand initially to induct Paul Anka into the Hall of Fame. When Anka got stranded somewhere in Colorado in a snow storm, he presented the Male Vocalist of the Year award to Burton Cummings.

» April 26, 1980 Canada's *Today Magazine* features Anne Murray on the cover with the heading "Anne Wins Big in Vegas... Nova Scotia's Snowbird is Suddenly Superstar" referring to her success at the Riviera Hotel.

» April 1980 In St. John's, Newfoundland, Terry Fox begins his Marathon of Hope, a cross-country run to raise money for cancer research. He is forced to abandon the run just outside of Thunder Bay, Ontario when it is discovered that his cancer has spread to his lungs.

» June 4, 1980 Rush begin live tapings of five SRO shows at London's Hammersmith Odeon as well as at later dates in Glasgow, Manchester and Newcastle.

» June 1980 An incident at Ontario Place in Toronto dubbed by some as "The Punk Rock Riot" during performances by Teenage Head and The Bob Segarini Band

results in the banning of "hard rock" at the venue for a number of years.

» June 18, 1980 The film *The Blues Brothers*, starring John Belushi and Dan Aykroyd of NBC-TV's *Saturday Night Live* as R&B fanatics Jake and Elwood Blues, premieres in New York.

» June 27, 1980 Bill C-36 in Canada's House of Commons designates "O Canada" as the country's official national anthem.

» July 2, 1980 The Montreal International Jazz Festival, established by Alain Simard and André Menard, is held for the first time, drawing 12,000 jazz fans to see and hear artists like Ray Charles, Chick Corea, Vic Vogel and Gary Burton. The 2004 edition of the festival enters the *Guinness Book of World Records* as the world's largest jazz festival.

» July 28, 1980 Rush and Max Webster get together at Phase One Studios in Toronto to record the track "Battlescar" for Max Webster's new album. During the session, lyricist Pye Dubois presents some lyrics to Rush he felt they might be able to use. They become the foundation for the Rush song "Tom Sawyer."

>> **August 8, 1980** The four-day Edmonton Folk Festival, established by Don Whalen, is held for the first time. It is now held annually during the second weekend of August.

>> **August 23, 1980** Heatwave, billed as "The 1980s Big Beat Rock and Roll Party," is produced at Mosport Park, Bowmanville, Ontario, just east of Toronto, by promoter, John Brower. Artists on the bill include The B-52s, Elvis Costello & the Attractions, The Kings, Teenage Head, The Pretenders, BB Gabor, Holly and the Italians, The Rumour (without Graham Parker), Rockpile with Nick Lowe and Dave Edmunds, ARKITEX (Vladymir Rogov) and Talking Heads.

>> **September 1980** Loverboy's self-titled debut album is released in the U.S.

>> **October 1, 1980** Paul Simon's semi-autobiographical film, *One Trick Pony*, which features an appearance by the Lovin' Spoonful, premieres in New York. The original members of the band, including Zal Yanovsky and John Sebastian, had reunited briefly in 1979 for a show at the Concord Hotel in the Catskill Mountains of New York, part of which was filmed for the movie.

>> **Winter 1980** Toronto singer/songwriter Eddie Schwartz has one of his biggest successes as Pat Benatar hits number nine on the Billboard chart with his song, "Hit Me With Your Best Shot."

>> **December 31, 1980** Loverboy make their U.S. debut in Seattle.

>> **1980** The first referendum on the separation of Québec results in the defeat of the proposition.

>> **1980** Rough Trade sign with Toronto-based True North Records. Their debut album for the label is *Avoid Freud*.

>> **1980** Vancouver's Young Canadians (formerly The K-Tels) play the Mabuhay Gardens in San Francisco. The night's performance is captured on the band's live album *Joyride on the Western Front* released in 2001.

>> **1980** Bryan Adams' debut album is recorded at Toronto's Manta Sound Studio with help from guest musicians

▲ Long John Baldry

▲ Rough Trade

Fred Turner (BTO), Jim Clench (April Wine, BTO) and Jeff "Skunk" Baxter (The Doobie Brothers).

>> **1980** Sharon, Lois & Bram make their American debut at the Lincoln Center Out-Of-Doors Festival in New York.

>> **1980** Long John Baldry, one of the mainstays of the British blues and R&B boom of the '60s and influential in the careers of artists like Rod Stewart and Elton John, becomes a Canadian citizen. He had taken up residence in Vancouver.

>> **1980** Burton Cummings makes his acting debut co-starring in the movie *Melanie*, for which he composes and performs the original soundtrack.

>> **1980** Bruce Cockburn has one of his biggest hits in the U.S. this year with "Wondering Where the Lions Are," which goes Top 25 on the Billboard single chart.

>> **1980** "Je ne suis qu'une chanson," written by Diane Juster and performed by Ginette Reno, becomes one of the biggest singles in Québec music history.

>> **1980** The Calgary Folk Music Festival has its beginnings as a 22-venue tour of Alberta by The Travelling Folk Festival and Goodtime Medicine Show, organized by Winnipeg Folk Festival founder Mitch Podolak as part of Alberta's 75th anniversary celebrations. In the years since, the festival has settled in at Prince's Island Park in Calgary, where it is held in late July each year.

>> **1980** The Ottawa Jazz Festival is founded by local musicians Bob Misener and Tony Pope, later joined by the late Bill Shuttleworth.

>> **1980** The non-profit Folk on the Rocks music festival is held for the first time on the shores of Long Lake in Yellowknife, Northwest Territories.

>> **1980** Groups formed this year include Barney Bentall and the Legendary Hearts, Vancouver; Barra MacNeils, Sydney Mines, NS; Images In Vogue from Vancouver; Leahy, Lakefield, ON; L'Étranger Toronto; Straight Lines, Vancouver; The Front, Toronto; The Rheostatics, Toronto.

>> 1981

>> **January 3, 1981** Vocalist, producer Bryan Russell (aka Brian Russell) marries

actress, singer Cheryl Ladd (Charlie's Angels).

» February 5, 1981. The 11th annual JUNO Awards are held at the O'Keefe Centre in Toronto, hosted by the pairings of John Candy and Andrea Martin, Ronnie Hawkins and Carroll Baker and Frank Mills and Ginette Reno. Anne Murray, who is again not on hand for the evening's festivities, is a four-time JUNO winner for the second year in a row. In the Singles category, she is part of the second tie in JUNO history as her hit "Could I Have This Dance" shares the spotlight with Martha and the Muffins' first chart-topper, "Echo Beach." There's a little unrehearsed and unexpected slapstick this year as co-hosts Ronnie Hawkins and Carroll Baker arrive on stage in a chauffeur-driven Rolls Royce. The door jams and, in the process of extricating himself from the car, Hawkins rips his tuxedo pants and almost does his "Bo Diddley" a mischief as he clambers out leaving a gaping hole and co-host Baker doubled up with laughter. Carrie and Jonathan Thomas, son and daughter of singer/songwriter Ian Thomas, introduce a video clip of kids singing songs from the nominated Children's Albums of the Year and take some good-natured ribbing from John Candy. Joni Mitchell [on being inducted into the JUNO Hall of Fame by Prime Minister Pierre Trudeau: "Well, the Hall of Fame... makes me feel like Boom Boom Geoffrion."

» March 1981 The Montréal Symphony Orchestra's first album *Daphnis et Chloé* is released.

▲ Bob & Doug Mackenzie. "Take off, eh?"

» April 2, 1981 Though April Wine had consciously put a harder edge to their rock sound, ironically it is the ballad "Just Between You and Me" that brings the group their first gold album in the U.S. for *Nature of the Beast*.

» May 1981 Raffi plays his first public concert in the U.S. in Portland, Oregon. The demand for tickets is such that a second show has to be added.

» May 20, 1981 Loverboy complete the recording of their sophomore album *Get Lucky* and are honoured with a party on 52nd Street in New York by Columbia Records in recognition of their first album going gold for U.S. sales in excess of 500,000 copies. In Canada, sales have passed the 300,000 mark. The group subsequently sets out on a two-month U.S. tour with ZZ Top.

» June 30, 1981 Loverboy make their live concert debut in New York opening for ZZ Top at the Dr. Pepper Music Festival.

» July 21, 1981 Vancouver club The Cave closes with a farewell performance by the Bobby Hales Orchestra.

» August 1, 1981 MTV debuts in the U.S. The first video played is "Video Killed the Radio Star" by The Buggles.

» August 15, 1981 Mary Bailey, who will become Shania Twain's manager in the late '80s, hits the Billboard Country chart in the U.S. as a recording artist in her own right with the single, "Too Much, Too Little, Too Late."

» September 2, 1981 Anne Murray, who appears at the CNE Grandstand in Toronto for the first time since 1972, receives the highest guarantee to this point for an appearance at the venue... a sum reportedly well in excess of $100,000.

» October 1981 Loverboy's *Get Lucky* album is released in the U.S. while the band is in the middle of a cross-country tour with Journey. Their self-titled debut album has at this point sold a million copies in the U.S. and over 400,000 in Canada.

» November 21, 1981 Tafelmusik make their New York debut at the Metropolitan Museum of Art as part of a wider North American tour.

▲ Loverboy

THEIR GREATEST HITS AND MORE - NOW AT PEPPERHORN COLLECTIONS!

>> **December 1, 1981** Bob and Doug McKenzie make their *Tonight Show* debut. On its release, *Great White North* featuring the McKenzie brothers (the alter egos of SCTV cast members Rock Moranis and Dave Thomas), becomes one of the fastest selling debut albums in the history of the Canadian recording industry. Rush, with Geddy Lee on vocals, guest on the duo's single "Take Off," which almost certainly helps with the impressive sales figures.

>> **December 31, 1981** Vancouver band 54-40 open for local punk legends D.O.A. at the Smilin' Buddah Cabaret in Vancouver.

>> **1981** Murray McLauchlan's song "If the Wind Could Blow My Troubles Away" becomes the theme for the International Year of Disabled Persons.

>> **1981** The U-Knows, awards for Canadian independent and alternative music, are first presented by Toronto radio station CFNY, later rebranded as 102.1 The Edge. The awards, an alternative to the mainstream JUNO Awards developed by CFNY Program Director David Marsden, are renamed the CASBYs (Canadian Artists Selected By You) in 1986.

>> **1981** David Clayton-Thomas takes part in a five-city tour with the Cincinnati Pops Orchestra in a Tribute to John Lennon that also includes Sarah Vaughan and Roberta Flack.

>> **1981** Rob McConnell and The Boss Brass make their first U.S. live appearance at the Monterey Jazz Festival in California.

>> **1981** A concert appearance at Toronto's Music Hall by Bruce Cockburn becomes the subject of the film Rumours of Glory.

>> **1981** Drummer, songwriter Skip Prokop (The Paupers, Lighthouse) produces an album for the late singer/songwriter Gene MacLellan, which is recorded at Attica State Prison.

>> **1981** Musician, composer Loreena McKennitt bases herself in Stratford, Ontario and opens her own independent record label, Quinlan Road.

>> **1981** Having attended the Berklee School of Music in Boston, Neil Osborne returns to Vancouver and forms the band 54-40 with Brad Merritt. Their initial recorded output is the four tracks included on the compilation album, *Things Are Still Coming Ashore*, released by local indie label, Mo-Da-Mu.

>> **1981** Grant McDonagh opens Zulu Records at West 4th Avenue and Burrard in Vancouver which bills itself as "Record Store and Community Centre since 1981." It will also become the home of a record label under the same name.

>> **1981** David Farrell and wife Patricia Dunn-Farrell found the Canadian music trade magazine, *The Record*. Music journalists Richard Flohil and Larry LeBlanc are early contributors to its success.

>> **1981** The Canadian Music Centre based in Toronto establishes the Centrediscs record label, the only one of its kind devoted entirely to Canadian concert music.

>> **1981** Groups formed this year include: 54-40, Tsawwassen, BC; Boys Brigade, Toronto; Deja Voodoo, Montréal; Honeymoon Suite, Niagara Falls, ON; Killer Dwarfs, Oshawa, ON; Lime, Montréal; Moev, Vancouver; The Arrows, Toronto; The Box, Montréal; The Breeding Ground, Toronto; The Jitters, Toronto.

>> 1982

>> **January 18, 1982** Los Angeles mayor Tom Bradley declares today Bob and Doug McKenzie Day in the city in honour of the two Canadian characters ("hosers") portrayed by Rick Moranis and Dave Thomas on the TV comedy program SCTV.

▲ Loreena McKennitt

Back bacon sandwiches and Molson Ale are served at the celebration.

>> **February 1982** Saga sell out a 12,000-seat concert hall in Budapest, Hungary as part of a triumphant European tour, during which they record their Munich, Germany date.

>> **February 1, 1982** NBC-TV's *Late Night with David Letterman* debuts. His side-kick and leader of The World's Most Dangerous Band is multi-talented musician and Thunder Bay, Ontario-native Paul Shaffer, who had previously worked on NBC-TV's *Saturday Night Live*.

>> **March 3, 1982** The re-formed Mamas and the Papas, with original members John Phillips and Denny Doherty and Phillips' actress daughter MacKenzie and Spanky McFarlane of '60s pop/folk group, Spanky and Our Gang, play the first show of their brief reunion tour at New York's Other End club.

>> **March 5, 1982** John Belushi, former *Saturday Night Live* cast member and Dan Aykroyd's partner in *The Blue Brothers*, dies of an accidental drug overdose at the Chateau Marmont Hotel in Los Angeles.

>> **March 28, 1982** Sass Jordan embarks on a solo singing career as the popular Montréal group The Pinups, which she has fronted as vocalist/bassist for over five years, play their last gig at The Pretzel in Montréal. Other members of the group included current Los Angeles-based video, TV commercial and movie director, David McNally; L.A. session singer and co-founder/producer of Vox Lumiere, Victoria Levy, and noted New York-based music marketing executive, David Hazan.

>> **April 14, 1982** The 12th annual JUNO Awards are held at Toronto Harbour Castle Hilton and hosted by Burton Cummings. Loverboy's self-titled debut album sets a new standard for most wins at the JUNOs. The project picks up six trophies, or a quarter of all the awards on offer that year. Anne Murray and Bruce Cockburn are both double winners. The Technics All-Star Band Award, voted on by record-buyers and fans and presented to outstanding Canadian musicians, is introduced. First winners are Ken "Spider" Sinnaeve (bass), Neil Young (rhythm guitar),

▲ Sass Jordan

Rob McConnell (trombone), Neil Peart (drums), Burton Cummings (keyboards), Rik Emmett (lead guitar), Moe Koffman (sax) and Mark Hasselbach (trumpet). Neil Young, on being inducted into the Hall of Fame by Francis Fox, Minister of Communications]: "I have this one feeling tonight. I'm proud to be a Canadian."

>> **May 1982** Loverboy appear in a segment of the TV soap opera, *Guiding Light*.

▲ The Nylons

>> **May 4, 1982** The Nylons make their concert debut at Toronto's Massey Hall.

>> **May 19, 1982** The National Film Board feature, *Anna and Kate McGarrigle*, airs on CBC-TV.

>> **Summer 1982** The Montréal duo of Rosalind Milligan Hunt and Lyn Cullerier, collectively known as Cheri, have a Top 40 U.S. hit with the single "Murphy's Law."

>> **July 7, 1982** Pianist Jane Vasey of Downchild Blues Band, who wrote the group's "Trying To Keep Her 88s Straight," which features her only vocal contribution to the band on record, dies of leukemia at age 33.

>> **September 11, 1982** Lighthouse play the first of a two-night reunion at Toronto's Ontario Place.

>> **October 1, 1982** The first digital Compact Disc (CD), Billy Joel's album *52nd Street*, is released in Japan.

>> **October 4, 1982** Pianist Glenn Gould dies at Toronto General Hospital following a severe stroke.

>> **November 6, 1982** "Up Where We Belong," written by Buffy Sainte-Marie, her husband Jack Nitzsche, and Will Jennnings, and performed by Joe Cocker and Jennifer Warnes, tops the Billboard singles chart. In 1983, the song is heard on the soundtrack of the movie *An Officer and a Gentleman* and wins an Academy Award as Best Song.

>> **November 21, 1982** Joni Mitchell marries bassist Larry Klein at the Malibu, California, home of her manager Elliot Roberts.

>> **1982** Canada adopts its new constitution, including a charter of rights and freedoms, after the U.K. transfers final legal powers over to Canada.

>> **1982** The Canadian Country Music Association (CCMA) holds its inaugural Canadian Country Music Awards ceremony in Halifax, Nova Scotia as part of Country Music Week. Prior to this, and starting in 1977, the RPM Big Country Awards had been presented.

>> **1982** Kathy Dawn Lang, who has appeared in the musical *Country Chorale* in Edmonton and had begun singing at the Sidetrack Cafe in the same city, answers an ad in a local newspaper placed by Larry Wanagas looking for a vocalist for a "Texas swing, twin-fiddle band." She gets the job, Wanagas becomes her manager, and she becomes k.d.lang, who will reign initially as the queen of "country cow-punk."

>> **1982** During the recording of the *Get It On Credit* album by Toronto, one of the songs that didn't make the cut was "What About Love," written by band members Brian Allen and Sheron Alton with outside collaborator, Jim Vallance. The song would become the "comeback" single for Heart in 1985, who took the song to the Top 10 of the Billboard chart. It was later issued by Toronto as a bonus track on the CD release of their album.

>> **1982** Platinum Blonde play the Toronto club circuit, initially as a tribute to The Police.

>> **1982** Zal Yanovsky and John Sebastian, formerly of the Lovin' Spoonful, reunite for the three-hour CBC TV special on Canadian pop music titled *Heart of Gold*, produced by Toronto-based Insight Productions. The Insight Heart of Gold project also results in a syndicated radio series and a book under the same title.

>> **1982** Bruce Cockburn receives the USC Gold Pin from the Unitarian Services Committee for his on-going work with Third World countries. He also wins an Edison Award

in the Netherlands for the album *Inner City Front* and makes a five-city tour of Italy.

>> **1982** Kim Mitchell of Max Webster embarks on a solo career.

>> **1982** Lisa Dalbello wins first and second prize at the American Song Festival in the Top 40 category with the songs "Can I Do It?" and "Don't Get Mad," co-written with Tim Thorney.

>> **1982** Celine Dion tours Japan, has a couple of hits in Germany and is a gold medal winner at Tokyo's World Popular Music Festival. She also appears on the French TV variety show *Champs Elysées* before returning to Montréal to sing with the Montréal Symphony Orchestra.

>> **1982** At age 17, cellist Ofra Harnoy becomes the youngest first prize winner in the history of the New York Concert Artists Guild Award.

>> **1982** The Robert Gordon cover of Windsor, Ontario-native Jack Scott's "The Way I Walk" is the catalyst for a reissue of Scott's early material by Attic Records.

>> **1982** The Montréal Jubilation Choir is formed by Trevor Payne for a concert commemorating the 75th anniversary of Union United Church, Montréal's oldest black community church.

>> **1982** David Farrell and his wife Patricia Dunn-Farrell, publishers of the Canadian music trade magazine *The Record*, with music marketing executive Neill Dixon as program director, launch The Record Music Industry Conference. In 1985, they introduce The Record Music Industry Awards for recognition of excellence in the areas of broadcasting, retailing, marketing, management and concert productions,

▲ Ofra Harnoy

among others. Dixon will take over the conference in 1993, adding a music showcase called Canadian Music Fest and incorporating an annual Broadcasting and Music Industry Awards, as it begins to evolve to the the current day Canadian Music Week, the most important event, outside of the JUNOs, on the Canadian music calendar each year.

» 1982 Groups formed this year include: Brighton Rock, Niagara Falls, ON; Cats Can Fly, Toronto; Chalk Circle, Newcastle, ON; Change of Heart, Toronto; Coney Hatch, Toronto; Eight Seconds, Ottawa; Haywire, Charlottetown, PEI; Jerry Jerry and the Sons of the Rhythm Orchestra, Edmonton; The Parachute Club, Toronto; Urgent, Toronto.

» 1983

» Early 1983 Corey Hart signs to Aquarius Records in his hometown of Montréal and heads for England to record his debut album. Eric Clapton guests on the track "Jenny Fay."

» January 1983 A&M Records releases Bryan Adams' *Cuts Like A Knife* album. Through the rest of the year, he tours with Aerosmith, Journey and The Police (in Australia and New Zealand) and headlines his own shows in Japan.

» February 14, 1983 Rush begin their first of two standing-room-only concerts at the Long Beach Arena. They become the first Canadian band to sell out four nights in the Los Angeles area when they complete the second of two SRO concerts at the Los Angeles Forum on February 18. The group draws close to 50,000 people over the four nights.

» February 1983 Bruce Cockburn and Nancy White travel to Nicaragua and Mexico on an Oxfam-sponsored, fact-finding tour. For Cockburn, it marks the beginning of a concentrated schedule of benefits and goodwill appearances on behalf of organizations that work for causes close to his heart. The effect on his music is predictable. His Nicaragua experience and subsequent anger explode in the 1984 song "If I Had A Record Launcher."

» April 1983 Brian MacLeod and Ab Bryant leave Chilliwack to become full-time members of The Headpins.

» April 1983 The Bruce Cockburn documentary film *Rumours of Glory — Bruce Cockburn Live*, with concert footage shot in 1981 at Ontario Place in Toronto, is screened at the Los Angeles Film Festival.

» April 5, 1983 The 13th annual JUNO Awards are held at the Toronto Hilton Harbour Castle Hotel in Toronto and hosted by Burton Cummings and Canadian comedic actor Alan Thicke. The Vancouver-based group Payola$ take home four JUNOs, including Most Promising Group and Best Single ("Eyes of a Stranger"). Bryan Adams wins his first JUNO Award. Anne Murray's absence from the show again causes a certain amount of controversy and on-stage comment. Alan Thicke, a friend of Murray's, comments sarcastically at one point: "Anne Murray is in Los Angeles, conducting herself, as usual, in a manner that does honour to the Canadian recording industry." Jazz legend Count Basie is on hand to introduce the nominees for Best Jazz Album. Carole Pope wins the award as Female Vocalist of the Year. It is the first time since 1978 that Anne Murray has been deposed from that title. Murray is named Country Female Vocalist for the fourth straight year. The Right Honourable Edward Schreyer, Governor General of Canada, inducts Glenn Gould into the Hall of Fame: "... it honours a man whose talent burned so brightly that he transcended all categories of craft and lifestyle, or even nationhood in the sense that his talent was truly of international caliber."

» April 29, 1983 Triumph's album *Never Surrender* premieres simultaneously at seven radio stations across Canada via the first nationwide live radio network of its type in Canada. In the April issue of *Hit Parader* magazine, the trio's guitarist Rik Emmett makes the Top 15 list of Great Guitar Heroes, along with players like Jeff Beck, Eric Clapton, Ritchie Blackmore and Jimi Hendrix.

>> **May 1983** A cover story in *Canadian Business* magazine on Anne Murray's business empire reveals that to this point she has sold more than 18 million records internationally for Capitol Records from the sale of 19 albums and 30 singles.

>> **May 4, 1983** "Metal Queen" Lee Aaron, with interim backing group Sam Thunder, debuts in England at London's Marquee Club.

>> **June 1983** The first digital Compact Discs are released in America by Denon, CBS and Telarc.

>> **June 2, 1983** Singer/songwriter Stan Rogers (33) dies in a plane fire aboard an Air Canada DC-9 at Cincinnati/North Kentucky International Airport in Hebron, Kentucky, on his way home to Toronto from the Kerrville Folk Festival in Texas. Rogers left a legacy of six highly-acclaimed albums recorded for his own Fogarty's Cave record label.

>> **June 16, 1983** Buzz Shearman (32), former lead singer of Toronto groups Leigh Ashford and Moxy, dies at Etobicoke General Hospital in Toronto after the motorcycle he was riding slams into the back of a tractor/trailer.

>> **June 19, 1983** BC Place Stadium opens in Vancouver.

>> **Summer 1983** Men Without Hats' techno-pop single "The Safety Dance" lands at number three on the Billboard Hot 100 chart. "The Safety Dance" ultimately becomes a Top 10 single in 20 countries and earns the group a Grammy nomination in January 1984 in the category of Best New Artist.

>> **Summer 1983** Vancouver-based group Powder Blues appear at the Montreux Jazz Festival in Switzerland. Portions of the concert are featured on the group's 1984 album *Live at Montreux*.

>> **Summer 1983** Major country music festival The Big Valley Jamboree is held for the first time in Craven, Saskatchewan.

>> **August 26, 1983** *Strange Brew*, the Bob and Doug McKenzie film, shot in "Hoserama" and written, directed and starring Bob and Doug's alter egos Dave Thomas and Rick Moranis, opens in the U.S. and Canada. Ian Thomas, Dave's brother, writes and performs the title song.

>> **Fall 1983** The video revolution is in full nova as Corey Hart's debut single "Sunglasses At Night" is released. The single will not make the charts in Canada until February of 1984, and even then peaking outside of the Top 20. In the U.S., where his video is getting high rotation play on MTV, the single soars into the Top 10.

>> **October 16, 1983** Loverboy Day is proclaimed in Shreveport, Louisiana.

▲ Rush

>> **October 1983** The National Library of Canada (now Library and Archives Canada) acquires Glenn Gould's private legacy from his estate.

>> **November 19, 1983** Loverboy appear as musical guests on NBC-TV's *Saturday Night Live*.

>> **1983** The Tommy Banks Quintet become the first foreign jazz group to tour in the People's Republic of China.

>> **1983** Singer, songwriter Norman Brooks, who has been billed as "The Voice That Lives Again" given his uncanny ability to replicate Al Jolson's singing style and sound, is heard on the soundtrack of the Woody Allen movie *Zelig* as Jolson singing "I'm Sitting On Top of the World."

>> **1983** Loverboy become the first international artist in CBS Records' history to sell over three million albums in the U.S. The band's sophomore album *Get Lucky* is at that point the biggest-selling album ever to come out of Canada.

>> **1983** Rush prove to be kings of the magazine polls as they place first in Britain's *Sounds* magazine's poll in the album (*Signals*) and group categories. Circus magazine in the U.S. also has them at number one in the same categories as well as in the categories of songwriters, bassist (Geddy Lee) and drummer (Neil Peart).

>> **1983** Gordon Lightfoot makes his silver screen debut in the Bruce Dern/Helen Shaver film, *Harry Tracy, Desperado*.

>> **1983** Rough Trade embark on a European tour after opening for David Bowie on a number of his Canadian dates.

>> **1983** Walter Ostanek is inducted into the International Polka Hall of Fame in Chicago.

>> **1983** London, Ontario-born impresario/manager Saul Holiff, who had managed Johnny Cash's career through the '60s and into the early '70s, graduates as a mature student from the University of Victoria in British Columbia with a BA after taking a double major in English and History.

>> **1983** Barney Bentall, who had recorded in the late '70s for A&M Records under the name Brandon Wolf, reverts back to his given name and begins working the British Columbia bar scene with The Revengers (later the Legendary Hearts).

>> **1983** Niagara Falls, Ontario group Honeymoon Suite take top prize in the Homegrown contest run by Toronto radio station, Q107.

▲ Martha Johnson, Mark Gane of M+M (Martha and the Muffins)

>> **1983** While in high school, guitarist Jeff Healey is chosen as a Canadian Stage Band Festival All-Star for two consecutive years.

>> **1983** The Arts Club Revue Theatre opens in Vancouver.

>> **1983** Groups formed this year include: Boulevard, Calgary; Buddy Wasisname and the Other Fellers, Newfoundland; Glass Tiger, Newmarket, ON; Idle Eyes, Vancouver; Partland Brothers, Colgan/Toronto, ON; The Grapes of Wrath, Kelowna, BC; The Jeff Healey Band, Toronto; and The Tragically Hip, Kingston, ON.

» 1984

>> **February 3, 1984** Vancouver Mayor Mike Harcourt declares this Dal Richards Day. Band leader Richards, "Vancouver's Swinging Legend," who had to that point been performing and touring for close to 50 years, is still active today and accepting bookings.

>> **February 14, 1984** Blue Rodeo play their first gig at the Rivoli in Toronto.

>> **March 31, 1984** Corey Hart makes his hometown concert debut opening for Culture Club at the Montréal Forum.

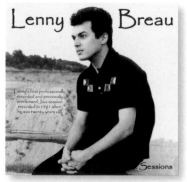

▲ Lenny Breau

>> **Spring 1984** M+M (formerly Martha and the Muffins) led by Martha Johnson and Mark Gane, find that social commentary and pop music do in fact mix as their single "Black Stations, White Stations" becomes a minor hit in Canada, as well as in the U.S. and the U.K. during the summer. The single is from their Daniel Lanois-produced *Mystery Walk* album.

>> **May 17, 1984** Commentator/author Gordon Sinclair (83), who in 1973 delivered his emotional commentary "The Americans (A Canadian's Opinion)," which led to recorded versions by himself, Byron McGregor and Tex Ritter, dies of a heart attack at Toronto's Queensway Hospital.

>> **July 14, 1984** The first Hillside Festival is held in Guelph, Ontario at the Riverside Park Bandshell. It later moves to Guelph Lake Island.

>> **July 24, 1984** Zenora Rose "Nora" Moore Hendrix, the grandmother of guitar legend Jimi Hendrix passes away in Vancouver at the age of 100.

>> **Summer 1984** Platinum Blonde causes a near-riot by female fans during a concert at Toronto's City Hall.

>> **August 12, 1984** Pioneering jazz guitarist Lenny Breau, who took the instrument's harmonic potential to new heights, is murdered in Ventura, California.

>> **August 15, 1984** Corey Hart, whose video exposure in the U.S. on MTV has brought him a significant following there, begins two and a half months of tour dates with Hall and Oates and Rick Springfield. He is later nominated by MTV as one of the hot new artists of 1984.

>> **August 31, 1984** *MuchMusic*, the Nation's Music Station, is launched and puts a face to Canadian music.

>> **September 17, 1984** Jane Siberry makes her American concert debut at the Ritz in New York.

>> **September 19, 1984** Men Without Hats kick off a European tour at The Venue in London.

>> **November 1984** Bryan Adams gives a free concert at the 2700-seat Orpheum Theatre in Vancouver in order to complete filming of his five-song video-cassette. Those who got in saw Adams film video footage for "Heaven" and "Kids Want To Rock" and then play a full set. Those outside were the beneficiaries of the $1000 worth of pizzas provided by Adams' manager, Bruce Allen.

>> **November 8, 1984** Bruce Cockburn's "If I Had A Rocket Launcher" is released, the day after Ronald Reagan was elected for a second term as President.

>> **November 9, 1984** Anne Murray plays the first of two nights at New York's Radio City Music Hall. It is her first appearance at the venue.

>> **November 1984** Rush tour Japan, Hawaii, Canada and the U.S. during their 100-date Grace Under Pressure tour.

>> **December 5, 1984** The 14th annual JUNO Awards are held at the Automotive Building, Exhibition Place, Toronto and hosted by Andrea Martin and Joe Flaherty. Bryan Adams, a relatively new face at the JUNOs, picks up four awards for his *Cuts Like A Knife* album project including Male Vocalist, Composer, Producer and Album. Parachute Club take the honours as Most Promising Group and for their single, "Rise Up." Anne Murray scores her fifth straight JUNO as Country Female Vocalist, which is accepted by Tommy Hunter on her behalf. Corey Hart's "Sunglasses At Night" video, directed by Rob Quartly, receives the first JUNO in the Best Video category. The inaugural Walt Grealis Special Achievement Award, named after the *RPM Weekly* publisher/editor and JUNO co-founder, is presented to executive J. Lyman Potts of the Canadian Talent Library. The induction of The Crew Cuts, The Diamonds and The Four Lads into the JUNO Hall of Fame becomes a show highlight as the 12 members of the three doo-wop groups take to the stage to perform a medley of their hits from the '50s. Carole Pope on winning Female Vocalist award: "I'd like to thank CBS and True North Records and my creator... Max Factor."

>> **December 15, 1984** Paul Shaffer appears with Robert Plant's group The Honeydrippers on NBC-TV's *Saturday Night Live*.

>> **December 26, 1984** Ron Tabak (31), former lead singer of Vancouver group Prism, dies from a brain hemorrhage after falling off his bicycle. He had originally been discharged from a Burnaby, BC hospital with no apparent symptoms, but when he turned violent he was arrested by two police officers who happened to be in the building and taken to the local lock-up. He was found unconscious in his cell the following day and was rushed to Vancouver General Hospital, where he died 24 hours later.

>> **December 26, 1984** Bryan Adams opens his North American tour in Chicago.

>> **December 28, 1984** Corey Hart plays a hometown concert at The Spectrum in Montreal, which causes quite a commotion among the local teeny-bop set.

>> **December 31, 1984** In the middle of an extensive North American tour, Bryan Adams takes time out to co-host MTV's New Year's Eve Bash.

▲ Fred Penner

>> **1984** Paul Shaffer makes his acting debut in the movie, *This Is Spinal Tap*.

>> **1984** Canada's first fully-animated video, "Can't Stand Still, " for The Extra's first single, is produced by Peter Sandler, who had worked on The Beatles' animated film, *Yellow Submarine*.

>> **1984** Honeymoon Suite tour North America with Jethro Tull.

>> **1984** Prime Minister Pierre Elliott Trudeau retires and the subsequent election is won by the Progressive Conservatives led by Brian Mulroney.

>> **1984** Daniel Lanois co-produces the soundtrack to Alan Parker's film *Birdy* with Peter Gabriel, who composes and performs the music.

>> **1984** k.d. lang makes her American debut at the Bottom Line in New York.

>> **1984** At age 10, Alanis Morissette is in the cast of the kids series, *You Can't Do That On Television*, seen on the Nickelodeon cable network in the U.S. She cuts an indie single titled "Fate Stay With Me."

>> **1984** After playing at a farewell party for Canada's U.S. Ambassador Ken Taylor in New York, The Nylons leave for a tour of the Far East, Australia and New Zealand.

>> **1984** Raffi undertakes his first tour of the U.S.

▲ Northern Lights For Africa ("Tears Are Not Enough")

>> **1984** Sharon, Lois & Bram's *Elephant Show* is first telecast by CBC-TV. It will be seen in the U.S. on the Nickelodeon cable channel beginning in 1987.

>> **1984** Fred Penner begins hosting the popular CBC-TV children's show *Fred Penner's Place*. The program is introduced in the U.S. on Nickelodeon in 1989.

>> **1984** Leonard Cohen, singer, musician, songwriter Lewis Furey and actress, singer Carole Laure collaborate on the film *Night Magic* in Montréal.

>> **1984** Before taking a two-year sabbatical from the music business to go through the image perception transformation from child star to mature recording artist, Céline Dion plays six weeks at the Olympia in Paris and sings at Montréal's Olympic Stadium for the Pope and an audience of 65,000 people.

>> **1984** Leonard Cohen's *Book of Mercy*, a collection of contemporary psalms, is published (October 12). Also this year, Cohen's long-form video, *I Am A Hotel* (Citytv), partly based on his song "The Guests" and featuring appearances by dancer/choreographer Ann Ditchburn and figure skater Toller Cranston, among others, wins the prestigious Golden Rose Award at the Montreux International Television Festival in Switzerland.

>> **1984** Tafelmusik becomes the first North American baroque orchestra to be invited to tour Europe.

>> **1984** Lisa Dalbello drops her first name professionally, moves to England and is managed by Roger Davies whose other clients include Olivia Newton-John and Tina Turner.

>> **1984** Singer, songwriter, actress Mylène Farmer, who moved to France from Pierrefonds, Québec with her family in 1969 at the age of eight years old, meets young film student Laurent Boutonnat and together they set the French music industry on its ear. Farmer would become one of the most successful recording artists of all time in France.

>> **1984** Alert Music Inc., which becomes the recording home of artists like Kim Mitchell and the Holly Cole Trio, is founded by President W. Tom Berry.

>> **1984** Duke Street Records is established in Toronto by Andrew Hermant and records artists like Willie P. Bennett, Jane Siberry, Art Bergmann, Manteca, Chalk Circle, Rik Emmett and FM.

>> **1984** Groups formed this year include: Annihilator, Ottawa; Blue Rodeo, Toronto; Fast Forward, Vancouver; Fifth Column, Toronto; Kashtin, Maliotenam Reserve, QC; One2One, Ottawa; Paradox, Grand-Mère, QC; Poisoned,

Vancouver; The Hanson Brothers, Victoria, BC; The Northern Pikes, Saskatoon, SK.

» 1985

» **January 2, 1985** Bryan Adams, with opening artist Luba, sets out on a 20-date Canadian tour.

» **February 4, 1985** Bruce Cockburn kicks off a five-week tour of Czechoslovakia, Austria and East and West Germany, which results in back-to-back dates in West and East Berlin on February 12 and 13.

» **February 10, 1985** "Tears Are Not Enough," a song written by Bryan Adams, Jim Vallance and David Foster — with the title conceived by Bob Rock and Paul Hyde and the French verse by Rachel Paiement — to raise funds for Ethiopian famine relief, is recorded at Toronto's Manta Sound Studios under the name Northern Lights For Africa. (10% of the net proceeds are donated to Canadian food banks.) Chief organizer is manager Bruce Allen with Maureen Jack working as the overall co-ordinator. In Toronto, the Canadian recording artists, entertainers and sports personalities involved include Bryan Adams, Carroll Baker, Veronique Beliveau, Salome Bey, Liona Boyd, John Candy, Robert Charlebois, Tom Cochrane, Burton Cummings, Dalbello, Paul Dean, Gordon Deppe (The Spoons), Claude Dubois, Robin Duke, Rik Emmett (Triumph), David Foster, Donny Gerrard, Brian Good (The Good Brothers), Corey Hart, Ronnie Hawkins, Dan Hill, Mark Holmes (Platinum Blonde), Tommy Hunter, Paul Hyde (The Payola$), Martha Johnson (Martha and the Muffins), Marc Jordan, Geddy Lee (Rush), Eugene Levy, Gordon Lightfoot, Baron Longfellow, Loverboy, Luba, Richard Manuel (The Band), Murray McLauchlan, Frank Mills, Joni Mitchell, Kim Mitchell, Anne Murray, Bruce Murray, the 1985 National Hockey League All-Stars, Aldo Nova, Catherine O'Hara, Rachel Paiement, Oscar Peterson, Colina Phillips, Carole Pope (Rough Trade), Mike Reno, Lorraine Segato (Parachute Club), Paul Shaffer, Graham Shaw, Leroy Sibbles, Jane Siberry, Liberty Silver, Wayne St. John, Alan Thicke, Dave Thomas, Ian Thomas, Sylvia Tyson, Jim Vallance, Sharon Lee Williams, Neil Young and Zappacosta. Bruce Cockburn made his audio and video contribution at a studio in Hamburg, Germany while on tour as Jim Vallance made a quick turnaround flight to Germany to oversee the recording and to return with the results so that they made the final production.

» **March 1985** Bryan Adams, who had teamed up with Tina Turner for a duet on the single "It's Only Love," appears on a double bill with her at London's Wembley Stadium as well as at a star-studded Prince's Trust Charity concert in London that summer.

» **March 16, 1985** Triumph set out from Vancouver on their 17-date Thunder Seven tour of Canada.

» **March 21, 1985** Rick Hansen, who had been paralyzed in June of 1973 in a vehicular accident, begins his around-the-world Man In Motion Tour by wheelchair at the Oakridge Mall in Vancouver.

» **March 31, 1985** k. d. Lang appears with the Edmonton Symphony Orchestra.

» **Spring 1985** Record executive Seymour Stein sees k.d. lang at New York's Bottom Line and signs her to his Sire record label, which at the time is also the home of Madonna.

» **Spring 1985** Corey Hart's single/video "Never Surrender" from his sophomore album *Boy In the Box* is released. It will become his first number one single in Canada and his biggest hit in the U.S., where it reaches number three.

» **April 1985** Vancouver group Agent becomes Virgin Records' first North America signing.

» **April 18, 1985** Toronto (aka Holly Woods and Toronto), one of only a handful of groups from Canada to have four straight platinum albums, play their last show in Hanover, Ontario.

» **June 15, 1985** Sheriff play their last gig... but it will not be the last heard of the band. Group members Arnold Lanni and Wolf Hassel later form the group Frozen Ghost.

» **June 22, 1985** Bryan Adams' single "Heaven," a song originally written by Adams and Jim Vallance for the 1983 film *A Night In Heaven* starring Lesley Ann Warren and Christopher Atkins, begins a two-week run at the top of the Billboard Hot 100 chart.

» **June 23, 1985** 329 people, including 280 Canadians, are killed in a bomb attack on an Air India flight traveling between Montréal and London.

» **July 13, 1985** Bryan Adams is one of the many acts involved in the Live Aid concert at JFK Stadium

▲ Kim Mitchell

in Philadelphia. He will later be part of the Amnesty International Conspiracy of Hope concerts with Sting, U2, Peter Gabriel, Lou Reed and Joan Baez, among others.

» **July 20, 1985** Corey Hart kicks off a 21-date arena tour of Canada.

» **August 16, 1985** Platinum Blonde set out on their Alien Invasion Tour '85 of Canada.

» **August 28, 1985** Kim Mitchell Day is proclaimed by Sarnia, Ontario.

» **September 1985** Dalbello tours Germany with local star, Udo Lindberg.

» **September 12, 1985** Jane Siberry opens a one-month U.S. tour in Chicago.

» **September 21, 1985** A Bryan Adams concert at the CNE Stadium in Toronto results in the largest gross by a Canadian artist in the Canadian marketplace in history ($914,163.50).

» **Fall 1985** Triumph bass player Mike Levine and manager Joe Owens set some kind of record as they personally deliver the group's *Stages* album to radio stations in seven cities across Canada, from Halifax to Vancouver, in one day.

» **October 31, 1985** Doug Johnson of Loverboy puts together a group of musicians and singers under the name Action to make a record and video with proceeds benefiting Canada's food banks. The single, "Action Speaks Louder Than Words" is recorded on this day.

» **November 1985** Loverboy receives a Crystal Globe Award in New York from Columbia Records for selling in excess of five million albums outside of the artist's country of origin (Canada).

» **November 1985** The Band, with The Revols, play a benefit in Stratford, Ontario for the Shakespeare Festival Theatre. This is the 25th anniversary reunion of the Rockin' Revols, with whom The Band's Richard Manuel began his career.

» **November 1, 1985** Offenbach play their last concert at the Montréal Forum after a career that spans 16 years and 13 albums. The recording *Le Dernier Show* and the film Merci subsequently document the event.

» **November 4, 1985** The 15th annual JUNO Awards are held at the Harbour Castle Convention Centre in Toronto with Andrea Martin and Martin Short co-hosting. With a leading three JUNO wins, a scorching live duet with Tina Turner on "It's Only Love" and his integral involvement in "Tears Are Not Enough," the song for Ethiopian famine relief honoured at this year's award show, Bryan Adams becomes the major story at the 15th anniversary edition of the JUNO Awards. Best R&B/Soul Recording and Best Reggae/Calypso Recordings JUNOs are introduced with Liberty Silver figuring in both awards in their inaugural year. k.d. lang makes a memorable dash for the stage to accept her award as Most Promising Female Vocalist in a frothy, white wedding dress and work boots. Prime Minister Brian Mulroney accepts a special JUNO to the Canadian people for their support of the Northern Lights For Africa initiative: "Tonight is a double celebration. A celebration of the tremendous generosity of the Canadian people inspired in many ways by the creativity of the Canadian artistic community, so I accept on behalf of the Canadian people this tremendous award, but tonight is also a celebration of the unique and splendid talent of Canada's recording artists and the strength and vibrancy of this industry."

▲ k.d. lang

>> **December 1985** The Payola$ play their last gig at Vancouver's Club Soda.

>> **December 1985** Jeff Healey meets future band mates Tom Stephens and Joe Rockman at Grossman's Tavern in Toronto.

>> **December 9, 1985** Bryan Adams receives a diamond award for sales of over one mllion copies of his Reckless album in Canada. It is a first for a Canadian artist.

>> **December 22, 1985** CBC-TV telecasts the 90 minute documentary on the making of *Tears Are Not Enough*.

>> **1985** Sarah McLachlan, at the age of 17, fronts the band The October Game in her hometown of Halifax. The first gig the band plays is as opening act for the Vancouver-based group, Moev. The group's guitar player, Mark Jowett, is impressed enough with McLachlan that over the next few years he stays in touch and finally signs her to the west coast label Nettwerk Records, of which he is co-founder.

>> **1985** Glass Tiger, formerly Tokyo, signs to Capitol Records and opens for Culture Club at Toronto's Maple Leaf Gardens.

>> **1985** The Kim Mitchell song "Go For Soda," co-written by Mitchell and lyricist Pye Dubois, is picked up by the Mothers Against Drunk Driving (M.A.D.D.) campaign as its theme.

>> **1985** The Tragically Hip is formed in Kingston, Ontario by Queen's University alumni Gord Downie, Bobby Baker and Gord Sinclair.

>> **1985** Ben Mink begins songwriting and production collaboration with k. d. Lang

>> **1985** Leonard Cohen embarks on a world tour in the wake of the release of his album, *Various Positions*.

>> **1985** Bryan Adams and Tina Turner win an MTV Video Award for their duet on the track, "It's Only Love."

>> **1985** The influential American music trade publication *Billboard* names Bryan Adams, the year's Top Male Singles Artist. The same publication names his manager Bruce Allen, Manager of the Year, as does the Canadian music industry publication, *The Record*.

>> **1985** Mark Jowett, a member of Vancouver group Moev, Terry McBride, the band's manager, and Ric Arboit, form Nettwerk Productions in Vancouver, which will become the umbrella company for Nettwerk Records, Management, Publishing, Soundtrack, Multimedia and Nettfilms. It will become one of the most successful independent companies in the music world during the next two decades.

>> **1985** Groups formed this year include 13 Engines from Toronto; Blvd. from Calgary; Bob's Your Uncle from Vancouver; Bourbon Tabernacle Choir from Toronto;

Cowboy Junkies from Toronto; Frozen Ghost from Toronto; The Look People from Toronto; The Pursuit of Happiness from Toronto.

>> 1986

>> **January 26, 1986** Corey Hart becomes only the second Canadian artist in history to sell over a million copies of an album (*Boy In the Box*) in Canada. Hart got the phrase "boy in the box" from Steve Anthony, an on-air personality at radio station CKGM Montréal, who used it to refer to himself in relation to his studio surroundings. Anthony would later become a national multimedia presence, beginning with his time as a veejay at *MuchMusic* from May 1987 to November 1995.

>> **January 26, 1986** Saga and Honeymoon Suite set out on a European tour.

>> **January 1986** Singer Michelle Wright heads for Nashville to record the songs for her debut album.

>> **February 4, 1986** Vancouver Mayor Mike Harcourt honours influential, locally-based manager Bruce Allen (Bachman-Turner Overdrive, Loverboy, Bryan Adams) by proclaiming this day as "Bruce Allen Day."

>> **February 22, 1986** Bruce Cockburn presents a check for $28,000 to the Council of Haida Nations following two concerts at Vancouver's Queen Elizabeth Theatre to help in their fight to stop logging on Lyell Island in the Queen Charlotte Islands (Haida Gwaii) on the north coast of British Columbia.

>> **April 24, 1986** The Glenn Gould Prize is inaugurated as "a tribute by the people of Canada to the life and work of Glenn Gould" and is awarded to recognize "an exceptional contribution to music and its communication through the use of any of the communications technologies."

>> **Spring 1986** Former Toronto carpet salesman turned successful comedian/actor, Howie Mandel, takes the plunge

into the music biz with the release of his album, *Fits Like A Glove*. The single is "I Do the Watusi"... and he does.

>> **May 2, 1986** The 1986 World Exposition on Transportation and Communication — or as it was more commonly known, Expo '86 — opens in Vancouver during the city's centennial year. It runs until October 13, 1986 and draws more than 22 million people.

>> **May 5, 1986** Honeymoon Suite appear on the *Solid Gold* TV show.

>> **May 9, 1986** Anne Murray co-hosts the CBC-TV music show, *Good Rockin' Tonight*.

>> **May 13, 1986** Producer/songwriter/musician David Foster is named Songwriter of the Year at the BMI Awards in New York.

>> **May 31, 1986** Peter Gabriel's *So* album, co-produced by Daniel Lanois, debuts at #1 on the British album chart.

>> **June 1986** Vancouver's 54-40 make their Toronto debut at the Diamond Club.

>> **June 4, 1986** Bryan Adams, U2, Sting, Peter Gabriel and Lou Reed open Amnesty International's A Conspiracy of Hope tour at the Cow Palace in San Francisco.

>> **July 1, 1986** Bilingual singer and songwriter Roch Voisine plays his first major concert.

>> **July 27, 1986** Nancy Wilson of Heart marries movie director, Cameron Crowe.

>> **August 18, 1986** Ian & Sylvia reunite for a concert at the Kingswood Music Theatre in Maple, Ontario. The historic show, which includes performances by guests Gordon Lightfoot, Judy Collins, Emmylou Harris and Murray McLauchlan, is filmed by the CBC.

>> **August 1986** The Loverboy song "Heaven In Your Eyes" is featured in the soundtrack of the film, *Top Gun*. The song is recorded without the participation of group member Doug Johnson, who believed that the promotion of the American military was wrong.

>> **September 2, 1986** French music video network *MusiquePlus*, sister station to *MuchMusic*, signs on in Québec.

>> **September 1986** *Throb*, a TV sitcom that takes a comedic look at the record business, is released to syndication. The theme is written by Paul Cooper of The Nylons and performed by the group, who make several guest appearances.

>> **October 11, 1986** Glass Tiger's "Don't Forget Me (When I'm Gone)" peaks at #2 on the Billboard Singles chart.

>> **October 1986** Molly Johnson, who has been referred to as "the Diva of Queen Street West" in Toronto, plays the prestigious Imperial Room of the Royal York Hotel in her hometown with her part-time group, Blue Monday.

>> **October 26, 1986** Honeymoon Suite are finalists at the Yamaha World Popular Music Festival in Tokyo with the Ray Coburn song, "Those Were the Days."

>> **November 10, 1986** The 16th annual JUNO Awards are held at the Harbour Castle Convention Centre in Toronto, hosted by comedian, Howie Mandel. It's a JUNO three-pack for Glass Tiger at this year's festivities. Though at times he seems completely lost, the appearance of Bob Dylan to induct Gordon Lightfoot into the Canadian Music Hall of Fame adds a touch of excitement to the proceedings that only a music legend can generate. Corey Hart performs "Can't Help Falling In Love With You," live via satellite from Amsterdam. Rick "The Man In Motion" Hansen, who inspired David Foster's hit song "St. Elmo's Fire," is on hand to present the Group of the Year Award to Honeymoon Suite. Howie Mandel, who descends from the ceiling on a harness to open the show says, "This is a weird coincidence. Here I am the host of the JUNOs and I have a Jew nose." Anne Murray, who has been a no-show at the JUNOs for years, quips, "So this is where you hold this thing every year! Finally found it! As some of you know, I've won a great many of these. I just want you to know that I'm proud of every one."

>> **November 1986** Comedians Martin Short, Dave Thomas, Rick Moranis and Eugene Levy, among others, collectively known as The Wankers, record the album, *Wankers Guide To Canada*.

>> **November 1986** Powder Blues win the W.C. Handy Award as Best Foreign Blues Group at the National Blues Foundation Convention in Memphis, Tennessee.

» **December 1986** The release of Rita MacNeil's indie album, *Flying On Your Own*, proves to be a major turning point in her career. She subsequently signs to Virgin Records and, in 1988, fellow Maritimer Anne Murray covers the album's title song as a single.

» **1986** Singer, actress Gisele MacKenzie is temporarily cast as Katherine Chancellor on the soap opera, *The Young and the Restless*.

» **1986** Jennifer Warnes, one of Leonard Cohen's former back-up singers, records an album of his songs titled *Famous Blue Raincoat*. The subsequent single/video, "First We Take Manhattan," creates a renewed surge of interest in Cohen and his music. He makes a TV appearance this year on the TV series *Miami Vice* as the head of Interpol.

» **1986** Randy Bachman joins the exclusive BMI Million-Air Club, which recognizes the broadcast of his songs over a million times on radio in North America.

» **1986** Long involved in the fund-raising efforts of the Canadian Cerebral Palsy Association, Neil Young and son Ben are featured on a poster released by the organization.

» **1986** The songs "Let It Go" and "The Best Is Yet To Come" by Montréal-based singer Luba are heard on the soundtrack of the Mickey Rourke/Kim Basinger film, *9 ½ Weeks*.

» **1986** Classical guitarist Liona Boyd looks to broaden her audience as she releases the album *Persona* featuring icons of the rock guitar, Eric Clapton and David Gilmour.

» **1986** The CASBY (Canadian Artists Selected By You) Awards, a rebranding of Toronto radio station CFNY's U-Know Awards, are launched.

» **1986** Canada and U.S. begin negotiations on a Free Trade Agreement.

» **1986** Rough Trade end their 14-year career with their *Deep Six* in 86 mini-tour with guests Dusty Springfield, Nona Hendryx and Taborah Johnson in a show at the RPM Club in Toronto.

» **1986** ruce Cockburn, having played two benefit concerts for Haida Gwaii earlier in the year, releases the album World of Wonders and sets off on a round the world trip that includes a month long visit to Nepal on behalf of the Unitarian Services Committee. Following the release of his *World of Wonders* album this same year, Cockburn sets off on a round the world trip that includes a month long visit to Nepal on behalf of the Unitarian Services Committee.

» **1986** Honeymoon Suite record the theme for the Mel Gibson film *Lethal Weapon*.

» **1986** The Coastal Jazz and Blues Society partners with Expo 86 in Vancouver to produce the first annual

▲ Leonard Cohen and Jennifer Warnes

Vancouver International Jazz Festival, which featured Miles Davis, Wynton Marsalis, Bobby McFerrin, Tito Puente, Tony Williams, Albert Collins and John Mayall and the Bluesbreakers.

» **1986** Festi Jazz International de Rimouski is held for the first time in Rimouski, Québec.

» **1986** Groups formed this year include Candi & the Backbeat from Toronto; Front Line Assembly fromVancouver; Grievous Angels from Toronto; Holly Cole Trio from Toronto; Tu from Toronto.

» 1987

» **February 7, 1987** Musicologist Ida Halpern dies in Vancouver at age 76.

» **April 2, 1987** k.d. lang appears at The Roxy in West Hollywood, California.

» **May 5, 1987** Vancouver Mayor Gordon Campbell declares this "Georgia Straight Day" as the often controversial publication releases its 1000th issue.

» **May 1987** Bruce Cockburn's *Waiting For A Miracle* becomes the first double CD to be issued by a Canadian artist. In November, he begins playing his first solo concerts (without a band) since the late '70s.

» **May 22, 1987** Rick Hansen's around-the-world Man in Motion Tour, which raises million for research on spinal cord injury, comes to a close at the Oakridge Mall in Vancouver. The achievement is the inspiration for the David Foster/John Parr composition "St. Elmo's Fire (Man In Motion)," which becomes a number one song when recorded by Parr.

» **June 3, 1987** Bryan Adams records a live version of "Run Rudolph Run" at the Marquee in London, England for inclusion on a Special Olympics charity album. A few days later, he joins George Harrison, Elton John, Ringo Starr and others in the fifth annual Prince's Trust Rock Gala at Wembley Arena.

June 28, 1987 Hometown boy Neil Young is reunited with members of his Kelvin High School day's group, The Squires, as he appears at the Shakin' All Over concert at Winnipeg's Main Street Club organized by writer/music historian, John Einarson. The event, which reunites ten of Winnipeg's early rock bands, features artists like Randy Bachman, Burton Cummings, Fred Turner, Chad Allan and Kurt Winter.

July 1, 1987 The first Edgefest held at Molson Park in Barrie, Ontario draws 25,000 people. Initially planned as a one-off tenth birthday party for Toronto radio station 102.1 The Edge and to celebrate Canada Day, it has become an annual festival that primarily promotes Canadian music.

July 1987 Liona Boyd becomes the first solo classical artist to go platinum in Canada for the album, *A Guitar For Christmas*.

Summer 1987 The SaskTel Saskatchewan Jazz Festival is first held in Saskatoon.

September 25, 1987 Corey Hart, who had canceled a major Canadian tour due to fatigue, appears in concert at the Montréal Forum, where he is filmed for a CBC-TV special.

September 1987 Pink Floyd's concert date at Toronto's Exhibition Stadium is the top-grossing concert of the year in North America at $3.7 million.

October 6, 1987 k.d. lang appears on Nashville's Grand Ole Opry for the first time.

November 2, 1987 The 17th annual JUNO Awards are held at the O'Keefe Centre in Toronto with comedian Howie Mandel as host. The inaugural Entertainer of the Year award, voted by the public, is won by Bryan Adams, who accepts with his band live from London, England. The category of Classical Composition also debuts. Kim Mitchell's *Shaking Like A Human Being* becomes the first release on a Canadian independent label (Alert) to win in the category of Album of the Year. Film clips take the viewing audience behind the scenes to look at the creative process behind the production of a record. It features a number of artists paying homage to their Canadian record producers including Daniel Lanois, Bryan Adams, Bruce Fairbairn, Terry Brown, Gino Vannelli and Chris Wardman. On her 26th birthday, k.d. lang is named Country Female Vocalist, deposing Anne Murray who has dominated the category since 1980. Randy Bachman, Burton Cummings, Garry Peterson and Jim Kale, the four original members of the night's Hall of Fame inductees, The Guess Who, inadvertently have their acceptance speeches cut off by a commercial break during the JUNO Awards telecast. The resulting kerfuffle results in the airing of a half-hour profile on the group by the CBC.

November 27, 1987 Cowboy Junkies' *The Trinity Sessions* album, recorded on this date at the Church of the Holy Trinity in Toronto pretty much live off the floor, produces a cover of Lou Reed's "Sweet Jane," which opens the floodgate of critical praise from the press on both sides of the Atlantic.

Late 1987 Dalbello tours Europe with Marillion.

Winter 1987 Celine Dion begins a 40-night stand at Montréal's Theatre St-Denis.

▲ Liona Boyd

>> **December 13, 1987** Honeymoon Suite singer Johnnie Dee is hit by a car at the Los Angeles airport, necessitating a lengthy period of recuperation.

>> **December 13, 1987** The Corey Hart TV concert special, shot at the Montréal Forum, airs on the CBC.

>> **1987** Bryan Adams' fourth album, *Into the Fire*, is released. Adams continues his hectic international touring schedule that includes four SRO nights at London's 10,000-seat Wembley Arena.

>> **1987** Dan Hill's "Can't We Try" is named the number one Adult Contemporary hit of the year by Billboard.

>> **1987** King Lou (Louis Robinson) and Capital Q (Frank Allert) become The Dream Warriors.

>> **1987** The Nylons headline Carnegie Hall in New York.

>> **1987** *MuchMusic*, with Britain's Sky Channel, organizes the first World Music Video Awards.

>> **1987** Peterborough, Ontario-native Sebastien Bierk (aka Sebastien Bach) joins American group Skid Row as vocalist.

>> **1987** Vancouver's Spirit of the West performs at the Edinburgh Folk Festival.

>> **1987** The track "Overload" by Toronto's Zappacosta is included on the soundtrack of the film *Dirty Dancing*, which sells over 10 million copies.

>> **1987** Ross Vannelli, who wrote the hit song "I Just Wanna Stop" for brother Gino, becomes the producer behind the California Raisin records that include the single, "I Heard It Through the Grapevine," with Buddy Miles on vocals. The recordings spawn a pre-Christmas CBS-TV special.

>> **1987** Vancouver's Skinny Puppy have their album *Cleanse, Fold and Manipulate* listed in the Top 10 of Melody Maker's year-end poll in the U.K.

>> **1987** The Nylons' "That Kind of Man" is heard on the soundtrack of the Disney film, *Tin Men*.

>> **1987** k.d. lang performs the old Patsy Cline classic, "Three Cigarettes and An Ash Tray," on *The Tonight Show* with Johnny Carson. Cline's producer Owen Bradley is watching that night and lang's entree into the Nashville country music community is assured as Bradley produces her third album there the following year. "Three Cigarettes and An Ash Tray" was also one of the songs that convinced Roy Orbison that k.d. lang was the singer with whom he would feel comfortable reviving his hit, "Crying," as a duet.

>> **1987** k.d. lang records her sophomore album, *Angel With A Lariat*, in England with Dave Edmunds in the producer's chair.

>> **1987** Daniel Lanois co-produces Robbie Robertson's self-titled debut solo album, for which he shares a JUNO Award.

>> **1987** Neil Peart of Rush heads out on an African safari.

>> **1987** After close to two years away from the music business, during which she completely rethinks her musical career, Céline Dion emerges with a more mature and sexy image as a dance music artist. She wins the Eurovision Song Contest with "Ne partez pas sans moi," which sells over 20,000 copies in Europe in a couple of days. Her album, *Incognito*, becomes one of the biggest sellers of the year in Québec.

>> **1987** The Academy of Country Music Entertainment (ACME) becomes the Canadian Country Music Association (CCMA). This same year, the Canadian Country Music Awards are televised nationally for the first time in partnership with CTV, a relationship that lasts until 1998 when the awards move to CBC TV with encore broadcasts on CMT Canada.

>> **1987** The Toronto Jazz Festival is co-founded by Executive Producer Patrick Taylor and former Artistic Director Jim Galloway.

>> **1987** Groups formed this year include Corky and the Juice Pigs from Windsor, ON; Delerium from Vancouver;; Doughboys from Montréal; Flying Bulgar Klezmer Band from Toronto; Hard Rock Miners from Vancouver; Harem Scarem from Toronto; Hart-Rouge from Willow Bunch, SK; Headstones from Kingston, ON; King Apparatus from London, ON/Toronto, ON.

>> 1988

>> **Winter 1988** The Jeff Healey Band sign a worldwide recording deal with Arista Records in New York.

>> **February 13, 1988** As part of the opening ceremonies for the 1988 Winter Olympic Games in Calgary, Ian Tyson and Gordon Lightfoot join together to sing Tyson's song "Four Strong Winds" and Lightfoot's "Alberta Bound." Liona Boyd performs with Rik Emmett of Triumph and Alex Lifeson of

Rush on "Hands Of Man," a song that marks the first time Boyd has sung her own lyrics on record. It won't be the last.

>> **February 28, 1988** k.d. lang performs a rousing version of "Round and Round" at the closing ceremonies of the 1988 Winter Olympics at Calgary's McMahon Stadium.

>> **February 1988** "Don't Shed A Tear," the Paul Carrack single co-written by Toronto-based songwriter/artist Eddie Schwartz, hits the Top 10 of the U.S. charts.

>> **February 1988** The Raffi video featuring songs like "Baby Beluga" and "Down By the Bay" is certified platinum after selling over 55,000 copies in the U.S.

>> **February 1988** Bryan Adams plays five sold-out shows before 65,000 people in Tokyo, Japan, where he is presented with a platinum record for his *Into the Fire* album.

>> **March 9, 1988** Leonard Cohen receives a Crystal Globe Award from CBS Records for the sale of over five million copies of his album, *I'm Your Man*, outside of America.

>> **March 10, 1988** k.d. lang is named Best New Female Performer by a *Rolling Stone* magazine poll.

>> **March 17, 1988** Blue Rodeo showcase at New York's Bottom Line club in the wake of the release of their debut CD, *Outskirts*. The single, "Try," becomes the thin-edge of the wedge for the critical acclaim and record sales that follow. In a head-turning tribute, *Rolling Stone* magazine states in their year-end wrap-up: "The best new American band of the year (1988) may very well be Canadian."

>> **March 25, 1988** Bruce Cockburn is honoured with a citation by the Dean of Boston's Berklee School of Music, where he had been a student, in recognition of his contribution to music.

>> **April 1988** Paul Cooper of The Nylons' song "Number One," co-written with David Foster, becomes a major hit in Japan for homegrown songstress, Seiko, backed by The Nylons.

>> **May 17, 1988** State-run Soviet TV runs their first paid commercials, among them, a Pepsi ad featuring guitarist Derry Grehan of Honeymoon Suite.

>> **June 3, 1988** Bruce Cockburn headlines a peace concert in Montréal with all the proceeds going to International Physicians for the Prevention of Nuclear War.

>> **June 11, 1988** Bryan Adams is on hand for Nelson Mandela's 70th Birthday Party concert at Wembley Stadium in London.

>> **June 16, 1988** The Roxy Theatre opens on Granville Street in Vancouver.

>> **July 21, 1988** The Parachute Club play its final concert at Toronto's Ontario Place.

>> **July 1988** Vancouver group 54-40 tours the U.S. with The Church.

>> **Summer 1988** Bryan Adams tour Europe during which time he plays both sides of the Iron Curtain in East and West Berlin.

>> **August 8, 1988** Québec mourns the loss of one of its cultural giants as singer/songwriter Félix Leclerc passes away in Saint-Pierre-de-L'ile-d'Orléans.

>> **August 1988** Kim Mitchell makes Toronto music history at the time as he sells out two shows at the Kingswood Music Theatre at Canada's Wonderland, north of Toronto, and is forced to add a third. He ultimately plays to close to 40,000 people.

>> **September 3, 1988** Though the group will go on, the original members of Triumph play their last concert at the Kingswood Music Theatre as guitarist Rik Emmett departs after the show.

>> **October 1988** After a false start in 1984, Toronto's Mary Margaret O'Hara has her debut album *Miss America* released. Though it meets with a lukewarm reception at home, in the U.K., O'Hara basks in the glow of wide critical acclaim and SRO concerts.

>> **November 1988** Bryan Adams' song "Remembrance Day" becomes the soundtrack of an anti-war video by David Maltby.

>> **November 1988** After a benefit show for Nashville's

▲ Blue Rodeo

songwriters, Anne Murray is presented with a Lifetime Achievement Award. She is also made an honourary citizen of Tennessee and given the key to Nashville.

>> **November 1988** Neil Young reunites with Crosby, Stills and Nash to record the album *American Dream*.

>> **December 1988** Chilliwack end their tour of Canadian military bases in Europe with a concert in Nicosia, Cyprus.

>> **December 1988** *The Anne Murray Christmas* special on CBC-TV draws an impressive 4.2 million viewers, the highest-rated entertainment TV show in the network's history to that point.

>> **1988** The sale of digital Compact Discs (CDs) overtakes vinyl album sales worldwide.

>> **1988** The Jeff Healey Band appear on *Late Night with David Letterman* and *The Tonight Show*.

>> **1988** Doug Bennett of Vancouver's Doug and the Slugs makes his stage debut in John Gray's musical *Rock and Roll* playing Parker, the plump lead singer of The Monarchs, a fictitious band from Nova Scotia.

>> **1988** Priscilla Wright becomes the first Canadian female singer to re-record a hit and place on the charts again. Her new version of her 1955 hit, "The Man In the Raincoat," is released and charts again.

>> **1988** Rita MacNeil appears with the Men of the Deeps at the Halifax Metro Centre to an audience of 10,000.

>> **1988** Toronto-based reggae band Messenjah appear in the film *Cocktail* and contribute to the soundtrack.

>> **1988** Walter Ostanek is inducted into the National Cleveland-Style Polka Hall of Fame in Euclid, Ohio.

>> **1988** Jane Siberry makes her European debut at the Institute of Contemporary Art in London.

>> **1988** Singer/songwriter Ian Thomas receives the Danny Kaye Medal from UNICEF in recognition of his fund-raising efforts over the years, during which he has been National Chairman for Music for UNICEF and participated in a program called the UNICEF challenge.

>> **1988** During a homecoming celebration for Lucille Starr in Coquitlan, BC, just east of Vancouver, a local street is named Lucille Starr Drive in her honour.

>> **1988** David Wilcox' "Hypnotizing Blues," is heard on the soundtrack of the Tom Cruise film *Cocktail* while his "Cabin Fever" is heard in *The Great*

▲ The Jeff Healey Band

▲ Rita MacNeil

Outdoors starring fellow Canadians Dan Aykroyd and the late John Candy.

>> **1988** Platinum Blonde, and specifically group frontman Mark Holmes get the acting bug. The four group members play alien bikers in an episode of *War of the Worlds* series, and in *Mr. T's T and T* series. Holmes is seen in the film *Eddie and the Cruisers II — Eddie Lives*.

>> **1988** This proves to be the most eventful year of k.d. lang's country career to date. Having teamed up with the late Roy Orbison to record his classic hit, "Crying," it subsequently becomes lang's first international hit and brings the duo a Grammy Award for the collaboration. She also appears with Orbison in the full-length concert film, *A Black and White Evening*. Lang, a major Patsy Cline fan, named her band The Reclines in tribute to the late country legend. She worked with Cline's producer Owen Bradley on her *Shadowland* album, which included the memorable collaboration with country icons Loretta Lynn, Kitty Wells and Brenda Lee on the "Honky Tonk Angels: Medley." lang

also traveled to the U.K. on the Country Music Association's Route 88 tour with Randy Travis and the Sweethearts of the Rodeo.

» **1988** Michel Lemieux is named Canadian ambassador to Expo 88 in Brisbane, Australia.

» **1988** Stompin' Tom Connors, newly-signed to Capitol Records, returns with the CD, *Fiddler and Song*, after a decade away.

» **1988** Groups formed this year include Alias from Toronto; Barenaked Ladies from Toronto; Crash Test Dummies from Winnipeg; Crash Vegas from Toronto; Dream Warriors from Toronto; Grim Skunk from Montréal, QC; Kon Kan from Toronto; The Smugglers from Vancouver.

» 1989

» **January 15, 1989** Bryan Adams' late-1987 tour of Europe produces the TV special, *Live In Belgium*, which airs on the CBC TV network in Canada.

» **February 4, 1989** Almost six years after it hit the Billboard chart, peaking at number 61, and four years after the group had broken up, Sheriff's single, "When I'm With You," hits the top of the charts in America. Arnold Lanni and Wolf Hassell, two of the original members of Sheriff, had moved on to form a new group, Frozen Ghost, which had already enjoyed some chart success on Billboard in May of 1987 with the single "Should I See." They had no interest in retracing their steps and reforming Sheriff. The success of the single was nonetheless the catalyst for vocalist Freddy Curci and guitarist Steve DeMarchi, former members of Sheriff, to get together with former Heart guitarist Roger Fisher to form the group Alias.

» **February 14, 1989** Cowboy Junkies appear on *Saturday Night Live*.

» **February 15, 1989** With the release of their sophomore album, *Diamond Mine*, Blue Rodeo showcase at Soho's Borderline Club in London, England.

» **February 22, 1989** k.d. lang and Roy Orbison win a Grammy for their collaboration on the international hit single, "Crying."

» **March 6, 1989** In the same year that The Jeff Healey Band are named Entertainers of the Year at the JUNO Awards, the group's album *See the Light* receives Holland's Edison Award for Best Foreign Rock Recording.

» **March 6, 1989** Bryan Adams is one of the featured artists on the Greenpeace album, *Rainbow Warriors*, released in the Soviet Union.

» **March 12, 1989** The 18th annual JUNO Awards are held at Toronto's O'Keefe Centre, hosted by Andre-Philippe Gagnon. As The Band is inducted into the Hall of Fame,

Robbie Robertson, winner of three JUNOs on the night, Garth Hudson and Rick Danko of the group perform "The Weight" with back-up provided by the members of Blue Rodeo, also three-time JUNO winners that year. There's a poignant moment when Paula and Josh, children of the late Richard Manuel, pick up the award on his behalf. Levon Helm acknowledges the honour on video from Little Rock, Arkansas. The show-stopper of the night is Rita MacNeil's performance of her song, "Working Man," with the Men of the Deeps male choir, who had flown in from Cape Breton. Emotions ran high when k.d. lang performed "Crying," her hit duet with the late Roy Orbison, and accepted the coveted Female Vocalist award: "Roy [Orbison] deserves a piece of this too," said a tearful lang. And when the tears wouldn't stop: "I feel like Wayne Gretzky when he got traded."

» **March 17, 1989** Tom Cochrane and Red Rider's performance with the Edmonton Symphony Orchestra is recorded as the group's final album, *The Symphony Sessions*.

» **March 29, 1989** Tom Cochrane and Red Rider appear on the *David Letterman show* before heading for Europe to open for German star, Herbert Gronmeyer.

» **Spring 1989** Brighton Rock play two sold-out shows at the Marquee in London, England.

» **Spring 1989** Kon Kan, the Toronto dance music duo of Barry Harris and Kevin Wynne, celebrate a #1 dance hit and a Top 15 Billboard hit with the single "I Beg Your Pardon," which freely samples the Lynn Anderson country hit, "Rose Garden."

» **April 14, 1989** Bryan Adams makes music history when he and guitarist Keith Scott perform "Kids Wanna Rock" with the Russian group Aureole live from Moscow on the internationally broadcast World Video Music Awards.

» **April 14, 1989** Rita MacNeil makes her U.S. concert debut at the Berklee Performance Centre to great critical praise.

>> **April 1989** Following two sold-out shows at London's Town and Country Club, the London Times calls Jeff Healey a "blues messiah."

>> **April 27, 1989** Vancouver bands 54-40 and The Scramblers play the first of two shows in Moscow as part of an exchange program called the Interchance 89 Festival.

>> **June 3, 1989** David Clayton-Thomas is among the featured performers at the opening of The Skydome in Toronto.

>> **June 14, 1989** Bruce Cockburn receives an honourary Doctor of Letters degree from Toronto's York University.

>> **July 28, 1989** The Anne Murray Centre opens in Murray's hometown of Springhill, Nova Scotia.

>> **July 1989** Blue Rodeo is one of the featured groups at the Montreux Jazz Festival in Switzerland while on a European tour with Edie Brickell and the New Bohemians. During this period, the group is selected by actress Meryl Streep and music director Howard Shore to play her back-up band in a climactic scene from the film, *Postcards From the Edge*.

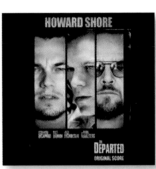

▲ Howard Shore

>> **July 1989** The Montréal Jazz Festival/Festival international de jazz de Montréal introduces the Prix Oscar Peterson for Canadian musicians of international renown. Peterson is honoured in its inaugural year.

>> **November 12, 1989** While touring Europe with Melissa Etheridge, Andrew Cash joins Etheridge, Joe Cocker and several German bands for a free concert at the Berlin Wall as citizens are allowed to move freely between East and West Germany.

>> **November 1989** The Roch Voisine single "Helène" tops the charts in France where he is quickly becoming a major star.

>> **December 8, 1989** Glass Tiger frontman Alan Frew appears in an episode of the TV series *Street Legal* as a musician fighting a paternity suit.

>> **December 15, 1989** Dan Hill appears at the NAACP 80th anniversary benefit gala in New York on a bill that includes Stevie Wonder.

>> **December 15, 1989** *See the Light*, a one-hour Global TV special on The Jeff Healey Band, airs.

>> **1989** Céline Dion tours Switzerland, Germany and France before starting work with producer David Foster on her first English-language album.

>> **1989** Crash Test Dummies get a little hometown love as the group plays the main stage of the Winnipeg Folk Festival.

>> **1989** The Diamonds join the Royalty of Doo Wop Tour with The Belmonts, The Chiffons, The Flamingos and The Silhouettes.

>> **1989** The Maritime Music Awards, forerunner of the East Coast Music Awards, are launched by Halifax-based impresario, Rob Cohn.

>> **1989** Roch Voisine sweeps the major categories at the annual L'ADISQ gala in Montréal, picking up Felix awards for Male Singer, Pop Song ("Helène"), Pop Rock Album (*Helène*) and Discovery. As a presenter, he hands Sass Jordan her Felix as Top Québec Artist Working In English.

>> **1989** Daniel Lanois, at this point critically acclaimed internationally as a producer following his work with artists like U2, Peter Gabriel, Robbie Robertson, Luba, Parachute Club, M+M, Bob Dylan and The Neville Brothers, releases his first album, *Acadie*.

>> **1989** Comedic actor Rick Moranis, former radio personality at CHUM-FM and CHFI-FM in Toronto, records the first album under his own name. The title track "You, Me, The Music and Me" is also a video in which Moranis revisits one of his alter-egos, the smooth-talking but vapid radio announcer, Gerry Todd.

>> **1989** A busy year for Toronto group The Pursuit of Happiness, who spend 80 days of it on the road in the U.S. opening for artists like Duran Duran, The Replacements, Mike and the Mechanics and Melissa Etheridge. Britain's Melody Maker has called the group's frontman Moe Berg, "Woody Allen with a groin."

▲ Tom Cochrane

>> **1989** *MuchMusic* Video Awards are established.

>> **1989** Soul Asylum, Nick Cave and Pixies are among the artists contributing to a tribute album to Neil Young titled *The Bridge To Neil Young*. The proceeds from the record benefit The Bridge, a California foundation for handicapped children, given guidance by Young and his wife, Peggy.

>> **1989** Gary Fjellgaard receives the Gram Award in The Netherlands as Most Promising New International Artist.

>> **1989** Barrie, Ontario-native Daniel MacMaster joins Bonham as lead vocalist.

>> **1989** The Jeff Healey Band appear in the film Road House starring Patrick Swaze, contributing four songs to the soundtrack.

>> **1989** Ofra Harnoy makes world premiere recordings of several Vivaldi Cello Concertos, which subsequently top the *Billboard* classical chart in the U.S.

>> **1989** Anne Murray appears on President George Bush's list of all-time favorite recording artists.

>> **1989** Sony introduces Digital Audio Tape (DAT) in the U.S.

>> **1989** The Beaches International Jazz Festival has its beginning with a number of top jazz artists playing the Kew Beach Bandshell in the lakeside "Beach" community of Toronto.

>> **1989** The non-profit Peterborough Folk Festival is held for the first time in Peterborough, Ontario.

>> **1989** Groups formed this year include Age of Electric from Lanigan, SK; Barstool Prophets from Cornwall, ON; Bootsauce from Montréal; By Divine Right from Toronto; Finger Eleven from Burlington; Furnaceface from Ottawa; Ghetto Concept from Toronto; Junkhouse from Hamilton; Lava Hay from Toronto; Leslie Spit Treeo from Toronto; Lost Dakotas from Toronto; The Gandharvas from London, ON; The Rankins from Mabou, NS; UHF from Vancouver; Wild Strawberries from Vancouver.

CHART-TOPPING CANADIAN SONGS 1980-1989

1980 **Daydream Believer** ANNE MURRAY
1980 **Could I Have This Dance** ANNE MURRAY
1981 **Blessed Are the Believers** ANNE MURRAY
1982 **Don't Let Him Know** PRISM
1982 **New World Man** RUSH
1984 **Almost Paradise... Love Theme From Footloose** MIKE RENO AND ANN WILSON
1985 **Heaven** BRYAN ADAMS

1985 **Never Surrender** COREY HART
1985 **Everything In My Heart** COREY HART
1985 **Tears Are Not Enough** NORTHERN LIGHTS
1985 **Crying Over You** PLATINUM BLONDE
1986 **Don't Forget Me (When I'm Gone)** GLASS TIGER
1987 **Can't Help Falling In Love** COREY HART
1987 **Pop Goes the World** MEN WITHOUT HATS
1988 **When I'm With You** SHERIFF

Oh What A Feeling

And I'm here to remind you
of the mess you left when you went away
It's not fair to deny me
The cross I bear that you gave to me
You, you, you oughta know . . .

— You Oughta Know

Lyrics & Music by Alanis Morissette and
Glen Ballard, performed by Alanis Morissette.

» 1990–1999

»1990–1999

ALANNAH MYLES
black velvet

» 1990

» **March 7, 1990** Montréaler Sass Jordan boosts the fortunes of the visiting side as she sings the national anthems prior to a Montréal Canadiens vs. Los Angeles Kings hockey game at the Great Western Forum in L.A. Montréal wins 5-2.

» **March 8, 1990** Music critics at Rolling Stone give Neil Young's *Freedom* the 1989 Critic's Award for Best Album.

» **March 18, 1990** The 19th annual JUNO Awards are held at the O'Keefe Centre in Toronto with Rick Moranis hosting, but this is Alannah Myles' night as she opens the show with "Still Got This Thing" and closes the show as she accepts the Album of the Year JUNO, her fifth award. She is the only multiple award winner. Six days later her recording of the Christopher Ward/Dave Tyson song "Black Velvet" tops the Billboard singles chart. The self-titled album on which the song appears goes on to sell over one million copies in Canada, making it the top-selling debut record for a Canadian artist in history to that point.

The Jeff Healey Band pick up their first JUNO — the prestigious Canadian Entertainer of the Year award, the only category voted on by the public. k.d. lang takes home her third trophy for Country Female Vocalist, confessing "for me, it has nothing to do with awards. It has nothing to do

with record sales. It has nothing to do with what category I'm in. I just love to sing." Kim Mitchell on accepting the Male Vocalist award: "I think of myself more as a white boy yelling." George Fox on accepting his Country Male Vocalist JUNO: "I'll tell you folks, a couple of years ago it was a big deal for me to take the cow into the vet." Milli Vanilli are destined to become the first act ever to have a JUNO Award revoked in the wake of the revelation later this year that group members Rob Pilatus and Fab Morvan did not sing on the duo's top-selling album, *Girl You Know It's True*. Singer, songwriter, producer, author and founder of the Centre for Child Honouring, Raffi (Cavoukian), receives the Walt Grealis Special Achievement Award.

» **April 16, 1990** Neil Young and Daniel Lanois are among the artists appearing at the Nelson Mandela International Tribute to a Free South Africa Concert at Wembley Stadium, London. The concert, held 2 months after the release of Mandela from a South African apartheid prison, is broadcast to more than 60 countries.

» **April 27, 1990** Cowboy Junkies perform "Cheap Is How I Feel" on *Late Night with David Letterman* and appear June 19 on *The Tonight Show starring Johnny Carson*.

» **May 27-29, 1990** When Madonna arrives in Toronto for concerts at the Skydome (now the Rogers Centre) during her Blond Ambition Tour, she is warned by the police to tone down the sexuality of her show (she doesn't) or face charges and cancellation of the concert (they don't). The incident is part of the *Truth or Dare* film that documents the tour.

>> **June 6, 1990** Alannah Myles picks up an Elvis Award as Best Newcomer at the 2nd International Rock Awards.

>> **Summer 1990** Kashtin make their U.S. debut at the New Music Seminar in New York. The duo of Claude McKenzie and Florent Vollant, singing in their native Innu-aimun (Montagnais) language, have great success during this period with songs like "Tipatshimun" ("Song of the Devil"), "E Uassiuian" ("My Childhood"), "Ish-kuess" ("Girl") and "Akua tuta" ("Take Care of Yourself"), which was widely heard on the soundtrack of popular TV series *Due South* and the TV documentary, *The Native Americans*, as well as on the associated "compilation" album Music for The Native Americans by Robbie Robertson in 1994.

▲ Luc Plamendon

>> **July 1990** Cattle-country radio stations in the U.S. drop k.d. lang's records after she participates in a Meat Stinks campaign for the Washington-based advocacy group, People For the Ethical Treatment of Animals (PETA). Folks back in Alberta aren't thrilled either and the sign that once identified Consort as lang's hometown is torched.

>> **July 18, 1990** The Québec music world loses one of its most-beloved "rockers" as Gerry Boulet, solo artist and singer with the band Offenbach, dies following a battle with cancer.

>> **July 21, 1990** Bryan Adams, Joni Mitchell and The Band are among those taking part in Roger Waters' performance of The Wall at the site of the Berlin Wall in Potsdamer Plaz, Berlin. The event is broadcast around the world and raises money for the Memorial Fund for Disaster Relief.

>> **September 6, 1990** Paul Anka becomes an American citizen in a Federal court ceremony in Las Vegas.

>> **September 10, 1990** Joni Mitchell's paintings comprise a major part of Canada In the City, an exhibition of Canadian art, music and culture at the Broadgate Centre in London.

>> **September 21, 1990** Celine Dion makes her first appearance on *The Tonight Show starring Johnny Carson*.

>> **September 22, 1990** Luc Plamondon and the late Michel Berger's rock opera *La Légende de Jimmy*, starring Diane Tell,

Renaud Hantson and Nanette Workman, premieres at the Théâtre Mogador in Paris. The rock opera, based on the life of James Dean, runs for 5 months.

>> **September 1990** The Family Brown give their final performance at the County Fair in Kanata, Ontario.

>> **October 1990** Neil Young is joined by Elvis Costello, Edie Brickell, Jackson Browne, Chris Isaak and Steve Miller at his fourth annual Bridge School benefit at the Shoreline Amphitheater near San Francisco.

>> **Late 1990** At a time when she is the best-selling country artist in Canada, Rita MacNeil becomes the first solo female recording artist with three albums on the Australian charts in a single year.

>> **Late 1990** Tom Cochrane and Canadian media personality Terry David Mulligan undertake a tour of four African countries with the international relief and development agency, World Vision Canada.

>> **December 1990** Stompin' Tom Connors, whose hit anthology *A Proud Canadian*, becomes the biggest-selling album of his career, completes a 70-city tour of Canada with two concerts at Toronto's Massey Hall.

>> **1990** The first year of the MuchMusic Video Awards (MMVAs), known then as the Canadian Music Video Awards. They are presented this first year as a week-long awards show that travels across Canada by train, stopping in towns and cities where the various invited artists perform at the station before the train moves on. Those performances and the hi-jinx and impromptu jams on-board were sent back to the studio in Toronto by way of a satellite dish affixed to the front of the train.

▲ Barenaked Ladies

» 1990 The Leonard Cohen song "Everybody Knows" is heard in the film *Pump Up the Volume*. It is the first of a handful of songs on film soundtracks in the early '90s, including Atom Egoyan's *Exotica* ("Everybody Knows") and *Natural Born Killers* ("Waiting For the Miracle," "The Future" and "Anthem").

» 1990 The Collapse of the Meech Lake Accord.

» 1990 Celine Dion launches an international career singing in English with the release of her first English album, *Unison*, produced by David Foster in Los Angeles, Chris Neal in London and Andy Goldmark in New York.

» 1990 The success of rap artist Maestro Fresh Wes' debut album, *Symphony in Effect*, and accompanying single/video "Let Your Backbone Slip" brings a sharp rise of interest in rap music in Canada, especially at the record company level.

» 1990 Musician/author Paul Quarrington, formerly with Joe Hall and the Continetal Drift, wins the Governor General's Award for fiction for his novel, *Whale Music*. The book is the basis for the critically-acclaimed film of the same name.

» 1990 Rush, Bryan Adams and k.d., lang are named artists of the decade ('80s) by the Canadian Recording Industry Association (CRIA).

» 1990 Vancouver's Spirit of the West tour the U.K. with Wonder Stuff.

» 1990 Roch Voisine becomes the first artist from Québec to play four nights at the Zenith in Paris.

» 1990 Tommy Hunter takes his place on Nashville's Country Music Hall of Fame Walkway of Stars.

» 1990 Alannah Myles opens for Robert Plant on his U.S. tour.

» 1990 David Clayton-Thomas sues the writers of Milli Vanilli's "All or Nothing," for not giving him credit (or paying royalties) given the song's similarity to his song "Spinning Wheel," which became a hit while Clayton-Thomas was vocalist for Blood, Sweat & Tears.

» 1990 Ofra Harnoy's recording of the *Vivaldi Concertos* is one of the biggest-selling classical albums of the year internationally.

» 1990 The Winnipeg International Jazz Festival (aka Jazz Winnipeg) is first held in Winnipeg, Manitoba.

» 1990 The Havelock Country Jamboree, now a four-day country music festival, is first held in the village of Havelock, Ontario.

» 1990 BMG Music Canada releases the 4-CD box set *Made In Canada: Our Rock 'N' Roll History*, which was compiled and produced by BMG executive Paul White. The set includes 69 classic pop recordings from the years 1960-1974.

» 1990 British computer scientist Sir Timothy Berners-Lee, having developed an effective information management system on the Internet, becomes the inventor of the World Wide Web.

» 1990 Phillips introduces a digital audio tape recorder (DAT).

» 1990 Groups formed this year include BKS, Toronto; Eric's Trip, Moncton; Glueleg, Toronto; Huevos Rancheros, Calgary; Infidels, Toronto; Les Colocs, Montréal, QC ; Lost and Profound, Calgary/Toronto; The Boomers, Ontario; The Irish Descendants, St. John's, NF; The Moffatts, Tumbler Ridge, BC; The Wyrd Sisters, Winnipeg; West End Girls, Vancouver; Wild T and the Spirit, Toronto; World On Edge, Québec.

» 1991

» January 20, 1991 Buffalo, New York-born pianist Stan Szelest, who had been a member of The Hawks and most recently was touring with The Band, suffers chest pains and dies on the way to hospital in Woodstock, New York. He had just co-written a tribute to the late Richard Manuel and Paul Butterfield with Jules Shear titled "Too Soon Gone," which is heard on The Band's album *Jericho* (1993).

» January 31, 1991 Vancouver-based heavy metal act Annihilator open a 45-date European tour with Judas Priest.

» January 1991 Mint Records is founded in Vancouver by former colleagues at the University of British Columbia radio station CITR-FM, Randy Iwata and Bill Baker.

» February 1991 The Dream Warriors embark on a 35-city European tour.

» February 10, 1991 David Foster and wife Linda Thompson-Jenner organize the recording of a charity record titled "Voices That Care" to benefit the American Red Cross Gulf Crisis Fund. More than 100 celebrities take part in the session.

» March 3, 1991 20th annual JUNO Awards are held at the Queen Elizabeth Building in Vancouver and hosted by Paul Shaffer, who enthuses, following Celine Dion's live performance of her hit song, "Where Does My Heart Beat Now": "Man, people say, 'You've been out of the country so long. Are you going to be able to do a Canadian music show?' This babe has the number four record on Billboard this week. I'm in a different country and I know who she is. I see Steven Tyler and Joe Perry sitting down here who write some of the best hooks in today's music digging her... right? Celine Dion, ladies and gentlemen! Unbelievable!"

Celine Dion, Colin James and songwriter/producer David Tyson are all double award winners as the JUNOs takes its show on the road for the first time. Blue Rodeo accept Group of the Year honors for the third year in a row, while The Tragically Hip see their extensive touring pay off as they are selected by the fans as Canadian Entertainers of the Year. One of the most riveting acceptance speeches in JUNO history comes with Leonard Cohen's acknowledgements following his induction into the Canadian Music Hall of Fame. His ex tempore reading of the lyrics to his song, "Tower of Song" sums up the moment and his career to perfection. The Rap Recording of the Year category is introduced with the album *Symphony In Effect* by Maestro Fresh Wes as the first winner. Earlier in the proceedings, singer/songwriter Murray McLauchlan expresses some of the on-going frustrations of many music creators: "While we are celebrating the successes of our industry here tonight, we shouldn't forget that the music that is created is constantly being commercially-exploited and stolen. All members of our industry urge the federal government to quickly pass new copyright legislation... The future of our industry depends on it." The Walt Grealis Special Achievement Award is presented to artist manager, producer Mel Shaw, the founding President of both the Canadian Academy of Recording Arts & Sciences (CARAS) and the Canadian Independent Record Production Association (CIRPA), now the Canadian Independent Music Association (CIMA).

» Spring 1991 Winnipeg's Crash Test Dummies have a Top Five hit in Canada with "Superman's Song" 53 years after Torontonian Joe Shuster created the comic book hero with Jerome Siegel.

» May 1991 Larry Good leaves The Good Brothers after 17 years and is replaced by Bruce Good's son, Travis. The group ultimately change their name to The Goods.

» May 25, 1991 "Rhythm of My Heart," co-written by Canadian songwriters Marc Jordan and John Capek and the first single from Rod Stewart's *Vagabond Heart* album, tops the charts in Canada. The duo are also the co-writers of the Stewart song "This" from his *Spanner In the Works* (1995) album.

» June 3, 1991 Bonnie Raitt releases the Shirley Eikhard song "Something to Talk About," which is included on her album *Luck of the Draw* (1991). It is one of the biggest songs of her career and leads to GRAMMY nominations for Record of the Year and Best Female Pop Vocal Performance, — the latter of which she won.

» June 1991 Ricky Van Shelton records the Charlie Major song, "Backroads" as the title track of his fifth studio album and takes it to number two on the Billboard Hot Country singles chart.

» July 27, 1991 Bryan Adams has his second consecutive number one single on the Billboard Hot 100 chart and, once again, it's with a song written specifically for a movie. The film was Robin Hood: Prince of Thieves and the song was "(Everything I Do) I Do It For You," co-written by Adams, Michael Kamen and his co-producer Robert John "Mutt" Lange. It holds down the penthouse position for an impressive seven consecutive weeks. In the U.K., the song's 16-week run at the top of the charts is unprecedented in British chart history. It will become one of the biggest-selling singles of all time with sales of more than 10 million.

» August 13, 1991 Blue Rodeo appear on NBC-TV's *The Tonight Show starring Johnny Carson.*

▲ Alanis Morissette

» September 1991 The annual Harvest Jazz & Blues Festival is first held in downtown Fredericton, New Brunswick.

» December 31, 1991 Barenaked Ladies are banned from the annual city-sponsored New Year's celebration in front of City Hall by the Toronto city council and Mayor June Rowlands because the group's name spooks them. The resulting publicity helps make the group a household name across the country even before their music has been widely heard.

» 1991 *Kick at the Darkness*, a tribute album to Bruce Cockburn, includes Barenaked Ladies' cover of the Cockburn song "Lovers in a Dangerous Time," which becomes the group's first hit.

» 1991 Rapper, singer, songwriter K'naan flees Mogadishu in Somalia with his mother and brothers as hostilities of the Somali Civil War begin. They initially move to New York before traveling to Canada and settling in the Rexdale area of Toronto where there is a large Somali community.

» 1991 The East Coast Music Association (ECMA) is formed in Halifax by Rob Cohn with Sheri Jones, Karen Byers, Lee Stanley, Mike Barkhouse, Peter Hendrickson and Tony Kelly.

» 1991 The MuchMusic Video Awards are held for the first time at the network's home in the CHUM Building at Queen & John Streets in Toronto.

» 1991 Canadian forces participate in the Gulf War following Iraq's invasion of Kuwait.

» 1991 Paul Anka briefly becomes one of the original owners of the Ottawa Senators' National Hockey League franchise.

» 1991 Michael Bublé first begins singing in nightclubs, thanks to his grandfather Demetrio Santagà, who would exchange his plumbing services to get his grandson time on the stage.

» 1991 An 87-year-old Wilf Carter announces that a nine-concert tour of Nova Scotia, New Brunswick, Ontario and Manitoba will be his last.

» 1991 [Leslie] Feist kicks off her musical career as founder and lead vocalist of the Calgary punk band Placebo.

» 1991 A number of international recording artists, including John Cale, Nick Cave, The Pixies and R.E.M., get together to record a tribute album to Leonard Cohen titled *I'm Your Fan*.

» 1991 Roch Voisine launches a European tour with two dates at the Palais Omnisports de Paris-Bercy in Paris.

» 1991 Exactly two decades after it was a hit for Ottawa's Five Man Electrical Band, Sacramento rockers Tesla top the charts with the song "Signs," which is included on their *Five Man Acoustical Jam* album. The song was written by Five Man Electrical Band member, Les Emmerson.

» 1991 Pianist Oscar Peterson is named Chancellor of York University in Toronto.

» 1991 JUNO Award-winning R&B, jazz and gospel singer and songwriter Billy Newton-Davis joins The Nylons.

» 1991 Alanis Morissette, known initially by just her first name, has her first, self-titled album, produced by Leslie Howe of the Ottawa group One2One, released by MCA Records in Canada. The dance/pop album goes on to sell more than 200,000 copies in the wake of the Top 10 single, "Too Hot." The 17-year-old Morissette graduates high school and then moves to Toronto from her hometown of Ottawa.

» 1991 Fiddle player Ashley MacIsaac emerges from Cape Breton, Nova Scotia for the first time to play the Memphis Celtic Festival and to play alongside the Rankin Family at the Mariposa Folk Festival in Toronto. Within the next few years, he will play and act in — and co-choreograph — the New York Shakespeare Festival's *Woyzeck*, record with Edie Brickell, perform with Paul Simon, The Chieftains, John McDermott and Ron Hynes, play Carnegie Hall twice and with both Symphony Nova Scotia and the Toronto Symphony.

» 1991 Inuk singer, songwriter Susan Aglukark gives her first live public performance at a festival in her hometown of Arviat, Nunavut, the first step on a career that would lead to command performances for HRH Queen Elizabeth, Canadian Prime Ministers Jean Chretien and Brian Mulroney, French President Jacques Chirac and Nelson Mandela, among others.

>> **1991** The Pacific Music Industry Association (now Music BC), launches Music West, an international conference, festival and exhibition held in Vancouver produced by Maureen Jack and Laurie Mercer.

>> **1991** Groups formed this year include Chixdiggit, Calgary; hHead, Toronto; I Mother Earth, Toronto; I Spy, Regina; King Cobb Steelie, Guelph; Len, Toronto; Love and Sas, Toronto; Lowest of the Low, Toronto; Our Lady Peace, Oshawa; Sloan, Halifax; The Arrogant Worms, Kingston, ON; The Boomtang Boys, Toronto; The Inbreds, Kingston, ON; Tristan Psionic, Hamilton.

>> 1992

>> **January 13, 1992** During a press conference in Sydney, Cape Breton, Nova Scotia prior to the start of the13-date Canadian leg of his Waking Up the World Tour, Bryan Adams lets fly a barrage of criticism at the Canadian music infrastructure. The outburst arises from a question about the status of some of his current songs, which had been labelled "Un-Canadian" because his collaboration with British/Zambian producer and songwriter Robert John "Mutt" Lange meant that they didn't meet the Content requirements for Canadian radio. His comments blow up in the media across the country but have no impact on the tour — it wraps at the Pacific Coliseum in Vancouver on January 31 having played to 135,000 fans across Canada — though it does influence the outlook of the Canadian Radio-television and Telecommunications Commission (CRTC), which in September changes one of the qualifications for Canadian Content to allow collaborations with non-Canadians.

>> **January 18, 1992** Robbie Robertson appears on *Saturday Night Live* with host Chevy Chase.

>> **Late January 1992** Roch Voisine, a certified superstar in Québec and the French-speaking countries of Europe, sets out on a three-month 50-city European tour, which includes four sold-out shows at the 16,000-seat Palais Omnisport de Paris-Bercy in Paris.

>> **February 25, 1992** At the 34th annual GRAMMY Awards held at Radio City Music Hall in New York and hosted by Whoopi Goldberg, Bryan Adams arrives having earned an impressive six nominations. On this night though, it is fellow-Canadian David Foster who spends more time at the podium, though Adams does pick up a trophy for "(Everything I Do) I Do It For You," which has also been nominated this year for an Oscar in the Best Original Song category.

>> **March 29, 1992** The 21st annual JUNO Awards are held at the O'Keefe Centre in Toronto with Rick Moranis as host. Tom Cochrane's Mad, Mad World and the hit single "Life Is A Highway" earns him four JUNOs. Moranis

▲ Ashley MacIsaac

quips, following Cochrane's performance of "Life Is A Highway": "A highway? Robbie [Robertson], for 15 years you've been telling me it's a carnival! Work it out!" The surprise of the night is Cochrane's win in the single category, which many thought was a lock for Bryan Adams and his international smash "(Everything I Do) I Do It For You." There is talk of a possible backlash from the industry to Adams' much-publicized comments that the Canadian Content regulations are the breeding ground for mediocrity, but he leaves town with three JUNOs, including the first ever Special Achievement Award. Adams and the Canadian music industry bury the hatchet. *The Globe & Mail* dubs the competition between Tom Cochrane and Bryan Adams as "the shootout at JUNO corral" though neither artist wants much to do with any gun-slinging. CBC Radio's Peter Gzowski is on hand to induct Ian & Sylvia into the Canadian Music Hall of Fame, as are Blue Rodeo and

▲ Susan Aglukark

musical guests Kashtin, Molly Johnson, Jane Siberry and Andy Maize, to perform a medley of the duo's best-known songs. Host Rick Moranis' closing remark: "Ian Tyson, would you please move your horse so Tom Cochrane can get his U-Haul out of here!" Music executive (BMI Canada Ltd.), songwriter William Harold Moon is honored with the Walt Grealis Special Achievement Award.

>> **April 27, 1992** Barenaked Ladies, whose independent cassette has already sold well over 50,000 copies in Canada, sign with Sire Records in the U.S..

>> **May 22, 1992** After 4531 episodes, *The Tonight Show* starring Johnny Carson, which debuted on October 1, 1962, has its last airing before NBC hands the time slot off to Jay Leno. Over the years, Carson and the show's producers had a number of favorite Canadian musical guests, including k.d. lang (Dec. 7, 1987 with Roy Orbison, June 24, 1987, May 13, 1988, July 29, 1988, June 9, 1989, Aug. 30, 1989, April 3, 1992), Anne Murray (Nov. 16, 1971 with Glen Campbell, Feb. 19, 1973 with Glen Campbell, June 12, 1975, Nov. 27, 1975, Dec. 9, 1977, June 23, 1980, Nov. 30, 1981): Paul Anka, who was responsible for "Johnny's Theme," the instantly recognizable musical opening to each show (April 23, 1963, Nov. 3, 1969, Dec. 10, 1973, July 15, 1974, Sept. 17, 1975, Aug. 23, 1978); Celine Dion (Sept. 21, 1990, Nov. 15, 1990, Jan. 29, 1991, July 10, 1991, Mar. 31, 1992); Robert Goulet (May 4, 1973, June 11, 1975, Oct. 8, 1975, Sept. 2, 1976): The Jeff Healey Band (Nov. 23, 1988, Dec. 20, 1990); Alias (Mar. 8, 1991), Blue Rodeo (Aug. 13, 1991); Liona Boyd (Dec. 19, 1984); David Clayton-Thomas (Dec. 29, 1972); Cowboy Junkies (May 4, 1989); and The Bells (Aug. 24, 1971).

>> **Late May 1992** Bryan Adams becomes the first Canadian artist to have two albums certified diamond in Canada as his *Waking Up the Neighbours* disc sells over one million copies.

>> **June 26, 1992** Tom Cochrane kicks off his cross-Canada Mad, Mad World tour in Victoria, B.C. following a full slate of concerts in the U.S. where his single "Life Is A Highway" has become a major hit.

>> **July 1, 1992** On Canada's 125th birthday, Molson Canadian Rocks and MCA Concerts present the Great Canadian Party at major venues in St. John's, Newfoundland; Molson Park, Barrie, Ontario and Vancouver, British Columbia. Artists featured on the all-day show, which was broadcast live by MuchMusic, include Kim Mitchell, The Tragically Hip, The Jeff Healey Band, Crash Test Dummies, Colin James, 54-40,

Sass Jordan, Lee Aaron, Chrissy Steele and Spinal Tap, who crossed five time zones during the day to perform in all three cities as part of their 1992 Break Like the Wind "reunion" tour.

>> **July 1, 1992** Roch Voisine is presented with the medal decorating him as a Chevalier dans l'Ordre des Arts et des Lettres by France's Ambassador to Canada. Later that day, Voisine premieres a new song co-written with David Foster, who joins him for the first live performance of "I'll Always Be There (You and I)."

>> **July 28, 1992** Barenaked Ladies' debut album, *Gordon* is released and debuts in the Top 10 on the Canadian charts on its way to an eight-week run at number one.

>> **August 8, 1992** The Guns N' Roses/Metallica Stadium Tour rolls into Montréal for a date at the Olympic Stadium and quickly becomes memorable for the chaos that ensues rather than the music. Metallica frontman James Hetfield was badly burned when he inadvertently moved into the line of fire of a pyrotechnics blast, forcing the cancellation of the second hour of the show. Things didn't go much better when Guns N' Roses took to the stage and cut their set short because of stage monitor issues and singer Axl Rose's sore throat. The angry crowd rioted, subsequently turning downtown Montréal into a war zone.

>> **August 14, 1992** Bryan Adams kicks off his cross-Canada Waking Up the Neighbours tour at Quidi Vidi Park in St. John's, Newfoundland. Support artists on the tour include the Steve Miller Band, Extreme and Arc Angels. This Canadian leg of his world tour ends with a free show at Brockton Oval in Vancouver on September 9.

>> **October 1, 1992** Michelle Wright makes her debut at the Grand Ole Opry in Nashville, where she is introduced to fellow-Canadian, Hank Snow.

>> **October 16, 1992** The Band perform "When I Paint My Masterpiece," the Dylan song heard on their *Cahoots*

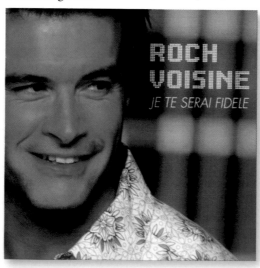

album, as part of a 30th anniversary tribute to Bob Dylan at New York's Madison Square Gardens. Neil Young, who performs the Dylan songs "Just Like Tom Thumb's Blue" and "All Along the Watchtower," meets Eddie Vedder of Pearl Jam for the first time. The group tours with Young the following year and appears with him at the MTV Video Awards.

>> **November 17, 1992** The Joe Cocker/Sass Jordan duet "Trust In Me" is included on the soundtrack

of the Whitney Houston/Kevin Costner film *The Bodyguard*, which has sold more than 45 million copies worldwide and is the best-selling soundtrack of all time.

>> **1992** The Governor General's Performing Arts Awards for Lifetime Artistic Achievement is initiated by Governor General Ray Hnatyshyn.

>> **1992** The annual Celtic Roots Festival is first held in Goderich, Ontario.

>> **1992** Mark Milne, Sandy MacIntosh and Tim Potocic of the band Tristan Psionic found the Sonic Unyon Recording Company, an independent label based in Hamilton, Ontario.

>> **1992** Phillips introduces the Digital Compact Cassette (DCC).

>> **1992** Canada, U.S. and Mexico finalize the terms of the North American Free Trade Agreement (NAFTA).

>> **1992** Groups formed this year include Cub, Vancouver; Dubmatique, Montréal; Econoline Crush, Vancouver; Ginger, Kelowna,; Hemingway Corner, Toronto; Jale, Halifax; The Killjoys, Hamilton; Thrush Hermit, Halifax; Treble Charger, Sault Ste. Marie; Zumpano, Vancouver.

>> 1993

>> **January 17, 1993** Bob Dylan, The Band, Ronnie Hawkins, Vassar Clements, Stephen Stills, Clarence Clemmons, Dr. John, Dicky Betts (Allman Bothers) and The Cate Brothers, with hosts Don Johnson and Melanie Griffith, are among the artists on hand for a concert dubbed The Absolutely Unofficial Blue Jeans Bash (For Arkansas) at the National Building Museum in Washington, DC, celebrating the presidential inauguration of Bill Clinton.

>> **February 1993** Brian Mulroney resigns as leader of the Progressive Conservative party but remains Prime Minister until June.

>> **March 1993** Toronto ragamuffin rapper Snow hits the top of the charts around the world with the single "Informer" from his debut *12 Inches of Snow* album. It sits at number one on the Billboard singles chart for seven weeks.

>> **March 21, 1993** The 22nd annual JUNO Awards are held at the O'Keefe

Centre in Toronto with Celine Dion hosting. "I've been very excited since I was asked to do this," Dion states. "I've been working hard on everything... polishing up my speeches and working on some very funny material and then, when I got here, they asked me to do it in English!" Celine Dion, k.d. lang and Leonard Cohen top the list of honourees with Dion taking home four, lang snagging three and Cohen, two. Bryan Adams becomes the first Canadian to win the JUNO in the category of Best-Selling Album (Foreign or Domestic). The Tragically Hip pick up their second Canadian Entertainer of the Year JUNO. The star-studded tribute to Anne Murray, as she is inducted into the Canadian Music Hall of Fame, includes well-wishes from Gordon Lightfoot, Burt Reynolds, Kenny Rogers, Glen Campbell, Gene MacLellan, Alan Thicke, k.d. lang, Rita MacNeil and Jerry Seinfeld. Ever the clowns, Barenaked Ladies actually dress the part during their performance of the tongue-in-cheek, "My Box Set." Leonard Cohen accepting Male Vocalist JUNO: "My cup runneth over. It's only in a country like this that I could get the Male Vocalist of the Year award... It was in 1972 after a concert I gave at the Isle of Wight, a journalist with the New Musical Express wrote: 'Leonard Cohen is a boring old drone and should get the 'F' back to Canada where he belongs.' Well, I did and I do and I thank you." Buffy Sainte-Marie introduces the Music of Aboriginal Canada category: "Canadians have been making music for a real long time... like 60 or 70,000 years." P.J. Perry accepts Best Jazz Album JUNO: "That's some deep shit! Wow, this is too much! This is the first time I've ever won anything." The Walt Grealis Special Achievement Award is presented to music industry executive (Canadian Academy of Recording Arts & Sciences) and theater and television producer (Governor General's Performing Arts Awards, Juno Awards) Brian Robertson.

>> **June 1993** Kim Campbell, who succeeds Brian Mulroney as leader of the Progressive Conservative party, becomes Canada's first female Prime Minister.

>> **July 5, 1993** Blue Rodeo begin recording their fifth album *Five Days In July*, on a farm northeast of Toronto. Sarah McLachlan is a guest performer on the CD.

>> **July 13, 1993** Keyboard whiz Bob Wiseman announces his intentions to acquire Prince's name after he discards

it in favour of a symbol. The letter from Prince's lawyer contains the word "actionable." Wiseman drops the idea.

>> **July 16, 1993** The Tragically Hip kick off the first of their cross-Canada Another Roadside Attraction tours at the Western Speedway, Victoria, BC with special guests Midnight Oil, Hothouse Flowers, Daniel Lanois and Crash Vegas. Subsequent concerts on the tour include Seabird Island and Agassiz (Chilliwack), BC (July 17), Thunder Bay, ON (July 21), Markham Fairgrounds, Markham, ON (July 23), Parc Therrien, Verdun, QC (July 25), Lansdowne Park, Ottawa, ON (July 26), Winnipeg Stadium, Winnipeg, MB (July 29), Calgary Raceway, Calgary, AB (July 31) and Clark Stadium, Edmonton, AB (August 1). Another Roadside Attraction tours are also undertaken in 1995 and 1997.

>> **July 1993** The Merritt Mountain Music Festival (Mountainfest) is first held in Merritt, British Columbia. On May 12, 2012 organizers announced the cancellation of the 2012 edition of the country music gathering due to low ticket sales. The festival had registered its largest crowd in 2005 when it hosted close to 150,000 country fans over the 6-day event.

>> **September 1993** Toronto vocalist Molly Johnson (Alta Moda, Infidels, Blue Monday) organizes the first of her annual Kumbaya Festivals, all broadcast by MuchMusic, to raise funds for Canadian AIDS hospices.

>> **October 1993** Election decimates the Progressive Conservative party, who win only two seats when they previously had 169. Kim Campbell subsequently resigns. Liberal Jean Chretien is elected Prime Minister.

>> **December 1993** *Billboard Magazine* names David Foster Top Singles Producer and Top R&B Singles Producer of the year.

>> **1993** Winnipeg band Crash Test Dummies enjoy international chart success with the debut single "Mmm Mmm Mmm Mmm" from their sophomore album *God Shuffled His Feet*. The song's cultural relevance is given a boost as Weird Al Yankovic records a parody version titled "Headline News."

>> **1993** Following the departure of Kevin Kane from Kelowna, BC-based band, The Grapes of Wrath, the group Ginger forms around the remaining members Tom and Chris Hooper and Vincent Jones. They release a debut EP and open for Sarah McLachlan on her career ground-breaking *Fumbling Towards Ecstasy* tour.

>> **1993** Canadian Parliament ratifies the North America Free Trade Agreement (NAFTA).

>> **1993** The CBC-TV special Anne Murray in Nova Scotia airs and attracts 2.67 million viewers, the best ratings of any English-language Canadian entertainment special this year.

>> **1993** Leonard Cohen publishes the book *Stranger Music: Selected Poems and Songs*.

>> **1993** In Montréal, Sam Roberts forms a group that evolves to William and, three years later, to Northstar. The band breaks up in 1999 after failing to make an impact nationally. Roberts' band-mate, drummer, vocalist George Donoso III, later has success as a member of Montréal group, The Dears.

>> **1993** The annual Halifax Pop Explosion, an amalgamation of a couple of other similar initiatives that put the spotlight on the success of local artists like Sloan, Jale, Thrush Hermit and The Super Friendz, is first held.

>> **1993** The annual Downtown Oakville Jazz Festival, coordinated by the Downtown Oakville Business Improvement Area, debuts in Oakville, Ontario.

>> **1993** Intel introduces the Intel Pentium processor at a time when three million people in the U.S. are connected to the Internet.

>> **1993** Groups formed this year include Bass Is Base, North York (Toronto), ON; Billy Talent, Mississauga, ON; Blinker the Star, Pembroke, ON; Captain Tractor, Edmonton; Gob, Langley, BC; Great Big Sea, St. John's. NF; La Chicane, Val d'Or, QC; Sons of Maxwell, Timmins, ON/ Halifax; soulDecision, Vancouver; The Hardship Post, St. John's/Halifax.

>> 1994

>> **January 1994** Anne Murray and Celine Dion, betting on the stock of The Bay, become TV spokespersons for the Canadian retail giant.

>> **February 19, 1994** Crash Test Dummies appear on *Saturday Night Live* with host Martin Lawrence.

>> **February 1994** In Los Angeles, Alanis Morissette begins her collaboration with Glenn Ballard, a protégé of producer

▲ Celine Dion

Quincy Jones and, among other things, the co-writer of Michael Jackson's single "Man In the Mirror."

>> **March 1, 1994** Singer, songwriter, musician, actor Justin Bieber (Justin Drew Bieber) is born in London, Ontario.

>> **March 5, 1994** At Nashville's Opryland Hotel, Surrey, BC-born country singer, songwriter Lisa Brokop brings the house down with a showcase performance at the Country Radio Seminar (CRS). The same month, *Harmony Cats*, the film in which Brokop plays the lead role, premieres in theaters across the U.S.

>> **March 15, 1994** Michelle Wright co-hosts The Nashville Network's top-rated *Music City Tonight* with Charlie Chase.

>> **March 20, 1994** The 23rd annual JUNO Awards are held at the O'Keefe Centre, Toronto with Roch Voisine as host. Cape Breton's The Rankin Family have this JUNO thing down to a fare-thee-well as these relative newcomers to the Canadian music scene walk off with four JUNOs, including the coveted Entertainer of the Year prize. Newcomer Jann Arden is the only other multiple winner, taking home the newly-introduced Best New Artist Award and sharing Best Video honours with Jeff Weinrich. Robbie Robertson is on hand to present the first ever Best Music of Aboriginal Canada Recording JUNO to Lawrence Martin (Wapistan). Once again, the Canadian Music Hall of Fame induction is a star-studded affair as Rush well-wishers include members of Soundgarden, Primus and Barenaked Ladies, Mike Myers, Sebastian Bach of Skid Row, Vernon Reid of Living Color, Kim Mitchell, Toronto Blue Jays baseball players Joe Carter and Paul Molitor, long-time manager Ray Danniels and Alexis Lifeson, son of Rush guitarist, Alex Lifeson. Recipient of the Walt Grealis Special Achievement Award is music industry executive John Mills (Composers, Authors and Publishers Association of Canada CAPAC).

>> **April 1, 1994** Bryan Adams plays to 17,000 fans in Durban, South Africa despite a declared state of emergency. Over the seven concert dates he plays in South Africa, he draws more than 100,000 people. Later, when asked by a journalist at fifa.com when playing concert dates in South Africa at the time of the 2010 Fifa World Cup football finals in that country what his impressions are of South Africa, he replied: "I've always loved it here, and the people have always been great to perform to. We were the first rock band to come into South Africa in 1994."

>> **April 1994** Randy Bachman donates various items of import to his career to what is now known as the Library and Archives Canada in Ottawa.

>> **May 9, 1994** On Hank Snow's 80th birthday, he is presented with an honorary Doctor of Letters from Saint Mary's University in Halifax.

▲ The Rankin Family

>> **Summer 1994** The soundtrack album *The Crow*, containing the Jane Siberry track "It Can't Rain All the Time," hits the top of the U.S. album charts.

>> **August 1994** Montréal-born bass player Melissa Auf Der Maur, daughter of local politician and Montréal Gazette columnist Nick Auf Der Maur, joins the Seattle band Hole fronted by Courtney Love.

>> **September 5, 1994** Blue Rodeo's *Five Days In July* album, the group's fifth consecutive platinum record in Canada, gets a U.S. release as they sign with Discovery Records.

>> **September 24, 1994** On its release, The Tragically Hip CD *Day For Night* becomes the band's first album to debut at number one on the Canadian album chart. It went on to sell more than 600,000 copies in Canada.

>> **September 29, 1994** Bryan Adams is on hand to perform live at MuchMusic's Canadian Music Video Awards in Toronto ,which also feature 54-40, Bass Is Base, Blue Rodeo, Moist, Jane Siberry, The Tea Party and Michelle Wright.

>> **September 1994** Erica Ehm, MuchMusic's first female veejay, calls it quits to pursue her already successful career as award-winning songwriter, author (*She Should Talk*), actress and lifestyle commentator on TV and radio. She would found the highly successful Erica Ehm's Yummy Mummy Club (yummymummyclub.ca) in 2006.

>> **September 1994** The annual Ottawa Folk Festival, which will be held in a number of different venues in the nation's capital over the years, is launched by the Festival's first Director, Max Wallace, Station Manager at Ottawa's community radio station CKCU-FM, and local singer/songwriter, Chris White. It is initially held on Victoria Island, moved to Britannia Park in 1995 and ultimately to its current location at Hog's Back Park in 2010.

>> **October 1994** The Rankin Family head out on a Canadian Maritimes homecoming tour.

>> **October 4, 1994** Celine Dion makes her U.K. debut at the Cambridge Theatre in Camden, London.

>> **October 29, 1994** Rita MacNeil's Gemini Award-winning, CBC-TV musical variety series *Rita and Friends,* which will run until 1997, debuts with guests Roch Voisine, Jann Arden, Real World and Punjabi By Nature. The show is a ratings winner drawing 1.7 million viewers.

>> **November 21, 1994** The Tragically Hip, whose CD *Day For Night* is released in the U.K., embarks on a three-week European tour.

>> **November 24, 1994** Rush guitarist Alex Lifeson opens Toronto nightspot, The Orbit Room.

>> **November 1994** Bryan Adams tours Europe with the Rolling Stones and is named Best Male Star over Prince, Seal and Bruce Springsteen at the publicly-voted European Music Awards in Berlin.

>> **November 1994** Beau Dommage reunion album is released.

>> **November 1994** Roch Voisine signs a worldwide record deal with BMG International. Voisine's first English-language album *I'll Always Be There* has to this point sold over 500,000 copies in Canada and over 1.5 million worldwide.

>> **Winter 1994** *Spin* Magazine calls Halifax band Sloan's *Twice Removed* CD "one of the Ten Best Albums You Didn't Hear in 1994."

>> **December 13, 1994** Vancouver band 54-40 become one of the first rock acts to launch themselves into cyberspace as they open a web site on the Internet.

>> **December 16, 1994** Following the release of her *Freedom Sessions* album, Sarah McLachlan has a private audience with the Pope as she takes part in the Christmas at the Vatican concert.

>> **December 17, 1994** Celine Dion marries her long-time manager Rene Angelil.

>> **1994** Celine Dion's CD, *The Colour of My Love,* is certified diamond in Canada

for sales of more than one million copies.

>> **1994** Leonard Cohen takes a five-year hiatus from the "music business" as he goes into seclusion at the Mt. Baldy Zen Center near Los Angeles where, by 1996, he is ordained as a Rinzai Zen Buddhist monk with the Dharma name Jikan (Silence).

>> **1994** Rush drummer Neil Peart produces an all-star tribute to drummer Buddy Rich titled *Burning for Buddy.*

>> **1994** k.d. lang and her co-writer Ben Mink provide the soundtack for the Gus Van Sant, Jr.-directed film, *Even Cowgirls Get the Blues,* based on the 1976 Tom Robbins novel.

>> **1994** The National Aboriginal Achievements Awards (NAAA) are presented for the first time. Inuk singer, songwriter Susan Aglukark is honoured with the first award in the Arts & Entertainment field.

>> **1994** The annual Ottawa Blues Fest, now one of the largest of its kind in North America, is first held, under the auspices of Executive and Artistic Director Mark Monahan, at Major's Hill Park in Ottawa.

>> **1994** Music Waste has its beginnings in Vancouver originally as an alternative to the annual New Music West Festival, which ultimately moves to Edmonton, Alberta in July of 2011.

>> **1994** PCs outsell TVs for the first time.

>> **1994** Groups formed this year include Big Wreck, Boston/Toronto; Eagle & Hawk, Winnipeg; Soul Attorneys, Québec City, QC; The Carpet Frogs, Toronto; The Super Friendz, Halifax.

>> 1995

>> **January 1, 1995** Country music and the arts in Canada get a significant boost with the launch of NCN — The New Country Network — and Bravo on Canadian cable systems. With the appearance of NCN, the Nashville-based CMT: Country Music Television is taken off the air and a cross-border trade war begins as CMT drops all Canadian country artists without U.S. recording deals off their playlist south of the border.

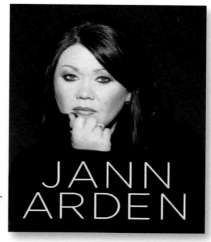

JANN ARDEN

» January 8, 1995 Ronnie Hawkins' 60th birthday bash is held at Toronto's Massey Hall, which features performances by Hawkins, Jerry Lee Lewis, Carl Perkins, The Band, Jeff Healey and Larry Gowan. The DVD and live album *Let It Rock*, released the same year, documents the event.

» January 19, 1995 Singer/songwriter Gene MacLellan, best known for his songs "Snowbird" and "Put Your Hand In the Hand," which were career-launching hits for Anne Murray and Ocean, respectively, dies at his rural Prince Edward Island home after an apparent suicide.

» January 23, 1995 Jann Arden, whose *Living Under June* CD has sold more than 100,000 copies in Canada, sets out on a three-week European tour.

» January 25, 1995 Vocalist/guitarist Colin James signs a worldwide deal with Warner Music/Elektra.

» January 1995 The Rankin Family kick off a tour of Scotland and England with an SRO concert in Glasgow as one of the headliners for the Celtic Connection Festival.

» February 1995 Charlie Major becomes the first country artist to have six number one songs from the same album in Canada as he hits the top of the country chart with "I'm Here" from his platinum album, *The Other Side*.

» March 25, 1995 The Tragically Hip are guests on *Saturday Night Live*, hosted by John Goodman with special guest and fellow Kingston, Ontario-native, Dan Aykroyd.

» March 26, 1995 The 24th annual JUNO Awards are held at Copps Coliseum in Hamilton, Ontario and hosted by Cathy Jones, Rick Mercer, Greg Thomey and Mary Walsh of the CBC-TV program *This Hour Has 22 Minutes*. The women are front and center at this year's JUNOs as artists like Jann Arden, Celine Dion and Susan Aglukark are all multiple award winners. Arden is the night's top honouree with three. Only The Tragically Hip make sure the men get a real sniff as they pick up their third Entertainer of the Year JUNO and take Group of the Year honours. This is the second JUNO Awards show presented outside of Toronto and the first in a venue the size of Hamilton, Ontario's Copps Colisuem: 8000 seats are made available to the fans to attend the show and the atmosphere is electric. An emotional tribute to Anne Murray's critically-ill manager, Leonard Rambeau, who receives a special Global Achievement

▲ Sarah McLachlan

Award, is balanced on the night by the joyous celebration that accompanies the induction of Buffy Sainte-Marie into the Canadian Music Hall of Fame and the on-target humor of the comedic wrecking crew from *This Hour Has 22 Minutes*. The Walt Grealis Special Achievement Award recipient is Grammy Award-winning composer, conductor and administrator Louis Applebaum.

» March 1995 The Rankin Family headline the 17-date Guinness Festival tour of Australia and New Zealand.

» April 13, 1995 Leonard Rambeau, long-time manager for Anne Murray, George Fox and Rita MacNeil, among others, passes away in Toronto following a lengthy battle with cancer.

» May 1995 Ian Tyson celebrates another milestone in his career as his *Cowboyography* album is certified platinum in Canada for sales of more than 100,000.

» May 1995 Hot on the heels of Michelle Wright's cross-Canada The Reasons Why Tour with guests John Berry and One Horse Blue, the CD for which the tour is named is certified platinum for sales of more than 100,000 copies in Canada. Mid-month she sets out on a European tour.

» June 27, 1995 Neil Young's 38th album, *Mirror Ball*, features Pearl Jam as his backing band.

» June 1995 The annual North by Northeast (NXNE) music and arts festival, modeled after the similar South by Southwest (SXSW) event in Austin, Texas, is held for the first time at multiple venues in Toronto with an emphasis on live music with as many as 800+ performers.

» July 11, 1995 Michelle Wright sings the Canadian national anthem at the All-Star baseball game in Arlington, Texas.

» July 13, 1995 The 1995 edition of The Tragically Hip's Another Roadside Attraction cross-Canada tour featuring

guests Ziggy Marley & the Melody Makers, Spirit of the West, Blues Traveler, Matthew Sweet, Rheostatics, Eric's Trip and The Inbred kicks off at Thunderbird Stadium in Vancouver, BC. Subsequent dates include Rocky Mountain Ranch, High River, AB (July 15), Big Valley site, Craven, SK (July 17), Assiniboia Downs Racetrack, Winnipeg, MB (July 18), Cayuga Speedway, Hagersville, ON (July 20), Parc Therrien, Verdun, QC (July 21), Markham Fairgrounds, Markham,

ON (July 22) and Capital City Speedway, Ottawa, ON (July 23).

» July 21, 1995 George Fox is immortalized in his hometown of Cochrane, Alberta as the civic leaders take the high road in recognizing his accomplishments by renaming a street in his honor — George Fox Trail.

» July 1995 Shania Twain becomes only the third Canadian artist to top the Billboard country singles chart in the U.S. as "Any Man of Mine" puts her into the select company of Anne Murray, who had hit the heights ten times, and Hank Snow, who had seven number one hits.

» July 1995 Bluesfest International, a blues and roots music festival, is founded by its producer Ted Boomer. The event is held annually at the Riverfront Festival Plaza on the banks of the Detroit River overlooking Windsor, Ontario.

» July 1995 The annual World Music festival SunFest, one of the largest of its kind in North America, is first held in Victoria Park in London, Ontario.

» August 5, 1995 The Bay's Big Sky — Canada Concert, a three-day celebration of Canadian rock, pop, folk and country music marks The Bay's 325th anniversary. The event, held at Rocky Mountain Ranch in High River, Alberta, features more than 30 Canadian artists, including Bryan Adams, Susan Aglukark, Jann Arden, Blue Rodeo, Burton Cummings, Celine Dion, David Foster, Colin James, Ashley MacIsaac, Sarah McLachlan, Anne Murray, Fred Penner, The Rankin Family, Buffy Sainte-Marie and Michelle Wright.

» August 28, 1995 "Only One Moon" becomes Prairie Oyster's fourth number one song from their album of the same name.

» September 15, 1995 Ronnie Hawkins launches his video and current CD, *Let It Rock*, with a concert at the Canadian Embassy Theatre in Washington, DC, with special guest Jeff Healey.

» September 19, 1995 General Motors Place in Vancouver opens with a concert by hometown rocker, Bryan Adams. An inaugural celebration takes place two nights later with a gala concert featuring David Foster, Shania Twain, Blue Rodeo, Sarah McLachlan, Michelle Wright, The Nylons, Sue Meldey, Ashley MacIsaac and Bass Is Base.

» September 28, 1995 21-year-old Alanis Morissette becomes the first Canadian woman to top Billboard's influential Top 200 albums chart in the U.S. as her CD *Jagged Little Pill* goes to number one. It

is driven, in part, by the success of the first single from the album, "You Oughta Know" and speculation about the identity of the male antagonist in the song. (Majority of the conjecture is that it is former boyfriend, comedic actor Dave Coulier, best known as Joey Gladstone in the ABC sitcom, *Full House*.) She is the first Canadian to reach that milestone since Bryan Adams' *Reckless* album hit the penthouse position of the same chart in 1984. *Jagged Little Pill* will stay in the Top 20 of the Billboard chart for more than a year as the album sells 16 million copies in the U.S. and 30 million worldwide, making it the most successful debut album of all time.

» September 1995 The Tragically Hip tour the U.S. with Page & Plant.

» September 1995 Tom Cochrane's *Mad Mad World* album is certified diamond for sales of over one million copies in Canada. He joins the select company of fellow Canadians Bryan Adams, Corey Hart, Alannah Myles and Celine Dion in reaching the milestone to that point.

» October 25, 1995 Alanis Morissette appears on *Saturday Night Live* with host Gabriel Byrne.

» October 30, 1995 A referendum in Québec rejects independence by a margin of only 1%.

» November 1995 Alanis Morissette appears on the cover of both *Rolling Stone* and *Spin* the same month.

» November 1995 In a triumphant return, Beau Dommage take home four Félix Awards at the 17th annual ADISQ Gala in Montréal.

» December 1, 1995 Calling themselves Canadian Recording Artists for Copyright Reform, Bryan Adams, Tom Cochrane, Bruce Cockburn, Celine Dion, k.d. lang, Anne Murray, Oscar Peterson, Rush, Buffy Sainte-Marie and Michelle Wright send an open letter to Prime Minister Jean Chretien and all federal MPs urging swift passage of revisions to the Copyright Act.

▲ Shania Twain

» 1995 As a student at Hants East Rural High School in Milford Station, Nova Scotia, rapper and producer Classified (Luke Boyd) releases his first album, *Time's Up Kid*.

» 1995 Recording artist Hagood Hardy makes an unsuccessful bid for election as Liberal party candidate in the riding of York South in the Ontario provincial elections.

» 1995 Lloyd Nishimura, former executive with Denon Canada, founds record label and distribution outlet, Outside Music.

>> **1995** The annual Woodstock en Beauce music festival is first held in St-Ephrem-de-Beauce, Québec. It features a variety of Canadian and international rock artists as well as some of the top French-speaking artists from Québec.

>> **1995** Microsoft launches Windows 95 and the browser, Internet Explorer.

>> **1995** Groups formed this year include Corb Lund and the Hurtin' Albertans, Edmonton; Destroyer, Vancouver; Tegan and Sara, Calgary; The Cash Brothers, Toronto; Emerson Drive, Grande Prairie, AB; Nickelback, Hanna, AB; The Dears, Montréal.

>> 1996

>> **January 1996** The first DVD (Digital Versatile Disc) is introduced at the Consumer Electronics Show in Las Vegas.

>> **February 28, 1996** At the 38th annual GRAMMY Awards at the Shrine Auditorium in Los Angeles, Alanis Morissette wins four GRAMMYs, including Album of the Year for *Jagged Little Pill*. Emmylou Harris' album *Wrecking Ball*, produced by Daniel Lanois, wins a GRAMMY in the category of Best Contemporary Folk Recording.

>> **March 10, 1996** The 25th annual JUNO Awards are held at Copps Coliseum in Hamilton with Anne Murray hosting and you oughta know that Alanis Morissette sweeps the awards, picking up five to go with the four Grammys she won the previous month for her angst-ridden, international career-launching album, *Jagged Little Pill*. It wasn't a clean sweep though as Shania Twain, who was a no-show at the awards due to illness, was named Entertainer of the Year, her only win out of seven nominations. A Canadian Music Hall of Fame Dinner and Gala was held the previous evening hosted by Burton Cummings, which honoured the year's five inductees: David Clayton-Thomas (Blood, Sweat & Tears), Denny Doherty (the Mamas and the Papas), John Kay (Steppenwolf), Domenic Troiano (Mandala, The Guess Who, James Gang) and Zal Yanovsky (The Lovin' Spoonful). Ronnie Hawkins receives the Walt Grealis Achievement Award as an industry builder. A 77-song 4-CD box set of the best of Canadian music, compiled by acclaimed music journalist, Larry Leblanc, a CHUM-FM-sponsored radio series co-created by noted radio producer Doug Thompson and a book, all under the name *Oh What A Feeling*, were released to commemorate the JUNO silver anniversary.

>> **Spring 1996** Ontario, Canada-born sisters Natalie (Mississauga, ON) and Nicole (Hamilton, ON) Appleton join with Shaznay Lewis and Melanie Blatt in London, England to launch the group All Saints.

>> **May 9, 1996** Rush becomes the first rock band to be honoured as a group as Officers of the Order of Canada.

>> **Early Summer 1996** The annual SCENE Music Festival (St. Catharines Event For New Music Entertainment), primarily featuring alternative artists, holds its inaugural event.

>> **July 12-14, 1996** Eden MusicFest at Mosport Park in Bowmanville, Ontario features a bill of more than 50 artists including Blinker the Star, Tracy Bonham, Bush, Buzzcocks, Ani DiFranco, Doughboys, Everclear, Gandharvas, Glueleg, Goo Goo Dolls, hHead, Howard Jones, Live, Love & Rockets, Holly McNarland, Merlin, Muse, Odds, Pluto, Porno for Pyros, Skydiggers, Sloan, Spin Doctors, Spirit of the West, Starkicker, Supergarage, The Cure, The Tragically Hip, The Watchmen and Universal Honey. It reportedly draws close to 90,000 ticketed and unticketed fans during the three-day festival The event comes with a couple of firsts. It boasts the largest attendance of any rock festival in Canada to that date and is one of the first major concerts to be streamed over the Internet.

>> **September 14, 1996** A concert by Sarah McLachlan, Paula Cole, Lisa Loeb and Michele McAdorey, formerly of Crash Vegas, in McLachlan's hometown of Vancouver, is dubbed Lilith Fair. (Lilith in Jewish folklore was Adam's first wife who was created as Adam's equal, unlike Eve who was created from one of Adam's ribs.) McLachlan plays four cities with an all-female bill during that period. "It was a way to get Sarah out of the house and back working again," recalls Nettwerk Music Group co-founder Terry McBride, her manager at the time. "This was back during the period of her writing the material for her *Surfacing* album. She had just come off the road in support of her *Fumbling Towards Ecstasy* project on which she had worked for three years, so she was really burnt out. When she arrived home things are not really going well because her life has slowed down. She was asking, 'How do I get to want to do music again? I said, 'You have to do some summer shows.' She said, 'I don't want to do summer shows. I don't want to have to put together a 90-minute set.' 'Well, why don't we make it a multi-artist bill so you only have to do a 45-minute set?' 'Well,

maybe. How about just doing three?' So, it came down to 'yes' to doing three shows. And then she went, 'Tell you what. If I do this as a multi-artist bill, they all have to be female.' It was like a challenge to me because I'd challenged her back. That's typical of the relationship between Sarah and I. I said, 'Okay. If that seals the deal... alright, I'll do it.' She went, 'Oh shit!' So we did a show in Detroit at this 15,000-seater with everyone going, 'It's never going to sell.' Sold out in one day. Everyone was shocked, utterly shocked. I knew that Sarah could sell it out by herself. She had a great time. So she said, 'Okay, I think I might be able to do some more of these, but next summer.' So that summer we went and did two more shows, one in Los Angeles and one in San Francisco. In the meantime, I suggested we also do Vancouver, which we did. Then I said, 'I tell you what, why don't we do this all next summer and why don't you figure out a name. And before we put the show up, she'd figured out a name for it... Lilith Fair. That's how it was born. It was not born out of any grandiose idea or play by any of the four partners, me, Sarah, Dan Fraser, who runs the management company and Marty Diamond, who's Sarah's agent. It was something that just happened and every good thing I think just happens when you do it for all the right reasons... and then it turned into something else."

» **Fall 1996** Singer/songwriter Roy Forbes and Paul Grant launch *Snap, Crackle, Pop*, "an occasionally regular" music/chat show on CBC Radio One.

» **October 1996** Buffy Sainte-Marie founds the Cradleboard Teaching Project to improve Native American students' participation in learning.

» **1996** Having moved east from Victoria to Toronto, singer, songwriter Nelly Furtado forms the short-lived trip-hop duo, Nelstar.

» **1996** Rainbow Butt Monkeys, a group that had formed at Lester B. Pearson High School in Burlington, Ontario, make a name change to Finger Eleven from a phrase in a version of their song, "Tip."

» **1996** Canadian sprinter Donovan Bailey wins 100-meter gold at the Summer Olympics.

» **1996** Shania Twain's sophomore album *The Woman In Me* rewrites country music history (for a while) as it becomes the best-selling album by a female country artists of all time, surpassing Patsy Cline's *Greatest Hits* album. *The Woman In Me* would subsequently enter the history books again as an unprecedented eighth hit single, an expanded version of "God Bless the Child" was released, an accomplishment unequalled by any other female country artist. *The Woman In*

Me is the best-selling country album in the U.S. in 1996, surpassing even perennial country best-seller Garth Brooks' *Fresh Horses* CD.

» **1996** Alanis Morissette heads out on a 18-month world tour to introduce folks far-and-wide to her *Jagged Little Pill* album.

» **1996** Art Bergmann plays himself in the Bruce McDonald film, *Hard Core Logo*.

» **1996** Vancouver's Econoline Crush record their sophomore album *The Devil You Know* following a period of steady touring in North America and Europe. In the wake of the album's release in 1997 — in the U.S. in 1998 — they hit the road with artists like Kiss, Foo Fighters, Green Day and The Tea Party while a number of their songs are heard on the tube in shows like *Melrose Place* and *Psi Factor.*

» **1996** Groups formed this year include Blackie and the Rodeo Kings, Hamilton, ON; Bran Van 3000, Montréal; Danko Jones, Toronto; Doc Walker, Portage La Prairie, MB; Enter the Haggis, Toronto; jacksoul, Toronto; Limblifter, Vancouver; Slainte Mhath, Cape Breton, NS; Supergarage, Thorold, ON; The Dudes, Calgary; Tricky Woo, Montréal; Tudjaat, Nunavut.

» 1997

» **January 1997** Fiddler Ashley MacIsaac, who is often as renowned for his penchant for mischief as his extraordinary playing, appears on the *Late Night with Conan O'Brien* TV show and performs "Sleepy Maggie." He is wearing a kilt with nothing under it and, late in the song, a high leg kick makes it plain that is the case. Though the censors were reportedly not impressed, it prompted slow motion replays and accompanying analysis by O'Brien and side-kick Andy Richter the following night.

» **February 1997** Each of the three members of Rush are honoured as Officers of the Order of Canada. This is the first time the Order of Canada is presented to a group rather than an individual.

» **March 9, 1997** The 26th annual JUNO Awards are held at Copps Coliseum in Hamilton, Ontario with multiple JUNO Award-winner Jann Arden as host. Celine Dion takes home four awards, including a special JUNO introduced this year as a tribute to the spectacular success at home and abroad of Dion as well as that of Alanis Morissette and Shania Twain, who also receive the trophy. The Tragically Hip win in the three of the six categories in which they are nominated, including the North Star Rock Album of the Year Award, which replaces the previous Entertainer of the Year Award as the category voted on by the public at

ROB McCONNELL & THE BOSS BRASS

ROB McCONNELL (1) valve trombone
MOE KOFFMAN (7) flute, soprano & alto saxophones
JOHN JOHNSON (3) flute, clarinet, soprano & alto saxophones

ALEX DEAN (20) flute, clarinet, tenor saxophone
RICK WILKINS (21) clarinet, tenor saxophone
BOB LEONARD (17) flute, clarinet, bass clarinet, baritone saxophone

ARNIE CHYCOSKI (13) lead trumpet, flugelhorn
STEVE McDADE (11) assoc. lead trumpet, flugelhorn
JOHN MacLEOD (15) trumpet, flugelhorn

GUIDO BASSO (9) trumpet, flugelhorn
DAVE WOODS (2) trumpet, flugelhorn
ALASTAIR KAY (12) lead trombone
BOB LIVINGSTON (14) trombone

JERRY JOHNSON (4) trombone, bass trombone on "Overtime"
ERNIE PATTISON (10) bass trombone
GARY PATTISON (16) french horn

JAMES MacDONALD (8) french horn
DAVID RESTIVO (5) piano
ED BICKERT (6) guitar
JIM VIVIAN (19) bass
TED WARREN (18) drums

this year's JUNOs. In a nod to Canada's vibrant jazz music community, the inductees to the Canadian Music Hall of Fame include jazz guitarist Lenny Breau, arranger/composer Gil Evans, big band leader/trumpet player Maynard Ferguson, woodwind player/jazzman Moe Koffman and big band leader/trombonist/arranger Rob McConnell. The Walt Grealis Special Achievement Award recipient is sound recordist, cinematographer and photographer Dan Gibson.

>> July 5, 1997 Sarah McLachlan officially founds the Lilith Fair tour as it kicks off its summer '97 tour through North America with a sold out concert before 20,000 at the Gorge Amphitheater in George, Washington. "Sarah embodies a lot of the qualities I like in people," Jana Lynne White of *MuchMoreMusic* notes as part of her Lilith Fair journal. "She has a great sense of humor, she thrives on creative expression, she has compassion, and she puts that compassion into action. And now, as we begin this historic rock and roll journey, I am reminded that this one woman has made a difference simply by having the courage to follow her instincts and be a catalyst for change. According to Sarah, the Lilith Fair concept was born in reaction to a promoter's comment that 'you can't book two chicks on the same [concert] bill.' According to him, that was a firm, long-standing booking rule. In other words, that's just the way things are done. Well, that isn't the way things are done anymore."

>> July 9, 1997 Bryan Adams opens the second incarnation of his Warehouse Studio in the old Oppenheimer Bros. Wholesale Grocers building at Powell & Columbia in Vancouver.

>> July 17, 1997 The 1997 edition of The Tragically Hip's cross-Canada music fest, Another Roadside Attraction, this time with special guests Sheryl Crow, Ashley MacIsaac, Wilco, Los Lobos, Change of Heart, The Mutton Birds, Ron Sexsmith and Van Allen Belt, kicks off at the Thunderbird Stadium in Vancouver, BC. Subsequent dates include Exhibition Grounds,

Camrose, AB (July 19), Saskatchewan Place, Saskatoon, SK (July 21), Assiniboia Downs, Winnipeg, MB (July 23), Franklin County Field, Highgate, Vermont, USA (July 26), Rideau Carleton Field, Ottawa, ON (July 28), Darien Lake Performing Arts Center, Buffalo, New York, USA (July 30), Molson Park, Barrie, ON (August 2).

>> July 1997 The annual three-day Stan Rogers Folk Festival (aka Stanfest), established in honour of the late Canadian singer, songwriter Stan Rogers, is first held in Canso, Nova Scotia.

>> August 24, 1997 The last of the Lilith Fair 1997 North American concert dates is in front of a crowd of 30,000 at the Thunderbird Stadium in Vancouver.

>> August 31, 1997 Diana, Princess of Wales, is fatally injured, along with companion Dodi Fayed and driver Henri Paul, in a car crash in the Pont de l'Alma road tunnel in Paris.

>> September 1, 1997 The CBC Radio Network is renamed CBC Radio One. The French Radio-Canada is renamed Première Chaîne.

>> September 22, 1997 The Rolling Stones' hit single "Anybody Seen My Baby?" is released and carries writing credits for k.d. lang and her co-writer, musician/producer Ben Mink, along with those of Mick Jagger and Keith Richards. Reportedly, after Jagger and Richards had recorded the song, they realized how similar the chorus was to one of the biggest songs in lang's repertoire, "Constant Craving." To avoid any legal problems, they give lang and Mink credits.

>> September 26, 1997 Bryan Adams' performance at the Hammerstein Ballroom, New York is recorded and released as the album, *MTV Unplugged*.

>> October 1997 The annual Celtic Colours International Festival is first held at venues around Cape Breton Island, Nova Scotia, featuring concerts by Celtic artists from around the world, workshops and art exhibitions. On its 10th anniversary

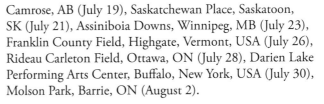

(2007), the Tourism Industry Association of Canada named it The Event of the Year.

≫ **November 4, 1997** Shania Twain's third studio album, *Come On Over*, released on this day, will become the best-selling country album, topping her album *The Woman In Me*, which previously held that distinction, and the best-selling studio album of all time by a female artist in any genre having sold more than 40 million copies worldwide.

≫ **November 22, 1997** Sarah McLachlan appears on *Saturday Night Live* with host Rudy Giuliani.

≫ **Late 1997** "My Heart Will Go On (Love Theme From Titanic)," recorded by Celine Dion and written by James Horner and Will Jennings, is released and subsequently becomes one of the top-selling singles of all time with reported sales of more than 15 million. The song earns Dion an Oscar, four Grammys, including Record and Song of the Year, and a Golden Globe Award. It results in historic worldwide sales for her album *Let's Talk About Love*.

≫ **1997** Nelly Furtado performs at the Honey Jam talent show in Toronto and comes to the attention of singer, songwriter Gerald Eaton of Toronto-group The Philosopher Kings. Over the next two years, Furtado, Eaton and Brian West of The Philosopher Kings write and produce the songs that lead to her record deal with Dreamworks in 1999 and her first single, "Party's Just Begun (Again)," which was included on the *Brokedown Palace* movie soundtrack.

≫ **1997** Following a career revival in Canada in 1996 with the release of his platinum self-titled CD and hit single "Black Cloud Rain," Corey Hart begins to work with fellow Montréaler Celine Dion, who includes two songs written and co-produced by Hart: "Miles To Go (Before I Sleep)" and "Where Is the Love" on *Let's Talk About Love*, one of the biggest selling albums in history.

≫ **1997** k.d. lang is heard on a number of soundtracks this year, including the James Bond film, *Tomorrow Never Dies*, in which she sings "Surrender" over the closing credits, and *Midnight in the Garden of Good and Evil* ("Skylark").

≫ **1997** Lawrence Gowan releases the song "Healing Waters" as a tribute to Diana, Princess of Wales, after her death.

≫ **1997** Singer, songwriter, actor Michael Bublé appears in the award-winning Bravo! documentary *Big Band Boom!*, directed by Mark Glover Masterson. Over the next seven years, he is also a frequent guest on Vicki Gabereau's national CTV network talk show.

≫ **1997** Liberal Jean Chretien is re-elected Prime Minister with a reduced majority.

≫ **1997** The New Pornographers form in Vancouver. Like Broken Social Scene in Toronto, the group is a prime example of the community and collaborative spirit of many artists of the late '90s and the new millennium, even across musical borders and art forms, as the infrastructure of the music industry changes drastically. Group co-founder Carl Newman says that he got the inspiration for their name from the Japanese film, *The Pornographers*, rather than from Reverend Jimmy Swaggart, Jerry Lee Lewis' cousin, who has called rock 'n' roll "the new pornography."

≫ **1997** Todd Kerns of Age of Electric/Limblifter stars in indie film, *Horsey*.

≫ **1997** Groups formed this year include High Valley, La Crete, AB; Les cowboys fringants, Repentigny, QC; Lillix, Cranbrook, BC; Love Inc., Toronto; McMaster & James, Winnipeg; The Ennis Sister (now Ennis), St. John's, NF; The New Pornographers, Vancouver; The Trews, Antigonish, NS.

≫ 1998

≫ **March 22, 1998** The 27th annual JUNO Awards, hosted by Canadian actor/producer Jason Priestley, a Vancouver native, are presented during the live CBC-televised award ceremonies from General Motors Place in Vancouver, British Columbia. It turns out to be a homecoming to remember for Vancouver's Sarah McLachlan, who picks up JUNOs in all four categories for which she had been nominated, while Our Lady Peace, Leahy and Paul Brandt, who wins both the Male Vocalist and Country Male Vocalist categories, take home two apiece. The Canadian Music Hall of Fame inductee is internationally-renowned musician, producer, composer and recording industry executive, David Foster. The Walt Grealis Special Achievement Award is presented to Vancouver-based agent and manager Sam Feldman (S.L. Feldman & Associates), who has been instrumental in transforming the touring and booking landscape in Canada over the years.

≫ **June 19, 1998** The second year of North American concert dates for Lilith Fair kicks off at the Civic Stadium in Portland, Oregon. They end on August 31 at the Thunderbird Stadium in Vancouver.

≫ **Summer 1998** Billed as "the world's largest, longing standing and original wakeboarding, action sports and music festival," Wakestock had its beginnings in Bala, Ontario in 1998 before moving to the Toronto Islands from

August 11-14, 2005. The festival moved to Collingwood, Ontario as of August 9, 2009.

» **August 23, 1998** Toronto band Our Lady Peace organize Summersault, a trio of multi-artist concert dates with a long list of guest artists who share the bill at Molson Park, Barrie on this date, Bowring Park, St. John's, NF (Sept. 3) and Parlee Beach, Shediac, NB (Sept. 5). Among those on the bill in Barrie are Garbage, I Mother Earth, The Crystal Method, Esthero, Hayden, Fuel, Gandharvas, Eve 6, Harvey Banger, Goldfinger, Johnny Favourite Orchestra and Bionic. The east coast dates feature Our Lady Peace with Moist, I Mother Earth, Esthero, BTK, Sloan and Bucket Truck (Shediac).

▲ Our Lady Peace

» **October 24, 1998** Alanis Morissette appears on *Saturday Night Live* with host Ben Stiller.

» **1998** Supreme court rules that if Quebec votes to secede, it can only carry out the policy with the federal government's consent. For its part, the federal government is obliged to negotiate on secession if a majority of Québec's citizens desires it.

» **1998** Having moved from Calgary to Toronto in 1996, [Leslie] Feist joins local group By Divine Right on rhythm guitar and tours with them until 2000.

» **1998** Singer, songwriter Rita MacNeil writes her memoirs, *On a Personal Note*, with Anne Simpson.

» **1998** A month-long trip to Mali by filmmaker Robert Lang and Bruce Cockburn, during which Cockburn jams with Grammy Award-winning blues musician Ali Farka Toure and kora master Toumani Diabate, is documented in the award-winning film, *River of Sand*.

» **1998** Econoline Crush tour North America with Kiss.

» **1998** Manager Bruce Allen (Bryan Adams, Bachman-Turner Overdrive, Loverboy etc.) climbs Mount Kilimanjaro in support of the Alzheimer Society of B.C.

» **1998** Groups formed this year include Down With Webster, Toronto; Fembots, Toronto; Metric, Toronto; Prozzak, Montréal; Sky, Montréal; The Guthries, Halifax; The Sadies, Toronto; The Weakerthans, Winnipeg; The Weekend, London, ON.

» 1999

» **February 6, 1999** Barenaked Ladies appear on *Saturday Night Live* with host Gwyneth Paltrow.

» **February 1999** The Tragically Hip inaugurate the newly-opened Air Canada Centre in Toronto by playing the first concert in the venue.

» **March 7, 1999** The 28th annual JUNO Awards are held at Copps Coliseum in Hamilton, Ontario hosted by comedian, TV personality Mike Bullard. Celine Dion dominates this year's edition of the JUNO Awards, picking up four major trophies plus a special International Achievement Award while performing twice during the CBC-televised show. The other big winners of the night were Barenaked Ladies, who won three JUNOs and performed and made their acceptance speeches by satellite from Melbourne, Australia. The Canadian Music Hall of Fame inductee is Montréal-based songwriter Luc Plamondon, known for his early work with Celine Dion and for co-writing popular French rock musicals like *Starmania* and *La Légende de Jimmy* with the late French composer, Michel Berger. He is the first and only Canadian artist in the Hall of Fame whose work is known primarily in French-speaking countries and the province of Québec. The Walt Grealis Special Achievement Awards recipient is Allan Waters, co-founder of Canadian media corporation, CHUM Limited, which in its heyday owned 33 radio stations, 12 TV stations and 21 specialty channels in Canada, including MuchMusic, MusiquePlus and Bravo.

» **May 17, 1999** Acclaimed producer/musician Bruce Fairbairn passes away in Vancouver.

» **March 18, 1999** 15-year-old Avril Lavigne, her artistic success still in the future, wins a contest to sing on stage with Shania Twain during her concert at the Corel Centre in Ottawa. With Twain handling the back-up vocal, Lavigne sings one of Twain's earliest hits, "What Made You Say That?"

» **May 1999** Lawrence Gowan joins the band Styx as lead vocalist and keyboardist replacing Dennis DeYoung. Gowan had opened for the group at Montréal's Molson Centre and Québec City's Colisée in 1997.

» **June 1999** Napster, the peer-to-peer file sharing web site that at the time enables mass-scale copyright infringement, is founded by Shawn Fanning, John Fanning and Sean Parker. It's a wake-up call for the music industry, which manages to get the site shut down by court order in July 2001, that it will not be business as usual in the digital era.

» **July 8, 1999** The third and final year of the Lilith Fair North American tour kicks off at the Thunderbird Stadium in Vancouver. The last show was at Edmonton's Commonwealth Stadium in Edmonton on Aug. 31. Lilith Fair had traveled 12,327 miles, played 139 shows and raised $600,000 for women's shelters. Sarah McLachlan looks back on the experience: "Women were already there.

▲ Chantal Kreviazuk

All we did was give them a platform in a summer touring market. I was so entwined in it emotionally and personally, so it's hard for me to have a true perspective on its impact. I know what it did for me, both personally and for my career. Obviously, it was a huge help for my career. I grew a lot from it. I forged a lot of great friendships. I learned an awful lot and had a great couple of summers playing great shows and getting to sing with a lot of my heroes, so for me it was fantastic. Certainly, on a larger scale, I think we definitely managed to change some attitudes. Whether they honestly changed or whether they just realized they had to accept this because it was not going away... maybe that's just me being skeptical."

» **July 8, 1999** Vancouver's The Be Good Tanyas play publicly for the first time as they busk outside Thunderbird Stadium in Vancouver during the first day of the Lilith Fair North American tour.

» **July 1999** The annual Rogers Sarnia Bayfest debuts in Centennial Park in downtown Sarnia, Ontario operated by the non-profit Bayfest Festival of Performing Arts.

» **August 9, 1999** The print edition of the Canadian music trade publication, *The Record*, ceases publication at Volume 18, No. 48.5 and briefly becomes an online magazine.

» **August 1999** The annual Edmonton Labatt Blues Fest is first held at the Heritage Amphitheatre in Hawrelak Park in Edmonton, Alberta.

» **December 19, 1999** Singer, pianist, songwriter Chantal Kreviazuk and singer, guitarist, songwriter Raine Maida (Our Lady Peace) are married at a private ceremony at the Sunnybrook Health Science Centre in Toronto.

» **1999** Kevin Kane and Tom Hooper reunite to record and perform as The Grapes of Wrath.

» **1999** Vancouver-born actress Joely Collins, adopted daughter of recording artist Phil Collins, is named Best Leading Actress for her role in the TV series, *Madison*.

» **1999** A turning point in the career of rapper, singer, songwriter K'naan, comes with the help of Toronto-based concert promoter Sol Guy, who secures a speaking engagement for him before the United Nations High Commissioner for Refugees at which he criticizes the U.N. for its failed aid missions to Somalia. In the audience is Senegalese singer Youssou N'Dour, who is so impressed with his courage and forthrightness that he later invites K'naan to contribute to his 2001 album project, *Building Bridges*.

» **1999** Sarah McLachlan founds the Sarah McLachlan Foundation.

» **1999** Territory of Nunavut is created in the Canadian far north. It is the first territory in Canada to have a majority indigenous population.

» **1999** Groups formed this year include 11:30, Montréal; Broken Social Scene, Toronto; Constantines, Guelph, ON; Hot Hot Heat, Victoria, BC; The Be Good Tanyas, Vancouver.

CHART-TOPPING CANADIAN SONGS 1990-1999

1990 More Than Words Can Say ALIAS
1990 Black Velvet ALANNAH MYLES
1991 (Everything I Do) I Do It For You BRYAN ADAMS
1991 Can't Stop This Thing We Started BRYAN ADAMS
1991 Life Is A Highway TOM COCHRANE
1992 Thought I'd Died and Gone To Heaven BRYAN ADAMS
1992 If You Asked Me To CELINE DION
1992 Song Instead of a Kiss ALANNAH MYLES
1993 All For Love BRYAN ADAMS, ROD STEWART & STING
1993 Please Forgive Me BRYAN ADAMS
1993 Informer SNOW
1994 The Power of Love CELINE DION
1995 Have You Ever Really Loved A Woman? BRYAN ADAMS
1995 Insensitive JANN ARDEN
1995 I Wish You Well TOM COCHRANE
1995 Hand In My Pocket ALANIS MORISSETTE
1995 You Oughta Know ALANIS MORISSETTE
1995 Any Man of Mine SHANIA TWAIN

1996 Let's Make A Night To Remember BRYAN ADAMS
1996 The Only Thing That Looks Good On Me Is You BRYAN ADAMS
1996 Because You Loved Me CELINE DION
1996 It's All Coming Back To Me Now CELINE DION
1996 Ironic ALANIS MORISSETTE
1996 You Learn ALANIS MORISSETTE
1996 Head Over Feet ALANIS MORISSETTE
1996 Ahead By A Century THE TRAGICALLY HIP
1997 Building A Mystery SARAH MCLACHLAN
1997 Clumsy OUR LADY PEACE
1998 Back To You BRYAN ADAMS
1998 On A Day Like Today BRYAN ADAMS
1998 One Week BARENAKED LADIES
1998 My Heart Will Go On (Love Theme from Titanic) CELINE DION
1998 I'm Your Angel R. KELLY & CELINE DION
1998 Thank U ALANIS MORISSETTE
1998 It's All Been Done BARENAKED LADIES
1999 Love Song SKY

OH WHAT A FEELING

Oh, you know it'll all turn out
And you'll make me work so we can work to work it out
And I promise you kid to give so much more than I get
Yeah, I just haven't met you yet

— Haven't Met You Yet

Lyrics & Music by Michael Bublé,
Alan Chang & Amy Foster-Gilles,
performed by Michael Bublé.

» 2000–2009

▲ Diana Krall

» 2000

» February 6, 2000 Randy Bachman and Fred Turner of Bachman-Turner Overdrive guest on the *Saddlesore Galactica* episode of *The Simpsons*. The Simpsons' creator, Matt Groening, whose father is from Winnipeg, is a long-time BTO fan.

» February 13, 2000 The first edition of the Wavelength Music Arts Projects, a weekly Canadian music series and annual festival founded by Jonny Dovercourt, Duncan "Doc Pickles" MacDonnell and Derek Westerholm, is held at Ted's Wrecking Yard in Toronto.

» March 12, 2000 The 29th annual JUNO Awards are held at the Skydome (now The Rogers Centre) in Toronto with The Moffatts (with vocal accompaniment by their screaming fans) as hosts and with a new design for the JUNO statuette created by artist/glass blower Shirley Elford. It was a night of surprises as Chantal Kreviazuk picks up two awards, including Female Vocalist of the Year, even though she was up against artists the stature of Celine Dion and Alanis Morissette. Similarly, Canadian Hip-Hop Pioneer Choclair

takes the honours in a Best Male Artist category that includes Bryan Adams and Tom Cochrane. Alanis Morissette takes home two JUNOs as does the Matthew Good Band. Diana Krall is the winner of the inaugural Best Vocal Jazz Album award. Vancouver-based Musician/Producer Bruce Fairbairn (Aerosmith, AC/DC, Bon Jovi, Motley Crue), who passed away on May 17, 1999 at age 49, is inducted into the Canadian Music Hall of Fame. The Walt Grealis Special Achievement Award posthumously honours record industry pioneer, Emile Berliner while Alanis Morissette presents Sarah McLachlan with the International Achievements Award, for her artistic and charitable work with Lilith Fair.

» May 6, 2000 Neil Young appears on *Saturday Night Live* with host John Goodman.

» August 4, 2000 The second edition of Summersault, a music festival organized by Toronto band Our Lady Peace, featuring a number of guest artists in concert with them in eight major venues across the country, kicks off at BC Place in Vancouver. Participating artists include The Smashing Pumpkins, Foo Fighters, I Mother Earth, Sum 41, A Perfect Circle, Eve 6, The Catherine Wheel, Treble Charger,

Finger Eleven and Deftones (Vancouver). Subsequent dates include the Commonwealth Stadium, Edmonton (August 6), Saskatchewan Place, Saskatoon(August 7), Winnipeg Stadium, Winnipeg (August 9), Molson Park, Barrie, ON (August 11), Parc Jean-Drapeau, Montréal(August 12), Rideau Carleton Raceway, Ottawa(August 13) and Citadel Hill, Halifax (August 16).

》 **August 4-5, 2000** Diana Krall and Tony Bennett, with the Los Angeles Philharmonic Orchestra, sell out two nights at the Hollywood Bowl in Los Angeles as part of a Krall/Bennett 20-city tour.

》 **October 2000** Nelly Furtado releases her debut album, *Whoa, Nelly!* which brings her international recognition, four Grammy nominations and a win for her debut single, "I'm Like A Bird."

》 **November 13, 2000** The last issue of Canadian music trade magazine *RPM Weekly* (Vol. 71, No. 7) is published.

》 **November 27, 2000** Bryan Adams performs the song "Behind Blue Eyes" with The Who at a concert at the Royal Albert Hall in London billed as The Who and Special Guests in aid of the Teenage Cancer Trust. The concert DVD's accompanying booklet features Adams' photographs of the band.

》 **November 30, 2000** Loverboy bass player Scott Smith, on his way from Mexico to Vancouver with friends on his 37-foot sailboat, is swept overboard by a 25-foot wave and lost at sea near San Francisco.

》 **December 31, 2000** There are 361 million Internet users in the world, 108 million of them in North America, 114.3 million in Asia, 4.5 million in Africa, 105 million in Europe, 3.3 million in the Middle East, 18 million in Latin America/Caribbean and 7.6 million in Oceania/Australia. (See June 30, 2012 by comparison)

》 **2000** *Flying On Her Own*, a stage play based on the life of singer, songwriter Rita MacNeil written by Charlie Rhindress, premieres at the Live Bait Theatre in Sackville, New Brunswick before being produced by the Neptune Theatre in Halifax in 2002.

》 **2000** Robbie Robertson joins DreamWorks Records as creative executive and is subsequently responsible for convincing Nelly Furtado to sign with the label.

》 **2000** Susan Aglukark's album *Unsung Heroes* includes the song, "Turn of the Century," a song about the creation of Nunavut, the newest Canadian territory (April 1, 1999), which comprises a major portion of Northern Canada and most of the Canadian Arctic Archipelago.

》 **2000** A pivotal year for Michael Bublé who picks up two Genie Award nominations for songs he wrote for the film

Here's To Life, plays a karaoke singer in the Gwyneth Paltrow film *Duet* and meets acclaimed producer David Foster after being invited to sing at the wedding of Prime Minister Brian Mulroney's daughter, Caroline. The contact resulted in Foster producing his debut album, the support of Foster's friend Paul Anka and a management deal with Bruce Allen, who Bublé had previously pursued.

》 **2000** At the turn of the Millennium, Feist (Leslie Feist) is working on her solo career in the wake of her 1999 debut album, *Monarch (Lay Your Jeweled Head Down)*, playing rhythm guitar in the Toronto band By Divine Right and working with a sock puppet under the name "Bitch Lap Lap" with Merrill Nisker, an electro-punk musician known as Peaches. During this period, they tour England together. She is guest vocalist on his album, *The Teaches of Peaches*, and is seen in his video for the song, "Lovertits."

》 **2000** The annual Evolve Festival, a musically diverse cultural event promoting sustainable living and environmental awareness, is first held near Antigonish, Nova Scotia. Founder of the festival is local resident Joe MacEachern, joined by Jim Dorey and Jay Cleary. Fredericton-native Jonas Colter joined the team in 2005.

》 **2000** Liberal Jean Chretien is again elected Prime Minister and in the process picks up votes in Québec, weakening support for Québec separatists.

》 **2000** The CBC Vancouver Orchestra becomes the CBC Radio Orchestra following the elimination of the other CBC radio orchestras in Halifax, Montreal, Toronto and Winnipeg due to federal budget cuts.

》 **2000** Groups formed this year include Fun 100, Abbotsford, BC; Stars, Montréal; The Stills, Montréal.

》 2001

》 **January 13, 2001** Nelly Furtado appears on *Saturday Night Live* with host Charlie Sheen.

》 **March 4, 2001** The 30th annual JUNO Awards are held at Copps Coliseum in Hamilton, Ontario with comedian

Nelly Furtado

▲ Avril Lavigne

Rick Mercer as host. Twenty-two-year-old Nelly Furtado has her coming out party this night, picking up four of the five JUNOs for which she had been nominated, including Best New Artist, Best Songwriter, Best Single ("I'm Like A Bird") and Best Producer, shared with Gerald Eaton and Brian West. Barenaked Ladies were coming off a pretty good year too and won in the categories of Best Group, Best Album and Best Pop Album (*Maroon*). Nickelback was named Best New Group. As the 15th anniversary of the inclusion of urban music categories at the JUNOs, it was a big year for the genre. Swollen Members took the Best Rap Recording JUNO for the third consecutive year, while the award for Best R&B/Soul Recording went to jacksoul (Haydain Neale), who took part in the warmly-received Urban Music Tribute featuring Jully Black, Choclair, Deborah Cox, Dream Warriors, Ghetto Concept, Maestro Fresh Wes, Michie Mee, Kardinal Offishall, Rascalz and Snow. The Walt Grealis Special Achievement Award was presented to Daniel Caudeiron, the ambassador of Canadian dance and urban music, while Gordon Lightfoot and David Suzuki were on hand to induct Bruce Cockburn into the Canadian Music Hall of Fame.

>> **April 2001** Leaders of countries from across the Americas meet in Canada at the Summit of the Americas. They reaffirm their commitment to setting up the world's largest free trade zone by 2005.

>> **May 8, 2001** Sum 41 release their second album, *All Killer, No Filler*. The first released single "Fat Lip" becomes the band's biggest hit, topping the charts in the U.S. and internationally.

>> **May 22, 2001** Rapper and producer Kardinal Offishall (Jason D. Harrow) releases his second album, *Quest for Fire: Firestarter, Vol. 1*, which moves him from Toronto's underground Hip-Hop scene into the mainstream. Often referred to as Canada's "Hip-Hop Ambassador," the album produced his first international hit, "BaKardi Slang," and added the term "T-dot" to the lexicon of slang in reference to Toronto.

>> **June 30, 2001** The Shania Twain Centre opens in Timmins, Ontario, where country singer/songwriter Shania Twain grew up.

>> **September 11, 2001** On the infamous "9/11," passenger airliners are used by terrorists to attack the World Trade Centre in New York, the Pentagon Building in Washington and the United States Capitol, the latter attack foiled by passengers on the plane, which crashes in Pennsylvania.

>> **October 6, 2001** Sum 41 appear on *Saturday Night Live* with host Seann William Scott.

>> **October 6, 2001** Big Wreck plays a special show at Toronto's Roy Thomson Hall with the Toronto Symphony, Uzume Taiko Drum Ensemble, Cirque Eloize along with musical friends Paul Langlois and Robby Baker of The Tragically Hip, Bernie Breen and Eric Johnson. The group had previously performed with the Edmonton Symphony.

>> **October 14, 2001** Canadian rapper, songwriter and actor Drake, working under his given name Aubrey Graham, is first seen in the role of Jimmy Brooks, the star basketball player from a wealthy family, in the first season of the Canadian serial teen drama TV series, Degrassi: The Next Generation. By the eighth season, which runs from October 5, 2008 to August 30, 2009, Graham and his character Jimmy Brooks are dropped to recurring status.

>> **November 29-December 2, 2001** Jazz pianist, vocalist Diana Krall plays a series of sold-out shows at Paris' Olympia as part of a world tour. A live album (Diana Krall: Live in Paris), and DVD documenting the shows are released on October 1, 2002.

>> **September, 21 2001** Neil Young performs John Lennon's "Imagine" and joins Eddie Vedder

Vedder and Mike McCready on the Pearl Jam song "Long Road," co-written by Young, as part of the America: A Tribute to Heroes benefit concert and telethon created by the major TV networks. During this period, he also releases the single "Let's Roll," which pays tribute to the victims of the 9/11 terrorist attacks and the courage of the passengers and crew of United Airlines Flight 93, which crashed in Pennsylvania.

» **October 21, 2001** Music Without Borders Live, a six-hour concert to raise funds for the United Nations Donor Alert Appeal to provide aid to refugees in and around Afghanistan, is held at the Air Canada Centre in Toronto featuring The Tragically Hip, Alanis Morissette, Our Lady Peace, Barenaked Ladies, Bruce Cockburn and Choclair. It airs live on MuchMusic and CBC-TV.

» **October 23, 2001** Shania Twain's *The Complete Limelight Sessions*, an album of songs recorded prior to her major label success, many of them written by Shania and Paul Sabu, is released in the U.S. with moderate sales and chart success.

» **2001** Win Butler and Josh Deu first begin performing as Arcade Fire in Boston before moving to Montréal, QC.

» **2001** By 2001, Feist (Leslie Feist) is spending time touring Europe with Gonzales, whom she met while working with electro-punk artist Peaches, and contributing vocals as a member of the Kevin Drew/Brendan Canning-formed group, Broken Social Scene in Toronto. While touring in Europe with Gonzales, she begins recording new versions of songs she had previously home-recorded as *The Red Demos*. They will be the basis of her 2004 album, *Let It Die*.

» **2001** Singer, songwriter Jimmy Rankin, who wrote the classic Celtic ballad, "Fare Thee Well Love," which became a signature song for The Rankins (aka The Rankin Family) and the title track of the group's five-times platinum debut album in Canada, releases his first solo album, *Song Dog*.

» **2001** Michael Bublé co-stars in the film *Totally Blonde* as nightclub singer/club owner Van Martin. He sings seven songs in the movie, which are released as a CD — much to Bublé's chagrin — as *Totally Bublé* in 2003.

» **2001** The Personal Computer (PC), which had its beginning back in 1981 with the first IBM PC featuring an Intel 8088 microprocessor as its "internal intelligence," turns 20 at a time when worldwide sales of PCs has reached 835 million.

» **2001** Groups formed this year include Alexisonfire, St. Catharines, ON; Arcade Fire, Boston/Montréal; Bedouin Soundclash, Toronto; Boys Night Out, Burlington, ON;

▲ Leslie Feist

Butterfinger, Saskatoon, SK; Death From Above 1979, Toronto; Femme Fatale, East York (Toronto); Fucked Up, Toronto; Sugar Jones, Toronto; Theory of a Deadman, Delta, BC; Wintersleep, Halifax, ON.

» 2002

» **February 26, 2002** *Under Rug Swept*, Alanis Morissette's fifth album, debuts at number one on album charts in 12 countries, including Canada and the U.S. The previous evening she appears on *The Late Show with David Letterman* for the first time.

» **February 27, 2002** Victoria, BC-native Nelly Furtado wins her first Grammy Award for her single "I'm Like A Bird."

» **March 26, 2002** k-os (Kevin Brereton) releases his debut album, *Exit*, and heads out on a tour of the U.S. with India. Arie. The album is released in the U.S. on January 28, 2003 and he subsequently earns the title of Best International Hip-Hop Artist at the Source Awards. A collaboration with The Chemical Brothers on their single, "Get Yourself High," results in a 2005 Grammy Award nomination for the song as Best Dance Recording.

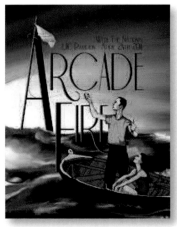

» **April 14, 2002** The 31st annual JUNO Awards are held at Mile One Stadium in St. John's, Newfoundland and Labrador with hosts Barenaked Ladies. This was the year that the JUNOs switched broadcast partners from CBC to CTV and began to take the show on the road across Canada. This was the first year for JUNO Fan Fare, JUNOFest and the Songwriters' Circle. It was also Melanie Berry's first year as President of the Canadian Academy of Recording Arts & Sciences (CARAS), the organization which oversees the JUNO Awards. The show in

St. John's, the most easterly city in Canada, was marked by the success of two artists from Canada's West Coast whose sound couldn't be more different. Diana Krall and Nickelback both won three JUNOs, Krall for Best Artist, Best Album and Best Jazz Vocal Album (*The Look of Love*) and Nickelback for Best Group, Best Rock Album (*Silver Side Up*) and Best Single ("How You Remind Me"). Renowned concert promoter Michael Cohl received the Walt Grealis Special Achievement Award and musician/producer Daniel Lanois was inducted into the Canadian Music Hall of Fame.

▲ k-os

» **June 4, 2002** 17-year-old Avril Lavigne releases her debut album *Let Go*, which peaks at number two on the Billboard album chart in the U.S. and goes to number one in Canada, Australia and the U.K., where, to that point, she is the youngest female solo artist to have a chart-topping album. By the end of the year, and in the wake of her career-launching debut single "Complicated," she is the best-selling female artist of the year with the top-selling debut album of 2002.

» **June 6, 2002** Mississauga, Ontario-born singer/actress Natalie Appleton of the British group, All Saints, marries Liam Howlett of British group, Prodigy.

» **September 2002** POP Montréal, an annual, five-day, not-for-profit "curated cultural event that champions independence in the arts by presenting emerging and celebrated artistic talents from around the world," is held for the first time. Founded by Daniel Seligman, Noelle Sorbara and Peter Rowan, the inaugural event takes place in 40 venues around Saint-Laurent Boulevard in Montréal. Among the artists performing are Broken Social Scene, Constantines, Hot Hot Heat, Julie Doiron, Martha Wainwright, Stars, The Dears and The Walkmen.

» **October 10, 2002** Oscar Peterson and The Tragically Hip are among the artists who perform during a gala concert at Toronto's Roy Thomson Hall for Queen Elizabeth II, who is touring Canada as part of her Golden Jubilee. Previously, in Winnipeg, the Queen and Prince Phillip attended a performance of the Royal Winnipeg Ballet accompanied by Lorenna McKennitt and the Winnipeg Symphony Orchestra.

» **2002** Bryan Adams is one of only 11 photographers commissioned to photograph Queen Elizabeth II during the Golden Jubilee. His portrait of the Queen is used on Canadian stamps issued in 2003 and 2004.

» **2002** Chad Kroeger of Nickelback collaborates with Josey Scott on "Hero," the theme song for the 2002 film, Spider-Man.

» **2002** Buffy Sainte-Marie sings at the Kennedy Space Center for Commander John Herrington, USN, a Chickasaw and the first Native American astronaut.

» **2002** Sass Jordan appears in the role of Janis Joplin in the off-Broadway production of *Love, Janis* at the Village Theater in New York. It runs until January 5, 2003.

» **2002** Nickelback singer, songwriter Chad Kroeger and attorney Jonathan Simkin found 604 Records in Vancouver, the recording home of such chart-topping acts as Carly Rae Jepsen, Marianas Trench, Theory of a Deadman, Faber Drive, Dallas Smith and My Darkest Days, among others.

» **2002** MapleMusic Recordings, which was originally founded in Toronto in 1999 by former management consultant, Grant Dexter, entrepreneur Mike Alkier (Ideaca) and Andy Maize of the band Skydiggers, makes an impact with its first signing, Sam Roberts. Other artists released by the label include Kathleen Edwards, David Usher, Colin James, The Dears, Martha Wainwright, Gord Downie, Joel Plaskett, Spirit of the West, Ridley Bent and Kinnie Starr.

» **2002** Avril Lavigne and her band are seen performing her song "Sk8er Boi" in a nightclub in an episode of the TV series *Sabrina, The Teenage Witch*.

» **2002** With the release of their debut album *No Pads, No Helmets... Just Balls*, Québec band Simple Plan are revealed as road warriors as they play a reported 300+ shows in support of the record. Beginning in 2003, the group become regular headliners on the annual Vans Warped Tour.

» **2002** Progressive house music producer and performer Joel Zimmerman makes the transformation to deadmau5 about three years prior to the release of his debut album, *Get Scraped*, in 2005.

» **2002** Groups formed this year include Crush, Newfoundland; Hey Romeo, Edmonton; Simple Plan, Québec; The Duhks, Winnipeg; The King Khan & BBQ Show, Montréal; The Wailin' Jennys, Winnipeg.

» 2003

» **January 11, 2003** Avril Lavigne appears on *Saturday Night Live* with host Jeff Gordon.

» **January 26, 2003** Shania Twain performs "Man I Feel Like A Woman" and "Up!" for the Half-Time Show at Super Bowl XXXVII (TB Buccaneers beat Oakland Raiders) at the Qualcomm Stadium in San Diego, California.

» **February 9, 2003** Kurt Nilsen, winner of Norwegian Idol, releases a cover of the Tal Bachman song, "She's So High." It becomes one of the biggest-selling singles in Norwegian history.

» **February 11, 2003** The self-titled debut album by Michael Bublé is released by David Foster's label 143 Records/Reprise and goes to number one in Australia and enters the Top 10 in Canada, the U.K. and South Africa.

» **March 20, 2003** Avril Lavigne appears on the cover of Rolling Stone magazine.

» **March 2003** Canada decides not to join the U.S.-led coalition against Iraq. The move sparks fierce domestic political debate and Prime Minister Chretien comes under fire from Washington.

» **March-April 2003** Toronto is hit by the largest outbreak of the flu-like SARS virus outside of Asia.

» **April 6, 2003** The 32nd annual JUNO Awards are held at the Corel Centre in Ottawa and hosted by Shania Twain, who takes home the coveted JUNO Fan Choice Award as well as plaudits for Artist of the Year and Country Recording ("I'm Gonna Getcha Good"). The big winner was Avril Lavigne, who had first met Twain when she won a talent contest organized by Twain in 1999 in each of the city's in which she played which offered as the first prize the opportunity to appear on stage with her. It was during a concert by Twain in this same Ottawa arena that a 14-year-old Lavigne experienced a dream come true. Lavigne's four JUNOs include Single of the Year ("Complicated"), New Artist, Pop Album and Album of the Year (*Let Go*). The Walt Grealis Special Achievement Award was presented to Canadian music indie stalwart and co-founder of Vancouver-based Nettwerk Productions, Terry McBride. Guitarist/vocalist Jeff Healey was on hand to induct Tom Cochrane into the Canadian Music Hall of Fame.

» **April 22, 2003** Chantal Kreviazuk performs the song "In This Life" on The *Tonight Show* with Jay Leno.

» **April 2003** The Liberal Party beats the Parti Québecois in provincial elections in Québec, ending 9 years of rule by the pro-independence party.

» **May 2003** Avril Lavigne's debut album *Let Go* is certified diamond for the sale of more than one million copies in Canada.

» **June 9, 2003** The first season of the TV reality show, *Canadian Idol*, part of the Pop Idol international franchise created initially in the U.K. by Simon Fuller, debuts on the CTV Network. The four featured judges include Farley Flex, Jake Gold, Sass Jordan and Zack Werner with Ben Mulroney as host. Co-presenter for the first three years is comedian/actor Jon Dore. The show is taped at the John Bassett Theatre in downtown Toronto. First season winner, announced on September 16, 2003, is Ryan Malcolm (Kingston, ON). Runner-up is Gary Beals (Dartmouth, NS).

» **June 17, 2003** Alternative rock band Finger Eleven release their eponymous album and have great multimedia success with the single "One Thing," which went to number 16 in the U.S. and was heard in a number of video games and TV series.'

» **July 30, 2003** Molson Canadian Rocks For Toronto (aka SARSfest), a benefit concert originally proposed by The Rolling Stones to help get Toronto back on its feet economically following the SARS outbreak and subsequent World Health Organization warning earlier in the year, is held at Downsview Park in Toronto. It becomes the largest outdoor ticketed-event in Canadian history with an estimated attendance of close to 500,000. Hosted by comedic actor Dan Aykroyd, the day-long event features performances by the Have Love Will Travel Revue (Aykroyd and James Belushi), Sam Roberts, Kathleen Edwards, La Chicane, The Tea Party, The Flaming Lips, Sass Jordan with Jeff Healey, The Isley Brothers, Blue Rodeo, Justin Timberlake, The Guess Who, Rush, AC/

DC and The Rolling Stones. Segments of the concert are broadcast by the CBC and MuchMusic/MusiquePlus and a documentary film titled Toronto Rocks is released in 2004.

>> August 14, 2003 The biggest power cut in North American history hits Toronto, Ottawa and other parts of Ontario as well as cities in the U.S.

>> Fall 2003 Last Gang Records is founded in Toronto by music industry attorney Chris Taylor, in the early '90s, founding member/vocalist of Toronto Reggae/Ska group, One, and Montréal-based concert promoter Donald Tarlton, initially to record the Toronto group Metric. Roster now includes Metric, Lindi Ortega, Mother Mother, Crystal Castles, Lights, Death From Above 1979, Hot As Sun, Purity Ring and Huoratron.

>> November 4, 2003 Sum 41 is one of the bands collaborating with Iggy Pop on his album *Skull Ring*, released on this date. The single/video from the set, "Little Know It All," features Sum 41, who perform the song with Iggy on *The Late Show with David Letterman* (November 6, 2003). The song also appears on the soundtrack of the video game, NASCAR Thunder 2004.

>> November 2003 Alanis Morissette appears in the off-Broadway play, *The Exonerated*, as Sunny Jacobs.

>> December 6, 2003 Jazz singer, songwriter, musician Diana Krall and singer, songwriter, producer Elvis Costello are married at Elton John's Old Windsor estate outside of London.

>> December 8, 2003 The first Canadian Songwriters Hall of Fame (CSHF)/Le pantheon des auteurs et compositeurs Canadiens (PACC) Gala is held at the Glenn Gould Studio in Toronto with Gordon Lightfoot and Hank Snow among the first inducted writers. Performers include Blue Rodeo, Murray McLauchlan, Tom Cochrane, Ron Sexsmith, Quartette, Sarah Slean, Marc Jordan, Measha Brueggergosman, Molly Johnson, Tobi-Legend Lark and the original Toronto cast of Hair. CSHF was founded in 1998 by music publisher, producer Frank Davies.

>> December 21, 2003 Tom Cochrane, Damhnait Doyle and Kevin Fox travel to Camp Julien in Kabul, Afghanistan with comedian Rick Mercer to shoot the CBC TV special *Christmas in Kabul*, which airs on this date.

>> December 21, 2003 Vancouver Mayor Larry Campbell declares this "D.O.A. Day" in honor of the pioneering "hardcore" punk band from the city.

>> December 2003 Jean Chretien retires after 10 years in office and former Finance Minister Paul Martin is sworn in as Prime Minister.

>> 2003 Robbie Robertson is awarded an honorary degree by Queen's University in Kingston, Ontario.

>> 2003 With the release of his album *Canto*, Gino Vannelli reveals an operatic side to his singing aspirations, tackling songs in French, Spanish, English and Italian, including the moving tribute to his father, "Parole per mio padre," reportedly a favorite of Pope John Paul II, for whom he was asked to perform during this period.

>> 2003 Jazz pianist, vocalist Diana Krall receives an honorary Ph.D (Fine Arts) from the University of Victoria (British Columbia).

>> 2003 Fiddler Ashley MacIsaac publishes his autobiography, *Fiddling With Disaster*.

>> 2003 The annual Red Rock Folk Festival is first held in Red Rock, Ontario.

>> 2003 The music company Arts & Crafts is founded in Toronto by former Virgin Records executive Jeffrey Remedios and Kevin Drew, founder with Brendan Canning of the group Broken Social Scene (BSS). Among the artists signed to the company are BSS and associated artists, including Feist and Stars.

>> 2003 Groups formed this year include: Great Lake Swimmers, Wainfleet, ON; Shaye, Maritimes/Toronto; Wolf Parade, Montréal.

>> 2004

>> February 2004 Scandal erupts over the alleged misuse of Liberal government money intended for advertising and sponsorship.

>> April 4, 2004 The 33rd annual JUNO Awards are held at Rexall Place in Edmonton, Alberta with host Alanis Morissette, who memorably appears at one point in a body suit with nipples and pubic hair that makes it appear, in a cartoonish way, that she is naked. This came in the wake of what Morissette felt was an over-reaction in the U.S. to the now famous Janet Jackson "nipple slip" incident at the Super Bowl half-time show that year. Montréaler Sam Roberts leads the pack this year picking up JUNOs in all three categories in which he and the band are nominated: Artist of the Year, Rock Album and Album of the Year (*We Were Born In A*

Flame). Sarah McLachlan is honored as Songwriter of the Year and for Pop Album (*Afterglow*). Nickelback wins this year's JUNO Fan Choice Award, and Michael Bublé was named New Artist of the Year. The JUNO Cup, a hockey game created by Jim Cuddy of Blue Rodeo, which pits past National Hockey League stars against a Rockers team of wannabe hockey players from the music world, is held for the first time during JUNO week. Producer/musician Bob Ezrin is inducted into the Canadian Music Hall of Fame by Alice Cooper, while Walt Grealis, publisher of *RPM Weekly*, the Canadian music trade magazine, posthumously receives the JUNO that bears his name, the Walt Grealis Special Achievement Award.

» **May 8, 2004** Avril Lavigne appears again on *Saturday Night Live* with host Snoop Dogg.

» **May 18, 2004** Feist's second album, *Let It Die*, recorded in Paris, where she had taken up residence, is released in Canada. During this period, she co-wrote the song "The Simple Story" and performed it as a duet with Jane Birkin, the expatriate English singer/actress living in France, on her album *Rendezvous*.

» **May 25, 2004** Avril Lavigne's sophomore studio album, *Under My Skin*, much of which was co-written with fellow Canadian singer, songwriter, musician Chantal Kreviazuk, debuts at number one in the U.S., Canada, the U.K., Australia, Mexico and Japan. The album is co-produced by Our Lady Peace front-man, Raine Maida.

» **May 2004** On a trip to the Democratic Republic of Congo with War Child Canada, Sum 41 get caught up in the country's civil war as fighting breaks out near their hotel in Bukavu. As they began to despair, U.N. peacekeeper Charles "Chuck" Pelletier came to the rescue with armored carriers that ferried the band and 40 other civilians to safety. On October 12, the band released an album titled *Chuck* in tribute to their rescuer. A documentary film on the trip, *Rocked: Sum 41 in Congo*, aired on MTV and was later

released in the U.S. and Canada on DVD on November 29, 2005.

» **June 2004** The annual Kingfest Music Festival is first held on the campus of Seneca College in King City, Ontario. In 2007, Kingfest launches a winter concert series with a varied music policy at the Newmarket Theatre in Newmarket, Ontario.

» **June 2004** Prime Minister Paul Martin is returned to power in general elections, but his Liberal party is stripped of its majority.

» **Summer 2004** Jay Ferguson of Sloan organizes the first Olympic Island Festival on one of the Toronto Islands in Lake Ontario, with Sloan headlining a line-up that includes Sam Roberts, Broken Social Scene, The Stills, Buck 65, Constantines, Death From Above 1979 and Arcade Fire.

» **Summer 2004** The annual three-day Rock In the Park, created by Jones Entertainment Group to support Bethany's Hope Foundation in progressing research for Metachromatic Leukodystrophy (MLD), is first held in Harris Park in London, Ontario.

» **July 4, 2004** Nelly Furtado performs her song "Força," which had become the official anthem of the 2004 European Football Championship being held in Portugal, at the final at Estadio da Luz in Lisbon during which Portugal lost to Greece 1-0.

» **July 2004** Alanis Morissette is seen in the Cole Porter biographical film *De-Lovely*. She performs the song "Let's Do It" and has a brief role as an anonymous stage performer.

» **July 2004** The annual Nakusp Music Fest, a classic rock music and arts festival, debuts in Nakusp, British Columbia with Randy Bachman, Trooper, Dr. Hook and Wide Mouth Mason, among others.

» **July 2004** The annual Montréal Reggae Festival, co-founded by Eric Blagrove, Ricardo Forbes and Cezar

Brumeanu, is first held at the Quays of the Old Port of Montréal.

>> **September 14, 2004** Arcade Fire's debut album *Funeral* is released.

>> **September 15, 2004** At the 16th annual World Music Awards, held in Las Vegas, Nevada for the first time rather than Monaco, Avril Lavigne picks up two awards as World's Best Pop/Rock Artist and World's Best-Selling Canadian Artist while Celine Dion is honored with the Chopard Diamond Award, which is presented to recording artists who have sold over 100 million albums worldwide during their career.

>> **September 16, 2004** The winner of the second season of *Canadian Idol*, which runs from June 1 to this date, is Kalan Porter (Medicine Hat, AB) with runner-up, Theresa Sokyrka (Saskatoon, SK). This season, the show earns the distinction of being the most-watched program on Canadian television with weekly viewership of more than 3 million. An Idol franchise first comes with a group performance of Gordon Lightfoot's "Canadian Railroad Trilogy" for which the final six accompanied themselves with their own instruments. This second season is notable for the emergence of third runner-up, Burnaby, B.C.-native Jacob Hoggard, who will go on to enjoy great success with his band Hedley. Kalan Porter's debut album *219 Days* sells more than 200,000 copies in Canada and earns him three JUNO nominations. He is voted Fan Favourite Canadian Artist at the MuchMusic Video Awards.

SOCAN

>> **November 2, 2004** The Shania Twain Centre in Timmins, Ontario is officially opened as hometown girl Shania Twain is in attendance for the ceremony. The Centre had been open for three years previously but this was the earliest Twain could fit this homecoming into her schedule.

>> **November 21, 2004** The Tragically Hip play the half-time show during the 92nd Grey Cup at Frank Clair Stadium in Ottawa.

>> **2004** Bryan Adams founds *Zoo Magazine*, a photography magazine based in Berlin, Germany, He is co-publisher.

>> **2004** While collaborating on an album (*Northey Valenzuela*), Craig Northey of Odds and Gin Blossoms guitarist Jesse Valenzuela record the theme song to the popular Canadian sitcom, *Corner Gas* (CTV).

>> **2004** Timmins, Ontario-born musician, writer, broadcaster Charlie Angus adds successful politician to his resume as he becomes the New Democratic Party MPP in the Ontario riding of Timmins-James Bay. He was well-suited as the party's parliamentary critic for Canadian Heritage from 2004-2007 before moving on to other portfolios.

>> **2004** JUNO Award-winning singer, songwriter, guitarist Kim Mitchell joins Toronto classic rock radio station Q107 (CILQ-FM) as on-air personality.

>> **2004** Groups formed this year include DAD OF, Black Mountain, Vancouver; Cancer Bats, Toronto; Crystal Castles, Toronto; Hedley, Vancouver; Holy Fuck, Toronto; State of Shock, Vancouver; You Say Party, Abbotsford, BC.

>> 2005

>> **January 13, 2005** Canada For Asia, a benefit concert in support of tsunami relief in Asia, originates from the CBC's Canadian Broadcasting Centre in Toronto. It features some of the biggest names in Canadian music, including Celine Dion, Anne Murray, Rush, The Tragically Hip, Oscar Peterson, Blue Rodeo, Bruce Cockburn and Tom Cochrane, who with his wife Kathleene and Alex Lifeson of Rush, are active in organizing the event which is broadcast on an unprecedented network of private and public TV and radio stations.

>> **January 22, 2005** Sum 41 and Ludacris appear on *Saturday Night Live* with host Paul Giamatti.

>> **February 11, 2005** Alanis Morissette becomes Canadian/American as she becomes a naturalized citizen of the U.S.

>> **February 15, 2005** Michael Bublé's sophomore studio album *It's Time*, not only includes a variety of pop standards, including a duet on "Quando Quando Quando" with fellow Canadian west coast artist, Nelly Furtado, but also the original song "Home," co-written by Bublé with Alan Chang and Amy Foster-Gilles. The album topped the Billboard Top Jazz chart for a record-breaking 78 weeks.

>> **March 29, 2005** Neil Young is treated in a New York hospital for a brain aneurism, from which, despite an alarming setback a few days later in which he passes out on a New York street from bleeding in an artery, he makes a full recovery, though he is forced to miss an appearance at the JUNO Awards in his former hometown of Winnipeg, Manitoba.

>> **March 26, 2005** *50 Tracks with Jian Ghomeshi*, the CBC Radio One morning program, airs its five-hour countdown show. The run-up shows featured a number of panellists from the music industry and the radio audience on a 10-week quest to compile a list of the 50 essential Canadian popular songs. The top song is "Four Strong Winds," the 1963 classic and unofficial anthem of Alberta written by Ian Tyson and performed by Ian & Sylvia. The runner-up is "If I Had $1000000" by Barenaked Ladies (1992).

>> **April 3, 2005** The 34th annual JUNO Awards are held at the MTS Centre in Winnipeg, Manitoba and hosted by comedic actor Brent Butt (*Corner Gas*). The awards were evenly distributed amongst the top winners this year. k-os picked up three JUNOs for Single of the Year ("Crabbuckit"), Rap Recording of the Year and Video of the Year ("B-Boy Stance" with Micah Meisner) as did Artist of the Year Avril Lavigne who won the JUNO Fan Choice Award and picked up a trophy for Pop Album (*Under My Skin*). Group of the Year Billy Talent also took the JUNO for Album of the Year (*Billy Talent*) and New Artist of the Year Feist won in the category of Alternative Album of the Year (*Let It Die*). One of the disappointments of the night came with the absence of Neil Young who was still dealing with the treatment for a brain aneurysm and advised not to travel. k.d. lang stepped into one of Young's performance spots and provided a highlight of the night with her rendition of the Leonard Cohen song, "Hallelujah." The Walt Grealis Special Achievement Award is presented to broadcaster, philanthropist Allan Slaight and The Tragically Hip are inducted into the Canadian Music Hall of Fame.

>> **April 4, 2005** Arcade Fire appear on the cover of *Time* magazine's Canadian edition.

>> **April 8, 2005** Michael Bublé, Jann Arden and Elvis Costello appear on the last edition of the CTV afternoon talk show hosted by Vicki Gabereau, which wraps after eight seasons. Bublé had been a regular guest on her show since 1997.

>> **May 1, 2005** Arcade Fire appear at the Coachella Valley Music & Arts Festival in Indio, California.

>> **May 30, 2005** The third season of *Canadian Idol* debuts on CTV.

>> **May 2005** The Liberal government wins a confidence motion in Parliament over the financial scandal by just one vote.

>> **June 23, 2005** Glass Tiger perform their hit "Don't Forget Me (When I'm Gone)" and cover Vertical Horizon's "Everything You Want" on the popular summer NBC TV show *Hit Me Baby One More Time*, losing to Thelma Houston on the audience vote but prevailing with online voters.

>> **June 2005** The annual Mondial Loto-Québec de Laval (Mondial Choral), one of the world's largest gatherings of choral groups, is first held in Laval, Québec. President and Artistic Director is Grégory Charles.

>> **July 2005** Senate approves a bill to legalize same-sex marriages.

>> **July 2, 2005** The Live 8 concert at Molson Park in Barrie, Ontario is one of nine concerts held simultaneously in nine major cities around the world, as well as at the Eden Project in Cornwall, England, to pressure the world leaders attending the G8 Summit to fight poverty in Africa by cancelling its debt. Performers at the Barrie show include Neil Young, Bryan Adams, The Tragically Hip (with co-host Dan Aykroyd), Bruce Cockburn, Tom Cochrane, Blue Rodeo, Simple Plan, Gordon Lightfoot, Barenaked Ladies, Our Lady Peace, Jann Arden, DobaCaracol (featuring K'naan), Great Big Sea, Sam Roberts, Chuck Berry, DMC, Motley Crue, Deep Purple, African Guitar Summit, Jet and Celine Dion (by satellite from Las Vegas). Sarah McLachlan performs her song "Angel" with Josh Groban at the Philadelphia Live 8 concert.

>> **July 21, 2005** Long John Baldry, a long-time resident of Vancouver, passes away after fighting a severe chest infection. He was 64.

>> **Summer 2005** Randy Bachman creates and hosts the weekly CBC Radio show, *Vinyl Tap*, which features selected classic rock, pop and jazz music, rock 'n' roll reminiscence, music lists and personal anecdotes from the Canadian guitar-playing legend who has earned a reputation as a story-teller.

>> **August 2005** Canada sends naval vessels to Churchill, an Arctic port, for the first time in 30 years. It is seen as a challenge to rival territorial claims.

>> **September 14, 2005** The third season of *Canadian Idol*, which kicked off on May 30, comes to an end as Calgary's Melissa O'Neil becomes the first female *Canadian Idol* winner. Runner-up is Rex Goudie of Burlington, Newfoundland.

>> **September 9, 2005** David Bowie joins Arcade Fire on their song "Wake Up" for the U.K./U.S. TV special *Fashion Rocks*. The BBC in the U.K. used "Wake Up" in an ad for their fall 2005 broadcast season, and U2 play the song prior to their shows during their 2005/2006 Vertigo Tour to pump up the crowd. The group appears on the long-running BBC TV music series, *Top of the Pops* (September 11).

>> **October 2005** A number of radio stations stop playing The Tragically Hip song "New Orleans Is Sinking" in deference to the victims of Hurricane Katrina.

>> **November 16, 2005** Bryan Adams, whose charity efforts would fill a book, topped himself in Qatar where he was guest of honor at the inaugural Reach Out To Asia

charity fundraiser in the capital city of Doha. Following the devastation of the tsunami in December of 2004, Adams began gathering signatures on a white Fender Stratocaster guitar with the intent of auctioning it off to raise money for tsunami relief in Asia. Ultimately, nearly 20 rock legends signed the guitar, including Mick Jagger, Keith Richards, Eric Clapton, Brian May, Jimmy Page, David Gilmour, Jeff Beck, Pete Townshend, Mark Knopfler, Ray Davies, Liam and Noel Gallagher of Oasis, Ronnie Wood, Tony Iommi, Angus and Malcolm Young of AC/DC, Paul McCartney, Sting, Ritchie Blackmore, Def Leppard and himself. The final bid... a reported US$2.7 million, a new Guinness World Record for the most expensive guitar in history with proceeds donated to the Reach Out To Asia Foundation. Adams returned to Doha on February 1, 2006 for a concert at Al Sadd Stadium with the proceeds going to Reach Out To Asia.

>> **November 2005** Paul Martin's minority Liberal government is brought down in a vote of no confidence.

>> **December 17, 2005** Neil Young appears on *Saturday Night Live* with host Jack Black.

>> **2005** Nickelback drummer Ryan Vikedal departs and is replaced by 3 Doors Down drummer Daniel Adair.

>> **2005** Canadian Hip-Hop pioneer Maestro records a cover of the Lawrence Gowan song "A Criminal Mind."

>> **2005** Lucille Starr is an honorary inductee into Canada's Aboriginal Music Hall of Fame.

>> **2005** Blue Rodeo mark the 20th anniversary of their first show by getting the original members of the band together to play one last gig filmed by noted Canadian documentary filmmaker, Ron Mann, for the retrospective DVD, *In Stereovision*.

>> **2005** Groups formed this year include Crash Parallel, Mississauga, ON; Die Mannequin, Toronto; Dragonette, Toronto; Hey Rosetta! St. John's, NF; My Darkest Days, Norwood, ON; The New Cities, Trois Rivieres, QC; Tokyo Police Club, Newmarket, ON; Yukon Blonde, Kelowna, BC.

>> 2006

>> **January 2006** Stephen Harper's Conservatives defeat Paul Martin in a general election, ending 12 years of Liberal government.

>> **Early 2006** Arcade Fire buy an old church in the small town of Farnham, Québec, just over an hour southeast of Montréal, and convert it into a recording studio.

>> **February 26, 2006** Avril Lavigne represents Canada at the closing ceremonies of the Torino Winter Olympics, during which she performs her song "Who Knows" as Vancouver moves into the spotlight as the host city for the 2010 Winter Olympics.

>> **April 2, 2006** The 35th annual JUNO Awards are held at the Halifax Metro Centre in Halifax, Nova Scotia with Pamela Anderson as host. Michael Bublé is the story this year as he picks up four JUNOs including Artist of the Year, Album and Pop Album of the Year (*It's Time*) and Single of the Year for the original song, "Home." Fellow West Coasters Nickelback, who had been nominated a leading six times, took home JUNOs as Group of the Year and for Rock Album of the Year (*All the Right Reasons*). The indie scenes in Toronto and Montréal get a little love as Broken Social Scene take the JUNO for their self-titled Alternative Album, Bedouin Soundclash is named New Group of the Year, while Arcade Fire earn the award as Songwriters of the Year. Chris Martin of Coldplay is on hand to induct Bryan Adams into the Canadian Music Hall of Fame as the British group's album *X&Y* is joint winner of the JUNO for International Album of the Year with Black Eyed Peas (*Monkey Business*). The JUNO's first Allan Waters Humanitarian Award, named after the late CHUM Limited broadcast executive, is presented to singer, songwriter, social activist Bruce Cockburn, while the Walt Grealis Special Achievement Award goes to Cockburn's manager and record executive (True North Records), Bernie Finkelstein.

>> **April 2006** Ra McGuire, singer, songwriter of the Vancouver group Trooper releases the book, *Here For A Good Time: On the Road with Trooper, Canada's Legendary Rock Band*.

>> **May 18, 2006** The anthology film *Paris, je t'aime*, 18 short films inspired by the various arrondissements that make up the city, premieres at the Cannes film festival. The soundtrack includes two songs sung by Feist: "La meme histoire" and "We're All In the Dance."

>> **May 19, 2006** Avril Lavigne is the voice of Heather, a Virginia Opossum, in the popular animated film, *Over the Hedge*.

>> **May 20, 2006** Nelly Furtado appears on *Saturday Night Live* with host Kevin Spacey.

>> **May 2006** MPs vote by a narrow margin to extend Canada's military deployment in Afghanistan.

>> **June 3, 2006** After divesting herself of most of her worldly possessions, Jane Siberry, now unencumbered and open to the life changes she has said she craves, travels to Europe where, on this date, she changes her name to Issa. She reverts back to Jane Siberry by 2009.

>> **June 29, 2006** 12-year-old jazz singer Nikki Yanofsky of Montréal wows the hometown crowd with her set at the Montréal International Jazz Festival, the beginning of her professional career.

>> **June 2006** Nelly Furtado's third album, *Loose*, on which she collaborates with renowned producer Timbaland, is destined to top the charts in Canada, the U.S. and internationally in the wake of songs like "Promiscuous," her first number one hit in the U.S., "Maneater," her first U.K. chart-topper, "Say It Right," her second number-one song and "All Good Things (Come To An End)," her most successful song in Europe.

>> **July 15, 2006** Avril Lavigne marries Sum 41 front-man Deryck Whibley at a private estate in Montecito, California.

>> **July 29, 2006** k.d. lang performs "Constant Craving" at the Outgames Opening Ceremonies in Montréal.

>> **August 2006** Singer, composer Loreena McKennitt is appointed as Honorary Colonel of 435 Transport and Rescue Squadron at 17 Wing Winnipeg, Manitoba.

>> **August 2006** Jimmie Rodgers Snow, son of Nova Scotia-born country music legend Hank Snow, resigns as pastor of Nashville's Evangel Temple after more than 40 years at what some have called, "The Church of the Country Stars" to return to the road preaching and singing. For many years, Snow was featured on video at the entrance of the Rock 'N' Roll Hall of Fame in Cleveland preaching loudly on the evils of "sex, drugs and rock 'n' roll."

>> **Summer 2006** The annual Sled Island Music and Arts Festival, founded by Zak Pashak, is held for the first time in over 30 venues in downtown Calgary.

>> **Summer 2006** The first edition of the annual Osheaga Festival Musique et Arts, a multi-day indie music festival, is held at Parc Jean-Drapeau on Île Sainte-Hélène (Montréal).

>> **Summer 2006** The annual SappyFest, an arts and music festival founded by Sappy Records, is first held on Bridge Street in the heart of downtown Sackville, New Brunswick.

>> **September 9-10, 2006** The inaugural Virgin Fest concert, which Virgin Group head Richard Branson had announced would take place yearly in a variety of cities in the U.S. and Canada — is canceled after the 2009's schedule of cross-Canada dates. It was first held at Toronto's Island Park featuring

▲ Nikki Yanofsky

more than 40 artists, including Broken Social Scene, The Flaming Lips, Gnarls Barkley, Muse, The Dears, Buck 65, Alexisonfire, Sam Roberts Band, The Strokes and illScarlett. Subsequent Canadian Virgin Festival sites include Vancouver (Thunderbird Stadium, May 20-21, 2007) with Billy Talent, My Chemical Romance, Jets Overhead, The Killers, Hot Hot Heat, Metric, Marianas Trench, Mother Mother etc., Toronto (Toronto Island Park, Sept. 8-9, 2007) with Bjork, Smashing Pumpkins, The Killers, Arctic Monkeys, k-os, Paolo Nutini, Hayley Sales, Metric, Stars, Tokyo Police Club etc. Calgary (Fort Calgary, Calgary, AB, June 21-22, 2008) with Three Days Grace, Corb Lund, The Flaming Lips, Stone Temple Pilots, The Tragically Hip, The Dudes, Hey Ocean, Chixdiggit, City and Colour, Matthew Good, Said the Whale, The New Pornographers etc. TORONTO (Toronto Island Park, Toronto, ON, Sept. 6-7, 2008) with Foo Fighters, Oasis, Paul Weller, Stereophonics, Silversun Pickups, The Weakerthans, Danko Jones, deadmau5, MGMT, Constantines, Wintersleep, The Midway State, Lights, etc. Montreal (Parc Jean-Drapeau, June 19-20, 2009) with Black Eyed Peas, Simple Plan, Hedley, Kreesha Turner, Carly Rae Jepsen, New Kids on the Bock, Akon, David Usher, Karl Wolf, Live, Lights etc.; Nova Scotia (Citadel Hill, Halifax, NS, July 4, 2009) with The Offspring, Metric, Handsome Furs, Dinosaur Jr., Hey Rosetta, Arkells, Plants and Animals etc. British Columbia (Deer Lake Park, Burnaby, BC, July 25-26, 2009) with Our Lady Peace, Broken Social Scene, k-os, Ben Harper & Relentless 7, Metric, Sonic Youth, Jarvis Cocker, De La Soul, Gomez, Carly Rae Jepsen etc.; Alberta (Canada Olympic Park, Calgary, AB, Aug. 8-9, 2009) with Pearl Jam, Wintersleep, Billy Talent, Metric, Arkells, Tokyo Police Club, Mother Mother, The Cliks etc.; Ontario (Molson Amphitheatre, Toronto, ON, Aug. 29-30, 2009) with The Pixies, Franz Ferdinand, Paolo Nutini, Sloan, Pitbull, Down With Webster, Nine Inch Nails, Pet Shop Boys, Our Lady Peace, Sean Kingston, Melanie Fiona etc.

>> **September 13, 2006** Two people are killed and 19 injured in the Dawson College shooting in Montreal.

>> **September 17, 2006** In a close vote, Gatineau, Québec-native Eva Avila is named winner as the *Canadian Idol* finals show

airs. Runner-up is Craig Sharpe of Carbonear, Newfoundland. Co-presenter/roving reporter on this year's show, which premiered on May 29, is a Season 2 semi-finalist, Elena Juatco.

>> **September 18, 2006** The Polaris Music Prize, a not-for-profit organization founded by its Executive Director Steve Jordan, a former A&R executive with Warner Music Canada and True North Records, is

▲ Drake

presented for the first time at a gala celebration at Toronto's Phoenix Concert Theatre. Inaugural winner is the album *He Poos Clouds* by Final Fantasy (Owen Pallett). The Polaris and $20,000 in prize money— raised to $30,000 in 2011 — is presented for the best full-length Canadian album based on artistic merit, regardless of genre, sales or record label. The award is adjudicated by selected music journalists, broadcasters and bloggers. Subsequent winners include *Closer to Paradise*, Patrick Watson (2007), *Andorra*, Caribou (2008), *The Chemistry of Common Life*, Fucked Up (2009), *Les Chemins de verre*, Karkwa (2010), *The Suburbs*, Arcade Fire (2011) and *Metals*, Feist (2012).

>> **October 10, 2006** k-os releases his third album, *Atlantis: Hymns For Disco*. He collaborated with Sam Roberts and Buck 65 (Richard Terfry). It debutes at number one on the Canadian Digital Albums chart.

>> **November 17, 2006** Avril Lavigne plays Alice, a high school student who is determined to free the cows in a slaughterhouse, in the film *Fast Food Nation*.

>> **2006** Neil Young is so angered by the disregard with which veterans of the U.S. invasion of Iraq and their families are being met with at home that in less than a month he writes and records the album *Living With War* that takes the government to task for its policies in this regard. Songs from the album, including the track "Let's Impeach the President," are performed during the Crosby, Stills, Nash & Young Freedom of Speech Tour '06 that summer.

>> **2006** Toronto rapper, songwriter Drake releases his first mix-tape *Room For Improvement*, featuring Trey Songz and Lupe Fiasco.

>> **2006** Groups formed this year include Arkells, Hamilton, ON; Beast, Montréal; Carmen & Camille, Vancouver; Handsome Furs, Montréal; The Burning Hell, Peterborough, ON; The Sheepdogs, Saskatoon, SK; Walk Off the Earth, Burlington, ON.

>> **2007**

>> **January 15-19, 2007** Barenaked Ladies set out on the first of their Ships and Dip fan cruises, which over the next four years will feature artists like Sarah McLachlan, Sloan, The New Odds, The Weakerthans, Jason Plumb, Guster, Luke Doucet, The Mountain Goats and comedians Sean Cullen and Harland Williams.

>> **January 19, 2007** Halifax-born Denny Doherty of The Mamas and the Papas dies in Mississauga, Ontario.

>> **February 3, 2007** Young Edmonton, Alberta-born First Nations singer Akina Shirt makes history as the first to perform the Canadian national anthem "O Canada" at a major league sporting event in an aboriginal language. She sang the anthem in the Cree language prior to a Calgary Flames/Vancouver Canucks NHL hockey game in Calgary on this date.

>> **February 16, 2007** Nelly Furtado embarks on her Get Loose Tour.

>> **February 18, 2007** Fiddler Ashley MacIsaac marries his partner Andrew Stokes on stage at the Cape Breton Rocks showcase during the East Coast Music Awards in Halifax, Nova Scotia.

>> **February 24, 2007** Arcade Fire appear on *Saturday Night Live* with host Rainn Wilson in advance of the release of the group's sophomore album, *Neon Bible,* which debuts at number one in Canada, Ireland and the U.K. and number two in the U.S. The group's 2007 Neon Bible Tour will play 122 shows in 75 cities in 19 countries.

>> **March 6, 2007** Finger Eleven's fifth studio album, titled *Them vs. You vs. Me,* produces "Paralyzer," the band's biggest single to date, which had gone to number one in Canada and, by November, had entered the Top 10 in the U.S.

>> **March 21, 2007** On the occasion of her homecoming concert in Victoria, British Columbia at Save-On-Foods Memorial Centre as part of her Get Loose Tour, civic leaders proclaim Nelly Furtado Day.

>> **March 30, 2007** The Rheostatics perform a farewell show at Toronto's Massey Hall.

>> **April 1, 2007** The 36th annual JUNO Awards are held at the Credit Union Centre in Saskatoon, Saskatchewan and

hosted by Nelly Furtado on a night she will not soon forget. From the moment she "flew" down from the arena's rafters in a black, feathered outfit with black knee-high boots, Furtado was rarely out of the spotlight. She had been nominated in five categories and swept all of them, including JUNO Fan Choice, Artist of the Year, Album, Pop Album (*Loose*) and Single of the Year ("Promiscuous" featuring Timbaland). Billy Talent, the other multiple award winner, took home JUNOs as Group of the Year and for Rock Album (*Billy Talent II*). The Tragically Hip inducts noted musician/producer Bob Rock (Motley Crue, Metallica, Bryan Adams) into the Canadian Music Hall of Fame, and Montréal-based impresario/record executive Donald Tarlton is presented with the Walt Grealis Special Achievement Award. Musician, actor, philanthropist Tom Jackson receives this year's Allan Waters Humanitarian Award for his "unwavering support to Canada's hungry and underprivileged."

» **April 14, 2007** Avril Lavigne appears on *Saturday Night Live* with host Shia LeBeouf.

» **April 16, 2007** Musician, TV/radio broadcaster, producer and author Jian Ghomeshi, former member of the Toronto band Moxy Fruvous, known for their political satire, becomes the host of *Q*, the highly-acclaimed arts and culture program he co-created on CBC Radio One. The show, also heard on more than 150 stations in the U.S., becomes the highest-rated show in its morning time slot in CBC history. He has managed the career of Juno Award-winning musician, songwriter Lights since 2001.

» **April 17, 2007** The release of Avril Lavigne's third album, *The Best Damn Thing*, produces the song "Girlfriend" that confirms her stature as an international star. It is her first number one single on the Billboard 100 singles chart and, for a time, both the album and the single top their respective Billboard charts. The song tops the charts around the world and is recorded in Spanish, French, Italian, Portuguese, German, Japanese and Mandarin.

According to stats from the International Federation of the Phonographic Industry (IFPI) later this year, "Girlfriend" is the most downloaded song worldwide in 2007.

» **April 30, 2007** Drake, who is still an independent artist at this point, has the video for his first single "Replacement Girl," featuring Trey Songz, featured as The New Joint of the Day on Black Entertainment Television (BET).

» **May 1, 2007** Michael Bublé's third album, *Call Me Irresponsible*, is released and debuts at number two on the Billboard 200 album chart before rising to the top spot the following week. It debuted at number one in Australia on its way to becoming the top selling album of 2007 Down Under.

» **May 1, 2007** Feist's third album, *The Reminder*, recorded in Europe and co-produced with frequent collaborator Gonzales, among others, is released. In September of this year, the track "1234," written by Australian artist Sally Seltmann (aka New Buffalo) and co-produced by the ubiquitous Canadian musician/producer Ben Mink, is heard in TV ads for Apple's third generation iPod nano. The exposure not only ignites interest in the song but also in Feist and the album. Later in the year, among many other accolades, including an Album of the Year JUNO Award, *Time* magazine ranks it number two in its countdown of the 10 Best Songs of 2007. The album topped the 2007 Best of lists of John Pareles and Kaleefah Saneh at the *New York Times*.

» **May 2007** Roch Voisine receives an honorary doctorate of music from the Université de Moncton in New Brunswick.

» **June 22, 2007** Canada's first officially-recorded F4 twister touched down in Elite, Manitoba. Despite the millions of dollars of damage, no one died and only six people were injured.

» **June 29, 2007** Canada Post issues four limited edition stamps portraying Canadian recording artists Paul Anka, Gordon Lightfoot, Joni Mitchell and Anne Murray.

» **July 1, 2007** Nelly Furtado performs "Say It Right," "I'm Like A Bird" and "Maneater" at the Concert For Diana at Wembley Stadium in London, England on the occasion of what would have been the late Diana, Princess of Wales' 46th birthday. The show hosted by Diana's sons Princes William and Harry was headlined by Elton John, who opened and closed the concert. CTV broadcast the show live in Canada reaching a reported 2.8 million viewers.

>> **July 24, 2007** Sum 41's album *Underclass Hero* debuts at number one on the Billboard Rock Albums chart, a first for the group, as are the number one peak positions on the Canadian Albums and Alternative Albums charts.

>> **August 3, 2007** Jacksoul singer Haydain Neale is taken to hospital in critical condition following a traffic accident in which a Honda Civic crashes into the Vespa scooter he is riding. It takes Neale more than two years to recover.

>> **September 9, 2007** Producer, musician Daniel Lanois premieres the documentary film *Here Is What Is*, which documents the recording of the album of the same name, at the Toronto Film Festival.

>> **September 11, 2007** As Season Five of Canadian Idol comes to a close, Hamilton, Ontario singer/songwriter Brian Melo is voted the winner over runner-up Jaydee Bixby of Drumheller, Alberta. Co-presenter of this year's series, which premiered on June 5, is Montréal-born actor Dave Kerr. Notably, third runner-up Carly Rae Jepsen will go on to have an international hit with the song, "Call Me Maybe," receive two Grammy Award nominations and win three JUNO Awards.

>> **September 24, 2007** The theme for the hit CBS TV series *The Big Bang Theory*, which premieres on this date, was written by Ed Robertson of Barenaked Ladies, who subsequently record it themselves.

>> **October 2007** During a tour of Canada with Finger Eleven and Die Mannequin, Sum 41's Deryck Whibley sustains a herniated disc, resulting in the cancellation of the rest of the dates. The injury will dog Whibley for the next few years.

>> **November 3, 2007** Feist appears on *Saturday Night Live* with host Brian Williams.

>> **November 29, 2007** Singer, songwriter, musician Tom Cochrane is invested as an Honorary Colonel with the Royal Canadian Air Force's 409 "Nighthawks" Tactical Fighter Squadron.

>> **December 2007** The legendary True North Records, founded in Toronto in 1969 by artist manager Bernie Finkelstein and recording home to artists like Bruce Cockburn, Murray McLauchlan, Rough Trade, Rheostatics, Stephen Fearing and Blackie and the Rodeo Kings, is acquired by Linus Entertainment. Finkelstein remains Chairman of the label and continues to manage Bruce Cockburn.

>> **2007** Nelly Furtado has her third U.S. number one single and second in the U.K. as she and Justin Timberlake are featured on the Timbaland chart-topper "Give It To Me."

>> **2007** Singer, songwriter, actor Alan Frew (Glass Tiger) publishes the motivational book, *Lessons From A Tour Bus*, presents *The Action Sandwich: A Six Step Recipe for Success by Doing What You're Already Doing*, co-written with Sharon Brennan.

>> **2007** Rather than play the major cities during their Canadian tour, The White Stripes opt to play small markets like Glace Bay, Nova Scotia, Whitehorse, Yukon and Iqaluit, Nunavut with the ambition of playing every Canadian province and territory. During the excursion, they shoot the video for their single "You Don't Know What Love Is (You Just Do As You're Told)" in Iqaluit.

>> **2007** K'naan's debut album, *Dusty Foot Philosopher*, which had been released in 2005, receives a BBC Radio 3 Award for World Music in the newcomer category.

>> **2007** Groups formed this year include Eleven Past One, Bowmanville, ON/New Brunswick; Hollowick, Oshawa, ON; Neverest, Toronto; Said the Whale, Vancouver; The Tenors, Victoria, BC; The Midway State, Collingwood/Wasaga Beach, ON.

>> 2008

>> **February 8, 2008** On her 14th birthday, Nikki Yanofsky plays Carnegie Hall in New York with noted composer, conductor Marvin Hamlisch, the opening night of a multi-city tour.

>> **February 10, 2008** At the 50th annual Grammy Awards held at the Staples Center in Los Angeles, The Band receive the Grammy Lifetime Achievement Award.

>> **February 23, 2008** The Tragically Hip are the first artists to perform at the newly-opened K-Rock Centre in their hometown of Kingston, Ontario.

>> **February 28, 2008** Bryan Adams, Josh Groban, Sarah McLachlan, Jann Arden and RyanDan perform at One Night Live, a fundraising concert at Toronto's Air Canada Centre to benefit the construction of two new floors for births, high-risk pregnancies and critically-ill newborns at the Sunnybrook Health Sciences Centre in Toronto.

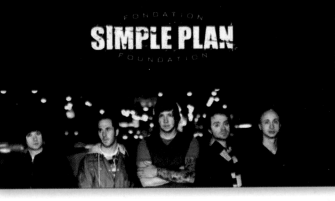

» February 2008 Tom Cochrane and John Mellencamp undertake a 12-date tour of Canada.

» March 10, 2008 Leonard Cohen is inducted into the Rock and Roll Hall of Fame at ceremonies at New York's Waldorf-Astoria.

» April 6, 2008 The 37th annual JUNO Awards are held at the Pengrowth Saddledome in Calgary, Alberta and hosted by Russell Peters. It was quite the homecoming for [Leslie] Feist, who two decades prior had danced during the opening ceremonies of the 1988 Winter Olympics in Calgary. On this night, she became the second artist in as many years to sweep all five categories in which she was nominated. Nelly Furtado accomplished that in 2007. Feist won in the categories of Artist, Single (*"1234"*), Songwriter, Album and Pop Album of the Year (*The Reminder*). Blue Rodeo won a trio of JUNOs, including Group of the Year, Adult Alternative Album (*Small Miracles*) and Video of the Year for the Christopher Mills-directed clip for "C'mon." Montréal indie collective Arcade Fire took the honors for Alternative Album (*Neon Bible*) and CD/DVD Artwork Design (*Neon Bible*). Hometown country music star Paul Brandt is presented with the JUNO for Country Recording of the Year (*Risk*) by country/cowboy music icon Ian Tyson and earns the 2008 Allan Waters Humanitarian Award. The JUNO Fan Choice Award is won by Michael Bublé. Innovative broadcast executive Moses Znaimer takes home the Walt Grealis Special Achievement Award and Canadian rock singer, songwriter Tom Cochrane inducts Toronto rock trio Triumph into the Canadian Music Hall of Fame.

» April 28, 2008 Feist appears on *The Colbert Report*, hosted by Stephen Colbert, and performs the song, "I Feel It All."

» May 23, 2008 Following tour dates in the U.S. in February and March of 2008 and her Coast-to-Coast — One Last Time tour of Canada in April and May, Anne Murray plays her final public concert in Toronto at the Sony Centre.

» June 8, 2008 Singer, songwriter, broadcaster Roy Forbes (aka Bim) receives an honorary arts degree from Northern Lights College in his hometown of Dawson Creek, BC. The following day, the town renames the stretch of 11th Street from 96th to 97th Avenue Roy Forbes Drive during a ceremony led by Mayor Calvin Kruk.

» June 2008 Through their charitable foundation, Simple Plan donates $100,000 to organizatons that aid children or families experiencing difficulties due to handicaps or

illness, and on July 1, 2008, following a period of extensive world touring, Simple Plan return home to play a free concert on Québec City's Plains of Abraham to a reported crowd of 150,000.

» July 16, 2008 Toronto trio Rush make their first appearance on American TV in more than 30 years as they guest on *The Colbert Report*, during which they are interviewed by Stephen Colbert and perform "Tom Sawyer."

» July 19, 2008 Nelly Furtado marries Cuban recording engineer Demacio "Demo" Castillon.

» July 2008 Avril Lavigne launches her line of clothing branded Abbey Dawn.

» Summer 2008 The World Trance Festival, which will become the World Electric Music Festival (WEMF), is established. It will subsequently be held each year at venues around Ontario, most notably in Madawaska, Ontario.

» Summer 2008 The annual Heavy MTL, a two-day heavy metal and hard rock music festival, is held for the first time at Parc Jean-Drapeau in Montréal. A similar event, Heavy TO, was established at Downsview Park in Toronto in 2011 on the same weekend.

» Summer 2008 CBC Radio Two airs the five part series, *The People's Music*, a history of folk music in English Canada, produced by Gary Cristall, co-founder of the Vancouver Folk Festival and proprietor of the Vancouver-based Festival Records and Aural Traditions Records.

» August 11, 2008 On an episode of *Sesame Street*, Feist spends time with The Muppets and performs a reworked version of her hit song *"1234"* to teach the kids to count to four. She makes a cameo appearance in the 2011 film, *The Muppets*.

» August 29, 2008 Reminiscent of the threat of a concert ban made to Madonna by Toronto city officials if she got too sexy on stage during her May 27-29, 1990 concert dates at the Skydome (Rogers Centre), the Pan-Malaysian Islamic Party tries to have Avril Lavigne's concert in Kuala Lumpur cancelled given over concerns that she would not be promoting values compatible with theirs on the eve of Malaysia's Independence Day on August 31. More than a week before the date, the Malaysian government confirmed the concert would go on as scheduled.

» September 6, 2008 "Move For Me," deadmau5's collaboration with Kaskade, hits number one on the

Billboard Dance/MixShow Airplay chart, the first of three to enjoy the same status, including "I Remember" with Kaskade and "Ghosts 'n' Stuff" with Rob Swire.

>> **September 7, 2008** The Hendrix House Concert, featuring a number of local Vancouver artists, including Randy Bachman, perform the music of Jimi Hendrix in tribute to his Vancouver connection at 827 East Georgia Street, the one-time home of Nora Hendrix, the legendary guitarist's grandmother. It is broadcast live on CBC Radio 2.

>> **September 9, 2008** Kardinal Offishall's fourth album, *Not 4 Sale*, released during his four-year collaboration with chart-topping R&B/Hip-Hop producer, recording artist, songwriter Akon, produces the most successful single of his career, "Dangerous," which peaks at number five on the Billboard Hot 100 chart. The album subsequently wins a JUNO Award as Rap Recording of the Year.

>> **September 10, 2008** The sixth and final season of *Canadian Idol*, which premiered on June 3, 2008, comes to a close with Theo Tams of Lethbridge, Alberta as winner. Runner-up is Port Hood, Nova Scotia-born Mitch MacDonald. This season, R&B singer, songwriter Jully Black acts as special correspondent and mentor to the contestants.

>> **September 30, 2008** Singer, songwriter Carly Rae Jepsen, who came third in the 2007 edition of *Canadian Idol*, releases her debut album, *Tug of War*. The title track is Jepsen's first single, released on iTunes on September 16, 2008.

>> **October 2008** The Conservatives improve their standing in early general election but still fall short of gaining overall majority.

>> **November 11, 2008** Jazz singer Nikki Yanofsky makes her orchestral debut at the age of 14 with the Edmonton Symphony Orchestra in Edmonton.

>> **November 23, 2008** Feist guests on the Stephen Colbert Christmas special, *A Colbert Christmas: The Greatest Gift of All!*

>> **December 11, 2008** Michael Bublé becomes a minority shareholder in the Vancouver Giants of the Western Hockey League. The ownership group also includes hockey legend Gordie Howe, former Vancouver Canucks and Toronto Maple Leafs coach Pat Quinn, majority owner Ron Toigo and co-owner Sultan Thiara.

>> **December 2008** Finger Eleven tours Europe with Kid Rock including a date at the Hammersmith Apollo in London.

>> **December 2008** Opposition parties unite to bring down the minority

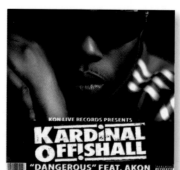

Conservative government but Prime Minister Stephen Harper asks Governor-General Michelle Jean to suspend parliament until January.

>> **2008** Justin Bieber, in his early teens and at home in Stratford, Ontario, has some performance videos posted on YouTube by his mother (Patricia "Pattie" Mallette). American artist manager Scooter Braun comes across them, is impressed and tracks him down. He subsequently introduces him to Atlanta, Georgia-based Usher [Raymond], one of the best selling artists in American music history. Usher likes him too and they sign Bieber to the Raymond Braun Media Group (RBMG) and subsequently arrange a record deal with Island Records through record executive, L.A. Reid.

>> **2008** New Orleans-based Hip Hop artist Lil Wayne invites Drake to join his crew, Young Money, and to tour with him after hearing some of his music.

>> **2008** Singer, songwriters Stephen Fearing, Catherine MacLellan, Murray McLauchlan and Paul Quarrington head out on their Canadian Songbook tour.

>> **2008** Singer, songwriter Susan Aglukark is appointed Distinguished Scholar in Residence at the University of Alberta.

>> **2008** Nanaimo, BC's Harbourfront Plaza undergoes a name-change to Diana Krall Plaza in honor of home girl, jazz pianist, vocalist Diana Krall.

>> **2008** Groups formed this year include Parallels, Toronto; Pardon My Striptease, Chilliwack, BC; Stereos, Edmonton, AB.

>> 2009

>> **January 21, 2009** Arcade Fire and Jay Z are the musical guests at President Barack Obama's Campaign Staff Ball at the DC Armory in Washington, DC, reportedly at the request of the President. Arcade Fire had played a number of free concerts for Obama prior to state Primaries in New Hampshire and North Carolina in the spring of 2008.

>> **February 1, 2009** Michael Bublé, Leslie Feist, Sting and former Fugees guitarist Wyclef Jean join host Daniel Levitin, neuroscientist, writer, producer and McGill University professor, in the CTV network film *My Musical Brain*, based on Levitin's best-selling book, *This Is Your Brain On Music*.

>> **February 13, 2009** Drake releases his third mixtape, *So Far Gone*, featuring the singles "Best I Ever Had" and "Successful." MTV refers to it as "The Hottest Mixtape of 2009 (So far)." Such is his reputation and stature as an artist, he begins working with a number of the biggest names in the genre, including Jay Z, Kanye West, Rihanna,

Eminem, Timbaland, Mary J. Blige, Jamie Foxx, Trey Songz, Alicia Keys and Dr. Dre.

» February 23-March 15, 2009 K'naan plays a free live show on the opening weekend of Arabesque: Arts of the Arab World, an international festival held at the John F. Kennedy Center for the Performing Arts in Washington, DC, which showcases the varied cultures of the 22 Arab nations that represent the Arabic-speaking world.

» February 24, 2009 Barenaked Ladies and group member Steven Page announce that, by mutual agreement, they had parted company.

» February 2009 Parliament passes a budget that includes a major stimulus package, thereby ensuring survival of the Conservative minority government in Canada.

» March 29, 2009 The 38th annual JUNO Awards are held at General Motors Place in Vancouver hosted by comedian Russell Peters. Nickelback carries the West Coast banner high as they lead the way by picking up three awards: Album of the Year, Group of the Year and Juno Fan Choice Award. Toronto-based rapper Kardinal Offishall takes home two JUNOs, one of which had a West Coast connection. "Dangerous," honoured as Single of the Year, was co-produced and co-written by hAZEL, the rap moniker of Ballet BC star Donald Sales. The Stills also pick up two awards: New Group of the Year and Alternative Album (*Oceans Will Rise*). Hometown heroes Loverboy are inducted into the Canadian Music Hall of Fame, and locally-based songstress Sarah McLachlan receives the Allan Waters Humanitarian Award. The Walt Grealis Special Achievement Award goes to long-time CHUM Limited broadcast executive, Fred Sherratt.

» March 2009 Glass Tiger and members of National Hockey League alumni visit Canadian Forces in Kandahar, Afghanistan.

» March 2009 Avril Lavigne launches Black Star, a perfume created by Procter & Gamble Prestige Products.

» Spring 2009 Carly Rae Jepsen tours western Canada with Marianas Trench and Shiloh. Both would be important in Jepsen's career. Josh Ramsay of Marianas Trench is the co-writer of Jepsen's first international hit, "Call Me Maybe" and Shiloh is the co-writer of her later hit single, "Tonight I'm Getting Over You." The same year, Jepsen undertakes a cross-Canada tour with Marianas Trench,

The New Cities and Mission District.

» Spring 2009 *Canadian Musician* magazine, founded in 1979 by publisher Jim Norris, the former drummer/vocalist with early '70s Toronto group, Sea Dog, celebrates its 30th anniversary.

» April 7, 2009 Neil Young releases the album *Fork In The Road*, in part a tribute to the automobile no doubt inspired by his current work on the production of a hybrid-engine 1959 Lincoln, which he dubs Lincvolt.

» July 2, 2009 Canada Post issues the second Canadian Recording Artist series of stamps, featuring Bryan Adams, Edith Butler, Robert Charlebois and Stompin' Tom Connors.

» July 4, 2009 Drake matches a chart milestone set earlier in the decade by fellow Canadian Nelly Furtado as his first two Top 10 hits, "Best I Ever Had" and "Every Girl," occur in the same week. In 2001, Furtado charted in the Top 10 with "I'm Like A Bird" the same week that Missy Elliott reached the same heights with "Get Ur Freak On," a remix which included a credited-contribution from Furtado.

» July 11, 2009 Broken Social Scene, including Feist, who appears with the band a number of times during this period, play a concert at Toronto's Harbourfront Centre. The concert, filmed by director Bruce Macdonald, is later released as the movie, *This Movie Is Broken*.

» August 10, 2009 Alanis Morissette first appears in the role of Dr. Audra Kitson in the popular TV series, *Weeds*.

» August 30-31, 2009 Shania Twain appears as a guest judge on *American Idol*.

» September 11, 2009 Nelly Furtado releases her fourth studio album, *Mi Plan*, her first in Spanish, on her own Nelstar Entertainment label. The album hits number one on the U.S. Latin Billboard chart and produces the single "Manos al Aire," which tops the charts and reportedly gives Furtado the distinction of being the first North American artist to have a number one record on the chart with an original Spanish song.

» September 21, 2009 Fucked Up's album *The Chemistry of Common Life* is the winner of the 2009 Polaris Prize.

» September 29, 2009 Sarah McLachlan releases the single "One Dream," the official theme song of the upcoming 2010 Winter Olympics in Vancouver.

>> **September 29, 2009** Diana Krall is in on a little recording history as producer of Barbra Streisand's album of jazz standards titled *Love Is the Answer*, on which she is also featured on piano. It becomes her ninth number one album on the Billboard 200 and gives Streisand the distinction of being the only artist to have a number one album in America in five different decades.

>> **October 5, 2009** Andrew Cash, who began his music career in the '80s in the Toronto punk band L'Étranger before signing to Island Records as a solo artist in 1986, is nominated as the New Democratic Party (NDP) candidate in the Toronto riding of Davenport. He was elected on May 2, 2011 and for a time sat in the House of Commons with fellow NDP Member of Parliament Charlie Angus, who was a bandmate of Cash's in L'Étranger.

>> **October 9, 2009** To launch his fourth studio album, *Crazy Love*, in the U.S., Michael Bublé appears on the *Oprah Winfrey Show* where he performs the debut single, "Haven't Met You Yet," a Bublé co-write.

>> **October 27, 2009** Anne Murray publishes her autobiography, *All of Me*, written in collaboration with author Michael Posner.

>> **October 2009** The Tom Cochrane song "Life Is A Highway" is voted the number one road song of all time in an Econo Lodge Travelin' Tunes online survey.

>> **November 17, 2009** Justin Bieber's debut record is released — an EP of seven songs with three co-written by Bieber titled *My World*. It debuts at number one on the Canadian Albums chart and peaks at number 5 in the U.S.

>> **December 5, 2009** In Mexico City, Avril Lavigne takes part in Latin America's biggest charity event, Teleton, an annual 24-hour TV and radio broadcast to raise money for children's rehabilitation centers.

>> **December 14, 2009** Nickelback are named Top Duo/Group of the decade by *Billboard Magazine* based on chart success. The group ranks number seven overall. The band's single "How You Remind Me" is named Top Rock Song of the decade and places at number four on the Top 10 Songs of the 2000s countdown.

>> **December 2009** The K'naan song "Wavin' Flag" is chosen by Coca-Cola as their anthem for the 2010 FIFA World Cup in South Africa. As part of Coca-Cola's FIFA World Cup Trophy Tour, K'naan performed the song live in 86 countries.

>> **December 2009** PM Stephen Harper prorogues parliament for two months.

>> **2009** Members of the group Hedley become ambassadors for *Free the Children*, an international charity.

>> **2009** Singer, songwriter, author, Dan Hill publishes his autobiography, *I Am My Father's Son: A Memoir of Love and Forgiveness*.

>> **2009** Groups formed this year include Audio Playground, Edmonton, AB; Crash Karma, Toronto; LeE HARVeY OsMOND, Ontario; The Heartbroken, Toronto.

CHART-TOPPING CANADIAN SONGS 2000-2009

2000 I'm Like A Bird NELLY FURTADO
2000 Faded Soul DECISION
2000 Bang Bang Boom THE MOFFATTS
2001 How You Remind Me NICKELBACK
2001 Completely Serial JOE
2001 Days Like That SUGAR JONES
2002 Canadian Man PAUL BRANDT
2002 Get Ready SHAWN DESMAN
2002 Hero CHAD KROEGER
2002 Hands Clean ALANIS MORISSETTE
2002 Movin' On THE BOOMTANG BOYS
2003 I Drove All Night CELINE DION
2003 Something More RYAN MALCOLM
2003 Someday NICKELBACK

2003 I'm Gonna Getcha Good SHANIA TWAIN
2004 Awake In A Dream KALAN PORTER
2005 On My Own HEDLEY
2005 Photograph NICKELBACK
2005 Alive MELISSA O'NEIL
2005 Paper Rain AMANDA STOTT
2006 Meant To Fly EVA AVILA
2006 Promiscuous NELLY FURTADO FEATURING TIMBALAND
2006 Say It Right NELLY FURTADO
2006 Bad Day DANIEL POWTER
2007 Give It To Me TIMBALAND FEATURING NELLY FURTADO AND JUSTIN TIMBERLAKE
2007 Girlfriend AVRIL LAVIGNE

OH WHAT A FEELING

You know you love me, I know you care
Just shout whenever, and I'll be there
You are my love, you are my heart
And we will never, ever, ever be apart...

— Baby

Featuring Ludacris, Lyrics & Music by
Justin Bieber, Christopher "Tricky"
Stewart, Terius "The-Dream" Nash,
Christopher Bridges and Christina
Milan. Performed by Justin Bieber.

»2010–2013

>> 2010

>> **January 12, 2010** A 7.1 magnitude earthquake devastates Haiti, claiming between 230,000 and 300,000 lives and leaving 1.5k million people homeless.

>> **January 18, 2010** Justin Bieber's single "Baby," featuring Ludacris, from the album *My World 2.0*, the second half of Bieber's debut opus, makes Bieber an international star as it charts in the Top 10 around the world. The video for the song, which features cameos from fellow Canadian recording artist Drake and Lil Twist, becomes the most-viewed video in YouTube history until November 24, 2012 when "Gangham Style" by PSY surpassed it.

>> **January 22, 2010** Neil Young performs "Long May You Run" on the final episode of *The Tonight Show* with Conan O'Brien. The same night, Young and Dave Matthews perform the song "Alone and Forsaken" for *Hope For Haiti Now: A Global Benefit for Earthquake Relief* charity telethon for the victims of the 2010 Haiti earthquake.

>> **January 22, 2010** The nationally-televised *Canada For Haiti/Ensemble pour Haiti* telethons, created jointly by Canadian networks CBC, CTV and Global and TVA, Société Radio-Canada and MusiquePlus to aid earthquake victims in that country, feature appearances by Geddy Lee (Rush) and opera/concert singer Measha Brueggergosman as well as performances from Nelly Furtado ("Try"), The Tragically Hip ("Fiddler's Green"), K'naan ("Wavin' Flag") and Metric ("Help, I'm Alive"). The Québec-based networks feature performers Daniel Boucher, Bruno Pelletier, Diane Dufresne, Gregory Charles, Pierre Lapointe, Marie-Jo Thério, Nomadic Massive, Roberto Lopez and La troupe Mapou Ginen, among others. Reportedly, the telethons raise $16 million, not including matching funds from the Canadian government.

>> **January 30, 2010** Michael Bublé appears on *Saturday Night Live* with host Jon Hamm.

>> **February 7, 2010** The Arcade Fire song "Wake Up," which has become a popular soundtrack for a variety of broadcast media, is heard in commercials that run during the broadcast of Super Bowl XLIV from Sun Life Stadium in Miami, Florida.

>> **February 12, 2010** The opening ceremony for the 2010 Winter Olympics is held at BC Place Stadium in

▲ Canada for Haiti/Ensemble pour Haiti

Vancouver which, along with Whistler, B.C., is hosting the Games. Among the Canadian artists who participate are 16-year-old Nikki Yanofsky, who sings an arrangement of the national anthem "O Canada," Bryan Adams and Nelly Furtado, who perform "Bang the Drum," written by Adams and songwriter/producer Jim Vallance as a tribute to the Olympic athletes, Sarah McLachlan, who performs her song "Ordinary Miracle," Loreena McKennitt, who performs the song "The Old Ways," as part of a tribute to the fiddling tradition of Canada, during which Cape Breton fiddler Ashley MacIsaac plays his version of the 19th-century strathspey, "Devil In the Kitchen," k.d. lang, who performs the Leonard Cohen song "Hallelujah," soprano Measha Brueggergosman, who sings the Olympic Hymn and Garou, who provide their rendition of the Jean-Pierre Ferland song, "Un peu plus haut, un peu plus loin" ("A Little Higher, A Little Faster") "I Believe," co-written by Stephan Moccio and Alan Frew (Glass Tiger) and sung by Nikki Yanofsky, is the official promotional song for CTV's coverage of these Winter Games as well as the 2012 Summer Olympics in London. There is also a French version "J'imagine", sung by Annie Villeneuve, and an instrumental recording by Moccio. The BBC in the U.K. uses the big-band jazz version of the song "Cry Me A River," which opens Michael Bublé's Crazy Love album, for their Olympic advertising/promotion and as the theme music for their coverage of the Games. Bryan Adams' "One World, One Flame" is used by German TV station ARD for their Olympic coverage.

>> **February 28, 2010** The closing ceremony of the 2010 Winter Olympics is held at BC Place Stadium in Vancouver.

A bilingual version of the Canadian national anthem sung by the Vancouver Youth Symphony Orchestra and Inward Eyes precedes the entrance of the flag bearers and the parade of the athletes and then the invitation to the festivities is delivered by Eva Avila, Derek Miller and Nikki Yanofsky with the song "Let's Have A Party." The Greek national anthem is sung by Canadian mezzo-soprano Ariana Chris while Canadian tenor, Ben Heppner, who had sung the Canadian national anthem at the 2006 closing ceremony in Torino, Italy, sings the Olympic Hymn. Neil Young sings "Long May You Run" as the Olympic Flame is being extinguished and the Games are declared closed. Following comedic monologues by actors William Shatner, Michael J. Fox and Catherine O'Hara on Canadian stereotypes, singer, songwriter Michael Bublé appears dressed as a Mountie performing an "arrangement" of "The Maple Leaf Forever." He was followed by La Bottine Souriante ("Envoyons d'l'avant nos gens"). The closing cultural section concert features Nickelback ("Burn It To the Ground"), Avril Lavigne, who performed "Who Knows" at the closing ceremony of the Torino Olympics, ("My Happy Ending" and "Girlfriend"), Alanis Morissette ("Wunderkind"), Hedley ("Cha-Ching"), Simple Plan ("Your Love Is A Lie"), Marie-Mai ("Emmène-moi"), k-os ("Eye Know Something") and Scrap Arts Music (excerpts from "Phonk"). The event, televised by CTV, is reportedly the second-most watched event in Canadian television history with 14.3 million viewers and a total of 24.5 million watching some part of the ceremonies. The most-watched television broadcast ever in Canada? — The gold medal hockey game at these same Olympics between Canada and the U.S., which draws an average audience of 16.6 million viewers to see Canada emerge victorious in overtime 3-2 on Sidney Crosby's golden goal. 80 percent of Canadians

▲ K'naan

watched some part of the game (26.5 million).

>> **March 12, 2010** A version of the K'naan song "Wavin' Flag," recorded on February 18 by more than 50 Canadian artists under the name Young Artists For Haiti, is released with all proceeds going to help the victims of the earthquake in Haiti. Produced by Bob Ezrin and recorded at Bryan Adams' Warehouse Studio in Vancouver, the song features K'naan and some of Canada's biggest stars, including Nelly Furtado, Avril Lavigne, Drake, Michael Bublé, Justin Bieber, Tom Cochrane, Jim Cuddy (Blue Rodeo), Pierre Bouvier (Simple Plan), Tyler Connolly (Theory of a Deadman), Deryck Whibley (Sum 41), Jacob Hoggard (Hedley), Serena Ryder, Kardinall Offishall, Nikki Yanofsky, Canadian Tenors, Sam Roberts and Emily Haines (Metric, Broken Social Scene). It becomes only the third single in history to debut at number one on the Canadian Hot 100 chart (March 27, 2010).

>> **March 26, 2010** Alanis Morissette marries rapper Mario "MC Souleye" Treadway in a private ceremony.

>> **April 18, 2010** The 39th annual JUNO Awards are held at the Mile One Centre in St. John's Newfoundland and Labrador under threat of disruption from an ash cloud that had formed from a volcanic eruption in Iceland and led to the closure of most European airports. Bryan Adams is forced to accept his Allan Waters Humanitarian Award by satellite after he is unable to fly in. But the festivities go on as Michael Bublé matches his 2006 domination of the JUNOs by taking home four awards, including Pop Album and Album of the Year (*Crazy Love*), Single of the Year ("Haven't Met You Yet") and the coveted JUNO Fan Choice Award. Bob Rock is named Producer of the Year for his work on the Bublé songs "Haven't Met You Yet" and "Baby (You've Got What It Takes)." The other multiple award winners

▲ Ben Heppner

include Drake in the categories of Rap Recording of the Year ("So Far Gone") and New Artist of the Year; K'naan is named Artist and Songwriter of the Year for songs on his *Troubadour* album; and Metric, who take the group honours, also have their disc *Fantasies* named Alternative Album of the Year. Barry Stock of Three Days Grace hosts April Wine's induction into the Canadian Music Hall of Fame, while the Walt Grealis Special Achievement Award is presented to the former head of Universal Music Canada and a founding board member of the Canadian Academy of Recording Arts & Sciences (CARAS), Ross Reynolds.

>> **April 24, 2010** *Rush: Beyond the Lighted Stage*, directed by Scot McFadyen and Sam Dunn, premieres at the Tribeca Film Festival in New York and wins the Festival's Audience Award.

>> **May 10, 2010** The tracks "Stop For A Minute" and "Looking Back" on the EP *Night Train* by British group Keane are collaborations with Somali/Canadian rapper K'naan.

>> **May 14, 2010** Alan Doyle of Great Big Sea is seen in the role of Alan A'Dayle in the Ridley Scott film *Robin Hood* co-starring with Cate Blanchett, Kevin Durand and Russell Crowe, with whom Doyle has been working as producer and co-writer on a number of Crowe's music projects.

>> **June 9, 2010** Shania Twain and producer Robert John "Mutt" Lange finalize their divorce.

>> **June 15, 2010** Drake releases his debut album, *Thank Me Later*, and celebrates with a free concert at New York's South Street Seaport that also features Hanson. The police risk a full-scale riot when they close it down because of the size of the crowd. *Thank Me Now* debuts at number one on the Billboard Hot 200 album chart.

>> **June 17, 2010** The Broken Social Scene concert film *This Movie is Broken* premieres during North By Northeast (NXNE) in Toronto.

>> **June 23, 2010** Justin Bieber kicks off his lengthy My World tour, his first as a headliner, at the XL Centre in Hartford, Connecticut. It will wrap at Estadio de Futbol de la USB in Caracas, Venezuela on October 11, 2011.

>> **June 25, 2010** Rush receive a star on the Hollywood Walk of Fame.

>> **June 27, 2010** Sarah McLachlan revives Lilith Fair with the intention of touring through North America followed by a two-week tour of Europe. The tour, which was modified due to poor ticket sales in some markets, kicks off at McMahon Stadium in Calgary on this date.

>> **June 2010** The annual Manitoba Electronic Music Exhibition (MEME), an electronic music and digital arts festival, is held for the first time featuring workshops and free outdoor concerts at The Cube in Old Market Square, part of the Exchange District in Winnipeg, Manitoba.

>> **August 2, 2010** Drake hosts the first annual OVO (October's Very Own) Festival/Concert in Toronto featuring Eminem, Jay Z, Rick Ross, Bun B, Fabolous, Kardinal Offishall and Young Jeezy.

>> **August 3, 2010** Arcade Fire's third album, *The Suburbs*, is released with eight different covers. It debuts at number one on the Billboard 200 chart and is a number one record in Canada and the U.K. On August 4 and 5, the group introduces the album to America with two sold-out shows at New York's Madison Square Gardens. The concert, which features opening artists Owen Pallett, Spoon and Britt Daniel, is webcast on YouTube on the second night, directed by writer, broadcaster and Monty Python alumnus, Terry Gilliam.

>> **August 5, 2010** Sum 41's Deryck Whibley is attacked by three men in a bar in Japan and is hospitalized after tests reveal that his back has been re-injured, having sustained a slipped disc a second time.

>> **August 2010** Arcade Fire explore the capabilities of the new technologies as they partner with Google (Google Maps and Google Chrome) in releasing an interactive video/film by Chris Milk, titled *The Wilderness Downtown*, which features the song "We Used To Wait." Viewers can personalize the film by inputting the address of the house in which they grew up and have the action unfold in their old neighbourhood with shots of the house incorporated.

>> **September 12, 2010** deadmau5 is named the house DJ for the 2010 MTV Video Music Awards at the Nokia Theater in Los Angeles during which he performs with Jason Derulo and Travie McCoy.

>> **September 20, 2010** Drake opens his Lights, Dreams and Nightmares Tour of North America in Miami. It wraps in Las Vegas on November 6.

>> **September 22, 2010** Avril Lavigne announces the launch of The Avril Lavigne Foundation, which supports children and youth living with disabilities and serious illnesses.

>> **September 23, 2010** Justin Bieber guest stars in the season premiere of the CBS crime drama

▲ Alan Doyle of Great Big Sea (far left) in the Ridley Scott film Robin Hood

CSI: Crime Scene Investigation. He appears in a subsequent episode of the show (February 17, 2011) in which his character (Jason McCann) is killed off.

>> **September 23, 2010** Vancouver band Marianas Trench make their U.S. debut at the Bowery Electric in Manhattan, New York.

>> **September 24, 2010** Ivan Doroschuk re-forms the band Men Without Hats and the following year they set out on the Dance If You Want Tour 2011.

>> **September 24-25, 2010** As his *Crazy Love* album tops the charts in Canada, the U.S. and Australia, Michael Bublé gets a whole lotta love from the Irish as he plays to a reported 95,895 fans over two nights at the Aviva Stadium in Dublin as part of his Crazy Love Tour. They are the first concerts at the venue which opened on May 14 of this year.

>> **September 26, 2010** Launch Party at Hugh's Room in Toronto for *World Jazz For Haiti*, a double CD compilation of 23 original songs produced to raise funds for the disaster relief effort in Haiti. Contributions come from Canadian artists living in Toronto, including David Clayton-Thomas, Guido Basso, Holly Cole, Jane Bunnett and John McDermott.

>> **October 2010** Jazz singer Nikki Yanofsky is the first recipient of the Allan Slaight Award presented as part of the Canada's Walk of Fame celebrations to a young Canadian for "making a positive impact in the fields of music, film, literature, visual or performing arts, sports, innovation or philanthropy." The latest receipients include Drake and Melanie Fiona.

>> **October 2010** The video game *DJ Hero 2* features deadmau5 as a playable avatar. He has a number of tracks in the game including "Ghosts 'N Stuff" in a mix with Lady Gaga's "Just Dance."

>> **November 4, 2010** Rush receive the 2010 Legends of Live award at the Billboard Touring Awards.

>> **November 11, 2010** At the 11th annual Latin Grammy Awards held at the Mandalay Bay Events Centre in Las Vegas, Nelly Furtado and Alex Cuba become the first Canadian recipients of a Latin Grammy: Furtado for Best Female Pop Vocal Album (*Mi Plan*) and Cuba as Best New Artist.

>> **November 13, 2010** Arcade Fire appear on *Saturday Night Live* with host Scarlett Johansson.

FACE THE MUSIC
TOUR
MARIANAS TRENCH

AVEC INVITÉS SPÉCIAUX

JEUDI 18 OCTOBRE
METRPOLIS

Billets: Metropolis - Admission/Ticketmaster - Cheap Thrills - Off The Hook - evenko.ca

>> 2011

>> **January 1, 2011** In Rincon, Puerto Rico, Shania Twain marries Nestlé executive Frédéric Thiébaud, the former husband of Twain's best friend who allegedly had an affair with her former husband, Robert John "Mutt" Lange.

>> **January 19, 2011** Alan Doyle of Great Big Sea guest stars with Russell Crowe, Kevin Durand and Scott Grimes in the third season opening episode of the CBC-TV series *Republic of Doyle*.

>> **February 10-20, 2011** Arcade Fire debut the short film, *Scenes From the Suburbs* by director Spike Jonze, at the 61st Berlin International Film Festival.

>> **February 11, 2011** *Justin Bieber: Never Say Never*, the 3D concert film/biopic which documents the 10-day countdown to his August 31, 2010 concert at New York's Madison Square Gardens and also includes a visit to his hometown of Stratford, Ontario, is released in the U.S. and Canada.

>> **February 13, 2011** Arcade Fire perform at the 53rd annual Grammy Awards at the Staples Center in Los Angeles at which the group had three nominations. They win the Grammy for Album of the Year (*The Suburbs*).

>> **February 15, 2011** K'naan is co-writer on the Bruno Mars single "The Lazy Song" which tops the chart in the U.K.

>> **February 19, 2011** Bryan Adams and his band become the first international artists to perform in Nepal as they play a concert in Kathmandu.

DJ Hero 2 features deadmau5 avatar

>> **March 6, 2011** The Prism song "Spaceship Superstar" provides the wake-up call for Space Shuttle Discovery crew members on the day that the Discovery departed the International Space Station and headed back to earth on its last mission.

>> **March 15, 2011** Simple Plan donate $10,000 to the Japan Red Cross relief efforts and rally their fans to give as well in the wake of the devastation in Japan as a result of a major earthquake, tsunami and nuclear power plant meltdown on March 11, 2011.

>> **March 27, 2011** The 40th annual JUNO Awards are held at the Air Canada Centre in Toronto and hosted by rapper Drake, who comes to the Awards with six nominations but remarkably leaves empty-handed. Arcade Fire makes the headlines this year as they win four JUNOs, including those for Album, Alternative Album (*The Suburbs*), Group and Best Songwriters. Neil Young, who is honoured with the Allan Waters Humanitarian Award, also picks up JUNOs as Artist of the Year and for Adult Alternative Album of the Year (*Le Noise*). JUNO Fan Choice award goes to Justin Bieber, who also picked up an award for Best Pop Album (*My World 2.0*). Of note, Deadmau5 wins his fourth consecutive JUNO for Dance Recording ("Sofi Needs A Ladder"). Deane Cameron, long-time president of EMI Music Canada, receives the Walt Grealis Special Achievement Award, while Shania Twain is inducted into the Canadian Music Hall of Fame. Marking the JUNO 40th anniversary milestone is the coffee-table book *Music From Far and Wide*, co-written by music journalists Karen Bliss, Nick Krewen, Larry LeBlanc and Jason Schneider, with a foreword by Jim Cuddy of Blue Rodeo.

>> **March 31, 2011** Michael Bublé marries Argentine model and actress Luisana Lopilato in Buenos Aires.

>> **May 3, 2011** Shania Twain releases her autobiography, *From This Moment On*.

>> **May 8, 2011** The TV series *Why Not?* with Shania Twain premieres on the Oprah Winfrey Network (OWN).

>> **May 10-11, 2011** As part of his solo Twisted Road tour, Neil Young plays two nights at Toronto's Massey Hall. It is the venue where 40 years ago, in 1971, he had introduced many of the songs at the heart of one of his most popular albums, *Harvest*. Portions of the concert are documented in Jonathan Demme's third film on Young titled *Neil Young Journeys*, which premieres at the Toronto International Film Festival in September of that year.

>> **June 2, 2011** Shania Twain is given a star on the Hollywood Walk of Fame.

>> **June 15, 2011** Sarah McLachlan receives an honorary degree from Vancouver's Simon Fraser University.

>> **August 1, 2011** Saskatoon, Saskatchewan-based band The Sheepdogs win *Rolling Stone* magazine's "Do You Wanna Be a Rock & Roll Star" competition, which includes getting onto the cover.

>> **September 10, 2011** Sarah McLachlan performs "I Will Remember You" and "Angel" at the dedication of the Flight 93 National Memorial in Shanksville, Pennsylvania, a tribute to the passengers and crew of hijacked United Airlines Flight 93 who resisted the hijackers causing the plane to crash. The action was thought to have saved thousands of lives in the nation's capital where the plane was headed. Presidents George W. Bush and Bill Clinton, Vice President Joe Biden and Speaker John Boehner are on hand for the ceremony.

>> **September 21, 2011** The release date of the Carly Rae Jepsen single "Call Me Maybe," co-written and produced by Josh Ramsay of the band Marianas Trench, the Canadian West Coast band who are her label mates at 604 Records. 604 had been founded by Chad Kroeger of Nickelback and music attorney Jonathan Simkin, her manager.

>> **October 15, 2011** Drake appears on *Saturday Night Live* with host Anna Faris.

>> **October 15, 2011** K'naan is one of eight performers at the Decade of Difference concert at the Hollywood Bowl in Los Angeles to celebrate President Bill Clinton's 65th birthday and the 10th anniversary of the Clinton Foundation. During his portion of the show, K'naan surprised the audience by bringing Bono of U2 on to the stage for a duet.

>> **November 15, 2011** Drake releases his fourth album, *Take Care*, the title track of which features Barbadian recording artist Rihanna and becomes his biggest hit internationally. The three number one hits from the album,": "Headlines," "Make Me Proud" (featuring Nicki Minaj) and "The Motto" (featuring Lil Wayne) help Drake reach the milestones of the most number one hits on the Billboard Hot Rap Songs chart with 13, and, as a rap artist, the most number one hits on the Billboard Hot R&B/Hip-Hop Songs chart, with ten.

>> **November 24, 2011** Nickelback perform "When We Stand Together" during halftime at the NFL Thanksgiving Day game at Ford Field in Detroit despite local football fans' protests backed up by an online petition with 55,000 signatures asking that they not play. Many felt that a Canadian band was not appropriate for this all-American game and holiday. The band played the halftime show of the Canadian Football League's 99th Grey Cup game in their hometown of Vancouver a few days later. (November 27).

>> **December 2, 2011** The cover of the posthumously-released Amy Winehouse album *Lioness: Hidden Treasures* is a portrait of the late singer in 2007 shot by Bryan Adams.

>> **December 17, 2011** Michael Bublé appears on *Saturday Night Live* with host Jimmy Fallon.

>> **2011** Bryan Adams is the voice of *Jock the Hero Dog* in the animated film of the same name which also features the voices of Donald Sutherland, Helen Hunt, Ted Danson, Desmond Tutu, Mandy Patinkin and William Baldwin. Adams also provides the soundtrack.

>> 2012

>> **January 2012** While on holiday in Canada, Justin Bieber and girlfriend Selena Gomez hear the Carly Rae Jepsen single "Call Me Maybe" on the radio. When both mentioned the song on twitter, the interest in Jepsen grew. In February, she finds herself in Los Angeles meeting with Bieber and his manager Scooter Braun.

>> **February 13, 2012** The Canadian Broadcasting Corporation launches *CBC Music* (cbcmusic.ca) and the *CBC Music App*, a free digital music service with an initial choice of 40 different web radio stations, 14 distinct genre-based communities and music from nearly 1000 major and independent music companies as well as more than 25,000 independent artists with thousands of songs available for play. *The CBC Music App* allows listeners to stream the service to their iPad, iPhone or iPod touch, including 40 web radio stations as well as CBC Radio 2 and CBC Radio 3.

>> **March 4, 2012** *Canada's Got Talent*, the Canadian version of the Simon Cowell-created "Got Talent" internationally-franchised TV shows, debuts on Citytv for its first and only season. The judges are soprano Measha Brueggergosman, composer Stephan Moccio and comedic actor Martin Short.

>> **March 12, 2012** *The Hunger Games* film soundtrack album, *The Hunger Games: Songs from District 12 and Beyond*, which contains the song "Abraham's Daughter" by Arcade Fire which had played over the film's end credits, debuts at number one on the Billboard 200 chart. The group also contribute "Horn of Plenty" (the national anthem of the fascist Capitol), one of the main themes heard as part of *The Hunger Games* original motion picture score.

>> **April 1, 2012** The 41st annual JUNO Awards are held at Scotiabank Place in Ottawa, Ontario and hosted by actor William Shatner. Feist wins a trio of awards including Artist of the Year, Adult Alternative Album (*Metals*) and Music DVD (*Feist: Look At What the Light Did Now*). The Sheepdogs from Saskatoon pick up their first JUNOs this year, prevailing in the categories of New Group, Single of the Year ("I Don't Know") and Rock Album (*Learn & Burn*). Blue Rodeo are inducted into the Canadian Music Hall of Fame with the help of Sarah McLachlan while broadcast executive Gary Slaight is the recipient of the Walt Grealis Special Achievement Award. Simple Plan, who earned their first and only JUNO in 2006 as the Fan Choice Award winners, are the recipients this year of the Allan Waters Humanitarian Award.

>> **April 17, 2012** Canadian music industry executive and artist manager (Bruce Cockburn) Bernie Finkelstein releases his autobiography, *True North: A Life in the Music Business*.

>> **May 19, 2012** Arcade Fire appear on *Saturday Night Live* as backing band for host/musical guest Mick Jagger on songs like "Last Time," She's A Rainbow" and "Ruby Tuesday." The group members wear carrés rouge (red squares) to show solidarity with the student protests back home in Québec.

>> **May 22, 2012** Alanis Morissette appears on the Ellen Degeneres Show which also features Katy Perry.

>> **June 12, 2012** Tom Cochrane receives the Key To the City of Winnipeg, Manitoba.

>> **June 19, 2012** Justin Bieber releases his third studio album, *Believe*, which debuts at number one on the Canadian Album chart. He kicks off The Believe Tour in support of the album at the Jobing.com Arena in Glendale, Arizona on September 2, 2012. It is scheduled to wrap at the Philips Arena in Atlanta, Georgia on August 10, 2013.

>> **June 21, 2012** Canadian Defence Minister Peter MacKay announces that singer, songwriter, actress Sass Jordan has been appointed as the next Honorary Colonel of 417 Combat Support (CS) Squadron based at 4 Wing Cold Lake, Alberta.

>> **June 30, 2012** There are 2.4 billion Internet users in the world, 273.8 million in North America, 167.3 million in Africa, 1.1 billion in Asia, 518.5 million in Europe, 90 million in the Middle East, 255 million in Latin America/Caribbean and 24.3 million in Oceania/Australia. (For comparison, see December 31, 2000)

>> **June 2012** Bryan Adams receives the German magazine trade's Lead Award for his fashion photos of British heiress and style icon Honourable Daphne Guinness. He had previously won a Lead Award in 2006 for a series of photographs titled "Mickey Rourke by Bryan Adams" shot in London the previous year.

>> **August 21, 2012** Avril Lavigne and Nickelback frontman Chad Kroeger announce their engagement.

>> **September 13, 2012** Jazz pianist and vocalist Diana Krall performs "Fly Me To the Moon" at the memorial service in Washington, D.C. for astronaut Neil Armstrong.

>> **September 18, 2012** Former Moxy Fruvous band member and host of CBC Radio One program *Q*, Jian Ghomeshi hits the top of the best-seller list in Canada with his first book, *1982*.

>> **September 18, 2012** Justin Bieber's mother, Pattie Mallette, releases her autobiography, *Nowhere But Up: The Story of Justin Bieber's Mom*.

>> **September 25, 2012** Neil Young releases his autobiography, *Waging Heavy Peace: A Hippie Dream*.

>> **September 2012** Marianas Trench undertake their first headline tour of Australia and, on their return home, they kick off their first Canadian headline arena tour with Down With Webster, Anami Vice and Jesse Giddings in Barrie, Ontario on October 12, 2012.

>> **October 2012** *Music Express* magazine, published and edited by Keith Sharp, is revived as an online publication, the latest installment of a publishing saga that began in 1976 in Calgary where the magazine had its beginnings as the *Alberta Music Express*. The story is documented in Sharp's 2013 book *Music Express: Rise and Fall of a Canadian Music Icon*.

>> **November 16, 2012** Feist writes the song "Fire in the Water" for the blockbuster film *The Twilight Saga: Breaking Dawn — Part 2* which is released on this date.

>> **December 1, 2012** Shania Twain premieres her Las Vegas production *Shania: Still the One* at the Colosseum at Caesar's Palace. The residency concert runs for 36 shows until June 1, 2013.

▲ Johnny Reid

>> **December 4, 2012** Jazz singer Nikki Yanofsky is one of the performers at an all-star tribute to Carole King at the Dolby Theatre in Los Angeles hosted by Quincy Jones, Jack Nicholson and Danny DeVito.

>> **December 2012** Carly Rae Jepsen's "Call Me Maybe," reportedly the best-selling single worldwide in 2012, tops most of the year-end music charts and lists. It is named Song of the Year for 2012 by MTV and, at Billboard, it ranks number two on the Hot 100 Songs, Digital Songs and Canadian Hot 100 charts.

>> **2012** Seven Canadian artists: Lights, Pierre Bouvier (Simple Plan), Jacob Hoggard (Hedley), Fefe Dobson, Kardinal Offishall, Alyssa Reid and Walk Off the Earth, join together under the banner Artists Against Bullying to record a version of the Cyndi Lauper hit, "True Colors." Proceeds are donated to Kids Help Phone, a Canadian counselling service for children and youth.

>> **2012** In commemoration of their 10th anniversary and to raise money for their foundation, Simple Plan release the book, *Simple Plan: The Official Story*.

>> **2012** Young jazz singer Nikki Yanofsky tours Canada as opening act for acclaimed singing quartet, Il Divo.

>> 2013

>> **January 22, 2013** The self-titled, third major label album by rapper Classified (Luke Boyd) — he has 15 albums overall at this point — debuts at number one on the Canadian Albums Chart. The first single "Inner Ninja" peaks at number 5 on the Canadian Hot 100 and earns Classified a JUNO Award for Rap Recording of the Year. The song also becomes his second platinum-selling single; "Oh... Canada" was his first.

>> **February 1, 2013** The Shania Twain Centre in Timmins, Ontario permanently closes. It is announced that it is to be demolished to become part of an open-pit gold mine. Many of the items of memorabilia had been removed in May of 2012 and relocated to Las Vegas where Twain has a long-term contract for shows.

>> **February 8, 2013** "I.S.S. (Is Somebody Singing?)," the song recorded by Barenaked Ladies' Ed Robertson and the glee choir of Wexford Collegiate School For the Arts, performing at the CBC Broadcast Centre in Toronto, and Canadian astronaut Chris Hadfield, making his contribution from the International Space Station in orbit, premieres on

CBCMusic.ca Co-written by Robertson and Hadley, the song was commissioned by CBCMusic.ca, The Coalition of Music Education and The Canadian Space Agency to promote and celebrate music education in schools across Canada.

>> **February 9, 2013** Justin Bieber appears on *Saturday Night Live*.

>> **April 13, 2013** Jazz singer Nikki Yanofsky sings a duet with Stevie Wonder on the song, "Let the Good Times Roll" at a star-studded gala event at the MGM Grand Garden Arena in Las Vegas to celebrate the 80th birthday of both producer, musician Quincy Jones and actor Sir Michael Caine.

>> **April 18, 2013** Rush is inducted into the Rock and Roll Hall of Fame in Cleveland, Ohio.

>> **April 21, 2013** The 42nd annual JUNO Awards are held at the Brandt Centre in Regina, Sakatchewan with Michael Bublé as host. Newcomer Carly Rae Jepsen wins in the categories of Album, Pop Album (*Kiss*) and Single of the Year ("Call Me Maybe"), co-written by Josh Ramsay, vocalist of the group Marianas Trench, while popular indie band Metric win for Alternative Album of the Year (*Synthetica*) which also gets the nod for Best Packaging and Producer of the Year (Jimmy Shaw). Leonard Cohen wins the fifth and sixth JUNOs of his career for Artist of the Year and Songwriter of the Year, presented and accepted by his son, Adam Cohen, due to Leonard's absence. Rush wins in the category of Best Rock Album (*Clockwork Angels*) but loses out to Marianas Trench as Group of the Year. Justin Bieber, a no-show on the night, wins his third straight JUNO Fan Choice award. k.d. lang is inducted into the Canadian Music Hall of Fame by Anne Murray. Recipient of the Walt Grealis Special Achievement Award is music journalist Larry LeBlanc.

>> **April 21, 2013** Michael Bublé has the fastest selling album of the year to this point — and of his own career — as his record *To Be Loved* becomes his fourth consecutive number one album on the Billboard 200 albums chart.

>> **April 2013** Canadian Astronaut and International Space Station

▲ Robert Michaels

Commander Col. Chris Hadfield and Ed Robertson of the Barenaked Ladies record the first duet performed simultaneously from Earth and Space. The title of the song "I.S.S. Is Somebody Singing?"

>> **Spring 2013** R&B singer, songwriter and actor Robin Thicke, son of popular Canadian TV host, actor and musician Alan Thicke, has a worldwide, chart-topping hit with the single/video "Blurred Lines" featuring T.I. and Pharrell, the title track from his sixth studio album released on July 30, 2013. Thicke has written songs for a number of top artists in the genre, including Christina Aguilera, Mary J. Blige and Jennifer Hudson.

>> **May 12, 2013** Accompanying himself on guitar, Col. Chris Hadfield performs the David Bowie song "Space Oddity" as he leaves the International Space Station.

>> **May 18, 2013** Montréal's newest concert venue, the 730-seat Théatre Symposia, opens with a concert by Chantal Kreviazuk on the occasion of her 40th birthday.

>> **June 1, 2013** JUNO and Canadian Country Music Award-winning singer and songwriter Johnny Reid, who remarkably held down a full 10 percent of the Country Top 50 album chart of Canadian and International best-sellers in Canada in the summer of 2012, receives an honorary law degree from his alma mater, Bishop's University, where he was, among other things, a football hero as place-kicker for the Gaiters. At the time, he was also putting the finishing touches on his highly-anticipated Christmas album, on which he is collaborating with award-winning producer and Canadian Music Hall of Fame inductee, Bob Ezrin (Pink Floyd, Alice Cooper, KISS).

>> **June 2013** The award-winning Los Angeles-based theatrical music company Vox Lumiere, co-founded by Montréal-born singer and songwriter Victoria Levy and her husband, acclaimed composer Kevin Saunders Hayes, is into pre-production on *Peter Pan*, the fifth in a series of productions the company has undertaken since its founding in 2000. Other productions have included *Metropolis*, *The Hunchback*

▲ Victoria Levy of Vox Lumiere

of Notre Dame, also a PBS TV special, *Phantom of the Opera* and *Intolerance*. Vox Lumiere combines the energy of a rock concert, featuring new Hayes-composed scores for the featured silent films projected on a huge screen on stage, with the dynamism and drama of live theatrical performance as the rock band, singers and dancers interact with the film.

>> **June 2013** Juno Award-winning guitarist and platinum-selling recording artist Robert Michaels completes work on his 8th album *Via Italia*, a musical tribute to his family's Italian roots featuring fresh arrangements of Italian vocal and instrumental standards, along with several new original compositions inspired by the music and culture of Italy.

>> **2013** "The Godfather of Canadian Hip Hop" Maestro (formerly Maestro Fresh Wes) (Wesley Williams) announces that his new album, *Orchestrated Noise*, is a "conceptual extension" of his 1989 debut album *Symphony In*

Effect, which was not only ground-breaking for Maestro as an artist but also for the Hip-Hop genre in general.

>> **July 1, 2013** Avril Lavigne and Chad Kroeger (Nickelback) are married just outside of Château de la Napoule, a 14th-century castle in the town of Mandelieu-la-Napoule on the French Riviera.

>> **July 4, 2013** 16-year-old Ebony Oshunrinde (aka WondaGurl) of Brampton, Ontario produces beat for the track "Crown" on Jay Z's platinum album *Magna Carta Holy* Grail released worldwide on this date. In an unprecedented marketing initiative, the album is made available as a digital download free to the first one million Samsung Galaxy S III, Galaxy X4 and Galaxy Note II users of the new Jay Z Magna Carta Samsung app.

▲ Col. Chris Hadfield, performing on board the International Space Station

CHART-TOPPING CANADIAN SONGS 2010-2013

2010 I Believe **NICKI YANOFSKY**
2010 Wavin' Flag **YOUNG ARTISTS FOR HAITI**
2012 Boyfriend **JUSTIN BIEBER**

2011 Call Me Maybe **CARLY RAE JEPSEN**
2012 Good Time **OWL CITY & CARLY RAE JEPSEN**

CANADIAN HIT SONGS LIST

Here is the real story of Canadian music, found in the country's songs. These are the "hits" — the songs that have become widely popular from sea to shining sea and have defined Canadian contemporary music and culture since 1900. Many were created and performed by Canadian artists, others were made popular through the vocal or instrumental talents of Canadian singers or musicians. This is Canada's hit parade with songs tracked, compiled and given rankings over the years on charts in such music industry publications as *RPM Weekly*, *The Record*, *Record Week* and *Billboard* in Canada and the U.S. It was shaped by generations of remarkable Canadian recording artists many of whom have not only made a lasting impact on their own country's musical heritage but also on the culture of music around the world. This is a list you can hum to.

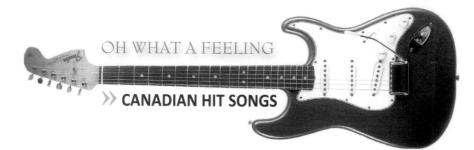

OH WHAT A FEELING

» CANADIAN HIT SONGS

CANADIAN HIT SONGS AT THE TURN OF THE CENTURY

» 1900

1900 Mandy Lee Harry Macdonough

1900 My Sunny Southern Home Harry Macdonough

1900 When We Are Married Harry Macdonough & Grace Spencer

1900 My Wild Irish Rose Harry Macdonough

1900 A Bird In A Gilded Cage Harry Macdonough

1900 I Can't Tell Why I Love You But I Do Harry Macdonough

1900 The Holy City Harry Macdonough

1900 I Love You Just the Same Harry Macdonough

» 1901

1901 **Tell Me, Pretty Maiden Har**ry Macdo**nough & Grace Spencer**

1901 When the Harvest Days Are Over Harry Macdonough

1901 Good-Bye, Dolly Gray Harry Macdonough

1901 Hearts and Flowers Harry Macdonough

1901 When You Were Sweet Sixteen Harry Macdonough

1901 Sweet Annie Moore Harry Macdonough & S.H. Dudley

1901 In the Shade of the Palm Harry Macdonough

1901 The Tale of the Bumble Bee Harry Macdonough

1901 Absence Makes the Heart Grow Fonder Harry Macdonough

1901 I've A Longing In My Heart For You, Louise Harry Macdonough

1901 I'll Be With You When the Roses Bloom Again Harry Macdonough

1901 The Wedding of Reuben and the Maid Harry Macdonough

» 1902

1902 Bye and Bye You Will Forget Me Harry Macdonough & S.H. Dudley

1902 Home, Sweet Home Harry Macdonough with Charles D'Almaine

1902 My Carolina Lady Harry Macdonough

1902 On A Sunday Afternoon Harry Macdonough

1902 Jennie Lee Harry Macdonough

1902 Josephine, My Jo Harry Macdonough

1902 The Mansion of Aching Hearts Harry Macdonough

1902 My Beautiful Irish Maid Harry Macdonough

» 1903

1903 The Rosary Henry Burr

1903 Come Down, Ma Ev'ning Star Henry Burr

1903 To My First Love Henry Burr

1903 In the Good Old Summer Time Harry Macdonough

1903 In the Sweet Bye and Bye Harry Macdonough & John Bieling

1903 Two Eyes Of Blue Harry Macdonough

1903 Heidelberg Harry Macdonough

1903 Since I First Met You Harry Macdonough

1903 Hiawatha **Harry Macdonough**

1903 Tessie Harry Macdonough & S.H. Dudley

1903 Beautiful Bird, Sing On Harry Macdonough with Joe Belmont

1903 When Kate and I Were Comin' Thro' the Rye Harry Macdonough

1903 By the Sycamore Tree Harry Macdonough

» 1904

1904 Sammy Henry Burr

1904 My Cosey Corner Girl Henry Burr

1904 Blue Bell Henry Burr

1904 Good-Bye, My Lady Love Henry Burr

1904 My Little Canoe Henry Burr

1904 I Love Only One Girl in the Wide, Wide World Harry Macdonough

1904 The Girl You Love Harry Macdonough

1904 Peggy Brady Harry Macdonough

1904 Navajo Harry Macdonough

1904 My San Domingo Maid Harry Macdonough

1904 Good-Bye, My Lady Love Harry Macdonough

» 1905

1905 Sing Me To Sleep Irving Gillette (aka Henry Burr)

1905 In the Shade of the Old Apple Tree Irving Gillette (aka Henry Burr)

1905 Oh Promise Me Irving Gillette (aka Henry Burr)

1905 In Dear Old Georgia Irving Gillette (aka Henry Burr)

1905 Sweet Thoughts of Home Harry Macdonough

1905 My Cozy Corner Girl Harry Macdonough

1905 Marguerite Harry Macdonough & John Bieling

1905 You and I Harry Macdonough & Florence Hayward

1905 Tale of the Turtle Dove Harry Macdonough

1905 Dearie Harry Macdonough

1905 In the Valley of Yesterday Harry Macdonough

» 1906

1906 Good Night, Little Girl, Good Night Henry Burr

1906 Love Me and the World Is Mine Henry Burr

1906 All Through the Night Henry Burr

1906 If A Girl Like You Loved A Boy Like Me Harry Macdonough

1906 When the Mocking Birds Are Singing In the Wildwood Harry Macdonough

1906 My Old Kentucky Home Harry Macdonough

1906 Where the River Shannon Flows Harry Macdonough

1906 Ain't You Coming Back To Old New Hampshire, Molly? Harry Macdonough

» 1907

1907 Won't You Come Over To My House Henry Burr

1907 Red Wing (An Indian Fable) Frank Stanley & Henry Burr

1907 When Summer Tells Autumn Good-Bye Frank Stanley & Henry Burr

1907 The Bully May Irwin

1907 In the Evening By the Moonlight, Dear Louise Harry Macdonough

1907 A Flower From Home, Sweet Home Harry Macdonough & John Bieling

1907 Almost Persuaded Harry Macdonough & Frank Stanley

1907 Because You're You Harry Macdonough & Elise Stevenson

1907 The Tale The Church Bell Tolled Harry Macdonough

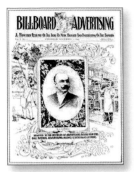

1907 Sweet Julienne Harry Macdonough

1907 Dreaming Harry Macdonough

1907 My Dear Harry Macdonough

1907 Messiah: Every Valley Shall Be Exalted Harry Macdonough

» 1908

1908 I Love and the World Is Mine Henry Burr

1908 As Long As the World Rolls On Henry Burr

1908 Kiss Duet Henry Burr and Elise Wood

1908 I Want You Henry Burr

1908 You Have Always Been the Same Old Pal Henry Burr

1908 She's the Fairest Little Flower Old Dixie Ever Grew Frank Stanley & Henry Burr

1908 Bye Bye Dearie Frank Stanley & Henry Burr

1908 Rainbow Frank Stanley & Henry Burr

1908 I Love You So Harry Macdonough & Elise Stevenson

1908 Some Day You'll Come Back To Me Harry Macdonough & Frank Stanley

1908 One Sweet Girl Harry Macdonough

1908 Maxim's Harry Macdonough

1908 Sweetheart Days   Harry Macdonough

1908 Kiss Duet (Sweetest Maid of All)   Harry Macdonough & Elise Stevenson

1908 Over the Hills and Far Away Harry Macdonough

1908 When Sweet Marie Was Sweet Sixteen Harry Macdonough & John Bieling

» 1909

1909 Then You'll Remember Me Henry Burr

1909 When You and I Were Young, Maggie Henry Burr

1909 To the End of the World With You Henry Burr

1909 I Wonder Who's Kissing Her Now Henry Burr

1909 Honey On Our Honeymoon Henry Burr

1909 In the Garden of My Heart Frank Stanley & Henry Burr

1909 Softly and Tenderly Frank Stanley & Henry Burr

1909 Shine On, Harvest Moon Frank Stanley & Henry Burr

CANADIAN HIT SONGS

1909 Beautiful Isle of Somewhere Harold Jarvis

1909 There Never Was A Girl Like You
Harry Macdonough

1909 Shine On, Harvest Moon Harry Macdonough
with Miss Walton"

1909 The Message of the Red Rose Harry
Macdonough with Miss Walton

CANADIAN HIT SONGS OF THE 1910s

» 1910

1910 My Southern Rose Henry Burr

1910 Where the River Shannon Flows Henry Burr

1910 Meet Me Tonight In Dreamland Henry Burr

1910 All That I Ask of You Is Love Henry Burr

1910 Every Little Movement Henry Burr and
Margaret Mahew

1910 We Shall Meet Bye and Bye Frank Stanley &
Henry Burr

1910 Silver Bell Frank Stanley & Henry Burr

1910 My Prairie Song Bird Frank Stanley & Henry Burr

1910 When I Marry You Harry Macdonough &
Elizabeth Wheeler

1910 Where the River Shannon Flows Harry
Macdonough

1910 Ring O' Roses Harry Macdonough &
Lucy Isabelle Marsh

1910 Every Little Movement Harry Macdonough &
Lucy Isabelle Marsh

1910 In the Valley of Yesterday Harry Macdonough

» 1911

1911 Day Dreams, Visions of Bliss Henry Burr and
Elise Stevenson

1911 Love Is Like A Red, Red Rose Henry Burr and Elise
Stevenson

1911 Save Up Your Kisses For A Rainy Day Henry Burr
and Elise Stevenson

1911 When You're In Town Henry Burr and Elise
Stevenson

1911 On Mobile Bay Henry Burr & Albert Campbell

1911 The Moonlight, The Rose and You Frank Stanley &
Henry Burr

1911 Down By the Old Mill Stream Harry Macdonough

» 1912

1912 I Love Love (I Love You, Dear) Henry Burr and
Caroline Vaughan

1912 Come To the Ball Henry Burr

1912 That's How I Need You Henry Burr

1912 Down In Sunshine Valley Henry Burr & Albert
Campbell

1912 When I Was Twenty-One And You Were Sweet
Sixteen Henry Burr & Albert Campbell

1912 In A Little While Henry Burr & Albert Campbell

1912 Sweetheart Sue Henry Burr & Albert Campbell

1912 I'd Love To Live In Loveland With A Girl Like You
Henry Burr & Albert Campbell

1912 Two Little Love Bees Christie MacDonald &
Reinald Werrenrath

1912 Day Dreams, Visions of Bliss Christie MacDonald
& Lyric Quartet

1912 When I Was Twenty-One and You Were Sweet
Sixteen Harry Macdonough & American
Quartet

» 1913

1913 When I Lost You Henry Burr

1913 To Have, To Hold, To Love Henry Burr

1913 Last Night Was the End of the World Henry Burr

1913 There's A Girl in the Heart of Maryland
Henry Burr and Edgar Stoddard

1913 Flow Gently Sweet Afton Henry Burr

1913 Peg o' My Heart Henry Burr

1913 The Trail of the Lonesome Pine Henry Burr &
Albert Campbell

1913 Sailing Down the Chesapeake Bay Henry Burr &
Albert Campbell

1913 The Angelus Christie MacDonald, Reinald
Werrenrath & Victor Male Chorus

1913 Sweethearts Christie MacDonald

1913 A Little Girl At Home Harry Macdonough &
Marguerite Dunlap

1913 When Irish Eyes Are Smiling Harry Macdonough

1913 There's A Girl In the Heart of Maryland (With A
Heart That Belongs To Me) Harry Macdonough

1913 On the Banks Of the Wabash Harry Macdonough
& American Quartet

» 1914

1914 On the Old Front Porch Ada Jones and Henry Burr

1914 Somewhere A Voice is Calling Harry McClaskey
(aka Henry Burr)

1914 Rebecca Of Sunny-brook Farm Irving Gillette (aka
Henry Burr) and Helen Clark

1914 Where Can I Meet You To-Night? Ada Jones and
Henry Burr

1914 The Song That Stole My Heart Away Henry Burr

1914 In the Heart of the City That Has No Heart
Henry Burr and Ada Jones

1914 In the Valley of the Moon Henry Burr and
Helen Clark

1914 You Planted A Rose In the Garden of Love
Henry Burr

1914 When You're A Long, Long Way From Home
Henry Burr

1914 I'm On My Way To Mandalay Henry Burr, Albert Campbell and Will Oakland

1914 Off With the Old Love, On With the New Henry Burr & Albert Campbell

1914 Dear Love Days Henry Burr, Albert Campbell and Will Oakland

1914 California and You Henry Burr & Albert Campbell

1914 When It's Apple Blossom Time In Normandy Harry Macdonough & Marguerite Dunlap

1914 You're Here and I'm Here Harry Macdonough & Olive Kline

1914 When It's Night Time Down In Burghandy George MacFarlane

1914 Can't You Hear Me Calling, Caroline? George MacFarlane

» 1915

1915 There's A Little Spark of Love Still Burning Henry Burr

1915 Maybe A Day, Maybe A Year Henry Burr

1915 There's A Little Lane Without A Turning (On the Way To Home Sweet Home) Henry Burr

1915 When I Leave the World Behind Henry Burr

1915 It's Tulip Time In Holland Henry Burr

1915 When My Ship Comes In Henry Burr & Albert Campbell

1915 In the Land of Love With the Songbirds Henry Burr & Albert Campbell with Joe Belmont

1915 My Little Girl Henry Burr & Albert Campbell

1915 Close To My Heart Henry Burr & Albert Campbell

1915 When It's Peach Picking Time In Delaware Henry Burr & Albert Campbell

1915 Sweet Kentucky Lady (Dry Your Eyes) Harry Macdonough

1915 Auf Wiedersehen Harry Macdonough & Alice Green" aka Olive Kline

1915 They Didn't Believe Me Harry Macdonough & Alice Green" aka Olive Kline

1915 A Little Bit Of Heaven ('Shure, They Call It Ireland') George MacFarlane

» 1916

1916 When You're In Love With Someone Who Is Not In Love With You Henry Burr and Miriam Clark

1916 M-O-T-H-E-R (A Word That Means the World To Me) Henry Burr

1916 My Mother's Rosary Henry Burr

1916 Memories Henry Burr

1916 What A Wonderful Mother You'd Be Henry Burr

1916 Good-Bye, Good Luck, God Bless You (Is All That I Can Say) Henry Burr

1916 Baby Shoes Henry Burr

1916 Is There Still Room For Me 'Neath the Old Apple Tree? Henry Burr & Albert Campbell

1916 The Wedding of the Sunshine and the Rose Henry Burr & Albert Campbell

1916 There's A Quaker Down In Quaker Town Henry Burr & Albert Campbell

1916 Through These Wonderful Glasses of Mine Henry Burr & Albert Campbell

1916 She Is the Sunshine of Virginia Henry Burr & Albert Campbell

1916 You Were Just Made To Order For Me Henry Burr & Albert Campbell

1916 On the South Sea Isle Sterling Trio (including Henry Burr)

1916 In Florida Among the Palms Sterling Trio (including Henry Burr)

1916 Araby Harry Macdonough

1916 The Girl On the Magazine Harry Macdonough

1916 My Own Home Town In Ireland George MacFarlane

1916 All I Want Is A Cottage, Some Roses and You Geoffrey O'Hara

1916 They Made It Twice As Nice As Paradise (And They Called It Dixieland) Geoffrey O'Hara

1916 Thais: Meditation Kathleen Parlow

» 1917

1917 Your Eyes, Your Lips, Your Heart Henry Burr

1917 All the World Will Be Jealous of Me Henry Burr

1917 Joan of Arc Henry Burr

1917 My Hawaiian Sunshine Henry Burr & Albert Campbell

1917 Where the Black-Eyed Susans Grow Henry Burr & Albert Campbell

1917 For Me and My Gal Henry Burr & Albert Campbell

1917 Lookout Mountain Henry Burr & Albert Campbell

1917 Shenandoah Henry Burr & Albert Campbell

1917 Hush-A-Bye Ma Baby (The Missouri Waltz) Henry Burr & Albert Campbell

1917 Hawaiian Butterfly Sterling Trio (Including Henry Burr)

1917 Babes In the Wood Harry Macdonough & Anna Howard aka Lucy Isabelle Marsh

» 1918

1918 Somewhere In France Is the Lily Henry Burr

1918 Life In A Trench In Belgium Lt. Gitz Rice and Henry Burr

1918 I'm Going To Follow the Boys Henry Burr and Elizabeth Spencer

CANADIAN HIT SONGS

1918 Just A Baby's Prayer At Twilight (For Her Daddy Over There) Henry Burr

1918 Are You From Heaven? Henry Burr

1918 I'm Sorry I Made You Cry Henry Burr

1918 There's A Little Blue Star in the Window (And It Means All the World To Me) Henry Burr

1918 Three Wonderful Letters From Home Henry Burr

1918 When You Come Home Henry Burr

1918 Your Lips Are No Man's Land But Mine Henry Burr & Albert Campbell

1918 One Day In June (It Might Have Been You) Henry Burr & Albert Campbell

1918 Belgian Rose Henry Burr & Albert Campbell

1918 After You've Gone Henry Burr & Albert Campbell

1918 Smiles Henry Burr & Albert Campbell

1918 Where the Morning Glories Grow Elizabeth Spencer & Sterling Trio (including Henry Burr)

1918 My Sunshine Jane Sterling Trio (including Henry Burr)

1918 When You Sang 'Hush-A-Bye' To Me Sterling Trio (including Henry Burr)

1918 When We Meet In the Sweet Bye and Bye Sterling Trio (including Henry Burr)

1918 Wait Till the Cows Come Home Harry Macdonough & Alice Green" aka Olive Kline

1918 Good-Bye, Mother Machree Harry Macdonough & Shannon Four

» 1919

1919 Oh, How I Wish I Could Sleep Until My Daddy Comes Back Home Henry Burr

1919 Don't Cry, Little Girl, Don't Cry Henry Burr

1919 Baby's Prayer Will Soon Be Answered Henry Burr

1919 Beautiful Ohio Henry Burr

1919 That Wonderful Mother of Mine Henry Burr

1919 Oh! What A Pal Was Mary Henry Burr

1919 They'll Be Mighty Proud In Dixie of Their Old Black Joe Henry Burr & Albert Campbell

1919 Hindustan Henry Burr & Albert Campbell

1919 Till We Meet Again Henry Burr & Albert Campbell

1919 I'm Forever Blowing Bubbles Henry Burr & Albert Campbell

1919 Somebody's Waiting For Someone Henry Burr & Albert Campbell

1919 Dreaming of Home, Sweet Home Sterling Trio (including Henry Burr)

1919 That Tumble-Down Shack In Athlone Sterling Trio (including Henry Burr)

1919 Friends Sterling Trio (including Henry Burr)

1919 Carolina Sunshine Sterling Trio (including Henry Burr)

CANADIAN HIT SONGS OF THE 1920s

» 1920

1920 Weeping Willow Lane Henry Burr and Frank Croxton

1920 Carolina Sunshine Henry Burr and John Meyer

1920 Just For Me and Mary Henry Burr

1920 I Never Knew Henry Burr and John Meyer

1920 Was There Ever A Pal Like You? Henry Burr

1920 When My Baby Smiles At Me Henry Burr

1920 Daddy, You've Been A Mother To Me Henry Burr

1920 Rose Of Washington Square Henry Burr

1920 I'm In Heaven When I'm In My Mother's Arms Henry Burr

1920 You're the Only Girl That Made Me Cry Henry Burr

1920 Dardanella Henry Burr & Albert Campbell

1920 Where the Lanterns Glow Henry Burr & Albert Campbell

1920 I'll Be With You In Apple Blossom Time Henry Burr & Albert Campbell

» 1921

1921 Old Pal Why Don't You Answer Me? Henry Burr

1921 You Made Me Forget How To Cry Henry Burr

1921 Feather Your Nest Henry Burr & Albert Campbell

1921 Mandalay Henry Burr & Albert Campbell

1921 Carolina Lullaby Henry Burr & Albert Campbell

1921 I Found A Rose In the Devil's Garden Sterling Trio (including Henry Burr)

» 1922

1922 You Made Me Forget How To Cry Henry Burr

1922 Time After Time Henry Burr

1922 My Buddy Henry Burr

1922 Georgia Rose Sterling Trio (including Henry Burr)

» 1923

1923 Mary Dear Henry Burr

1923 You Remind Me Of My Mother Henry Burr

1923 Faded Love Letters Henry Burr

1923 You Know You Belong To Somebody Else (So Why Don't You Leave Me Alone) Henry Burr

1923 Just A Girl That Men Forget Henry Burr

1923 Carry Me Back To My Carolina Home Henry Burr & Albert Campbell

» 1924

1924 Wonderful One Henry Burr

1924 What'll I Do? Henry Burr and Marcia Freer

1924 She's Everybody's Sweetheart (But Nobody's Gal) Henry Burr

1924 I'm Sitting Pretty In A Pretty Little City Henry Burr & Albert Campbell

» 1925

1925 Honest and Truly Henry Burr

1925 West of the Great Divide Henry Burr

1925 Alone At Last Henry Burr

1925 At the End of the Road Henry Burr & Albert Campbell

» 1926

1926 You Forgot To Remember Henry Burr

1926 I Wonder Where My Baby Is Tonight Henry Burr and Billy Murray

1926 Always Henry Burr

1926 I Wish I Had My Old Gal Back Again Henry Burr

1926 The Prisoner's Sweetheart Henry Burr

» 1927

1927 Because I Love You Henry Burr

1927 Are You Lonesome Tonight? Henry Burr

1927 Charmaine! Guy Lombardo & His Royal Canadians

» 1928

1928 Memories of France Henry Burr

1928 Coquette Guy Lombardo & His Royal Canadians

1928 Beloved Guy Lombardo & His Royal Canadians

1928 Japansy Guy Lombardo & His Royal Canadians

1928 Sweethearts On Parade Guy Lombardo & His Royal Canadians

» 1929

1929 High Up On A Hilltop Guy Lombardo & His Royal Canadians

1929 Where the Shy Little Violets Grow Guy Lombardo & His Royal Canadians

1929 I Get the Blues When It Rains Guy Lombardo & His Royal Canadians

1929 You Made Me Love You (Why Did You?) Guy Lombardo & His Royal Canadians

1929 College Medley Fox Trot (The Big Ten) Guy Lombardo & His Royal Canadians

1929 A Little Kiss Each Morning (A Little Kiss Each Night) Guy Lombardo & His Royal Canadians

1929 Singin' In the Bathtub Guy Lombardo & His Royal Canadians

CANADIAN HIT SONGS OF THE 1930s

» 1930

1930 Have A Little Faith In Me Guy Lombardo & His Royal Canadians

1930 Cryin' For the Carolines Guy Lombardo & His Royal Canadians

1930 Under A Texas Moon Guy Lombardo & His Royal Canadians

1930 Lazy Lou'siana Moon Guy Lombardo & His Royal Canadians

1930 A Cottage For Sale Guy Lombardo & His Royal Canadians

1930 With You Guy Lombardo & His Royal Canadians

1930 You're the Sweetest Girl This Side of Heaven Guy Lombardo & His Royal Canadians

1930 Rollin' Down the River Guy Lombardo & His Royal Canadians

1930 Singing A Song To the Stars Guy Lombardo & His Royal Canadians

1930 Swingin' In A Hammock Guy Lombardo & His Royal Canadians

1930 Confessin' (That I Love You) Guy Lombardo & His Royal Canadians

1930 Go Home and Tell Your Mother Guy Lombardo & His Royal Canadians

1930 I Still Get A Thrill (Thinking of You) Guy Lombardo & His Royal Canadians

1930 Baby's Birthday Party Guy Lombardo & His Royal Canadians

1930 You're Driving Me Crazy! (What Did I Do?) Guy Lombardo & His Royal Canadians

» 1931

1931 Heartaches Guy Lombardo & His Royal Canadians

1931 By the River St. Marie Guy Lombardo & His Royal Canadians

1931 Running Between the Rain-Drops Guy Lombardo & His Royal Canadians

1931 Whistling In the Dark Guy Lombardo & His Royal Canadians

1931 (There Ought To Be A) Moonlight Saving Time Guy Lombardo & His Royal Canadians

1931 Without That Gal Guy Lombardo & His Royal Canadians

1931 Sweet and Lovely Guy Lombardo & His Royal Canadians

1931 Begging For Love Guy Lombardo & His Royal Canadians

1931 Now That You're Gone Guy Lombardo & His Royal Canadians

1931 Goodnight, Sweetheart Guy Lombardo & His Royal Canadians

1931 You Try Somebody Else (We'll Be Back Together Again) Guy Lombardo & His Royal Canadians

» 1932

1932 Too Many Tears Guy Lombardo & His Royal Canadians (#1 U.S.)

1932 Paradise Guy Lombardo & His Royal Canadians

1932 My Extraordinary Gal Guy Lombardo & His Royal Canadians

1932 Lawd, You Made the Night Too Long Guy Lombardo & His Royal Canadians

1932 Sharing (My Love For You) Guy Lombardo & His Royal Canadians

1932 We Just Couldn't Say Goodbye Guy Lombardo & His Royal Canadians

1932 I'll Never Be the Same Guy Lombardo & His Royal Canadians

1932 I Guess I'll Have To Change My Plan (The Blue Pajamas Song) Guy Lombardo & His Royal Canadians

1932 Puh-Leeze, Mr. Hemingway Guy Lombardo & His Royal Canadians

1932 How Deep Is the Ocean (How High Is the Sky?) Guy Lombardo & His Royal Canadians

1932 Pink Elephants Guy Lombardo & His Royal Canadians

1932 I'm Sure of Everything But You Guy Lombardo & His Royal Canadians

1932 Just A Little Home For the Old Folks (A Token From Me) Guy Lombardo & His Royal Canadians

1932 Waltzing In A Dream Guy Lombardo & His Royal Canadians

» 1933

1933 Street of Dreams Guy Lombardo & His Royal Canadians

1933 Going, Going, Gone! Guy Lombardo & His Royal Canadians

1933 Maybe It's Because I Love You Too Much Guy Lombardo & His Royal Canadians

1933 Lover Guy Lombardo & His Royal Canadians

1933 You'll Never Get Up To Heaven That Way Guy Lombardo & His Royal Canadians

1933 Stormy Weather (Keeps Rainin' All the Time) Guy Lombardo & His Royal Canadians

1933 Shadow Waltz Guy Lombardo & His Royal Canadians

1933 Don't Blame Me Guy Lombardo & His Royal Canadians

1933 Time To Go Guy Lombardo & His Royal Canadians

1933 This Time It's Love Guy Lombardo & His Royal Canadians

1933 By A Waterfall Guy Lombardo & His Royal Canadians

1933 The Last Round-Up Guy Lombardo & His Royal Canadians

1933 Did You Ever See A Dream Walking? Guy Lombardo & His Royal Canadians

» 1934

1934 Annie Doesn't Live Here Anymore Guy Lombardo & His Royal Canadians

1934 I Raised My Hat Guy Lombardo & His Royal Canadians

1934 Night On the Water Guy Lombardo & His Royal Canadians

1934 Inka Dinka Doo Guy Lombardo & His Royal Canadians

1934 Little Dutch Mill Guy Lombardo & His Royal Canadians

1934 Riptide Guy Lombardo & His Royal Canadians

1934 How Do I Know It's Sunday? Guy Lombardo & His Royal Canadians

1934 The Sweetest Music This Side of Heaven Guy Lombardo & His Royal Canadians

1934 Fare Thee Well, Annabelle Guy Lombardo & His Royal Canadians

1934 My Old Flame Guy Lombardo & His Royal Canadians

1934 Stars Fell On Alabama Guy Lombardo & His Royal Canadians

1934 Love In Bloom Guy Lombardo & His Royal Canadians

1934 Stay As Sweet As You Are Guy Lombardo & His Royal Canadians

1934 Winter Wonderland Guy Lombardo & His Royal Canadians

1934 Tumbling Tumbleweeds Sons Of the Pioneers

» 1935

1935 June In January Guy Lombardo & His Royal Canadians

1935 What's the Reason (I'm Not Pleasin' You) Guy Lombardo & His Royal Canadians

1935 Down By the River Guy Lombardo & His Royal Canadians

1935 Would There Be Love? Guy Lombardo & His Royal Canadians

1935 Everything's Been Done Before Guy Lombardo & His Royal Canadians

1935 Seein' Is Believin' Guy Lombardo & His Royal Canadians

1935 Cheek To Cheek Guy Lombardo & His Royal Canadians

1935 Broadway Rhythm Guy Lombardo & His Royal Canadians

1935 Red Sails In the Sunset Guy Lombardo & His Royal Canadians

1935 I'm Sittin' High On A Hill Top Guy Lombardo & His Royal Canadians

1936 The Broken Record Guy Lombardo & His Royal Canadians

1936 Alone At A Table For Two Guy Lombardo & His Royal Canadians

1936 I'm Putting All My Eggs In One Basket Guy Lombardo & His Royal Canadians

1936 Lost Guy Lombardo & His Royal Canadians

1936 When Did You Leave Heaven? Guy Lombardo & His Royal Canadians

1936 The Way You Look Tonight Guy Lombardo & His Royal Canadians

1936 A Fine Romance Guy Lombardo & His Royal Canadians

1936 You Do the Darndest Things, Baby Guy Lombardo & His Royal Canadians

1936 Sweetheart, Let's Grow Old Together Guy Lombardo & His Royal Canadians

1936 When My Dream Boat Comes Home Guy Lombardo & His Royal Canadians

1936 Gone Guy Lombardo & His Royal Canadians

» 1937

1937 Rainbow On the River Guy Lombardo & His Royal Canadians

1937 Boo Hoo Guy Lombardo & His Royal Canadians

1937 I Can't Lose That Longing For You Guy Lombardo & His Royal Canadians

1937 September In the Rain Guy Lombardo & His Royal Canadians

1937 It Looks Like Rain Cherry Blossom Lane Guy Lombardo & His Royal Canadians

1937 Toodle-oo Guy Lombardo & His Royal Canadians

1937 The Love Bug Will Bite You Guy Lombardo & His Royal Canadians

1937 A Sailboat In the Moonlight Guy Lombardo & His Royal Canadians

1937 Gone With the Wind Guy Lombardo & His Royal Canadians

1937 I Know Now Guy Lombardo & His Royal Canadians

1937 The Folks Who Live On the Hill Guy Lombardo & His Royal Canadians

1937 Can I Forget You? Guy Lombardo & His Royal Canadians

1937 So Rare Guy Lombardo & His Royal Canadians

1937 You Can't Stop Me From Dreaming Guy Lombardo & His Royal Canadians

1937 When the Mighty Organ Played 'Oh Promise Me' Guy Lombardo & His Royal Canadians

1937 I See Your Face Before Me Guy Lombardo & His Royal Canadians

» 1938

1938 Bei Mir Bist Du Schoen Guy Lombardo & His Royal Canadians

1938 It's Easier Said Than Done Guy Lombardo & His Royal Canadians

1938 Ti-Pi-Pin Guy Lombardo & His Royal Canadians

1938 Let's Sail To Dreamland Guy Lombardo & His Royal Canadians

1938 In My Little Red Book Guy Lombardo & His Royal Canadians

1938 Two Bouquets Guy Lombardo & His Royal Canadians

1938 So Little Time Guy Lombardo & His Royal Canadians

1938 Little Lady Make Believe Guy Lombardo & His Royal Canadians

1938 Girl Friend of the Whirling Dervish Guy Lombardo & His Royal Canadians

1938 I Must See Annie Tonight Guy Lombardo & His Royal Canadians

1938 It's A Lonely Trail (When You're Travelin' All Alone) Guy Lombardo & His Royal Canadians

1938 The Girl In the Bonnet of Blue Dick Todd

1938 Love Doesn't Grow On Trees Dick Todd

1938 When Paw Was Courtin' Maw Dick Todd

1939 I Ups To Her and She Ups To Me (And the Next Thing I Knows I'm In Love) Guy Lombardo & His Royal Canadians

1939 Deep Purple Guy Lombardo & His Royal Canadians

1939 Penny Serenade Guy Lombardo & His Royal Canadians (#1 U.S.)

1939 Little Sir Echo Guy Lombardo & His Royal Canadians

1939 Easter Parade Guy Lombardo & His Royal Canadians

1939 St. Louis Blues Guy Lombardo & His Royal Canadians

1939 Cinderella, Stay In My Arms Guy Lombardo & His Royal Canadians

1939 South American Way Guy Lombardo & His Royal Canadians

1939 I'm Sorry For Myself Guy Lombardo & His Royal Canadians

1939 In An 18th Century Drawing Room Guy Lombardo & His Royal Canadians

1939 South of the Border (Down Mexico Way) Guy Lombardo & His Royal Canadians

1939 Little Sir Echo Dick Todd

1939 It's A Hundred To One (I'm In Love) Dick Todd

CANADIAN HIT SONGS OF THE 1940s

1940 Confucius Say Guy Lombardo & His Royal Canadians

1940 When You Wish Upon A Star Guy Lombardo & His Royal Canadians

1940 Now I Lay Me Down To Dream Guy Lombardo & His Royal Canadians

1940 Notre Dame Medley Guy Lombardo & His Royal Canadians

1940 To You, Sweetheart, Aloha Dick Todd

1940 The Gaucho Serenade Dick Todd

1940 Angel In Disguise Dick Todd

1940 The Singing Hills Dick Todd

1940 Make Believe Island Dick Todd

1940 All This And Heaven, Too Dick Todd

» 1941

1941 A Nightingale Sang In Berkeley Square Guy Lombardo & His Royal Canadians

1941 We'll Meet Again Guy Lombardo & His Royal Canadians

1941 The Moon Fell In the River Guy Lombardo & His Royal Canadians

1941 The Band Played On Guy Lombardo & His Royal Canadians

1941 Intermezzo (Souvenir de Vienne) Guy Lombardo & His Royal Canadians

1941 Ma! I Miss Your Apple Pie Guy Lombardo & His Royal Canadians

1941 Cool Water Sons Of the Pioneers

» 1942

1942 Johnny Doughboy Found A Rose In Ireland Guy Lombardo & His Royal Canadians

1942 Beale Street Blues Guy Lombardo & His Royal Canadians

» 1943

1943 For Me And My Gal Guy Lombardo & His Royal Canadians

1943 Where Or When Guy Lombardo & His Royal Canadians

» 1944

1944 Speak Low (When You Speak, Love) Guy Lombardo & His Royal Canadians

1944 Take It Easy Guy Lombardo & His Royal Canadians

1944 It's Love, Love, Love Guy Lombardo & His Royal Canadians

1944 Long Ago (And Far Away) Guy Lombardo & His Royal Canadians

1944 Humoresque Guy Lombardo & His Royal Canadians

1944 Together Guy Lombardo & His Royal Canadians

1944 Meet Me In St. Louis Guy Lombardo & His Royal Canadians

» 1945

1945 The Trolley Song Guy Lombardo & His Royal Canadians

1945 Always Guy Lombardo & His Royal Canadians

1945 A Little On the Lonely Side Guy Lombardo & His Royal Canadians

1945 Oh! Moytle Guy Lombardo & His Royal Canadians

1945 Poor Little Rhode Island Guy Lombardo & His Royal Canadians

1945 Bell Bottom Trousers Guy Lombardo & His Royal Canadians

1945 Stars In Your Eyes Guy Lombardo & His Royal Canadians

1945 No Can Do Guy Lombardo & His Royal Canadians

» 1946

1946 Symphony Guy Lombardo & His Royal Canadians

1946 Seems Like Old Times Guy Lombardo & His Royal Canadians

1946 Shoo-Fly Pie and Apple Pan Dowdy Guy Lombardo & His Royal Canadians

1946 Give Me the Moon Over Brooklyn Guy Lombardo & His Royal Canadians

1946 I'd Be Lost Without You Guy Lombardo & His Royal Canadians

1947 Mangua, Nicaragua Guy Lombardo & His Royal Canadians

1947 Anniversary Song Guy Lombardo & His Royal Canadians

1947 April Showers Guy Lombardo & His Royal Canadians

1947 I Wonder, I Wonder, I Wonder Guy Lombardo & His Royal Canadians

1947 The Echo Said 'No,' Guy Lombardo & His Royal Canadians

» 1948

1948 I'm My Own Grandpaw Guy Lombardo & His Royal Canadians

» 1949

1949 Red Roses For A Blue Lady Guy Lombardo & His Royal Canadians

1949 Everywhere You Go Guy Lombardo & His Royal Canadians

1949 Down By the Station Guy Lombardo & His Royal Canadians

1949 Merry-Go-Round Waltz Guy Lombardo & His Royal Canadians

1949 The Four Winds and the Seven Seas Guy Lombardo & His Royal Canadians

1949 Hop-Scotch Polka (Scotch Hot) Guy Lombardo & His Royal Canadians

1949 Room Full of Roses Sons Of the Pioneers

CANADIAN HIT SONGS OF THE 1950s

» 1950

1950 Enjoy Yourself (It's Later Than You Think) Guy Lombardo & His Royal Canadians

1950 The Third Man Theme Guy Lombardo & His Royal Canadians

1950 Dearie Guy Lombardo & His Royal Canadians

1950 Our Little Ranch House Guy Lombardo & His Royal Canadians

1950 All My Love Guy Lombardo & His Royal Canadians

1950 Harbor Lights Guy Lombardo & His Royal Canadians

1950 Tennessee Waltz Guy Lombardo & His Royal Canadians

1950 Daddy's Little Girl Dick Todd

1950 I'm Movin' On Hank Snow & The Rainbow Ranch Boys

» 1951

1951 If Guy Lombardo & His Royal Canadians

1951 Because of You Guy Lombardo & His Royal Canadians

» 1952

1952 Crazy Heart Guy Lombardo & His Royal Canadians

1952 Blue Tango Guy Lombardo & His Royal Canadians

1952 Auf Wiederseh'n Sweetheart Guy Lombardo & His Royal Canadians

1952 Half As Much Guy Lombardo & His Royal Canadians

1952 La Fiacre Gisele MacKenzie

1952 Adios Gisele MacKenzie

1952 Don't Let the Stars Get In Your Eyes Gisele MacKenzie

» 1953

1953 Hello Sunshine Norman Brooks

1953 You Shouldn't Have Kissed Me the First Time Norman Brooks

1953 Somebody Wonderful Norman Brooks

1953 Seven Lonely Days Gisele MacKenzie

1953 Till I Waltz Again With You Dick Todd

» 1954

1954 Hernando's Hideaway Guy Lombardo & His Royal Canadians

1954 I Don't Hurt Anymore Hank Snow & The Rainbow Ranch Boys

» 1955

1955 My Boy Flat Top Dorothy Collins

1955 Earth Angel The Crew Cuts

1955 Ko Ko Mo (I Love You So) The Crew Cuts

1955 Don't Be Angry The Crew Cuts

1955 Chop Chop Boom The Crew Cuts

1955 A Story Untold The Crew Cuts

1955 Gum Drop The Crew Cuts

1955 Angels In the Sky The Crew Cuts

1955 Moments To Remember The Four Lads

1955 Hard To Get Gisele MacKenzie

1955 The Man In the Raincoat Priscilla Wright

» 1956

1956 Seven Days Dorothy Collins

1956 Mostly Martha The Crew Cuts

1956 Seven Days The Crew Cuts

1956 Why Do Fools Fall In Love The Diamonds

1956 The Church Bells May Ring The Diamonds

1956 Love, Love, Love The Diamonds

1956 Soft Summer Breeze The Diamonds

1956 Ka-Ding-Dong The Diamonds

1956 No Not Much The Four Lads

1956 Standing On the Corner The Four Lads

1956 My Little Angel The Four Lads

1956 A House With Love In It The Four Lads

1956 The Bus Stop Song (A Paper of Pins) The Four Lads

1956 Graduation Day The Rover Boys

» 1957

1957 Diana Paul Anka

1957 Young Love The Crew Cuts

CANADIAN HIT SONGS

1957 Little Darlin' The Diamonds
1957 Words of Love The Diamonds
1957 Zip Zip The Diamonds
1957 Silhouettes The Diamonds
1957 Who Needs You The Four Lads
1957 I Just Don't Know The Four Lads
1957 Put A Light In the Window The Four Lads

»1958
1958 You Are My Destiny Paul Anka
1958 Crazy Love Paul Anka
1958 Let the Bells Keep Ringing Paul Anka
1958 The Teen Commandments Paul Anka with
      George Hamilton IV and Johnny Nash
1958 The Stroll The Diamonds
1958 High Sign The Diamonds
1958 Kathy-O The Diamonds
1958 Walking Along The Diamonds
1958 There's Only One of You The Four Lads
1958 Enchanted Island The Four Lads
1958 The Mocking Bird The Four Lads
1958 The Swingin'
      Shepherd Blues
      Moe Koffman
      Quartette
1958 My True Love Jack Scott
1958 Leroy Jack Scott
1958 With Your Love Jack Scott
1958 Goodbye Baby Jack Scott

»1959
1959 (All of a Sudden) My Heart Sings Paul Anka
1959 I Miss You So Paul Anka
1959 Lonely Boy Paul
      Anka
1959 Put You Head On
      My Shoulder Paul
      Anka
1959 It's Time To Cry
Paul Anka
1959 She Say (Ooom
Dooby Doom) The
      Diamonds
1959 Mary Lou Ronnie
      Hawkins
1959 The Way I Walk
      Jack Scott

CANADIAN HIT
SONGS OF THE
1960s

»1960
1960 Puppy Love Paul
      Anka

1960 My Home Town Paul Anka
1960 Hello Young Lovers Paul Anka
1960 I Love You in the Same Old Way Paul Anka
1960 Summer's Gone Paul Anka
1960 Clap Your Hands The Beau-Marks
1960 The Theme From A Summer Place Percy Faith and
      His Orchestra
1960 Theme for Young Lovers Percy Faith and His
      Orchestra
1960 What In the World's Come Over You Jack Scott
1960 Burning Bridges Jack Scott
1960 Oh Little One Jack Scott
1960 It Only Happened Yesterday Jack Scott
1960 The Blamers Les Vogt

»1961
1961 The Story of My Love Paul Anka
1961 Tonight My Love, Tonight Paul Anka
1961 Dance On Little Girl Paul Anka
1961 Kissin' On the Phone Paul Anka
1961 One Summer Night The Diamonds

»1962
1962 Love Me Warm and Tender Paul Anka
1962 A Steel Guitar and a Glass of Wine Paul Anka
1962 Eso Beso (That Kiss!) Paul Anka

»1963
1963 Love (Makes the World Go 'Round) Paul Anka
1963 Remember Diana Paul Anka
1963 Charlena Ritchie Knight and the Mid-Knights

»1964
1964 We'll Sing In the Sunshine Gale Garnett
1964 My Love, Forgive Me (Amore, Scusami)
      Robert Goulet
1964 Ringo Lorne Greene
1964 Unless You Care Terry Black
1964 Come Home Little Girl Bobby Curtola
1964 Las Vegas Scene Wes Dakus
1964 Lovin' Place Gale Garnett

»1965
1965 Shakin' All Over The Guess Who
1965 Tossin' and Turn in' The Guess Who
1965 Hey Ho The Guess Who
1965 Remember the Face Allan Sisters
1965 Easy Come, Easy Go Barry Allen
1965 It's Alright With Me Now Barry Allen
1965 Put You Down Big Town Boys
1965 It Was I Big Town Boys
1965 Say It Again Terry Black

1965 Little Liar Terry Black

1965 Only Sixteen Terry Black

1965 Poor Little Fool Terry Black

1965 Leaning On the Lampost Bradfords

1965 Baby Ruth Butterfingers

1965 S.O.S. (Sweet On Susie) Kenny Chandler

1965 Alone and Lonely Bobby Curtola

1965 It's About Time Bobby Curtola

1965 Mean Woman Blues Bobby Curtola

1965 Walkin' With My Angel Bobby Curtola

1965 Makin' Love Bobby Curtola

1965 Forget Her Bobby Curtola

1965 Hobo Wes Dakus

1965 Take the First Train Home Dee & the Yeomen

1965 So Many Other Boys Esquires

1965 Cry Is All I Do Esquires

1965 Love's Made A Fool Of You Esquires

1965 Ringo Deer Gary Ferrier

1965 Give Me Lovin' Great Scots

1965 That Weepin' Willow Tree Ray Griff

1965 Bluebirds Over the Mountain Ronnie Hawkins

1965 Goin' To the River Ronnie Hawkins

1965 Think About Me Pat Hervey

1965 He Belongs To Yesterday Pat Hervey

1965 The Time Has Come Dianne James

1965 My Guy Dianne James

1965 One Good Reason Ritchie Knight

1965 Ain't Love A Funny Thing Robbie Laine

1965 Sandy Robbie Laine

1965 Won't Be A Lovely Summer Diane Leigh

1965 I'm Not Sayin' Gordon Lightfoot

1965 Just Like Tom Thumb's Blues Gordon Lightfoot

1965 Sloopy Little Caesar and the Consuls

1965 You Really Got A Hold On Me Little Caesar and the Consuls

1965 Must I Tell You Liverpool Set

1965 If You Don't Want My Love/It's Been One Of Those Days Today Jack London and the Sparrows

1965 I'll Be the Boy Jack London and the Sparrows

1965 Our Love Has Passed Jack London and the Sparrows

1965 Because You're Gone Nocturnals

1965 Hard Times With the Law The Sparrows

1965 Small Town Girl The Staccatos

1965 Move To California The Staccatos

1965 Walk That Walk David Clayton Thomas & the Shays

1965 Out of the Sunshine David Clayton Thomas & the Shays

1965 Don't Say Goodbye Townsmen

»1966

1966 Off To Dublin In the Green Abbey Tavern Singers

1966 Dream Boy Allan Sisters

1966 Love Drops Barry Allen

1966 Turn Her Down Barry Allen

1966 Blue Lipstick Patrician Anne

1966 Hey Girl Go It Alone Big Town Boys

1966 Rainbow Terry Black

1966 The Merry Ploughboy Carlton Showband

1966 We Will Break Your Heart Counts

1966 While I'm Away Bobby Curtola

1966 Real Thing Bobby Curtola

1966 Wildwood Days Bobby Curtola

1966 Hoochie Coochie Coo Wes Dakus

1966 Love Like Mine Dee & the Yeomen

1966 Baby It's All Worthwhile Dee & the Yeomen

1966 In A Minute Or Two Dee & the Yeomen

1966 A Bit Of Love Jimmy Dybold

1966 Hurting Each Other The Guess Who

1966 Believe Me The Guess Who

1966 Clock On the Wall The Guess Who

1966 And She's Mine The Guess Who

1966 1-2-5 Haunted

1966 That's Why I Love You Joey Hollingsworth

CANADIAN HIT SONGS

1966 Rose Marie Ray Hutchinson

1966 I'm A Loner Jaybees

1966 Please Forget Her Jury

1966 Soldier Boy Debbie Lori Kaye

1966 I Can't Explain King Beez

1966 That's Alright Ritchie Knight

1966 Walk On By Bobby Kris

1966 What Am I Gonna Do Robbie Lane

1966 I Symbolize You Last Words

1966 Toodle-oo Kangaroo Larry Lee

1966 Spin Spin Gordon Lightfoot

1966 You Laugh Too Much Little Caesar and the Consuls

1966 Mercy Mr. Percy Little Caesar and the Consuls

1966 Oh Gee Girl Liverpool Set

1966 Until It's Time For You To Go Catherine McKinnon

1966 Whatcha Gonna Do About It The Modbeats

1966 All Of My Life Don Norman

1966 Going Down Tom Northcott

1966 Walking the Dog Jerry Palmer

1966 Like A Dribblin' Fram Race Marbles

1966 Don't Cry For Me Marti Shannon

1966 Another Man The Shondels

1966 C'mon Everybody The Staccatos

1966 Let's Run Away The Staccatos

1966 It's A Long Way Home The Staccatos

1966 Brainwashed David Clayton Thomas & the Bossmen

1966 Bound To Fly 3's A Crowd

1966 My Kinda Guy Willows

»1967

1967 For What It's Worth (Stop, Hey What's That Sound) Buffalo Springfield

1967 Bluebird Buffalo Springfield

1967 Rock 'n' Roll Woman Buffalo Springfield

1967 Armful of Teddy Bears Barry Allen

1967 Somebody Help Me The British Modbeats

1967 Looking At A Baby The Collectors

1967 Fisherwoman The Collectors

1967 It's Not Funny Honey Bobby Curtola

1967 Give Me A Reason To Stay Bobby Curtola

1967 Multitude of Sins Esquires

1967 Labourer 49th Parallel

1967 My Girl Gettysburg Address

1967 His Girl The Guess Who

1967 Pretty Blue Eyes The Guess Who

1967 This Time Long Ago The Guess Who

1967 Flying On the Ground Is Wrong The Guess Who

1967 Lovin' Sound Ian & Sylvia

1967 Think Of Her Jaybees

1967 Bring It Down Front Jon & Lee and the Checkmates

1967 Playground Debbie Lori Kaye

1967 Give Me Time Last Words

1967 Hang On To Me Baby Lynda Layne

1967 Go Go Round Gordon Lightfoot

1967 The Way I Feel Gordon Lightfoot

1967 Cornflakes and Ice Cream Lords of London

1967 A Little Bit of Oh Yeah Martin Martin

1967 Next To Nowhere MG & the Escorts

1967 Sunny Goodge Street Tom Northcott

1967 I Believe In Sunshine A Passing Fancy

1967 If I Call You By Some Name The Paupers

1967 Simple Deed The Paupers

1967 Ship Of Dreams Quiet Jungle

1967 I Take It Back The Shondels

1967 Half Past Midnight The Staccatos

1967 Catch the Love Parade The Staccatos

1967 Got To Get You Into My Life The Stitch In Tyme

1967 New Dawn The Stitch In Time

1967 Canada Sugar Shoppe

1967 Don't Make Promises Susan Taylor

1967 Gaslight The Ugly Ducklings

1967 Diamonds and Gold Willie & the Walkers

1967 I'll Forget Her Tomorrow Witness Inc.

1967 Jezebel Witness Inc.

1967 Canada Young Canada Singers

1968 The Unicorn The Irish Rovers

1968 How'd We Ever Get This Way Andy Kim

1968 Shoot'em Up, Baby Andy Kim

1968 Born To Be Wild Steppenwolf

1968 Magic Carpet Ride Steppenwolf

1968 Does Your Mama Know About Me Bobby Taylor & the Vancouvers

1968 The Weight The Band

1968 Expecting To Fly Buffalo Springfield

1968 Bitter Green Gordon Lightfoot

1968 Everlasting Love Love Affair

1968 Love-Itis Mandala

1968 Morning Magic The Stampeders

1968 Does Your Mama Know About Me? Bobby Taylor & the Vancouvers

1968 Alone In My Room Willie & the Walkers

»1969

1969 Goodnight My Love Paul Anka
1969 Up On Cripple Creek The Band
1969 These Eyes The Guess Who
1969 Laughing The Guess Who
1969 Undun The Guess Who
1969 Rainbow Ride Andy Kim
1969 Baby, I Love You Andy Kim
1969 So Good Together Andy Kim
1969 When I Die Motherlode
1969 Rock Me Steppenwolf
1969 Move Over Steppenwolf
1969 It's Never Too Late Steppenwolf
1969 Faster Than the Speed of Life Mars Bonfire
1969 Pack It In Buckstone Hardware
1969 Private Train Five Man Electrical Band
1969 Twilight Woman 49th Parallel
1969 Now That I'm A Man 49th Parallel
1969 Hey Little Man Happy Feeling
1969 Better Watch Out McKenna Mendelson
   Mainline
1969 When I Die Motherlode
1969 Memories of a Broken Promise Motherlode
1969 Which Way You Goin' Billy? The Poppy
   Family
1969 Me & You The Regents
1969 Cruel War Sugar 'N' Spice
1969 So Come With Me Witness Inc.

CANADIAN HIT SONGS OF THE 1970s

»1970

1970 No Time The Guess Who
1970 American Woman The Guess Who
1970 No Sugar Tonight The Guess Who
1970 **Hand Me Down World The Guess Who**
1970 Share the Land The Guess Who
1970 A Friend In the City Andy Kim
1970 Be My Baby Andy Kim
1970 As the Years Go By Mashmakhan
1970 Snowbird Anne Murray
1970 One Tin Soldier The Original Caste
1970 Which Way You Goin' Billy? Poppy Family
   featuring Susan Jacks
1970 That's Where I Went Wrong
   Poppy Family featuring Susan Jacks
1970 Monster Steppenwolf
1970 Hey Lawdy Mama Steppenwolf

1970 Who Needs Ya Steppenwolf
1970 Only Love Can Break Your Heart Neil Young
1970 Rag Mama Rag The Band
1970 Time To Kill The Band
1970 Fly Little White Dove Fly The Bells
1970 Higher and Higher Canada Goose
1970 Jean Bobby Curtola
1970 You, Me and Mexico Edward Bear
1970 You Can't Deny It Edward Bear
1970 Doctor Tom Freedom
1970 To Love Means To Be Free Green & Stagg
1970 Living On A Wishbone Bobby G. Griffith
1970 Sacroiliac Boop Happy Feeling
1970 Down In the Alley Ronnie Hawkins
1970 Bitter Green Ronnie Hawkins
1970 I'm Gonna Capture You Terry Jacks
1970 You're My Life David Jensen
1970 Corrina, Corrina King Biscuit Boy
1970 We're All In This Together Tobi Lark
1970 Me and Bobby McGee Gordon Lightfoot
1970 The Chant Lighthouse
1970 You Make Me High Luke & the Apostles
1970 I Believe In Sunshine Madrigal
1970 I Love Candy Marshmallow Soup Group
1970 As Years Go By Mashmakhan
1970 Big Yellow Taxi Joni Mitchell
1970 Goin' Down Allan Nicholls

CANADIAN HIT SONGS

1970 The Rainmaker Tom Northcott

1970 Crazy Jane Tom Northcott

1970 One Tin Soldier Original Caste

1970 Mr. Monday Original Caste

1970 Country Song Original Caste

1970 Ain't That Tellin' You People Original Caste

1970 Mr. Pride Pepper Tree

1970 Lookin' Round Poor Souls

1970 That's Where I Went Wrong The Poppy
Family

1970 Beautiful Second Hand Man Ginette Reno

1970 I've Got A Feeling Sands of Time

1970 Ten Pound Note Steel River

1970 Indiana Wants Me R. Dean Taylor

1970 If You're Lookin' Tranquility Base

1970 Yankee Lady Jesse Winchester

1970 Cinnamon Girl Neil Young

»1971

1971 Stay Awhile The Bells

1971 I Love You Lady Dawn The Bells

1971 Sweet Sound of Music The Bells

1971 For Better Or Worse The Bells

1971 Signs Five Man Electrical Band

1971 Absolutely Right Five Man Electrical Band

1971 Hang On To Your Life The Guess Who

1971 Albert Flasher The Guess Who

1971 Rain Dance The Guess Who

1971 If You Could Read My Mind Gordon
Lightfoot

Billboard®

1971 Talking In Your Sleep Gordon Lightfoot

1971 Summer Side Of Life Gordon Lightfoot

1971 Hats Off (To the Stranger) Lighthouse

1971 One Fine Morning Lighthouse

1971 Put Your Hand In the Hand Ocean

1971 We Got A Dream Ocean

1971 Fast Train April Wine

1971 Life Is A Carnival The Band

1971 Chick-A-Boom Big Gee

1971 Build A Tower Brahman

1971 Crazy Arms, Crazy Eyes Brave Belt

1971 Do You Know What You're Doing Terry Bush

1971 I Say A Little Prayer/Phoenix Glen Campbell
and Anne Murray

1971 Lonesome Mary Chilliwack

1971 Oh What A Feeling Crowbar

1971 One More Mountain To Climb Dr. Music

1971 Signs Five Man Electical Band

1971 Absolutely Right Five Man Electrical Band

1971 Turned 21 Fludd

1971 It's Been A Long Time Green & Stagg

1971 Jodie Joey Gregorash

1971 Down By the River Joey Gregorash

1971 Just A Little Lovin' Hagood Hardy

1971 Man From the City Humphrey & the
Dumptrucks

1971 Run Run John & Francois James

1971 Bow Down (To the Dollar) Jericho

1971 I Wish I Were Here Andy Kim

1971 I Been Moved Andy Kim

1971 Dickens Leigh Ashford

1971 Children of the Sun Mashmakhan

1971 Hello Mom. The Mercey Brothers

1971 Carey Joni Mitchell

1971 Sing High, Sing Low Anne Murray

1971 A Stranger In My Place Anne Murray

1971 It Takes Time Anne Murray

1971 Talk It Over In the Morning Anne Murray

1971 I Think It's Gonna Rain Tom Northcott

1971 Sault Ste. Marie Original Caste

1971 Lovin' You Ain't Easy Pagliaro

1971 You're My People Pepper Tree

1971 Where Evil Grows The Poppy Family

1971 I've Got To Have You Ginette Reno

1971 Glory Glory Smyle

1971 A Country Boy Named Willie Spring

1971 Carry Me The Stampeders

1971 Sweet City Woman Stampeders

1971 Devil You The Stampeders

1971 Walk By the River Steel River

1971 Southbound Train Steel River

1971 Snowblind Friend Steppenwolf

1971 Ride With Me Steppenwolf

1971 For Ladies Only Steppenwolf

1971 Tillicum Syrinx

1971 Love Me Brother Tapestry

1971 Ain't It A Sad Thing R. Dean Taylor

1971 Gotta See Jane R. Dean Taylor

1971 Rosaline Russell Thornberry

1971 Band Bandit Tundra
1971 You're Gonna Miss Me Wishbone
1971 Garden of Ursh Karen Young
1971 Going To the Country Neil Young
» 1972
1972 Strawberry Wine April Wine
1972 You Could Have Been A Lady April Wine
1972 Bad Side of the Moon April Wine
1972 Drop Your Guns April Wine
1972 Don't Do It The Band
1972 Take It Slow Lighthouse
1972 Sunny Days Lighthouse
1972 You Turn Me On, I'm A Radio Joni Mitchell
1972 Mister Can't You See Buffy Sainte-Marie
1972 Heart of Gold Neil Young
1972 Old Man Neil Young
1972 Goodbye Farewell Abraham's Children
1972 Do I Love You Paul Anka
1972 Jubilation Paul Anka
1972 Oh My Love The Bells
1972 We Gotta Make It Together Marty Butler
1972 Time Marty Butler
1972 Fly Away Crowbar
1972 Sun Goes By Dr. Music
1972 Long Time Comin' Home Dr. Music
1972 Julia Get Up Rich Dodson
1972 Fly Across the Sea Edward Bear
1972 Masquerade Edward Bear
1972 Smiling Wine Shirley Eikhard
1972 Feelin' Better Already Everyday People
1972 Julianne Five Man Electrical Band
1972 Money Back Guarantee Five Man Electrical Band
1972 Get Up, Get Out, Move On Fludd
1972 (Make Me Do) Anything You Want A Foot In Coldwater
1972 Get That Ball Patsy Gallant
1972 New York Is Closed Tonight Greenfield
1972 My Love Sings Joey Gregorash
1972 Take the Blindness Joey Gregorash
1972 Sour Suite The Guess Who
1972 Life In the Bloodstream The Guess Who
1972 Heartbroken Bopper The Guess Who
1972 Running Back To Saskatoon The Guess Who
1972 House On Holly Road David Idema
1972 Concrete Sea Terry Jacks
1972 Saskatchewan Sunrise Rick Jones

1972 I'm Movin' On John Kay
1972 Who Has the Answers Andy Kim
1972 Beautiful Gordon Lightfoot
1972 Bloodshot Eyes Lucifer

1972 Get Down To McKenna Mendelson Mainline
1972 Love Is Mashmakhan
1972 The Theme Robbie McDougall
1972 Jesus Please Don't Save Me Murray McLauchlan
1972 I Can Smell That Funky Music Eric Mercury
1972 Love Me Love Me Love Frank Mills
1972 Poor Little Fool Frank Mills
1972 Reflections of My Childhood Frank Mills
1972 Cotton Jenny Anne Murray
1972 Robbie's Song For Jesus Anne Murray
1972 Little Old Rock 'n' Roll Band Billy Mysner
1972 One More Chance Ocean
1972 Rainshowers Pagliaro
1972 Some Sing, Some Dance Pagliaro
1972 Tell Me Who Pinky
1972 Don't Send Someone Pinky
1972 No Good To Cry The Poppy Family
1972 Good Friends The Poppy Family
1972 Out Of My Mind Rain
1972 Listen To These Words Roger Rodier
1972 Storm Warning Bob Ruzicka
1972 Mister Can't You See Buffy Sainte-Marie
1972 Strawberry Wine Spice
1972 Monday Morning Choo Choo/Then Came the White Man The Stampeders
1972 Wild Eyes The Stampeders
1972 Mexican Lady Steel River
1972 Taos New Mexico R. Dean Taylor
1972 Africa Thundermug
1972 Riverboat Ladies Timothy
1972 Dream No. 2 Ken Tobias
1972 Rock and Roll Song Valdy
1972 War Song Neil Young and Graham Nash
» 1973
1973 Basketball Jones featuring Tyrone Shoelaces Cheech & Chong

CANADIAN HIT SONGS

1973 Sister Mary Elephant (Shudd-Up!) Cheech & Chong

1973 Heartbeat It's A Lovebeat DeFranco Family featuring Tony DeFranco

1973 Last Song Edward Bear

1973 Close Your Eyes Edward Bear

1973 Danny's Song Anne Murray

1973 What About Me? Anne Murray

1973 Send A Little Love My Way Anne Murray

1973 Wildflower Skylark

1973 Painted Ladies Ian Thomas

1973 Gypsy Abraham's Children

1973 Thank You Abraham's Children

1973 Song of Love Alabama

1973 Highway Driving Alabama

1973 Lady Run, Lady Hide April Wine

1973 Gimme Your Money/Little Candy Dancer Bachman-Turner Overdrive

1973 Blue Collar Bachman-Turner Overdrive

1973 He Was Me, He Was You The Bells

1973 The Singer The Bells

1973 Once Loved Woman, Once-Loved Man/Love Vibrations Marty Butler

1973 Make My Life A Little Brighter Chester

1973 Groundhog Chilliwack

1973 You're Still the One Copperpenny

1973 Sitting On A Poor Man's Throne Copperpenny

1973 Happy Dreamer Jack Cornell

1973 Living Without You Creamcheeze Goodtime Band

1973 Power To All Our Old Friends Cal Dodd

1973 Flip Flop & Fly Downchild Blues Band

1973 Come And Join Us Dublin Corporation

1973 Last Song Edward Bear

1973 Close Your Eyes Edward Bear

1973 Walking On Back Edward Bear

1973 Uncle Dad and Auntie Mom Cliff Edwards

1973 Carpenter of Wood Cliff Edwards

1973 Carry On Cliff & Ann Edwards

1973 Control of Me Les Emmerson

1973 Cry Your Eyes Out Les Emmerson

1973 Ice On the Road Fergus

1973 I'm A Stranger Here Five Man Electrical Band

1973 Always Be Thinking Of You Fludd

1973 Yes Fludd

1973 Old Enough To Break My Heart Flying Circus

1973 Bondi Junction Peter Foldy

1973 In My Life A Foot In Coldwater

1973 Love Is Coming A Foot In Coldwater

1973 Could You Ever Love Me Again Gary & Dave

1973 Bit of Both/Underneath the Twilight David George

1973 Tell the People Joey Gregorash

1973 Sound of Peace Bobby G. Griffith

1973 Follow Your Daughter Home The Guess Who

1973 Orly The Guess Who

1973 Glamour Boy The Guess Who

1973 Daytime Nighttime Keith Hampshire

1973 The First Cut Is the Deepest Keith Hampshire

1973 Sign Of the Gypsy Queen Lorence Hud

1973 Bongo Rock Incredible Bongo Band

1973 You Don't Know What Love Is Susan Jacks

1973 I'm Gonna Love You Too Terry Jacks

1973 Moonshine (Friend of Mine) John Kay

1973 Oh What A Day Andy Kim

1973 Goodbye Superdad Bill King

1973 Give Me Love Bill King

1973 All Things Come From God Tony Kosinec

1973 Touch of Magic James Leroy

1973 You Look Good In Denim James Leroy

1973 You Are What I Am Gordon Lightfoot

1973 Can't Depend On Love Gordon Lightfoot

1973 You Girl Lighthouse

1973 Broken Guitar Blues Lighthouse

1973 Pretty Lady Lighthouse

1973 Dance A Little Step Mashmakhan

1973 Pretty City Lady Bob McBride

1973 Treasure Song Bob McBride

1973 Farmer's Song Murray McLauchlan

1973 It Wouldn't Have Made Any Difference Tom Middleton

1973 The Beatles' Thing Moran

1973 Goodbye Mama Dave Nicol

1973 West Coast Woman Painter

1973 Lost Mickey Posner

1973 Find Yourself A Boy Tammy Rafferty

1973 Everyday Working Man Ginette Reno

1973 Clear Night Riverson

1973 Lately Love (Laughter Don't Come Easy) Bob Ruzicka

1973 Holding Your Hand Seadog

1973 Wildflower Skylark

1973 Johnny Lightning The Stampeders

1973 Oh My Lady The Stampeders

1973 Minstrel Gypsy The Stampeders

1973 Rosalie Michael Tarry

1973 Orbit Thundermug

1973 I Just Want To Make Music Ken Tobias

1973 Fly Me High Ken Tobias

1973 Love Can Bless the Soul of Anyone Ian Tyson

1973 Good Song Valdy

1973 Simple Life Valdy

1973 Day and Night The Wackers

1973 Last Kiss Wednesday

1973 Isn't That So? Jesse Winchester

»1974

1974 Let Me Get To Know You Paul Anka

1974 (You're) Having My Baby Paul Anka with Odia Coates

1974 One Man Woman/One Woman Man Paul Anka with Odia Coates

1974 Let It Ride Bachman-Turner Overdrive

1974 Takin' Care of Business Bachman-Turner Overdrive

1974 You Ain't Seen Nothing Yet Bachman-Turner Overdrive

1974 Earache My Eye featuring Alice Bowie Cheech & Chong

1974 Abra-Ca-Dabra DeFranco Family featuring Tony DeFranco

1974 Save the Last Dance For Me DeFranco Family featuring Tony DeFranco

1974 Star Baby The Guess Who

1974 Clap For the Wolfman The Guess Who

1974 Dancin' Fool The Guess Who

1974 Seasons In the Sun Terry Jacks

1974 If You Go Away Terry Jacks

1974 Rock Me Gently Andy Kim

1974 Fire, Baby I'm On Fire Andy Kim

1974 Sundown Gordon Lightfoot

1974 Carefree Highway Gordon Lightfoot

1974 Americans Byron MacGregor

1974 Help Me Joni Mitchell

1974 Free Man In Paris Joni Mitchell

1974 Love Song Anne Murray

1974 You Won't See Me Anne Murray

1974 The Americans (A Canadian's Opinion) Gordon Sinclair

1974 Straight Shootin' Woman Steppenwolf

1974 People Gotta Move Gino Vannelli

1974 Goddess of Nature Abraham's Children

1974 Virginia (Touch Me Like You Do) Bill Amesbury

1974 Weeping Widow April Wine

1974 Ain't Got No Home The Band

1974 Molly Bearfoot

1974 Passing Time Bearfoot

1974 Finally (With You) Cooper Brothers

1974 Good To Be By You Jack Cornell

1974 Million Dollar Weekend Crowbar

1974 Same Old Feeling Edward Bear

1974 Freedom For the Stallion Edward Bear

1974 Werewolf Five Man Electrical Band

1974 Long Gone Debbie Fleming

1974 I Am What I Am Lois Fletcher

1974 Cousin Mary Fludd

1974 Brother and Me Fludd

1974 I Fell In Love With You Sometime Gary & Dave

1974 It Might As Well Rain Until September Gary & Dave

1974 I May Never See You Gary & Dave

1974 This Is Your Song Don Goodwin

1974 Time To Cry Don Goodwin

1974 The Badger's Song Bobby G. Griffith

1974 Big Time Operator Keith Hampshire

1974 Forever and Ever (Baby I'm Gonna Be Yours) Keith Hampshire

1974 I Thought Of You Again Susan Jacks

1974 Just As Bad As You Shawne Jackson

1974 Make It All Worthwhile James Leroy

1974 Can You Feel It Lighthouse

1974 Shelley Made Me Smile Lisle

1974 Do It Right Bob McBride

1974 Hurricane of Change Murray McLauchlan

1974 Linda Won't You Take Me In Murray McLauchlan

1974 One More Chance Tom Middleton

1974 Love Song Anne Murray

1974 You Won't See Me Anne Murray

1974 Just One Look Anne Murray

1974 Summer Girl Craig Ruhnke

1974 She Southcote

1974 Dirty Work Songbird

1974 Running Wild The Stampeders

CANADIAN HIT SONGS

1974 Me and My Stone The Stampeders

1974 Ramona The Stampeders

1974 Carrie's Song J.C. Stone

1974 Come the Sun Ian Thomas

1974 Teen Angel Wednesday

1974 Roses Are Red Wednesday

1974 Walk On Neil Young

»1975

1975 I Don't Like To Sleep Alone Paul Anka with Odia Coates

1975 (I Believe) There's Nothing Stronger Than Our Love Paul Anka with Odia Coates

1975 Times of Your Life Paul Anka

1975 Roll On Down the Highway Bachman-Turner Overdrive

1975 Hey You Bachman-Turner Overdrive

1975 Quick Change Artist Bachman-Turner Overdrive

1975 Rainy Day People Gordon Lightfoot

1975 Big Yellow Taxi (Live) Joni Mitchell

1975 I Wouldn't Want To Lose Your Love April Wine

1975 Cum Here the Band April Wine

1975 Oowatanite April Wine

1975 Back Up (Against Your Persuasion) Terry Black & Laurel Ward

1975 Dancin' On A Saturday Night Bond

1975 When You're Up, You're Up Bond

1975 You Beat Me To the Punch Charity Brown

1975 Take Me In Your Arms Charity Brown

1975 Crazy Talk Chilliwack

1975 Keep Our Love Alive Patricia Dahlquist

1975 Watching the World Go By Les Emmerson

1975 What An Animal Fludd

1975 (Make Me Do) Anything You Want/Paradice A Foot In Coldwater

1975 Dancin' Fool The Guess Who

1975 Loves Me Like A Brother The Guess Who

1975 I Can't Live Without You The Guess Who

1975 The Homecoming Hagood Hardy

1975 You Make Me Want To Be Dan Hill

1975 Rock and Roll (I Gave You the Best Years Of My Life) Terry Jacks

1975 Christina Terry Jacks

1975 The Essence of Joan Andy Kim

1975 California Jam Klaatu

1975 Lady Ellen James Leroy

1975 I'm Running After You Major Hoople's Boarding House

1975 Linda Put the Coffee On Ray Materick

1975 Do You Dream of Being Somebody Murray McLauchlan

1975 Down By the Henry Moore Murray McLauchlan

1975 Little Dreamer Murray McLauchlan

1975 Day Tripper Anne Murray

1975 Uproar Anne Murray

1975 Can You Give It All To Me Myles & Lenny

1975 Good Feeling (To Know) Octavian

1975 Round and Round Octavian

1975 What the Hell I Got Pagliaro

1975 In the Mood Rush

1975 Fly By Night Rush

1975 I Can Dance Shooter

1975 Hit the Road Jack The Stampeders

1975 New Orleans The Stampeders

1975 Make Me Your Baby Suzanne Stevens

1975 Mother Earth Ian Thomas

1975 Every Bit Of Love Ken Tobias

1975 Baby Woncha Please Come Home Trooper

1975 Renaissance (Let's Dance That Old Dance) Valdy

1975 Powerful People Gino Vannelli

1975 Fly Away Wednesday

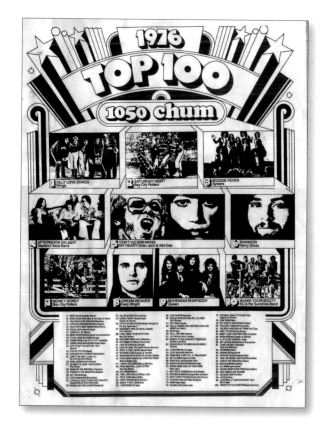

1975 Here Today, Gone Tomorrow Wednesday

1975 Things That Go Bump In the Night Willi

»1976

1976 Anytime (I'll Be There) Paul Anka

1976 Down To the Line Bachman-Turner Overdrive

1976 Take It Like A Man Bachman-Turner Overdrive

1976 Looking Out For Number One Bachman-Turner Overdrive

1976 Gimme Your Money Please Bachman-Turner Overdrive

1976 Stand Tall Burton Cummings

1976 Crazy On You Heart

1976 Magic Man Heart

1976 The Wreck of the Edmund Fitzgerald Gordon Lightfoot

1976 Hit the Road Jack Stampeders

1976 Tell Me Airlift

1976 The Whole World's Goin' Crazy April Wine

1976 Gimme Love April Wine

1976 Like A Lover, Like A Song April Wine

1976 Anyway You Want It Charity Brown

1976 High In the Rockies Brussel Sprout

1976 Linda Write Me A Letter Choya

1976 Suspicious Love Copperpenny

1976 It's Alright (This Feeling) Crack of Dawn

1976 Having A Party Crescent Street Stompers

1976 Dance Deja Vu

1976 Say You Love Me Shirley Eikhard

1976 Roxanne Peter Foldy

1976 My Lady Fullerton Dam

1976 Wow Andre Gagnon

1976 New York to L.A. Patsy Gallant

1976 Late Night Lovin' Man Hammersmith

1976 (Love Theme From) Missouri Breaks Hagood Hardy

1976 Old Time Movie Lisa Hartt Band

1976 Growin' Up Dan Hill

1976 Santa Jaws Homemade Theatre

1976 Anna Marie Susan Jacks

1976 Memories Are Made of You Susan Jacks

1976 Y' Don't Fight the Sea Terry Jacks

1976 You Can't Dance Jackson Hawke

1976 Harlem Andy Kim

1976 Dolly Liverpool

1976 On the Boulevard Murray McLauchlan

1976 One Night Lovers Tom Middleton

1976 In France They Kiss On Main Street Joni Mitchell

1976 Lazy Love New City Jam Band

1976 I'm Easy Ron Nigrini

1976 Roll You Over Marty Simon

1976 Playing In the Band The Stampeders

1976 Sweet Love Bandit The Stampeders

1976 Sweeney Todd Folder Sweeney Todd

1976 Roxy Roller Sweeney Todd

1976 Cowboys To Girls Sweet Blindness

1976 Sweet Blindness (Music You Can Ride On) Sweet Blindness

1976 Liars Ian Thomas

1976 (Theme From) SWAT THP Orchestra

1976 Clap Your Hands and Stomp Your Feet Thundermug

1976 Give A Little Love Ken Tobias

1976 General Hand Grenade Trooper

1976 Two For the Show Trooper

1976 Loving You Baby Wednesday

1976 Looking For A Love Neil Young

»1977

1977 Gonna Fly Now (Theme From Rocky) Maynard Ferguson

1977 Barracuda Heart

1977 Sometimes When We Touch Dan Hill

1977 Your Love Gets Me Around Ronney Abramson

1977 Happier Paul Anka

1977 Make It Up To Me In Love Paul Anka and Odia Coates

1977 Forever For Now April Wine

1977 You Won't Dance With Me April Wine

1977 Fly At Night Chilliwack

1977 I'm Scared Burton Cummings

1977 Timeless Love Burton Cummings

1977 My Own Way To Rock Burton Cummings

1977 Dazz John Ellison & Soul Brothers Six

1977 Are You Ready For Love Patsy Gallant

1977 Sugar Daddy Patsy Gallant

1977 Calling Occupants of Interplanetary Earth Klaatu

1977 Party Song Lavender Hill Mob

1977 Race Among the Ruins Gordon Lightfoot

1977 Heaven On the Seventh Floor Mighty Pope

1977 Que Sera Sera The Raes

1977 Fightin' On the Side of Love THP Orchestra

1977 It Always Happens This Way Toulouse

1977 A.P.B. Toulouse

CANADIAN HIT SONGS

1977 Santa Maria Trooper
1977 We're Here For A Good Time Trooper
1977 Mr. Love Vehicle
1977 Once In A Long Time Christopher Ward
1977 Ride Me Wednesday

»1978

1978 This Is Love Paul Anka
1978 Hot Child In the City Nick Gilder
1978 Heartless Heart
1978 Straight On Heart
1978 The Circle Is Small (I Can See It In Your Eyes) Gordon Lightfoot

FACTOR
THE FOUNDATION ASSISTING CANADIAN TALENT ON RECORDINGS
WITH SUPPORT FROM CANADA'S PRIVATE RADIO BROADCASTERS

1978 Daylight Katy Gordon Lightfoot
1978 You Needed Me Anne Murray
1978 I Will Still Love You Stonebolt
1978 I Just Wanna Stop Gino Vannelli
1978 Rock 'n' Roll Is A Vicious Game April Wine
1978 Comin' Right Down On Top Of Me April Wine
1978 Arms of Mary Chilliwack
1978 Break It To Them Gently Burton Cummings
1978 Mama Let Him Play Doucette
1978 Let the Song Last Forever Dan Hill
1978 All I See Is Your Face Dan Hill
1978 You and I Rick James
1978 Music Box Dancer Frank Mills
1978 Walk Right Back Anne Murray
1978 Flyin' Prism
1978 Closer To the Heart Rush
1978 Love Is In the Air Martin Stevens
1978 I Will Still Love You Stonebolt
1978 Coming Home Ian Thomas
1978 Oh Pretty Lady Trooper
1978 Raise A Little Hell Trooper
1978 Round Round We Go Trooper
1978 Maybe Your Heart Christopher Ward

»1979

1979 Roller April Wine
1979 Dog & Butterfly Heart
1979 Sweet Lui-Louise Ironhorse
1979 Come To Me France Joli

1979 Music Box Dancer Frank Mills
1979 I Just Fall In Love Again Anne Murray
1979 Shadows In the Moonlight Anne Murray
1979 Broken Hearted Me Anne Murray
1979 So Good, So Right Brenda Russell
1979 Hold On Triumph
1979 Heartaches BTO
1979 (Boogie Woogie) Dancin' Shoes Claudja Barry
1979 Boogie Tonight Claudja Barry
1979 Soul Man Blues Brothers
1979 Rubber Biscuit Blues Brothers
1979 Wondering Where the Lions Are Bruce Cockburn
1979 The Dream Never Dies Cooper Brothers
1979 I Will Play A Rhapsody Burton Cummings
1979 Nobody Doucette
1979 Here Comes the Night Nick Gilder
1979 (You Really) Rock Me Nick Gilder
1979 Please Come Back To Me Good Brothers
1979 Get Up and Boogie Freddie James
1979 Little People (Une Monde Enchanteur) Bob Liddell
1979 Let Go the Line Max Webster
1979 Whispering Rain Murray McLauchlan
1979 Peter Piper Frank Mills
1979 Armageddon Prism
1979 Your Place Or Mine Private Eye
1979 A Little Lovin' (Keeps the Doctor Away) The Raes
1979 I Only Want To Get Up and Dance The Raes
1979 Dancer Gino Soccio
1979 Midnight Magic Martin Stevens
1979 Hold On Triumph
1979 We All Need Love Domenic Troiano
1979 The Moment That It Takes Trooper
1979 The Boys In the Bright White Sports Car Trooper
1979 Wheels Of Life Gino Vannelli

CANADIAN HIT SONGS OF THE 1980s

»1980

1980 Wondering Where the Lions Are Bruce Cockburn
1980 Even It Up Heart
1980 Tell It Like It Is Heart
1980 Daydream Believer Anne Murray

1980 Could I Have This Dance Anne Murray
1980 Say Hello April Wine
1980 Gimme Some Lovin' Blues Brothers
1980 Tokyo Bruce Cockburn
1980 Fine State of Affairs Burton Cummings
1980 Too Bad Doug & the Slugs
1980 Tiny Thing Jenson Interceptor
1980 The Kid Is Hot Tonight Loverboy
1980 Echo Beach M+M (Martha and the Muffins)
1980 Paradise Skies Max Webster
1980 Doin' It Right Powder Blues Band
1980 Night To Remember Prism
1980 Young and Restless Prism
1980 White Hot Red Rider
1980 The Spirit of Radio Rush
1980 Can I Come Near Graham Shaw
1980 Under My Thumb Streetheart
1980 Somethin' On My Mind Teenage Head
1980 Even the Score Toronto
1980 Three Dressed Up As A Nine Trooper
1980 Janine Trooper

»1981
1981 Just Between You and Me April Wine
1981 Sign of the Gypsy Queen April Wine
1981 My Girl (Gone, Gone, Gone) Chilliwack
1981 You Saved My Soul Burton Cummings
1981 Turn Me Loose Loverboy
1981 Lady of the '80s Loverboy
1981 Blessed Are the Believers Anne Murray
1981 Living Inside Myself Gino Vannelli
1981 Say What Jesse Winchester
1981 Who's Making Love Blues Brothers
1981 My Girl (Gone, Gone, Gone) Chilliwack
1981 Coldest Night of the Year Bruce Cockburn
1981 You Saved My Soul Burton Cummings
1981 Innocence Harlequin
1981 Thinking of You Harlequin
1981 Happy Birthday Kid Geoff Hughes
1981 The Love Of A Woman Klaatu
1981 Women Around the World At Work M+M (Martha and the Muffins)
1981 If the Wind Could Blow My Troubles Away Murray McLauchlan
1981 Thirsty Ears Powder Blues Band
1981 Lovin' Kissin' and Huggin' Powder Blues Band

1981 Don't Let Him Know Prism
1981 What Have You Got To Do? (To Get Off Tonight) Red Rider
1981 Fashion Victim Rough Trade
1981 High School Confidential Rough Trade
1981 All Touch Rough Trade
1981 Wasn't That A Party Rovers
1981 Limelight Rush
1981 Tom Sawyer Rush
1981 Does A Fool Ever Learn Eddie Schwartz
1981 Hold On Ian Thomas
1981 Chains Ian Thomas
1981 Magic Power Triumph
1981 In the Mood Wildroot Orchestra
1981 Say What Jesse Winchester
1981 For You Zon

»1982
1982 Murphy's Law Cheri
1982 I Believe Chilliwack
1982 Working For the Weekend Loverboy
1982 When It's Over Loverboy
1982 Take Off Bob & Doug McKenzie featuring Geddy Lee
1982 Fantasy Aldo Nova
1982 Don't Let Him Know Prism
1982 New World Man Rush
1982 All Our Tomorrows Eddie Schwartz
1982 Fits Ya Good Bryan Adams
1982 Enough Is Enough April Wine
1982 Tell Me Why April Wine
1982 I Believe Chilliwack
1982 Whatcha Gonna Do (When I'm Gone) Chilliwack
1982 Hey Operator Coney Hatch
1982 Pretty Bad Boy Goddo
1982 Superstitious Feeling Harlequin
1982 I Did It For Love Harlequin
1982 Don't It Make Ya Feel Headpins
1982 Fantasy Aldo Nova
1982 Foolin' Yourself Aldo Nova
1982 Eyes Of A Stranger The Payola$
1982 Soldier The Payola$
1982 Boys of Autumn David Roberts
1982 New World Man Rush
1982 Wind Him Up Saga
1982 All Our Tomorrows Eddie Schwartz

CANADIAN HIT SONGS

1982 Over the Line Eddie Schwartz
1982 You Remind Me Sheriff
1982 Nova Heart Spoons
1982 Arias & Symphonies Spoons
1982 Hiding From Love Rosetta Stone
1982 Letting Go Straight Lines
1982 What Kind of Love Is This? Streetheart
1982 Some Kinda Fun Teenage Head
1982 Your Daddy Don't Know Toronto
1982 Start Tellin' the Truth Toronto
1982 Say Goodbye Triumph
1982 Only A Fool Trooper

»1983

1983 Straight From the Heart Bryan Adams
1983 Cuts Like A Knife Bryan Adams
1983 This Time Bryan Adams
1983 Hold Me 'Til the Mornin' Comes Paul Anka
1983 Hot Girls In Love Loverboy
1983 Queen of the Broken Hearts Loverboy
1983 The Safety Dance Men Without Hats
1983 On the Loose Saga
1983 OK Blue Jays Bat Boys
1983 Don't Stop Chilliwack
1983 Who Knows How To Make Love Stay Doug & the Slugs
1983 Making It Work Doug & the Slugs
1983 Celebration Headpins
1983 Love In the Shadow Dan Hill
1983 Every Time I See Your Picture Luba
1983 Danseparc (Every Day It's Tomorrow) M+M (Martha and the Muffins)
1983 The Safety Dance Men Without Hats
1983 Sign of the Times Mens Room
1983 Rise Up Parachute Club
1983 Never Said I Loved You The Payola$ & Carole Pope
1983 Video Kids Prototype
1983 Human Race Red Rider
1983 Crimes of Passion Rough Trade
1983 Subdivisions Rush
1983 When I'm With You Sheriff
1983 Smiling In Winter Spoons
1983 Old Emotions Spoons
1983 Kiss In the Dark Strange Advance
1983 Worlds Away Strange Advance
1983 Start Again Surrender
1983 Tornado Teenage Head

1983 Sheriff The Tenants
1983 Twenty Questions Tic Toc
1983 Girls Night Out Toronto
1983 All I Need Toronto

»1984

1984 Run To You Bryan Adams
1984 Sunglasses At Night Corey Hart
1984 It Ain't Enough Corey Hart
1984 Almost Paradise... Love Theme From Footloose Mike Reno and Ann Wilson
1984 Meet Me In the Middle Arrows
1984 Walk Away The Box
1984 Melody Boys Brigade
1984 Lovers In A Dangerous Time Bruce Cockburn
1984 Just One More Time Headpins
1984 Rock You Helix
1984 New Girl Now Honeymoon Suite
1984 The Curly Shuffle Jump In the Saddle
1984 I Want You Back Sherry Kean
1984 The Curly Shuffle The Knuckleheads
1984 Let It Go Luba
1984 Black Stations/White Stations M+M (Martha and the Muffins)
1984 Where Do the Boys Go? Men Without Hats
1984 Go For Soda Kim Mitchell
1984 Doesn't Really Matter Platinum Blonde
1984 Standing In the Dark Platinum Blonde
1984 Listen To the Radio The Pukka Orchestra
1984 Young Thing, Wild Dream (Rock Me) Red Rider
1984 Almost Paradise Mike Reno & Ann Wilson
1984 Scratching the Surface Saga
1984 All Right Now Santers
1984 Strike Eddie Schwartz
1984 Tell No Lies Spoons
1984 Ready To Make Up Toronto
1984 New Romance Toronto

»1985

1985 Christmas Time Bryan Adams
1985 Somebody Bryan Adams
1985 Heaven Bryan Adams
1985 Summer of '69 Bryan Adams
1985 One Night Love Affair Bryan Adams
1985 It's Only Love Bryan Adams and Tina Turner
1985 Love Theme From St. Elmo's Fire David Foster
1985 Lamp At Midnight Corey Hart
1985 Never Surrender Corey Hart

1985 Boy In the Box Corey Hart
1985 Everything In My Heart Corey Hart
1985 Wasn't That A Party The Rovers
1985 Lovin' Every Minute of It Loverboy
1985 Talk Talk Arrows
1985 Mona With the Children Doug Cameron
1985 If I Had A Rocket Launcher Bruce Cockburn
1985 Just Like You FM
1985 Let Me In Nick Gilder
1985 A Criminal Mind Gowan
1985 (You're A) Strange Animal Gowan
1985 Guerilla Soldier Gowan
1985 (Make Me Do) Anything You Want Helix
1985 Stay In the Light Honeymoon Suite
1985 Tokyo Rose Idle Eyes
1985 Go To Pieces Paul Janz
1985 Storm Before the Calm Luba
1985 Tears Are Not Enough Northern Lights
1985 At the Feet of the Moon Parachute Club
1985 You're the Only Love Paul Hyde & the Payola$
1985 Not In Love Platinum Blonde
1985 Crying Over You Platinum Blonde
1985 Situation Critical Platinum Blonde
1985 One More Colour Jane Siberry
1985 We Run Strange Advance
1985 Black Car Gino Vannelli
1985 Hurts To Be In Love Gino Vannelli

»1986

1986 Don't Forget Me (When I'm Gone) Glass Tiger
1986 Thin Red Line Glass Tiger
1986 Someday Glass Tiger
1986 I Am By Your Side Corey Hart
1986 Feel It Again Honeymoon Suite
1986 This Could Be the Night Loverboy
1986 Heaven In Your Eyes Loverboy
1986 For Tonight Nancy Martinez
1986 Somebody's Out There Triumph
1986 Action Speaks Louder Action
1986 L'Affair Dumoutier The Box
1986 Flippin' To the 'A' Side Cats Can Fly
1986 April Fool Chalk Circle
1986 People See Through You Bruce Cockburn
1986 The Best Of Me David Foster and Olivia
        Newton-John
1986 Cosmetics Gowan
1986 Eurasian Eyes Corey Hart
1986 I Am By Your Side Corey Hart

1986 Bad Bad Boy Haywire
1986 What Does It Take Honeymoon Suite
1986 Anything For Love Gordon Lightfoot
1986 Stay Loose Gordon Lightfoot
1986 How Many (Rivers To Cross) Luba
1986 Song In My Head M+M (Martha and the
        Muffins)
1986 Patio Lanterns Kim Mitchell
1986 Alana Loves Me Kim Mitchell
1986 Now and Forever (You and Me) Anne Murray
1986 There Was A Time One To One
1986 Angel In My Pocket One To One
1986 Love Is Fire Parachute Club
1986 Soul City Partland Brothers
1986 Somebody, Somewhere Platinum Blonde
1986 Boy Inside the Man Tom Cochrane & Red Rider
1986 When I Fall In Love Again Zappacosta

»1987

1987 Heat of the Night Bryan Adams
1987 Hearts on Fire Bryan Adams
1987 Victim of Love Bryan Adams

CANADIAN HIT SONGS

1987 I Will Be There Glass Tiger
1987 Can't Help Falling In Love Corey Hart
1987 Dancing With My Mirror Corey Hart
1987 Too Good To Be Enough Corey Hart
1987 Can't We Try Dan Hill with Vonda Sheppard
1987 Notorious Loverboy
1987 Pop Goes the World Men Without Hats
1987 Kiss Him Goodbye The Nylons
1987 Soul City Partland Brothers
1987 Only Human Lee Aaron
1987 Try Blue Rodeo
1987 Closer Together The Box
1987 Ordinary People The Box
1987 Rain Michael Breen
1987 This Mourning Chalk Circle
1987 20th Century Boy Chalk Circle
1987 Waiting For A Miracle Bruce Cockburn
1987 Kiss You (When It's Dangerous) Eight Seconds
1987 Dream Girl FM
1987 Should I See Frozen Ghost
1987 You're What I Look For Glass Tiger
1987 I Will Be There Glass Tiger
1987 Moonlight Desires Gowan
1987 Awake the Giant Gowan
1987 Together (The New Wedding Song) Joey Gregorash
1987 Dance Desire Haywire
1987 Can't We Try Dan Hill
1987 Last of the Red Hot Fools Jitters
1987 Walkin' A Fine Line Johansen
1987 Notorious Loverboy
1987 Flying On Your Own Rita MacNeil
1987 For Tonight Nancy Martinez
1987 Pop Goes the World Men Without Hats
1987 Easy To Tame Kim Mitchell
1987 Only Love Sets You Free Patrick Norman
1987 Teenland Northern Pikes
1987 Kiss Him Goodbye The Nylons
1987 Contact Platinum Blonde
1987 I'm An Adult Now Pursuit of Happiness
1987 Dirty Water Rock & Hyde
1987 I Will Rock & Hyde
1987 Time Stand Still Rush
1987 Just One Night Triumph
1987 Stay With Me Tu
1987 Wild Horses Gino Vannelli
1987 Make A Move On Me Véronique
1987 Nothing Could Stand In Your Way Zappacosta

»1988

1988 I'm Still Searching Glass Tiger
1988 In Your Soul Corey Hart
1988 Piano In the Dark Brenda Russell
1988 When I'm With You Sheriff
1988 Julian Alta Moda
1988 Come Back To Me Barney Bentall
1988 Something To Live For Barney Bentall
1988 Into the Night Big Bang
1988 Day After Day Blue Rodeo
1988 Never Give Up Blvd
1988 Far From Over Blvd
1988 Dream On Blvd
1988 Crying Out Loud For Love The Box
1988 Dancing Under A Latin Moon Candi
1988 Smile Me Down Andrew Cash
1988 Ain't Good Lovin' Diamond In the Rough
1988 Tomcat Prowl Doug & the Slugs
1988 Savin' Myself Eria Fachin
1988 Winter Games David Foster
1988 And When She Danced David Foster and Marilyn Martin
1988 Round and Round Frozen Ghost
1988 I'm Still Searching Glass Tiger
1988 Diamond Sun Glass Tiger
1988 My Song Glass Tiger
1988 Do You Know What I Mean Myles Goodwin and Lee Aaron
1988 In Your Heart Corey Hart
1988 Spot You In A Coalmine Corey Hart
1988 Black and Blue Haywire
1988 Thinkin' About the Years Haywire
1988 Never Thought (I Could Live) Dan Hill
1988 Carmelia Dan Hill
1988 It's Over Now Honeymoon Suite
1988 Love Changes Everything Honeymoon Suite
1988 Lookin' Out For Number One Honeymoon Suite
1988 Voodoo Thing Colin James
1988 Believe In Me Paul Janz
1988 Here We Go Again Johansen
1988 When A Man Loves A Woman Luba
1988 Walk On Through Rita MacNeil
1988 Moonbeam Men Without Hats
1988 My Secret Place Joni Mitchell
1988 Flying On Your Own Anne Murray
1988 Hold Me Now One To One
1988 Connect Me Platinum Blonde

1988 Fire Platinum Blonde
1988 Big League Tom Cochrane & Red Rider
1988 Showdown At Big Sky Robbie Robertson
1988 Shangri-La Roman Grey
1988 IBU Roman Grey
1988 Gimme Some Kind of Sign The Sattalites
1988 Let It Begin Tonight Liberty Silver
1988 Love Becomes Electric Strange Advance
1988 Hands Up (Give Me Your Heart) Sway
1988 Levity Ian Thomas

»1989

1989 Miss You 54-40
1989 Whatcha Do To My Body Lee Aaron
1989 The House of Love Barney Bentall
1989 She's My Inspiration Barney Bentall
1989 Shooting From My Heart Big Bamboo
1989 How Long Blue Rodeo
1989 Diamond Mine Blue Rodeo
1989 House of Dreams Blue Rodeo
1989 One More Try Brighton Rock
1989 Under Your Spell Candi
1989 Missing You Candi
1989 Love Makes No Promises Candi
1989 What Am I Gonna Do With These Hands Andrew Cash
1989 Boomtown Andrew Cash
1989 Sons & Daughters Chalk Circle
1989 Don't Feel Your Touch Bruce Cockburn
1989 If A Tree Falls Bruce Cockburn
1989 Misguided Angel Cowboy Junkies
1989 Sweet Jane Cowboy Junkies
1989 Tango Dalbello
1989 My Sensation Eye Eye
1989 Pauper In Paradise Frozen Ghost
1989 Dream Come True Frozen Ghost
1989 We Close Our Eyes David Gibson
1989 Send Your Love Glass Tiger
1989 (Watching) Worlds Crumble Glass Tiger
1989 All the Things I Wasn't Grapes of Wrath
1989 Still In Love Corey Hart
1989 Angel Eyes The Jeff Healey Band
1989 Unborn Heart Dan Hill
1989 Still Lovin' You Honeymoon Suite
1989 America Is Sexy Paul Hyde
1989 Blue Train Idle Eyes
1989 Hard Sun Indio
1989 Five Long Years Colin James

1989 Dream of Satin Colin James
1989 Why'd You Lie Colin James
1989 Tell Somebody Sass Jordan
1989 Double Trouble Sass Jordan
1989 So Hard Sass Jordan
1989 Stranger Than Paradise Sass Jordan
1989 Harry Houdini Kon Kan
1989 I Beg Your Pardon Kon Kan
1989 Giving Away A Miracle Luba
1989 Hey Men Men Without Hats
1989 Rock 'N' Roll Duty Kim Mitchell
1989 Rocklandwonderland Kim Mitchell
1989 Love Is Alannah Myles
1989 Still Got This Thing Alannah Myles
1989 I Can't Take It Billy Newton-Davis
1989 Can't Live With You Billy Newton-Davis
1989 Hopes Go Astray Northern Pikes
1989 Love Child One To One
1989 Do You Believe One To One
1989 Another Day Paradox
1989 Waterline Paradox
1989 Beautiful White Pursuit of Happiness
1989 She's So Young Pursuit of Happiness
1989 Victory Day Tom Cochrane & Red Rider
1989 Good Times Tom Cochrane & Red Rider
1989 Another Man's Gun Ray Lyell & the Storm
1989 Give Me Your Love Roman Grey
1989 Woman's Work Sheree
1989 Waterline Spoons
1989 Blow At High Dough The Tragically Hip
1989 Back To Square One Ian Thomas
1989 Boy With A Beat Trooper
1989 It Doesn't Matter Coleman Wilde
1989 Rockin' the Free World Neil Young

CANADIAN HIT SONGS OF THE 1990s

»1990

1990 Hands On Lee Aaron
1990 Haunted Heart Alias
1990 More Than Words Can Say Alias
1990 Crime Against Love Barney Bentall and the Legendary Hearts
1990 Life Could Be Worse Barney Bentall and the Legendary Hearts
1990 Til I Am Myself Again Blue Rodeo
1990 Crazy Life Boulevard
1990 Lead Me On Boulevard

1990 The World Just Keeps On Turning Candi and the Backbeat

1990 Don't Wanna Fall In Love Jane Child

1990 Rock and Bird Cowboy Junkies

1990 Sun Comes Up, It's Tuesday Morning Cowboy Junkies

1990 Inside Out Crash Vegas

1990 Take One Away Burton Cummings

1990 Unison Celine Dion

1990 Big Lie Rik Emmett

1990 When A Heart Breaks Rik Emmett

1990 Heart In Pieces Tim Feehan

1990 All the Lovers In the World Gowan

1990 Lost Brotherhood Gowan

1990 Do You Want To Tell Me? Grapes of Wrath

1990 What Was Going Through My Head Grapes of Wrath

1990 A Little Love Corey Hart

1990 Bang! (Starting Over) Corey Hart

1990 Good To the Last Drop Helix

1990 Just Came Back Colin James

1990 Keep On Lovin' Me Baby Colin James

1990 Every Little Tear Paul Janz

1990 Hold Me Tender Paul Janz

1990 Rocket To My Heart Paul Janz

1990 Stand Paul Janz

1990 Edge of the World Marc Jordan

1990 Rescue Me Sass Jordan

1990 Little Salvation Luba

1990 No More Words Luba

1990 Don't Look Back Kenny MacLean

1990 Rescue Me Kenny MacLean

1990 Drop the Needle Maestro Fresh Wes

1990 Let Your Backbone Slip Maestro Fresh Wes

1990 Dangerous Times Sue Medley

1990 Love Thing Sue Medley

1990 That's Life Sue Medley

1990 In the 21st Century Men Without Hats

1990 Expedition Sailor Kim Mitchell

1990 I Am A Wild Party Kim Mitchell

1990 I'll Watch Over You Mae Moore

1990 Where Loveliness Lives Mae Moore

1990 Black Velvet Alannah Myles

1990 Lover of Mine Alannah Myles

1990 Girl With A Problem Northern Pikes

1990 Kiss Me You Fool Northern Pikes

1990 She Ain't Pretty Northern Pikes

1990 Honest Man Partland Brothers

1990 Untouched Partland Brothers

1990 Carry Me Ray Lyell & the Storm

1990 Cruel Life Ray Lyell & the Storm

1990 This Is Love Regatta

1990 Wherever You Run Regatta

1990 Show Don't Tell Rush

1990 The Pass Rush

1990 Stealin' Fire Lorraine Segato

1990 Before We Fall Sheree

1990 Forever You, Forever Me Sheree

1990 I Will Give You Everything Skydiggers

1990 Carry On The Box

1990 Inside My Heart The Box

1990 Temptation The Box

1990 I Think I Love You Too Much The Jeff Healey Band

1990 While My Guitar Gently Weeps The Jeff Healey Band

1990 The Bridge Is Burning The Jitters

1990 Til the Fever Breaks The Jitters

1990 New Language The Pursuit of Happiness

1990 Two Girls In One The Pursuit of Happiness

1990 38 Years Ago The Tragically Hip

1990 Boots or Hearts The Tragically Hip

1990 White Hot Tom Cochrane & Red Ryder

1990 The Time of Day Gino Vannelli

1990 Still Beating World On Edge

1990 Letter Back Zappacosta

»1991

1991 Call Me Acosta-Russell

1991 Never Change My Mind Acosta-Russell

1991 (Everything I Do) I Do It For You Bryan Adams

1991 Can't Stop This Thing We Started Bryan Adams

1991 Feel Your Love Alanis

1991 Too Hot Alanis

1991 Walkaway Alanis

1991 Waiting For Love Alias

1991 I Gotta Go Barney Bentall and the Legendary Hearts

1991 Faithlessly Yours Art Bergmann

1991 After the Rain Blue Rodeo

1991 Trust Yourself Blue Rodeo

1991 What Am I Doing Here Blue Rodeo

1991 Everyone's A Winner Bootsauce

1991 Friends Forever Candi and the Backbeat

1991 Good Together Candi and the Backbeat

1991 Life Is A Highway Tom Cochrane

1991 No Regrets Tom Cochrane

1991 A Dream Like Mine Bruce Cockburn

1991 Superman's Song Crash Test Dummies

1991 The Ghosts That Haunt Me Crash Test Dummies

1991 Have A Heart Celine Dion

1991 Where Does My Heart Beat Now Celine Dion

1991 (If There Was) Any Other Way Celine Dion

1991 Saved By Love Rik Emmett

1991 World of Wonder Rik Emmett

1991 Hold On Joey Ferrera

1991 Animal Heart Glass Tiger

1991 My Town Glass Tiger

1991 Rescued (By the Arms of Love) Glass Tiger

1991 The Rhythm of Your Love Glass Tiger

1991 Out of A Deeper Hunger Gowan

1991 I Am Here Grapes of Wrath

1991 Let Her Go Gregory Hoskins and the Stickpeople

1991 Neighbourhood Gregory Hoskins and the Stickpeople

1991 Slowly Slipping Away Harem Scarem

1991 I Fall All Over Again Dan Hill

1991 Say You Don't Know Me Honeymoon Suite

1991 100 Watt Bulb Infidels

1991 Just Another Day Keven Jordan

1991 No Sign of Rain Keven Jordan

1991 True Believers Keven Jordan

1991 Powerdrive Longfellow

1991 Conductin' Thangs Maestro Fresh Wes

1991 Into the Fire Sarah McLachlan

1991 The Path of Thorns Sarah McLachlan

1991 Maybe the Next Time Sue Medley

1991 Sideways Men Without Hats

1991 Cry To Me Darby Mills

1991 Come In From the Cold Joni Mitchell

1991 Red Clay Hills Mae Moore

1991 Dream Away Northern Pikes

1991 Kiss Me On the Lips Paradox

1991 What About Now Robbie Robertson

1991 Dreamline Rush

1991 Roll the Bones Rush

1991 The Answer's Electric Brett Ryan

1991 Boomerang Spunkadelic

1991 Runaround Glen Stace

1991 Love You Too Much The Boomers

1991 How Long Can A Man Be Strong The Jeff Healey Band

1991 How Much The Jeff Healey Band

1991 Love Is the Subject Odds

1991 Little Bones The Tragically Hip

1991 Twist My Arm The Tragically Hip

1991 Refuse To Die Too Many Cooks

1991 American Dream Trooper

1991 Cry of Love Gino Vannelli

1991 If I Should Lose This Love Gino Vannelli

1991 Not Like Kissing You West End Girls

1991 Say You'll Be Mine West End Girls

1991 Little Lack of Love World On Edge

1991 Only the Lonely World On Edge

1991 Standing Push and Fall World On Edge

1991 Wash the Rain World On Edge

1991 Weight of the World Young Saints

1991 I'll Be the One Zappacosta

1991 Simple Words To Say Zappacosta

»1992

1992 Music Man 54-40

1992 Nice To Luv You 54-40

1992 She-La 54-40

1992 Deep In My Soul Acosta Russell

1992 You're So Tempting Acosta Russell

1992 There Will Never Be Another Tonight Bryan Adams

1992 Thought I'd Died and Gone To Heaven Bryan Adams

1992 Do I Have To Say the Words Bryan Adams

1992 An Emotion Away Alanis

1992 Ghosts Kerri Anderson

1992 Enid Barenaked Ladies

1992 Lovers In A Dangerous Time Barenaked Ladies

1992 Doin' Fine Barney Bentall

1992 Livin' In the '90s Barney Bentall

1992 Baby Dolls Big House

1992 Lost Together Blue Rodeo

1992 Rain Down On Me Blue Rodeo

1992 One Little Word The Boomers

1992 Love Monkey #9 Bootsauce

1992 The Sweater Meryn Cadell

1992 Life Is A Highway Tom Cochrane

1992 Mad, Mad World Tom Cochrane

1992 Sinking Like A Sunset Tom Cochrane

1992 Washed Away Tom Cochrane

CANADIAN HIT SONGS

1992 Great Big Love Bruce Cockburn

1992 Somebody Touched Me Bruce Cockburn

1992 Southern Rain Cowboy Junkies

1992 Beauty and the Beast Celine Dion and Peabo Bryson

1992 If You Asked Me To Celine Dion

1992 Nothing Broken But My Heart Celine Dion

1992 Bang On Rik Emmett

1992 Head Over Heels Frozen Ghost

1992 Cry (If You Want To) Frozen Ghost

1992 Head Over Heels Frozen Ghost

1992 92 Days of Rain Corey Hart

1992 Always Corey Hart

1992 Baby When I Call Your Name Corey Hart

1992 Buzz Haywire

1992 Get Back Haywire

1992 Wanna Be the One Haywire

1992 Is It Really Love Dan Hill

1992 Celebrate Infidels

1992 Without Love Infidels

1992 This Love Is Forever Paul Janz

1992 Wind Me Up Paul Janz

1992 Goin' Back Again Sass Jordan

1992 I Want To Believe Sass Jordan

1992 Make You A Believer Sass Jordan

1992 You Don't Have To Remind Me Sass Jordan

1992 Constant Craving k.d. lang

1992 In Your Eyes Leslie Spit Treeo

1992 Brand New Set of Lies Lost and Profound

1992 Don't Stop Now Love & Sas

1992 One In A Lifetime Love & Sas

1992 Inside Out Sue Medley

1992 Jane's House Sue Medley

1992 When the Stars Fall Sue Medley

1992 It's No Secret Stan Meissner

1992 River of Fire Stan Meissner

1992 Give It All Up Darby Mills

1992 America Kim Mitchell

1992 Find the Will Kim Mitchell

1992 Pure As Gold Kim Mitchell

1992 Some Folks Kim Mitchell

1992 Tear It All Down Monkeywalk

1992 Bohemia Mae Moore

1992 Song Instead of a Kiss Alannah Myles

1992 Twister Northern Pikes

1992 Someday Aldo Nova

1992 King of the Heap Odds

1992 Friends One2One

1992 Memory Lane One2One

1992 Peace of Mind (Love Goes On) One2One

1992 Go Back To Your Woods Robbie Robertson

1992 Shake This Town Robbie Robertson

1992 Ghost of a Chance Rush

1992 Fallen Angels Buffy Sainte-Marie

1992 The Big Ones Get Away Buffy Sainte-Marie

1992 I Run To You Scott Dibble & Watertown

1992 A Penny More Skydiggers

1992 White Lies/Black Truth Slik Toxic

1992 Cruel Little Number The Jeff Healey Band

1992 Fare Thee Well Love The Rankin Family

1992 Locked In the Trunk of a Car The Tragically Hip

1992 Show Me the Way West Ends Girls

1992 My Temptation Vivienne Williams

1992 Goodbye World On Edge

1992 Harvest Moon Neil Young

1992 War of Man Neil Young

» 1993

1993 More 13 Engines

1993 All For Love Bryan Adams, Rod Stewart & Sting

1993 Change (Is Never A Waste of Time) Alanis

1993 No Apologies Alanis

1993 If You Believe In Me April Wine

1993 Voice In My Heart April Wine

1993 I'm Not Your Lover Jann Arden

1993 I Would Die For You Jann Arden

1993 Will You Remember Me Jann Arden

1993 Prairie Town Bachman

1993 The Truth Banned In the U.K.

1993 If I Had $1,000,000 Barenaked Ladies

1993 What A Good Boy Barenaked Ladies

1993 If This Is Love Barney Bentall

1993 5 Days In May Blue Rodeo

1993 Already Gone Blue Rodeo

1993 Flying Blue Rodeo

1993 It's Just the Rain Alexander Caplin

1993 Bigger Man Tom Cochrane

1993 Hard To Explain Cowboy Junkies

1993 Mmm, Mmm. Mmm, Mmm Crash Test Dummies

1993 Did You Give Enough Love Celine Dion

1993 Love Can Move Mountains Celine Dion

1993 When I Fall In Love Celine Dion and Clive Griffin

1993 Heaven In Your Heart Rik Emmett

1993 'Til the Last Teardrop Falls Exchange with Marc Jordan and Amy Sky

1993 Touch of Your Hand Glass Tiger

1993 Say You Will Gogh Van Go

1993 When There's Time (For Love) Lawrence Gowan

1993 Dance of the Vulnerable Gregory Hoskins and the Stick People

1993 I Want (Cool, Cool Love) Corey Hart

1993 Man On A Mission Hemingway Corner

1993 So Long JFK Hemingway Corner

1993 Healing Power of Love Dan Hill

1993 Let Me Show You Dan Hill

1993 I Can See Clearly Now Holly Cole Trio

1993 Cadillac Baby Colin James

1993 Amazon Rain Paul Janz

1993 Miss My Love Sheree Jeacocke

1993 Serious Sheree Jeacocke

1993 Waiting For A Miracle Marc Jordan

1993 Who Do You Think You Are Sass Jordan

1993 Out of My Head Junkhouse

1993 Just Keep Me Moving k.d. lang

1993 The Mind of Love (Where Is...) k.d. lang

1993 Lot of Love To Give Daniel Lanois

1993 Gypsy Wind Ray Lyell

1993 Possession Sarah McLachlan

1993 Heading West Mitsou

1993 Big Money Monkey House

1993 Lazy Nina Monkey House

1993 Because of Love Mae Moore

1993 Coat of Shame Mae Moore

1993 The Wish Mae Moore

1993 Stuck In the '90s Moxy Fruvous

1993 Make Love To Me Anne Murray

1993 Living On A Memory Alannah Myles

1993 Our World Our Dream Alannah Myles

1993 Sonny Say You Will Alannah Myles

1993 Believe Northern Pikes

1993 Worlds Away Northern Pikes

1993 Blast Pure

1993 Informer Snow

1993 Girl, I've Been Hurt Snow

1993 And If Venice Is Sinking Spirit of the West

1993 Love Don't Live Here Anymore Sven Gali

1993 Remedy The Band

1993 Darling Be Home Soon The Barra MacNeils

1993 Row, Row, Row The Barra MacNeils

1993 Art of Living The Boomers

1993 You've Got To Know The Boomers

1993 Lost In Your Eyes The Jeff Healey Band

1993 Lift Me Up The Partland Brothers

1993 Cigarette Dangles The Pursuit of Happiness

1993 North Country The Rankin Family

1993 Rise Again The Rankin Family

1993 The River The Tea Party

1993 Save Me The Tea Party

1993 At the Hundredth Meridien The Tragically Hip

1993 Courage The Tragically Hip

1993 Fifty Mission Cap The Tragically Hip

1993 Colder Than You The Waltons

1993 In the Meantime The Waltons

1993 Naked Rain The Waltons

1993 Missing Persons Tim Thorney

1993 I'll Always Be There Roch Voisine

1993 Oochigeas (Indian Song) Roch Voisine

1993 Look Me In the Eye Vivienne Williams

1993 Long May You Run Neil Young

» 1994

1994 Blame Your Parents 54-40

1994 Ocean Pearl 54-40

1994 Please Forgive Me Bryan Adams

1994 Could I Be Your Girl Jann Arden

1994 Alternative Girlfriend Barenaked Ladies

1994 Jane Barenaked Ladies

1994 Bad Timing Blue Rodeo

1994 Hasn't Hit Me Yet Blue Rodeo

1994 Listen For the Laugh Bruce Cockburn

1994 Scanning These Crowds Bruce Cockburn

1994 Anniversary Song Cowboy Junkies

1994 Afternoons and Coffeespoons Crash Test Dummies

1994 God Shuffled His Feet Crash Test Dummies

1994 Mmm Mmm Mmm Mmm Crash Test Dummies

1994 Swimming In Your Ocean Crash Test Dummies

1994 Brown-Eyed Girl Freddy Curci

1994 Misled Celine Dion

1994 Only One Road Celine Dion

1994 The Power of Love Celine Dion

1994 Think Twice Celine Dion

1994 Healing Hands Alan Frew

1994 So Blind Alan Frew

1994 Solid Ground Ginger

1994 Dancing On My Own Ground Lawrence Gowan

1994 Soul's Road Lawrence Gowan

CANADIAN HIT SONGS

1994 Your Stone Walls Lawrence Gowan
1994 King of New York Hemingway Corner
1994 Love, Love, Love Hemingway Corner
1994 Ride It Out Hemingway Corner
1994 Tell Me Why Hemingway Corner
1994 In Your Eyes Dan Hill and Rique Franks
1994 Sometimes When We Touch Dan Hill and Rique Franks
1994 So Gently We Go I Mother Earth
1994 Breakin' Up the House Colin James
1994 Surely (I Love You) Colin James
1994 Broadway Joe Keven Jordan
1994 High Road Easy Sass Jordan
1994 Sun's Gonna Rise Sass Jordan
1994 Prayin' For Rain Junkhouse
1994 The Sky Is Falling Junkhouse
1994 Hush Sweet Lover k.d. lang
1994 Invitation Lost and Profound
1994 Miracles Happen Lost and Profound
1994 One More Moment Julie Masse
1994 Good Enough Sarah McLachlan
1994 I Had A Dream Carol Medina
1994 Acrimony Kim Mitchell
1994 Believe Me Moist
1994 Silver Moist
1994 Change Your Mind Neil Young and Crazy Horse
1994 Starseed Our Lady Peace
1994 Angels Real World
1994 Throwin' It All Away Real World
1994 We All Need Real World
1994 Toy Train Rhymes with Orange
1994 Bad Intentions Robbie Robertson
1994 Cold Fire Rush
1994 Nobody's Hero Rush
1994 Missing You Richard Samuels
1994 Coax Me Sloan
1994 In the Wink of an Eye The Barra MacNeils
1994 Daydream The Earthtones
1994 You're Coming Home The Jeff Healey Band
1994 Time of the Season The Nylons
1994 Borders and Time The Rankin Family
1994 Save Me The Tea Party
1994 Grace Too The Tragically Hip
1994 Greasy Jungle The Tragically Hip
1994 All Uncovered The Watchmen
1994 Boneyard Tree The Watchmen

1994 Am I Wrong Roch Voisine
1994 Lost Without You Roch Voisine
1994 She Picked On Me Roch Voisine
1994 Shout Out Loud Roch Voisine
1994 There's No Easy Way Roch Voisine
1994 Bet You Think I'm Lonely Wild Strawberries
1994 Cryin' Shame Wild Strawberries
1994 Loveland Wild T and the Spirit

»1995

1995 Have You Ever Really Loved A Woman? Bryan Adams
1995 O Siem Susan Aglukark
1995 Insensitive Jann Arden
1995 Wonderdrug Jann Arden
1995 Unloved Jann Arden with Jackson Browne
1995 Good Mother Jann Arden
1995 Wonderdrug Jann Arden
1995 Life In A Nutshell Barenaked Ladies
1995 You Love, You Gain John Bottomley
1995 I Wish You Well Tom Cochrane
1995 Sentimental Deborah Cox
1995 The Ballad of Peter Pumpkinhead Crash Test Dummies
1995 How Strong Doucette
1995 Tell Me Groove Kings
1995 I'm Not Sass Jordan
1995 Tell Me You Love Me Carol Medina
1995 Hand In My Pocket Alanis Morissette
1995 You Oughta Know Alanis Morissette
1995 Truth Untold Odds
1995 She Forgot To Laugh Rhymes With Orange
1995 Bourbon Street Eddie Schwartz
1995 Shade of Your Love Laura Smith
1995 We Celebrate The Barra MacNeils
1995 Move This Night The Earthtones
1995 I Got A Line On You The Jeff Healey Band
1995 Love T.K.O. The Nylons
1995 The Bazaar The Tea Party
1995 Fire In the Head The Tea Party
1995 Nautical Disaster The Tragically Hip
1995 Any Man of Mine Shania Twain
1995 Prime of Life Neil Young

»1996

1996 Let's Make A Night To Remember Bryan Adams
1996 The Only Thing That Looks Good On Me Is You Bryan Adams

1996 I Finally Found Someone Barbra Streisand & Bryan Adams

1996 Looking For It (Finding Heaven) Jann Arden

1996 Digging A Hole Big Sugar

1996 If I Had My Way Big Sugar

1996 Open Up Baby Big Sugar

1996 Who Do U Love Deborah Cox

1996 Because You Loved Me Celine Dion

1996 It's All Coming Back To Me Now Celine Dion

1996 Raygun Matthew Good Band

1996 Ironic Alanis Morissette

1996 You Learn Alanis Morissette

1996 Head Over Feet Alanis Morissette

1996 Ahead By A Century The Tragically Hip

»1997

1997 Crossing A Canyon 54-40

1997 I'll Always Be Right There Bryan Adams

1997 Remote Control Age of Electric

1997 Uh La La La Alexia

1997 The Sound Of Jann Arden

1997 Last of the Big Game Hunters Barstool Prophets

1997 You Should Be Having Fun Barney Bentall

1997 If I Had My Way Big Sugar

1997 The Oaf Big Wreck

1997 Drinking In L.A. Bran Van 3000

1997 Peace Joe Brooks

1997 It Should Be Change of Heart

1997 Good Man, Feeling Bad Tom Cochrane

1997 Night Train Bruce Cockburn

1997 My Own Sunrise Crash Test Dummies

1997 Euphoria (Firefly) Delerium

1997 All By Myself Celine Dion

1997 To Love You More Celine Dion

1997 Jumping the Shadows Damhnait Doyle

1997 All That You Are Econoline Crush

1997 Here With Me Ginger

1997 Ordinary Day Great Big Sea

1997 When I'm Up (I Can't Get Down) Great Big Sea

1997 Tell Me Corey Hart

1997 Third of June Corey Hart

1997 Cubically Contained Headstones

1997 I've Just Seen A Face Holly Cole Trio

1997 It's OK, It's Alright Gavin Hope

1997 Raspberry I Mother Earth

1997 Open Your Eyes Ivan

1997 Super Bad Girls Ivan

1997 Do What I Can Sass Jordan

1997 Pearly White Junkhouse

1997 Believer Chantal Kreviazuk

1997 Surrounded Chantal Kreviazuk

1997 Wayne Chantal Kreviazuk

1997 Angels & Ordinary Men Wendy Lands

1997 My Addiction Dayna Manning

1997 Making Love Out of Nothing At All M-Appeal

1997 Dark Horse Amanda Marshall

1997 Sitting On Top of the World Amanda Marshall

1997 Trust Me Amanda Marshall

1997 Everything Is Automatic Matthew Good Band

1997 Indestructible Matthew Good Band

1997 Building A Mystery Sarah McLachlan

1997 Sweet Surrender Sarah McLachlan

1997 Numb Holly McNarland

1997 Got 'Til It's Gone Janet featuring Q-Tip and Joni Mitchell

1997 Gasoline Moist

1997 Tangerine Moist

1997 Bad 4 You Alannah Myles

1997 Make You Mad Odds

1997 Automatic Flowers Our Lady Peace

1997 Clumsy Our Lady Peace

1997 Superman's Dead Our Lady Peace

1997 Bad Time To Be Poor Rheostatics

1997 Half the World Rush

1997 Empty Cell Rusty

1997 The Lines You Amend Sloan

1997 Chevrolet Way Tariq

1997 Saving Face The Boomers

1997 No Regrets The Breits

1997 Look Like Me The Killjoys

1997 Can't Get Excited The Monoxides

1997 I Am the Man The Philosopher Kings

1997 Temptation The Tea Party

1997 Just To See You Again TRU-G2

1997 Love Gets Me Every Time Shania Twain

1997 Flamenco The Tragically Hip

1997 Springtime in Vienna The Tragically Hip

1997 Friend of Mine Treble Charger

1997 Deliver Me Roch Voisine

1997 Kissing Rain Roch Voisine

1997 Shed A Light Roch Voisine

CANADIAN HIT SONGS

1997 Midnight Rain Wide Mouth Mason
1997 Lost Highway Lori Yates
1997 Heavy Zuckerbaby

»1998

1998 Since When 54-40
1998 Back To You Bryan Adams
1998 I'm Ready Bryan Adams
1998 On A Day Like Today Bryan Adams
1998 Don't Wreck It Age of Electric
1998 Wishing That Jann Arden
1998 I Know You Jann Arden
1998 Ode To A Friend Jann Arden
1998 One Week Barenaked Ladies
1998 Friend of Mine Barstool Prophets
1998 Shoulder of the Road Barney Bentall
1998 Better Get Used To It Big Sugar
1998 The Scene Big Sugar
1998 Blown Wide Open Big Wreck
1998 Under the Lighthouse Big Wreck
1998 Falling Down Blue Blue Rodeo
1998 Everywhere Bran Van 3000
1998 You're Easy On the Eyes Terri Clark
1998 Nobody's Supposed To Be Here Deborah Cox
1998 Immortality Celine Dion with the Bee Gees
1998 My Heart Will Go On (Love Theme from Titanic) Celine Dion
1998 Tell Him Celine Dion & Barbra Streisand
1998 To Love You More Celine Dion
1998 I'm Your Angel R. Kelly & Celine Dion
1998 Adam's Rib Melanie Doane
1998 All That You Are Econoline Crush
1998 I'm Still Searching Glass Tiger
1998 It's the End of the World Great Big Sea
1998 Summer Long Emm Gryner
1998 Falling Bruce Guthro
1998 Carmelia Dan Hill
1998 Onion Girl Holly Cole Trio
1998 Love Changes Everything Honeymoon Suite
1998 Let's Shout (Baby Work It Out) Colin James
1998 If I Could Joee
1998 Desire Sass Jordan
1998 Shine Junkhouse
1998 Hands Chantal Kreviazuk
1998 Leaving On A Jet Plane Chantal Kreviazuk
1998 Broken Bones Love Inc.

1998 You're A Superstar Love Inc.
1998 Believe In You Amanda Marshall
1998 Apparitions Matthew Good Band
1998 Rico Matthew Good Band
1998 The Mummers' Dance Loreena McKennitt
1998 Sweet Surrender Sarah McLachlan
1998 Adia Sarah McLachlan
1998 Angel Sarah McLachlan
1998 Coward Holly McNarland
1998 U.F.O. Holly McNarland
1998 Uninvited Alanis Morissette
1998 Thank U Alanis Morissette
1998 Spaceman Bif Naked
1998 London Rain Heather Nova
1998 4AM Our Lady Peace
1998 Goodbye Girl Pluto
1998 Omobolasire Prozzak
1998 The Spirit of Radio Rush
1998 Piano In the Dark Brenda Russell
1998 Carry Sandbox
1998 Some Kinda Wonderful Sky
1998 Love, Pain and the Whole Damn Thing Amy Sky
1998 Money, City Maniacs Sloan
1998 Love Becomes Electric Strange Advance
1998 Hands of Time Temperance
1998 Picture Me Leaving You TRU G2
1998 Don't Be Stupid (You Know I Love You) Shania Twain
1998 You're Still the One Shania Twain
1998 From This Moment Shania Twain with Bryan White
1998 Letting Time Pass The New Meanies
1998 Three Seeds The New Meanies
1998 I'll Be There The Moffatts
1998 Miss You Like Crazy The Moffatts
1998 Cry The Philosopher Kings
1998 Hurts To Love You The Philosopher Kings
1998 Psychopomp The Tea Party
1998 Release The Tea Party
1998 Fireworks The Tragically Hip
1998 Poets The Tragically Hip
1998 Any Day Now The Watchmen
1998 Forest Fire David Usher
1998 It's Just My Luck V.I.P.
1998 The Game Wide Mouth Mason
1998 This Mourning Wide Mouth Mason
1998 Trampoline Wild Strawberries
1998 Your Love Jim Brickman & Michelle Wright
1998 Shampoo Zuckerbaby

»1999

1999 Thinkin' About You 2 Rude featuring Latoya
1999 Best of Me Bryan Adams
1999 Cloud #9 Bryan Adams
1999 When You're Gone Bryan Adams with Mel C

1999 She's So High Tal Bachman
1999 Strong Enough Tal Bachman
1999 Call and Answer Barenaked Ladies
1999 Get In Line Barenaked Ladies
1998 It's All Been Done Barenaked Ladies
1999 Better Get Used To It Big Sugar
1999 Girl Watcher Big Sugar
1999 Turn the Lights On Big Sugar
1999 Somebody Waits Blue Rodeo
1999 Willie Dixon Said Tom Cochrane
1999 We Can't Be Friends Deborah Cox with R.L. from Next
1999 Get You In the Morning Crash Test Dummies
1999 Keep A Lid On Things Crash Test Dummies
1999 Never Never D-Cru
1999 Silence Delerium with Sarah McLachlan
1999 That's the Way It Is Celine Dion
1999 Human Direct Nature
1999 Goliath Melanie Doane
1999 Waiting For the Tide Melanie Doane
1999 Consequence Free Great Big Sea
1999 The Ultimate Love Song Gavin Hope
1999 Arriba Joee
1999 Do You Right Joee
1999 Before You Chantal Kreviazuk
1999 Anywhere But Here k.d. lang
1999 Steal My Sunshine LEN
1999 Homeless Love Inc.
1999 Who Do U Love Love Inc.
1999 416/905 Maestro
1999 If I Didn't Have You Amanda Marshall
1999 Love Lift Me Amanda Marshall
1999 Hello Time Bomb Matthew Good Band
1999 Load Me Up Matthew Good Band
1999 Ice Cream Sarah McLachlan
1999 I Will Remember You (Live) Sarah McLachlan
1999 Love Wins Everytime McMaster & James
1999 Breathe Moist
1999 Underground Moist
1999 Joining You Alanis Morissette
1999 So Pure Alanis Morissette
1999 That I Would Be Good Alanis Morissette
1999 Unsent Alanis Morissette
1999 Heart and Shoulder Heather Nova
1999 Sucks To Be You Prozzak
1999 Weightless See Spot Run
1999 Mistake Serial Joe
1999 All I Want Sky
1999 Love Song Sky
1999 Push Sky
1999 12 Years Old Kim Stockwood
1999 You & Me Kim Stockwood

1999 Dancing In the Key Of Love Temperance
1999 Pictures The Boomtang Boys featuring Kim Esty
1999 Popcorn The Boomtang Boys featuring Fred
1999 Squeeze Toy The Boomtang Boys featuring Kim Esty
1999 Girl Of My Dreams The Moffatts
1999 Misery The Moffatts
1999 Until You Loved Me The Moffatts
1999 Heaven Coming Down The Tea Party
1999 The Messenger The Tea Party
1999 Bobcaygeon The Tragically Hip
1999 Say Something The Watchmen
1999 That Don't Impress Me Much Shania Twain
1999 Man! I Feel Like A Woman!" Shania Twain
1999 You've Got A Way Shania Twain
1999 Why Wide Mouth Mason

CANADIAN HIT SONGS AT THE TURN OF THE MILLENNIUM

»2000

2000 Ole Ole 11:30
2000 Casual Viewin' 54-40
2000 As If Jason All
2000 I Caught You Crying Jason Allan
2000 Sleepless Jann Arden
2000 Into the Sun Jann Arden
2000 Dream About You B2-Krazy
2000 Something To Say B2-Krazy
2000 Get Down b4-4
2000 Go Go b4-4
2000 Pinch Me Barenaked Ladies
2000 Both Sides Now Boomtang Boys
2000 Let's Ride Choclair
2000 Pride Simon Collins
2000 I Will Be Waiting D-Cru
2000 Keepin' It Real D-Cru
2000 Heaven's Earth Delerium
2000 That's the Way It Is Celine Dion
2000 Tattooed Damhnait Doyle
2000 I Will Love Again Lara Fabian
2000 I'm Like A Bird Nelly Furtado
2000 The Hampsterdance Hampton the Hamster
   (created by Canadian art student Deidre LaCarte)
2000 Can't Stop jacksoul
2000 Somedays jacksoul
2000 Listen To My Heart Jacynthe
2000 Let Me Know Jake
2000 Better Man J Gaines & Soul Attorneys
2000 I Don't Believe You Joee
2000 Dear Life Chantal Kreviazuk

CANADIAN HIT SONGS

2000 Souls Chantal Kreviazuk
2000 If I Could Lorraine Lawson
2000 Here Comes the Sunshine Love Inc.
2000 Is She A Lot Like Me Luba
2000 If I Fall Tara Maclean
2000 Shades of Grey Amanda Marshall
2000 Why Don't You Love Me Amanda Marshall
2000 Strange Days Matthew Good Band
2000 I Understand McMaster & James
2000 Thank You McMaster & James
2000 Whatcha Got? Carlos Morgan
2000 Europa Prozzak
2000 www.nevergetoveryou Prozzak
2000 Sunshine Rubber
2000 Look At Us Now Sarina
2000 Superhero Sky
2000 Everybody Wants To Be Like You Snow
2000 Faded Soul Decision
2000 Gravity Soul Decision
2000 No One Does It Better Soul Decision
2000 Ooh It's Kinda Crazy Soul Decision
2000 Both Sides Now The Boomtang Boys
2000 Bang Bang Boom The Moffatts
2000 Just Another Phase The Moffatts
2000 If I Ever Lose This Heaven The
    Philosopher Kings
2000 The Message The Tea Party
2000 Walking Around The Tea Party
2000 My Music @ Work The Tragically Hip
2000 When Shania Twain

»2001
2001 Moola Moola Jordy Birch
2001 Astounded Bran Van 3000 & Curtis
    Mayfield
2001 Erotic Century CURL
2001 Innocente (Falling In Love) Delerium
    featuring Leigh Nash
2001 Oh Canada David Foster and

Lara Fabian
2001 I'm Like A Bird Nelly Furtado
2001 Turn Off the Light Nelly Furtado
2001 Sous le vent Garou & Celine Dion
2001 Christmas Blues Holly Cole Trio
2001 Money (Part 1) Jelleestone (David Carty)
2001 Raygun Matthew Good Band
2001 How You Remind Me Nickelback
2001 Orchestral Pop Noir Romantique
    The Dears
2001 Completely Serial
    Joe
2001 Days Like That
Sugar Jones
2001 Lullaby The Tea Party
2001 Soulbreaking The
    Tea Party

»2002
2002 Dear M.F. Big Sugar
2002 Canadian Man Paul Brandt
2002 Just Like Ali Tom Cochrane
2002 Skunk Choclair
2002 Underwater Delerium featuring Rani
2002 A New Day Has Come
    Celine Dion
2002 I'm Alive Celine Dion
2002 I Should Be Sleeping Emerson
    Drive
2002 Hero Chad Kroeger
2002 Complicated Avril Lavigne
2002 Sk8er Boi Avril Lavigne
2002 I'm With You Avril Lavigne
2002 Marry Me Amanda Marshall
2002 Hands Clean Alanis Morissette
2002 Precious Illusions Alanis Morissette
2002 Supersexworld One Ton
2002 Perry Preal Réal Béland
2002 Legal Snow
2002 Bring It Home Swollen Members
2002 I'm Gonna Getcha Good! Shania Twain
2002 Movin' On The Boomtang Boys
2002 Nothing Could Come Between Us
    Theory of a Deadman
2002 Soul Breaking The Tea Party
2002 It's Good Life The Tragically Hip
2002 I'm Gonna Getcha Good
    Shania Twain
2002 Don't Say Sarah Wave

»2003

2003 Love Is the Only Soldier Jann Arden

2003 Another Postcard Barenaked Ladies

2003 Unpredictable Keshia Chanté

2003 I Just Wanna Be Mad Terri Clark

2003 Centre of My Heart Aselin Debison

2003 After All Delerium featuring Jael

2003 Meme les anges Audrey de Montigny

2003 Shook Shawn Desman

2003 I Drove All Night Celine Dion

2003 Tout l'or des hommes Celine Dion

2003 Bye Bye Boyfriend Fefe Dobson

2003 Fall Into Me Emerson Drive

2003 Waitin' On Me Emerson Drive

2003 Pedal To the Metal Kazzer

2003 I'm With You Avril Lavigne

2003 Something More Ryan Malcolm

2003 In A Word Called Catastrophe Matthew Good Band

2003 Someday Nickelback

2003 Where Have All the People Gone? Sam Roberts

2003 Still Waiting Sum 41

2003 Billy S. Skye Sweetnam

2003 Officially Missing You Tamia

2003 Make Up Your Mind Theory of a Deadman

2003 Every Inambition The Trews

2003 Forever and For Always Shania Twain

2003 Up! Shania Twain

2003 Time Of Our Lives David Usher

2003 Anger As Beauty Hawksley Workman

»2004

2004 Follow the Waves Auf der Maur

2004 Spiderman Theme Michael Bublé

2004 I Wanna Do It All Terri Clark

2004 Girls Lie Too Terri Clark

2004 I'm Out My Hood Suni Clay

2004 We Rebuilt This City Closet Monster

2004 With God On Our Side Burton Cummings

2004 Life Aselin Debison

2004 Silence Delerium with Sarah McLachlan

2004 Truly Delerium featuring Nerina Pallot

2004 Don't Go (Girls and Boys) Fefe Dobson

2004 Take Me Away Fefe Dobson

2004 Miracle Matt Dusk

2004 O.G. Bitch Esthero

2004 One Thing Finger Eleven

2004 Sing For the Enemy Hostage Life

2004 B-boy Stance k-os

2004 Temptation Diana Krall

2004 Don't Tell Me Avril Lavigne

2004 My Happy Ending Avril Lavigne

2004 Fallen Sarah McLachlan

2004 Ti Peyi A Luck Mervil

2004 Everything Alanis Morissette

2004 Awake In A Dream Kalan Porter

2004 Chu pas plus pouvri qu'un aut Dufort Jean Rene

2004 Perfect Simple Plan

2004 Tangled Up In Me Skye Sweetnam

2004 Party For Two Shania Twain

2004 Watch Your Money The Waking Eyes

» 2005

2005 Neighbourhood #2 (Laika) Arcade Fire

2005 Neighbourhood #3 (Power Out) Arcade Fire

2005 Rebellion (Lies) Arcade Fire

2005 Wake Up Arcade Fire

2005 Stand By Me Jann Arden

2005 Where No One Knows Me Jann Arden

2005 Fastlane Esthero

2005 On My Own Hedley

2005 Christmas Blues Holly Cole Trio

2005 I'm With You Avril Lavigne

2005 Crazy Alanis Morissette

2005 Si t'achetes pas tu creves Jérôme Minière

2005 Photograph Nickelback

2005 Alive Melissa O'Neil

2005 Ghetto Love Original 3

2005 Jimmy Gets High Daniel Powter

2005 Paper Rain Amanda Stott

2005 Don't Shania Twain

2005 Forever and For Always Shania Twain

2005 I Ain't No Quitter Shania Twain

2005 Shut Up Simple Plan

2005 Welcome To My Life Simple Plan

unison benevolent fund

CANADIAN HIT SONGS

» 2006

2006 Meant To Fly Eva Avila
2006 You Gotta Believe To Believe Frank D'Angelo
2006 No Heaven DJ Champion
2006 Crier la vie Moby & Mylene Farmer
2006 All Good Things Nelly Furtado
2006 Maneater Nelly Furtado
2006 Promiscuous Nelly Furtado featuring
    Timbaland
2006 Say It Right Nelly Furtado
2006 Keep Holding On Avril Lavigne
2006 Say Anything Marianas Trench
2006 Far Away Nickelback
2006 If Everyone Cared Nickelback
2006 Savin' Me Nickelback
2006 Bad Day Daniel Powter

» 2007

2007 Keep the Car Running Arcade Fire
2007 Bring the Boys Home Jann Arden
2007 Surrender Billy Talent
2007 Seven Day Fool Jully Black
2007 Call Me (I'll Be Around) Bran Van 3000
2007 Lost Michael Bublé
2007 Melody Day Caribou
2007 Angelicus Delerium featuring Isabel
    Bayrakdarian
2007 Lost and Found Delerium featuring Jael
2007 Taking Chances Celine Dion
2007 Tongue Tied Faber Drive
2007 1,2,3,4 Feist
2007 I'll Keep Your Memory Vague Finger Eleven
2007 Paralyzer Finger Eleven
2007 Do It Nelly Furtado
2007 Give It To Me Timbaland featuring Nelly
    Furtado and Justin Timberlake
2007 For the Nights I Can't Remember Hedley
2007 Into the Night Santana & Chad Kroeger
2007 Girlfriend Avril Lavigne
2007 Hot Avril Lavigne
2007 When You're Gone Avril Lavigne
2007 Shaketramp Marianas Trench
2007 All I Ever Wanted Brian Melo
2007 If Everyone Cared Nickelback
2007 Rockstar Nickelback
2007 When I'm Gone Simple Plan
2007 Money Honey State of Shock
2007 Me Tamia

2007 Met A Man On Top Of the Hill The Midway
    State
2007 Never Too Late Three Days Grace

» 2008

2008 Give Me the Music Eva Avila
2008 Turn Your Back Billy Talent and Anti-Flag
2008 Until I Stay Jully Black
2008 Lay It On the Line Divine Brown
2008 Islands In the Stream Constantines
2008 Beautiful UR Deborah Cox
2008 World We Know Crash Parallel
2008 The Prayer Celine Dion and Josh Groban
2008 Unlove You Elise Estrada
2008 The End Andrew F
2008 When I'm With You Faber Drive
2008 Fantasy Danny Fernandes
2008 Private Dancer Danny Fernandes
2008 In God's Hands Nelly Furtado
2008 Never Too Late Hedley
2008 Old School Hedley
2008 Drive My Soul Lights
2008 U Want Me? Sarah McLachlan
2008 Help I'm Alive Metric
2008 Never Again Midway State
2008 Underneath Alanis Morissette
2008 Gotta Be Somebody Nickelback
2008 If Today Was Your Last Day Nickelback
2008 Numba 1 (Tide Is High) Kardinal Offishall
2008 Dangerous Kardinal Offishall featuring Akon
2008 Beautiful Akon featuring Colby O'Donis and
    Kardinall Offishall
2008 Them Kids Sam Roberts
2008 Operator (A Girl Like Me) Shiloh
2008 Save You Simple Plan
2008 Your Love Is A Lie Simple Plan
2008 Best I Ever Had State of Shock
2008 Hearts That Bleed State of Shock
2008 With Me Sum 41
2008 All Or Nothing Theory of a Deadman
2008 Hold Me In Your Arms The Trews
2008 Don't Call Me Baby Kreesha Turner

» 2009

2009 Young Cardinals Alexisonfire
2009 Favorite Girl Justin Bieber
2009 Love Me Justin Bieber
2009 One Less Lonely Girl Justin Bieber
2009 One Time Justin Bieber
2009 Rusted From the Rain Billy Talent
2009 Running Jully Black
2009 Sunglasses Divine Brown
2009 Haven't Met You Yet Michael Bublé
2009 Dust In Gravity Delerium featuring Kreesha Turner
2009 Rich Girl $ Down With Webster
2009 Pick Up the Phone Dragonette
2009 Best I Ever Had Drake
2009 Forever Drake & Kanye West
2009 G-Get Up and Dance Faber Drive
2009 Give It To Me Right Melanie Fiona
2009 Jump FloRida & Nelly Furtado
2009 Morning After Dark Timbaland & Nelly Furtado
2009 Cha Ching Hedley
2009 Don't Talk To Strangers Hedley
2009 Perfect Hedley
2009 Bucket Carly Rae Jepsen
2009 Tug Of War Carly Rae Jepsen
2009 Wavin' Flag K'naan
2009 Saviour Lights
2009 All To Myself Marianas Trench
2009 Beside You Marianas Trench
2009 Cross My Heart Marianas Trench
2009 Supergirl Suzie McNeil
2009 Burn It To the Ground Nickelback
2009 I'd Come For You Nickelback
2009 If Today Was Your Last Day Nickelback (recharted)
2009 Never Gonna Be Alone Nickelback
2009 All You Did Was Save My Life Our Lady Peace
2009 Too Pretty State of Shock
2009 Get With You Stereos & Far East Movement
2009 Summer Girl Stereos
2009 Throw Ya Hands Up Stereos
2009 Dead End Countdown The New Cities
2009 Love Is A First The Tragically Hip
2009 Break Three Days Grace
2009 Africa Karl Wolf
2009 Carrera Karl Wolf
2009 Yalla Habibi Karl Wolf Rime & Kaz Money

CANADIAN HIT SONGS TO 2013

» 2010

2010 Ready To Start Arcade Fire
2010 You Run Away Barenaked Ladies
2010 Somebody To Love Justin Bieber
2010 Baby Justin Bieber & Ludacris
2010 Never Say Never Justin Bieber & Jaden Smith
2010 Eenie Meenie Sean Kingston & Justin Bieber
2010 Hollywood Michael Bublé
2010 Oh Canada Classified
2010 Electric/Night Like This Shawn Desman
2010 Shiver Shawn Desman
2010 Ghost Fefe Dobson
2010 Stutterin' Fefe Dobson
2010 Whoa Is Me Down With Webster
2010 Your Man Down With Webster
2010 Find Your Love Drake
2010 Over Drake
2010 Forever Drake & Kanye West
2010 What's My Name? Rihanna & Drake
2010 Give Him Up Faber Drive
2010 Living In A Dream Finger Eleven
2010 Night Is Young Nelly Furtado
2010 Take A Minute K'naan
2010 Hallelujah k.d. lang
2010 Alice Avril Lavigne
2010 Naala Yeessi Les Colocs
2010 Celebrity Status Marianas Trench
2010 Good To You Marianas Trench
2010 Porn Star Dancing My Darkest Days
2010 This Afternoon Nickelback
2010 Babybounce Kardinal Offishall
2010 Today I'm Gonna Try and Change Johnny Reid
2010 Bu2b Rush
2010 Caravan Rush
2010 Turn It Up Stereos
2010 Feel It In My Bones Tiesto and Tegan & Sara
2010 J'imagine Annie Villeneuve
2010 I Believe Nicki Yanofsky
2010 Lullaby of Birdland Nicki Yanofsky
2010 Wavin' Flag Young Artists For Haiti

» 2011

2011 Brand New Chick Anjulie
2011 Famous Audio Playground
2011 The Christmas Song Justin Bieber
2011 Mistletoe Justin Bieber
2011 Next To You Chris Brown & Justin Bieber
2011 Home Michael Bublé

CANADIAN HIT SONGS

2011 Fragile Bird City & Colour

2011 Aural Psynapse Deadmau5

2011 She's Dope Down With Webster

2011 Headlines Drake

2011 Make Me Proud Drake

2011 Take Care Drake & Rihanna

2011 She Will Lil Wayne & Drake

2011 Moment 4 Life Nicki Minaj & Drake

2011 Shut Up and Dance Victoria Duffield

2011 Hit Me Up Danny Fernandes

2011 Heaven's Gonna Wait Hedley

2011 Invincible Hedley

2011 One Life Hedley

2011 Call Me Maybe Carly Rae Jepsen

2011 Just Let Me Go Ketsia

2011 Running On Empty Ketsia

2011 Smile Avril Lavigne

2011 What the Hell Avril Lavigne

2011 Let's Play Kristina Maria

2011 By Now Marianas Trench

2011 Fallout Marianas Trench

2011 Haven't Had Enough Marianas Trench

2011 Bottoms Up Nickelback

2011 When We Stand Together Nickelback

2011 Pray (for LJ) Pardon My Striptease

2011 Alone Again Alyssa Reid

2011 Jet Lag Simple Plan

2011 Lowlife Theory of a Deadman

2011 We're Here For A Good Time Trooper

2011 Today Is Your Day Shania Twain

2011 Somebody That I Used To Know Walk Off the Earth

2011 Ghetto Love Karl Wolf & Kardinal Offishall

» 2012

2012 You and I Anjulie

2012 True Colors Artists Against Bullying

2012 All Around the World Justin Bieber & Ludacris

2012 As Long As You Love Me Justin Beiber & Big Sean

2012 Beauty and A Beat Justin Bieber

2012 Boyfriend Justin Bieber

2012 Die In Your Arms Justin Bieber

2012 Turn To You Justin Bieber

2012 Live My Life Far East Movement & Justin Bieber

2012 Canadian Girls Dean Brody

2012 The Veldt Deadmau5

2012 Days Turn Into Night Delerium featuring Michael Logen

2012 Monarch Delerium featuring Nadine

2012 Dum Da Dum Shawn Desman

2012 Nobody Does It Like You Shawn Desman

2012 Let It Go Dragonette

2012 Motto Drake

2012 Take Care Drake

2012 Break My Heart Victoria Duffield

2012 She's My Kind of Crazy Emerson Drive

2012 Big Hoops (Bigger the Better) Nelly Furtado

2012 Kiss You Inside Out Hedley

2012 Curiosity Carly Rae Jepsen

2012 This Kiss Carly Rae Jepsen

2012 Beautiful Carly Rae Jepsen & Justin Bieber

2012 Good Time Owl City & Carly Rae Jepsen

2012 Hurt Me Tomorrow K'naan

2012 Is Anybody Out There? K'naan

2012 Moi + Toi Les Académiciens

2012 Our Song Comes On Kristina Maria

2012 Fallout Marianas Trench

2012 Stutter Marianis Trench

2012 Youth Without You Metric

2012 Turn It Up Kardinal Offishall & Karl Wolf

2012 Stompa Serena Ryder

2012 Summer Paradise Simple Plan & K'naan

2012 Closer Tegan & Sara

2012 Somebody That I Used To Know Walk Off the Earth

2012 DJ Gonna Save Us Karl Wolf

2012 Mash It Up Karl Wolf & Three 6 Mafia

» 2013

2013 That Power Will.i.am & Justin Bieber

2013 It's A Beautiful Day Michael Bublé

2013 Inner Ninja Classified & David Myles

2013 Started From the Bottom Drake

2013 The World Is Ours Eleven Past One

2013 Karma Kristina Maria

2013 What I Wouldn't Do Serena Ryder

2013 Kiss Goodnight Tyler Shaw

2013 I Was A Fool Tegan & Sara

2013 Red Hands Walk Off the Earth

CANADIAN MUSIC HALL OF FAME PROFILES

(1978-2013)

The Canadian Music Hall of Fame was first established by the Canadian Academy of Recording Artists (CARAS), and the first induction ceremonies were staged at the 8th annual JUNO awards in 1978, held at the Harbour Castle Convention Centre in Toronto and hosted by comedian David Steinberg. Receiving this newly-minted honour for their musical and humanitarian achievements at home and abroad were veteran musicians Guy Lombardo and Oscar Peterson. Since then the Canadian Music Hall of Fame has grown to 46 members, who are profiled in this section of *Oh What A Feeling*. We have included not only the facts but also career milestones and insights into the special talent of each artist, in the words of various music pundits and the artists themselves.

OH WHAT A FEELING

>> **HALL OF FAME**

CANADIAN MUSIC HALL OF FAME MEMBER LIST

»GUY LOMBARDO

Gaetano Alberto Lombardo

Violinist, Band leader

Inducted 1978

b. June 19, 1902, London, Ontario

d. November 5, 1977, Houston, Texas

SIGNATURE SONGS

Auld Lang Syne, Boo Hoo

MILESTONES

Lombardo's live *New Year's Eve Party* broadcasts from the Roosevelt Hotel in New York City, and later from New York's Waldorf Astoria, set a record as the longest-running annual radio special. Guy Lombardo and His Royal Canadians is the only dance band in the world to have sold more than 100 million records... and reportedly that figure could be as high as 300 million. The Guy Lombardo Bridge was dedicated in London, Ontario (1977), and Lombardo Avenue in north London also pays tribute to the band leader. Canada Post has issued a Guy Lombardo commemorative stamp (December 1999).

INSIGHTS

"The sweetest music this side of heaven"
— Ashton Stevens, *Chicago Tribune*

"The sweetest jazzmen on any stage this side of heaven."
— Music critic, *Chicago Herald & Examiner*

"Modest, gentlemanly, Guy Lombardo, the favorite band of Louis Armstrong. He cherished that idea. Guy believed for his audiences every night should be like

New Year's Eve. As Papa Lombardo had told him, 'give the people more than they pay for and they will always invite you back.' For 49 straight years North America has invited Mr. New Year's Eve, Guy Lombardo, back into their living room. This New Year's Eve, Guy is making the sweetest music both sides of heaven." — Lee Jordan, *Tribute to Guy Lombardo*, 1977

"Should Guy Lombardo and his Royal Canadians fail to play 'Auld Lang Syne' at midnight, New Year's Eve, a deep uneasiness would run through a large segment of the American populace, a conviction that despite the evidence on every calendar, the New Year has not really arrived." — *Life*

»BIOPICS: CBC Life and Times: *Guy Lombardo: When We Danced* (1998)
»BOOKS: *The Lombardo Story* by Beverly Fink Cline (1979)

»OSCAR PETERSON

Oscar Emmanuel Peterson

Jazz Pianist, Composer, Human rights activist

Inducted 1978

b, August 15, 1925, Montréal, Québec

d. December 23, 2007 Mississauga, Ontario

SIGNATURE COMPOSITION

Canadiana Suite

MILESTONES

Impresario Norman Granz arranged for Oscar Peterson to make a surprise guest appearance at his 1949 Jazz at the Philharmonic concert at New York's Carnegie Hall. Peterson's performance launched his career internationally. The Oscar Peterson Trio with bassist Ray Brown and guitarist Herb Ellis was formed in 1953. Oscar is the first ever non-classical musician to receive the Glenn Gould Prize (1993). He received the Lifetime Achievement Grammy Award in 1997. Canada Post has issued a commemorative Oscar Peterson stamp, the first living person (other than a monarch) to be honoured that way (August 15, 2005). The Oscar Peterson Public School was named for Peterson in Mississauga, Ontario (September 6, 2005).

INSIGHTS

"The Maharaja of the keyboard." — Duke Ellington

"Peterson really put Montréal on the map of jazz. … I believe that on a grander scale, the impact he had on the black community and on the whole musical community was huge. He broke out of Canada. He's one of the first people. We talk of Celine Dion and Shania Twain and Alanis Morissette and Bryan Adams. Oscar Peterson did what they did years ago as a black person. So what he's done is incredible." — Tracy Biddle, CBC

"The music field was the first to break down racial barriers because in order to play together, you have to love the people you are playing with, and if you have any racial inhibitions, you wouldn't be able to do that." — Oscar Peterson

»BIOPICS: *Oscar Peterson: Music in the Key of Oscar* (1995); *Oscar Peterson: The Life of a Legend* (1996)

>>HANK SNOW

Clarence Eugene Snow
aka Hank, The Yodeling Ranger or Hank Snow, The Singing Ranger
Country Music Singer & Songwriter
Inducted 1979
b. May 9, 1914 Brooklyn, Nova Scotia
d. December 20, 1999 Rainbow Ranch, Madison, Tennessee

SIGNATURE SONGS

I'm Movin' On (1950), *I've Been Everywhere* (1962)

MILESTONES

"I'm Movin' On" has been recorded by The Rolling Stones, Steppenwolf among many others. The song spent an unprecedented 21 weeks at the top of the Billboard chart in 1950. A mentor to Elvis Presley, Hank has also been inducted into the Nashville Songwriters Hall of Fame (1978) and the Country Music Hall of Fame in Nashville (October 8, 1979). The Hank Snow Country Music Centre has been established in Liverpool, Nova Scotia (early 1990s).

INSIGHTS

"[After the war] I had saved enough money in Canada and I had a tent show. I believed in putting up a big front, so I purchased a 1947 Cadillac. I didn't even have the money to change the oil on that thing. Those days, I would go to Wheeling, West Virginia for the winter and then in the summer I would tour across Canada. Then I got this stupid idea... On the strength of some encouragement from some very close friends, I went to Los Angeles and almost starved to death." — Hank Snow

"I wasn't doing too good at that point [when first appearing on the Opry in 1950]. I wasn't too prestigious. In the first place, I didn't have a hit record. Back then, you had to come to the Opry with a hit record and I was hardly known. But then, as I always say, the good Lord stepped in and guided my pen as I wrote 'I'm Movin' On.' That saved the day and helped to establish me around the world." — Hank Snow.

"The recorded legacy of Hank Snow is one of the largest and most impressive in country music history. It spans the early makeshift studios of depression-era Canada to the digital sophistication of contemporary Nashville, and its formats run the gamut of fragile old 78s through the earliest 'doughnut' discs of the 45 rpm age, from the eight-track tape to the compact disc. Hank Snow's music has, over the years, appeared on every recorded format except possibly the old Edison cylinder. The complexity of the Snow discography testifies not only to the quality and variety and richness of his repertoire, but also to the impact he has made on listeners in both the United States and Canada and in many other countries where his records have been released." — Charles K. Wolfe

>>BOOKS: *The Hank Snow Story* by Hank Snow with Jack Ownbey and Bob Burris (1994)

»PAUL ANKA

Paul Albert Anka
Songwriter, Singer, Musician, Actor
Inducted 1980
b. July 30, 1941, Ottawa, Ontario

SIGNATURE SONGS/COMPOSITION

Diana (1957), *Johnny's Theme* aka *It's Really Love* and *Toot Sweet,* the theme song for NBC's *The Tonight Show with Johnny Carson* (1962), *My Way* (1969)

MILESTONES

Paul Anka signed with ABC-Paramount Records and hit number one with the single, "Diana" (1957). Anka's theme for the movie *The Longest Day*, in which he also starred, was nominated for an Academy Award (1962). Frank Sinatra's recording of "My Way," with lyrics by Anka and music by Claude François, became his signature song (1969). Canada Post has issued a postage stamp commemorating Anka's recording career (June 2007).

INSIGHTS

"There are probably very few 13 year olds with great voices. Mine was terrible. There was a lot of emotion. I was just a nice little squeaky teenager with some appeal and got very lucky... Certainly I had the desire — I took some training — but to honestly sit here and tell you that I know how it all happened at that age, other than being very hungry and liking what I did. There was always a gnawing in my brain that this was a God-given gift — and I know sometimes that sounds just a little too syrupy — but what do you know at 13? There's a bigger design for all of us on this planet. Some do some things, some do others. My 'others' was entertaining; banging out a song. I had a crush on a girl named Diana. Did I really know what I was doing? It was just shear pain, guts and desire." — Paul Anka

"We lived and breathed rock and roll. Your life was rock and roll. Your life was pop music. You were on busses with your contemporaries, you were at a piano the next day, you were talking to managers and record companies everyday. You lived it 24 hours a day. There was no other life. All you were concerned about was the next project, the next performance, how to get ready for it, what were you going to write, what was the concept of the next album? There was no break from that. Maybe you took a vacation for a week, but that was it. It was intense." — Paul Anka

"... I first met Paul Anka, the singer and songwriter, in 1957 at Paramount Records. I was young. He was younger. Fifteen,16 years old. This was before his first song was released. The president of the label pulled me into an office to listen to it. And there was Paul, performing to a half-dozen suits. He was a sweet kid, baby-faced, singing his heart out in a nothing office in Midtown. But he had that thing — you could see it right away. The rock-star thing, the movie-star thing. Of all the great crooners of that era, only a handful survived: Frank Sinatra, Tony Bennett, Paul. He had written his song back home in Canada. It was a love ballad for a teen crush, three years his senior. Genius! What kid doesn't want to make it with an older girl? It was called "Diana," and it went straight to No. 1... It was the beginning of an incredible run that made Paul an icon, one of the great songwriters in pop-music history: 125 records, 900 songs, 60 million albums sold." — Legendary film producer/movie executive Jerry Weintraub, *Vanity Fair*

»BIOPICS: *Lonely Boy* (1962); *Destiny* (2004); *Music Man: The Authorized Biography* (2006).

»BOOKS: *My Way* by Paul Anka (2013)

»JONI MITCHELL

Roberta Joan Anderson
Songwriter, Singer, Musician, Painter
Inducted 1981
b. November 7, 1943, Fort Macleod, Alberta

SIGNATURE SONGS

Both Sides Now (1968), *Woodstock*
(1970), *Help Me* (1974), *Free Man In
Paris* (1974), *Big Yellow Taxi* (1975)

MILESTONES

Joni Mitchell initially came to prominence through
Judy Collins' recording of her song "Both Sides
Now" (1968). Mitchell's album *Blue*, listed by *Time*
magazine in November 2006 as among the "All-Time
100 Albums," was released in 1971. She has won the
Billboard Century Award (1995) and was inducted into
the Rock and Roll Hall of Fame (1997). She received
the Grammy Lifetime Achievement Award (2002), and
Canada Post commemorated Mitchell's career with a
postage stamp (June 2007). Mitchell has been inducted
into the Canadian Songwriters Hall of Fame (2007).

INSIGHTS

" 'I don't care who writes your laws, if only I can write
your songs.' The poet who said that understood well
what makes a country and how songs and music impact
on its destiny. The essence of living in a country is to
promote freedom so that each man and woman and
child can be free to fulfill himself to the utmost...
and the essence of songs and music is freedom... A
Canadian, who makes us very proud to be Canadian,
who sings of many things — liberty and freedom being
important themes in her songs. She expresses those
things admirably well. She wrote in one of her songs,
'We love our loving, but not like we love our freedom.'
She is a great singer, a great artist, a great composer, a
great songwriter, a great painter. She is Joni Mitchell

and I will present to her the Hall of Fame Award."
— Prime Minister Pierre Trudeau at 1981 JUNOs
"When the dust settles, Joni Mitchell may stand as
the most important and influential female recording
artist of the late 20th century. Uncompromising and
iconoclastic, Mitchell confounded expectations at every
turn; restlessly innovative, her music evolved from
deeply personal folk stylings into pop, jazz, avant-garde,
and even world music." — Jason Ankenny, *AllMusic*

"I sing my sorrow and I paint my joy." — Joni Mitchell

"My style of songwriting is influenced by cinema. I'm a
frustrated filmmaker. A fan once said to me, 'Girl, you
make me see pictures in my head!' and I took that as a
great compliment. That's exactly my intention." — Joni
Mitchell

»BIOPICS: American Masters: *Joni Mitchell —
Woman of Heart and Mind*

»BOOKS (SELECTED): *Will You Take Me As I
Am: Joni Mitchell's Blue Period* by Michelle Mercer
(2009); *Joni: The Creative Odyssey of Joni Mitchell* by
Katherine Monk (2012); *Gathered Light: The Poetry of
Joni Mitchell's Songs* by Joni Mitchell, edited by Lisa
Sornberger and John Sornberger.

»NEIL YOUNG

Neil Percival Young
Singer, Songwriter, Musician, Filmmaker
Inducted 1982
b. November 12, 1945, Toronto, Ontario

SIGNATURE SONGS

Ohio (1970), *Helpless* (1970), *Southern Man* (1970), *Heart of Gold* (1972), *Old Man* (1972), *Long May You Run* (1976), *Hey Hey, My My (Into the Black)* (1979), *This Note's For You* (1988), *Rockin' in the Free World* (1989)

MILESTONES

Neil Young co-founded the group Buffalo Springfield (1966), as well as the group Crazy Horse. He joined Crosby, Stills & Nash as the fourth member of the group (1969). He is one of the founders of Farm Aid (1985). Young and his wife Pegi (nee Morton) helped found The Bridge School (1986). "Philadelphia," from the soundtrack of the movie of the same name, was nominated for an Academy Award (1993). Young has been inducted into Rock and Roll Hall of Fame twice: for his solo work (1995) and as a member of Buffalo Springfield (1997). He is known as the "Godfather of Grunge."

INSIGHTS

"I've done a lot of different kinds of music and some people find it hard to understand how I can supposedly be the godfather of grunge and still be into Hank Williams, but to me it's all music and I don't care about labels." — Neil Young

"Young has consistently demonstrated the unbridled passion of an artist who understands that self-renewal is the only way to avoid burning out. For this reason, he has remained one of the most significant artists of the rock and roll era." — Rock and Roll Hall of Fame

"One of the most enigmatic songwriters, singers and guitarists to emerge in the sixties, Young had recorded more than twenty solo albums by the end of the century. Although his songs consistently expressed a melancholic and pessimistic view of personal and political relationships, Young's music veered into heavy rock, fifties rock 'n' roll and electronic synthesizer sounds, while retaining a country undertow." — Phil Hardy, *The Faber Companion to 20th Century Popular Music.*

»BIOPICS: *Neil Young: Heart of Gold* (2006); *Neil Young — Don't Be Denied* (2009); *The Neil Young Trunk Show* (2009); *Neil Young Journeys* (2011)

»BOOKS: *Waging Heavy Peace: A Hippie Dream* by Neil Young (September 25, 2012)

»GLENN GOULD

Glenn Herbert Gold

Classical Pianist, Composer, Conductor, Writer, Broadcaster

Inducted 1983

b. September 25, 1932, Toronto, Ontario

d. October 4, 1982, Toronto, Ontario

SIGNATURE RECORDING

Bach: The Goldberg Variations (1981)

MILESTONES

Glenn Gould's first radio recital on CBC Radio in 1950 was his first experience with broadcasting and recording, both of which he would embrace with a passion after retiring from concert performance. The Glenn Gould Foundation and associated Glenn Gould Prize was established in Toronto in 1983. The Glenn Gould Studio, a combined recording studio and public concert venue, opened in the Canadian Broadcasting Centre in Toronto on September 25, 1992. Canada Post honoured Gould with a postage stamp (December 17, 1999). He has received the Grammy Lifetime Achievement Award (2013). Conductor George Szell once declared, "That nut's a genius!"

INSIGHTS

"Glenn was a very modern, very North American, and more specifically, Canadian man ... Modern because the microphone, electronic tape, radio, television and film were indispensable means whereby the anachronism of a 'great pianist' (which one automatically hears joined with 'concert pianist') dispensing with his audience, could be resolved. This was only possible in our own days. But being Glenn, this solution became a creative challenge; it became an art in which all possible recording techniques were integrated into the very fabric of his musical conception and re-cast in a superior way." — Yehudi Menuhi, *Glenn Gould Variations*

"Since Gould's death, the world of music... has witnessed significant changes. Most notable of these is the ease of access to recorded music and its related consequence, the global jumbling of musical materials. Both are developments Gould would have welcomed: the first for its assumption of primacy in recorded music over performance and the second for its overturning of narratives of *musical progress*. What we should call the post-historical musical world — our world — is the one that Gould anticipated and advocated. At the same time, he was a self-declared puritan about art and frequently lamented music's corruption by commerce. Such are just the beginnings of his kaleidoscopic, contradictory, febrile, and brilliant mind." — Mark Kingwell

»BIOPICS: Francois Girard's *Thirty Two Short Films About Glenn Gould* (1993)

»BOOKS: *Glenn Gould Variations* (1983); *Glenn Gould: The Ecstasy and Tragedy of Genius* by Peter Ostwald (1998); *Glenn Gould, Extraordinary Canadians* by Mark Kingwell (2009)

»THE CREW CUTS

Vocal Quartet

Inducted 1984

b. Rudi Maugeri, January 27, 1931, Toronto, Ontario (baritone)

d. Rudi Maugeri, May 7, 2004, Las Vegas, Nevada

b. John Perkins, August 28, 1931, Toronto, Ontario (lead)

b. Ray Perkins, November 28, 1932, Toronto, Ontario (bass)

b. Pat Barrett, September 15, 1933, Toronto, Ontario (tenor)

SIGNATURE SONGS

Crazy 'Bout You Baby (1954), *Sh-Boom* (1954), *Earth Angel* (1955), *Ko Ko Mo (I Love You So)* (1955), *Gum Drop* (1955)

MILESTONES

In 1953, the group appeared on the Gene Carroll TV show in Cleveland and came to the attention of influential local deejay, Bill Randle, who not only got them to change their name from The Canadaires to The Crew Cuts but also arranged for an audition at Mercury Records in Chicago, who sign them shortly after.

In April 1954, the group had their first hit with the Maugeri/Barrett-penned, "Crazy 'Bout You Baby." On July 28, 1954, the group's cover of The Chords' r&b hit, "Sh'Boom," hits number one in America, where it remains for 9 weeks. It is considered to be one of the first rock and roll songs. The success of the cover version of "Sh'Boom" was a main factor in the subsequent interest by the music industry in having other pop artists' cover proven black r&b hits and "sanitize" them for mainstream white audiences. The group performed the song on Ed Sullivan's *Toast of the Town* TV show (aka *The Ed Sullivan Show*) on December 12, 1954.

INSIGHTS

"The Crew Cuts, riding high currently with 'Crazy 'Bout You Baby,' could get a lot of attention with this swinging new side. The tune is a peppery novelty which has broken through in the r&b field, and this pop version is sung neatly by the boys. Watch it: it could grab coins." — Initial *Billboard* magazine review of the single, "Sh-Boom," June 19, 1954

»THE DIAMONDS

Vocal Quartet

Inducted 1984

b. Dave Somerville (Lead), October 2, 1933, Guelph, Ontario

b. Ted Kowalski (Tenor), May 16, 1931, Whitby, Ontario. Evan Fisher replaces Kowalski1958

d. Ted Kowalski, August 8, 2010, Whitby, Ontario

b. Phil Levitt (Baritone), July 9, 1935. Mike Douglas replaces Levitt in 1957

b. Mike Douglas (Michael Dlugosz), April 23, 1934, Saskatchewan

d. Mike Douglas, July 2, 2012, Pinellas County, Florida

b. Bill Reed (bass) January 11, 1936. John Felton replaces Reed in 1958

d. Bill Reed, October 22, 2004

d. John Felton, May 17, 1982.

SIGNATURE SONGS

Why Do Fools Fall In Love? (1956), *Little Darlin'* (1957), *Silhouettes* (1957), *The Stroll* (1957)

MILESTONES

The Diamonds formed at the University of Toronto in 1954 and subsequently were heard on a number of CBC radio shows, including one hosted by Elwood Glover, one of their earliest boosters. The group made their TV debut on the CBC show *Pick the Stars* in 1955. During an engagement at the Alpine Village Club in Cleveland in 1955, local deejay Bill Randle saw the group and introduced them to Mercury Records in Chicago, who signed them. In the spring of 1957, The Diamonds had their biggest hit with "Little Darlin'," a cover version of the song written and originally recorded by Maurice Williams and his group The Gladiolas. The group also had great success with "The Stroll," a song inspired by the short-lived dance craze of the same name. In July 1958, the film (or video) as a music marketing tool was born as Mercury Records produced two three-minute promotional clips for the Diamonds and The Platters. The Diamonds appeared in the movie musical, *The Big Beat*.

INSIGHTS

"R&B singer Chuck Willis, known for a time as 'King of The Stroll,' kicked off the dance in black communities with his record 'C.C. Rider.' In *American Graffiti*, there's a scene where The Stroll is danced to the song of the same name by the Canadian doo-woppers The Diamonds (who also had a huge hit in 'Little Darlin"). The Stroll was just catching on at the time, and the group's manager remarked about it to Dick Clark. Dick told him there was no song for this particular dance yet, and within a month, the Diamonds had recorded 'The Stroll' – a classic with a rhythm and arrangement as low-down and ominous in its own way as Link Wray's downright-scary 'Rumble.'"

— Michael Shore in *The History of American Bandstand*

»THE FOUR LADS

Vocal Quartet

Inducted 1984

b. Corrado "Connie" Codarini, Toronto, Ontario (bass)

d. Corrado Codarini, April 28, 2010, Concord, North Carolina

b. John Bernard "Bernie" Toorish, March 2, 1931, Toronto, Ontario (tenor)

b. James F. "Jimmy" Arnold, January 4, 1932, Toronto, Ontario (lead)

d. James Arnold, June 15, 2004, Sacramento, California

b. Frank Busseri, Toronto, Ontario (baritone)

SIGNATURE SONGS

Istanbul (Not Constantinople)(1953), *Skokiaan* (1954), *Moments To Remember* (1955), *No, Not Much!* (1956), *Standing On the Corner* (1956), *Who Needs You* (1957), *Put A Light In the Window* (1957), *There's Only One of You* (1958)

MILESTONES

The Four Lads, ex-choirboys at Toronto's St. Michael's Cathedral School, toured Canada in 1949 for *Canadian Cavalcade*, a national radio show hosted by Elwood Glover. The group's first big break comes at the Casino Theatre in Toronto (Queen & Bay), where they meet Orlandus "Dad" Wilson of The Golden Gate Quartet, who asked them to sing for him. He was impressed enough to introduce them to his manager Mike Stewart in New York. On April 5, 1950, the group took the train from Toronto to the Big Apple, where they ended up with a regular booking at that city's Le Ruban Bleu club and made frequent appearances on radio and TV (including the *Perry Como Show*). In 1951, Columbia Records executive Mitch Miller, who had seen the group at Le Ruban Bleu, put them together with singer Johnnie Ray, who they backed on his two hit singles, "Cry" and "Little White Cloud That Cried." They worked with a number of other Columbia artists, including Frankie Laine and Doris Day, and signed with the label in 1952.

INSIGHTS

"Mitch Miller did almost everything. He wanted us to record with Doris Day or Frankie Laine. That was his choice. We enjoyed it. We loved it. He also picked our material. See, what happened is, when we recorded with Johnnie Ray, right away we became the magic back-up group. It's like, make a record with The Four Lads and you're gonna have a hit. You know how you get pegged with that stuff. So, it was no problem for us to go in and record with whoever. They didn't mind, and we loved it. It was great for us." — Frank Busseri to Gary James, classicbands.com

»WILF CARTER

Wilfred Arthur Charles Carter (aka Montana Slim)
Country Singer & Songwriter
Inducted 1985
b. December 18, 1904, Port Hilford, Nova Scotia
d. December 5, 1996, Scottsdale, Arizona

SIGNATURE SONGS

My Swiss Moonlight Lullaby,
Blue Canadian Rockies

MILESTONES

In 1932, Wilf Carter recorded the 78 rpm record, "My Swiss Moonlight Lullaby"/"The Capture of Albert Johnson" at RCA Victor in Montréal, the first Canadian hit recorded domestically. He has also been inducted into the Nashville Songwriters Hall of Fame (1971) and Canadian Country Music Hall of Fame (1984).

INSIGHTS

"The Father of Canadian Country Music." — Author Unknown

"One day in the early '20s, I gets the wanderbug and I get on the rods going west. It must have been a long-winded train that I caught because it just never stopped. Well, finally, when it did and I jumped off, I sees a fella way out there and I says, 'Hey bud, where am I?' He says, 'You're in Calgary, Alberta, son!' So, hey, hey man, there I was."— Wilf Carter

"Vancouver Island in the wartime '40s; no country music stations as such and the relentless grasp of television still ten years away. When a Wilf Carter song came soaring out of that wooden radio, it was a high octane blast of blue glacial energy. Energy so focused, echo so pure, you'd swear it was recorded high in some lost canyon under a full Alberta moon. At that time, Wilf Carter was quite literally the sound of the west, the sound against which all others were measured. In later high school logging years, we would gather at the Alberta Legion for pool and beers and listen to some young fellow with a guitar take a run at the latest Carter classic. Such was his influence, it never occurred to them not to imitate the master's every lick and yodel. Some of 'em came pretty close. The following year, I got my first real wrangling job at Mt. Assinaboine, 40 horseback miles out of Banff. They had a wind-up Victrola and four or five 78 RPM records: one was The Sons of the Pioneers singing 'Everlasting Hills of Oklahoma,' the others were Wilf Carter. As the thunder boomed and rolled on Assinaboine that season, we wound up that Victrola and wore those records out."
— Ian Tyson

»BIOPICS: *The Last Round-Up: The Wilf Carter Story* (2000)

»GORDON LIGHTFOOT

Gordon Meredith Lightfoot Jr.,
Singer, Songwriter, Actor
Inducted 1986
b. November 17, 1938, Orillia, Ontario.

SIGNATURE SONGS

Early Morning Rain (1966), *Canadian Railroad Trilogy* (1967), *If You Could Read My Mind* (1970), *Sundown* (1974), *Carefree Highway* (1974), *The Wreck of the Edmund Fitzgerald* (1976)

MILESTONES

Marty Robbins topped the country charts in the U.S. with the Gordon Lightfoot song "Ribbon of Darkness" (1965). The same year, Lightfoot signed a management contract with Albert Grossman, Bob Dylan's manager. Lightfoot's song "Black Day In July," about the Detroit riots of 1967, was banned on many radio stations in the U.S. The CBC commissioned Lightfoot to write the "Canadian Railroad Trilogy" during Canada's Centennial Year (1967). In 1974, Lightfoot accomplished the rare double on the Billboard charts as his single "Sundown" reached number one the same week the album of the same name topped the Billboard album chart (1974). "The Wreck of the Edmund Fitzgerald," a song written about the November 10, 1975 sinking of the SS *Edmund Fitzgerald* during a raging storm on Lake Superior with the loss of all 29 crewmen, reached number 2 in the U.S. In 1980, he was named Canadian Male Recording Artist of the Decade ('70s). Lightfoot was inducted into the Canadian Songwriters Hall of Fame (2003). Canada Post issued a commemorative Gordon Lightfoot stamp (June 29, 2007). He has been inducted into the New York-based Songwriters Hall of Fame (June 14, 2012).

INSIGHTS

"It was Gordon Lightfoot who etched the idyllic and lasting picture of the Canadian experience into the annals of that particular music style [folk]. Lightfoot, in the final analysis, has to be considered the definitive folksinger/songwriter. In the years when Bob Dylan, Joan Baez, Pete Seeger and others were documenting the realities of 'The American Dream,' Lightfoot was writing odes to the 'verdant country' whose 'wild majestic mountains,' 'green dark forests' and 'wide prairies' were a source of constant awe and inspiration to him... This country's very culture and history were molded by the vastness and solitude described in 'Canadian Railroad Trilogy.' He captured the essence of that reality in a song." — Martin Melhuish (*Billboard*)

"Almost all of the songs he sings are his own inspirations. The thoughts behind them are not unique, but they are firmly rooted in his own experience and, out of the private truths he finds, there comes an understanding in which we all can share. The result, the lyrics, are free from both clichés and obscure symbolism; the lines of communication are wide open. Likewise the melodies. Lightfoot uses a few quite unusual chord progressions; the tunes themselves are not surprising. Somehow though, most of them continue to be fresh and distinctively his. They are likeable, singable tunes, not so much catchy as evocative and memorable." — Wilder Penfield III, *Toronto Star*

»BOOKS: *Gordon Lightfoot* by Alfrieda Gabiou (1979); *If You Could Read His Mind* by Maynard Collins (1988); *Writing Gordon Lightfoot: The Man, the Music, and the World in 1972* by Dave Bidini (2011)

>>THE GUESS WHO

Pop/Rock Group

Inducted 1987

b. Randy Bachman, September 27, 1943, Winnipeg, Manitoba (guitar)

b. Burton Cummings, December 31, 1947, Winnipeg, Manitoba (vocals, keyboards)

b. Jim Kale, August 11, 1943, Winnipeg, Manitoba (bass)

b. Garry Peterson, May 26, 1945, Winnipeg, Manitoba (drums)

b. Chad Allan (Allan Kowbel), March 29, 1943, Winnipeg, Manitoba. Vocals: replaced by Burton Cummings in 1966)

b. Bob Ashley, St. Vital, Manitoba. Piano: replaced by Burton Cummings in 1966

b. Kurt Winter, April 2, 1946, Winnipeg, Manitoba. Guitar: replaced Randy Bachman in 1970

d. Kurt Winter, December 14, 1997

b. Greg Leskiw, August 5, 1947, Winnipeg, Manitoba. Guitar: replaced Randy Bachman in 1970

b. Bill Wallace, May 18, 1949, Winnipeg, Manitoba. Bass: replaced Jim Kale for a time in early '70s

b. Donnie McDougall, November 5, 1948, Winnipeg, Manitoba. Guitar: replaced Greg Leskiw in early '70s

b. Domenic Troiano, January 17, 1946, Modugno, Italy. Guitar: replaced Kurt Winter in 1974

d. Domenic Troiano, May 25, 2005, Toronto, Ontario.

SIGNATURE SONGS

Shakin' All Over (1965), *These Eyes* (1969), *Laughing* (1969), *Undun* (1969), *No Time* (1970), *American Woman/No Sugar Tonight* (1970), *Share the Land* (1970), *Sour Suite* (1971), *Clap For the Wolfman* (1974).

MILESTONES

In 1965, Winnipeg, Manitoba-band Chad Allan and the Expressions had their new single "Shakin' All Over" released under the name The Guess Who in order to disguise the fact that they were a Canadian band and liable to be rejected at Canadian radio stations as second-rate. The name stuck. The group hosted the weekly Thursday Winnipeg episodes of CBC-TV's national teen series *Let's Go* (1967-68). The group was first seen by producer Jack Richardson on *Let's Go,* and legend has it that he mortgaged his house to record and market the group's 1968 album, *Wheatfield Soul,* on his Toronto-based Nimbus 9 record label. The group's breakthrough single internationally was "These Eyes," a Top 10 hit for the group in 1969. The group topped the Billboard singles chart for 3 weeks beginning the week of May 9, 1970 with the single "American Woman"/ "No Sugar Tonight." The group's principle songwriters, Randy Bachman and Burton Cummings, were inducted into the Canadian Songwriters Hall of Fame (2005). A commemorative stamp ing the group has been issued by Canada Post (July 19, 2013). Randy Bachman would go on to equally great success with his band, Bachman-Turner Overdrive (BTO). Burton Cummings has enjoyed a successful solo career. The band has reunited from time to time.

INSIGHTS

"Rock royalty in their native country, the Guess Who did everything well. While they churned out a steady stream of radio hits, their albums may be the best listening of the Rock era, right next to the Beatles. For, like the Beatles' LPs, Guess Who albums contained classic cuts from almost every genre of music, each group managing to forge a couple of hit singles from each long player while avoiding filler and sameness on the rest of the cuts. And, no other group compared to the Beatles when it came to meshing humor into their recordings." — Phil Marder, *Goldmine*

"One of rock's most consistently fascinating maverick bands, with a succession of meritorious songs that has few equals among contemporary North American groups." — Ken Barnes, *Rolling Stone*

>>BOOKS: *American Woman: The Story of the Guess Who* by John Einarson (1995)

»THE BAND

Rock Group

Inducted 1989

b. Robbie Robertson (Jaime Robbie Robertson), July 5, 1944, Toronto, Ontario (guitar, vocals)

b. Levon Helm (Mark Lavon Helm), May 26, 1940, Marvell, Arkansas (drums, vocals, mandolin)

d. Levon Helm, April 19, 2012, New York, New York

b. Richard Manuel, April 3, 1943, Stratford, Ontario (piano, vocals)

d. Richard Manuel, March 4, 1986, Winter Park, Florida

b. Rick Danko (Richard Clarke Danko), December 29, 1943, Green's Corner, Ontario (bass, vocals, violin, guitar)

d. Rick Danko, December 10, 1999

b. Garth Hudson (Eric Garth Hudson), August 2, 1937, London, Ontario (organ, keyboards, saxophone, accordion, horns)

SIGNATURE SONGS

The Weight/I Shall Be Released (1968), *Up On Cripple Creek/The Night They Drove Old Dixie Down* (1969), *The Shape I'm In* (1970), *Life Is A Carnival* (1971), *When I Paint My Masterpiece* (1971), *Acadian Driftwood* (1976), *Ophelia* (1976)

MILESTONES

In 1958, Levon Helm arrived in Canada with Ronnie Hawkins as a member of his group, The Hawks, who initially played the club and bar circuit in and around Toronto and Hamilton, Ontario. As the original members of The Hawks began heading back to the southland, they were replaced with a number of local musicians. In 1963, the group, including Levon, left Hawkins to set out on their own as The Canadian Squires and then Levon and the Hawks.

In 1964, John Hammond Jr. heard the group and recruited them to tour and record with him. They come to the attention of Bob Dylan in the summer of 1965 and subsequently accompanied Dylan on a world tour. They later moved to Woodstock, New York to be close to Dylan who, on July 29, 1966, was involved in a near-fatal motorcycle accident. While Dylan is recovering, the group now referring to themselves as The Band — that's what everyone in the town of Woodstock called them — worked on their own material while living in a house known as Big Pink. The group's debut album, *Music From Big Pink*, entered the Billboard albums chart on August 10, 1968. The Band played their first concert on April 17, 1969 at San Francisco's Winterland. On August 31, 1969, they appeared with Bob Dylan at the Isle of Wight Pop Festival in England just over a month prior to the release of their widely-acclaimed, self-titled sophomore album. On January 12, 1970, the group appeared on the cover of *Time* under the banner "The New Sound of Country Rock." In the fall of 1973, they worked in the studio with Bob Dylan on his *Planet Waves* album, and on January 3, 1974, they opened a six week tour of North America with him in Chicago, during which Dylan's *Before the Flood* live album is recorded. On Thanksgiving Day, November 25, 1976, The Band returned to San Francisco's Winterland, where they had played their first concert as The Band, to play their final show — at least with all the original members — which famously becomes known at The Last Waltz.

INSIGHTS

"We wanted to have all players and singers and no front man. There was a terminology used back then: 'front man' and 'sideman.' A sideman was a player in the band that made a hell of a lot less money than the front man, who couldn't play a damn thing and took all the bouquets at the same time. So, that was our goal. We wanted to handle all the playing and all the singing and all the money. The goal was to be a real player on a level with these people whose records we listened to. Like when Muddy Waters came up to Woodstock to make a record. I'd been working 25 years to finally get good enough to get to play with Muddy Waters. That was the place you aimed for, to play with a Muddy Waters or a Bonnie Raitt or somebody who's a real music maker. The theatrics or showmanship, that was something that you kind of laughed at and pushed off to the side. That didn't count." — Levon Helm, *The Band: The Authorized Video Biography*

"*Music From Big Pink*, I think, was one of the best albums of all time. It totally broke away from the traditional. My first recollection of it must have been August or September of 1968. I came into New York from California and I was in the same hotel as Jimi Hendrix and Eric Clapton... Eric had just come from meeting with Robbie [Robertson] and some of The Band. He had a cassette — or it could have been an acetate — of *Big Pink*. He was saying, you've got to hear this! We played it over and over again. I liked it a lot and was very impressed with the variation. It had all these different singers, different sounds, different types of songs... it was much more organic sounding. Not as clinical as a studio." — George Harrison, *The Band: The Authorized Video Biography*

"I had a good smoke and I listened to this thing and I went off into a 5th dimension and never really came back. I listened to this album and thought, 'This is it! This is where music is supposed to have gone for a long time now. Now, someone's gone and done it'... They amalgamated all the influences with songwriting and musicianship and this is what it's about. And I'm in the wrong place with the wrong people doing the wrong thing and it had all kinds of effects on me. It stimulated me, it moved me and it upset me and made me discontent all at the same time. And it had a similar effect on a lot of people, especially musicians, who were struggling to find their way." — Eric Clapton, *The Band: The Authorized Video Biography*

»BIOPICS: *The Band: The Authorized Video Biography* (1995)

»BOOKS: *Across the Great Divide: The Band and America* by Barney Hoskyns (1993); *This Wheel's On Fire: Levon Helm and the Story of The Band* by Levon Helm with Stephen Davis (1993)

»MAUREEN FORRESTER

Maureen Kathleen Stewart Forrester
Operatic contralto
Inducted 1990
b, July 25, 1930, Montréal, Québec
d. June 16, 2010, Toronto, Ontario

SIGNATURE PERFORMANCES

Maureen Forrester was acclaimed for her Gustav Mahler performances, including *Das Lied von der Erde, Mahler's Second Symphony (Resurrection) Des Knaben Wunderhorn*.

MILESTONES

Maureen Forrester made her professional debut with the Montréal Elgar Choir at the Salvation Army Citadel (December 8, 1951). In 1953, she began working with German-born Montréal pianist/ accompanist/coach John Newmark, with whom she has toured the world during the course of her career. Forrester made her recital debut with Newmark at the Montréal YMCA (March 29, 1953). At the Salle Gaveau in Paris she first performed in Europe on February 14, 1955. On November 12, 1956, she sang with the New York Philharmonic at Carnegie Hall in Mahler's Second Symphony. In 1957, she appeared with both the Royal Philharmonic in London and the Berlin Philharmonic. She made her Metropolitan Opera debut in the role of Erda in Das Rhiengold on February 10, 1975. Forrester was Chair of the Canada Council for five years (1983-88).

INSIGHTS

"She was a big woman, magnificent on the platform (always gorgeously gowned and coiffed) and charismatic on the operatic stage. She was always supremely present for her audience; your eye couldn't leave her and, when she sang, neither could your ear. Her voice, arguably an opulent and capacious mezzo-soprano, officially a contralto, was famous in Mahler, ideal in Brahms and Dvorak, supple and agile in Bach and Handel, intimate in the most delicate lied and mélodie, simple or rude or funny in folksong or operetta. Her embodiment of earth-mother, reigning queen and good sport made her the shining model of what Canadians want a diva to be." — Ken Winters, *The Globe & Mail*

"Maureen Forrester was born into a Canada where culture was a commodity that was most often imported and, like so many of her generation, she devoted her talent, her career and much of her life to transforming it to something we not only made here, but exported as well. And while she deserves to be remembered as one of the greatest voices Canada has ever produced, we should never lose sight of the fact that she was a cultural pioneer as well." — John Coulbourn, QMI Agency/Sun Media

"I have a real feeling about modern composers. I go around preaching to young people that the performer is the mouth of the composer. You must see that the composers in your country get a hearing. When I travel and do recitals, I always program a big piece of Canadian music." — Maureen Forrester, *Boston Globe*

»BIOPICS: CBC-TV Life and Times — *Maureen Forrester: The Diva In Winter* (2000).

»BOOKS: *Out of Character: A Memoir* by Maureen Forrester with Marci McDonald (1986)

»LEONARD COHEN

Leonard Norman Cohen
Singer, Songwriter, Poet, Novelist
Inducted 1991
b. September 21, 1934, Montréal, Québec

SIGNATURE SONGS

Suzanne (1968), Hey That's No Way To Say Goodbye (1968), So Long Marianne (1968), Bird On A Wire (1969), Dance Me To the End of Love (1984), Hallelujah (1984), Ain't No Cure For Love (1988), First We Take Manhattan (1988), Everybody Knows (1988), Closing Time (1992), The Future (1993)

MILESTONES

Judy Collins recorded Leonard Cohen's song "Suzanne" on her *In My Life* album, giving Cohen his first major exposure as a songwriter (1966). Jennifer Warnes, a former back-up singer for Cohen, released an album of his songs titled *Famous Blue Raincoat* in 1986, which resulted in a renewed interest in Cohen's music, particularly in North America. Columbia Records presented Cohen with the Crystal Globe Award for his album *I'm Your Man* as an artist who has sold more than five million copies of an album in foreign territories (1988). Cohen retreated to the Mt. Baldy Zen Center near Los Angeles, where he served as personal assistant to century-old Japanese Rinzai Zen teacher, Kyozan Joshu Sasaki Roshi and was ordained as a Rinzai Zen Buddhist (1994-1999). He has been inducted into the Canadian Songwriters Hall of Fame (2006) and into the Rock and Roll Hall of Fame in 2008 by Lou Reed. Later that year, two different versions of his song "Hallelujah" placed in the Top 10 of the U.K. charts.

INSIGHTS

"Cohen falls into the odd category of underrated legend. To his fans, including many songwriters, he is about as good as it gets, but he has never enjoyed a hit single or (outside his native Canada and, for some reason, Norway) a platinum album. He has said that a certain image of him has been 'put into the computer': the womanising poet who sings songs of 'melancholy and despair' enjoyed by those who wish they could be (or be with) womanising poets too. These days the database will also note that he wrote 'Hallelujah,' a neglected song on a flop album that, via an unlikely alliance of Jeff Buckley, Shrek and The X Factor, eventually became a kind of modern hymn." — Dorian Lynskey, *The Guardian*

"Leonard Cohen is the dude as far as I'm concerned. It's so funny how times change. I remember a point in high school, upon really first listening to Leonard Cohen, not liking his voice…and then today: 'Oh, the voice of Leonard Cohen, kill me now!!'" — Singer, songwriter Damhnait Doyle

"You go to a Leonard Cohen concert and he spends two hours singing what most people call 'black songs'… and everyone's grinning, ear to ear. Why are they so happy coming out of a Leonard Cohen concert?

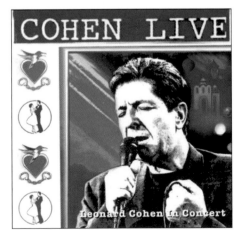

Because it's cathartic; it's great emotional psychic therapy." — Singer, songwriter, record executive Tom Northcott, who recorded the album, *Joyful Songs of Leonard Cohen* (1997).

"Right around the time that I had my kid, we were shopping at the mall and I'd seen *The Best of Leonard Cohen* album. Something made me want to hear it again and I bought it. I took it home and I just got it right away. It was just like this bolt of light. It changed everything for me because I started to appreciate his words… the power of words. The way a song like 'That's No Way To Say Goodbye,' in its two simple verses, can say something that's really moving and I wanted to do that." — Singer, songwriter Ron Sexsmith.

»BOOKS: *Various Positions: A Life of Leonard Cohen* by Ira Bruce Nadel (1996); *I'm Your Man: The Life of Leonard Cohen* by Sylvie Simmons (2012)

»BIOPICS: *Ladies and Gentlemen... Mr. Leonard Cohen* (1965), *Bird On A Wire* (1974/2010), *The Song of Leonard Cohen* (1980), *Songs from the Life of Leonard Cohen* (1988), *Leonard Cohen: Spring 96* (1997), *Leonard Cohen: I'm Your Man* (2006), *Leonard Cohen: Under Review* 1934-1977 (2007), *Leonard Cohen: Under Review* 1978-2006 (2008), *Leonard Cohen: Live at the Isle of Wight 1970* (2009)

»IAN & SYLVIA

Ian Tyson and Sylvia Fricker
Singer Songwriters
Inducted 1991
b. Ian Tyson, September 25, 1933, Victoria, British Columbia
b. Sylvia Tyson (Sylvia Fricker), September 19, 1940, Chatham, Ontario

SIGNATURE SONGS

Four Strong Winds (1963), You Were On My Mind (1964), Early Morning Rain (1965), Lovin' Sound (1967)

MILESTONES

Ian and Sylvia met in Toronto and began performing together in 1959. They moved to New York a few years later, where they signed with manager Albert Grossman (Peter, Paul & Mary, Bob Dylan) and released their eponymous debut album on the Vanguard label in 1962. The title track of the duo's sophomore album "Four Strong Winds" (1964) became Ian Tyson's best known song and a classic of the folk genre. Ian and Sylvia married in 1964, the same year that Sylvia's "You Were On My Mind," and Ian's "Someday Soon," were heard on their album *Northern Journey*. We Five had an international hit with "You Were On My Mind" in 1965. "Early Morning Rain," and "For Lovin' Me" gave Gordon Lightfoot his first major exposure. Their 1969 album *Great Speckled Bird*, produced by Todd Rundgren, marked their first foray into the nascent country/rock music scene as they named their band Great Speckled Bird. In 1970, the *Ian Tyson Show* (aka *Nashville North*) debuted on CTV and ran until 1975. Following their separation in the mid-'70s, Sylvia hosted the award-winning CBC radio show *Touch the Earth* (1974-1980), embarked on a successful solo recording career, worked with the group Quartette and became an author/novelist. Ian moved west to a ranch south of Calgary and in the '80s released a series of acclaimed albums documenting the cowboy lifestyle on the Plains. He also authored a young-adult fiction books.

INSIGHTS

"Kettle of Fish on MacDougal Street [Greenwich Village] was our bar. Bob Dylan was bringing in songs daily and he sang me one. I say it was 'Blowin' In The Wind,' but I don't know if it was or not. It was probably 'Masters of War'… and I thought, 'Shit, I can do that!' I remember it very well. I asked Albert [Grossman] if I could use his apartment. He said, 'Sure!'… and he gave me the keys. He had an apartment on the Lower East Side. It was a rainy, autumn late-afternoon in New York and I went over there and sat down and thought about Alberta, and this and that, and half an hour later, there she was." — Ian Tyson, on writing "Four Strong Winds"

"People are always terribly surprised, unless they've known me for a long time, that I wrote, 'You Were on My Mind.' Nanci Griffith was going to put that song on a compilation and she said to my friend Tom Russell, 'Oh, I'm putting an Ian Tyson song on my new album…' Tom said, 'Oh, which one?' She replied, 'You Were on My Mind.' Tom said, 'Excuse me!?'" — Sylvia Tyson

"Photographs of Sylvia [Tyson] playing autoharp, while Ian [Tyson] plays guitar are the most romantic evocations of the coffeehouse era." — Music journalist, photographer Gene Wilburn

"When I saw that combination of folk and country music, I knew it was what I had been looking for. It was like seeing the light of day." — Gordon Lightfoot

»BOOKS: *Four Strong Winds: Ian and Sylvia, Their Story* by John Einarson (2011)

»ANNE MURRAY

Morna Anne Murray
Singer
Inducted 1993
b. June 20, 1945, Springhill, Nova Scotia

SIGNATURE SONGS

Snowbird (1970), *Danny's Song* (1973), *Love Song* (1974), *You Won't See Me* (1974), *You Needed Me* (1978), *I Just Fall In Love Again* (1979), *Shadows In the Moonlight* (1979), *Broken Hearted Me* (1979), *Daydream Believer* (1980), *Could I Have This Dance?* (1980), *Blessed Are the Believers* (1981), *A Little Good News* (1983), *Just Another Woman In Love* (1984), *Nobody Loves Me Like You Do* (1984), *Now and Forever (You and Me)* (1986)

MILESTONES

Anne Murray joined the cast of the popular CBC-TV series *Singalong Jubilee* on May 30, 1966. "Snowbird," written by fellow Maritimer Gene MacLellan, became one of the most played songs in North America in 1970. The song also gave Murray the distinction of being the first solo Canadian female artist to earn a gold record in the U.S. During this period, she becomes a regular on *The Glen Campbell Goodtime Hour* in the U.S. "He Thinks I Still Care" (1974) is the first of Murray's 10 number one songs on Billboard's country chart.

Anne Murray married TV producer/performer Bill Langstroth in 1975. Having previously formed the company Balmur Ltd. with Murray, the late Leonard Rambeau became her exclusive manager in 1977. "You Needed Me" became the biggest single of Murray's career and brought her the second of her four Grammy Awards (1978).

The Anne Murray Centre opened in Springhill, Nova Scotia, in 1989. Murray was inducted into the Canadian Country Music Hall of Fame (2002) and received the Legacy Award from the Canadian Songwriters Hall of Fame (2006). Canada Post issued the limited edition Anne Murray stamp (June 29, 2007). The first annual Anne Murray Charity Golf Classic in support of Colon Cancer Canada was held in May 2009.

INSIGHTS

"Bill Langstroth called me from the CBC building in Halifax and said, 'You have to come over here! I've got this guy singing these songs.' [Gene MacLellan was guesting on the *Don Messer Show*, which Langstroth produced] 'Wait 'til you hear this guy!' So I went right over and we were in a little conference room somewhere upstairs and Gene sang 'Snowbird.' He sang about four or five songs. Well, I was just flabbergasted. And he just gave them to me. He said, 'Well, if you like them so much, you have them.' I said, 'Okay!' I sang them all summer, sang them for my parents, friends and relatives. Everybody told me how great the songs were. So, Brian [Ahern] and I went in the studio that fall and recorded the *Snowbird* album. We went in with the blessing of Capitol Records who gave us *carte blanche*. I thought, 'Why would they do that? But it worked." — Anne Murray

"Anne Murray's recording of 'Snowbird' was Elvis' favorite record. We used to listen to it all the time. He loved the depth of feeling that Anne has — and her vocal range." — Linda Thompson, Elvis Presley's girlfriend in the last years of his life.

"I know two things about Canada: hockey and Anne Murray." — Elton John

"In the late '80s when I would look out at the marquees in Las Vegas — and those marquees are huge — there would be Frank Sinatra up there. And I'd look out the window and see my name up there and go, 'Nah!' It's the same reaction I have sometimes if I'm getting an encore. I'll be standing in the wings and the people will be applauding and standing and I almost look over my shoulder and go, 'What?! It's just me!' But you have to pinch yourself from time to time, because it's quite a business and the adulation can sometimes become too much. You have to come home to Nova Scotia, get your feet planted firmly on the ground and go back at it again." — Anne Murray

»BOOKS: *Snowbird: The Story of Anne Murray* by Barry Grills (1996*); Anne Murray: All of Me* by Anne Murray with Michael Posner (2009)

»RUSH

Rock trio

Inducted 1994

b. Geddy Lee (Gary Lee Weinrib), July 29, 1953, Toronto, Ontario (bass, vocals).

b. Alex Lifeson (Aleksandar Zivojinovic), August 27, 1953, Fernie, British Columbia (guitar).

b. Neil Peart (Neil Ellwood Peart), September 12, 1952, Hamilton, Ontario (drums).

b. John Rutsey (John Howard Rutsey), July 23, 1952, Toronto, Ontario (drums – early member)

d. John Rutsey, May 11, 2008, Toronto, Ontario.

SIGNATURE SONGS

In the Mood (1974), *Fly By Night* (1975), *Closer To the Heart* (1977), *Entre nous* (1980), *Spirit of Radio* (1980), *Limelight* (1981), *Tom Sawyer* (1981), *YYZ* (1981), *New World Man* (1982), *Subdivisions* (1982), *Body Electric* (1984), *Big Money* (1985).

MILESTONES

Rush released their self-titled debut album in March 1974. In 2010, the year the group received a star on the Hollywood Walk of Fame (June 25), Billboard presented the group with the 2010 Legends of Live award (November 4, 2010), while Classic Rock magazine honour the group as the 2010 Living Legends (November 10, 2010). In 2012, Rush is presented with the Governor General's Performing Arts Awards for Lifetime Artistic Achievement (March 5). The band's 20th studio album *Clockwork Angels* debuted at number one on the charts in Canada and number two in the U.S. Rush, who at this point are third behind The Beatles and The Rolling Stones for most consecutive gold or platinum studio albums by a rock band — they have 24 gold and 14 platinum (three multi-platinum) albums — were inducted into the Rock and Roll Hall of Fame in Cleveland, Ohio (April 18, 2013). A Rush commemorative stamp was issued by Canada Post (July 19, 2013).

INSIGHTS

"In 1974, Toronto radio was going through its 'wimpy mellow-jello' phase, and hard rock got little airplay. The group [Rush] had put out their own record, as a result, on Moon Records. As a courtesy to [Bob] Roper [A&M Records Canada executive], who didn't normally send me something he didn't personally believe in, I put the album on my record library turntable. I dropped the needle on a track called 'Working Man,' and suddenly I understood why Roper believed the band had potential. The vocalist — I didn't know their names then — sounded a bit like a Led Zeppelin clone. But the band had a certain energy that I knew was perfect for our audience. When I listened to another track, 'Finding My Way,' I was convinced of it. I took the record downstairs and walked in on Denny Sanders' show. Denny also had a good ear. I asked him to listen to something — it was 'Working Man.' It didn't take long for him to have the same reaction I had. My love of Canadian music was a standing joke at the station, but in this instance, Denny agreed 100% that this album deserved to be played NOW. And he did play it. That is how I can say with certainty that the first Rush song ever played in the U.S. was in fact 'Working Man' because I was there. Almost immediately, the phones lit up…" — Donna Halper, Former Music Director of WMMS-FM, Cleveland

"Rock and roll is supposed to be an escape from the suburbs into a more vital world. But Rush did it in a bookish, middle-class way, opening up worlds into Greek mythology on *Hemispheres* or black holes on 'Cygnus X-1.' It wasn't an escape into the energizing working-class culture that critics valued, like what the Rolling Stones did. It was an escape for people who wanted to think about big ideas, but didn't necessarily want to read Tolstoy." — Chris McDonald, from *Rush, Rock Music and the Middle Class.*

"Rush fans have been very angry for a very long time. Not at the long-lived Canadian prog-rock trio — no, they worship them unequivocally. The "world's biggest cult band" has a fanatical following heavily composed of dudes, and in the last decade, those dudes have been pissed, ranting about the Rock and Roll Hall of Fame's perceived slight of their beloved band. It's taken more than 10 years, but Rush finally got what they didn't really care about in the first place: an induction into the Rock and Roll Hall of Fame, class of 2013." — Katherine Turman, The Village Voice

»BIOPICS: *Rush: Beyond the Lighted Stage* (2010).

»BOOKS: *Rush* by Brian Harrigan (1982); *Rush Visions: The Official Biography* (1990); *Ghost Rider: Travels On the Healing Road* by Neil Peart (2002); *Contents Under Pressure: 30 Years of Rush At Home and Away* (2004); *Rush, Rock Music and the Middle Class* by Chris McDonald (2009)

»BUFFY SAINTE-MARIE

Singer, Songwriter, Social activist, Digital Artist
Inducted 1995
b. Beverly Sainte-Marie, February 20, 1941, Piapot
Reserve, Qu'Appelle Valley, Saskatchewan

SIGNATURE SONGS

Cod'ine (1963), *Universal Soldier* (1964), *Now That the Buffalo's Gone* (1964), *My Country 'Tis of Thy People You're Dying* (1964), *Until It's Time For You To Go* (1965), *I'm Gonna Be A Country Girl Again* (1968), *He's An Indian Cowboy In the Rodeo* (1971), *Soldier Blue* (1971), *Mister Can't You See* (1972), *Up Where We Belong* (1982)

MILESTONES

"Universal Soldier," a song Buffy Sainte-Marie had written in the basement of the Purple Onion coffee house in Toronto's Yorkville Village in the early '60s, became an international hit for Donovan in 1965. The use of Michael Tchaikovsky's Bouccla synthesizer on her 1969 album *Illuminations* established Sainte-Marie as an electronic music pioneer. In the early '80s, Sainte-Marie was also one of the first artists to use computers (Apple II and Macintosh) for recording. In 1975, Sainte-Marie began a 6-year relationship with the hit children's TV series *Sesame Street*, during which the birth of her son Cody is chronicled. She is seen breast-feeding him during an 1977 episode.

"Up Where We Belong," co-written by Sainte-Marie, Jack Nitzsche and Will Jennings, was a number one hit in the U.S. for 3 weeks beginning November 6, 1982. The song, which is heard in the film *An Officer and Gentleman*, subsequently won an Oscar, Golden Globe and BAFTA Film Award as Best Original Song. Joe Cocker and Jennifer Warnes won a Grammy Award with the song for Best Pop Performance by a Duo or Group with Vocal in 1983. The Cradleboard Teaching Project, founded in 1997 and financed in part by Sainte-Marie's Nihewan Foundation for American Indian Education which she set up in 1968, "has developed a curriculum that aims to raise self-identity and self-esteem in present and future generations of Indian children by introducing them to enriching, accurate information about Native American people and cultures."

INSIGHTS

"The Vietnam War, and the climate around the Vietnam War, certainly had a lot to do with the music that was being made [in the '60s]. But it was more than that. Our generation of students was interested in Civil Rights. I was about the only one who was covering the base of Native Rights; that's what I wanted to do. I didn't feel like being Joan Baez. I wasn't showing up for photo-ops at the Civil Rights rallies because I thought that was being done very well. But no one was talking about Aboriginal Rights; nobody was going to the reservations and inspiring and organizing people and supporting their grass roots efforts to make things better." — Buffy Sainte-Marie (*Four Strong Winds: A Celebration of Canadian Singer/Songwriters*)

"I traveled alone with my guitar, feeling lonely, misunderstood, exploited, disconnected, yet also special and happy. My gender, Indian-ness and my own naiveté led to misunderstandings with the men who controlled show business. They wanted Pocahontas in fringe and I gave them activism and hot love songs, and they didn't know what to do with me. On the other hand, I was successful in achieving the real goals I had: to travel and learn, to spend time with lots of Indigenous people, and to participate in making the social changes that were necessary. — Buffy Sainte-Marie (to *J Poet of Native Peoples* magazine).

»BIOPICS: *Buffy Sainte-Marie: A Multimedia Life* (2006)

≫JOHN KAY

Joachim Fritz Krauledat

Lead singer, Songwriter, Guitarist

Member of Steppenwolf

Inducted 1996

b. April 12, 1944, Tilsit, East Prussia, Germany

SIGNATURE SONGS

Born To Be Wild (1968), *Magic Carpet Ride* (1968), *The Pusher* (1968), *Sookie Sookie* (1968), *Monster* (1969), *Move Over* (1969), *Rock Me* (1969), *It's Never Too Late* (1969), *Hey Lawdy Mama* (1970), *Who Needs Ya* (1970), *Snow Blind Friend* (1970), *For Ladies Only* (1971), *Ride With Me* (1971), *Screaming Night Hog* (1971), *Straight Shootin' Woman* (1974)

MILESTONES

John Kay arrived in Toronto from Germany in March 1958. Kay was initially inspired by Ronnie Hawkins and his band, The Hawks. He subsequently traveled through the U.S. as a solo artist playing acoustic blues in clubs and bars. Kay returned to Toronto in 1965 and joined the group The Sparrows (later The Sparrow) at The Devil's Den in the city's Yorkville Village. By the summer of 1966, Kay and the group had moved to San Francisco and were briefly part of the Bay Area music scene before breaking up and re-emerging in Los Angeles as Steppenwolf in 1967.

The band's fortunes are given a major boost in 1969 as the songs "Born To Be Wild," written by Mars Bonfire (aka Dennis Edmonton), and "The Pusher" are heard as part of the soundtrack of the popular film, *Easy Rider*. "Born To Be Wild" reached the number two position on the Billboard Hot 100 chart in the summer of 1968 as it sold over one million copies.

The lineup has been in constant flux since the late '60s. In 1980, Kay launched John Kay and Steppenwolf and began touring extensively in response to former band members using the group's name for "low-rent club gigs... and tarnishing the legacy." In 2004, John Kay and his wife Jutta Maue Kay formed The Maue Kay Foundation, which "supports individuals and organizations engaged in the protection of wildlife, the environment and human rights."

INSIGHTS

"As we speak here, some cab driver in Bangkok is listening to the song ["Born To Be Wild"]. This is a song that has been up in the space shuttle twice. This tune has literally become a global anthem, not just for the bikers who have been with us since the early days because of Easy Rider, but also because of every kid that gets behind the wheel of daddy's car or some jalopy... but the context is far broader than that." — John Kay, *Steppenwolf Tower of Song: An Epic Story of Canada and Its Music.*

"Heavy metal rock is said to have adopted its name from a line in 'Born To Be Wild.' Science fiction writer William S. Burroughs first used the term 'heavy metal' in his novels *The Soft Machine* (1962) and *Nova Express* (1964) in referring to one of his characters as Uranium Willy, the Heavy Metal Kid. Mars Bonfire conjured the compellingly descriptive phrase 'heavy metal thunder' later in the decade as the pop sounds of the mid-'60s were giving way to the bombast and harder edge of rock music." — Martin Melhuish (*Music Publisher Canada*).

"In the summer of 1969, Steppenwolf returned home to Toronto in triumph to play in front of 40,000 rock fans from all over North America at Varsity Stadium... One particular poetic description of the event came from a Toronto writer who was on hand and had obviously been deeply-inhaling the cloud of incense and pot smoke that wafted around the stadium. 'They were,' she wrote, 'unlikely and motley Caesars returning from triumphal forays in foreign lands, who followed their leader onto the stage like a flock of fierce sheep

led by a Neanderthal man.' Newsweek said that the band's lead singer sounded 'like a bullfrog whose mate had found a better lily pad.' Well, that so-called Neanderthal man with the bullfrog voice is one of tonight's honored Hall of Fame inductees... John Kay!'"
— Buffy Sainte-Marie introducing John Kay at 1996 Canadian Music Hall of Fame Gala in Toronto.

»BOOKS: *Magic Carpet Ride: The Autobiography of John Kay and Steppenwolf* by John Kay and John Einarson (1994)

>>DAVID CLAYTON-THOMAS

David Henry Thomsett,
Singer, Songwriter, Musician
Member of Blood, Sweat & Tears
Inducted 1996
b. September 13, 1941, Kingston upon Thames, Surrey, U.K.

SIGNATURE SONGS

Walk That Walk (1965, David Clayton-Thomas and the Shays), *Brainwashed* (1966, David Clayton-Thomas and the Bossmen), *You've Made Me So Very Happy* (1969, B,S &T), *Spinning Wheel* (1969, B,S&T), *And When I Die* (1969 – B,S&T), *Hi-De-Ho* (1970, B,S&T), *Lucretia Mac Evil* (1970, B,S&T), *Go Down Gamblin'* (1971, B,S&T).

MILESTONES

David Clayton-Thomas' musical career began in the early '60s on Toronto's fabled Yonge Street Strip at venues like the Club Bluenote and the Coq d'Or (with Ronnie Hawkins) before forming his own groups, David Clayton-Thomas and the Shays and David Clayton-Thomas and the Bossmen (with pianist Tony Collacott). In New York, Clayton-Thomas joined the second incarnation of Blood, Sweat & Tears, which debuted at the Cafe Au Go Go on June 18, 1968. The group's self-titled album hit number one on the album chart, where it remained for 7 weeks, and produced three Top two singles — "You've Made Me So Very Happy"and "And When I Die" — and Clayton-Thomas' composition "Spinning Wheel." At the Grammys, the record beat out The Beatles' *Abbey Road* as Album of the Year. The follow-up album, *Blood, Sweat & Tears 3* (1970), also topped the album chart

INSIGHTS

"We [Blood, Sweat & Tears] went back into the Cafe Au Go Go, the same place that I went when John Lee Hooker didn't show up, and became the house band there again. We developed a repertoire, some of it left over from Al Kooper — 'You Made Me Very Happy' and some of the other songs from the album *Child Is Father To the Man* — and we developed a set. And then something very strange started happening. This club seated maybe 300 people and I went down there one night and there were five thousand people lined up and down Bleecker Street. We hadn't recorded yet and we had developed this underground following in the Village. We went into the studio and basically recorded the set we were playing at the Cafe Au Go Go and 6 weeks later it was the number one record in the world. It just exploded and we were still playing a 300-seat club. That's how fast it happened." — David Clayton-Thomas

"Innocuous is not a word that has ever been used to describe David Clayton-Thomas... gigantic charisma, positive or negative. David is either hated or loved; there is no middle ground with David because he asserts himself. He knows exactly what he wants and he makes his feelings known. Some people are not comfortable with that. He's an interesting man, no doubt, always has been. He's a powerful figure. I have never heard a disparaging word with respect to his singing ability. The one thing I can tell you about David is that on stage he is another personality. His fantasies become reality when he is performing and people are cheering for him. You get the best of David in that situation, so being in a band with him was a delight. Even when he was deathly ill, there was never a night that he would not go out on stage and kill. He was absolutely great!" — Drummer Bobby Colomby, (former Blood, Sweat & Tears member).

"[David Clayton-Thomas] comes clean about the drugs, the cutthroat business dealings and the ego clashes that went on within the band [Blood, Sweat & Tears] during its platinum-plated 1970s peak and its subsequent dissolution into Clayton-Thomas and a revolving cast of hired-gun musicians half his age, not to mention the fatal 1978 overdose in Amsterdam of his friend and bandmate Greg Herbert. And he comes clean about how the staunch will to succeed that elevated him from the streets into pop music's elite was, for decades, a strain on his health, his family and his interpersonal relationships. There's also, however, a genuinely inspirational rags-to-riches story to be found in the life of a self-made man who, as Clayton-Thomas

recalls, once "walked out of Millbrook Penitentiary with 20 bucks in my pocket, a mail-order guitar and a dream.'" — Ben Raynor, The Toronto Star (Review of book *David Clayton-Thomas: Blood, Sweat & Tears*)

»**BIOPICS:** CBC Life and Times — David Clayton-Thomas: Rollercoaster (2002)

»**BOOKS:** *David Clayton-Thomas: Blood, Sweat & Tears* by David Clayton-Thomas (2010)

»ZAL YANOVSKY

Zalman Yanovsky
Guitarist, Vocalist, Restaurateur
Member of The Lovin' Spoonful
Inducted 1996
b. December 19, 1944, Toronto, Ontario.
d. December 13, 2002, Kingston, Ontario.

SIGNATURE SONGS

Do You Believe In Magic? (1965), You Didn't Have To Be So Nice (1965), Daydream (1966), Did You Ever Have To Make Up Your Mind? (1966), Summer In the City (1966), Rain On the Roof (1966), Nashville Cats (1966), Darling Be Home Soon (1967).

MILESTONES

Zal Yanovsky launched his career by playing in coffee houses in Toronto's Yorkville Village, before leaving for Israel where he worked on a kibbutz and busked on the streets of Tel Aviv. On returning to Toronto, he became accompanist for the group The Colonials from Halifax, which included vocalist Denny Doherty. The group's name subsequently was changed to The Halifax Three as they toured extensively through North America. When The Halifax Three broke up, Yanovsky and Doherty worked as bartenders and waiters at Max's Pipe and Drum in Washington, DC, where they also performed as a duo called The Noise. Zanovsky and Doherty subsequently formed a quartet, with Cass Elliot and James Hendricks, called The Mugwumps.

For a generation of aspiring poets, singers, songwriters, folkies and rock and rollers in the mid-'60s, all roads led to Greenwich Village in New York. It was here that Yanovsky met singer/songwriter John Sebastian at the Village apartment of Cass Elliott (later of The Mamas and the Papas) who has invited a few friends over to watch The Beatles' first TV appearance on The Ed Sullivan Show on that memorable Sunday night in February of 1964. The Lovin' Spoonful subsequently

came together around Sebastian and Yanovsky at a rehearsal space in the basement of the Albert Hotel, the infamous musician's hangout of the day, and through nightly performances at the legendary Night Owl Cafe on West 3rd Street (now Bleecker Bob's Records) in the Village. They were soon signed to Kama Sutra Records and, in the two-year span between 1965 and 1967, the Lovin' Spoonful made a lasting mark on pop music history when they created soundtrack music for the debut films of Woody Allen (*What's Up, Tiger Lily?*, 1966) and Francis Ford Coppola (*You're a Big Boy Now*, 1967). In the mid-'60s, The Lovin' Spoonful were never far from the top of the charts even in the face of an assault on the radio airwaves by The Beatles and the other artists of so-called British Invasion. In their relatively short career, the Spoonful contributed seven top ten hits to the soundtrack of the '60s.

Yanovsky quit the group on June 1, 1967 and returned to Canada where he launched a solo career and spent some time as a member of Kris Kristofferson's backing band. By the late '70s, Yanovsky had left the music business and was working as a chef at The Golden Apple in Gananoque, Ontario and Dr. Bull's in Kingston, Ontario, before opening the popular Kingston restaurant, Chez Piggy, with his second wife

Canadian Music Hall of Fame

Rose Richardson. They opened the Pan Chancho Bakery in the same city in 1994. The original Lovin' Spoonful members, including Yanovsky, re-united in 1980 to perform a cameo in Paul Simon's film, *One Trick Pony*. On March 6, 2000, they were together again for the band's induction into The Rock and Roll Hall of Fame.

INSIGHTS

"I heard all these strengths in Zally. He could play like Elmore James, he could play like Floyd Cramer, he could play like Chuck Berry. He could play like all these people, yet he still had his own overpowering personality. Out of this we could, I thought, craft something with real flexibility." — John Sebastian in *Rolling Stone*.

"In the Spoonful, he [Zal] was the zany guy, the one who sang 'On the Road Again' and 'Bald-Headed Lena' and was such fun to watch that you sometimes forgot how well he played the guitar. The artists he loved ran from Basie to Chuck Berry, Floyd Cramer, Jerry Lee, Hank Williams and Johnny Cash. All the right ones, and all right there in the grooves of Spoonful records. My friends and I probably would have found the Spoonful without radio. But hearing them on the radio made it easier and a whole lot more fun — because for all the abuse radio takes, there's nothing like hearing a great record over the radio. Not then, not now. Zal Yanovsky was 58 when he died, a successful restaurateur, who said this summer that he still regularly picked up his guitar and thought that if he just had the time, he'd love to get serious about playing like Charlie Christian. Yanovsky was as much of a character as his image suggested. He was a very funny. He had a razor-sharp tongue. He could be a hustler. He joked that he liked being in the Rock and Roll Hall of Fame because it gave him a free trip to New York. He loved sports. He was still pals with Sebastian... Most music, by the time it's 40, has been or is being evicted from most of its radio digs. But Zal, he left behind some magic." — David Hinckley, *New York Daily News*.

»DOMENIC TROIANO

Domenic Michele Antonio Troiano
Guitarist, Producer, Songwriter, Composer
Member of Mandala, Bush, The James Gang,
The Guess Who
Inducted 1996
b. January 17, 1946, Modugno, Italy
d. May 25, 2005, Toronto, Ontario.

SIGNATURE SONGS

Opportunity (1967, Mandala), *Love-itis* (1968, Mandala), *I Can Hear You Calling* (1970, Bush), *We All Need Love* (1979), *It's You* (1979)

MILESTONES

As a high school student, Troiano played with Robbie Lane and the Disciples and Ronnie Hawkins' back-up group in Toronto before joining The Rogues (later the Five Rogues), who were the house band at Club Bluenote and for a time David Clayton-Thomas' group. They became Mandala in 1966 and caused quite a stir on the local scene with their "Soul Crusade" fronted by singer George Olliver. Bo Diddley saw the group at The Hawk's Nest in Toronto, became a fan and introduced them to Chess Records in the U.S. The group record their signature song "Opportunity" at the original Chess Studios at 2120 South Michigan Avenue with the Dells singing back-up vocals. Mandala evolved to Bush, the member of which spend the summer of 1969 writing and rehearsing in Scottsdale, Arizona. Troiano turned down lucrative offers to join Iron Butterfly and Edgar Winter during this period. Bush signed with Three Dog Night's manager (Reb Foster) and record label, an affiliation that led to the Bush song "I Can Hear You Calling" becoming the b-side of Three Dog Night's biggest single, "Joy To the World." It was one of the highlights of the band's short-lived career, though their album met with much critical praise for showcasing the group's unique approach to the fusion of rock, R&B and funk styles.

The group broke up in June of 1971 and Troiano went on to record a couple of solo albums and replace Joe Walsh in The James Gang, which he joined with ex-Mandala and Bush vocalist Roy Kenner. He would later join The Guess Who with whom he would tour and record two albums. Troiano returned to Toronto at the end of 1975 and put together the Domenic Troiano Band, which released three albums. He formed the group Black Market in 1981 before beginning a successful career in scoring for television and film. His credits included TV series like *Night Heat*, *Diamonds*, *Hot Shots*, *Airwaves* and the film *Gunfighters*. As a producer, his credits include his former wife of 11 years, Shawne Jackson, Moe Koffman, Kilowatt, Patria, David Gibson and John Rutledge.

INSIGHTS

"It was surreal. You'd go to school Monday to Friday, play with Ronnie [Hawkins] Friday and Saturday at Le Coq d'Or with 800 hookers, 400 gangsters, three million parties, and then go back to school on Monday." — Domenic Troiano

"In the early '60s, a musical force from the east end of Toronto burst onto the scene and things would never quite be the same. Through music, his infamous Telecaster, Domenic Troiano had discovered the perfect way to expose emotions he found difficult to verbalize. His roots were heavy doses of the blues, R&B, jazz, a smattering of country, and almost immediately upon hitting the stage, he began to influence others. No one who had the pleasure of hearing him live will soon forget the almost ferocious intensity and unique style of his playing. It caressed. It inspired. It disturbed, but mostly it just plain smacked you upside the head. Many would ask: 'How the hell does he do that?' Well, do it, he did... with the Five Rogues, which begat Mandala, which begat Bush, then with the James Gang, the Guess Who and numerous self-produced solo projects along the way. He has played with the greats and near greats — plus a few ingrates. With a single-mindedness, just bordering on obsessive, Troiano has constantly strived to create, to innovate. More concerned with the respect of his peers than with commercial acceptance, he was, and is, the quintessential musician's musician."

— Singer, musician Roy Kenner inducts Domenic Troiano into the Canadian Music Hall of Fame.

»DENNY DOHERTY

Dennis Gerrard Stephen Doherty
Singer, Songwriter, Musician, TV personality, Actor
Member of The Mamas and the Papas
Inducted 1996
b. November 29, 1940, Halifax, Nova Scotia.
d. January 19, 2007, Mississauga, Ontario.

SIGNATURE SONGS

California Dreamin' (1966), *Monday Monday* (1966), *I Saw Her Again* (1966), *Words of Love* (1966), *Dedicated To the One I Love* (1967), *Creeque Alley* (1967)

MILESTONES

Denny Doherty became a member of Montréal-based folk act The Colonials (1960), which, a few years later, changed their name to the Halifax Three, a group which also featured Toronto guitarist Zal Yanovsky. In 1964, Doherty and Yanovsky briefly joined Cass Elliot and James Hendricks in the folk/rock group, thc Mugwumps. Following that group's demise, The Mamas and the Papas formed around Denny Doherty, Cass Elliot and John and Michelle Phillips of The Journeymen in 1965. They released a number of hit singles that helped to define the California Sound — *Monday, Monday*, and *California Dreamin'*, to name two.

The group folded in 1969, and Doherty embarked on a solo career in the '70s. In 1978, Doherty hosted *Denny's Sho'* at CBC Halifax. The Mamas and the Papas were revived in 1980 by Doherty, John Phillips, his daughter MacKenzie Phillips and Spanky McFarlane, formerly of Spanky and Our Gang. From July 5, 1993 to October 12, 2001, Doherty played the Harbourmaster in the popular children's TV series, *Theodore Tugboat*, for which he received a Gemini Award nomination in 1997. The Mamas and the Papas were inducted into the Rock and Roll Hall of Fame that same year.

INSIGHTS

"I had to have him. I'm sort of a background guy. I don't like to sing lead. I like to write songs. I like to do arrangements, tell the band what to do... I'm not crazy about standing up front. Denny just had this velvet, liquid voice. It was insane to me, someone like Bing Crosby, so good... Denny is one of the great singers of the entire world." — John Phillips, The Mamas and the Papas.

"I remember we [The Journeymen] were on tour as part of a Hootenanny tour and we played all over the Deep South. We were traveling by bus and I don't remember exactly where we were but I do remember the first time I heard Denny's voice. We all came up around the side of the stage and said to each other, 'My God, listen to this guy sing!' When the Journeymen broke up, we heard through the grapevine that The Halifax Three had also broken up and we jumped in there and tried to find Denny as quickly as possible because we knew someone was going to snag him. Finding Denny was really the beginning of The Mamas and the Papas. I was a true novice at that point but when I started to sing with Denny, I started to learn how to sing because, for the first time, somebody could actually carry a tune. He sang effortlessly with a beautiful, powerful voice and you were swept up in his singing and everyone else sang better too. There was no question in our minds that Denny was a hit maker, though he remained the least-known member of the group. He did that to himself. He chose to remain practically anonymous in the group. I'm told that tends to be a Canadian trait. He did not seek out the limelight like Cass or John or, ultimately, as I did, so many people aren't aware that Denny sang lead on most of our biggest hits including 'California Dreamin' and 'Monday Monday.'"
— Michelle Phillips, The Mamas and the Papas.

»BIOPICS: *Straight Shooter: The Story of John Phillips and The Mamas and the Papas* (1988)

»GIL EVANS

Ian Ernest Gilmore Evans (nee Green)
Jazz pianist, Arranger, Composer, Band
leader
Inducted 1997
b. May 13, 1912, Toronto, Ontario
d. March 20, 1988, Cuernavaca, Mexico

SIGNATURE ALBUMS

Birth of the Cool (1957, Miles Davis), *Miles
Ahead* (1957, Miles Davis), *Porgy and Bess*
(1958, Miles Davis), *Sketches of Spain* (1960,
Miles Davis), *Out of the Cool* (1960)

MILESTONES

While working as an arranger for the Claude Thornhill
Orchestra in New York in the '40s, Gil Evans' modest
basement apartment behind a Chinese laundry on
West 55th Street became a hangout for musicians,
including Charlie Parker, Gerry Mulligan, John Lewis
and John Carisi, who were experimenting with new
stylistic approaches to jazz. He met and worked with
Miles Davis during this period, laying the foundation
for a Davis-led nonet, which, in September of 1948,
appeared at the Royal Roost during the intermission
of Count Basie Orchestra shows. Capitol Records
recorded the ensemble in 1949 and 1950 and later
reissued the results in 1957 as the
landmark Miles Davis album, *Birth of
the Cool*. Evans continued to be Davis'
arranger of choice during his Columbia
Records years in the '50s and the
collaboration produced the albums *Miles
Ahead* (1957), *Porgy and Bess* (1958) and
Sketches of Spain (1960), all of which
benefited from Evans' cutting edge and adventurous
arrangements as much as Davis' musicianship.

Evans began recording under his own name in the late
'50s. In 1961, Evans' 19-piece orchestra performed
with Miles Davis at Carnegie Hall, a concert recorded
for a live album. In 1970, Evans began performing
weekly at the Village Vanguard in New York, usually
with large ensembles. It was a schedule that ran for
more than a decade. In 1972, Evans was named a
founding artist of the John F. Kennedy Center for the
Performing Arts. It was a period in which Evans had
begun to spend more time on tour abroad and was
embracing some of the iconic rock repertoires at the
time in themed concerts — Jazz In the Rock Age, Gil
Evans Retrospective and The Music of Hendrix —
presented by the New York Jazz Repertory Company.
Evans had planned to record with Hendrix in 1970, the
year of the legendary guitarist's death.

INSIGHTS

"Evans's originality does not require original compositions for its demonstration. His arrangements of other people's compositions simply sparkle with his individualism; they overflow with invention... His tastes have been unencumbered by convention or bias, and his career has been almost untouched by self-promotion or self-aggrandizement. And he has managed, on his own terms and at his own pace, to produce a body of work that holds its own proud place in Jazz." — Jazz biographer Jack Chambers

"He knows what can be done, what the possibilities are." — Miles Davis

"Almost every aspect of Gil Evans' extraordinary career reversed the normal pattern. He was virtually unknown and unseen until, at the age of 45, he recorded his first full-blooded masterpiece (*Miles Ahead*) with Miles Davis. Although a competent pianist, he was not a virtuoso, and he only began playing professionally in 1952, when he was forty. He did not lead bands of his own until he was almost fifty; his most intense period of public performance began ten years later and showed no sign of diminishing in his seventies, until illness and death intervened." — Ian Carr, *Jazz: The Rough Guide*

"With hindsight, we can make the claim that this [the nonet that played the Royal Roost in New York] was the most important jazz band in the world in the late summer of 1948 ... If you were constructing a family tree for modern jazz in the second half of the 20th century, almost all of the milestone events could be traced back to this one ensemble. It may have been a commercial failure, but it changed the course of American music." — Jazz critic and music historian, Ted Gioia

»BOOKS: *Milestones: The Music and Times of Miles Davis* by Jack Chambers; *Gil Evans: Out of the Cool — His Life and Music* by Stephanie Stein Crease (2002)

»LENNY BREAU

Leonard Harold Breau

Guitarist, Music educator

Inducted 1997

b. August 5, 1941, Auburn, Maine

d. August 12, 1984, Los Angeles, California

SIGNATURE ALBUMS

Guitar Sounds From Lenny Breau (1968), *The Velvet Touch of Lenny Breau Live!* (1969), *The Livingroom Tapes – Volumes 1 & 2* (1978), *Live At Bourbon Street* (1983)

MILESTONES

By the age of 14, Lenny Breau was playing lead guitar in the country and western band of his parents, Harold "Hal Lone Pine" Breau and Betty Cody (nee Betty Coté), billed as "Lone Pine Junior — The Guitar Wizard" (1955). In 1957, the Breau family move to Winnipeg, Manitoba and begin touring as the CKY Caravan, named after the local radio station on which they were heard on Saturday mornings. In 1959, Breau left his parents band and discovered the local jazz scene and venues like Rando Manor and the Stage Door. He is mentored during this period by pianist Bob Erlendson. Breau moved to Toronto in 1962 and formed the jazz group Three with singer/actor Don Francks and bassist Eon Henstridge. The trio, which was featured in the National Film Board documentary *Toronto Jazz*, recorded a live album at the Village Vanguard in New York and appeared on a number of U.S. variety shows, including the Jackie Gleason and Joey Bishop shows. Returning to Winnipeg, Breau became a regular on CBC TV with his own *Lenny Breau Show* and appeared on Music Hop and Teenbeat. Guitar legend Chet Atkins was instrumental in getting Breau signed to a contract with RCA Records (1968). Breau briefly joined Anne Murray's backing band, Richard, for a tour that kicked off in Winnipeg on June 1, 1972. Guitarist Randy Bachman (The Guess Who, Bachman-Turner Overdrive) founded the record label Guitarchives Music Inc. in the '90s, initially to release "hundreds of hours of Lenny's playing from a multitude of sources."

INSIGHTS

"I grew up with Lenny as a funny kind of friend. He never really got close to anyone. I used to go and see him play with his mom and dad at the time. They had an act known as the Hal Lone Pine Caravan with Betty Cody. Lenny was known as Hal Lone Pine, Jr. He used to live across the street from my girlfriend, so some days I'd play hooky from school and, after having lunch with her, I'd go over and visit with Lenny. He wouldn't give me lessons, but he'd let me sit there in the room and watch him figuring out all these Chet Atkins records he had. Wherever he'd put his hand on the guitar neck, I'd memorize it and then later I'd run all the way home, which was about two miles away, get my little guitar, and try to copy what he'd done. I remember I bought the same orange Gretsch guitar that he had and learned his finger style." — Randy Bachman

"Best known for his stunning, crystalline octave harmonic arpeggios, Lenny Breau possessed one of the most comprehensive musical vocabularies in the history of the instrument. Although he will no doubt be most remembered for his talents as a solo artist, he was an expert ensemble player who felt equally comfortable with bebop, fusion, rock, and funk. In a solo improvisational context, he could transform a familiar jazz standard into an extended tonal painting, complete with changes in meter and mood, rich harmonies, and introspective sections offset by formidable technical displays. A student of jazz, classical, and country styles, as well as more exotic forms such as flamenco and East Indian music, he had a vast array of sounds and textures at his disposal. One of the cornerstones of the Breau style was his uncanny ability to play chords with his right-hand thumb and first two fingers, while superimposing single-note lines with the third finger and pinky. Early explorations of Chet Atkins' right-hand approach led him to master the coordination of two distinct parts and develop the skill to emphasize a voice at will. He occasionally added a bass line to this concept, resulting in a mind-boggling three-voice tapestry that made an indelible impression on all who heard it." — Jim Ferguson, *Guitar Player Magazine*

"Breau's ability to accompany himself gives his playing a sense of interior dialogue that makes other jazz guitarists sound incomplete by comparison." — *Washington Post*

"I think if Chopin had played guitar, he would have sounded like Lenny Breau." — Chet Atkins.

»BIOPICS: *The Genius of Lenny Breau* (1999).

»BOOKS: *One Long Tune: The Life and Music of Lenny Breau* by Ron Forbes-Roberts (2006)

»ROB MCCONNELL

Robert Murray Gordon McConnell
Valve trombonist, Band leader, Composer, Arranger, Music educator
Inducted 1997
b. February 14, 1935, London, Ontario.
d. May 1, 2010, Toronto, Ontario.

SIGNATURE ALBUMS

The Jazz Album (1976), *Big Band Jazz* (1977), *Present Perfect* (1979), *All In Good Time* (1982), *Boss Brass & Woods* (1985), *The Brass Is Back* (1991), *Brassy and Sassy* (1992), *Our 25th Year* (1993), *Overtime* (1994), *Three For the Road* (1997, with Ed Bickert, Don Thompson), *The Rob McConnell Tentet* (2000)

MILESTONES

The story goes that Rob McConnell began playing valve trombone at Northern Secondary School in Toronto because all the trumpets were taken. A six-time JUNO Award winner, McConnell ultimately gained international notoriety as valve trombonist, bandleader, arranger and composer with the 16-piece progressive big band he formed in Toronto in 1968, The Boss Brass. (He expanded the group to 22-pieces in the '70s as he added a saxophone section and brought in a fifth trumpet.) He travelled to Edmonton, Alberta in 1954 and joined saxophonist Don Thompson's band, a stint he has said was the beginning of his music career. Early on, McConnell even played piano for a time, before returning to the valve-trombone and becoming one of the most in-demand session players, arrangers and composers on the Toronto music scene. In the mid-'60s, McConnell worked and recorded briefly with fellow Canadian Music Hall of Fame inductee Maynard Ferguson in New York before returning to Toronto to join Phil Nimmons' group, Nimmons 'N' Nine Plus Six in the late '60s. In 1987, McConnell and the band cut the first of two albums with famed jazz vocalist, Mel Torme. (The second, *Velvet & Brass*, was recorded in 1995.) McConnell spent a year teaching at the Dick Grove School of Music in California in 1988. A perennial Grammy nominee in the U.S., McConnell has been honored with that award three times with the latest coming in 1995 in the category of Best Instrumental Arrangement with Accompanying Vocal for "I Get A Kick Out of You." In 1997, he formed the Rob McConnell Tentet, which not only featured many of the stalwarts from The Boss Brass but also showcased the talents of some of the up-and-coming players on the local jazz scene.

INSIGHTS

"Rob McConnell, founder of the Boss Brass, was a big guy who thought big, especially when it came to bands. It didn't deter him that by the late sixties, the big band sound was heading into the realm of nostalgia or that there weren't a lot of places for big bands to play in Toronto, or that making music is a tough livelihood at the best of times. It was music he loved, and especially music made by the likes of George Gershwin, Duke Ellington, Cole Porter and Glenn Miller. So he went forward with the big band sound — way forward — and brought some of Canada's best musicians along with him. When he died... he had built an international reputation as a valve trombonist, as the leader of Canada's premier big band of the 1970s and '80s and as an arranger on par with the best in the business. The musicians who played in the Boss Brass were considered Canada's finest. And many stayed with McConnell for decades." — Susan Smith, *The Globe and Mail*

"[Rob McConnell was] a true renaissance man in the genre of jazz. A trombonist, band leader, composer/arranger, songwriter, and music educator, he wore many hats and all contributed to his great body of work and his unwavering devotion to the music he loved. His sense of storytelling and humour infused his dynamic career, which will be remembered and appreciated for generations to come." — Neil Portnow, President/CEO of the Recording Academy, organizers of the Grammys.

»MOE KOFFMAN

Morris Koffman
Jazz musician, Composer, Arranger, Flutist, Saxophonist,
Clarinetist, Booking agent
Inducted 1997
b. December 28, 1928, Toronto, Ontario
d. March 28, 2001, Orangeville, Ontario

SIGNATURE COMPOSITION

Swingin' Shepherd Blues (1958)

SIGNATURE ALBUMS

Hot and Cool Saxophone (1957), *Moe's Curried Soul with Doug Riley and Lenny Breau* (1969), *Moe Koffman Plays Bach* (1971),
Vivaldi's Four Seasons (1972), *Solar Explorations* (1974), *Live At George's* (1975), *Museum Pieces* (1977), *Oop Pop A Da featuring Dizzy Gillespie* (1989)

MILESTONES

Moe Koffman initially studied the violin before switching to the alto saxophone in his early teens. As his style developed, he gravitated towards the bebop movement in jazz popularized in the '40s by players like Coleman Hawkins, Dizzy Gillespie, Charlie Parker and Thelonious Monk. Through the early '50s, Moe Koffman worked in the U.S. with bands led by Sonny Durham, Buddy Morrow, Jimmy Dorsey, Ralph Flanagan and Tex Beneke before returning to Toronto, where he formed the Moe Koffman Quartet. He subsequently recorded the international hit, "Swingin' Shepherd Blues" (1958), a Koffman composition previously known as "Blues a la Canadiana." The song, and the notoriety it brought, helped to popularize the flute as a jazz instrument. Beginning in 1956, Koffman spent almost 40 years as music director/booking agent for the renowned Toronto jazz venue, George's Spaghetti House, where he regularly appeared with his band. (He moved to The Senator after George's.) Like fellow Hall of Famer Maynard Ferguson, Koffman was open to influences from the rock and pop worlds, which had the effect of broadening his fan base. In the '70s, in collaboration with producer/arranger Doug Riley, Koffman recorded a series of albums featuring contemporary arrangement of music by Bach, Berlioz, Debussy, Gluck, Greig, Mozart and Vivaldi, a number of which were best sellers in Canada. Through the '80s and into the early '90s, the Koffman quintet played several concerts a year with legendary jazz trumpeter Dizzy Gillespie and acclaimed vibraphonist, Peter Appleyard while making their own forays into the U.S., Australia, South America, and Germany. Koffman's last public performance was in June 2000 at Toronto's Downtown Jazz Festival. The character of jazzman Bernie, played by Michael Ironside in the 2009 film *The Jazzman*, is based on Moe Koffman according to director Josh Koffman, Moe's grandson.

INSIGHTS

"Moe Koffman's contribution to jazz in this country and the world is unique and lasting. He had a playing career that spanned over 60 years before his death in 2001, releasing over 30 albums in that time. As a player and a business man, he was instrumental in shaping the sound of the jazz scene in Canada. He was determined, motivated, and above all, blessed with a true feeling of humility and kindness." — Ross Porter, President/CEO Jazz.FM91

"As a flutist he married a pure, 'classical' tone to the breezy rhythmic and melodic freedom of jazz; as an alto saxophonist he remained faithful to the bebop tradition and demonstrated with the Boss Brass and Dizzy Gillespie his standing among Canada's most vivid stylists in that idiom." — Betty Nygaard King, *The Encyclopedia of Music in Canada*

»DAVID FOSTER

David Walter Foster

Musician, Producer, Composer, Songwriter, Singer, Arranger,
Record executive

Inducted 1998

b. November 1, 1949, Victoria, British Columbia

SIGNATURE COMPOSITIONS

The Best of Me (1986), Love Theme From St. Elmo's Fire (1985), Winter Games (1988)

SIGNATURE ALBUMS

The Best of Me (1983), *David Foster* (1986) *The Symphony Sessions* (1988), *The Christmas Album* (1993), *Hit Man: David Foster and Friends* (2008), *Hit Man Returns: David Foster and Friends*

NOTABLE PRODUCTIONS

"After the Love Has Gone" (1979, Earth, Wind and Fire), *Dreamgirls* (1982, Various Artists), "Hard To Say I'm Sorry" (1982, Chicago), *Can't Slow Down* (1983, Lionel Richie), *Chicago 17 (*1984, Chicago), "Glory of Love" (1986, Peter Cetera), *The Best Years of Our Lives (*1988, Neil Diamond), *Unison* (1990, Celine Dion), "Unforgettable" (1991, Natalie Cole), *The Bodyguard* (1992, Various Artists), *The Colour of My Love* (1993, Celine Dion), *Falling Into You* (1996, Celine Dion), *Josh Groban* (2001, Josh Groban), *Call Me Irresponsible* (2007, Michael Bublé), *My Christmas* (2009, Andrea Bocelli), *Passione* (2013, Andrea Bocelli).

MILESTONES

David Foster began playing piano as early as age four, putting that talent to practical use in his teens as he dropped out of high school and headed for the U.K. in a band that would back Chuck Berry on a British tour. In 1973, as keyboard player for the Vancouver group Skylark, he had his first brush with pop music success as the group's song "Wildflower" went to number nine on the Billboard chart in 1973. That success took Foster to Los Angeles where he would become an in-demand session musician, songwriter and producer. In 1979, he won the first of his 16 Grammy Awards for Best R&B Song ("After the Love Has Gone," Earth, Wind & Fire). Along the way, he has also picked up an Emmy Award, a Golden Globe, and three Oscar nominations for Best Original Song. In 1985, he created the David Foster Foundation to provide financial support to families in British Columbia with children in need of life-saving organ transplants. In June 2010, Foster was inducted into the Songwriter's Hall of Fame. He was named Chairman of Universal's Verve Music Group in 2012.

INSIGHTS

"More than his work with established artists, Foster's greatest gift to the world is his ability to recognize and nurture new singing talent. He helped make international stars of a French-Canadian child prodigy who didn't start learning English until she was 18 (Celine Dion), an Irish family band complete with fiddles (The Corrs), a 17-year-old LA kid whom Foster first heard on a tape sent by a voice coach (Josh Groban) and a young man from a family of Canadian fishermen who was 'doing lots of forties stuff' (Michael Bublé). With a highly commercial artist roster like that, Foster will never be a favorite of music critics and hipsters. He produces popular music — really popular music for the masses. And as long as he keeps forging gold and platinum, he sees no reason to kowtow to music snobs. Romance is his forte, and he knows it will never lose its appeal. 'I can't be Bruce Springsteen,' writes Foster, 'much as I might fantasize about being a rocker. I can only be who I am, and who I am is a guy who writes music that people make babies to — and I'm not going to apologize for it.'" — Charles Alexander, Huffington Post, reviews the David Foster book, *Hit Man.*

"Superstars like Barbra Streisand, Celine Dion, Whitney Houston, Michael Jackson, Madonna, Andrea Bocelli, Michael Bublé, Josh Groban, Rod Stewart and Stevie Wonder have trusted him with their voices and to help them realize their musical dreams. Indeed, few other songwriters and producers have had their fingerprints on more major moments in all of popular music. Foster has created hit songs and award-winning gold and platinum albums for a diverse array of artists including Earth, Wind & Fire, Natalie Cole, Michael Bolton, Seal, Chaka Khan, Kenny Rogers, Dolly Parton, Chicago, Hall & Oates, Brandy, 'N Sync, Boz Scaggs and Gloria Estefan; propelled singers who have straddled both pop and classical styles like Andrea Bocelli and Josh Groban into the mainstream; created culture-defining soundtracks for blockbuster films like *The Bodyguard, Urban Cowboy* and *St. Elmo's Fire*; and crafted timeless holiday classics, including perennial best-sellers like *Josh Groban's Noel,* Michael Bublé's *Christmas,* Celine Dion's *These Are Special Times,* Rod Stewart's *Merry Christmas Baby* and Andrea Bocelli's *My Christmas.*" — Hollywood Chamber of Commerce on David Foster's accomplishments re: his star on the Hollywood Walk of Fame (May 31, 2013).

"Quincy Jones said to me, 'If something isn't exactly the way you think it should be, don't put your name on it.' His words of advice had a great impact on me, and since then I've always fought for my artistic vision. I don't always win, but I know when an artist hires me, it's my job to push them towards greatness, and to get something out of them they didn't know was there. My personal motto has become, 'compromise breeds mediocrity.'" — David Foster

On taking a pass on producing the soundtrack for the hit movie, *Flashdance*: "Welder by day, disco dancer by night? Are you fucking kidding me?" — David Foster, *Hit Man*

»BOOKS: *Hit Man: Forty Years Making Music, Topping the Charts, and Winning Grammys* by David Foster and Pablo F. Fenjves (2009).

≫LUC PLAMONDON

Luc Plamondon,
Lyricist, Producer
Inducted 1999
b. March 2, 1942, Saint-Raymond de Portneuf, Québec

SIGNATURE SONGS

J'ai rencontré l'homme de ma vie, Diane Dufresne (1972, music: François Cousineau), *Les hauts et les bas d'une hôtesse de l'air,* Diane Dufresne (1975, music: François Cousineau), *Blues du businessman,* Claude Dubois (1978, music: Michel Berger), *Le monde est stone,* Fabienne Thibeault (1978, music: Michel Berger), *J'ai douze ans maman,* Diane Dufresne (1979, music: Germaine Gauthier), *L'amour existe encore,* Celine Dion (1992, music: Richard Cocciante)

MILESTONES

Luc Plamondon, the first artist from Québec to be inducted into the Canadian Music Hall of Fame, had already begun writing theatrical plays and songs for his own amusement by the time he was 16. There followed a period of travel during which he spent a year in the U.S. and, along the way, experienced the musical Hair during a stay in San Francisco. It was inspirational. Returning to Montréal, Plamondon's first success came in 1970 with the song "Les chemins d'été" recorded by Steve Fiset. By 1972, Plamondon was working with a number of female singers in Québec including Emmanuelle, Monique Leyrac, Renée Claude and Diane Dufresne. His first major success in musical theatre came with *Starmania*, the rock opera, which he co-wrote with the late composer Michel Berger. It opened in Paris at the Palais des Congrès on April 10, 1979 with Tom O`Horgan, who had directed *Hair* and *Jesus Christ Superstar* on Broadway, at the helm. Plamondon and Berger also collaborated on the 1990 musical, *La Légende de Jimmy*, which ran for six months in Paris before moving to Montréal the following year. In 1982, he co-wrote his first song for Celine Dion ("Le piano fantôme") who a decade later would record a best-selling album of songs in tribute to Plamondon titled *Dion chante Plamondon*. He made a triumphant return to musical theatre with *Notre Dame de Paris*, a collaboration with composer Richard Cocciante, which had a successful run in Paris and in Québec. An English version was also produced in London. Plamondon, who was inducted into the Canadian Songwriters Hall of Fame in 2011, is the jury Chair for the Freddie Mercury Live Music Awards which are held in Montreux, Switzerland. Plamondon is also a co-founder with Diane Juster and Lise Aubut of the Société professionelle des auteurs et des compositeurs du Québec (SPACQ) an advocacy organization for francophone songwriters and composers.

INSIGHTS

"I didn't really think I could make a go of it [writing] so I let the fates decide for me. I went on studying and learned modern languages because I wanted to be a teacher in that subject or an international journalist. I travelled to Spain, German, Italy and England, spending time in each country and learning the language. Diane Dufresne and I had become good friends when I was 20 and we were both in Paris studying. I never told her then that I was secretly writing songs. She used to tell me that one day she would be singing at the Olympia in Paris. I thought she was crazy." — Luc Plamondon

"[Composer Michel Berger] wanted me to do a rock opera with him because he knew Diane Dufresne's albums. He said, 'You can write about violence; you can write about a lot of different things and you write like no other French lyricist writes.' I was flattered and really amazed when I got the phone call because to me a French composer who wanted to do a rock opera was strange. He had produced Veronique Sanson's first two albums that I liked very much so I came to Paris and met him. For some reason, we were sort of terrified by each other in the beginning. It was very different working with a French composer because there was a kind of censorship imposed that he didn't want me to impose on myself. He often told me not to censor myself because he wanted my style of writing. 'I don't want you to write like a French lyricist,' he would say, but then if I used a word he wouldn't use or a Québec expression or an Americanized French expression, he would say, 'Oh no, you can't write that!'" — Luc Plamondon on the writing of *Starmania*.

››BRUCE FAIRBAIRN

Bruce Earl Fairbairn

Producer, Trumpet player

Inducted 2000

b. December 30, 1949, Vancouver, British Columbia

d. May 17, 1999, Vancouver, British Columbia

NOTABLE PRODUCTIONS

Loverboy (1980, Loverboy), *Get Lucky* (1981, Loverboy), *Keep It Up* (1983, Loverboy), *Slippery When Wet* (1986, Bon Jovi), *Permanent Vacation* (1987, Aerosmith), *New Jersey* (1988, Bon Jovi), *Pump* (1989, Aerosmith), *The Razor's Edge* (1990, AC/DC), *Flesh & Blood* (1990, Poison), *AC/DC – Live* (1991, AC/DC), *Get A Grip* (1993, Aerosmith), *Balance* (1995, Van Halen), *To the Faithful Departed* (1996, The Cranberries)

MILESTONES

When Bruce Fairbairn began playing trumpet at the age of 5, he would have had no concept of how far the instrument would take him, beginning with his first band The Spectres, founded while he was attending Vancouver's Prince of Wales Secondary School. Remarkably, the group was managed by Bruce Allen (Bryan Adams, Loverboy, Michael Bublé), and their relationship lasted through the years. By the early '70s, Fairbairn was playing trumpet and horns and handling production chores for the group Sunshyne, which for a time also featured prolific songwriter Jim Vallance, who would soon begin a successful writing collaboration with Bryan Adams. Sunshyne became Prism in the mid-'70s, and Fairbairn was in the producer's chair for the band's first four best-selling albums.

Fairbairn began an internationally successful relationship with Vancouver group Loverboy in the late-'70s as he began working out of the now-closed Little Mountain Sound in Vancouver with acts that included AC/DC, Aerosmith, Motley Cru, Poison, and Bon Jovi's *Slippery When Wet* album, which sold more than 12 million copies. This was the most commercially-successful production of the band and Fairbairn's career. His protégés during this period included several talented local engineer/producers: fellow Canadian Music Hall of Famer Bob Rock, Randy Staub and Mike Plotnikoff, who received a major career boost from the association, as Vancouver became the go-to city for big-budget rock recording. In 1995, Fairbairn bought Vancouver's Armoury Studios from his old band-mate Jim Vallance, and from this base of operations he continued to work with a number of high-profile artists, including The Cranberries, Van Halen and INXS, who recorded their last album with Fairbairn, who had been working with the British band Yes at the time of his passing in the spring of 1999. Over the years, Fairbairn earned three JUNO Awards for his production work beginning with the Prism album *Young and Restless* back in 1980.

INSIGHTS

"Bruce was very much about music being the soul of what he did in the studio. He didn't want [sessions] buggered up by business or by technology. He didn't believe in Pro-Tools. He still chopped tape with a razor blade. I used to want to cut harder [production] deals, but he wouldn't let me. He'd say, 'No. The band needs this or that. I don't care about the advance. We'll make it on the upside [producer's royalty].'" — Manager Bruce Allen to *Billboard*'s Larry LeBlanc.

"Record producers can create their own sound a la Phil Spector or do their utmost to enable artists to shine like George Martin with the Beatles. The Canadian producer Bruce Fairbairn, often called the 'king' of heavy metal producers or 'the schoolteacher' for his focused, methodical approach, belonged to the enabling school." — Pierre Perrone, *The Independent*.

"His accomplishments aside, Fairbairn was a man who always put his wife, Julie, and three sons, Scott, Kevin and Brent, first. In an industry where this is not always the case, he was known as a true family man and excellent role model who always instilled people with his 'go for it' attitude. His natural leadership and organization, combined with an uncanny musical ear, gave him the ability to bring the best out of people." — Tim Moshansky, *MIX magazine*.

»BRUCE COCKBURN

Bruce Douglas Cockburn
Singer, Songwriter, Social activist
Inducted 2001
b. May 27, 1945, Ottawa, Ontario

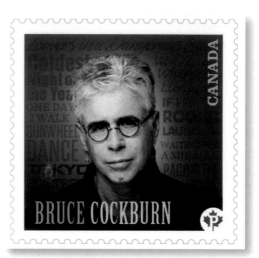

SIGNATURE SONGS

Going To the Country (1970), *Musical Friends* (1970), *Prenons le mer* (1978), *Wondering Where the Lions Are* (1979), *Tokyo* (1980), *The Coldest Night of the Year* (1981), *Fascist Architecture (I'm Okay)* (1981), *The Trouble With Normal* (1983), *Lovers In A Dangerous Time* (1984), *If I Had A Rocket Launcher* (1984), *People See Through You* (1984), *Call It Democracy* (1985), *Waiting For A Miracle* (1987), *If A Tree Falls* (1989), *A Dream Like Mine* (1991), *Listen For the Laugh* (1994), *Night Train* (1997), *Last Night of the World* (1999), *Tried and Tested* (2003), *The Iris of the World* (2011

MILESTONES

At the age of 18, and with music already firmly established as his calling in life, Bruce Cockburn dropped out of grade 13 at Nepean High School and headed for Europe to hang out in the continental style as a street musician. He returned to Ottawa, stayed long enough to pack his bags and headed for Boston to enrol at the Berklee School of Music, where he spent his extracurricular time in a jug band known as Walker Thompson and His Boys. By 1966, Cockburn was back in Ottawa playing organ with local group The Children, the first in a succession of bands he would be associated with through the late '60s in his hometown and Toronto, including Heavenly Blue, The Esquires, The Flying Circus (later Olivus) and 3's A Crowd. By late 1969, Cockburn had embarked on a solo career, beginning lengthy associations with producer Eugene Martynec, a former member of Toronto band Kensington Market, who has worked on 13 of Cockburn's 14 albums to 1983, and manager/True North Records executive Bernie Finkelstein, who is still Cockburn's business and creative confidant. In 1980, Cockburn had his biggest hit single in the U.S. with "Wondering Where the Lions Are" at a time when he had begun to schedule more benefits and goodwill appearances on behalf of organizations that work for causes close to his heart. A trip to Nicaragua and Mexico in 1983 to visit refugee camps on a two-week Oxfam-sponsored fact-finding tour angered him so much that his emotional response was the surprisingly militant song "If I Had Rocket Launcher." He has remained an eloquent and persistent voice in support of human rights and respect for the environment in lyric and deed. His 1987 album Waiting For A Miracle was the first double CD to be issued by a Canadian artist. On June 30, 2011, Canada Post issued a Bruce Cockburn stamp as part of its Canadian Recording Artists series.

INSIGHTS

"I'm not sure I can accurately address what makes my music unique, but certainly, spirituality plays a big part in what I do. My relationship to the divine is the most important thing in my life and I think that's true for everybody, although everybody has their own way of approaching it. But I do pay attention to it and I find it showing up in songs all the time in different ways. Not that all the songs are about that issue, but I can't talk about anything without including that kind of notion in there, some sense of the sort of spiritual order of things." — Bruce Cockburn

"My job is to try and trap the spirit of things in the scratches of pen on paper, in the pulling of notes out of metal. These become songs and the songs become fuel. They can become fuel for romance, for protest, for spiritual discovery, or for complacency. That's where you all come in. You decide how a song will be heard and felt. I'm filled with gratitude that so many of you have let my songs touch you. To all of you who have done me the honor of listening to what I have to say, thank you. I love my job; I can't wait to see what I'm gonna do next. I love you." — Bruce Cockburn during his induction to the Canadian Music Hall of Fame by David Suzuki and Gordon Lightfoot.

»BIOPICS: *Rumours of Glory — Bruce Cockburn Live* (1983); *My Beat: The Life and Times of Bruce Cockburn* (2001); *Bruce Cockburn: Pacing the Cage* (2013)

≫DANIEL LANOIS

Producer, Musician
Inducted 2002
b. September 19, 1951, Hull, Québec

SIGNATURE ALBUMS

Acadie (1989), *For the Beauty of Wynona* (1993), *Cool Water* (1994), *Sweet Angel Mine* (1996), *Lost in Mississippi Soundtrack* (1996), *Sling Blade Soundtrack* (1996), *Shine* (2003), *Rockets* (2004), *Belladonna* (2005), *Here Is What Is* (2007), *The Omni Series* (2008, Steel, Purple Vista and Santiago), *Black Dub* (2010)

NOTABLE PRODUCTIONS

More Singable Songs (1977, Raffi), *This Is the Ice Age* (1981, Martha and the Muffins), *Danseparc* (1982, Martha and the Muffins), *Ambient 4/On Land* (1982, Brian Eno), *Parachute Club* (1983, Parachute Club), *Apollo: Atmosphere and Soundtracks* (1983, Brian Eno), *The Pearl* (1984, Harold Budd and Brian Eno), *Mystery Walk* (1984, M+M), *The Unforgettable Fire* (1984, U2), *Thursday Afternoon* (1985, Brian Eno), *Birdy* (1985, Peter Gabriel), *So* (1986, Peter Gabriel), *The Joshua Tree* (1987, U2), *Robbie Robertson* (1987, Robbie Robertson), *Oh Mercy* (1989, Bob Dylan), *Yellow Moon* (1989, Neville Brothers), *Home* (1990, Hothouse Flowers), *Achtung Baby* (1991, U2), Us (1992, Peter Gabriel), *Ron Sexsmith* (1994, Ron Sexsmith), *Wrecking Ball* (1995, Emmylou Harris), *Time Out of Mind* (1997, Bob Dylan), *Teatro* (1998, Willie Nelson), *All That You Can't Leave Behind* (2000, U2), *No Line On the Horizon* (2009, U2), *Le Noise* (2010, Neil Young), *Battle Born* (2012, The Killers)

MILESTONES

Multiple Grammy Award-winner Daniel Lanois' early music influences were formed as part of his French Canadian upbringing and, in that tradition, his father's violin playing, though it was the recorder and later the pedal steel guitar that became his initial instruments of choice. His parents divorced when he was 11 and he moved with his mother, his older brother Robert and sister Jocelyne to Ancaster, Ontario. Through high school, Lanois played guitar in a number of bands, including local stalwarts, Tranquility Base, and even toured one summer backing a "strip-tease" show. By the time he was 17, Lanois and brother Robert had opened a studio in the basement laundry room of their mother's home — she was a singer herself which may explain her tolerance — and had begun to record local artists. A decade later, in the early '80s, they emerged from the basement and opened the Grant Avenue Studios in nearby Hamilton, Ontario. It was here that Lanois honed his production skills working with artists like the Parachute Club, Ian Tyson, Raffi, Simply Saucer and Martha and the Muffins (aka M+M), in which his sister Jocelyne played bass. His association with Brian Eno also began here and resulted in the pair co-producing a number of ground-breaking albums with Irish band U2, including *The Joshua Tree*, *The Unforgettable Fire* and the Grammy Award-winning *Achtung Baby*. During the course of the next two decades, Lanois also produced a number of career-significant albums for artists with the stature of Peter Gabriel, Bob Dylan, Neil Young, Emmylou Harris, Willie Nelson, Robbie Robertson, The Neville Brothers and his frequent collaborator, Brian Eno. *Rolling Stone* magazine called Lanois "the most important record producer to emerge in the '80s." Lanois is also an acclaimed recording artist in his own right having

debuted with the album *Acadie* in 1989, the first of more than a dozen albums including his recent project *Black Dub*.

INSIGHTS

"I just chose to go with the new frontier. I wanted to be an innovator. I was hanging out with Brian Eno, and it was all about pushing the boundaries. Interfacing — in school you're taught that this goes here, then you plug into that, then over here, and that's the way it is. And you challenge conventional interface and that's when you start stumbling onto the cool sounds. It's like, 'OK, we'll take this thing that's normally the last thing in the chain and put it in front,' and so on. So by monkeying around with the rules, myself and Brian Eno were able to hit on some pretty cool stuff." — Daniel Lanois speaking with Olivia Mather, Jonathan Greenberg, Echo, UCLA.

»BIOPICS: *Rocky World* (1993), *Here Is What Is* (2007)

»BOOKS: *Soul Mining: A Musical Life* (2010)

≫TOM COCHRANE

Thomas William Cochrane

Singer-Songwriter, Guitarist, Producer, Social activist

Inducted 2003

b. May 14, 1953, Lynn Lake, Manitoba

SIGNATURE SONGS

You're Driving Me Crazy (1973, Cochrane), *White Hot* (1980, Tom Cochrane & Red Rider), *Lunatic Fringe* (1981, Tom Cochrane & Red Rider), *Human Race* (1983, Tom Cochrane & Red Rider), *Young Thing, Wild Dreams* (Rock Me)" (1984, Tom Cochrane & Red Rider), *Boy Inside the Man* (1986, Tom Cochrane & Red Rider), *Big League*" (1988, Tom Cochrane & Red Rider), *Good Times* (1989, Tom Cochrane & Red Rider), *Victory Day* (1989, Tom Cochrane & Red Rider), *Life Is A Highway* (1991), *No Regrets* (1991), *Sinking Like A Sunset* (1992), *I Wish You Well* (1995), *Wildest Dreams* (1995), *Dreamer's Dream* (1996)

MILESTONES

Tom Cochrane has been a songwriter from the time he could pick up a pen. By the early '70s, Cochrane was already creating a buzz as a folksinger on the coffee house circuit. During the early years of his solo career (1973), he worked with the group Harvest that included bassist Rick Nickerson and drummer Deane Cameron, who in 1988, at the age of 35, became president of Capitol Records-EMI of Canada Ltd. Cochrane released his first album during that decade and spent time in Los Angeles writing film music.

It wasn't until the late '70s, when Cochrane joined the group Red Rider, that his reputation as a songwriter of note took on international dimensions. Cochrane, whose writing in those days showcased many of his literary influences like poet/adventurer Jean Arthur Rimbaud and Chilean poet Pablo Neruda, set the tone for Red Rider from the start. "White Hot," a single for the group in 1980 and 1989, referenced Rimbaud's gun-running days in Africa and the group's mid-'80s album *Neruda* was a tribute to the South American literary figure. Most of Red Rider's early material was atmospheric in the tradition of band's like Pink Floyd and in the early '80s, the track "Lunatic Fringe" was one of the favorite rock tracks in America, second only to Pink Floyd's "Money." The song was heard no less than eight times on the hit TV series *Miami Vice*.

In the early '90s, having departed Red Rider and embarked on a solo career, Cochrane made a number of fact-finding trips to Africa for the famine relief organization World Vision. His experiences during that period would inspire the album *Mad Mad World* and what has become his signature tune, "Life Is A Highway." A subsequent album, *Ragged Ass Road*, produced the hit single "I Wish You Well," which was reportedly the first song in Canadian radio history to enter the both the sales and airplay charts at number one simultaneously. In November 2007, the seven-time JUNO winner was formally invested as an Honorary Colonel by the Royal Canadian Air Force's 409 "Nighthawks" Tactical Fighter Squadron. Cochrane was the 2013 recipient of the Allan Waters Humanitarian Award for his work with World Vision and other NGOs.

INSIGHTS

"Some of my better songs have two different layers to them and 'Life Is A Highway' is an example of one. It was spawned out of a trip to Africa actually and Mozambique was one of the countries. That country impacted me a lot. It was the first time I saw somebody die in front of me and we got shot at and it was a pretty exhausting ordeal. But I wouldn't trade it for anything because I matured a lot through that trip. I was mentally and physically exhausted when I got home and this song came out as a pep talk to myself. I used to think songs could make these big broad changes to the world. You can't, but what you can do is change individuals, one by one, through your songs or through whatever you do in life. When you meet people, the goodwill you pass on is contagious, it gets passed on and that's how you change the world. And when somebody comes to me and says even as something as simple as, 'Life is a Highway' was the summer of '92 for me. That was the summer of my life. And that song was the number one song for the soundtrack of that summer.' That is such a great feeling, that someone says a song pulled them through a tough time or got them through a tough relationship. That's what fuels the batteries. That's what makes you feel like you're doing something as an artist." — Tom Cochrane.

"Music is a trust between the artist and the audience. It's something that validates the idea that there is a human spirit, a force that can really change the world. It's not to be violated by posturing or pandering or commerciality." — Tom Cochrane.

»BOB EZRIN

Robert Alan Ezrin,
Producer, Musician, Songwriter, Composer, Music educator,
Inducted 2004
Social activist
b. March 25, 1949, Toronto, Ontario

NOTABLE PRODUCTIONS

Love It To Death (1971, Alice Cooper), *Killer* (1971, Alice Cooper), *School's Out* (1972, Alice Cooper), *Billion Dollar Babies* (1973, Alice Cooper), *Berlin* (1973, Lou Reed), *Flo and Eddie* (1973, Flo and Eddie), *Get Your Wings* (1974, Aerosmith), *Welcome To My Nightmare* (1975, Alice Cooper), *Destroyer* (1976, KISS), *The Babys* (1977, The Babys), *Peter Gabriel* (1977, Peter Gabriel), *The Wall* (1979, Pink Floyd, co-producer with David Gilmour and Roger Waters), *The Kings Are Here* (1980, The Kings), *Storm Warning* (1981, Murray McLauchlan), *Dure Limite* (1982, Téléphone), *About Face* (1984, David Gimour, co-produced by David Gilmour), *Rod Stewart* (1986, Rod Stewart), *A Momentary Lapse of Reason* (1987, Pink Floyd, co-producer with David Gilmour), *Revenge* (1992, KISS), *The Division Bell* (1994, Pink Floyd, co-producer with David Gilmour), *Strays* (2003, Jane's Addiction, co-producer with Brian Virtue), "Wavin' Flag" (2010, Young Artists For Haiti), *Some Lessons Learned* (2011, Kristin Chenoweth), In2uition (2013, 2Cellos), *Christmas* (2013, Johnny Reed)

MILESTONES

Hearing potential where others seemed baffled, Bob Ezrin's production career had a promising start in the early '70s when his creative collaboration with Alice Cooper resulted in the hit single "Eighteen" from the group's sophomore album, *Love It To Death* (1971). From 1972-1975, Ezrin was in the producer's chair for three of the band's Top Five albums including *School's Out*, the chart-topping *Billion Dollar Babies* and *Welcome To My Nightmare*. Given Ezrin's hands-on style, he was a co-writer, arranger and musician on the sessions as well. In 1976, Ezrin worked with KISS on their classic album, *Destroyer*, on his way to becoming one of the most successful producers of the rock era in working with artists like Pink Floyd, Peter Gabriel, Rod Stewart, Lou Reed, Nine Inch Nails, Jane's Addiction, Dr. John, Nils Lofgren, The Darkness, The Jayhawks, Kristin Chenoweth, Julian Lennon, The Deftones, Kansas, 2Cellos, K'naan, Hanoi Rocks, Taylor Swift and 30 Seconds To Mars, among others.

In November 2005, Ezrin was co-founder, with The Edge of U2 and Henry Juszkiewicz of Gibson Musical Instruments, of Music Rising, an initiative to rescue the music culture of the Central Gulf Region of the United States, which had been devastated by the hurricanes of the summer of 2005, by replacing the musical instruments lost or destroyed in the deluge. Five years later, on February 18, 2010, Ezrin was producer of a rendition of Canadian hip hop star K'naan's "Wavin'

Flag" recorded by 50 Canadian artists, which raised US$2 million for the victims of the Haiti earthquake. It was honored with a JUNO as Single of the Year in 2011. Ezrin is also active with Mr. Holland's Opus Foundation and Canada's MusiCounts — dedicated to promoting music in schools by donating musical instruments. In 2009, with partners Garth Richardson and Kevin Williams, Ezrin co-founded the Nimbus School of Recording Arts in Vancouver with the stated goal of providing new engineers and producers with the hands-on teaching experience which he believed was no longer available from tradition recording studios.

INSIGHTS

"I've been into music my whole life. I started studying music when I was five and I took classical piano, jazz piano, and composition lessons. I really taught myself how to orchestrate. I bought a couple of books and called a couple of friends when I had questions. I also learned a lot just by doing it. Some of the world's most expensive demo sessions happened by simply deciding that on an Alice Cooper album we were going to have a string section and a couple of horns! I didn't tell anybody at the time that I really didn't know how to write for them, but that I was going to learn by the day of the session." — MadeLoud.com

"There aren't very many 'real artists.' There are a lot of singers, songwriters, great performers, and terrific emcees and great DJs, but, artists? Not necessarily. When you run into an artist, they are always motivated by the right thing. A true artist has an absolute burning compulsion to express something. They can't help themselves; it's beyond their control. And sometimes it is to their great personal peril that they pursue this, but they have no choice. They're born with it. And those people are motivated always by the right things. Everybody else — the rest of us mere mortals who are doing it because we love music — I think our motivations have been polluted somewhat by modern marketing and modern media. We're much more interested in the fame before we actually ever spend any time on the craft or on the "art" itself, and that's kind of sad. I wish that it was like a driver's license: that you had to pass a certain level of proficiency before you got a license to get out into the real world and create. But there is no such thing; it's now completely democratic. So the good news is that anybody can do it. The bad news is that anybody can do it." — Bob Ezrin to Scot Buchanan, 2011 Long & McQuade Gear Guide

»THE TRAGICALLY HIP

Rock Group

Inducted 2005

b. Gordon Edgar Downie: February 6, 1964, Amherstview, Ontario (Singer, Songwriter, Actor)

b. Paul Langlois: August 24, 1964 (Guitar, Backing vocals)

b. Rob Baker, 1975, Kingston, Ontario (Guitar)

b. Gord Sinclair: May 27, 1969, (Bass, Backing vocals)

b. Johnny Fay, April 30, 1966, Kingston, Ontario (Drums, Percussion)

SIGNATURE SONGS

Blow At High Dough (1989), *New Orleans Is Sinking* (1989), *Fifty Mission Cap* (1992), *Courage* (1993), *At the Hundredth Meridien* (1993), *Grace Too* (1994), *Ahead By A Century* (1996), *Poets* (1998), *Fireworks* (1998), *Bobcaygeon* (1999), *Vaccination Scar* (2004), *In View* (2006), *Love Is A First* (2009), *At Transformation* (2012).

MILESTONES

The Tragically Hip, a name inspired by the use of the phrase in the Michael Nesmith film *Elephant Parts*, formed in the early '80s at Queen's University in Kingston, Ontario, and by the mid-'80s they had developed a musical sound and energy perfectly matched to Gord Downie's impressionistic lyrics. Jake Gold and Allan Gregg signed to manage the band, and an 1987 appearance at The Horseshoe Tavern in Toronto earned The Hip their first record deal with Bruce Dickinson at MCA.

An eponymous debut EP was released followed by the group's first full-length album *Up To Here* in 1989, which featured two signature Hip songs, "Blow At High Dough" and "New Orleans Is Sinking." By the time of the release of their *Road Apples* album in 1991, the Hip had not only established themselves as fan favourites in Canada — they won the publicly voted Canadian Entertainer of the Year JUNO Award in 1991, 1993 and 1995. They had also developed a significant enough following in Australia to tour there during this period. On July 16, 1993, The Tragically Hip kicked off the first of their cross-Canada Another Roadside Attraction tours in Victoria, BC, with special guests Midnight Oil, Hothouse Flowers, Daniel Lanois and Crash Vegas. Another Roadside Attraction tours were also undertaken in 1995 and 1997. On its release on September 24, 1994, The Tragically Hip album *Day For Night* became the band's first album to debut at number one in Canada. More than 600,000 copies sold in Canada. On March 25, 1995, the group were guests on *Saturday Night Live*, hosted by John Goodman with special guest and fellow Kingston, Ontario-native, Dan Aykroyd.

On February 1999, The Tragically Hip played the first concert at the newly-opened Air Canada Centre in Toronto, and on October 10, 2002, Oscar Peterson and The Tragically Hip were among the artists who performed during a gala concert at Toronto's Roy Thomson Hall for Queen Elizabeth II, who was touring Canada as part of her Golden Jubilee. In 2012, the city of Kingston announced that a one-block segment of Barrack Street would be named Tragically Hip Way. On July 19, 2013 a commemorative stamp featuring the band was issued by Canada Post.

INSIGHTS

"The songs. It's the things we've made together that keep us together and, maybe more than that, it's the vague promise of what we might still make together. Everyone is listening for the same thing, from an old songwriter or from a new one: potential. A great song's greatest attribute is how it hints at more. The Hip has always had a strong curiosity to see what's around the next corner. To see what more we can do, what more

we can say — to each other, primarily. We try and serve the song. If we're any good at all it's because we're together on that."— Gord Downie to Joseph Boyden in *Maclean's*

"Gord Downie....possibly one of the best song writers in the world; a poet of the people. I just like the way he writes. He can write a song that you just can't see through ..." — Mike Michi, Ottawa street busker

»BOOKS: *Coke Machine Glow. Poems* by Gord Downie.

»BRYAN ADAMS

Bryan Guy Adams

Singer, Songwriter, Musician, Photographer

Inducted 2006

b. November 5, 1959, Kingston, Ontario

SIGNATURE SONGS

Straight From the Heart (1983), *Cuts Like A Knife* (1983), *Run To You* (1984), *Heaven* (1984) *Somebody* (1985), *Summer of '69* (1985), *It's Only Love* (1985, with Tina Turner), *Heat of the Night* (1987), *(Everything I Do) I Do It For You* (1991), *Do I Have To Say the Words?*(1992), *Please Forgive Me* (1993), *All For Love* (1993, with Rod Stewart and Sting), *Have You Ever Really Loved A Woman?* (1995), *The Only Thing That Looks Good On Me Is You* (1996), *Let's Make A Night To Remember* (1996), *I Finally Found Someone* (1996, with Barbra Streisand), *Back To You* (1997), *I'm Ready* (1998), *On A Day Like Today* (1998), *When You're Gone* (1998, with Melanie C), *Cloud Number Nine* (1999), *The Best of Me* (1999), *Here I Am* (2002), *Open Road* (2004)

MILESTONES

Bryan Adams, the gravel-voiced rocker, clad in the now trademark blue jeans and white T-shirt, used his songs (most co-written with Jim Vallance) to impress rather than elaborate stage gimmicks. Linking up with Vancouver-based manager, Bruce Allen, who was quoted early and often that Adams was his retirement policy, Adams emerged internationally as one of the top rock performers and songwriters of the last two decades of the 20th century. Having moved to Vancouver with his mother following his parents' divorce, he formed his first band while attending Sutherland Junior High School in North Vancouver. Adams joined JUNO-winning group Sweeney Todd in 1976 as vocalist. In January 1978, Adams was introduced to musician/songwriter Jim Vallance, who had played drums in the group Prism under the pseudonym Rodney Higgs and was now writing songs for the group. As they began writing songs together, they discovered the creative chemistry that was destined to make them one of the hottest songwriting partnerships in rock music history. One of the songs, "Let Me Take You Dancing" (1979) caught the ear of A&M Records Canada executive Michael Godin and he had Adams recorded it as a disco song. By the release of his second album for A&M titled *You Want It, You Got It* (1981), Adams was keeping the gruelling touring schedule punctuated by periods of songwriting that would mark most of his career. The the release of his fourth album, *Reckless* (1984), firmly established Adams as a star of international magnitude, topping the charts in North America, producing the number one single "Heaven" and eventually becoming the first album by a Canadian artist to sell over one million copies in Canada.

1985 was a heady year for Adams. He was in Toronto on February 10 to be part of the recording session and video shoot for the song "Tears Are Not Enough," which he co-wrote with Jim Vallance, David Foster and Rachel Paiement with the royalties going to benefit famine victims in Ethiopia. Adams was one of the acts involved in the Live Aid concert at JFK Stadium in Philadelphia (July 13, 1985). Through the final half of the '80s decade, Adams became a regular presence on the big stadium shows, many of them benefits, including two Wembley Stadium shows with

Tina Turner (March 1985), the Prince's Trust Charity Concert (Summer 1985), The Amnesty International Conspiracy of Hope concerts with Sting, U2, Peter Gabriel, Lou Reed and Joan Baez, among others, four SRO nights at London's Wembley Arena where, that summer (June 5, 1987), he had joined Ringo Starr and George Harrison on stage for the finale of the second annual Prince's Trust rock gala and the June 11, 1988 Nelson Mandela 70th Birthday Party at Wembley Stadium. Into the '90s, Adams released the album *Waking Up the Neighbours*, a big album internationally and an even bigger single — "(Everything I Do) I Do It For You," which topped the U.K. chart in 1991, where it remained for an unprecedented 16 consecutive weeks, breaking the 1955 record held by Slim Whitman with "Rose Marie." Adams took up photography with the same zeal with which he approached music, and used the proceeds from the vocation for charity. In 2002, Adams photographed Queen Elizabeth II during her Golden Jubilee and one of the images was used as a Canadian postage stamp in both 2003 and 2004. On July 2, 2009, Canada Post issued a commemorative Bryan Adams stamp.

INSIGHTS

"I always knew I'd be in music in some sort of capacity. I didn't know if I'd be successful at it, but I knew I'd be doing something in it. Maybe get a job in a record store. Maybe even play in a band. I never got into this to be a star. The idea of being 'famous' wasn't part of the plan. When I was fifteen or sixteen, buying records and listening to The Who was all the escapism I needed. Nothing else seemed to matter. School seemed unimportant, music being the only thing that gave me something to look forward to. There were a lot of years sitting on a bus or a station wagon, slipping on black ice, touring across America and Canada before things started to happen... I remember those times... there have been many more since then." — Bryan Adams, Introduction to his book, *Bryan Adams*

"My focus was music, and I was 100 per cent blinkered. And then about 10 years ago, I pulled the blinkers off.' Why? 'I'd been round the world a hundred times and had started to forget where I'd been. I knew I'd been there: it said it on the tour map. I could remember the name of the city but I couldn't remember what it was like — it was a massive blur. I was on tour for three, nearly four years, and people in the crew were getting married and divorced, and there was this Peyton Place/ Somerset Maugham backstage scenario going on, and I thought, 'Right: this has got to stop.'" — Bryan Adams to David Jenkins, *The Telegraph* (2008)

»BOOKS: *Bryan Adams: Everything He Does* by Sorelle Saidman (1993); *Bryan Adams* by Bryan Adams, photography Andrew Catlin (1995); *Made In Canada* by Bryan Adams (1999); *American Women* by Bryan Adams and Fabien Baron (2005); *Bryan Adams Exposed* (2012)

»BOB ROCK

Robert Jens Rock
Producer, Sound engineer, Mixer, Musician
Inducted 2007
b., April 19, 1954, Winnipeg, Manitoba

SIGNATURE SONGS

Eyes Of A Stranger (1982, Payola$), *Never Said I Love You* (1983, Payola$ with Carole Pope), *You're the Only Love* (1985, Paul Hyde and the Payola$), *Dirty Water* (1987, Rock and Hyde).

NOTABLE PRODUCTIONS

*Introducing The Payola$* (1980, The Payola$), *Get Lucky* (1981, Loverboy), *Slippery When Wet* (1986, Bon Jovi), *Permanent Vacation* (1987, Aerosmith), *Sonic Temple* (1989, The Cult), *Dr. Feelgood* (1989, Motley Crue), *Metallica* (1991, Metallica), *Keep the Faith* (1992, Bon Jovi), *Load* (1996, Metallica), *Eight Arms To Hold You* (1997, Veruca Salt), *On A Day Like Today* (1998, Bryan Adams), *St. Anger* (2003, Metallica), *World Container* (2006, The Tragically Hip), *Call Me Irresponsible* (2007, Michael Bublé), *Crazy Love* (2009, Michael Bublé), *Christmas* (2011, Michael Bublé)

MILESTONES

Bob Rock's musical beginnings were with a succession of bands in Vancouver formed in partnership with Paul Hyde, including The Payola$, which had their biggest hit with the 1982 single "Eyes of a Stranger." Other incarnations of the group were known as Paul Hyde and the Payola$ and simply Rock & Hyde.

Rock's beginnings as a producer can be traced back to his work in the late '70s with Vancouver bands Young Canadians, The Subhumans and Pointed Sticks. By the late '80s and into the '90s, Rock had begun working with Blue Murder, The Cult, Motley Crue, David Lee Roth and Metallica. He had his greatest chart successes with Metallica and Motley Crue, whose *Dr. Feelgood* album was a number one record in 1989. In 1991, Rock vacated the producer's chair for a while and formed the group Rockhead with former Payola$ and Rock and Hyde bandmate Chris Taylor. Rock produced the band's only album, which received a lukewarm reception and shortly after he returned to production working with artists like David Lee Roth, Cher, Bon Jovi, Skid Row, Veruca Salt, Bryan Adams, Tal Bachman, Our Lady Peace, The Tea Party, The Tragically Hip, Michael Bublé, Ron Sexsmith, Jann Arden and Nelly Furtado.

INSIGHTS

"There were times I thought I needed to pick up the big circus hammer, swing, and ring the bell. But Bob would come in and gently remind me, 'You don't need to do that.' He didn't want to lose the intensity at all. I was very challenged but very happy in the studio with Bob pushing me. With some producers, the singer can tend to get treated a bit like the goalie: the coach has no end of things to say to the forwards and defencemen. But when it comes to the goalie, coach is at a bit of a loss. 'And you!? Umm, you go over there and . . . stretch.' Bob is a great producer, editor and friend. He takes the task to heart more than anyone I've known, to create beautiful songs. He would say that that's really all it's ever about." — Gord Downie to Joseph Boyden in *Maclean's*

"I'm an artist-driven producer. I've always sided with artists. You have to give them the records they want. I don't care about managers or record companies — the artist has to be happy. Whatever the weaknesses are, I try to shore them up, and I try to play up the strengths. Some people say I've got a sound, but really, I just want a great sound and an album that keeps going." — Bob Rock to Joe Bosso, musicradar.

»TRIUMPH

Rock Group
Inducted 2008
b. Rik Emmett (Richard Gordon Emmett), July 10, 1953, Toronto, Ontario (Guitarist, vocals)
b. Gil Moore, October 4, 1953, Toronto, Ontario (Drums, vocals)
b. Mike Levine (Michael Stephen Levine), June 1, 1949, Toronto, Ontario (Bass, keyboards)

SIGNATURE SONGS

24 Hours A Day (1976), *Rock & Roll Machine* (1977), *Hold On* (1979), *Lay It On the Line* (1979), *Allied Forces* (1981), *Magic Power* (1981), *Follow Your Heart* (1984), *Somebody's Out There* (1986)

MILESTONES

Rock power trios came to define a slice of Toronto music history in the mid-'70s beginning with bands like Rush — they were actually out of the Toronto bar scene by the summer of 1974 — Goddo and Triumph, who stood out for their industrial strength approach to playing local rock venues like The Gasworks, Piccadilly Tube, Abbey Road Pub and Larry's Hideaway, initially as a Led Zeppelin cover band. In short order, Triumph was showcasing their own songs and building a live show that brought the flashpod bombast and "blinding light show" of an arena rock spectacle into the clubs. The group had formed in the mid-'70s and within a year had released their self-titled debut album through local indie label, Attic Records. Though the album met with little success in Canada, when Billboard magazine Canadian Editor David Farrell sent a copy off to the late Joe Anthony at radio station KISS-FM in San Antonio, Texas, the city once dubbed "The Heavy Metal Capital of the World," he gave it some airplay and Triumph suddenly found themselves with a regional following in the Lone Star State. It allowed the group to tour there and brought them to the attention of RCA Records in the U.S. who re-issued

the debut album and released their 1977 sophomore opus, *Rock & Roll Machine*, which contained one of the group's first singles to make an impression, a cover of Joe Walsh's "Rocky Mountain Way." The group's 1979 album *Just A Game* was notable for the tracks "Hold On" and "Lay It On the Line." Into the '80s, Triumph placed five albums in the Top 35 of the Billboard chart by mid-decade and had created a body of signature songs that included "Magic Power," "Follow Your Heart" and "Somebody's Out There." In 1988, Rik Emmett left the band to pursue a solo career and was replaced by Aldo Nova/Frozen Ghost alumnus Phil X. Guitarist, keyboardist, vocalist Rick Santers toured as part of the group for a decade beginning in the mid-'80s.

The group split up in the mid-'90s but in 2007, with the announcement of their induction into the Canadian Music Hall of Fame, the original members put past differences aside and re-united for a couple of high profile international gigs the following year, including Rocklahoma in Pryor, Oklahoma, where they co-headlined on the third day with Extreme, and a festival gig in Norje (Solvesborg), Sweden, which was released as the CD/DVD Live at Sweden Rock Festival. Gil Moore is the owner of Metalworks Studios and founder of Metalworks Institute for Sound and Music Production in Mississauga, Ontario.

INSIGHTS

"My bread gets buttered because of 'Lay It on the Line,' the song that was on the *Just A Game* album. And there's stuff that was on that *Just A Game* album that I'm proud of. That was a big record in my life, a big record in the career of the band... When Triumph did the reunion, Gil said, 'We've got to do 'Never Surrender.' I think that's one of the best lyrics you ever wrote.' I hadn't really thought about that tune. I've started to put it back in my set now, because it was a pretty good lyric. I'd kind of forgotten about it, but it's kind of a cool song.'" — Rik Emmett to Trevor Morelli of *Songfacts*

"The idea was really practical that we only wanted three musicians. We thought,' there's never going to be a tie vote'. (Laughs) That sounds crazy but that was part of it. The whole idea about what we wanted to do musically, we were looking at bands like ZZ Top, Cream, Zeppelin…generally dealing with no rhythm guitar and no keyboards. That was part of the philosophy of what we wanted to do musically. We knew the limitations. I use to always say,' In a three piece band there is no place to hide'." — Gil Moore, hennemusic.com

"By the time we started making records in 1976, we started to have some really good success in Canada in '77, and '78, and a big success in America in '79 with our recordings. I think we were just different than any other band. We weren't a heavy metal band per say, we weren't a pop band, we weren't a progressive band. We were a miss-mash of all that stuff. So, Triumph had its own identity, so I think that helped us get successful, because Triumph was different than anybody else. They tried to compare us with Aerosmith, that didn't work, they tried to compare us with AC/DC, that wouldn't work, they tried to compare us with Journey, that didn't work… so, we had our own little button hole, a niche where we were trying to fit into. Radio stations adopted our music as part of their format. Without that we wouldn't have had the big success. We would have done okay, but we were staples on radio in North America for many, many years because of our style. We were part of the fount of radio. It was different because whenever a song went on the radio it was Triumph, it couldn't be anybody else…" — Mike Levine, rockpages.gr

»LOVERBOY

Rock/Power Pop Group
Inducted 2009
b. Paul Dean, February 19, 1946, Vancouver, British Columbia (Guitar)
b. Mike Reno, (Joseph Michael Rynoski), January 8, 1955, New Westminster, British Columbia (Vocals)
b. Matt Frenette, March 7, 1954, Calgary, Alberta (Drums)
b. Scott Smith (Donald Scott Smith), February 13, 1955, Winnipeg, Manitoba (Bass)
d. Scott Smith, November 30, 2000, off the coast of San Francisco
b. Doug Johnson, December 19, 1957, New Westminster, British Columbia (Keyboards)
b. Ken "Spider" Sinnaeve (Kenneth Sinnaeve), (Bass — replaced Scott Smith in 2000)

SIGNATURE SONGS

Turn Me Loose (1981), *The Kid Is Hot Tonite* (1981), *Working For the Weekend* (1981), *When It's Over* (1982), *Hot Girls In Love* (1983), *Queen of the Broken Hearts* (1983), *Lovin' Every Minute of It* (1985), *This Could Be the Night* (1986), *Heaven In Your Eyes* (1986).

MILESTONES

Loverboy came together at The Refinery in Calgary in the late '70s where club owner Lou Blair had provided a haven for a number of musicians and singers intent on turning a new corner in their careers. Guitarist Paul Dean arrived in Calgary having been with a succession of bands, including Fox (aka Canada), Scrubbaloe Caine, the Great Canadian River Race and Streetheart, from which he had just been fired. Matt Frenette, who had been in the latter two bands with Dean, arrived soon after. Then Mike Reno, formerly of Moxy and Hammersmith, dropped by for a jam session during this period and never left. The songwriting chemistry between Dean and Reno soon became apparent, and Loverboy, which also included bass player Steve Smith and keyboardist Matt Johnson, was born. A combination of compelling songs, musicianship and management played a significant role in the band's early success. Lou Blair was joined by established Vancouver-based manager Bruce Allen (Bachman-Turner Overdrive, Bryan Adams) in guiding the band's career, which got its initial boost when CBS Records Canada (Columbia) executive Jeff Burns signed the group to a recording deal.

Loverboy recorded their self-titled debut album with fellow Hall of Famer members producer Bruce Fairbairn and engineer Bob Rock on March 20, 1980. The record made an immediate impact, selling an unprecedented 600,000+ copies in Canada alone on its way to selling four million copies internationally. The band made its live debut with KISS at the Pacific Coliseum in Vancouver on November 19, 1979 as they geared up for the heavy touring schedule of arenas and stadiums with artists like ZZ Top, Cheap Trick, Kansas and Def Leppard that was a trademark of their early career. The group's sophomore album, *Get Lucky* (1981) met with similar success, as the group took home an unprecedented six JUNO Awards in 1982. Over the course of the band's next two albums, *Keep It Up* and *Lovin' Every Minute of It*, they continued their grueling international touring schedule and, by the mid-'80s, were one of the top five grossing touring acts. They were also presented with Columbia Records' prestigious Crystal Globe Award for selling more than five million records in foreign markets. "Almost Paradise... Love Theme from Footloose," a duet by Mike Reno and Ann Wilson of Heart, hit number seven on the Billboard singles chart in 1984. Loverboy's last big hit was "Heaven In Your Eyes" from the *Top Gun* soundtrack in 1986 and, following the release of the album *Wildside* in 1987 and the touring surrounding it, the band decided to take a break. They re-united in 1992 for a benefit performance for cancer-stricken friend, guitarist Brian "Too Loud" McLeod, and subsequently decided that they would begin touring and recording again. With the tragic death at sea of bass player Scott Smith on November 30, 2000, bass player Ken "Spider" Sinnaeve (Streetheart, Tom Cochrane etc.), joined the group.

INSIGHTS:

"Fate brought me and Matt [Frenette] together... I think more me and Matt than Mike [Reno]. But just the way it worked out. I mean, meeting Matt was way more convoluted. Mike, I was just in a warehouse and Mike walked in. I was flying all over the country. I was desperate to find a band. My band had just broken up, I was almost on welfare. We were right at the bottom. My girl was still working, thankfully, but we were hurting. So I phoned up an agent that lived in Toronto, and I knew this agent from Calgary. He was a drummer that I knew, and now he's an agent. I said, 'Do you know any bands, any drummers, anybody that I could maybe audition with? I'm desperate. I need to get a job.' And he says, 'I'm loving this band up in Edmonton, called Headpins,' he said. 'Got a killer drummer. Why don't you go up and talk to them?' So I did and met Matt and listened to him play and went, 'Okay. He's definitely in my groove.'" — Paul Dean to Dan MacIntosh of *Songfacts*

"We turned in three videos the week they [video network MTV] opened [August 1, 1981], and MTV didn't have much content. So, just by process of elimination, it was like, 'What have we got?' and they said, 'Well, we've got these three Loverboy videos.' [I believe it was 'Turn Me Loose,' 'Working For the Weekend' and 'Lucky Ones.'] Actually, back then, we didn't really know what to call them — they were music performances that were filmed. We didn't even have the term 'video' back then. But it was great that we did three, which we did all in one weekend in Albany, New York, and we handed them to MTV and became TV heroes, I guess." — Mike Reno to Mike Ragogna of *Huffington Post*

>>APRIL WINE

Rock, Power Pop Group

Inducted 2010

b. Myles Goodwyn (Miles Francis Goodwyn), June 23, 1948, Woodstock, New Brunswick (Vocals, guitar, producer)

b. David Henman, April 6, 1948, Charlottetown, Prince Edward Island (Guitar)

b. Ritchie Henman, August 8, 1949, Bridgewater, Nova Scotia (Drums)

b. Jim Henman, April 5, 1947, Amherst, Nova Scotia (Bass)

b. Jim Clench (James Patrick Clench), May 1, 1949 (Bass)

d. Jim Clench, November 3, 2010, Montréal, Québec.

b. Steve Lang, March 24, 1949, Montréal, Québec (Bass)

b. Gary Moffet, June 22, 1949, Montréal, Québec (Guitar)

b. Jerry Mercer (Gerald Mercer), April 27, 1939, Newfoundland (Drums)

b. Brian Greenway (Brian Gilbert Greenway), October 1, 1951, Hawkesbury, Ontario (Guitar).

SIGNATURE SONGS

You Could Have Been A Lady (1972), *Bad Side Of Man* (1972), *Lady Run, Lady Hide* (1973), *I Wouldn't Want To Lose Your Love* (1974), *Tonight Is A Wonderful Time To Fall In Love* (1975), *Oowatanite* (1975), *Cum Hear the Band* (1975), *The Whole World's Goin' Crazy* (1976), *Like A Lover, Like A Song* (1976), *You Won't Dance With Me* (1977), *Roller* (1979), *Just Between You and Me* (1981), *Enough Is Enough* (1982), *If You Believe In Me* (1993).

MILESTONES

The origins of April Wine go back to Waverley, Nova Scotia in December of 1969 when the initial incarnation of the group formed, including Myles Goodwyn (formerly in the local group Woody's Termites) Pam Marsh, David and Ritchie Henman, and their cousin, Jimmy Henman. The group relocated to Montréal on April Fool's Day 1970 after believing that a nicely-worded rejection of a demo tape they had sent to Terry Flood was in fact a couched invitation to come west to Québec. Terry Flood and promoter Donald Tarlton ran Aquarius Records and the Laugh-In Club in Montréal. Aquarius took pity on the stranded band and put them up at The Band House in Montréal North and a ski chalet in the Laurentians north of the city. They were eventually booked into The Laugh In Club, where they made enough of an impression to be signed to Aquarius Records and have their self-titled debut album recorded and released in 1971. In 1972, the band's cover of the song "You Could Have Been A Lady," a British hit by Hot Chocolate from their sophomore album, *On Record*, marked the group's earliest visit to the U.S. charts. By 1973, the Henmans had all taken their leave and had been replaced by Jim Clench (Allison Gross and Coven), Jerry Mercer (Mashmakhan, Roy Buchanan) and Gary Moffet (The Vegetable Band, Pops Merrily). With the release of the *Electric Jewels* album in 1973, April Wine became one of the first Canadian bands to headline in arenas across Canada playing in 80 towns and cities across the country on their Electric Adventure Tour. The excursion resulted in a live album, recorded in Halifax and produced by fellow Canadian Gene Cornish and Dino Danelli, former members of The Young Rascals. In 1975, Myles Goodwyn, the principle songwriter for the band, took control of the production of the group's records and the resulting *Stand Back* album, with its rockier edge, was a best-seller in Canada. Jim Clench left the group and was replaced by Steve Lang (Mashmakhan) during this period. In 1976, the year of the Summer Olympics in Montréal, the album *The Whole World's Going Crazy* became the first Canadian album to be released as a platinum record with shipments of more than 100,000 copies. It was accompanied by a cross-Canada tour that grossed over $1 million. On March 4, 1977, the group played the first of two shows with The Rolling Stones (appearing as The Cockroaches) at the El Mocambo club in

Toronto. *Live at the El Mocambo* became the second live album by April Wine (1977). On July 4, 1978, they opened for The Stones at Rich Stadium in Buffalo, New York in front of more than 60,000 people. With the release of the single "Roller" from their 1978 album *First Glance*, the band returned to the U.S. charts and continued their lean toward a much tougher rock sound that had begun with the addition of guitarist Brian Greenway a year earlier. In 1979, they toured the U.S. for the time as support act for artists like Rush, The Tubes, Squeeze and Styx. Ironically, it was a ballad, "Just Between You and Me" (1981), that brought April Wine their first gold record in the U.S. for *Nature of the Beast*. Their 1982 album *Power Play* reached the Top 40 of the U.S. charts. The group continued to tour and recorded two more albums — *Animal Grace* and *Walking Through Fire* — but by the mid-'80s, Myles Goodwyn had moved to The Bahamas with his family and opted for a solo career. The band, with Goodwyn, Greenway, Mercer, Clench and new member, guitarist Steve Segal, got back together in 1992 to tour and record. The line-up produced two albums: *Attitude* (1993) and *Frigate* (1994). April Wine was inducted into the Canadian Music Industry Hall of Fame and awarded the CMW Lifetime Achievement Award on March 13, 2009.

INSIGHTS

"We work a lot. We generate more money with our touring now than we ever have and we work a little less than we used to. We live in an ideal world. I don't know how it happened. I saw a guy in the supermarket today, I am hitting the road tomorrow, so I was just grabbing something for tonight. He says, 'Do you guys still play?' I said, 'I am going down to Missouri tomorrow for the weekend.' He said, 'I wasn't sure if you still played.' I told him, 'We don't stop. We record and then we play, and we play, and we play'." — Myles Goodwyn to Jeb Wright, Classic Rock Revisited (2009)

"I think it was right around *Stand Back* that Myles really came into his own as a song writer. At least he knew what sound he was comfortable with and wanted to move in that direction. With Myles, he's always had a vision and in truth April Wine is his vehicle for that vision. That's why, early on there were a lot of changes in the band — he wanted to find just the right guys that understood where he wanted this thing to go." — Brian Greenway to Todd K. Smith, The Cutting Edge

»SHANIA TWAIN

Eileen Regina Edwards
Singer, Songwriter
Inducted 2011
b. August 28, 1965, Windsor, Ontario

SIGNATURE SONGS

Whose Bed Have Your Boots Been Under? (1995), *Any Man Of Mine* (1995), *The Woman In Me (Needs the Man In You)* (1995), *(If You're Not In It For Love) I'm Outta Here!* (1995), *You Win My Love* (1996), *No One Needs To Know* (1996), *Home Ain't Where His Heart Is Anymore* (1996), *God Bless the Child* (1996), *Love Gets Me Every Time* (1997), *Don't Be Stupid (You Know I Love You)* (1997), *You're Still the One* (1998), *From This Moment On* (1998), *When* (1998), *Honey, I'm Home* (1998), *That Don't Impress Me Much* (1998), *Man! I Feel Like A Woman* (1999), *You've Got A Way* (1999), *Come On Over* (1999), *I'm Gonna Getcha Good!* (2002), *Up!* (2003), *Forever and For Always* (2003), *Party For Two* (2004: with Billy Currington/Mark McGrath),

MILESTONES

By the mid-'90s, country — or New Country, as it was then being labeled — was the most popular form of music in North America, and Shania Twain had become its biggest star. Twain, with her saucy and sassy stage and video presence, infectious melodies and lyrics that took a tongue-in-cheek look at the state of relations between men and women in the '90s, broke down the barriers between country and pop music. Twain's sexy image may have brought her a large following among the male population, but that was more than counterbalanced by assertive songs like her career-launching single "Any Man of Mine," to which women could relate...and they did, in large numbers.

By the end of the millennium, her *Come on Over* album, the follow-up to her sophomore blockbuster,

The Woman in Me, had sold more than 18 million copies in the U.S., making it not only the best-selling country album of all time, but also the best-selling album by a female artist, surpassing Whitney Houston's *The Bodyguard* soundtrack album.

The second of five children, Twain was born in Windsor, Ontario, but raised in Timmins, Ontario, by her mother, Sharon, and adoptive father, Gerald Twain. Here, as a teen, she worked with her father on various reforestation projects while being encouraged to develop her obvious singing talents, which had been influenced by everything from the pop hits of the day to the country music her parents played at home. When Twain was 21, her parents were killed in an automobile accident and she was left to take care of her brothers and sisters. To support the family, she worked at the Deerhurst Resort in Huntsville, Ontario, where she did everything from musical cabaret to Andrew Lloyd Webber to Gershwin. As her siblings began to grow up and move away, Twain finally had the freedom to pursue her dream of becoming a recording artist. Her self-titled debut album served to introduce her to the world of country music and to Robert John "Mutt" Lange, the man who would become her creative soul-mate and husband. Lange, who co-wrote and produced Twain's *The Woman in Me* and *Come on Over* albums, was already a legend in rock circles having produced artists like AC/DC, Foreigner, The Cars, Def Leppard, Tina Turner and The Backstreet Boys. His Canadian connection began with rocker Bryan Adams before he first saw and heard Twain on the country music network, CMT, which at the time was available in Europe. Twain first met Lange in person in Nashville at the Fan Fair event in 1993.

In the summer of 2001, Twain's hometown of Timmins, Ontario, where she worked at a McDonalds in her teens, opened the 4000-square-foot Shania Twain Centre on the site of the current Timmins Underground Gold Mine Tour. Until its recent closing, it showcased more than a million dollars' worth of Shania Twain memorabilia, including awards, clothing from her tours. Her 2002 album, *Up!* which was released with three different discs — country/acoustic (green CD), pop/rock (red CD) and world/dance (blue CD) — expanded Twain's popularity internationally.

Twain made her first television appearance since her split with her husband "Mutt" Lange as a presenter at the *42nd CMA Awards* on November 12, 2008. Her TV show *Why Not? with Shania Twain* debuted on the Oprah Winfrey Network (OWN) on May 8, 2011 and on December 1, 2012 her two-year residency at Caesar's Palace in Las Vegas with the show *Still the One* began.

INSIGHTS

"I was born in 1965 and the first seven years I remember pretty specifically what was going on musically. I was wearing the bell-bottoms — really colourful, tight hip-huggers — even as a kid. It was just at the very end of that era really, but I remember very clearly the Mamas and Papas and the Carpenters, who were big for me, and Stevie Wonder, Gladys Knight and all of that Motown stuff. I loved that period and I was really into music. My parents were big fans of country and that's all they listened to, and as far as my career went as a child, the only music that we had in the house for me to learn from were 8-track country tapes. When we had people over, it was country music they listened to and that's what I sang for them, so it was natural that country music became my career, though I was influenced by many other styles of music." — To Martin Melhuish, *Canada's Hot New Country Stars*

"Before my parents died, I was still really searching for my musical direction whether it was R&B or rock or pop or whatever. After [my parents] accident, I even did an off-Broadway musical theatre show for three years … Everyone along the way always asked, 'Wow, have you every sung country? You've really got this country thing in your voice. You'd really sound good singing country.' And I'd say to myself, 'Oh my God! I'm trying to make a living singing whatever kind of music happens to pay the bills.' I guess it was just one of those things that wouldn't go away no matter how much I tried to ignore it." — To Martin Melhuish, *Canada's Hot New Country Stars*

"Nashville's an industry town; let's face it. If you can record a barking dog and sell a million records, they don't care. You know, she was incredibly, economically important to the city and to country music so on that level I think she's universally respected as far as her impact as an artist… her financial impact as an artist.

I think musically, there was quite a bit of eyebrow-raising about: is that country music? My point of view is that it is. In some mysterious and ineffable way that I can't explain, it somehow works for me." — Robert K. Oermann, *Shania: Respect*, CMT Canada.

"She has done so much for country music, for the women in country music. She has added a breath of life, a breath of fresh air into everything. She's different, she's beautiful and she's added a great spark that we've all needed." — Reba McEntire, The Case For Shania, CMT Canada

»BOOKS: *Shania Twain: Up and Away* by Jim Brown; *From This Moment On* by Shania Twain (2011).

»BLUE RODEO

Roots Rock Band

Inducted 2012

b. Jim Cuddy (James G. Cuddy), December 2, 1955, Toronto, Ontario (Guitar, vocals)

b. Greg Keelor (J. Gregory Keelor), August 29, 1954, Inverness County, Nova Scotia (Guitar, vocals)

b. Cleave Anderson, Toronto, Ontario (Drums)

b. Bazil Donovan, Halifax, Nova Scotia (Bass)

b. Bobby Wiseman (Robert Neil Wiseman), Winnipeg, Manitoba (Keyboards)

Mark French (Drums)

Glenn Milchem (Drums)

Bob Egan (Multi-instrumentalist)

James Gray (Keyboardist)

Michael Boguski (Keyboardist)

Bob Packwood (Keyboardist)

Kim Deschamps (Multi-instrumentalist)

SIGNATURE SONGS

Try (1987), *Diamond Mine* (1989), *Til I Am Myself Again* (1990), *What Am I Doing Here?* (1991), *Lost Together* (1992), *Rain Down On Me* (1992), *5 Days In May* (1993), *Hasn't Hit Me Yet* (1994), *Side of the Road* (1995), *Better Off As We Are* (1995), *It Could Happen To You* (1997)

MILESTONES

Blue Rodeo is a country/rock hybrid from Toronto's Queen Street West scene, where they virtually held house-band status at The Horseshoe Tavern in the mid-'80s. They were hardly the overnight success story they appeared. Founded by Jim Cuddy and Greg Keelor, who had played football together while attending Toronto's North Toronto Collegiate Institute, Blue Rodeo took more than a decade and a succession of musical influences before being acclaimed. In the mid-'70s, Cuddy and Keelor worked in Toronto-based bands, The Tears and The Hi-Fis. 1981 found them in the group Fly To France, which spent some time in New York and brought Cuddy and Keelor into contact with New York 'new country" singer Ned Sublette, who became an early influence. Returning to Toronto in 1984, they recruited drummer Cleave Anderson (The Battered Wives, Sharks, Gamma Gamma, Sidewinders), Bazil Donovan (Sharks) and Bobby Wiseman to form the band Blue Rodeo. They initially recorded for the independent label Risque Disque founded by manager John Caton, an ex-member of The Arrows.

In early 1987, Blue Rodeo signed with Warner and on March 17, 1988, they played New York's Bottom Line club in the wake of the release of their debut album, *Outskirts*, and the single "Try," which brought the band universal critical praise. With the release of their second album, *Diamond Mine*, and a showcase at Soho's Borderline Club in London, England on February 15, 1989, drummer Cleave Anderson left the group and was replaced by Mark French (The Cartwrights, Johnnie Lovesin, Streetwalkin' Barbie). That year Blue Rodeo was a featured group at the Montreux Jazz Festival in Switzerland as part of their European tour with Edie Brickell and the New Bohemians. They were also selected by actress Meryl Streep and music director Howard Shore to play her back-up band in a climactic scene from the movie, *Postcards From the Edge.*

As CARAS noted prior to the group's induction into the Canadian Music Hall of Fame which represented their 12th JUNO Award: "Spanning nearly three decades, Blue Rodeo has sold in excess of four million records and won an unprecedented 11 JUNO Awards, establishing themselves as one of the premier groups in Canadian music history."

INSIGHTS

"Don't you think that's a funny thing in itself that we picked up a rural sound in New York? Greg [Keelor] and I are the product of kids who listened to the British invasion; grew up on rock and roll and then, along the way, there was Dylan and Lightfoot and, for me, Jackson Browne — and all those little country rock things that came in. We go to New York to be a pop band and just learn to loathe that scene… And we get smitten by this kind of urban-countrified thing that's going on. A guy named Ned Sublette's doing it; he's this transplant from Oklahoma and he does these crazy kind of word poetry things with a band — sometimes he's got a tuba for the bass, sometimes a steel… and we're off. Also, seeing a band like NRBQ [made a great impression]. And NRBQ is a band that, without pause, could break into different styles; they were totally wacky and you couldn't figure out whether they could actually play some of the instruments or whether it was a modern approach to it… That band just floored us when we saw them. So, when we came back to Toronto,

it was already a scene and it was urban, but it was all about rural life or about the lost highway or the pill poppin' guys like Johnny Cash and writing songs, those crazy songs… I think what it did was unleash our most natural inclination toward songs. The rest had been a bit of an imposition; learning to play reggae or pop or Talking Heads kinds of stuff was not that natural to us." — Jim Cuddy to Martin Melhuish, *Four Strong Winds: A Celebration of Canadian Singer/Songwriters.*

"I started playing guitar in the winter of '75 in Lake Louise when I was working at the Chateau there. My roommate had a guitar — and he had songbooks — and I'd pick it up and try a Gordon Lightfoot song or an Everly Brother's tune, that sort of thing. The next summer, I was working on a Great Lakes freighter and, at Three Rivers, I bought my first guitar. That night, my very first night sitting in that cabin, I wrote my first song. And that was definitely one of those epiphany evenings for me, as my life would unfold. And writing that song, there was whatever that feeling is of self-expression and the sort of communing with all the previous self-expressers. That night, I just sort of made a little artistic manifesto for myself, looking out my little porthole saying to myself that I wanted to live a life where I was around creative people and that sort of scene. I wanted to be creating and around creative people." — Greg Keelor to Martin Melhuish, *Four Strong Winds: A Celebration of Canadian Singer/Songwriters.*

"The best new American band of the year [1988] may very well be Canadian." — *Rolling Stone*

Canadian Music Hall of Fame

»k.d. lang

Kathryn Dawn Lang

Singer, Songwriter, Social activist, Actress

Inducted 2013

b., November 2, 1961, Edmonton, Alberta

SIGNATURE SONGS

Hanky Panky (1984), *Rose Garden* (1984), *Three Cigarettes in an Ashtray* (1987), *Crying* (1987: with Roy Orbison), *Honky Tonk Angels Medley* (1988: with Brenda Lee, Loretta Lynn and Kitty Wells), *I'm Down To My Last Cigarette* (1988), *Full Moon of Love* (1989), *Three Days* (1989), *Luck In My Eyes* (1990), *Constant Craving* (1992), *Miss Chatelaine* (1992), *Calling All Angels* (1992: with Jane Siberry), *Lifted By Love* (1994), *If I Were You* (1995), *Sexuality* (1996), *Summerfling* (2000), *Hallelujah* (2010: Vancouver Winter Games Version), *I Confess* (2011), *Sing It Loud* (2011)

MILESTONES

Shania Twain wasn't the first Canadian artist to give the Nashville establishment a bad case of the wriggles. k.d. lang's brief fling with country music between 1987 and 1992 earned her a number of Grammy Awards and a special place in the country music history books for her undeniable vocal talents and capricious ways right out of a L'il Abner comic strip. By the late '80s, as the Urban Cowboy craze, prompted by the John Travolta movie of the same name, began to lose its appeal and the new traditionalists began to emerge, the country world wondered if it had indeed seen it all. k.d. lang wasn't long in providing the answer. lang hit Nashville's Music Row in the late '80s and, despite some raised eyebrows, was greeted with enthusiasm by those pundits who believed that there was room for lang — "torch and twang" vocals, androgynous image, and all — in their universe. The recording of her Grammy-winning *Shadowland* album, which saw Owen Bradley, Patsy Cline's producer and Nashville legend, come out of retirement to oversee the project, and which also included a collaboration with country divas Kitty Wells, Brenda Lee, and Loretta Lynn on the track "Honky Tonk Angels Medley," was just the beginning. In the few short years she spent in the embrace of the country community, she did as much to broaden the appeal of country music as any of the so-called outlaw country acts like Waylon Jennings and Willie Nelson. Endorsing a "meat stinks" campaign by an animal rights group and "coming out" to great media fanfare was the very definition of "outlaw" in the world of country music.

lang's next album, *Absolute Torch and Twang*, spent two years on the U.S. country album charts, but by 1992 lang was bound for movin' on. She was named one of Canada's Artists of the Decade alongside Rush and Bryan Adams. The release of her Grammy Award-winning album *Ingénue* confirmed her broad appeal in the pop world. The single "Constant Craving" was so ubiquitous at the time that Mick Jagger and Keith Richards of The Rolling Stones unwittingly wrote a song ("Anybody Seen My Baby?") with a chorus remarkably similar to lang's song and voluntarily listed her as co-writer. lang, a four-time Grammy Award winner, who also has nine JUNO Awards to her credit, was universally acclaimed for her performance of the Leonard Cohen song, "Hallelujah," long a signature song for her, at the opening of the 2010 Winter Olympics in Vancouver. In March 2013, she topped the list of the Top 25 Canadian singers as voted on by a panel of CBC producers and show hosts. "She's not precious," they commented, "she doesn't indulge in diva-like vocal tricks — lang sings from the gut and the heart, and it's perfection."

INSIGHTS

"The startlingly original debut by k.d. lang and the reclines gives country music a tornado of a swirl that could send a few rhinestones flying into the 21st century. Put away the telescopes, Music Row. This angel from left field just tossed a lariat around the future and pulled it into view." — Michael McCall, *Nashville Banner*

"Few singers command such perfection of pitch. Her voice, at once beautiful and unadorned and softened with a veil of smoke, invariably hits the middle of a note and remains there. She discreetly flaunted her technique, drawing out notes and shading them from sustained cries into softer, vibrato-laden murmurs. She balanced her commitment to the material with humor, projecting a twinkling merriment behind it all." — Stephen Holden, *New York Times*

"I think the fact that I'm standing here receiving this award says more about Canada than it does about me. Only in Canada could there be such a freak as k.d. lang receiving this award… So I am here to tell you, my friends and my countrymen, that it is okay to be you. It is okay to let your freak flags fly. Embrace the quirkmeister that is inside all of us." — k.d. lang at 2013 JUNO Awards, as she was inducted into the Canadian Music Hall of Fame

»BOOKS: *k.d. lang: An Illustrated Biography* by David Bennahum (2013)

JUNO AWARD WINNERS ROLL

Remarkably, more than 2700 JUNO Awards, which honour excellence and sales success in the Canadian music industry, have been presented in their various categories since the first awards were handed out on February 22, 1971 at St. Lawrence Hall in Toronto. It was an intimate, family affair in those days, during which Anne Murray, Gordon Lightfoot, The Guess Who and Stompin' Tom Connors were among those who were honoured with the 17 awards presented that evening.

Today, the annual JUNO Awards ceremony, under the auspices of the Canadian Academy of Recording Arts & Sciences (CARAS), is a movable gala which plays out in the biggest venues in Canada with enthusiastic public and civic participation in each city and a high-profile national broadcast on the CTV Network. Winners of at least one JUNO Award are listed with the number of nominations they have received over the years.

* An asterisk indicates that it is the official number but includes at least one RPM Gold Leaf Award, forerunner to the JUNOs, from 1970.

MULTIPLE AWARD WINNERS

»BRYAN ADAMS (19)

2010: Allan Waters Humanitarian Award
2006: Canadian Music Hall of Fame
2000: Best Male Artist
1999: Best Songwriter ("On A Day Like Today," Co-Songwriter Phil Thornalley; "When You're Gone," Co-Songwriter, Eliot Kennedy)
1997: Male Vocalist of the Year
1993: Best Selling Album (Foreign or Domestic) (Waking Up the Neighbours)
1992: Canadian Entertainer of the Year
1992: International Achievement Award
1992: Producer of the Year (Robert John "Mutt" Lange, Co-Producer for "(Everything I Do) I Do It For You"; "Can't Stop This Thing We Started" from Waking Up the Neighbours, Bryan Adams)
1987: Canadian Entertainer of the Year
1987: Male Vocalist of the Year
1986: Male Vocalist of the Year
1985: Composer of the Year (with Jim Vallance)
1985: Male Vocalist of the Year
1984: Album of the Year (Cuts Like A Knife)
1984: Composer of the Year (with Jim Vallance)
1984: Male Vocalist of the Year
1984: Producer of the Year (Cuts Like A Knife by Bryan Adams)
1983: Male Vocalist of the Year

»SUSAN AGLUKARK (3)

2004: Aboriginal Recording of the Year (Big Feeling)
1995: Best Music of Aboriginal Canada Recording (Arctic Rose)
1995: Best New Solo Artist

»JAVIER AGUILERA (2)

1999: Best Video (Javier Aguilera, David Usher – "Forestfire," David Usher)

1998: Best Video (Javier Aguilera, Moist – "Gasoline," Moist)

»BRIAN AHERN (4)

1973: Best Produced MOR Album (Annie, Anne Murray)
1972: Best Produced MOR Album (Talk It Over In the Morning, Anne Murray)
1971: Best Produced MOR Album (Honey, Wheat & Laughter, Anne Murray)
1971: Best Produced Single ("Snowbird," Anne Murray

»KIRAN AHLUWALIA (2)

2012: World Music Album of the Year (Aam Zameen: common ground)
2004: World Music Album of the Year (Beyond Boundaries)

»LILLIAN ALLEN (2)

1989: Best Reggae/Calypso Recording (Conditions Critical)
1986: Best Reggae/Calypso Recording (Revolutionary Tea Party)

»ALPHA YAYA DIALLO (3)

2005: World Music Album of the Year (Mighty Popo, Madagascar Slim, Donné Robert, Alpha Ya Ya Diallo, Adam Solomon, Pa Joe – African Guitar Summit)
2002: Best Global Album (The Journey)
1999: Best Global Album (The Message)

»PAUL ANKA (2)

1980: Canadian Music Hall of Fame
1975: Composer of the Year

»ARCADE FIRE (6)

2011: Album of the Year (*The Suburbs*)
2011: Alternative Album of the Year (*The Suburbs*)
2011: Group of the Year
2011: Songwriter of the Year ("Ready To Start," "We Used To Wait," "Sprawl II (Mountains Beyond Mountains)," Arcade Fire)
2008: Alternative Album of the Year (*Neon Bible*)
2006: Songwriter of the Year ("Wake Up," "Rebellion (Lies)," "Neighbourhood #3 (Power Out)," Arcade Fire)

»JANN ARDEN (8)

2002: Best Songwriter ("Never Mind," "Thing For You" (co-writer Russell Broom), Jann Arden)
2001: Best Female Artist
1996: Best Video (Jeth Weinrich, Jann Arden – "Good Mother," Jann Arden)
1995: Entertainer of the Year
1995: Single of the Year ("Could I Be Your Girl," Jann Arden)
1995: Songwriter of the Year
1994: Best New Solo Artist
1994: Best Video (Jeth Weinrich, Director – "I Would Die For You," Jann Arden)

»ARKELLS (2)

2012: Group of the Year
2010: New Group of the Year

»GARNET ARMSTRONG (2)

2006: CD/DVD Artwork Design of the Year (Rob Baker: Director/Illustrator; Garnet Armstrong, Director/Designer; Susan Michalek, Designer; Will Ruocco, Illustrator – *Hipeponymouse*, The Tragically Hip)
2004: Album Design of the Year (Garnet Armstrong, Susan Michalek, Director/Designer; Andrew MacNaughtan, Photographer – *Love Is the Only Soldier*, Jann Arden)

»RANDY BACHMAN (11)

1987: Canadian Music Hall of Fame (with The Guess Who)
1976: Best Selling Album (*Four Wheel Drive*, Bachman-Turner Overdrive)
1976: Best Selling Single ("You Ain't Seen Nothin' Yet," Bachman-Turner Overdrive)
1976: Group of the Year (Bachman-Turner Overdrive)
1975: Best Selling Album (Bachman-Turner Overdrive, *Not Fragile*)
1975: Group of the Year (Bachman-Turner Overdrive)
1975: Producer of the Year
1974: Contemporary Album of the Year (Bachman-Turner Overdrive)
1974: Most Promising Group of the Year (Bachman-Turner Overdrive)
1971: Top Vocal Instrumental Group (The Guess Who)
1970: Top Vocal Instrumental Group (The Guess Who)

»TAL BACHMAN (2)

2000: Best New Solo Artist
2000: Best Producer (Tal Bachman & Bob Rock – "She's So High," "If You Sleep," Tal Bachman)

»BACHMAN-TURNER OVERDRIVE (7)

1976: Best Selling Album (*Four Wheel Drive*)
1976: Best Selling Single ("You Ain't Seen Nothin' Yet")
1976: Group of the Year
1975: Best Selling Album (*Not Fragile*)
1975: Group of the Year
1974: Contemporary Album of the Year (Bachman-Turner Overdrive)
1974: Most Promising Group of the Year

»CARROLL BAKER (3)

1979: Country Female Vocalist of the Year
1978: Country Female Vocalist of the Year
1977: Country Female Vocalist of the Year

»ROB BAKER (2)

2006: CD/DVD Artwork Design of the Year (Rob Baker, Director/Illustrator; Garnet Armstrong, Director/Designer; Susan Michalek, Designer; Will Ruocco, Illustrator – *Hipeponymouse*, The Tragically Hip)
1999: Best Album Design (Rob Baker/Brock Ostram, Creative Director; Andrew MacLachlan, Graphic Artist/Creative Director; Bernard Clark/David

Ajax, Photographer, Phantom Power, The Tragically Hip)

»BARENAKED LADIES (8)

2009: Children's Album of the Year (*Snacktime!*)
2001: Best Album (*Maroon*)
2001: Best Group
2001: Best Pop Album (*Maroon*)
1999: Best Group
1999: Best Pop Album (*Stunt*)
1999: Best Single ("One Week")
1993: Group of the Year

»ISABEL BAYRAKDARIAN (4)

2007: Classical Album of the Year: Vocal or Choral Performance (Isabel Bayrakdarian, Michael Schade, Russell Braun, Canadian Opera Company Orchestra, Richard Bradshaw, *Mozart: Arie e Duetti*)
2006: Classical Album of the Year: Vocal or Choral Performance (Isabel Bayrakdarin, Serouj Kradjian – Viardot-Garcia: *Kieder Chansons Canzone Mazurkas*)
2005: Classical Album of the Year: Vocal or Choral Performance (Isabel Bayrakdarian, Tafelmusik Baroque Orchestra – *Cleopatra*)
2004: Classical Album of the Year: Vocal or Choral Performance (Isabel Bayrakdarian, James Parker, Cello Ensemble – *Azulao*)

»DANIEL BÉLANGER (2)

2008: Francophone Album of the Year (*L'échec du materiel*)
2003: Francophone Album of the Year (*Rêver mieux*)

»STEVE BELL (2)

2001: Best Album (*Simple Songs*)
1998: Best Gospel Album (*Romantics & Mystics*)

»MARIO BERNARDI (3)

2004: Classical Album of the Year: Large Ensemble or Soloist with Large Ensemble Accompaniment (André Laplante, piano; Christopher Millard, Bassoon; Robert Cram, flute; Joaquin Valdepenas, clarinet, CBC Radio Orchestra, Mario Bernardi, Conductor, Concertos: Music of Jacquest Hétu)
2003: Classical Album of the Year: Large Ensemble or Soloist with Large Ensemble Accompaniment

(James Ehnes, Mario Bernardi, Orchestre symphoique due Montréal–Bruch Concertos: *Vol.II*)
1998: Best Classical Album: Large Ensemble or Soloist with Large Ensemble Accompaniment (James Somerville, CBC Vancouver Orchestra, Mario Bernardi – *Mozart Horn Concertos*)

»JUSTIN BIEBER (4)

2013: JUNO Fan Choice Award
2012: JUNO Fan Choice Award
2011: JUNO Fan Choice Award
2011: Pop Album of the Year (*My World 2.0*)

»BILLY TALENT (7)

2010: Rock Album of the Year (*Ill*)
2008: Music DVD of the Year (Billy Talent, Pierre & Francois Lamoureux, Pierre Tremblay, Steve Blair – *666 Live*, Billy Talent)
2007: Group of the Year
2007: Rock Album of the Year (*Billy Talent II*)
2005: Album of the Year (*Billy Talent*)
2005: Group of the Year
2004: New Group of the Year

»BLUE RODEO (12)

2012: Canadian Music Hall of Fame
2009: Music DVD of the Year (Blue Rodeo, Chirstopher Mills, Geoff McLean for Blue Rodeo by Blue Rodeo)
2008: Adult Alternative Album of the Year (*Small Miracles*)
2008: Group of the Year
2008: Video of the Year (Blue Rodeo, Christopher Mills for *C'mon* by Blue Rodeo)
2005: Music DVD of the Year (Ron Mann, Blue Rodeo for *In Sterovision* by Blue Rodeo)
1996: Group of the Year
1991: Group of the Year
1990: Group of the Year
1989: Best Video (Michael Buckley, Blue Rodeo for "Try" by Blue Rodeo)

»BILL BOURNE (2)

2001: Best Roots & Traditional Album: Group (*Tri-Continental, Tri-Continental*)
1991: Best Roots & Traditional Album (Bill Bourne & Alan MacLeod, *Dance & Celebrate*)

≫LIONA BOYD (5)

1996: Instrumental Artist of the Year
1984: Instrumental Artist of the Year
1983: Instrumental Artist of the Year
1982: Instrumental Artist of the Year
1979: Instrumental Artist of the Year

≫RICHARD BRADSHAW (2)

2007: Classical Album of the Year: Vocal or Choral Performance (Isabel Bayrakdarian, Micahel Schade, Russell Braun, Canadian Opera Company Orchestra, Richard Bradshaw – *Mozart: Arie e Duetti*)
1998: Best Classical Album: Vocal or Choral Performance (Michael Schade, Tenor; Russell Braun, Baritone; Canadian Opera Company Orchestra, Richard Bradshaw – *Soirée française*)

≫DAVID BRAID (2)

2012: Traditional Jazz Album of the Year (*Verge*)
2005: Traditional Jazz Album of the Year (*Vivid: The David Braid Sextet Live*)

≫PAUL BRANDT (8)

2008: Allan Waters Humanitarian Award
2008: Country Recording of the Year (*Risk*)
2001: Best Country Male Artist
2000: Best Country Male Artist
1999: Bet Country Male Vocalist
1998: Country Male Vocalist of the Year
1998: Male Vocalist of the Year
1997: Country Male Vocalist of the Year

≫RUSSELL BRAUN (3)

2007: Classical Album of the Year: Vocal or Choral Performance (Isabel Bayrakdarian, Micahel Schade, Russell Braun, Canadian Opera Company Orchestra, Richard Bradshaw – *Mozart: Arie e Duetti*)
2001: Best Classical Album: Vocal or Choral Performance (Karina Gauvin, Russell Braun, Les Violons du Roy – G.F. Handel: Apollo e Dafne, Silete Venti)
1998: Best Classical Album: Vocal or Choral Performance (Michael Schade, Tenor; Russell Braun, Baritone; Canadian Opera Company Orchestra, Richard Bradshaw – *Soirée française*)

≫BROKEN SOCIAL SCENE (2)

2006: Alternative Album of the Year (*Broken Social Scene*)
2003: Alternative Album of the Year (*You Forget It In People*)

≫MEASHA BRUEGGERGOSMAN (2)

2008: Classical Album of the Year: Vocal or Choral Performance (*Surprise*)
2005: Classical Album of the Year: Vocal or Choral Performance (Measha Brueggergosman, Manitoba Chamber Orchestra, "So Much To Tell."

≫MICHAEL BUBLÉ (11)

2012: Album of the Year (*Christmas*)
2010: Album of the Year (*Crazy Love*)
2010: JUNO Fan Choice Award
2010: Pop Album of the Year (*Crazy Love*)
2010: Single of the Year ("Haven't Met You Yet")
2008: JUNO Fan Choice Award
2006: Album of the Year (*It's Time*)
2006: Artist of the Year
2006: Pop Album of the Year (*It's Time*)
2006: Single of the Year ("Home")
2004: New Artist of the Year

≫BUCK 65 (2)

2006: Video of the Year (Buck 65, Micah Meisner, Rich Terfry – "Devil's Eyes," *Buck 65*)
2004: Alternative Album of the Year (*Talkin' Honky Blue*)

≫JANE BUNNETT (4)

2009: Contemporary Jazz Album of the Year (*Embracing Voices*)
2006: Contemporary Jazz Album of the Year (*Radio Guantanamo – Guantanamo Blues Project Vol. 1*)
2001: Best Global Album (*Jane Bunnett & the Spirits of Havana – Ritmo + Soul*)
1993: Best World Beat Recording (*Spirits of Havana*)

JUNO WINNERS

JIM BYRNES (3)

2011: Blues Album of the Year (*Everywhere West*)
2007: Blues Album of the Year (*House of Refuge*)
1996: Best Blues/Gospel Album (*That River*)

CANADIAN OPERA COMPANY ORCHESTRA (2)

2007: Classical Album of the Year: vocal or Choral Performance (Isabel Bayrakdarian, Michael Shade, Russell Braun, Canadian Opera Company Orchestra, Richard Bradshaw – *Mozart: Arie e Duetti*)
1998: Best Classical Album: Vocal or Choral Performance (Michael Shade, Tenor; Russell Braun, Baritone; Canadian Opera Company Orchestra, Richard Bradshaw – *Soirée Française*)

GEORGE CANYON (2)

2007: Country Recording of the Year (*Somebody Wrote Love*)
2005: Country Recording of the Year (*One Good Friend*)

CAPITOL RECORDS (4)

1973: Canadian Content Company of the Year
1971: Top Record Company
1971: Top Record Company in Promotional Activities
1970: Top Record Company in Promotional Activities

PEGI CECCONI (2)

2011: Music DVD of the Year (Rush, Scot McFadyen, Sam Dunn, Pegi Cecconi, Noah Segal, Shelley Nott, John Virant – *Rush: Beyond the Lighted Stage*)
2004: Music DVD of the Year (Rush, Andrew MacNaughtan, Dan Catullo: Directors; Allan Wenrib, Pegi Cecconi, Ray Danniels: Producers – *Rush in Rio, Rush*)

CHAN KA NIN (2)

2002: Best Classical Composition ("Par-çi, par-la")
1994: Best Classical composition (Chan Ka Nin – AMICI: Joaquin Valdepenas, clarinet, David Hetherington, cello, Patricia Parr, piano – "Among Friends")

CHOCLAIR (4)

2004: Rap Recording of the Year ("Flagrant")
2000: Best Rap Recording ("Ice Cold")
1999: Best Rap Recording (Rascalz featuring Choclair, Kardinal Offishal, Thrust and Checkmate – "Northern Touch")
1997: Best Rap Recording ("What It Takes")

KEVIN CHURKO (4)

2013: Recording Engineer of the Year (Kevin Churko, co-engineer Kane Churko – "Blood," In This Moment, Blood; "Coming Down," American Capitalist – *Five Finger Death Punch*)
2011: Recording Engineer of the Year ("Let It Die," "Life won't Wait," Ozzy Osbourne)
2009: Recording Engineer of the Year ("Disappearing," "The Big Bang," Simon Collins)
2008: Recording Engineer of the Year ("I Don't Wanna Stop," "God Bless the Almighty Dollar," Ozzy Osbourne)

CITY AND COLOUR (3)

2012: Songwriter of the Year (Dallas Green – "Fragile Bird," "We Found Each Other," "Weightless," Little Hell, City and Colour)
2009: Songwriter of the Year (Dallas Green – "Waiting…," "Sleeping Sickness," "The Girl," City and Colour)
2007: Alternative Album of the Year (City and Colour, *Sometimes*)

TERRI CLARK (3)

2012: Country Album of the Year (*Roots and Wings*)
2001: Best Country Female Artist
1997: Best New Solo Artist

CLASSICAL KIDS (3)

1999: Best Children's Album (Susan Hammond's Classical Kids – *Mozart's Magnificent Voyage*)
1994: Best Children's Album (Susan Hammond/ Classical Kids – *Tchaikovsky Discovers America*)
1992: Best Children's Album (Classical Kids, Susan Hammond, producer – *Vivaldi's Ring of Mystery*)

» DAVID CLAYTON-THOMAS (2)

1996: Canadian Music Hall of Fame
1973: Outstanding Contribution to the Canadian Music Scene

» TOM COCHRANE (8)

2013: Allan Waters Humanitarian Award
2003: Canadian Music Hall of Fame
1992: Album of the Year (*Mad Mad World*)
1992: Male Vocalist of the Year
1992: Single of the Year ("Life Is A Highway")
1992: Songwriter of the Year
1989: Composer of the Year
1987: Group of the Year (Tom Cochrane & Red Rider)

» BRUCE COCKBURN (11)

2012: Roots & Traditional Album of the Year: Solo (*Small Source of Comfort*)
2006: Allan Waters Humanitarian Award
2001: Canadian Music Hall of Fame
2000: Best Roots & Traditional Album: Solo (*Breakfast in New Orleans, Dinner in Timbuktu*)
1982: Folk Artist of the Year
1982: Male Vocalist of the Year
1981: Folk Artist of the Year
1981: Male Vocalist of the Year
1973: Folksinger of the Year
1972: Folksinger of the Year
1971: Top Folksinger

» LEONARD COHEN (6)

2013: Artist of the Year
2013: Songwriter of the Year
1994: Songwriter of the Year
1993: Best Video (Curtis Wehrfritz, Leonard Cohen – "Closing Time," Leonard Cohen)
1993: Male Vocalist of the Year
1991: Canadian Music Hall of Fame

» COLDPLAY (2)

2009: International Album of the Year
2006: International Album of the Year

» HOLLY COLE (2)

2004: Vocal Jazz Album of the Year (*Shade*)
1994: Best Contemporary Jazz Album (*Don't Smoke In Bed, Holly Cole Trio*)

» SONIA COLLYMORE (2)

2005: Reggae Recording of the Year (*WYSIWYG What You See Is What You Get*)
2003: Reggae Recording of the Year ("You Won't See Me Cry")

» STOMPIN' TOM CONNORS (6)

1975: Country Male Vocalist of the Year
1974: Country Album of the Year (*To It and At It*)
1974: Country Male Vocalist of the Year
1973: Male Country Singer of the Year
1972: Male Country Singer of the Year
1971: Top Country Singer, Male

» DEBORAH COX (3)

1999: Best R&B/Soul Recording (*One Wish*)
1998: Best R&B/Soul Recording (*Things Just Ain't the Same*)
1996: Best R&B/Soul Recording (Deborah Cox)

» JIM CUDDY (13)

2009: Music DVD of the Year (Blue Rodeo, Christopher Mills, Geoff McLean for *Blue Road* by Blue Rodeo)
2008: Adult Alternative Album of the Year (*Small Miracles* by Blue Rodeo)
2008: Group of the Year (Blue Rodeo)
2008: Video of the Year (Blue Rodeo, Christopher Mills for "C'mon" by Blue Rodeo)
2007: Adult Alternative Album of the Year (*The Light That Guides You Home*)
2005: Music DVD of the Year (Ron Mann, Blue Rodeo for *In Stereovision* by Blue Rodeo)
1999: Best Male Vocalist
1996: Group of the Year (Blue Rodeo)
1991: Group of the Year (Blue Rodeo)
1990: Group of the Year (Blue Rodeo)
1989: Best Video (Michael Buckley, Blue Rodeo for "Try" by Blue Rodeo)

1989: Group of the Year (Blue Rodeo)
1989: Single of the Year ("Try" by Blue Rodeo)

›› BURTON CUMMINGS (7)

1987: Canadian Music Hall of Fame
1980: Male Vocalist of the Year
1979: Best Selling Album (*Dream of a Child*)
1977: Male Vocalist of the Year
1977: Most Promising Male Vocalist of the Year
1971: Top Vocal Instrumental Group (The Guess Who)
1970: Top Vocal Instrumental Group (The Guess Who)

›› ANDREW DAVIS (2)

1996: Best Classical Album: Vocal or Choral Performance (Ben Heppner, Tenor, Toronto Symphony Orchestra, Andrew Davis, Conductor – *Ben Heppner Sings Richard Strauss*)
1986: Best Classical Album: Large Ensemble or Soloist with Large Ensemble Accompaniment (Toronto Symphony Orchestra, Andrew Davis, Conductor – *Holst: The Planets*)

›› DEADMAU5 (4)

2011: Dance Recording of the Year ("Sofi Needs A Ladder")
2010: Dance Recording of the Year ("For Lack of a Better Name")
2009: Dance Recording of the Year ("Random Album Title")
2008: Dance Recording of the Year (Billy Newton-Davis vs. Deadmau5 – "After Hours")

›› PAUL DEAN (2)

1982: Composer of the Year (Mike Reno & Paul Dean – "Turn Me Loose," Loverboy)
1982: Producer of the Year (Paul Dean/Bruce Fairbairn – "Working For the Weekend," "It's Over," Loverboy)

›› JACK DE KEYZER (2)

2010: Blues Album of the Year (*The Cooktown Sessions*)
2003: Blues Album of the Year (*6 String Lover*)

›› DELERIUM (2)

2000: Best Dance Recording ("Silence")
1998: Best Dance Recording ("Euphoria – Rabbit in the Moon Mix")

›› CELINE DION (20)

1999: Best Album (*Let's Talk About Love*)
1999: Best Female Vocalist
1999: Best Selling Album (Foreign or Domestic) (*Let's Talk About Love*)
1999: Best Selling Francophone Album (*S'il suffisait d'aimer*)
1999: International Achievement Award
1997: Best Selling Album (Foreign or Domestic) (*Falling Into You*)
1997: Best Selling Francophone Album (*Live a Paris*)
1997: Female Vocalist of the Year
1997: International Achievement Award
1996: Album of the Year (*Colour of My Love*)
1996: Best Selling Francophone Album (*D'eux*)
1995: Best Selling Album (Foreign or Domestic) (*Colour of My Love*)
1994: Female Vocalist of the Year
1993: Best Dance Recording ("Love Can Move Mountains" – Club Mix)
1993: Best Selling Francophone Album (*Dion chante Plamondon*)
1993: Female Vocalist of the Year
1993: Single of the Year ("Beauty and the Beast" – with Peabo Bryson)
1992: Female Vocalist of the Year
1991: Album of the Year (*Unison*)
1991: Female Vocalist of the Year

›› DOWNHERE (4)

2012: Contemporary Christian/Gospel Album of the Year (*On the Altar of Love*)
2009: Contemporary Christian/Gospel Album of the Year (*Ending Is Beginning*)
2007: Contemporary Christian/Gospel Album of the Year (*Wide-Eyed and Mystified*)
2002: Best Gospel Album – (*Downhere*)

›› KEVIN DOYLE (3)

1999: Best Recording Engineer (Stanstill, Various Artists; "Soul On Soul," Amy Sky)

1994: Recording Engineer of the Year ("Old Cape Cod," "Cry Me A River," Anne Murray)

1990: Recording Engineer of the Year ("Black Velvet," Alannah Myles)

»DRAKE (4)

2013: Video of the Year (Director X – HYFR, DRAKE)

2012: Rap Recording of the Year ("Take Care")

2010: New Artist of the Year

2010: Rap Recording of the Year ("So Far Gone")

»SAM DUNN (2)

2011: Music DVD of the Year (Rush, Scot McFadyen, Sam Dunn, Pegi Cecconi, Noah Segal, Shelley Nott, John Virant – *Rush: Beyond the Lighted Stage*)

2010: Music DVD of the Year (Iron Maiden, Sam Dunn, Scott McFadyen, Rod Smallwood, Stefan Demetriou, Andy Taylor – *Iron Maiden Flight 666*, Iron Maiden)

»CHARLES DUTOIT (7)

1997: Best Classical Album: Vocal or Choral Performance (Choeur et orchestra symphonique de Montréal , Charles Dutoit, Conductor – Berlioz : *La Damnation de Faust*)

1996: Best Classical Album : Large Ensemble or Soloist with Large Ensemble Accompaniment (Orchestre symphonique de Montréal, Charles Dutoit, Conductor – Shostakovich: *Symphonies 5 & 9*)

1995: Best Classical Album : Vocal or Choral Performance (Vocal Soloists, Choeur et Orchestre symphonique de Montréal, Charles Dutoit, Conductor – Berlioz: *Les Troyens*)

1992: Best Classical Album : Large Ensemble or Soloists with Large Ensemble Accompaniment (Orchestre symphonique de Montréal, Charles Dutoit, Conductor – Debussy: *Pelleas et Melisande*)

1989: Best Classical Album: Large Ensemble or Soloist with Large Ensemble Accompaniment (Orchestre symphonique de Montréal, Charles Dutoit, Conductor – Bartok: *Concerto for Orchestra; Music for Strings and Percussion and Celesta*).

1985: Best Classical Album – Large Ensemble (Orchestre symphonique de Montréal, Charles Dutoit, Conductor – Ravel: *Ma mere l'oye/Pavane pour un infant debunte/Tombeau de Couperin and Valses nobles et sentimentale*).

1982: Best Classical Album of the Year (Orchestre symphonique de Montréal, Charles Dutoit, Conductor – Ravel: *Daphnis et Chloe*).

»PHIL DWYER (2)

2012: Contemporary Jazz Album of the Year (Phil Dwyer Orchestra featuring Mark Fewer, *Changing Seasons*)

1994: Best Mainstream Jazz Album (Dave Young/Phil Dwyer Quartet, *Fables and Dreams*)

»EDDIE EASTMAN (2)

1983: Country Male Vocalist of the Year

1981: Country Male Vocalist of the Year

»JAMES EHNES (7)

2013: Classical Album of the Year: Large Ensemble or Soloist with Large Ensemble Accompaniment (Tchaikovsky: *Violin Concerto*)

2009: Classical Album of the Year: Solo or Chamber Ensemble (*Homage*)

2008: Classical Album of the Year: Large Ensemble or Soloist with Large Ensemble Accompaniment (James Ehnes, Bramwell Tovey, Vancouver Symphony Orchestra – Korngold, Barber & Walton Violin Concertos)

2007: Classical Album of the Year: Large Ensemble or Soloist with Large Ensemble Accompaniment (James Ehnes, Mozart Anniversary Orchestra – Mozart: *Violin Concerti*)

2003: Classical Album of the Year: Large Ensemble or Soloist with Large Ensemble Accompaniment (James Ehnes, Mario Bernardi, Orchestre symphonique de Montréal – Bruch Concertos: *Vol II*)

2002: Classical Album of the Year: Large Ensemble or Soloist with Large Ensemble Accompaniment (James Ehnes, violin, Orchestre symphonique de Québec, Yoav Talmi, Conductor – Concert Français/ French Showpieces)

2001: Best Classical Album: Solo or Chamber Ensemble (Bach: *The Six Sonatas & Partitas for Solo Violin*)

»SHIRLEY EIKHARD (2)

1974: Best Country Female Artist
1973: Female Country Singer of the Year

»EMINEM (2)

2003: International Album of the Year (*The Eminem Show*)
2001: Best Selling Album – Foreign or Domestic (*The Marshall Mathers LP*)

»BRUCE FAIRBAIRN (4)

2000: Canadian Music Hall of Fame
1990: Producer of the Year (Pump, Aerosmith)
1982: Producer of the Year ("Working For the Weekend," "It's Over" by Loverboy, co-producer, Paul Dean)
1980: Producer of the Year (*Armageddon*, Prism)

»FATHEAD (2)

2008: Blues Album of the Year (*Building Full of Blues*)
1999: Best Blues Album (*Blues Weather*)

»STEPHEN FEARING (2)

2007: Roots & Traditional Album of the Year: Solo (*Yellowjacket*)
2000: Best Roots & Traditional Album: Group (Blackie and the Rodeo Kings, *Kings of Love*)

»FEIST (11)

2012: Adult Alternative Album of the Year (*Metals*)
2012: Artist of the Year
2012: Music DVD of the Year (Anthony Seck, Jannie McInnes, Chip Sutherland for Feist: *Look At What the Light Did Now* by Feist)
2009: Video of the Year (Feist, Anthony Seck for "Honey Honey" by Feist)
2008: Album of the Year (*The Reminder*)
2008: Artist of the Year
2008: Pop Album of the Year (*The Reminder*)
2008: Single of the Year ("1234")
2008: Songwriter of the Year ("My Moon My Man" – Co-writer Gonzales; "1234" – Co-writer Sally Seltmann; "I Feel It All" by Feist)
2005: Alternative Album of the Year (*Let It Die*)
2005: New Artist of the Year

»GERALD FINLEY (2)

2011: Classical Album of the Year (*Great Operatic Arias*)
1999: Best Classical Album: Vocal or Choral Performance (Gerald Finley, baritone; Stephen Rails, piano – *Songs of Travel*)

»MALCOLM FORSYTH (3)

1998: Best Classical Composition ("Electra Rising," Electra Rising, Music of Malcolm Forsyth)
1995: Best Classical Composition ("Sketches from Natal," Milhaud – Maurice Forsyth & Sowande, CBC Vancouver Orchestra)
1987: Best Classical Composition ("Atayoskewin," Forsyth-Freedman)

»DAVID FOSTER (6)

1998: Canadian Music Hall of Fame
1989: Instrumental Artist of the Year
1987: Instrumental Artist of the Year
1986: Instrumental Artist of the Year
1986: Producer of the Year (*St. Elmo's Fire Soundtrack*, Various Artists)
1985: Producer of the Year (*Chicago 17, Chicago*)

»GEORGE FOX (3)

1992: Country Male Vocalist of the Year
1991: Country Male Vocalist of the Year
1990: Country Male Vocalist of the Year

»DAVID FRANCEY (3)

2008: Roots & Traditional Album of the Year: Solo (*Right of Passage*)
2004: Roots & Traditional Album of the Year: Solo (*Skating Rink*)
2002: Best Roots & Traditional Album: Solo (*Far End of Summer*)

»MIKE FRASER (2)

1992: Recording Engineer of the Year ("Thunderstruck," "Money Talks," The Razor's Edge, AC/DC)
1989: Recording Engineer of the Year ("Calling America," "Different Drummer", Tom Cochrane & Red Rider)

›› NELLY FURTADO (10)

2007: Album of the Year (*Loose*)
2007: Artist of the Year
2007: JUNO Fan Choice Award
2007: Pop Album of the Year (*Loose*)
2007: Single of the Year ("Promiscuous" by Nelly Furtado ft Timbaland)
2004: Single of the Year ("Powerless (Say What You Want)")
2001: Best New Solo Artist
2001: Best Producer (Gerald Eaton/Brian West/Nelly Furtado for "I'm Like A Bird," "Turn Off the Lights" by Nelly Furtado)
2001: Best Single ("I'm Like A Bird")
2001: Best Songwriter ("Turn Off the Light," "I'm Like A Bird" and "... On the Radio (Remember the Days)")

›› ANDRÉ GAGNON (3)

1995: Instrumental Artist of the Year
1978: Instrumental Artist of the Year
1977: Best Selling Album (*Neiges*)

›› KARINA GAUVIN (2)

2013: Classical Album of the Year: Vocal or Choral Performance (*Prima Donna*)
2001: Best Classical Album: Vocal or Choral Perfroamcne (Karina Gauvin, Russell Braun, Les Violons du Roy – G.F. Handel: *Apollo e Dafne Silete Venti*)

›› GHETTO CONCEPT (2)

1996: Best Rap Recording ("E-Z on the Motion")
1995: Best Rap Recording ("Certified")

›› NICK GILDER (2)

1979: Best Selling Single ("Hot Child In the City")
1979: Most Promising Male Vocalist of the Year

›› GLASS TIGER (5)

1989: Canadian Entertainer of the Year
1987: Single of the Year ("Someday")
1986: Album of the Year ("The Thin Red Line")
1986: Most Promising Group of the Year
1986: Single of the Year ("Don't Forget Me (When I'm Gone)")

›› MATTHEW GOOD (4)

2011: Rock Album of the Year (*Vancouver*)
2003: Video of the Year (Ante Kovac & Matthew Good – "Weapon," Matthew Good)
2000: Best Group
2000: Best Rock Album (*Beautiful Midnight*)

›› GLENN GOULD (4)

1984: Best Classical Album of the Year (Brahms: Ballades Op. 10, Rhapsodies Op. 79)
1983: Best Classical Album of the Year (Bach: *The Goldberg Variations*)
1983: Canadian Music Hall of Fame
1979: Best Classical Album of the Year (Glenn Gould & Roxolana Roslak – *Hindersmith, Das Marienleben*)

›› DALLAS GREEN (2)

2012: Songwriter of the Year (Dallas Green – "Fragile Bird," "We Found Each Other," "Weightless," Little Hell, City and Colour)
2009: Songwriter of the Year (Dallas Green – "Waiting...," "Sleeping Sickness," "The Girl," City and Colour)

›› DAVID GREENE (2)

1980: Recording Engineer of the Year (Hoffert: *Concerto for Contemporary Violin*)
1978: Recording Engineer of the Year (*Big Band Jazz*, Rob McConnell & the Boss Brass)

›› GRT OF CANADA (2)

1974: Canadian Content Company of the Year
1972: Canadian Content Company of the Year

›› JACK GRUNSKY (3)

2007: Children's Album of the Year (*My Beautiful World*)
2001: Best Children's Album (*Sing & Dance*)
1993: Best Children's Album (*Waves of Wonder*)

›› EMILY HAINES (2)

2010: Alternative Album of the Year (*Metric, Fantasies*)
2010: Group of the Year (*Metric*)

›› MARC-ANDRÉ HAMELIN (7)

2012: Classical Album of the Year: Solo or Chamber Ensemble (*Liszt Piano Sonata*)

2008: Classical Album of the Year: Solo or Chamber Ensemble (*Alkan Concerto for Solo Piano*)

2006: Classical Album of the Year: Solo of Chamber Ensemble (Albéniz: *Iberia*)

2003: Classical Album of the Year: Solo or Chamber Ensemble (Liszt: *Paganini Studies & Schubert March Transcriptions*)

1998: Best Classical Album: Solo or Chamber Ensemble (*Marc-André Hamelin Plays Franz Liszt*)

1997: Best Classical Album: Solo or Chamber Ensemble (Scriabin: *The Complete Piano Sonatas*)

1996: Best Classical Album: Solo or Chamber Ensemble (Marc-André Hamelin, piano – Alkan: *Grand Sonate/Sonatine/Le festin d'Esope*)

›› SUSAN HAMMOND (5)

2002: Best Children's Album (*A Classical Kids Christmas*)

1999: Best Children's Album (Susan Hammond's Classical Kids – *Mozart's Magnificent Voyage*)

1994: Best Children's Album (Susan Hammond/ Classical Kids – *Tchaikovsky Discovers America*)

1992: Best Children's Album (Classical Kids: Susan Hammond, producer – *Vivaldi's Ring of Mystery*)

1990: Best Children's Album (Susan Hammond/ Barbara Nichol – *Beethoven Lives Upstairs*)

›› HAGOOD HARDY (3)

1977: Instrumental Artist of the Year
1976: Composer of the Year ("The Homecoming")
1976: Instrumental Artist of the Year

›› SARAH HARMER (2)

2007: Music DVD of the Year (Sarah Harmer, Andy Keen, Patrick Sambrook, Bryan Bean – Escarpment Blues, Sarah Harmer)

2005: Adult Alternative Album of the Year (*All Of Our Names*)

›› OFRA HARNOY (5)

1994: Instrumental Artist of the Year
1993: Instrumental Artist of the Year
1991: Instrumental Artist of the Year

1989: Best Classical Album: Solo or Chamber Ensemble (Schubert: *Arpeggione Sonata*)

1987: Best Classical Album: Solo or Chamber Ensemble (The Orford String Quartet, Ofra Harnoy, Cello – Schubert, Quintet in C)

›› COREY HART (2)

1985: Single of the Year ("Never Surrender")

1984: Best Video (Rob Quartly, Corey Hart – "Sunglasses at Night," Corey Hart)

›› HATIRAS (2)

2006: Dance Recording of the Year (Hatiras & Macca featuring Shawna B., "Spanish Fly")

2002: Best Dance Recording ("Space Invader")

›› CHRISTOS HATZIS (2)

2008: Classical Composition of the Year ("Constantinople")

2006: Classical Compoisition of the Year ("String Quartet No. 1 – The Awakening")

›› RONNIE HAWKINS (2)

1996: Walt Grealis Special Achievement Award
1982: Country Male Vocalist of the Year

›› CRYSTAL HEALD (2)

1998: Best Album Design (John Rummen – Creative Director/Graphic Artist, Crystal Heald, Graphic Artist, Stephen Chung, Andrew MacNaughtan, Justin Zivojinovich, Photographers – *Songs of a Circling Spirit*, Tom Cochrane)

1997: Best Album Design (John Rummen, Creative Director; Crystal Heald, Graphic Artist – Decadence, Ten Years of Nettwerk, Various Artists)

›› HEDLEY (2)

2012: Pop Album of the Year (*Storms*)

2011: Video of the Year (Hedley, Kyle Davison, director – "Perfect")

›› BEN HEPPNER (3)

2002: Best Classical Album: Vocal or Choral Performance (*Airs Français*)

2000: Best Classical Album: Vocal or Choral

Performance (*German Romantic Opera*)

1996: Best Classical Album: Vocal or Choral Performance (Ben Heppner, Tenor; Toronto Symphony Orchestra, Andrew Davis, Conductor – *Ben Heppner sings Richard Strauss*)

ANGELA HEWITT (3)

2005: Classical Album of the Year: Solo or Chamber Ensemble (Bach: *The English Suites*)

2002: Best Classical Album: Solo or Chamber Ensemble (Bach *Arrangements*)

1999: Best Classical Album: Solo or Chamber Ensemble (Bach: *Well-Tempered Clavier – Book 1*)

DAN HILL (5)

1979: Composer of the Year (Dan Hill, co-composer Barry Mann – "Sometimes When We Touch," Dan Hill)

1978: Best Selling Album (*Longer Fuse*)

1978: Composer of the Year (Dan Hill, co-composer Barry Mann – "Sometimes When We Touch," Dan Hill)

1978: Male Vocalist of the Year

1976: Most Promising Male Vocalist of the Year

BRIAN HOWES (2)

2012: Jack Richardson Producer of the Year ("Heaven's Gonna Wait," Storms, Hedley; "Trying Not To Love You," co-producer Nickelback – *Here and Now*, Nickelback)

2007: Jack Richardson Producer of the Year ("Trip," Hedley; "Lips of an Angel," Hinder.)

TERRY JACKS (4)

1975: Best Selling Single ("Seasons In the Sun")

1974: Contemporary Single of the Year ("Seasons In the Sun")

1974: Male Vocalist of the Year

1974: Pop Music Single of the Year ("Seasons In the Sun")

JACKSOUL (Haydain Neale) (3)

2010: R&B/Soul Recording of the Year ("Lonesome Highway")

2007: R&B/Soul Recording of the Year (mySOUL)

2001: Best R&B/Soul Recording (*Sleepless*)

COLIN JAMES (6)

1999: Best Producer (Colin James, co-producer, Joe Hardy – "Let's Shout," "C'mon With the C'mon," Colin James)

1998: Best Blues Album (*National Steel*)

1996: Male Vocalist of the Year

1991: Male Vocalist of the Year

1991: Single of the Year ("Just Came Back")

1989: Most Promising Male Vocalist of the Year

CARLY RAE JEPSEN (3)

2013: Album of the Year (*Kiss*)

2013: Pop Album of the Year (*Kiss*)

2013: Single of the Year ("Call Me Maybe")

OLIVER JONES (2)

2009: Traditional Jazz Album of the Year (*Second Time Around*)

1986: Best Jazz Album (*Lights of Burgundy*)

CONNIE KALDOR (3)

2005: Children's Album of the Year (*A Poodle in Paris*)

2004: Children's Album of the Year (*A Duck in New York City*)

1989: Best Children's Album (Connie Kaldor & Carmen Champagne – *Lullaby Berceuse*)

GREG KEELOR (11)

2009: Music DVD of the Year (Blue Rodeo, Christopher Mills, Geoff McLean for *Blue Road* by Blue Rodeo)

2008: Adult Alternative Album of the Year (*Small Miracles* by Blue Rodeo)

2008: Group of the Year (Blue Rodeo)

2008: Video of the Year (Blue Rodeo, Christopher Mills for "C'mon" by Blue Rodeo)

2005: Music DVD of the Year (Ron Mann, Blue Rodeo for *In Stereovision* by Blue Rodeo)

1996: Group of the Year (Blue Rodeo)

1991: Group of the Year (Blue Rodeo)

1990: Group of the Year (Blue Rodeo)

1989: Best Video (Michael Buckley, Blue Rodeo for "Try" by Blue Rodeo)

1989: Group of the Year (Blue Rodeo)

1989: Single of the Year ("Try" by Blue Rodeo)

ANDY KEEN (2)

2013: Music DVD of the Year (Andy Keen, Bernie Breen, Patrick Sambrook, Shawn Marino, The Tragically Hip – *Bobcaygeon*, The Tragically Hip)

2007: Music DVD of the Year (Sarah Harmer, Andy Keen, Patrick Sambrook, Bryan Bean – *Escarpment Blues*, Sarah Harmer)

KINNEY MUSIC OF CANADA (2)

– see also WEA Music of Canada Ltd.

1972: Record Company of the Year
1972: Top Record Company in Promotional Activities

K'NAAN (3)

2010: Artist of the Year
2010: Songwriter of the Year (B. Mars, P. Lawrence & J. Daval, co-writers – "Wavin' Flag"; G. Eaton & B. West, co-writers – "Take A Minute"; G. Eaton & B. West, K'naan, co-writers – "Rap Gets Jealous")

k-os (3)

2005: Rap Recording of the Year ("Joyful Rebellion")
2005: Single of the Year ("Crabbuckit")
2005: Video of the Year (*The Love Movement* featuring k-os & Micah Meisner – "B-Boy Stance," k-os)

DIANA KRALL (8)

2007: Vocal Jazz Album of the Year (*From This Moment On*)
2006: Vocal Jazz Album of the Year (*Christmas Songs*)
2005: Vocal Jazz Album of the Year (*The Girl In the Other Room*)
2003: Vocal Jazz Album of the Year (*Live In Paris*)
2002: Best Album (*The Look of Love*)
2002: Best Artist
2002: Best Vocal Jazz Album (*The Look of Love*)
2000: Best Vocal Jazz Album (*When I Look Into Your Eyes*)

CHANTAL KREVIAZUK (2)

2000: Best Female Artist
2000: Best Pop/Adult Album (*Colour Moving and Still*)

LA BOTTINE SOURIANTE (3)

2002: Best Roots & Traditional Album: Group (*Cordial*)
1993: Best Roots & Traditional Album (*Jusqu'aux p'tites heures*)
1990: Best Roots & Traditional Album (*Je voudrais changer d'chapeau*)

JEANNE LAMON (5)

2005: Classical Album of the Year: Large Ensemble or Soloist with Large Ensemble Accompaniment (Jean Lamon, Tafelmusik Baroque Orchestra – *Dardanus/ Le temple de la gloire: Music of Jean-Phillipe Rameau*)
1999: Best Classical Album: Large Ensemble or Soloist with Large Ensemble Accompaniment (Tafelmusik, Jeanne Lamon: Musical Director – Handel: *Music for the Royal Fireworks*)
1995: Best Classical Album: Large Ensemble or Soloist with Large Ensemble Accompaniment (Bach: *Brandenburg Concertos Nos. 1-6*)
1994: Best Classical Album: Large Ensemble or Soloist with Large Ensemble Accompaniment (Tafelmusik, Jeanne Lamon: Director – Handel: *Concerti Grossi, Op. 3, No. 1-6*)
1993: Best Classical Album: Large Ensemble or Soloists with Large Ensemble Accompaniment (Tafelmusik with Alan Curtis, Catherine Robbin, Linda Maguire, Nancy Argenta, Ingrid Attrot and Mel Braun; Jeanne Lamon, Leader – Handel: *Excerpts from Floridante*)

k.d. lang (9)

2013: Canadian Music Hall of Fame
1993: Album of the Year (*Ingenue*)
1993: Producer of the Year (k.d. lang & Ben Mink, co-producer Greg Penny – "Constant Craving," "The Mind of Love" – k.d. lang
1993: SOCAN JUNO For Songwriter of the Year (k.d. lang/Ben Mink)
1990: Country Female Vocalist of the Year
1989: Country Female Vocalist of the Year
1989: Female Vocalist of the Year
1987: Country Female Vocalist of the Year
1985: Most Promising Female Vocalist of the Year

»DANIEL LANOIS (8)

2011: Jack Richardson Producer of the Year ("Hitchhiker," Neil Young; "I Believe In You," Black Dub)

2009: Jack Richardson Producer of the Year ("Here Is What Is," "Not Fighting Anymore," Daniel Lanois)

2006: Instrumental Album of the Year (*Belladonna*)

2002: Canadian Music Hall of Fame

2002: Jack Richardson Best Producer (Daniel Lanois, co-producer Brian Eno – "Beautiful Day," "Elevation," U2)

1990: Most Promising Male Vocalist

1989: Producer of the Year (Daniel Lanois & Robbie Robertson – "Big Sky," "Somewhere Down the Crazy River," Robbie Robertson)

1987: Producer of the Year (Daniel Lanois, co-producer Peter Gabriel – So, Peter Gabriel and The Joshua Tree, U2)

»AVRIL LAVIGNE (7)

2005: Artist of the Year

2005: JUNO Fan Choice Award

2005: Pop Album of the Year (Under My Skin)

2003: Album of the Year (Let Go)

2003: New Artist of the Year

2003: Pop Album of the Year (Let Go)

2003: Single of the Year ("Complicated")

»LEAHY (3)

1999: Best Country Group or Duo

1998: Best New Group

1998: Instrumental Artist of the Year

»LES VIOLONS DU ROY (3)

2007: Classical Album of the Year: Solo or Chamber Ensemble (Les Violons de Roy, Jean-Marie Zeitouni – *Piazzolla*)

2003: Classical Album of the Year : Vocal or Choral Performance (*Mozart Requiem*)

2001: Best Classical Album: Vocal or Choral Performance (Handel: *Apollo e Dafne*)

»LE VENT DU NORD (2)

2011: Roots & Traditional Album of the Year: Group (*La part du feu*)

2004: Roots & Traditional Album of the Year : Group (*Mauditte Moisson!*)

»EXCO LEVI (2)

2013: Reggae Recording of the Year (*Storms of Life*)

2012: Reggae Recording of the Year (*Bleaching Shop*)

»GORDON LIGHTFOOT (13)*

1986: Canadian Music Hall of Fame

1978: Folksinger of the Year

1977: Composer of the Year ("The Wreck of the Edmund Fitzgerald")

1977: Folksinger of the Year

1976: Folksinger of the Year

1975: Folksinger of the Year

1975: Male Vocalist of the Year

1974: Folk Album of the Year (*Old Dan's Records*)

1973: Composer of the Year

1973: Male Vocalist of the Year

1972: Male Vocalist of the Year

1971: Top Male Vocalist

1970: Top Folksinger (or Group)

»LIGHTHOUSE (2)

1973: Vocal Instrumental Group of the Year

1972: Outstanding Performance of the Year: Group

»COLIN LINDEN (3)

2002: Best Blues Album (*Big Mouth*)

2000: Best Roots & Traditional Album: Group (Blackie and the Rodeo Kings – *Kings of Love*)

1994: Best Blues/Gospel Album (*South at Eight/North at Nine*)

»OSCAR LOPEZ (2)

2005: Instrumental Album of the Year (*Mi Destino/My Destiny*)

2002: Best Instrumental Album (*Armando's Fire*)

»MYRNA LORRIE (2)

1972: Female Country Singer of the Year

1971: Top Country Singer Female

»LOUIS LORTIE (3)

1994: Best Classical Album: Solo or Chamber Ensemble (Beethoven: *Piano Sonatas, Opus 10, No. 1-3*)

1993: Best Classical Album: Solo or Chamber Ensemble (Beethoven: *Piano Sonatas*)

1992: Best Classical Album: Solo or Chamber Ensemble (Liszt: *Annees de Pelerinage*)

»ALEXINA LOUIE (2)

2000: Best Classical Composition ("Shattered Night, Shivering Stars")

1989: Best Classical Composition ("Songs of Paradise," Songs of Paradise)

»LOVE & SAS (2)

1993: Best R&B/Soul Recording (*Once In a Lifetime*)

1992: Best R&B/Soul Recording (*Call My Name*)

»LOVE INC. (2)

2001: Best Dance Recording ("Into the Night")

1999: Best Dance Recording ("Broken Bones")

»LOVERBOY (7)

2009: Canadian Music Hall of Fame

1984: Group of the Year

1983: Album of the Year (*Get Lucky*)

1983: Group of the Year

1982: Album of the Year (*Loverboy*)

1982: Group of the Year

1982: Single of the Year ("Turn Me Loose")

»LUBA (3)

1987: Female Vocalist of the Year

1986: Female Vocalist of the Year

1985: Female Vocalist of the Year

»ASHLEY MACISAAC (3)

1997: Instrumental of the Year

1996: Best New Solo Artist

1996: Best Roots & Traditional Album: Solo (*Hi How Are You Today?*)

»ANDREW MACNAUGHTAN (4)

2004: Album Design of the Year (Garnet Armstrong/ Susan Mchalek, Director/Designer, Andrew MacNaughtan, photographer – *Love Is the Only Soldier*, Jann Arden)

2004: Music DVD of the Year (*Rush*, Andrew MacNaughtan/Dan Catullo, directors; Allan Weinrib/Pegi Cecconi/Ray Danniels, producers)

1998: Best Album Design (John Rummen, Creative Director/Graphic Artist, Crystal Heald, Graphic Artist, Stephen Chung, Andrew MacNaughtan, Justin Zivojinovich, Photographers – *Songs of a Circling Spirit*, Tom Cochrane)

1995: Best Album Design (Andrew MacNaughtan, Our Lady Peace – *Naveed*, Our Lady Peace)

»RITA MACNEIL (3)

1991: Country Female Vocalist of the Year

1990: Female Vocalist of the Year

1987: Most Promising Female Vocalist of the Year

»MADAGASCAR SLIM (3)

2005: World Music Album of the Year, presented in honour of Billy Bryans. (Mighty Popo, Madagascar Slim, Donné Robert, Alpha Ya Ya Diallo, Adam Solomon, Pa Joe – *African Guitar Summit*)

2001: Best Roots & Traditional Album: Group (*Tri-Continental*, Tri-Continental)

2000: Best Global Album (*Omnisource*)

»MADONNA (2)

1991: International Single of the Year (*Vogue*)

1987: International Album of the Year (*True Blue*)

»MAESTRO FRESH-WES (2)

1991: Best Video (Joel Goldberg, Maestro Fresh-Wes – "Drop the Needle," Maestro Fresh-Wes)

1991: Rap Recording of the Year (*Symphony in Effect*)

»MARGARET MALANDRUCCOLO (2)

2003: Album Design of the Year (Steve Goode, director/designer; Marina Dempster, Nelson Garcia and Margaret Malandruccolo, illustrator/ photographer – *exit*, k-os)

2001: Best Album Design (Stuart Chatwood, creative director; Antine Moonen, graphic artist; James St. Laurent, Margaret Malandruccolo, Nik Sarros, photographer – *Tangents: The Tea Party Collection*, The Tea Party)

»CHARLIE MAJOR (3)

1996: Country Male Vocalist of the Year

1995: Country Male Vocalist of the Year

1994: Country Male Vocalist of the Year

DAN MANGAN (2)

2012: Alternative Album of the Year (*Oh Fortune*)
2012: New Artist of the Year

PIERRE MARCHAND (3)

2004: Songwriter of the Year (Sarah McLachlan, Pierre Marchand – "World On Fire," "Fallen," "Stupid")
1998: Producer of the Year (Building A Mystery, Sarah McLachlan)
1998: Songwriter of the Year (Sarah McLachlan, Pierre Marchand – "Building A Mystery," Sarah McLachlan

SHAWN MARINO (2)

2013: Music DVD of the Year (Andy Keen, Bernie Breen, Patrick Sambrook, Shawn Marino, The Tragically Hip for *Bobcaygeon*)
2006: Music DVD of the Year (The Tragically Hip, Pierre Lamoureux, Christopher Mills, Gord Downie, Allan Reid, Shawn Marino for *Hipeponymouse*)

GENE MARTYNEC (2)

1981: Producer of the Year ("Tokyo," Bruce Cockburn; "High School Confidential," Carole Pope and Rough Trade)
1973: Best Produced Single ("Last Song," Edward Bear)

MATTHEW MCCAULEY (2)

1978: Producer of the Year (Matthew McCauley/Fred Mollin – *Longer Fuse*, Dan Hill)
1978: Producer of the Year: Single (Matthew McCauley/Fred Mollin – "Sometimes When We Touch," Dan Hill)

ROB MCCONNELL (6)

2001: Best Traditional Jazz Album – Instrumental (*The Rob McConnell Tentet*)
1997: Canadian Music Hall of Fame
1992: Best Jazz Album (*The Brass Is Back*, Rob McConnell & the Boss Brass)
1984: Best Jazz Album (*All In Good Time*, Rob McConnell & the Boss Brass)
1981: Best Jazz Album (*Present Perfect*, Rob McConnell & the Boss Brass)

1978: Best Jazz Album (*Big Band Jazz*, Rob McConnell & the Boss Brass)

SCOT MCFADYEN (2)

2011: Music DVD of the Year (Rush, Scot McFadyen, Sam Dunn, Pegi Cecconi, Noah Segal, Shelley Nott, John Virant – *Rush: Beyond the Lighted Stage*)
2010: Music DVD of the Year (Iron Maiden, Sam Dunn, Scott McFadyen, Rod Smallwood, Stefan Demetriou, Andy Taylor – *Iron Maiden Flight 666*, Iron Maiden)

KATE & ANNA MCGARRIGLE (2)

1999: Best Roots & Traditional Album: Group (*The McGarrigle Hour*)
1997: Best Roots & Traditional Album: Group (*Matapedia*)

LOREENA MCKENNITT (2)

1995: Best Roots & Traditional Album (*The Mask and Mirror*)
1992: Best Roots & Traditional Album (*The Visit*)

BOB & DOUG MCKENZIE (2)

1984: Comedy Album of the Year (*Strange Brew*)
1982: Comedy Album of the Year (*The Great White North*)

SARAH MCLACHLAN (8)

2004: Pop Album of the Year (*Afterglow*)
2004: Songwriter of the Year (Sarah McLachlan, Pierre Marchand – "World On Fire," "Fallen," "Stupid.")
2000: International Achievement Award
1998: Album of the Year (*Surfacing*)
1998: Female Vocalist of the Year
1998: Single of the Year ("Building A Mystery")
1998: Songwriter of the Year (Sarah McLachlan, Pierre Marchand – "Building A Mystery," Sarah McLachlan)
1992: Best Video (Phil Kates, Sarah McLachlan – "Into the Fire," Sarah McLachlan)

MURRAY MCLAUCHLAN (11)

1989: Country Male Vocalist of the Year
1986: Country Male Vocalist of the Year

1985: Country Male Vocalist of the Year
1984: Country Male Vocalist of the Year
1980: Country Male Vocalist of the Year
1979: Folksinger of the Year
1977: Country Male Vocalist of the Year
1976: Country Male Vocalist of the Year
1974: Best Songwriter
1974: Country Single of the Year ("Farmer's Song")
1974: Folk Single of the Year ("Farmer's Song")

» MICHAEL MEISNER (2)

2006: Video of the Year (Buck 65, Micah Meisner, Rich Terfry – "Devil's Eyes," Buck 65)
2005: Video of the Year (*The Love Movement* featuring k-os & Micah Meisner – "B-Boy Stance," k-os)

» METALWOOD (2)

1999: Best Classical Composition (*Metalwood 2*)
1998: Best Contemporary Jazz Album (*Metalwood*)

» METRIC (3)

2013: Alternative Album of the Year (*Synthetica*)
2010: Alternative Album of the Year (*Fantasies*)
2010: Group of the Year

» SUSAN MICHALEK (2)

2006: CD/DVD Artwork Design of the Year (Rob Baker, Director/Illustrator; Garnet Armstrong, Director/Designer; Susan Michalek, Designer; Will Ruocco, Illustrator – *Hipeponymouse*, The Tragically Hip)
2004: Album Design of the Year (Garnet Armstrong, Susan Michalek, Director/Designer; Andrew MacNaughtan, Photographer – *Love Is the Only Soldier*, Jann Arden)

» DEREK MILLER (2)

2008: Aboriginal Recording of the Year (*The Dirty Looks*)
2003: Aboriginal Recording of the Year ("Lovesick Blues," Music Is the Medicine)

» CHRISTOPHER MILLS (3)

2009: Music DVD of the Year (Blue Rodeo, Christopher Mills, Geoff McLean – Blue Rodeo, Blue Rodeo)

2008: Video of the Year (Blue Rodeo, Christopher Mills – "C'mon," Blue Rodeo)
2006: Music DVD of the Year (The Tragically Hip, Pierre Lamoureux/Christopher Mills, Gord Downie/ Allan Reid/Shawn Marino – *Hipeponymouse*, The Tragically Hip)

» FRANK MILLS (2)

1981: Instrumental Artist of the Year
1980: Instrumental Artist of the Year

» BEN MINK (2)

1993: Producer of the Year (k.d. lang & Ben Mink, co-producer Greg Penny – "Constant Craving," "The Mind of Love," k.d. lang
1993: SOCAN JUNO for Songwriter of the Year (k.d. lang/Ben Mink)

» JONI MITCHELL (4)

2008: Jack Richardson Producer of the Year ("Hana," "Bad Dream," Joni Mitchell)
2001: Best Vocal Jazz Album
1981: Canadian Music Hall of Fame
1976: Female Vocalist of the Year

» KIM MITCHELL (3)

1990: Male Vocalist of the Year
1987: Album of the Year (*Shakin' Like A Human Being*)
1983: Most Promising Male Vocalist of the Year

» MOIST (2)

1998: Best Video (Javier Aguilera, Moist – "Gasoline," Moist)
1995: Best New Group

» FRED MOLLIN (2)

1978: Producer of the Year – Album (Matthew McCauley/Fred Mollin – *Longer Fuse*, Dan Hill)
1978: Producer of the Year – Single (Matthew McCauley/Fred Mollin – "Sometimes When We Touch," Dan Hill)

» OSKAR MORAWETZ (2)

2001: Best Classical Composition (*From the Diary of Anne Frank*)

1990: Best Classical Composition (*Concerto for Harp and Chamber Orchestra*)

➤➤ ALANIS MORISSETTE (13)

2009: Pop Album of the Year (*Flavors of Entanglement*)

2003: Jack Richardson Producer of the Year ("Hands Clean," "So Unsexy" – Alanis Morissette)

2000: Best Album (*Supposed Former Infatuation Junkie*)

2000: Best Video ("So Pure")

1997: International Achievement Award

1997: Single of the Year ("Ironic")

1997: Songwriter of the Year (Glen Ballard, Co-Songwriter)

1996: Album of the Year (*Jagged Little Pill*)

1996: Best Rock Album (*Jagged Little Pill*)

1996: Female Vocalist of the Year

1996: Single of the Year ("You Oughta Know")

1996: Songwriter of the Year

1992: Most Promising Female Vocalist of the Year (known as Alanis)

➤➤ MIKE MURLEY (3)

2013: Traditional Jazz Album of the Year (Murley Bickert Wallace, *Test of Time*)

2002: Best Traditional Jazz Album – Instrumental (Murley, Bickert & Wallace: *Live at the Senator*)

1991: Best Jazz Album (*Two Sides*)

➤➤ ANNE MURRAY (24)

1971: Top Female Vocalist

1972: Female Vocalist of the Year

1973: Female Vocalist of the Year

1974: Pop Music Album of the Year (*Danny's Song*)

1974: Country Female Vocalist of the Year

1975: Female Vocalist of the Year

1975: Country Female Vocalist of the Year

1976: Country Female Vocalist of the Year

1979: Female Vocalist of the Year

1979: Best Children's Album (*There's A Hippo In My Tub*)

1980: Single of the Year ("I Just Fall In Love Again")

1980: Female Vocalist of the Year

1980: Country Female Vocalist of the Year

1980: Album of the Year (*New Kind of Feeling*) – Sponsored by Music Canada

1981: Single of the Year ("Could I Have This Dance")

1981: Female Vocalist of the Year

1981: Country Female Vocalist of the Year

1981: Album of the Year (*Greatest Hits*) – Sponsored by Music Canada

1982: Female Vocalist of the Year

1982: Country Female Vocalist of the Year

1983: Country Female Vocalist of the Year

1984: Country Female Vocalist of the Year

1985: Country Female Vocalist of the Year

1993: Canadian Music Hall of Fame

➤➤ ALANNAH MYLES (3)

1990: Album of the Year (*Alannah Myles*)

1990: Most Promising Female Vocalist of the Year

1990: Single of the Year ("Black Velvet")

➤➤ BILLY NEWTON-DAVIS (4)

2008: Dance Recording of the Year (Billy Newton-Davis vs. Deadmau5 – "After Hours")

1990: Best R&B/Soul Recording ("Spellbound")

1986: Best R&B/Soul Recording ("Love Is A Contact Sport")

1986: Most Promising Male Vocalist of the Year

➤➤ NICKELBACK (12)

2009: Album of the Year (*Dark Horse*)

2009: Group of the Year

2009: JUNO Fan Choice Award

2006: Group of the Year

2006: Rock Album of the Year (*All the Right Reasons*)

2004: Group of the Year

2004: JUNO Fan Choice Award

2003: Songwriter of the Year (Chad Kroeger/Nickelback – "Hero," Chad Kroeger ft. Josey Scott; "Too Bad," "How You Remind Me" – Nickelback)

2002: Best Group

2002: Best Rock Album (*Silver Side Up*)

2002: Best Single ("How You Remind Me")

2001: Best New Group

➤➤ PAUL NORTHFIELD (2)

2000: Best Recording Engineer (Paul Northfield & Jagori Tanna – "Summertime in the Void," "When Did You Get Back From Mars?" I Mother Earth)

1997: Recording Engineer of the Year ("Another Sunday," I Mother Earth and "Leave It Alone," Moist)

>> KARDINAL OFFISHALL (3)

2009: Rap Recording of the Year ("Not 4 Sale")
2009: Single of the Year ("Dangerous")
1999: Best Rap Recording (Rascalz featuring Choclair, Kardinal Offishall, Thrust and Checkmate – "Northern Touch")

>> OLD MAN LUEDECKE (2)

2011: Roots & Traditional Album of the Year: Solo (*My Hands Are On Fire and Other Love Songs*)
2009: Roots & Traditional Album of the Year: Solo (*Proof of Love*)

>> ORCHESTRE SYMPHONIQUE DE MONTRÉAL (12)

2012: Classical Album of the Year: Large Ensemble or Soloists with Large Ensemble Accompaniment (Alexandra Da Costa/Orchestre symphonique de Montréal – Daugherty: *Fire and Blood*)
2009: Classical Album of the Year: Large Ensemble or Soloists with Large Ensemble Accompaniment (Orchestre symphonique de Montréal, Kent Nagano – Beethoven: *Ideals of the French Revolution*)
2003: Classical Album of the Year: Large Ensemble or Soloists with Large Ensemble Accompaniment (James Ehnes/Mario Bernardi/Orchestre symphonique de Montréal – Bruch Concertos: *Vol. 2*)
2000: Best Classical Album: Large Ensemble or Soloists with Large Ensemble Accompaniment (Respighi: *La Boutique fantasque*)
1997: Best Classical Album: Vocal or Choral Performance (Choeur et orchestra symphonique de Montréal, Charles Dutoit, Conductor – Berlioz: *La damnation de Faust*)
1996: Best Classical Album: Vocal or Choral Performance (Orchestra symphonique de Montréal, Charles Dutoit, Conductor – Shostakovich: *Symphonies 5 & 9*)
1995: Best Classical Album: Vocal or Choral Performance (Vocal Soloists, Choeur et Orchestre symphonique de Montréal, Charles Dutoit, Conductor – Berlioz: *Les Troyens*)
1992: Best Classical Album : Large Ensemble or Soloists with Large Ensemble Accompaniment (Orchestre symphonique de Montréal, Conductor – Debussy: *Pelleas et Melisande*)
1989: Best Classical Album: Large Ensemble or Soloists with Large Ensemble Accompaniment (Orchestra symphonique de Montréal, Charles Dutoit, Condusctor – Bartok: Concerto for Orchestra: *Music for Strings and Percussion and Celesta*)
1987: Best Classical Album: Large Ensemble or Soloists with Large Ensemble Accompaniment (Orchestre symphonique de Montréal, Charles Dutoit, Conductor – Holst: *The Planets*)
1985: Best Classical Album (Large Ensemble) (Orchestre Symphonique de Montréal, Charles Dutoit, Conductor – Ravel: *Ma mere l'oye/Pavane pour un infant debunte/Tombeau de Couperin and Valses nobles et sentimentale*)
1982: Best Classical Album of the Year (Orchestre symphonique de Montréal, Charles Dutoit, Conductor – Ravel: *Daphnis et Chloe*)

>> OUR LADY PEACE (4)

2003: Rock Album of the Year (*Gravity*)
1998: Rock Album of the Year (*Clumsy*)
1998: Group of the Year
1995: Best Album Design (Andrew MacNaughtan/Our Lady Peace – *Naveed*, Our Lady Peace)

>> PARACHUTE CLUB (4)

1987: Best Video (Ron Berti, Parachute Club – "Love Is Fire," Parachute Club)
1985: Group of the Year
1984: Most Promising Group of the Year
1984: Single of the Year ("Rise Up")

>> PAYOLA$ (2)

1983: Most Promising Group of the Year
1983: Single of the Year ("Eyes Of a Stranger")

>> FRED PENNER (2)

2003: Children's Album of the Year (*Sing with Fred*)
1989: Best Children's Album (*Fred Penner's Place*)

>> GREG PENNY (2)

1994: Producer of the Year (Steven MacKinnon, Marc Jordan, co-producer Greg Penny – "Waiting For a

Miracle," Marc Jordan)
1993: Producer of the Year (k.d. lang & Ben Mink, co-producer Greg Penny – "Constant Craving," "The Mind of Love," k.d. lang)

›› OSCAR PETERSON (2)

1987: Best Jazz Album (The Oscar Peterson Four, If You Could See Me Now)
1978: Canadian Music Hall of Fame

›› PINK FLOYD (2)

1981: International Album of the Year (*The Wall*)
1981: International Single of the Year ("Another Brick in the Wall")

›› CAROLE POPE (3)

1984: Female Vocalist of the Year
1983: Female Vocalist of the Year
1981: Most Promising Female Vocalist of the Year

›› PRAIRIE OYSTER (6)

1996: Country Group or Duo of the Year
1995: Country Group or Duo of the Year
1992: Country Group or Duo of the Year
1991: Country Group or Duo of the Year
1987: Country Group or Duo of the Year
1986: Country Group or Duo of the Year

›› RONNIE PROPHET (2)

1979: Country Male Vocalist of the Year
1978: Country Male Vocalist of the Year

›› QUALITY RECORDS (2)*

1971: Top Canadian Content Company
1970: Top Canadian Content Company

›› ROB QUARTLY (2)

1985: Best Video (Rob Quartly, Gowan – "You're A Strange Animal," Gowan)
1984: Best Video (Rob Quartly, Corey Hart – "Sunglasses At Night," Corey Hart

›› RAFFI (2)

1995: Best Children's Album (*Bananaphone*)
1990: Walt Grealis Special Achievement Award

›› RASCALZ (2)

1999: Best Rap Recording (Rascalz featuring Choclair, Kardinal Offishall, Thrust and Checkmate, Northern Touch)
1998: Best Rap Recording (*Cash Crop*)

›› JOHNNY REID (3)

2013: Country Album of the Year (*Fire It Up*)
2011: Country Album of the Year (*A Place Called Love*)
2010: Country Album of the Year (*Dance With Me*)

›› GINETTE RENO (4)*

2001: Best Selling Francophone Album (*Un Grand Noel d'amour*)
1973: Outstanding Performance of the Year Female
1972: Outstanding Performance of the Year Female
1970: Top Female Vocalist

›› KIM RICHARDSON (2)

1987: Best R&B/Soul Recording (*Peek-A-Boo*)
1986: Most Promising Female Vocalist of the Year

›› SAM ROBERTS aka SAM ROBERTS BAND (6)

2009: Artist of the Year
2009: Rock Album of the Year (*Love At the End of the World*)
2007: Video of the Year (Sam Roberts, Duplex aka Dave Pawsey and Jonathan Legris – "Bridge To Nowhere," Sam Roberts)
2004: Album of the Year (*We Were Born In A Flame*)
2004: Artist of the Year
2004: Rock Album of the Year (*We Were Born In A Flame*)

›› ROBBIE ROBERTSON (5)

1999: Best Music of Aboriginal Canada Recording (*Contact from the Underworld of Redboy*)
1995: Producer of the Year ("Skin Walker," "It Is a Good Day To Die," Robbie Robertson & the Red Road Ensemble
1989: Album of the Year (Robbie Robertson)
1989: Male Vocalist of the Year

JUNO WINNERS

▶▶ BOB ROCK (9)

2010: Jack Richardson Producer of the Year ("Haven't Met You Yet," "Baby (You've Got What It Takes)" – Michael Bublé)

2007: Canadian Music Hall of Fame

2005: Jack Richardson Producer of the Year ("Welcome To My Life," Simple Plan, "Some Kind of Monster," Metallica)

2000: Best Producer (Tal Bachman & Bob Rock – "She's So High," "If You Sleep," Tal Bachman)

1983: Composer of the Year (Bob Rock, Paul Hyde – "Eyes Of a Stranger," Payola$)

1983: Most Promising Group of the Year – (Payola$)

1983: Recording Engineer of the Year (*No Stranger To Danger*, Payola$)

1983: Single of the Year ("Eyes Of a Stranger," Payola$)

1982: Recording Engineer of the Year (Keith Stein, Bob Rock – "When It's Over," "It's Your Life," Loverboy)

▶▶ RENEE ROSNES (3)

2003: Traditional Jazz Album of the Year (*Life On Earth*)

1997: Best Mainstream Jazz Album (*Ancestors*)

1992: Best Jazz Album (*For the Moment*)

▶▶ JOHN RUMMEN (2)

1998: Best Album Design (John Rummen, Creative Director/Graphic Artist, Crystal Heald, Graphic Artist, Stephen Chung, Andrew MacNaughtan, Justin Zivojinovich, Photographers – *Songs of a Circling Spirit*, Tom Cochrane)

1997: Best Album Design (John Rummen, Creative Director; Crystal Heald, Graphic Artist – *Decadence*, Ten Years of Nettwerk, Various Artists)

▶▶ RUSH (9)

2013: Rock Album of the Year (*Clockwork Angels*)

2011: Music DVD of the Year (Rush, Scot McFadyen, Sam Dunn, Pegi Cecconi, Noah Segal, Shelley Nott, John Virant – *Rush: Beyond the Lighted Stage*)

2004: Music DVD of the Year (Rush, Andrew MacNaughtan, Dan Catullo: Directors; Allan Weinrib, Pegi Cecconi, Ray Danniels: Producers – *Rush in Rio*, Rush)

1994: Canadian Music Hall of Fame

1992: Hard Rock Album of the Year (*Roll the Bones*)

1991: Best Hard Rock/Metal Album (*Presto*)

1979: Group of the Year

1978: Group of the Year

1975: Most Promising Group of the Year

▶▶ SERENA RYDER (4)

2013: Adult Alternative Album of the Year (*Harmony*)

2010: Video of the Year (Serena Ryder, Marc Ricciardelli – "Little Bit of Red," Serena Ryder)

2009: Adult Alternative Album of the Year (*Is it o.k.*)

2008: New Artist of the Year

▶▶ DIMO SAFARI (2)

1986: Best Album Graphics (Hugh Syme/Dimo Safari – *Power Windows*, Rush)

1985: Best Album Graphics (Rob MacIntyre/Dimo Safari – *Strange Animal*, Gowan)

▶▶ BUFFY SAINTE-MARIE (3)

2009: Aboriginal Recording of the Year (*Running For the Drum*)

1997: Best Music of Aboriginal Canada Recording (*Up Where We Belong*)

1995: Canadian Music Hall of Fame

▶▶ PATRICK SAMBROOK (2)

2013: Music DVD of the Year (Andy Keen, Bernie Breen, Patrick Sambrook, Shawn Marino, The Tragically Hip – *Bobcaygeon*, The Tragically Hip)

2007: Music DVD of the Year (Sarah Harmer, Andy Keen, Patrick Sambrook, Bryan Bean – *Escarpment Blues*, Sarah Harmer)

▶▶ SATTALITES (2)

1996: Best Reggae Recording ("Now and Forever")

1990: Best Reggae/Calypso Recording ("It's Too Late To Turn Back Now")

▶▶ MICHAEL SCHADE (2)

2007: Classical Album of the Year: Vocal or Choral Performance (Isabel Bayrakdarian, Micahel Schade, Russell Braun, Canadian Opera Company Orchestra, Richard Bradshaw – Mozart: *Arie e Duetti*)

1998: Best Classical Album: Vocal or Choral Performance (Michael Schade, Tenor; Russell Braun, Baritone; Canadian Opera Company Orchestra, Richard Bradshaw – *Soirée française*)

R. MURRAY SCHAFER (4)

2011: Classical Composition of the Year (*Duo for Violin and Piano*)
2004: Classical Composition of the Year (*String Quartet No. 8*)
1993: Best Classical Composition (*Concerto for Flute and Orchestra*)
1991: Best Classical Composition (*String Quartet No. 5 – 'Rosalind'*)

BART SCHOALES (2)

1976: Best Album Graphics (*Joy Will Find A Way*)
1975: Best Album Graphics (*Night Vision*)

EDDIE SCHWARTZ (2)

1982: Most Promising Male Vocalist of the Year
1981: Composer of the Year ("Hit Me With Your Best Shot," Pat Benatar)

ANTHONY SECK (2)

2012: Music DVD of the Year (Anthony Seck, Jannie McInnes, Chip Sutherland – Feist: *Look At What the Light Did Now*, Feist)
2009: Video of the Year (Feist, Anthony Seck – "Honey Honey," Feist

RON SEXSMITH (2)

2005: Songwriter of the Year ("Whatever It Takes," "Not About To Lose," "Hard Bargain," Ron Sexsmith)
1998: Best Roots & Traditional Album: Solo (*Other Songs*)

SHARON, LOIS & BRAM (3)

2000: Best Children's Album (*Skinnamarink TV*)
1981: Best Children's Album (*Singing 'n Swinging*)
1980: Children's Album of the Year (*Smorgasbord*)

JAMES SHAW (3)

2013: Jack Richardson Producer of the Year ("Youth Without Youth," "Breathing Underwater" – SYNTHETICA, Metric)
2010: Alternative Album of the Year (*Fantasies, Metric*)
2010: Group of the Year (*Metric*)

MEL SHAW (2)

1991: Walt Grealis Special Achievement Award
1972: Best Produced Single ("Sweet City Woman," The Stampeders)

LIBERTY SILVER (2)

1985: Best R&B/Soul Recording ("Lost Somewhere Inside Your Love")
1985: Best Reggae/Calypso Recording (Liberty Silver & Otis Gayle, "Heaven Must Have Sent You")

SIMPLE PLAN (2)

2012: Allan Waters Humanitarian Award
2006: JUNO Fan Choice Award

CHARLES SPEARIN (2)

2011: Recording Package of the Year (Justin Peroff, Charles Spearin, Robyn Kotyk & Joe McKay, art directors/designers; Jimmy Collins & Elisabeth Chicoine, photographers – Forgiveness Rock Record Vinyl Box Set, Broken Social Scene)
2010: Contemporary Jazz Album of the Year (*The Happiness Project*)

JAYME STONE (2)

2009: World Music Album of the Year, presented in honour of Billy Bryans (Jayme Stone & Mansa Sissko, *Africa To Appalachia*)
2008: Instrumental Album of the Year (*The Utmost*)

SUM 41 (2)

2005: Rock Album of the Year (*Chuck*)
2003: Group of the Year

SWOLLEN MEMBERS (4)

2007: Rap Recording of the Year ("Black Magic")
2003: Rap Recording of the Year ("Monsters In the Closet")

2002: Best Rap Recording ("Bad Dreams")
2001: Best Rap Recording ("Balance")

▷▷ HUGH SYME (4)

1992: Best Album Design (*Roll the Bones*, Rush)
1990: Best Album Design (*Presto*, Rush)
1989: Best Album Design (*Levity*, Ian Thomas)
1986: Best Album Graphics (Hugh Syme/Dimo Safari – *Power Windows*, Rush)

▷▷ TAFELMUSIK BAROQUE CHAMBER ORCHESTRA (9)

2006: Children's Album of the Year (Tafelmusik Baroque Orchestra – Baroque Adventure: *The Quest for Arundo Donax*)
2006: Classical Album of the Year: Large Ensemble or Soloist with Large Ensemble Accompaniment (Tafelmusik Baroque Orchestra, Bruno Weil – Beethoven: *Symphonies Nos. 5 et 6*)
2005: Classical Album of the Year: Large Ensemble or Soloist with Large Ensemble Accompaniment (Jean Lamon, Tafelmusik Baroque Orchestra – Dardanus/ *Le temple de la gloire: Music of Jean-Phillippe Rameau*)
2005: Classical Album of the Year: Vocal or Choral Performance (Isabel Bayrakdarian, Tafelmusik Baroque Orchestra – *Cleopatra*)
1999: Best Classical Album: Large Ensemble or Soloist with Large Ensemble Accompaniment (Tafelmusik, Jeanne Lamon: Musical Director – Handel: *Music for the Royal Fireworks*)
1995: Best Classical Album: Large Ensemble or Soloist with Large Ensemble Accompaniment (Bach: *Brandenburg Concertos Nos. 1-6*)
1994: Best Classical Album: Large Ensemble or Soloist with Large Ensemble Accompaniment (Tafelmusik, Jeanne Lamon: Director – Handel: *Concerti Grossi, Op. 3, No. 1-6*)
1993: Best Classical Album: Large Ensemble or Soloists with Large Ensemble Accompaniment (Tafelmusik with Alan Curtis, Catherine Robbin, Linda Maguire, Nancy Argenta, Ingid Attrot and Mel Braun; Jeanne Lamon, Leader – Handel: *Excerpts from Floridante*)
1990: Best Classical Album – Large Ensemble (Tafelmusik Baroque Orchestra – Boccherini: *Cello Concertos and Symphonies*)

▷▷ THE BOSS BRASS (4)

1992: Best Jazz Album (*The Brass Is Back*, Rob McConnell & the Boss Brass)
1984: Best Jazz Album (*All In Good Time*, Rob McConnell & the Boss Brass)
1981: Best Jazz Album (*Present Perfect*, Rob McConnell & the Boss Brass)
1978: Best Jazz Album (*Big Band Jazz*, Rob McConnell & the Boss Brass)

▷▷ THE FAMILY BROWN (2)

1990: Country Group or Duo of the Year
1985: Country Group of the Year

▷▷ THE GOOD BROTHERS (8)

1984: Country Group of the Year
1983: Country Group of the Year
1982: Country Group of the Year
1981: Country Group of the Year
1980: Country Group of the Year
1979: Country Group or Duo of the Year
1978: Country Group or Duo of the Year
1977: Country Group or Duo of the Year

▷▷ THE GRYPHON TRIO (2)

2011: Classical Album of the Year: Solo or Chamber Ensemble (Beethoven: Piano Trios Op. No. 1, Ghost & No. 2: *Op. 11*)
2004: Classical Album of the Year: Solo or Chamber Ensemble (Murphy, Chan, Hatzis, Kulescha Canadian Premieres)

▷▷ THE GUESS WHO (3)*

1987: Canadian Music Hall of Fame
1971: Top Vocal Instrumental Group
1970: Top Vocal Instrumental Group

▷▷ THE HUGH FRASER QUINTET (2)

1998: Best Mainstream Jazz Album (*In the Mean Time*)
1989: Best Jazz Album (Looking Up)

▷▷ THE MERCEY BROTHERS (6)*

1976: Country Group or Duo of the Year
1974: Country Group of the Year

1973: Country Group of the Year
1972: Country Group of the Year
1971: Top Country Instrumental Vocal Group
1970: Country Group of the Year

≫ THE ORFORD STRING QUARTET (3)

1991: Best Classical Album: Solo or Chamber Ensemble (Schafer: *Five String Quartets*)
1987: Best Classical Album: Solo or Chamber Ensemble (The Orford String Quartet, Ofra Harnoy, cello – Schubert: *Quintet in C*)
1985: Best Classical Album: Solo or Chamber Ensemble (*W.A. Mozart String Quartets*)

≫ THE RANKIN FAMILY aka THE RANKINS (6)

2000: Best Country Group of Duo
1997: Country Group or Duo of the Year
1994: Canadian Entertainer of the Year
1994: Country Group or Duo of the Year
1994: Group of the Year
1994: Single of the Year ("Fare Thee Well Love")

≫ THE SHEEPDOGS (3)

2012: New Group of the Year
2012: Rock Album of the Year (*Learn & Burn*)
2012: Single of the Year ("I Don't Know")

≫ THE SOUND BLUNTZ (2)

2004: Dance Recording of the Year (*Something About You*)
2003: Dance Recording of the Year (*Billie Jean*)

≫ THE STILLS (2)

2009: Alternative Album of the Year (*Oceans Will Rise*)
2009: New Group of the Year

≫ THE TRAGICALLY HIP (14)

2013: Music DVD of the Year (Andy Keen, Bernie Breen, Patrick Sambrook, Shawn Marino, The Tragically Hip for *Bobcaygeon*)
2006: Music DVD of the Year (The Tragically Hip, Pierre Lamoureux, Christopher Mills, Gord Downie, Allan Reid, Shawn Marino for *Hipeponymouse*)

2005: Canadian Music Hall of Fame
2001: Best Rock Album (*Music @ Work*)
2000: Best Single ("Bobcaygeon")
1999: Best Rock Album (*Phantom Power*)
1997: Album of the Year (*Trouble At the Henhouse*)
1997: Group of the Year
1997: North Star Rock Album of the Year (*Trouble At the Henhouse*)
1995: Entertainer of the Year
1995: Group of the Year
1993: Canadian Entertainer of the Year
1991: Canadian Entertainer of the Year
1990: Most Promising Group of the Year

≫ THE WEEKND (2)

2013: Breakthrough Artist of the Year
2013: R&B/Soul Recording of the Year (*Trilogy*)

≫ DON THOMPSON (3)

2006: Traditional Jazz Album of the Year (Don Thompson Quartet, *Ask Me Later*)
1985: Best Jazz Album (*A Beautiful Friendship*)
1980: Best Jazz Recording (Ed Bickert and Don Thompson, *Sackville 405*)

≫ TORONTO SYMPHONY ORCHESTRA (4)

2001: Best Classical Album: Large Ensemble or Soloist with Large Ensemble Accompaniment (Toronto Symphony Orchestra, Jukka-Pekka Saraste, Conductor – Sibelius: *Lemminkainen Suite, Night Ride and Sunrise*)
1996: Best Classical Album: Vocal or Choral Performance (Ben Heppner, Tenor, Toronto Symphony Orchestra, Andrew Davis, Conductor, *Ben Heppner Sings Richard Strauss*)
1986: Best Classical Album: Large Ensemble or Soloist with Large Ensemble Accompaniment (Toronto Symphony Orchestra, Andrew Davis, Conductor – Holst: *The Planets*)
1978: Best Classical Album of the Year (*Three Bordodin Symphonies*)

≫ BRAMWELL TOVEY (2)

2008: Classical Album of the Year: Large Ensemble or Soloist with Large Ensemble Accompaniment

(James Ehnes, Bramwell Tovey, Vancouver Symphony Orchestra – *Korngold, Barber & Walton Violin Concertos*)

2003: Classical Composition of the Year ("Requiem for a Charred Skull")

SHANIA TWAIN (13)

2011: Canadian Music Hall of Fame
2004: Country Recording of the Year (*Up!*)
2003: Artist of the Year
2003: Country Recording of the Year ("I'm Gonna Getcha Good")
2003: JUNO Fan Choice Award
2000: Best Country Female Artist
2000: Best Songwriter ("Man! I Feel Like A Woman," "You've Got A Way," "That Don't Impress Me Much" – Co-songwriter Robert John "Mutt" Lange)
1999: Best Country Female Vocalist
1998: Country Female Vocalist of the Year
1997: Country Female Vocalist of the Year
1997: International Achievement Award
1996: Country Female Vocalist of the Year
1996: Entertainer of the Year

DAVID TYSON (3)

1991: Producer of the Year ("Baby, It's Tonight," Jude Cole; "Don't Hold Back Your Love," Hall and Oates)
1991: Songwriter of the Year
1990: Composer of the Year (David Tyson/Christopher Ward)

IAN TYSON (2)

1992: Canadian Music Hall of Fame
1987: Country Male Vocalist of the Year

U2 (2)

1993: International Entertainer of the Year
1989: International Entertainer of the Year

DAVID USHER (4)

2002: Best Pop Album (*Morning Orbit*)
1999: Best Video (Javier Aguilera, David Usher – "Forestfire," David Usher)
1998: Best Video (Javier Aguilera, Moist – "Gasoline," Moist)
1995: Best New Group (Moist)

JOAQUIN VALDAPENAS (2)

2004: Classical Album of the Year: Large Ensemble or Soloist with Large Ensemble Accompaniment (André Laplante, piano; Christopher Millard, bassoon; Robert Cram, flute; Joaquin Valdepenas, clarinet, CBC Radio Orchestra, Mario Bernardi, Conductor – Concertos: Music of Jacques Hétu)
1994: Best Classical Composition (Chan Ka Nin – AMICI : Joaquin Valdepenas, clarinet, David Hetherington, cello, Patricia Parr, piano – "Among Friends")

VALDY (2)

1974: Folksinger of the Year
1973: Outstanding Performance of the Year – Folk

JIM VALLANCE (4)

1987: Composer of the Year
1986: Composer of the Year
1985: Composer of the Year (Bryan Adams/Jim Vallance)
1984: Composer of the Year (Bryan Adams/Jim Vallance – "Cuts Like a Knife," Bryan Adams)

GINO VANNELLI (7)

1991: Recording Engineer of the Year (Gino Vannelli/Joe Vannelli – "The Time of Day," "Sunset On L.A.," Gino Vannelli
1987: Recording Engineer of the Year (Gino Vannelli/Joe Vannelli – "Wild Horses," "Young Lover," Gino Vannelli
1986: Recording Engineer of the Year (Joe Vannelli/Gino Vannelli – "Black Cars," Gino Vannelli)
1979: Male Vocalist of the Year
1979: Producer of the Year (Gino Vannelli/Joe Vannelli/Ross Vannelli – Brother To Brother, Gino Vannelli)
1976: Male Vocalist of the Year
1975: Most Promising Male Vocalist of the Year

JOE VANNELLI (4)

1991: Recording Engineer of the Year (Gino Vannelli/Joe Vannelli – "The Time of Day," "Sunset On L.A.," Gino Vannelli
1987: Recording Engineer of the Year (Gino Vannelli/Joe Vannelli – "Wild Horses," "Young Lover," Gino Vannelli

1986: Recording Engineer of the Year (Joe Vannelli/ Gino Vannelli – "Black Cars," Gino Vannelli)

1979: Producer of the Year (Gino Vannelli/Joe Vannelli/Ross Vannelli – *Brother To Brother*, Gino Vannelli)

VARIOUS ARTISTS (3)

1992: Best Roots & Traditional Album (*Saturday Night Blues*)

1992: Best World Beat Recording (*The Gathering*)

1989: Best Selling International Album (*Dirty Dancing*)

CASSANDRA VASIK (2)

1994: Country Female Vocalist of the Year

1992: Country Female Vocalist of the Year

ROCH VOISINE (2)

1995: Best Selling Francophone Album (*Coup de tête*)

1994: Male Vocalist of the Year

RUFUS WAINWRIGHT (2)

2002: Best Alternative Album (*Poses*)

1999: Best Alternative Album (Rufus Wainwright)

WEA MUSIC OF CANADA LTD. (2) – see also Kinney Music of Canada

1974: Canadian Top Record Company (Manufacturer and Distributor)

1973: Record Company of the Year

JETH WEINRICH (3)

1997: Best Video (Jeth Weinrich, Junkhouse – "Burned Out Car," Junkhouse)

1996: Best Video (Jeth Weinrich, Jann Arden – "Good Mother," Jann Arden)

1994: Best Video (Jeth Weinrich, director; Jann Arden, artist – "I Would Die For You")

JENNY WHITELEY (2)

2005: Roots & Traditional Album of the Year: Solo (*Hopetown*)

2001: Best Roots & Traditional Album: Solo (Jenny Whiteley)

TOM WILSON (2)

2000: Best Roots & Traditional Album: Group (Blackie and the Rodeo Kings, *Kings of Love*)

1996: Best Album Design (Tom Wilson/Alex Wittholz – "Birthday Boy," Junkhouse)

MICHAEL PHILLIP WOJEWODA (2)

1998: Recording Engineer of the Year ("Armstrong and the Guys," "Our Ambassador," Spirit of the West)

1996: Producer of the Year ("End of the World," Waltons; "Beaton's Delight," Ashley MacIsaac)

JEFF WOLPERT (3)

2004: Recording Engineer of the Year (Mike Haas, Dylan Heming, Jeff Wolpert – "Heat Wave," "Something Cool" – Holly Cole)

2001: Best Recording Engineer ("Make It Go Away," "Romantically Helpless," Holly Cole)

1993: Recording Engineer of the Year (Jeff Wolpert & John Whynot – "The Lady of Shallott," Loreena McKennitt)

MICHELLE WRIGHT (2)

1995: Country Female Vocalist of the Year

1993: Country Female Vocalist of the Year

NEIL YOUNG (9)

2011: Adult Alternative Album of the Year (*Le Noise*)

2011: Allan Waters Humanitarian Award

2011: Artist of the Year

2006: Adult Alternative Album of the Year (*Prairie Wind*)

2006: Jack Richardson Producer of the Year ("The Painter," Neil Young)

2001: Best Male Artist

1995: Male Vocalist of the Year

1995: Album of the Year (*Harvest Moon*)

1982: Canadian Music Hall of Fame

JESSE ZUBOT (2)

2011: Instrumental Album of the Year (*Fond of Tigers, Continent & Western*)

2003: Roots & Traditional Album of the Year: Group (Zubot and Dawson, *Chicken Scratch*)

SINGLE JUNO WINNERS WITH (NUMBER OF NOMINATIONS)

Gary Gray 5
Antoine Gratton 1
Great Uncles of the Revolution 1
Green Day 1
Joey Gregorash 1
Grimes 2
Mike Haas 1
George Hamilton IV 1
MC Hammer 1
Lenn Hammond 2
Jeannette Hanna 1
Jeff Harrison 2
Jeff Healey 9
Heart 4
Tim Hecker 1
Dylan Heming 1
Bill Henderson 3
Joe Henderson 1
John Herberman 3
David Hetherington 1
Rob Heydon 1
Hilario Duran Trio 2
Hilario Duran and His Latin Jazz Big
    Band 1
Jim Hillman 1
Saul Holiff 1
Holly Cole Trio 2
Hometown Band 1
Honeymoon Suite 7
Charlie Hope 2
Whitney Houston 1
Humble 2
Tommy Hunter 3
Paul Hyde 4
I Mother Earth 3
I Musici de Montréal 7
In Essence 1
Infidels 1
Iron Maiden 1
I Sorenti 1
Chin Injeti 3
Chad Irschick 5
D.D. Jackson 5
Michael Jackson 5
Tom Jackson 3
JackSoul 4
Paul Janz 2
Jayson & Friends 1
Ingrid Jensen 4

Jive Bunny & The Mastermixers 1
Elton John 3
John MacLeod's Rex Hotel Orchestra 1
Carolyn Dawn Johnson 4
Martha Johnson 3
Molly Johnson 4
Sonia Johnson 1
France Joli 1
Jon Ballantyne Trio 2
Mike Jones 4
Keven Jordan 1
Marc Jordan 6
Sass Jordan 4
A. Hugh Joseph 1
Judy & David 5
Pierre Juneau 1
Junkhouse 3
Karkwa 3
Phil Kates 1
John Kay 1
Sherry Kean 3
James Keelaghan 4
KEN mode 1
Andy Kim 4
Kings of Leon 1
Lorraine Klaasen 1
Deborah Klassen 1
Chester Knight 3
Moe Koffman 9
Kon Kan 2
B. Kool 3
Korexion 3
Robyn Kotyk 4
Ante Kovac 1
Serouj Kradjian 1
Chad Kroeger 1
Anton Kuerti 7
Pat LaBarbera 1
La Chicane 3
Francois Lamoureux 4
Pierre Lamoureux 5
Robert John «Mutt» Lange 1
André LaPlante 2
Pierre Lapointe 3
Greg Lawson 1
Lazo 3
Robert Lebeuf 4
Claudette Leblanc 1
Larry LeBlanc 1

Wilfred Le Bouthiller 1
Ranee Lee 5
Alain Lefèvre 3
Dianne Leigh 1
John Lennon 1
Peter Lenton 1
André LeRoux 1
Glenn Lewis 6
Lhasa 3
Lights 3
Andrea Lindsay 1
Rich Little 1
Judy Loman 2
Guy Lombardo 1
London Mozart Players 2
Lonesome Daddy 1
Chloe Lum 1
Corb Lund 4
Macca 1
Andrew P. MacDonald 1
Kirk MacDonald 3
Rob MacIntyre 1
Steven MacKinnon 1
Gene MacLellan 1
Alan MacLeod 1
Brian MacLeod 2
Natalie MacMaster 7
Fraser MacPherson 3
Linda Maguire 1
Malajube 3
Dominic Mancuso 1
Eval Manigat 1
Manitoba Chamber Orchestra 2
Ron Mann 1
Manteca 4
Vincent Marcone 1
Marianas Trench 5
M.A.R.R.S. 1
Carla Marshall 2
Martha & the Muffins 3
Lawrence Martin 3
Garrett Mason 2
Julie Masse 3
Greg Masuak 2
Matthew Good Band 12
Tracy Maurice 2
Bob McBride 1
Terry McBride 1
Paul McCartney 3

Jannie McInnes 3
Joe McKay 1
Andrew McLachlan 1
Geoff McLean 2
Nana McLean 3
Holly McNarland 3
Colin McPhee 2
Sue Medley 1
Men At Work 1
Messenjah 4
Robert Michaels 3
Mighty Popo 3
Lynn Miles 3
Christopher Millard 1
Joel Miller 1
Milli Vanilli 1
John Mills 1
Sophie Milman 3
François Miron 1
Mobile 2
Ariane Moffatt 3
MonkeyJunk 1
Monster Truck 1
Monster Voodoo Machine 1
Montréal Jubilation Gospel
    Choir 4
Wm. Harold Moon 1
Antoine Moonen 2
Carlos Morgan 1
Dean Motter 6
Emilie Mover 1
Mozart Anniversary Orchestra 1
Marjan Mozetich 3
Mumford & Sons 1
Robert Munsch 2
Murley, Bickert and Wallace 1
Myles & Lenny 1
Kent Nagano 1
John Naslen 6
Nathan 2
A.C. Newman 3
Olivia Newton-John 3
Barbara Nichol 2
Dave Nichol 1
Phil Nimmons 2
NOJO 5
Shelley Nott 1
Opus 1
Orchestre Symphonique Bienne 1
Orchestre Symphonique de
    Québec 4
Brock Ostrom 1

Arthur Ozolins 2
Paul Pagé 3
Pa Joe 2
Jill Paquette 1
Paper Lace 1
Kevin Parent 5
James Parker 2
Patricia Parr 2
Hayward Parrott 3
Paulo Ramos Group 1
Anouk Pennel 1
Justin Peroff 2
Katy Perry 1
P.J. Perry 4
François Pérusse 3
Colleen Peterson 6
Adrianne Pieczonka 2
Phil Dwyer Orchestra 1
Phil Dwyer Quartet 1
Philosopher Kings 7
Luc Plamondon 1
Joel Plaskett 5
Stéphane Poirier 1
Murray Porter 2
J. Lyman Potts 1
Powder Blues 3
Daniel Powter 1
Tracey Prescott 2
Prism 7
Pugs & Crows 1
Quanteshia 1
Joel Quarrington 1
Lester Quitzau 2
Stephen Ralls 1
Jeszcze Raz 1
RCA Ltd. 1
RCA Records 1
Red Light 1
Red Rider 11
Allan Reid 2
Mike Reno 2
Marc Ricciardelli 2
Garth Richardson 2
Jack Richardson 4
Kim Ridgewell 1
Rihanna 2
Catherine Robbin 5
Donné Roberts 2
Mike Roberts 1
Brian Robertson 1
Eric Robertson 1
Rose Chronicles 1

Roxolana Roslak 1
Thomas Rösner 1
Walter Rossi 2
Will Ruocco 1
Saga 2
Doug Sahm 1
Said The Whale 2
Gordie Sampson 4
Ivana Santilli 5
Jukka-Pekka Saraste 5
Nik Sarros 1
Leo Sayer 1
Bob Schneider 2
Oliver Schroer 5
Joe Sealy 4
George Seara 2
Noah Segal 2
Shad 2
Shadowy Men On A Shadowy Planet 2
Shaggy 1
Remy Shand 4
Sharon Riley and Faith Chorale 2
Graham Shaw 1
Crystal Shawanda 3
Shawna B. 1
Elaine Lil'Bit Shepherd 2
Leroy Sibbles 4
Floria Sigismondi 6
Al Simmons 3
Simply Majestic 4
Mansa Sissko 1
Sisters Euclid 1
Sky 1
Skydiggers 1
Slik Toxik 2
Sloan 9
Rod Smallwood 1
Meaghan Smith 1
Sam Sniderman 1
Snow 10
Hank Snow 2
Adam Solomon 2
Harry Somers 6
James Sommerville 1
Spice Girls 2
Shari Spier 1
Bruce Springsteen 2
Standard Broadcasting 1
Erroll Starr 3
Randy Staub 10
Keith Stein 1
Suzanne Stevens 2

JUNO WINNERS

Benoit St-Jean 1
Lara St. John 1
Scott St. John 1
James St. Laurent 1
St. Lawrence String Quartet 2
Streetheart 3
Stretch Orchestra 1
Steve Strongman 1
Supertramp 1
Survivor 1
Chip Sutherland 1
Tomi Swick 2
Taima 1
Yoav Talmi 3
Jagori Tanna 1
Andy Taylor 1
Lydia Taylor 1
TBTBT 1
Rich Terfry 1
The Air Farce 1
The Band 1
The Brass Connection 2
The Captain and Tennille 1
The Chris Tarry Group 1
The CHUM Group 1
The City Harmonic 1
The Cranberries 1
The Crewcuts 1
The Diamonds 1
The Duhks 4
The Four Lads 1
The Irish Descendants 1
The Jeff Healey Band 7
The Killjoys 2
The Legendary Hearts 2
The Leslie Spit Treeo 1
The Love Movement 3
The McDades 1
The Medicine Beat 1

The Merlin Factor 2
The New Pornographers 2
Theory of a Deadman 3
The Oscar Peterson Four 1
The Paperboys 3
 The Police 2
The Poppy Family 1
The Road Hammers 2
The Rob McConnell Tentet 2
The Rolling Stones 1
The Rugrats 1
The Sadies 2
The Spirits of Havana 1
The Stampeders 7
The Tenors 1
The Waltons 1
The Wilkinsons 5
The Wooden Stars 1
Marie-Élaine Thibert 2
Ian Thomas 3
T.H.P. Orchestra 3
Thrust 2
Tiga 1
Sweeney Todd 2
Tommy Banks Big Band 1
Toronto Mass Choir 2
Denis Tougas 3
Sebastien Toupin 4
John Travolta 1
Martin Tremblay 1
Pierre Tremblay 1
Tri-Continental 1
Triumph 6
Domenic Troiano 2
Trooper 7
True North Records 1
Valerie Tryon 2
Sean Michael Turrell 2
Sylvia Tyson 8

Shari Ulrich 4
Richard Underhill 3
Bill Usher 1
Michel Valois 1
Vancouver Symphony Orchestra 6
Vanilla Ice 1
Ross Vannelli 3
John Virant 1
VOCM, St. John's,
   Newfoundland 1
Florent Vollant 2
Christopher Ward 2
Allan Waters 1
Kenny "Blues Boss" Wayne 4
Curtis Wehrfritz 8
Bruno Weil 4
Allan Weinrib 4
Brian West 3
John Whynot 3
Widelife 1
Amanda Wilkinson 6
Frankie Wilmot 1
Wintersleep 2
Alex Wittholz 2
Stevie Wonder 2
Woods of Ypres 1
Hawksley Workman 4
Michael Wrycraft 5
Zal Yanovsky 1
Young Artists for Haiti 1
Ritchie Yorke 1
Cathy Young 2
Dave Young 7
L. Stu Young 2
Zappacosta 1
Jean-Marie Zeitouni 1
Justin Zivojinovich 1
Zubot and Dawson 3

RECORD OF BIRTHS & DEATHS

You'll be hearing from me baby
long after I'm gone,
I'll be speaking to you sweetly
from a window in the tower of song

— Leonard Cohen, The Tower of Song

O ur earliest hand-written histories were records of family births and deaths, known in ancient cultures as "The Book of the Dead." This chapter of *Oh What A Feeling* constitutes a Book of the Dead for the Canadian music family, dating from 1800 to the second decade of the 21st century. Glancing through these vital records, patterns begin to emerge — odd peer groupings, possible musical influences, and strange demographic trivia — for example, the *Geist National Playlist Map*. Curiosities aside, this particular list is a tribute to each of the artists who make up the family of Canadian musicians. *Oh What a Feeling* celebrates their achievements and commemorates their passing through the Tower of Song.

»1800-1900

(B) 1819 • Poet, **Joesph M. Scriven**, Ballymoney Lodge, Banbridge, Ireland.

(B) April 5, 1830 • Canadian songwriter, poet and school headmaster, **Alexander Muir**, Lesmahagow, Scotland.

(B) October 1, 1842 • Poet and Inventor, **Charles Cros** (Émile-Hortensius Charles Cros), Fabrezan, Aude, France.

(B) February 11, 1847 • Inventor, **Thomas Alva Edison**.

(B) May 20, 1851 • Inventor, record executive, **Emile Berliner**, Hanover, Germany.

(B) November 9, 1858 • Composer, pianist and conductor, **John Stromberg** (John Stramberg), Milton, PEI.

(B) October 6, 1866 • "Father of Radio Broadcasting," **Reginald Aubrey Fessenden**, Knowlton, QC.

(B) March 30, 1871 • Tenor, and record executive, **Harry MacDonough** (John Scantlebury MacDonald), Hamilton, ON.

(B) September 15, 1871 • Lyricist, **Alfred Bryan**, Brantford, ON.

(B) February 1, 1873 • "The Prince of Fiddlers," **Joseph Allard** (aka Maxime Toupin), Woodland, Maine, USA.

(B) August 1, 1878 • "The Girl Who Made Vaudeville Famous," **Eva Tanguay**, Marbleton, QC.

(B) August 22, 1878 • Operatic tenor, **Edward Johnson** (aka Edoardo Di Giovanni), born Guelph, ON.

(B) January 15, 1882 • Tenor, **Henry Burr** (Harry H. McClaskey), St. Stephen, NB.

(B) September 13, 1882 • Record executive, **Herbert Samuel Berliner**, born Cambridge, MA.

(B) May 4, 1886 • Composer, vaudeville performer, **Shelton Brooks**, born Amherstburg, ON.

((D) August 9, 1888 • Poet and inventor, **Charles Cros**, (Émile-Hortensius Charles Cros), Paris, France.

▲ Alexander Muir

D) August 10, 1888, **Joesph M. Scriven**, Bewdley, Rice Lake, ON.

(B) December 6, 1888 • Composer, ragtime and jazz pianist, **William Eckstein**, Pointe St-Charles (Montréal), QC.

(B) November 14, 1890 • Lyricist, **Raymond B. Egan**, Windsor, ON.

(B) May 29, 1894 • Singer/actress, **Beatrice Lillie**, Toronto, ON.

(B) June 4, 1894 • Singer/musician, **Madame Bolduc** or La Bolduc (Mary Travers), Québécois, Newport, QC.

(B) June 20, 1896 • Conductor/pianist/composer/music educator, **Wilfrid Pelletier**, Montréal, QC.

»1901-1950

(B) June 19, 1902 • Bandleader/violinist, **Guy Lombardo**, (Gaetano Alberto Lombardo), London, ON.

(D) July 5, 1902 • Composer, pianist, conductor, **John Stromberg**, Long Island, NY.

(B) August 21, 1902 • Band leader,

THIS GARDEN
IS A TRIBUTE TO THE MEMORY OF
ALEXANDER MUIR
AUTHOR OF OUR NATIONAL SONG
"THE MAPLE LEAF FOREVER"
AND WAS MADE POSSIBLE BY
PUBLIC SUBSCRIPTION

trumpet player, violinist, **Charlie Pawlett**, Nanaimo, BC.

(B) July 16, 1903 • Vocalist/composer/saxophonist **Carmen Lombardo**, London, ON.

(B) December 18, 1904 • Country singer/songwriter, **Wilf Carter**, (aka Montana Slim), Port Hilford, NS.

(D) June 26, 1906 • Canadian songwriter, poet and school headmaster, **Alexander Muir**, Toronto, ON.

(B) April 7, 1908 • Band leader, arranger, composer, **Percy Faith**, Toronto, ON.

(B) April 13, 1908 • Singer, songwriter, actor, **Bob Nolan**, (Robert Clarence Nobles) (Sons of the Pioneers), born Winnipeg, MB.

(B) May 9, 1909 • Fiddler, TV personality, **Don Messer**, (Donald Charles Frederick Messer), Tweedside, NB.

(B) January 11, 1910 • Singer, arranger, saxophonist, pianist, **Art Hallman**, (Arthur Garfield Hallman), Kitchener, ON.

(B) March 7, 1910 • Band leader, **Mart Kenney**, born Tweed, ON.

(B) May 13, 1912 • Jazz pianist, arranger, composer, band leader, **Gil Evans**, Toronto, ON.

(B) February 1, 1914 • Canadian West Coast recording pioneer, **Al Reusch**, Yorkton, SK.

(B) May 9, 1914 • Country singer and songwriter, **Hank Snow**, (Clarence Eugene "Hank" Snow), Brooklyn, NS.

(B) August 2, 1914 • Singer, songwriter, poet, actor, political activist, **Félix Leclerc**, La Tuque, QC.

(B) August 4, 1914 • "The Canadian Crosby," **Dick Todd** (Dick Tohd), Montréal, QC.

(B) January 15, 1918 • "The King of Swing," **Dal Richards** (Dal Murray Richards), Vancouver, BC.

(B) November 12, 1919 • Blues musician, singer, **Jackie Washington**, Hamilton, ON.

(B) June 7, 1921 • Accordionist, **Marc Wald** (The Rhythm Pals), Bismarck, ND.

(B) June 26, 1921 • "Canada's King of Yodelers," **Donn Reynolds**, (Stanley Beresford Reynolds), Winnipeg, MB.

(B) June 3, 1923 • Band leader, clarinetist, **Phil Nimmons**, Kamloops, BC.

THE EDISON HOMESTEAD

On this site stood the home of Samuel Edison, a Loyalist from New Jersey who had moved to Nova Scotia in 1783 and settled here in 1811. During the War of 1812 he served as a captain in the 1st Middlesex Militia. Tradition maintains that this community was named Vienna at his suggestion. One of his sons Samuel Jr. supported the reform movement in Upper Canada, and after taking part in the Rebellion of 1837 fled to the United States. He settled in Milan, Ohio, where on February 11, 1847 his son, the noted inventor Thomas Alva Edison was born. As a boy Thomas Edison visited his grandfather here in Vienna.

Erected by the Ontario Archaeological and Historic Sites Board.

(B) August 16, 1924 • **Vocalist Jack Jensen** (The Rhythm Pals), Prince Rupert, BC.

(B) October 18, 1924 • Renowned Cape Breton fiddler, **Buddy McMaster** (Hugh Alan McMaster), Timmins, ON.

(B) August 15, 1925 • Pianist, composer, **Oscar Peterson** (Oscar Emmanuel Peterson), Montréal, QC.

(B) September 11, 1925 • Composer **Harry Somers**, Toronto, ON.

(B) December 22, 1925 • Vocalist, bass player **Mike Ferby** (The Rhythm Pals), Saskatoon, SK.

(B) July 28, 1926 • Jazz bassist **Charlie Biddle** (Charles Reed Biddle), Philadelphia, PA.

(B) October 29, 1926 • Heldentenor **Jon Vickers** (Jonathan Stewart Vickers), Prince Albert, SK.

(B) November 18, 1926 • Singer/actress **Dorothy Collins** (Marjorie Chandler), Windsor, ON.

(B) January 10, 1927 • Singer/radio-TV host/violinist **Gisele MacKenzie** (Gisèle Marie-Louise Marguerite LaFleche), Winnipeg, MB.

(B) July 6, 1927 • Pianist, composer "Hockey Night in Canada Theme" **Dorothy Clamans**, Vancouver, BC.

(B) August 26, 1927 • Vocalist, TV personality **Juliette** (Juliette Augustina Sysak), St. Viral, (Winnipeg), MB.

(B) December 12, 1927 • Jazz pianist **Chris Cage**, Regina, SK.

(B) April 10, 1928 • Jazz musician **Fraser MacPherson**, St. Boniface, MB.

▲ Martyrdom of the Jesuits, Jean de Brébeuf (right)

BIRTHS & DEATHS

(B) May 4, 1928 • Jazz musician, band leader **Maynard Ferguson** (Walter Maynard Ferguson), Verdun, QC.

(B) August 19, 1928 • Singer/ songwriter/actor/pianist **Norman Brooks** (nee Norman Joseph Arie), Montréal, QC.

(B) October 27, 1928 • Poet, singer, songwriter, political activist **Gilles Vigneault**, Natashquan, QC.

(B) December 18, 1928 • Composer (Hair), pianist **Galt MacDermot**, Montréal, QC.

(B) December 28, 1928 • Jazz musician, composer **Moe Koffman** (Morris Koffman), Toronto, ON.

(B) February 18, 1929 • *RPM Weekly* magazine publisher **Walt Grealis**, Toronto, ON

(D) August 3, 1929 • Inventor, record executive **Emile Berliner**, Washington, DC.

B) March 17, 1930 • Flautist, multi-instrumentalist **Paul Horn**, New York, NY.

(B) July 25, 1930 • Operatic contralto **Maureen Forrester** (Maureen Kathleen Stewart Forrester), Montréal, QC.

(B) January 21, 1931 • Baritone singer **Rudi Maugeri** (The Crew Cuts), Toronto, ON.

(B) March 2, 1931 • Tenor singer/arranger **John Bernard** "Bernie" Toorish (The Four Lads), Toronto, ON.

(B) March 13, 1931 • Singer, songwriter, musician **Bob Regan** (Bob Frederickson), Rolla, BC.

(B) May 16, 1931 • Tenor **Ted Kowalski** (The Diamonds).

(B) August 28, 1931 • Singer **John Perkins** (The Crew Cuts), Toronto, ON.

(D) September 26, 1931 • Tenor **Harry MacDonough** (John S. MacDonald), New York, NY.

(B) January 4, 1932 • Tenor **James F. "Jimmy" Arnold** (The Four Lads), Toronto, ON.

(B) April 29, 1932 • Producer/*RPM Weekly* co-founder **Stan Klees**, Toronto, ON.

(D) July 22, 1932 • "Father of Broadcasting"

Reginald Aubrey Fessenden, Bermuda.

(B) September 25, 1932 • Pianist **Glenn Gould** (Glenn Herbert Gould), Toronto, ON.

(B) November 10, 1932 • Jazz pianist **Paul Bley**, Montréal, QC.

(B) November 24, 1932 • Bass singer **Ray Perkins** (The Crew Cuts), Toronto, ON.

(B) November 29, 1932 • Jazz guitarist **Ed Bickert** (Edward Isaac Bickert), Hochfeld, MB.

(B) January 19, 1933 • Country vocalist **Stu Phillips**, Montréal, QC.

(B) September 15, 1933 • Tenor vocalist **Pat Barrett** (The Crew Cuts), Toronto, ON.

(B) September 25, 1933 • Singer, songwriter **Ian Tyson**, Victoria, BC.

(B) October 2, 1933 • Tenor vocalist **Dave Somerville** (The Diamonds), Guelph, ON.

(B) November 26, 1933 • Vocalist, actor **Robert Goulet** (Robert Gerard Goulet), Lawrence, MA.

(B) February 18, 1934 • Vocalist, songwriter, producer **Bobby Taylor** (Bobby Taylor and the Vancouvers), NC.

(B) August 9, 1934 • Bandleader, trumpet player **Bobby Hales**, Avonlea, SK.

(B) September 11, 1934 • Pianist, organist, composer, arranger **Oliver Jones** (Oliver Theophilus Jones), Little Burgundy, Montréal, QC.

(B) September 21, 1934 • Singer/songwriter **Leonard Cohen** (Leonard Norman Cohen), Westmount, Montréal, QC.

(B) January 8, 1935 • Singer/actor **Elvis Presley**, Tupelo, MS.

(B) January 10, 1935 • Rockabilly singer/"Legend in his spare time" **Ronnie Hawkins**, Huntsville, AK.

(B) February 14, 1935 • Jazz valve trombonist, band leader, composer, arranger music educator **Rob McConnell** (Robert Murray Gordon McConnell), London, ON.

(B) April 20, 1935 • "Canada's Polka King," **Walter Ostanek** (Ladislav Walter Ostanek), Duparquet, QC.

(B) July 9, 1935 • Baritone **Phil Levitt** (The Diamonds).

B) January 11, 1936 • Bass vocalist **Bill Reed** (The Diamonds).

(B) January 24, 1936 • Vocalist, songwriter **Jack Scott** (Giovanni Domenico Scafone Jr.), Windsor, ON.

(B) February 6, 1936 • Preacher/recording artist Jimmie **Rodgers Snow** (son of Hank Snow).

(B) February 9, 1936 • Country singer, songwriter **Stompin' Tom Connors** (Thomas Charles Connors), Saint John, NB.

(B) May 7, 1936 • Trumpet player **Arnie Chycoski**, New Westminster, BC.

(B) December 3, 1936 • Pianist, composer **John Arpin**, Port Nichol, ON.

(B) February 26, 1937 • Composer, arranger, multi-instrumentalist **Hagood Hardy**, Angola, IN.

(B) March 20, 1937 • "Canada's Country Gentleman" **Tommy Hunter** (Thomas James Hunter), London, ON.

(B) March 30, 1937 • Broadcaster **Red Robinson** (Robert Robinson), Comox, BC.

(B) August 2, 1937 • Multi-instrumentalist/producer **Garth Hudson** (The Band), London, ON.

(B) January 24, 1938 • Singer, recording artist **Jack Scott**, Windsor, ON.

(B) February 2, 1938 • Singer, songwriter **Gene MacLellan**, Val d'Or, QC.

(B) May 24, 1938 • Musician, comedian, actor, writer, director, social activist **Tommy Chong** (Thomas B. Kin Chong) (Cheech & Chong), Edmonton, AB.

(B) November 17, 1938 • Singer/songwriter **Gordon Lightfoot** (Gordon Meredith Lightfoot Jr.), Orillia, ON.

(B) December 16, 1938 • "Canadian Godfather of Celtic Music" **John Allan Cameron**, Inverness County, Cape Breton Island, NS.

(B) April 27, 1939 • Drummer **Jerry Mercer** (Gerald Mercer) (April Wine), NL.

(B) May 11, 1939 • Singer, songwriter, producer **R. Dean Taylor** (Richard Dean Taylor), Toronto, ON.

(B) August 2, 1939 • Musician, composer, arranger **André Gagnon**, Saint-Pacôme-de-Kamouraska, QC.

(B) August 28, 1939 • Composer/flautist **Robert Aitken** (Robert Morris Aitken), Kentville, NS.

(B) January 18, 1940 • Multi-instrumentalist jazz musician **Don Thompson**, Powell River, BC.

(B) May 24, 1940 • Comedian, musician, social activist **Tommy Chong** (Bobby Taylor & the Vancouvers, Cheech & Chong), Edmonton, AB.

(B) May 26, 1940 • Drummer, vocalist, multi-instrumentalist **Levon Helm** (The Band), Marvell, AK.

(B) August 10, 1940 • Singer, songwriter, actor **Brent Titcomb** (3's A Crowd), Vancouver, BC.

(B) September 19, 1940 • Singer, songwriter, musician, broadcaster **Sylvia Tyson** (Sylvia Fricker), Chatham, ON.

(B) November 13, 1940 • Singer, songwriter, guitarist **Bonnie Dobson**, Toronto, ON.

(B) November 29, 1940 • Vocalist, songwriter **Denny Doherty** (Dennis Gerrard Stephen Doherty) (The Mamas and the Papas), Halifax, NS.

(B) January 12, 1941 • Blues vocalist **Long John Baldry**, (John William Baldry), East Haddon (London), England.

(B) February 20, 1941 • Singer, songwriter, musician, composer, visual artist, educator, social activist **Buffy Sainte-Marie**, Piapot Cree Reserve, Qu'Appelle Valley, SK.

(D) February 20, 1941 • Singer/musician **Madame Bolduc** or La Bolduc (nee Mary Travers), Montréal, QC.

(D) April 6, 1941 • Tenor **Henry Burr** (nee Harry H. McClaskey), Chicago, IL.

(B) July 30, 1941 • Singer/actor **Paul Anka** (Paul Albert Anka), Ottawa, ON.

(B) August 15, 1941 • Guitarist **Lenny Breau** (Leonard Harold Breau), Auburn, ME.

(B) September 13, 1941 • Vocalist, musician, songwriter, producer **David Clayton-Thomas** (David Henry Thomsett) (Blood, Sweat & Tears), Kingston-upon-Thames, Surrey, U.K.

(B) November 26, 1941 • Guitarist, multi-instrumentalist, author **Amos Garrett**, Detroit, MI.

(B) December 2, 1941 • Alto sax player **P.J. Perry** (Paul John Guloien), Calgary, AB.

(B) March 2, 1942 • Lyricist **Luc Plamondon**, Saint-Raymond, QC.

(B) March 11, 1942 • Singer, songwriter **David Wiffen**, Redhill, Surrey, England.

(B) June 27, 1942 • Pianist **Frank Mills**, Toronto, ON.

(B) June 30, 1942 • Broadcaster, actor, writer **Terry David Mulligan**, New Westminster, BC.

(B) July 17, 1942 • Singer, songwriter, writer, actress **Gale Garnett** (Gale Zoe Garnett), Auckland, NZ.

(B) September 30, 1942 • Drummer **Dewey Martin** (Buffalo Springfield), Chesterville, ON.

(B) November 22, 1942 • Drummer **Floyd Sneed** (Three Dog Night), Calgary, AB.

(B) December 29, 1942 • Bassist, vocalist, multi-instrumentalist **Rick Danko** (The Band), Green's Corners near Simcoe, ON.

(B) 1942 • Jazz vocalist, musician **Ranee Lee**, New York, NY.

(B) 1942 • Broadcaster, actor, social activist **Moses Znaimer** (CityTV, MuchMusic, MusiquePlus, Zoomer Media), Kulyab, Tjikistan, Soviet Union.

(B) March 29, 1943 • Singer/musician **Chad Allan** (Allan Kowbel), Winnipeg, MB.

(B) April 3, 1943 • Pianist, vocalist, composer, multi-instrumentalist **Richard Manuel** (The Band), Stratford, ON.

(B) April 17, 1943 • Singer **Bobby Curtola** (Robert Allen Curtola), Port Arthur (now Thunder Bay), ON.

(B) April 21, 1943 • Musician, songwriter **Dennis Edmonton** aka Mars Bonfire (Dennis Eugene McCrohan) (Steppenwolf), Oshawa, ON.

(B) July 5, 1943 • Guitarist, vocalist, producer, songwriter, actor **Robbie Robertson** (Jaime Robert Klegerman) (The Band), Toronto, ON.

(B) August 11, 1943 • Bass player **Jim Kale** (Michael James Kale) (The Guess Who), Winnipeg, MB.

(B) September 27, 1943 • Singer, guitarist, songwriter, broadcaster, record executive **Randy Bachman** (Randolph Charles Bachman) (The Guess Who, Bachman-Turner Overdrive), Winnipeg, MB.

(B) October 16, 1943 • Bass player, vocalist **Fred Turner** (Charles Frederick "C.F." Turner), Winnipeg, MB.

(B) November 7, 1943 • Singer, songwriter, painter **Joni Mitchell** (Roberta Joan Anderson), Fort Macleod, AB.

(B) March 29, 1944 • Singer, songwriter, fisherman, environmentalist **Terry Jacks** (Terrence Ross Jacks), Winnipeg, MB.

(B) April 12, 1944 • Singer, songwriter, guitarist **John Kay** (Joachim Fritz Krauledat) (Steppenwolf), Tilsit, East Prussia, Germany.

(B) May 17, 1944 • Singer, songwriter, musician **Jesse Winchester** (James Ridout Winchester), Bossier City, LA.

(B) May 28, 1944 • Singer, songwriter **Rita MacNeil**, Big Pond, Cape Breton, NS.

(B) June 25, 1944 • Singer, songwriter, actor **Robert Charlebois**, Montréal, QC.

(B) July 30, 1944 • Singer, songwriter, guitarist, painter, political activist **Mendelson Joe** (Birrel Josef Mendelson), Maple, ON.

(B) August 12, 1944 • Music executive, personal manager, author **Bernie Finkelstein** (The Paupers, Bruce Cockburn, Murray McLauchlan, Dan Hill), Toronto, ON.

(B) November 6, 1944 • Singer, songwriter, musician, producer, environmentalist **Bill Henderson** (William A. Henderson) (The Collectors, Chilliwack, UHF), Vancouver, BC.

(B) December 19, 1944 • Guitarist, vocalist, restaurateur **Zal Yanovsky** (Zalman Yanovsky) (The Lovin' Spoonful), Toronto, ON.

(B) 1944 • Singer, songwriter, composer, producer **Salome Bey**, U.S.

(B) March 1, 1945 • Singer, songwriter, guitarist, actor **Sneezy Waters** (Peter Hodgson), Ottawa, ON.

(B) May 2, 1945 • Keyboardist **Goldy McJohn** (John Raymond Goadsby) (Steppenwolf), Toronto, ON.

(B) May 19, 1945 • Personal manager, broadcaster **Bruce Allen** (Bachman-Turner Overdrive, Bryan Adams, Anne Murray, Michael Bublé), Vancouver, BC.

(B) May 26, 1945 • Drummer **Garry Peterson** (Garry Denis Peterson) (The Guess Who), Winnipeg, MB.

(B) May 27, 1945 • Singer, songwriter, guitarist, social activist **Bruce Cockburn** (Bruce Douglas Cockburn), Ottawa, ON.

(B) June 20, 1945 • Singer **Anne Murray** (Morna Anne Murray), Springhill, NS.

(B) July 25, 1945 • Singer, songwriter **Ken Tobias** (Kenneth Wayne Paul Tobias), Saint John, NB.

(B) September 1, 1945 • Singer, songwriter, social activist **Valdy** (Paul Valdemar Horsdal), Ottawa, ON.

(B) October 21, 1945 • Broadcaster Fred Latremouille, Nanaimo, BC.

(B) November 12, 1945 • Singer/songwriter **Neil Young** (Neil Percival Young), Toronto, ON.

(B) November 20, 1945 • Singer, songwriter, actress, model **Nanette Workman** (Nanette Joan Workman), Brooklyn, New York, NY.

(B) February 6, 1946 • Singer/songwriter **Kate McGarrigle** (Kate & Anna McGarrigle), Montréal, QC.

(B) February 18, 1946 • Pedal steel guitarist **Buddy Cage** (New Riders of the Purple Sage), Toronto, ON.

(B) February 19, 1946 • Guitarist, songwriter **Paul Dean** (Paul Warren Dean) (Loverboy), Vancouver, BC.

(B) March 1, 1946 • Vocalist, songwriter **Gerry Boulet** (Joseph Gaetan Robert Gérald Boulet), Saint-Jean-sur-Richelieu, QC.

(B) April 2, 1946 • Guitarist/songwriter **Kurt Winter** (The Guess Who), Winnipeg, MB.

(B) April 28, 1946 • Singer, songwriter, actress **Ginette Reno**, Montréal, QC.

(B) May 19, 1946 • Musician, producer **Trevor Veitc**h (3's A Crowd), Vancouver, BC.

(B) May 23, 1946 • Vocalist **Donna Warner** (3's A Crowd), Edmonton, AB.

(B) June 17, 1946 • Guitarist, songwriter **Domenic Troiano** (Domenic Michele Antonio Troiano), Modugno, Italy.

(B) September 9, 1946 • Bass player **Bruce Palmer** (Buffalo Springfield), Liverpool, NS.

(B) October 18, 1946 • Academy Award-winning composer **Howard Shore** (Howard Leslie Shore), Toronto, ON.

(B) October 24, 1946 • Drummer **Jerry Edmonton** (Gerald McCrohan) (Steppenwolf), Oshawa, ON.

(B) December 5, 1946 • Singer, songwriter **Andy Kim** (Andrew Youakim), Montréal, QC.

(D) January 11, 1947 • "The Girl Who Made Vaudeville Famous," **Eva Tanguay**, Hollywood, CA.

(B) January 31, 1947 • Singer, songwriter, musician **Matt Minglewood** (Roy Alexander Batherson), Moncton, NB.

(B) April 24, 1947 • Singer, songwriter **Claude Dubois** (Claude André Dubois), Montréal, QC.

(B) May 10, 1947 • Composer, soundscape researcher **Barry Truax**, Chatham, ON.

(B) August 5, 1947 • Guitarist **Greg Leskiw** (The Guess Who), Winnipeg, MB.

(D) November 14, 1947 • "The Prince of Fiddlers" **Joseph Allard** (aka Maxime Toupin), near Montréal, QC.

(B) December 31, 1947 • Singer, songwriter, musician **Burton Cummings**, Winnipeg, MB.

(B) January 26, 1948 • Drummer **Corky Laing** (Laurence Gordon Laing) (Mountain), Montréal, QC.

(B) March 3, 1948 • News director CKLW/recording artist **Byron MacGregor** (Gary Lachlan Mack), Calgary, AB.

(B) June 23, 1948 • Vocalist, songwriter, guitarist, producer

▲ Glenn Gould, captured in bronze, wearing his favourite coat, outside of the CBC in Toronto

Myles Goodwyn (Myles Francis Goodwyn) (April Wine), Woodstock, NB.

(B) June 30, 1948 • Singer, songwriter, musician **Murray McLauchlan** (Murray Edward McLauchlan), Paisley, Scotland.

(B) July 8, 1948 • Children's entertainer, songwriter **Raffi** (Raffi Cavoukian), Cairo, Egypt.

(B) July 21, 1948 • Musician, songwriter **Allan Fraser** (Fraser & DeBolt), St. Stephen, NB.

(B) August 15, 1948 • Singer, musical theatre actress **Patsy Gallant**, Campbellton, NB.

(B) August 19, 1948 • Singer **Susan Jacks** (Susan Pesklevits) (The Poppy Family), Saskatoon, SK.

(B) November 5, 1948 • Guitarist **Donnie McDougall** (The Guess Who).

(B) November 9, 1948 • Singer, songwriter, guitarist **Michel Pagliaro** (Michel Armand Guy Pagliaro), Montréal, QC.

(B) December 16, 1948 • Singer **Denise McCann**, Clinton, IA.

(B) 1948 • Singer, musician, songwriter **B.B. Gabor** (Gabor Hegedus), Hungary.

(B) 1948 • Vocalist, musician, songwriter **Trevor Payne** (Trevor Winston Payne), Black Rock, Barbados.

(B) February 21, 1949 • Singer, songwriter, broadcaster **Jim Corcoran** (James Ashley Corcoran), Sherbrooke, QC.

(B) March 4, 1949 • Country singer **Carroll Baker** (Carroll Anne Baker), Bridgewater, NS.

(B) March 17, 1949 • Singer, songwriter **Daniel Lavoie**, Dunrea, MB.

(B) March 24, 1949 • Bassist **Steve Lang** (April Wine), Montréal, QC.

(B) March 25, 1949 • Producer, keyboardist **Bob Ezrin** (Robert Allan Ezrin), Toronto, ON.

(B) March 29, 1949 • Guitarist, songwriter **Brian "Smitty" Smith** (Trooper).

(B) April 8, 1949 • Singer, songwriter, keyboardist **Brenda Russell** (Brenda Gordon), Brooklyn, NY.

(B) May 1, 1949 • Bassist **Jim Clench** (James Patrick Clench) (April Wine), Montréal, QC.

(B) May 18, 1949 • Bassist **Bill Wallace** (The Guess Who), Winnipeg, MB.

(B) June 7, 1949 • Composer, singer, violinist, pianist, actor, director **Lewis Furey** (Lewis Greenblatt), Montréal, QC.

(B) July 5, 1949 • **Dave Beckett** (David Lloyd George Beckett) (Gary & Dave), Newmarket, ON.

(B) July 11, 1949 • Classical guitarist, vocalist, "The First Lady of the Guitar," **Liona Boyd** (Liona Marie Carolynne Boyd), London, England.

(B) July 13, 1949 • Guitarist, singer **David Wilcox** (David Karl Williams Wilcox), Montréal, QC.

(B) July 30, 1949 • Composer **Alexina Louie**, Vancouver, BC.

(B) November 1, 1949 • Musician, producer, composer, arranger **David Foster** (David Walter Foster), Victoria, BC.

(B) November 28, 1949 • Musician, composer, actor, comedian, author **Paul Shaffer** (Paul Allen Wood Shaffer), Thunder Bay, ON.

(B) November 29, 1949 • Singer, songwriter, musician **Stan Rogers** (Stanley Allison Rogers), Hamilton, ON.

(B) December 30, 1949 • Producer, musician **Bruce Fairbairn** (Bruce Earl Fairbairn), Vancouver, BC.

(B) 1949 • Bass player, keyboardist, vocalist **Mike Levine** (Triumph).

(B) 1949 • Singer, actor **Terry Black**, North Vancouver, BC.

»1951-2000

(B) May 22, 1950 • Vocalist **Gary Weeks** (Gary & Dave), Charlottetown, PEI.

(B) June 13, 1950 • Singer, songwriter **Ra McGuire** (Trooper), Vancouver, BC.

(B) July 23, 1950 • Guitarist **Blair Thornton** (Crosstown Bus, Bachman-Turner Overdrive), Vancouver, BC.

(B) July 23, 1950 • Singer, songwriter, actor, author **Ian Thomas** (Ian Campbell Thomas), Hamilton, ON.

(B) November 14, 1950 • Singer, songwriter **Colleen Peterson** (Colleen Susan Peterson), Peterborough, ON.

(B) December 18, 1950 • Singer, songwriter **Martha Johnson** (Martha and the Muffins), Toronto, ON.

(B) January 22, 1951 • Songwriter, multi-instrumentalist, producer **Ben Mink**, Toronto, ON.

(B) April 26, 1951 • Singer, songwriter **Billy Newton Davis**, Shaker Heights (Cleveland), OH.

(B) August 1, 1951 • Guitarist **Tim Bachman** (Bachman-Turner Overdrive), Winnipeg, MB.

(B) August 5, 1951 • Singer, actress **Carole Laure**, Shawinigan, QC.

(B) September 19, 1951 • Producer, guitarist, songwriter, vocalist **Daniel Lanois**, Hull, QC.

(B) October 1, 1951 • Guitarist, vocalist **Brian Greenway** (Brian Gilbert Greenway) (April Wine, Mashmakhan, The Dudes), Hawkesbury, ON.

(B) October 17, 1951 • Singer, songwriter, multi-instrumentalist, actress, music educator **Shari Ulrich** (Sharon Ulrich), San Rafael, CA.

(B) October 26, 1951 • Singer, songwriter, mandolin, harmonica player **Willie P. Bennett** (William Patrick Bennett), Toronto, ON.

(B) November 7, 1951 • Guitarist, songwriter, producer **Kevin MacMichael** (Kevin Scott MacMichael) (Cutting Crew), Saint John, NB.

(B) December 21, 1951 • Singer, songwriter **Nick Gilder** (Nicholas George Gilder), Vancouver, BC.

(B) December 29, 1951 • Singer, composer, multi-instrumentalist, author, broadcaster **Georges Thurston** (Boule Noir), Bedford, QC.

(B) April 17, 1952 • Singer, songwriter, musician, actor, producer **Gilles Valiquette**, Montréal, QC.

(B) May 31, 1952 • Songwriter, musician, arranger, producer **Jim Vallance** (James Douglas Vallance), Chilliwack, BC.

(B) June 1, 1952 • Singer, songwriter, poet **Ferron** (Debby Foisy).

(B) June 16 1952 • Singer, songwriter, musician, producer **Gino Vannelli**, Montréal, QC.

(B) June 25, 1952 • Guitarist, multi-instrumentalist, songwriter, producer **Brian "Too Loud" MacLeod** (Brian Oliver MacLeod) (Chilliwack, Headpins), Halifax, NS.

(B) July 1, 1952 • Comedian, singer, actor, screenwriter **Dan Aykroyd** (Daniel Edward Aykroyd), Ottawa, ON.

(B) July 10, 1952 • Singer, guitarist, broadcaster **Kim Mitchell** (Joseph Kim Mitchell), Sarnia, ON.

(B) September 12, 1952 • Drummer, lyricist **Neil Peart** (Neil Ellwood Peart) (Rush), Hamilton, ON.

(D) October 13, 1952 • Lyricist **Raymond B. Egan**, Westport, CT.

(B) 1952 • Guitarist, vocalist **Jerry Doucette**, Montréal, QC.

B) February 8, 1953 • Singer, songwriter, Canadian punk rock pioneer **Art Bergmann** (Arthur Frank Bergmann), Vancouver, BC.

(B) February 12, 1953 • Singer, songwriter, broadcaster **Roy Forbes** aka Bim, Dawson Creek, BC.

(B) February 18, 1953 • Drummer **Robbie Bachman** (Robin Bachman) (BTO), Winnipeg, MB.

(B) March 21, 1953 • Singer, actress **Taborah "Tabby" Johnson**, Toronto, ON.

(B) April 18, 1953 • Actor, comedian, broadcaster (as Rick Allan), musician **Rick Moranis** (Frederick Allan Moranis), Toronto, ON.

(B) May 9, 1953 • Singer, songwriter **Connie Kaldor** (Connie Isabelle Kaldor), Regina, SK.

(B) May 14, 1953 • Drummer **John Rutsey** (John Howard Rutsey) (Rush), Toronto, ON.

(B) May 14, 1953 • Singer, songwriter, musician **Tom Cochrane**, Lynn Lake, MB.

(B) July 7, 1953 • Bass player, vocalist **Jim Bescott** (Shmorgs, K-Tels, Young Canadians), San Francisco, CA.

(B) July 10, 1953 • Guitarist, vocalist **Rik Emmett** (Richard Gordon Emmett), Toronto, ON.

(B) July 11, 1953 • Guitarist **Benny DeFranco** (The DeFranco Family), Port Colborne, ON.

(B) July 15, 1953 • Operatic tenor **Richard Margison** (Richard Charles Margison), Victoria, BC.

(B) July 29, 1953 • Bassist, vocalist, songwriter **Geddy Lee** (Gary Lee Weinrib) (Rush), North York, ON.

(B) August 27, 1953 • Guitarist **Alex Lifeson** (Aleksandar Zivojinovic) (Rush), Fernie, BC.

(B) September 5, 1953 • Singer, songwriter **Paul Piché**, Montréal, QC.

(B) September 20, 1953 • Bass player, vocalist **Jeff Jones** (Rush, Ocean, Red Rider), Chicago, IL.

(B) October 4, 1953 • Drummer, vocalist, studio executive **Gil Moore** (Triumph), Toronto, ON.

(B) December 18, 1953 • Guitarist, composer, producer **Jim West** (James "kimo" West) (Weird Al Yankovic), Toronto, ON.

(B) 1953 • Singer, songwriter **Alfie Zappacosta** (Alfredo Peter Zappacosta), Sora, Italy.

(B) March 7, 1954 • Drummer **Matt Frenette** (Streetheart/Loverboy), Calgary, AB.

B) April 12, 1954 • Guitarist, singer, keyboardist **Pat Travers** (Patrick Henry Travers), Toronto, ON.

(B) April 19, 1954 • Producer, musician, songwriter, singer **Bob Rock** (Robert Jens Rock) (The Payola$, Rock & Hyde), Winnipeg, MB.

(B) July 23, 1954 • Keyboardist **Marisa DeFranco** (DeFranco Family), Port Colborne, ON.

(B) August 29, 1954 • Vocalist, songwriter, guitarist **Greg Keelor** (J. Gregory Keelor) (Blue Rodeo), Inverness County, NS.

(B) November 17, 1954 • Singer, songwriter **David Francey**, Ayrshire, Scotland.

(B) November 20, 1954 • Guitarist, vocalist, songwriter **Frank Marino** (Francesco Antonio Marino) (Mahogany Rush), Montréal, QC.

(B) June 3, 1954 • Singer, songwriter **Dan Hill** (Daniel Grafton Hill), Toronto, ON.

(B) 1954 • Guitarist, music educator, producer, arranger **Norbert Kraft**, Linz, Austria.

(B) 1954 • Flamenco guitarist **Oscar Lopez**, Santiago, Chile.

(B) January 8, 1955 • Vocalist, songwriter **Mike Reno** (Joseph Michael Rynoski) (Loverboy), New Westminster, BC.

(B) February 13, 1955 • Bassist **Scott Smith** (Donald Scott Smith) (Loverboy), Winnipeg, MB.

(B) May 21, 1955 • Singer, guitarist, keyboardist **Paul Hyde** (Paul Reginald Nelson), Yorkshire, England.

(B) May 1955 • Singer, songwriter **Garnet Rogers**.

(B) June 30, 1955 • Singer **Brian Vollmer**, Listowel, ON.

(B) October 12, 1955 • Singer, songwriter **Jane Siberry** aka Issa (Jane Stewart), Toronto, ON.

(B) October 19, 1955 • Guitarist **Nino DeFranco** (DeFranco Family), Port Colborne, ON.

(B) December 2, 1955 • Vocalist, songwriter, guitarist **Jim Cuddy** (James G. Cuddy) (Blue Rodeo), Toronto, ON.

(B) January 14, 1956 • Tenor **Ben Heppner**, Murrayville, BC.

B) March 1956 • Singer, songwriter **Barney Bentall** (Barnard Franklin Bentall) (Barney Bentall and the Legendary Hearts), Toronto, ON.

(B) June 3, 1956 • Multi-instrumentalist **Geoffrey Kelly** (Spirit of the West), Dumfries, Scotland.

(B) June 17, 1956 • Singer, songwriter, social activist, filmmaker **Lorraine Segato** (Lorraine Christine Segato) (The Parachute Club), Hamilton, ON.

(B) November 13, 1956 • Guitarist, vocalist, producer **Aldo Nova** (Aldo Capouscio), Montréal, QC.

(B) November 22, 1956 • Musician, singer, songwriter **Lawrence Gowan** (Lawrence Henry Gowan), Glasgow, Scotland.

(B) July 9, 1957 • Singer, songwriter, musician **Fred Eaglesmith** (Frederick John Elgersma), Castor Centre, ON.

(B) July 20, 1957 • Drummer **Merlina DeFranco** (DeFranco Family), Port Colborne, ON.

(B) December 19, 1957 • Keyboardist **Doug Johnson** (Loverboy), New Westminster, BC.

(D) April 1, 1958 • Lyricist **Alfred Bryan**, Gladstone, NJ.

(B) May 22, 1958 • Vocalist, songwriter, multi-instrumentalist **Dalbello** (Lisa Dalbello), Weston (Toronto), ON.

(B) September 20, 1958 • Academy Award-winning Composer **Mychael Danna**, Winnipeg, MB.

(B) 1958 • Singer, songwriter, musician **Luba** (Lubomira Kowalchyk), Montréal, QC.

(B) January 4, 1959 • Singer, songwriter, dancer, actress, model **Vanity** aka Denise Matthews-Smith aka D.D. Winters (Denise Katrina Matthews), Niagara Falls, ON.

(B) March 22, 1959 • Singer, songwriter, producer **Moe Berg** (The Pursuit of Happiness), Edmonton, AB.

(B) April 27, 1959 • Classical pianist **Louis Lortie**, Montréal, QC.

(D) April 29, 1959 • Canadian operatic tenor/Metropolitan Opera GM **Edward Johnson**, Guelph, ON.

(B) April 30, 1959 • Actor, producer, director, singer, writer **Paul Gross** (Paul Michael Gross), Calgary, AB.

(B) August 10, 1959 • Singer, songwriter **Florent Vollant** (Kashtin), Maliotenam, QC.

(B) August 31, 1959 • Singer, producer **Tony DeFranco** (DeFranco Family), Port Colborne, ON.

(B) October 28, 1959 • Singer, songwriter **James Keelaghan**, Calgary, AB.

(B) November 5, 1959 • Singer, songwriter, musician, producer, photographer **Bryan Adams** (Bryan Guy Adams), Kingston, ON.

(B) December 25, 1959 • Classical pianist **Jon Kimura** Parker, Vancouver, BC.

(B) February 19, 1960 • Singer, songwriter, guitarist **Steve Poltz**, Halifax, NS.

(B) March 23, 1960 • Singer, songwriter **George Fox**, Calgary, AB.

(D) July 6, 1960 • Nurse, songwriter **Elizabeth Clarke**, West Vancouver, BC.

(B) September 17, 1960 • Singer, songwriter **John Bottomley**.

(B) September 24, 1960 • Singer, songwriter, producer, broadcaster, actress **Amy Sky**, Toronto, ON.

(B) November 19, 1960 • Guitarist **Don Ross** (Donald James Ross), Montréal, QC.

(B) 1960 • Singer, composer, producer, broadcaster **Mary Jane Lamond**, Kingston, ON.

(B) January 27, 1961 • Singer **Margo Timmins** (Cowboy Junkies), Montréal, QC.

(B) May 14, 1961 • Singer, songwriter, author **Jean Leclerc** aka Jean Leloup, Sainte-Foy, QC.

(B) July 1, 1961 • Singer, songwriter **Michelle Wright**, Chatham, ON.

(B) August 31, 1961 • Singer, songwriter **Bruce Guthro**, Cape Breton Island, NS.

(B) September 12, 1961 • Vocalist, songwriter, actress, author **Mylène Farmer** (Mylène Jeanne Gautier), Pierrefonds (Montréal), QC.

(B) November 2, 1961 • Vocalist, songwriter, actress **k.d. lang** (Kathryn Dawn Lang), Edmonton, AB.

(B) February 9, 1962 • Singer, songwriter, producer, composer, musician **Craig Northey** (The Odds), Port Moody, BC.

(B) March 27, 1962 • Singer/songwriter **Jann Arden** (Jann Arden Anne Richards), Calgary, AB.

(B) April 13, 1962 • Musician, writer, broadcaster **Jaymz Bee** (James Terrence Doyle).

(B) May 31, 1962 • Singer, songwriter, producer, musician **Corey Hart** (Corey Mitchell Hart), Montréal, QC.

(B) May 31, 1962 • Singer, songwriter, producer, musician **Corey Hart** (Corey Mitchell Hart), Montréal, QC.

(B) July 21, 1962 • Rock and jazz singer, songwriter **Lee Aaron** (Karen Lynn Greening), Belleville, ON.

(B) July 22, 1962 • Singer **Martine St-Clair** (Martine Nault), Montréal, QC.

(D) July 25, 1962 • Broadway musical star **Christie MacDonald**.

(B) September 18, 1962 • Singer, musician, songwriter, actor **John Mann** (John Fraser Mann) (Spirit of the West), Calgary, AB.

(B) November 14, 1962 • Writer, musician, broadcaster, politician **Charlie Angus** (Charles Joseph Angus), Timmins, ON.

(B) December 23, 1962 • Singer, songwriter, broadcaster, actress **Sass Jordan** (Sarah Jordan), Birmingham, England.

(B) 1962 • Singer **Liberty Silver**, Detroit, MI.

(B) January 26, 1963 • Singer **France Joli**, Montréal, QC.

(B) March 26, 1963 • Singer, songwriter, actor, broadcaster **Roch Voisine** (Joseph Armand Roch Voisine), Edmundston, NB.

(B) September 11, 1963 • Musician, songwriter, author, broadcaster **Dave Bidini** (Rheostatics), Etobicoke (Toronto), ON.

(D) September 23, 1963 • Ragtime and jazz pianist, composer **William Eckstein**, Montréal, QC.

(B) 1963 • Singer, songwriter **Stephen Fearing**, Vancouver, BC.

(B) January 8, 1964 • Singer, songwriter **Ron Sexsmith** (Ronald Eldon Sexsmith), St. Catharines, ON.

(B) January 10, 1964 • Singer, songwriter, guitarist **Brad Roberts** (Bradley Kenneth Roberts) (Crash Test Dummies), Winnipeg, MB.

(B) February 6, 1964 • Vocalist, songwriter, musician **Gord Downie** (Gordon Edgar Downie) (The Tragically Hip), Amherstview, ON.

(B) August 17, 1964 • Singer, songwriter, guitarist, producer **Colin James** (Colin James Munn), Regina, SK.

(B) November 16, 1964 • Jazz pianist, vocalist **Diana Krall** (Diana Jean Krall), Nanaimo, BC.

(D) December 27, 1964 • Jazz pianist **Chris Cage**, North Vancouver, BC.

(B) January 31, 1965 • Cellist **Ofra Harnoy**, Hadera, Israel.

(B) August 28, 1965 • Country/pop singer, songwriter **Shania Twain** (Eilleen Regina Edwards), Windsor, ON.

(B) November 11, 1965 • Singer, musician, songwriter **Kim Stockwood**, St. John's, NF.

(B) December 17, 1965 • Jazz saxophonist, pianist, composer, producer, music educator **Phil Dwyer** (Philip Richard Dwyer), Vancouver Island, BC.

(B) 1965 • Singer, guitarist, songwriter **Ron Hawkins** (Ronald James Hawkins) (Lowest of the Low), Toronto, ON.

(B) March 10, 1966 • Guitarist, vocalist **Phil X** (Theofilis Xenidis), Toronto, ON.

(B) March 25, 1966 • Guitarist, vocalist, broadcaster, musicologist **Jeff Healey** (Norman Jeffrey Healey), Toronto, ON.

(B) April 24, 1966 • Singer, songwriter, social activist **David Usher** (Moist), Oxford, England.

(D) August 9, 1966 • Record executive **Herbert Samuel Berliner**, Montréal, QC.

(B) January 27, 1967 • Singer/songwriter **Susan Aglukark**, Churchill, MB.

B) May 22, 1967 • Singer, multi-instrumentalist **Sean McCann** "The Shantyman" (Great Big Sea), Gulf Island, NF.

(B) June 9, 1967 • Broadcaster, musician, songwriter, producer **Jian Ghomeshi** (Moxy Fruvous), London, England.

(B) July 1, 1967 • Actress **Pamela Anderson**, Ladysmith, Vancouver Island, BC.

(B) September 21, 1967 • Drummer **Tyler Stewart** (Tyler Joseph Stewart) (Barenaked Ladies), Toronto, ON.

(B) November 15, 1967 • Drummer, songwriter, guitarist **Andrew Scott** (Andrew Walter Gibson Scott) (Sloan), Ottawa, ON.

(B) December 19, 1967 • Singer, songwriter, musician, actress, music educator **Melanie Doane**, Halifax, NS.

(B) January 8, 1968 • Singer, songwriter **Gil Grand** (Gilles Lagrandeur), Sudbury, ON.

(B) January 28, 1968 • Singer, songwriter, musician **Sarah McLachlan** (Sarah Ann McLachlan), Halifax, NS.

(D) February 3, 1968 • Operatic contralto **Portia White**, Toronto, ON.

(B) March 29, 1968 • Blues singer, guitarist **Sue Foley**, Ottawa, ON.

(B) March 30, 1968 • Singer **Céline Dion**, Charlemagne, QC.

(B) March 31, 1968 • Rapper, producer, actor "Godfather of Canadian Hip Hop" **Maestro Fresh Wes** (Wesley Williams), Toronto, ON.

(B) April 3, 1968 • Vocalist **Sebastian Bach** (Sebastian Philip Bierk) (Skid Row), Detroit, MI.

(B) April 14, 1968 • Musician, singer, songwriter **A.C. Newman** (Allan Carl Newman) (The New Pornographers), Vancouver, BC.

(B) July 5, 1968 • Broadcaster, musician **Nardwuar the Human Serviette** (John Ruskin), Vancouver, BC.

(B) August 11, 1968 • Singer, songwriter **Veda Hille**, Vancouver, BC.

(B) August 13, 1968 • Singer, songwriter, musician **Tal Bachman** (Talmage Bachman), Winnipeg, MB.

(B) October 14, 1968 • Musician, songwriter, **Jay Ferguson** (Sloan), Halifax, NS.

(B) November 7, 1968 • Bassist, multi-instrumentalist, songwriter **Chris Murphy** (Sloan), Charlottetown, PEI.

(B) December 24, 1968 • Singer, songwriter, broadcaster **Tariq Hussain**, Cowansville, QC.

(B) January 23, 1969 • Singer, songwriter, multi-instrumentalist **J.P. Cormier** (John Paul Cormier), London, ON.

(B) May 17, 1969 • Vocalist, musician, songwriter, producer, actor **Alan Doyle** (Great Big Sea), Petty Harbour, NF.

(B) July 3, 1969 • Keyboardist **Kevin Hearn** (Kevin Neil Hearn) (Rheostatics, Barenaked Ladies, Kevin Hearn and Thin Buckle), Grimsby, ON.

(B) July 7, 1969 • Singer **Nathalie Simard**, Ile d'Orléans, QC.

(B) July 7, 1969 • Actress, musician, voice actress **Cree Summer** (Cree Summer Francks), Los Angeles, CA.

(B) September 20, 1969 • Singer, multi-instrumentalist, songwriter **Patrick Pentland** (Sloan), Newtownards, County Down, Northern Ireland.

(B) September 28, 1969 • Singer, musician **Éric Lapointe**, Point-aux-Trembles, QC.

(B) October 2, 1969 • Guitarist, singer, songwriter **Jeff Martin** (Jeffrey Scott Martin) (The Tea Party), Windsor, ON.

(B) October 30, 1969 • Singer, rapper, songwriter, producer **Snow** (Darrin Kenneth O'Brien), North York (Toronto), ON.

(D) December 2, 1969 • Impresario **Lily Laverock**, Duncan, BC.

(B) 1969 • Multi-instrumentalist **Brendan Canning** (Broken Social Scene), Toronto, ON.

(B) February 18, 1970 • Singer, songwriter, musician **Raine Maida** (Michael Anthony Maida of Our Lady Peace), Weston (Toronto), ON.

(B) June 4, 1970 • Techno musician **Richard "Richie" Hawtin**, Banbury, England.

(B) June 16, 1970 • Singer, actress **Camille Henderson** (West End Girls), Vancouver, BC.

(B) June 22, 1970 • Singer, songwriter, guitarist **Steven Page** (Steven Jay Page) (Barenaked Ladies), Scarborough (Toronto), ON.

(B) September 1, 1970 • Singer, broadcaster, actress **Mitsou** (Mitsou Annie Marie Gélinas), Loretteville, QC.

(B) September 3, 1970 • Singer, songwriter **Haydain Neale** (jacksoul), Hamilton, ON.

(D) September 18, 1970 • Guitarist, singer **Jim Hendrix**, London, England.

(B) October 25, 1970 • Singer, songwriter, guitarist **Ed Robertson** (Lloyd Edward Elwyn Robertson), Scarborough (Toronto), ON.

(B) December 5, 1970 • Singer, songwriter, musician, producer **Rick White**, Moncton, NB.

(B) 1970 • **King Lou** (Louie Robinson) (Dream Warriors), Jamaica.

(B) 1970 • **Capital Q** (Frank Allert) (Dream Warriors), Trinidad.

(B) 1970 • Rapper, actress **Michie Mee** (Michelle McCullock), Toronto, ON.

(B) 1970 • Singer, songwriter **Kinnie Starr** (Alida Kinnie Starr Pierre), Calgary, AB.

(B) February 12, 1971 • Singer, songwriter **Hayden** (Paul Hayden Desser), Thornhill, ON.

(B) February 25, 1971 • Singer, songwriter **Daniel Powter** (Daniel Richard Powter), Vernon, BC.

(B) January 14, 1971 • Singer, songwriter **Jennifer Whiteley,** Toronto, ON.

(D) April 17, 1971 • Vocalist/composer/saxophonist **Carmen Lombardo**, Miami, FL.

(B) April 30, 1971 • Singer, songwriter **Carolyn Dawn Johnson**, Grande Prairie, AB.

(B) June 15, 1971 • Singer, songwriter, actress, motivational speaker **Bif Naked** (Beth Torbert), New Delhi, India.

(B) June 29, 1971 • Singer, songwriter, musician **Matthew Good** (Matthew Good Band), Burnaby, BC.

(B) July 30, 1971 • Vocalist, broadcaster, writer **Grant Lawrence** (The Smugglers), Vancouver, BC.

(B) July 30, 1971 • Singer, songwriter, producer **Gordie Sampson**, Big Pond, NS.

(B) February 20, 1972 • Singer, rapper, songwriter, producer **k-os** (Kevin "Kheaven" Brereton), Toronto, ON.

(B) March 17, 1972 • Singer, songwriter, multi-instrumentalist **Torquil Campbell** (Broken Social Scene, Stars).

(B) May 5, 1972 • Singer, songwriter, guitarist **Devin Townsend** (Devin Garret Townsend), New Westminster, BC.

(B) May 17, 1972 • Bass player, singer, songwriter, photographer **Auf der Maur** (Melissa Auf der Maur), Montréal, QC.

B) June 13, 1972 • Fiddler **Natalie MacMaster**, Troy, Cape Breton, NS.

(B) June 26, 1972 • Singer, songwriter **Garou** (Pierre Garand), Sherbrooke, QC.

(B) July 21, 1972 • Singer, songwriter **Paul Brandt** (Paul Rennée Belobersycky), Calgary, AB.

(B) July 21, 1972 • Guitarist, singer, songwriter **Ian Thornley** (Big Wreck), Toronto, ON.

(B) August 16, 1972 • Broadcaster (MuchMusic, CBC, CNN) **George Stroumboulopoulos** (George Mark Paul Stroumboulopoulos), Malton (Mississauga/Toronto), ON.

(B) August 29, 1972 • Singer **Amanda Marshall** (Amanda Meta Marshall), Toronto, ON.

(D) March 26, 1973 • Fiddler, TV personality **Don Messer** (Donald Charles Frederick Messer), Halifax, NS.

(B) May 18, 1973 • Singer, songwriter, pianist, guitarist **Chantal Kreviazuk** (Chantal Jennifer Kreviazuk), Winnipeg, MB.

(B) July 22, 1973 • Singer, songwriter, composer **Rufus Wainwright** (Rufus McGarrigle Wainwright), Rhinebeck, NY.

(B) October 20, 1973 • Singer, songwriter **Reid Jamieson** (Reid Allan Jamieson), Toronto, ON.

(B) October 25, 1973 • Singer, songwriter **Tara MacLean** (Tara Margaret Charity MacLean), Charlottetown, PEI.

(B) November 14, 1973 • Hip-hop artist **Moka Only** (Daniel Denton), Langford, BC.

(B) November 14, 1973 • Multi-instrumentalist, singer, songwriter, entrepreneur **Mark Sultan** (Mark Antonio Pepe) (BBQ, The King Khan & BBQ Show), Montréal, QC.

(B) December 3, 1973 • Singer, songwriter, guitarist **Amy Millan** (Stars, Broken Social Scene), Toronto, ON.

(B) January 25, 1974 • Singer, songwriter **Emily Haines** (Metric), New Delhi, India.

(B) June 1, 1974 • Singer, songwriter, producer, actress **Alanis Morissette** (Alanis Nadine Morissette), Ottawa, ON.

(B) October 2, 1974 • Singer, songwriter **Sam Roberts**, Westmount, (Montréal), QC.

(B) October 29, 1974 • Guitarist, singer, songwriter **Derek Miller**, Six Nations, (Brantford), ON.

(B) November 15, 1974 • Singer, songwriter, guitarist, producer **Chad Kroeger** (Chad Robert Kroeger) (Nickelback), Hanna, AB.

(B) 1974 • DJ, musician, graphic novelist **Kid Koala** (Eric San), Vancouver, BC.

(B) February 24, 1975 • Fiddler **Ashley MacIsaac** (Ashley Dwayne MacIsaac), Creignish, Cape Breton, NS.

(B) March 4, 1975 • Singer, songwriter, producer **Hawksley Workman**, Huntsville, ON.

(B) March 13, 1975 • R&B, soul singer, songwriter **Glenn Lewis** (Glenn Ricketts), Toronto, ON.

(B) April 18, 1975 • Singer, songwriter, musician, producer Joel Plaskett, Lunenburg, NS.

(B) May 9, 1975 • R&B singer, songwriter **Tamia** (Tamia Marilyn Hill), Windsor, ON.

(D) September 6, 1975 • Composer, Vaudeville performer **Shelton Brooks**, Los Angeles, CA

(B) September 9, 1975 • Singer **Michael Bublé**, Burnaby, BC.

(B) October 23, 1975 • Singer, songwriter, musician **Holly McNarland**, The Pas, MB.

(B) December 9, 1975 • Singer, songwriter **Damhnait Doyle** (Shay, The Heartbroken), Labrador City, NF.

(D) February 9, 1976 • Band leader, arranger, composer **Percy Faith**, Encino, CA.

(B) February 13, 1976 • Singer, songwriter, multi-instrumentalist **Feist** (Leslie Feist), Amherst, NS.

(B) May 8, 1976 • Singer, songwriter **Martha Wainwright**, Montréal, QC.

(B) May 12, 1976 • Rapper, producer, **Kardinal Offishall** (Jason D. Harrow), Toronto, ON.

(B) September 9, 1976 • Musician, songwriter **Kevin Drew** (Broken Social Scene), Toronto, ON.

(B) September 14, 1976 • Musician, songwriter, producer **Simon Collins**, Hammersmith (London), England.

(B) October 15, 1976 • Rock/pop singer **Suzie McNeil** (Susan Jane McNeil), Mississauga, ON.

(B) 1976 • Experimental electronic artist **Mark Templeton**, Edmonton, AB.

(B) January 7, 1977 • Pianist, composer, vocalist, arranger **Michael Kaeshammer**, Offenburg, Germany.

(B) June 21, 1977 • Singer, songwriter, musician, visual artist, actress **Sarah Slean** (Sarah Hope Sloan), Pickering, ON.

(B) August 18, 1977 • Multi-instrumentalist, vocalist **Régine Chassagne** (Arcade Fire). Montréal, QC.

(B) October 4, 1977 • Multi-instrumentalist, composer, producer **Richard Reed Parry** (Arcade Fire), Toronto, ON.

(D) November 5, 1977 • Bandleader/violinist **Guy Lombardo** (Gaetano Alberto Lombardo), Houston, TX.

(B) December 13, 1977 • Rapper/producer **Classified** (nee Luke Boyd), Enfield, NS.

(B) 1977 • Inuk throat singer **Tanya Tagaq** (Tanya Tagaq Gillis), Cambridge Bay (Ikaluktuutiak), NU.

B) March 6, 1978 • Rapper, singer, producer **Saukrates** (Karl Amani Walloo), Toronto, ON.

(D) March 23, 1978 • Tenor **Bill Kenny** (The Ink Spots), Vancouver, BC. (Kenny who had left The Ink Spots in 1953, moved to Vancouver in 1961.)

(B) February 1, 1978 • Rapper, singer, songwriter, poet, musician **K'naan** (Keinan Abdi Warsame), Mogadishu, Somalia.

(B) June 6, 1978 • Drummer, multi-instrumentalist **Jeremy Gara** (Arcade Fire), Ottawa, ON.

(B) July 11, 1978 • Singer, songwriter, musician **Kathleen Edwards**, Ottawa, ON.

(B) November 19, 1978 • Jazz musician, vocalist **Matt Dusk** (Matthew Aaron Dusk), Toronto, ON.

(B) December 2, 1978 • Singer, songwriter, actress **Nelly Furtado** (Nelly Kim Furtado), Victoria, BC.

(B) December 23, 1978 • Singer, songwriter **Esthero** (Jenny-Bea Englishman), Stratford, ON.

(B) 1978 • Composer, musician, producer **Caribou** (Daniel Victor Snaith), Dundas, ON.

(B) 1978 • R&B/soul singer **Remy Shand** (Remy David Shand), Winnipeg, MB.

(B) 1978 • Rapper, producer **Berris Smith**, St. Boniface, MB.

(B) April 18, 1979 • Singer, songwriter, producer **Karl Wolf**, Beirut, Lebanon.

(B) July 16, 1979 • Singer, songwriter **Nathan Rogers**, Hamilton, ON.

(B) August 10, 1979 • Singer, songwriter **Matt Mays** (The Guthries, Matt Mays & El Torpedo), Hamilton, ON.

(B) August 27, 1979 • Violinist **Sarah Neufeld** (Arcade Fire), Courtenay, BC.

(B) October 13, 1979 • Singer **Ryan Malcolm**, Kingston, ON.

(B) 1979 • Singer, songwriter **Patrick Watson**, Montréal, QC.

(B) April 14, 1980 • Multi-instrumentalist, vocalist, songwriter **Win Butler** (Arcade Fire), Carson, CA.

(D) June 16, 1980 • Singer, songwriter, actor **Bob Nolan** (Sons of the Pioneers), Newport Beach, CA.

(D) January 4, 1981 • Pianist, songwriter **Ruth Lowe**, Toronto, ON.

(D) April 9, 1982 • Conductor/pianist/composer/music educator **Wilfrid Pelletier**, Wayne, PA.

(B) October 6, 1982 • Multi-instrumentalist **Will Butler** (William Pierce Butler)(Arcade Fire), Northern CA.

(B) May 21, 1983 • **Anjulie** (Anjulie Persaud), Oakville, ON

(D) June 2, 1983 • Singer, songwriter **Stan Rogers**, Air Canada flight 797, Hebron, Kentucky (Cincinnati/North Kentucky International Airport).

(B) July 4, 1983 • **Melanie Fiona** (Melanie Fiona Hallim), Toronto, ON.

(B) July 9, 1984 • Singer, songwriter **Jacob Hoggard** (Hedley), Burnaby, BC.

(D) August 12, 1984 • Guitarist **Lenny Breau**, Ventura, CA.

(B) July 12, 1985 • Singer **Theo Tams** (Theo Tyler Tams), Lethbridge, AB.

(B) September 16, 1985 • Singer and songwriter **Danny Fernandes**, Toronto, ON.

(B) November 21, 1985 • Singer and songwriter **Carly Rae Jepsen**, Mission, BC.

(D) March 4, 1986 • Pianist, vocalist, songwriter **Richard Manuel** of The Band, apparently in a fit of depression, hangs himself in the bathroom of the Winter Park Holiday Inn, after a gig with the group in Winter Park, Florida. Robbie Robertson dedicates future solo track, "Fallen Angel," to him. Eric Clapton's tribute to Manuel is "Holy Mother." His funeral service is held five days later in Stratford, ON.

(B) October 24, 1986 • Rapper, songwriter, actor **Drake** (Aubrey Drake Graham), Toronto, ON.

(D) March 20, 1988 • Jazz pianist, arranger, composer, band leader **Gil Evans**, Cuernavaca, Mexico.

(B) June 16, 1988 • Singer, songwriter, model, actress **Keshia Chanté** (Keshia Chanté Harper), Ottawa, ON.

(D) January 20, 1989 • Singer/actress **Beatrice Lillie**, Henley-On-Thames, England, Alzheimer's Disease.

(B) May 14, 1989 • **Kristina Maria** (nee Kristina Maria Chaloub), Ottawa, ON.

(D) March 5, 1990 • Guitarist **Bob Regan** (The Canadian Sweethearts).

(B) June 27, 1990 • Singer **Aselin Debison**, Glace Bay, NS.

(D) July 18, 1990 • Vocalist, songwriter **Gerry Boulet**, Montréal, QC.

(B) August 14, 1990 • Singer **Jaydee Bixby**, Drumheller, AB.

(B) December 8, 1990 • Singer, Host, Dancer **Martha Joy** (Martha Joy Lim-Fiuza), Toronto, ON.

(B) December 28, 1990 • Pop/rock singer, songwriter **Andrew F**, Calgary, AB.

(B) March 15, 1993 • **Alyssa Reid** (Alyssa Ashley Reid), Edmonton, AB.

(B) April 8, 1993 • Singer **Tyler Shaw**, Coquitlam, BC.

(B) April 25, 1993 • Rock/pop singer, songwriter **Shiloh** (Shiloh Hoganson), Abbotsford, BC.

(D) November 28, 1993 • Drummer **Jerry Edmonton** (Steppenwolf), Santa Barbara, CA.

(B) 1993 • **Tyler Shaw**, Coquitlam, BC.

(B) February 8, 1994 • Jazz singer **Nikki Yanofsky** (Nicole Yanofsky), Montréal, QC.

(B) March 1, 1994 • Singer, songwriter, musician, actor **Justin Bieber** (Justin Drew Bieber), London, ON.

(D) July 21, 1994 • Singer/actress **Dorothy Collins**, Watervliet, NY.

(D) December 5, 1994 • Singer, arranger, saxophonist, pianist **Art Hallman**, Richmond Hill, ON.

(B) January 3, 1995 • Singer, actress, dancer **Victoria Duffield**, Abbotsford, BC.

(D) January 3, 1995 • Former CKLW Windsor/Detroit News Director/recording artist **Byron MacGregor**.

(D) January 19, 1995 • Singer, songwriter **Gene MacLellan**, Summerside, PEI.

(D) October 9, 1996 • Singer, songwriter **Colleen Peterson**, Toronto, ON.

Richard Manuel of The Band

(D) December 5, 1996 • Country singer/songwriter **Wilf Carter** (aka Montana Slim), Scottsdale, AZ.

(D) January 1, 1997 • Composer, arranger, multi-instrumentalist **Hagood Hardy**, Hamilton, ON.

(D) August 16, 1997 • "Canada's King of Yodelers" **Donn Reynolds**, Toronto, ON.

(D) March 9, 1999 • Composer **Harry Somers**, Toronto, ON.

(D) May 17, 1999 • Producer, musician **Bruce Fairbairn**, Vancouver, BC.

(D) December 10, 1999 • Bassist, vocalist, multi-instrumentalist **Rick Danko** (The Band), Marbletown, NY.

(D) December 20, 1999 • Country music legend **Hank Snow**, Madison, TN.

(D) December 31, 1999 • Blues singer **Richard "Hock" Walsh** (Downchild Blues Band), Toronto, ON.

(D) January 16, 2000 • Cape Breton fiddle player **John Morris Rankin** (The Rankins), Mabou, Cape Breton, NS.

(B) July 17, 2000 • Singer, musician **Maria Aragon** (Maria Lourdes Aragon), Winnipeg, MB.

(D) November 30, 2000 • Bassist **Scott Smith** (Loverboy), Off the coast of San Francisco, CA.

(D) March 28, 2001 • Jazz musician, composer **Moe Koffman**, Orangeville, ON.

(D) January 21, 2002 • Singer, songwriter **Wade Hemsworth**, Montréal, QC.

BIRTHS & DEATHS

(D) December 13, 2002 • Guitarist/restaurateur **Zal Yanovsky** (The Lovin' Spoonful), Kingston, ON.

(D) December 31, 2002 • Guitarist **Kevin MacMichael** (Cutting Crew), Halifax, NS.

(D) February 4, 2003 • Jazz bassist **Charlie Biddle**, Montréal, QC.

(D) June 27, 2003 • Bass player, vocalist **Mike Ferbey** (The Rhythm Pals), Kelowna, BC.

(D) September 5, 2003 • Singer/radio-TV host/actress **Gisele MacKenzie**.

(D) September 17, 2003 • Organist, arranger, producer **Robbie King**, Vancouver, BC.

(D) January 20, 2004 • *RPM Weekly* publisher **Walt Grealis**, Toronto, ON.

(D) May 7, 2004 • Vocalist **Rudi Maugeri** (The Crew Cuts), Las Vegas, NV.

(D) June 15, 2004 • Vocalist **Jimmy Arnold** (The Four Lads).

(D) October 1, 2004 • Bass player **Bruce Palmer** (Buffalo Springfield), Belleville, ON.

(D) October 22, 2004 • Vocalist **Bill Reed** (The Diamonds), Whitby, ON.

(D) May 25, 2005 • Guitarist/songwriter **Domenic Troiano**, Toronto, ON.

(D) July 15, 2005 • Drummer, bodhran player **Polly "Lolly" Lawton** (The Paperboys, The Irish Rovers).

(D) July 21, 2005 • Blues vocalist **Long John Baldry**, Vancouver, BC.

(D) August 31, 2005 • Bass player, vocalist **Jim Bescott** (K-Tels, Young Canadians), Kitsilano (Vancouver), BC.

(D) August 23, 2006 • Jazz musician, band leader **Maynard Ferguson**, Ventura, CA.

(D) September 14, 2006 • Singer Norman Brooks, Montréal, QC.

(D) November 22, 2006 • "Canadian Godfather of Celtic Music" **John Allan Cameron**, Toronto, ON.

(D) December 23, 2006 • Singer, guitarist, pianist **Dutch Mason** (Norman Byron Mason), Truro, NS.

(D) January 10, 2007 • Original founding member of The Rankins **Geraldine Coyne** (Geraldine Rankin), Calgary, AB.

(D) January 19, 2007 • Vocalist **Denny Doherty** (The Mamas & the Papas), Mississauga, ON.

(D) February 17, 2007 • Singer **Dermot O'Reilly** (Ryan's Fancy), St. John's, NF.

(D) June 15, 2007 • Pianist **Richard Bell** (Janis Joplin's Full Tilt Boogie Band/The Band), Toronto, ON.

(D) June 18, 2007 • Singer, composer, multi-instrumentalist, broadcaster **Georges Thurston** (Boule Noir), Montréal, QC.

(D) September 25, 2007 • Bassist **Patrick Bourque** (Emerson Drive), Montréal, QC.

(D) October 30, 2007 • Vocalist, actor **Robert Goulet**, Los Angeles, CA.

(D) November 8, 2007 • Pianist, composer **John Arpin**, Toronto, ON.

(D) December 23, 2007 • Pianist, composer **Oscar Peterson** (Oscar Emmanuel Peterson), Mississauga, ON.

(D) January 4, 2008 • Electronic music pioneer **Mort Garson**, San Francisco, CA.

(D) February 15, 2008 • Singer, songwriter, multi-instrumentalist **Willie P. Bennett**, Peterborough, ON.

(D) March 2, 2008 • Guitarist, vocalist, broadcaster, musicologist **Jeff Healey**, Toronto, ON.

(D) May 11, 2008 • Drummer **John Rutsey** (Rush), Toronto, ON.

(D) July 3, 2008 • Fiddler **Oliver Schroer**, Toronto, ON.

(D) September 10, 2008 • Trumpet player **Arnie Chycoski**, Olympia, WA.

(D) January 31, 2009 • Drummer **Dewey Martin** (Buffalo Springfield), Van Nuys, CA.

(D) March 15, 2009 • Baritone, actor **Edmund Hockridge**, Peterborough, England.

(D) March 22, 2009 • Folklorist **Archie Green**, San Francisco, CA.

(D) May 3, 2009 • Classical pianist **Renée Morisset**, Québec City, QC.

(D) June 27, 2009 • Blues musician, singer **Jackie Washington**, Hamilton, ON.

(D) October 28, 2009 • Folk singer **Taylor Mitchell** (Taylor Luciow), Halifax, NS.

(D) November 22, 2009 • Singer, songwriter **Haydain Neale** (jacksoul), Toronto, ON.

(D) January 1, 2010 • Folk singer **Lhasa de Sela**, Montréal, QC.

(D) January 18, 2010 • Singer/songwriter **Kate McGarrigle** (Kate & Anna McGarrigle), Montréal, QC.

(D) January 21, 2010 • Novelist (Whale Music), musician (Porkbelly Futures) **Paul Quarrington**, Toronto, ON.

(D) February 9, 2010 • Composer, music educator **Jacques Hétu**, St-Hippolyte, QC.

(D) March 15, 2010 • Guitarist, studio owner **Dan Achen** (Junkhouse), Hamilton, ON.

(D) April 18, 2010 • Drummer **Devon Clifford** (You Say Party!), Vancouver, BC.

(D) April 22, 2010 • Lyricist, music critic biographer **Gene Lees**, Ojai, CA.

(D) April 28, 2010 - Vocalist **Corrado "Connie" Codarini** (The Four Lads), Concord, NC.

(D) May 1, 2010 • Jazz valve trombonist, band leader, composer, arranger, music educator **Rob McConnell**, Toronto, ON.

(D) June 16, 2010 • Operatic contralto **Maureen Forester**, Toronto, ON.

(D) July 27, 2010 • Country rock singer, songwriter **Edward Gamblin**, Winnipeg, MB.

(D) August 8, 2010 • Vocalist **Ted Kowalski** (The Diamonds).

(D) November 3, 2010 • Bassist **Jim Clench** (April Wine), Montréal, QC.

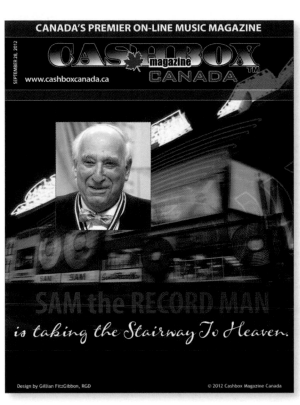

(D) April 6, 2011 • Singer, songwriter **John Bottomley**, Brackendale, BC.

(D) May 13, 2011 • Legendary record producer **Jack Richardson**, London, ON.

(D) May 28, 2011 • Jazz singer **Alys Robi**, Montréal, QC.

(D) June 9, 2011 • Chansonnier, composer **Claude Léveillé**, Saint-Benoit-de-Mirabel, QC.

(D) June 23, 2011 • Guitarist **Gaye Delorme**, Calgary, AB.

(D) August 7, 2011 • Jazz and Swing Pianist **Jiri Traxler**, Edmonton, AB.

(D) January 25, 2012 • Photographer, music video director **Andrew MacNaughtan**, Los Angeles, CA.

(D) February 21, 2012 • Film and broadcast executive, 1st CRTC Chairman **Pierre Juneau.**

(D) April 19, 2012 • Drummer, vocalist, multi-instrumentalist, actor **Levon Helm** (The Band), New York, NY.

(D) April 23, 2012 • Percussionist, record producer **Billy Bryans** (Parachute Club), Toronto, ON.

(D) August 23, 2012 • Vocalist **Phil Levitt** (The Diamonds).

(D) September 23, 2012 • Legendary record retailer **Sam Sniderman** (Sam the Record Man), Toronto, ON.

(D) September 30, 2012 • Vocalist **Raylene Rankin** (The Rankins), Halifax, NS.

(D) January 15, 2013 • Conductor, cellist, music educator **Yuli Turovsky**, Montréal, QC.

(D) March 6, 2013 • Country singer, songwriter **Stompin' Tom Connors**, Ballinafad, ON.

(D) April 16, 2013 • Singer, songwriter, TV personality **Rita MacNeil**, Sydney, Cape Breton, NS.

(D) May 8, 2013 • TV producer, performer **Bill Langstroth**, Moncton, NB.

TOP 10 EMERGING ARTISTS PREVIEWS

So who is going to generate those Oh What A Feeling music moments in the future? To close the book, we are showcasing a selection of emerging Canadian artists from various music genres we feel you should meet… if you haven't already. We looked at a variety of artists from across the country, especially those who have recently enjoyed wide acclamation in categories like "Rising Star," "Breakthrough" and "Best New" at music award shows. In the end, though, it was the author's limb to go out on in creating the final list of ten, arranged alphabetically without ranking.

As a quick aside, the Canadian Urban Music Conference has taken a unique approach to its annual award show by only honouring future stars as part of their "One to Watch" Music Awards. For the record, their most recent list of 14 includes A-Game, Lincoln Blanche, Chach, Culture Shock, Fito Blanko, Lil JaXe, Lina Luztono, Quanche, Queen of Hearts, SheKing, Lucas Teague, Devon Tracy, Shi Wisdom and Zolo.

So, taking a page from their book, let's just say that the emerging Canadian artists listed here are the ones to watch. It has been said that to be given the designation of "Most Promising" is the kiss of death. What's that old saying? — "Better to have been kissed and lost than to never have been kissed at all." For better or worse, the following ten Canadian artists — have been well and truly smooched.

OH WHAT A FEELING

>> EMERGING ARTISTS

TOP 10 EMERGING ARTIST PREVIEWS

JULY 30 2010 — EMERGING CANADIAN ARTISTS — Billboard

AIRPLAY MONITORED BY nielsen BDS — SALES DATA COMPILED BY nielsen SoundScan

TW	LW	WKS ON CHART	ARTIST/LABEL	TITLE	HOT 100 RANK
1	3	7	K'NAAN A&M/OCTONE/UNIVERSAL ★★ No. 1 (1 week) ★★	Take A Minute	22
2	1	27	DOWN WITH WEBSTER UNIVERSAL MOTOWN/UNIVERSAL	Your Man	26
3	4	13	JUSTIN BIEBER SCHOOLBOY/RAYMOND BRAUN/ISLAND/UNIVERSAL	Somebody To Love	35
4	5	25	MARIANAS TRENCH 604/UNIVERSAL	Celebrity Status	36
5	2	41	K'NAAN A&M/OCTONE/UNIVERSAL	Wavin' Flag	39
6	6	11	STEF LANG HIPJOINT/UNIVERSAL	Mr. Immature	47
7	7	11	ASH KOLEY NETTWERK/SONY MUSIC	Don't Let Your Feet Touch Ground	55
8	10	4	MY DARKEST DAYS 604/UNIVERSAL	Porn Star Dancing	62
9	12	3	ANDREW ALLEN ANDREW ALLEN	Loving You Tonight	83
10	8	7	JUSTIN BIEBER FEATURING JADEN SMITH SCHOOLBOY/RAYMOND BRAUN/ISLAND/UNIVERSAL	Never Say Never	89
11	9	27	JUSTIN BIEBER FEATURING LUDACRIS SCHOOLBOY/RAYMOND BRAUN/ISLAND/UNIVERSAL	Baby	90
12	13	5	RAGHAV CORDOVA BAY	So Much	98
13	11	44	DEADMAU5 FEATURING ROB SWIRE MAUSTRAP/ULTRA/EMI	Ghosts 'N Stuff	-
14	14	24	LAURELL NECTAR/PACIFIC/WARNER	Can't Stop Falling	-
15	26	3	KETSIA E-TRAIN	Possible	-
16	16	43	DOWN WITH WEBSTER UNIVERSAL MOTOWN/UNIVERSAL	Rich Girl\$	-
17	18	10	HAIL THE VILLAIN WARNER MUSIC CANADA/WARNER	Take Back The Fear	-
18	21	6	LUCKY UKE VEGA	Cum On Feel The Noize	-
19	15	12	GORD DOWNIE AND THE COUNTRY OF MIRACLES WIENER ART/UNIVERSAL	The East Wind	-
20	19	2	CHAD BROWNLEE 306 RECORDINGS	Hood Of My Car	-
21	17	26	NIKKI YANOFSKY CTV/UNIVERSAL	I Believe	-
22	22	7	ALEESIA INDUSTRY CONNS. INC.	Headlights	-
23	20	11	CRASH KARMA EI	Fight	-
24	23	8	KO WARNER MUSIC CANADA/WARNER	Capable	-
25	30	3	DOWN WITH WEBSTER UNIVERSAL	Whoa Is Me	-
26	24	13	HIGH VALLEY OPEN ROAD/UNIVERSAL	I Will Stand By You	-
27	27	5	METRIC LAST GANG	Stadium Love	-
28	NEW	1	ONE MORE GIRL EMI	The Day I Fall	-
29	RE-ENTRY	32	DOMAN & GOODING FEATURING DRU & LINCOLN REVERB	Runnin'	-
30	29	52	JUSTIN BIEBER RAYMOND BRAUN/ISLAND/UNIVERSAL	One Time	-

1

BEN CAPLAN

(aka Ben Caplan & The Casual Smokers)

Singer, Songwriter

b. Halifax, Nova Scotia

NOTABLE RECORDINGS AND SONGS:

In the Time of the Great Remembering (2011)

Down To the River (2011), *Stranger* (2011)

INSIGHTS:

"I'm interested in the context of ideas and development of a vast world video. I think what I try to do lyrically and musically is to understand my own world view and my own mythologies. Recently my songs have had a political bend to them just because of the political reality in Canada and other places around the world. Since those are the things I'm thinking about and experiencing right now, that's what I'm writing about." — Ben Caplan, Interview with Emily Johnson, Aesthetic Magazine

"If a man's musical prowess can be judged by the superiority of his beard, then before opening his mouth, Caplan is a god of a songwriter. Remarkably, his performance exceeds such expectations, Caplan delivering heartfelt folk tales with a powerful and gravelly voice. There's an intimacy between his words and delivery that is rare, and echoes of both Jeff Buckley and Tom Waits (the latter, certainly, informs aspects of Caplan's sound)." — Cai Trefor of clashmusic.com on Caplan's performance at the 2013 Glastonbury Festival in the U.K.

PLAUDITS:
- Hamilton Music Awards Roots Recording of the Year winner (2012)
- ECMA Rising Star Recording of the Year Award winner (2013)

2

NICK JOHNSTON

Guitarist

b. June 18, 1987, Georgetown, Ontario.

NOTABLE RECORDINGS AND SONGS

Public Display of Infection (2011), *In A Locked Room On the Moon* (2013)

INSIGHTS

"When I was a young boy, a guitar was a mystical magic machine of infinite power and potential. I always had strange attraction to it, finding it terrifying and mesmerizing at the same time. Eventually I worked up the courage to ask for one for my 14th birthday. After that, I quit playing all sports, and my parents noticed a significant plunge in my academic life. Basically, playing guitar ruined my life! I formed The Nick Johnston Band in 2010 to facilitate the live performance of the music that would become my first record. Playing live is to me, the single most important thing as a guitar player and a musician. The ability to properly execute your own music in front of an audience is a skill I've always tried hard to develop." — Nick Johnston, *Chapman Guitars website*

"While there is no denying this is a riff heavy, aggressive record of instrumental rock that leans toward the metal side [Public Display of Infection], it incorporates several things that separate it from a boring mash of shredding. Johnston proves to be an electric listener and player by throwing in dabs of other genres, as on the title cut, with its island feel and a solo that delves into a Middle Eastern mindset before heading back to reggae territory." — John Heidt, *Vintage Guitar Magazine*

"Johnston's… Public Display of Infection is an instrumental recording of 10 songs that show off his exceptional, versatile guitar gifts — gifts that would justifiably intimidate not only a guitar beginner, but even some seasoned players. I like the guitar gods — Satriani, Steve Vai, Jeff Beck and Stevie Ray Vaughan — and there are a lot of those influences on this CD. On a technical level, the young virtuoso is getting up there with the best of them." — Rob O'Flanagan, *Guelph Mercury*

3

HILL KOURKOUTIS

Singer, Songwriter, Multi-instrumentalist, Producer, Filmmaker (frequently performs as Hill & the Sky Heroes)

b. January 23, 1988, Toronto, Ontario.

NOTABLE RECORDINGS *Drowning Girl* (2008), *11:11* (2012).

INSIGHTS

"Multi-dimensional rock and roll. Planetarily aligned surf rock. Dreamy, heart piercing and mind bending melodies… if Gwen Stefani and Dalbello had a love child, this is what they would sound like." — Singer, songwriter Serena Ryder

"I've watched Hill from the time that she was about 17 years old rock out with an intensity and focus mostly spoken about in biographies of geniuses that have made a huge impact on music. It was such a pleasure, honor and hella fun to work with Hill." — Singer, songwriter Saidah Baba Talibah

"Hill Kourkoutis… is something of a staple in the Canadian industry. Having worked with everyone from Weeknd to Martha & the Muffins, her voice on this track ["Doctor, Doctor"] reveals exactly why. Some people simply have IT. Everything from her lyrics and their delivery to her overall aesthetic is just so, so bang'n." — Broadcaster Alan Cross

"There's a good chance you've seen Hill Kourkoutis on stage playing kcys, bass and guitar with acts like the Weeknd, the Cliks, Saidah Baba Talibah and many others, but she was usually backing up other musicians rather than taking the spotlight herself. Given her eclectic resumé, it's no surprise that her solo tunes are a similar grab bag of influences, mixing surf, pop, soul, glam and dub into a deceptively cohesive sound." — Benjamin Boles, *Now Magazine*

4

BARBRA LICA

Jazz singer, Songwriter

Hometown: Markham, Ontario.

NOTABLE RECORDINGS AND SONGS

That's What I Do (2012).

INSIGHTS

"Lica is a sweet, smilin' surprise in jazz. In fact, she's the brightest new light on the Canadian scene. That's why I recently named her one of 'Canada's Top 5 Female Jazz Singers'… Jazz is too often a 'serious business.' But Lica lightens it up with her smile. That's rare in jazz…"
— Tim Tamashiro, Jazz Evangelist, CBC Radio

"For someone so young, she has an impressive level of musical maturity. Many singers spend years trying to find their vocal 'sweet spot.' Barbra's already there."
— Ross Porter, CEO of Jazz.FM91 to Trish Crawford of the *Toronto Star*

"[She has the] ability to deliver a song with clarity, wit and deftness. Perennially upbeat, all the songs on That's What I Do have a sheen of positivity even when delving into what could be dark topics like being a starving artist, as she does on her own composition 'Scarlett O'Hara.' Many of the strongest songs on the disc — and the least jazzy — are the originals, which Lica wrote mostly with her partner and guitar player Colin Story." — Cathy Riches, *The WholeNote*

5

DAN MANGAN

Singer, Songwriter

b. Daniel Mangan, April 28, 1983, Smithers, British Columbia

NOTABLE RECORDINGS AND SONGS

Roboteering (2009 EP), *Nice, Nice, Very Nice* (2009), *Oh Fortune* (2011), *Radicals* (2012 EP), *Robots* (2009), *Road Regrets* (2009), *About As Helpful As You Can Be Without Being Any Help At All* (2011), *Post War Blues* (2011), *Oh Fortune* (2011), *Rows of Houses* (2011)

INSIGHTS

"Nobody starts by being Van Gogh, there is this learning curve, and [in] my particular experience my music has grown weirder and less accessible as my audience has grown. I feel like now that I have everyone's attention, I ask myself what I really want to say. What I try to avoid are shrill political folk songs, that are really poignant in that they mention politicians by name or are overly dogmatic, it's like that type of writing gives the opposition to your opinion something with which to discredit what you are saying and in a sense you begin to preach to the choir. Instead one could think of their opposition as an opportunity to use language and metaphor to paint a picture for them that could perhaps allow for them to begin seeing things my way... At this point I am not fighting this urge to get my message out there. At the heart of it, I want to have a really long career and diverse body of work. I love how people talk about how they loved Tom Waits in the '80 or '90s. I appreciate that people have followed musicians like Tom Waits and others for their whole careers. I just really want to keep trying to push myself

and do something that is relevant to me... Music can be fun but at the end of the day I just want to make music that matters. Candy pop music is fun, but it's fleeting and most of the music that I love and continue to love has a weight to it." — Dan Mangan, Interview with Laura Necochea, *Vancouver Weekly*

PLAUDITS

• Named Artist of the Year at the Verge Music Awards (2009)

• Album *Nice, Nice, Very Nice* short-listed for the Polaris Music Prize (2010)

• Album *Nice, Nice, Very Nice* named iTunes Album of the Year in the Singer/Songwriter category (2010)

• Winner of three Western Canadian Music Awards for Independent Album, Roots/Solo Album and

Songwriter of the Year (2010),

- "Robots" named Best Song by the CBC Radio 3 Bucky Awards (2010)

- Winner of JUNOs in the categories of New Artist of the Year and Alternative Album of the Year for *Oh Fortune* (2012)

- Nominated as Songwriter of the Year for "About As Helpful As You Can Be Without Being Any Help At All," "Post-War Blues" and "Oh Fortune" and for Video of the Year for "Rows of Houses" by Jon Busby (2012)

- Album *Oh Fortune* is long-listed for the Polaris Music Prize (2012)

- Winner of three Western Canadian Music Awards in the categories of Rock Album, Independent Album and Songwriter of the Year (2012)

- "Rows of Houses" named "Best Song" by the CBC Radio 3 BUCKY Awards, the only artist to be a multiple winner in that category and the only artist to have been honoured with a BUCKY five times.

6

MONSTER TRUCK

Rock group

Band members: Jon Harvey (Vocals, bass), Jeremy Widerman (Guitar), Brandon Bliss (Keyboardist), Steve Kiely (Drums)

Hometown: Hamilton, Ontario

NOTABLE RECORDINGS AND SONGS

Monster Truck (2010 EP), *The Brown EP* (2011), *The Don't Fuck With the Truck Collection* (2012), *Furiosity* (2013), *Seven Seas Blues* (2011), *Righteous Smoke* (2011), *Sweet Mountain River* (2013)

INSIGHTS

"Over the past two years — on the basis of eight songs issued on two free EPs — Monster Truck has risen to the top of the Canadian rock pile. The band's unabashed dedication to the riff rock of a previous generation caught on with young people who grew up listening to their parent's records — Deep Purple,

Thin Lizzy, Metallica, Lynryd Skynrd, Allman Brothers and Led Zeppelin. Songs like Seven Seas Blues and Righteous Smoke became rock radio favourites. The successful independent label Dine Alone (Alexisonfire, City And Colour, Arkells) signed Monster Truck. High profile tours followed, opening for Deep Purple, Slash, The Sheepdogs and Billy Talent." — Graham Rockingham, thespec.com (*Hamilton Spectator*)

PLAUDITS

• JUNO Award for Breakthrough Group of the Year (2013)

7

LINDI ORTEGA

Roots music singer, Songwriter, Painter

Hometown: Pickering, Ontario

NOTABLE RECORDINGS AND SONGS

The Drifter EP (2008), *Little Red Boots* (2011), *Cigarettes & Truckstops* (2012). "Little Lie" (2011), "Angels" (2011), "Black Fly" (2011), "The Day You Die" (2012), "Cigarettes & Truckstops" (2012), "Murder of Crows" (2012).

INSIGHTS

"Hot Throwback #1, though you probably guessed that from the title [*Cigarettes & Truckstops*], or the cover, or the first 20 seconds, her voice pouring into your ear in a startling Dolly/Tammy/Loretta reverie, like the smell of nicotine on your grandmother's breath. OG country and sassy rockabilly that never descends into wax-museum listlessness or painted-flames-on-an-upright-bass self-parody. The whispers and wails of 'Murder of Crows' will scare off any stray cats or Stray Cats in the area." — *Spin*

"In the flesh, Lindi Ortega is electrifying. Armed with a burgundy-coloured guitar and fetching cherry-red cowboy boots, she sounds like a giddy mix of Dolly Parton, Linda Ronstadt and a more upbeat Chris Isaak… and, most crucially of all, her voice is a truly magnificent instrument." — Ben Walsh, *The Independent*

"That little quiver you hear in Ortega's voice — the one that suggests she'll burst into tears any minute now — is real. Conjuring the sass of country spitfires past (Loretta Lynn) and present (Neko Case), this Canadian singer-songwriter could also turn tender and bewitching with a line like 'If you want to get your fix/ Darlin', use me.'" — James Reed, boston.com

"One of the most important new artists of the year [2012]." — *San Francisco Examiner*

PLAUDITS

• JUNO nominations, New Artist and Roots & Traditional Album, Solo (2012)

• *Little Red Boots* long-listed nominee for 2012 Polaris Music Prize

• *Cigarettes & Truckstops* #12 on *Spin* magazine Top 20 Country Albums of the Year list (2013)

• Sirius XM Indies Award nomination as Folk/Roots Artist of the Year (2013)

• *Cigarettes & Truckstops* long-listed nominee for 2013 Polaris Music Prize

8

ALYSSA REID

Singer, Songwriter

b. Alyssa Ashley Reid, March 15, 1993, Edmonton, Alberta

NOTABLE RECORDINGS AND SONGS

The Game (2011), *Alone Again* (2011 featuring P Reign), *The Game* (2011 featuring Snoop Dogg), *Talk Me Down* (2012), *Running Guns* (2013)

INSIGHTS

"I did a lot of contests when I was little, because I didn't understand how to get myself out there and I thought that that was the only way. Looking back at it now I think that show, as well as all the other contests that I did, were just that — they were just contests. I think what actually shaped me into becoming the artist I am right now has been just writing and playing piano and getting to work with other writers and performing. Because all that is the experience that I needed, the other stuff was just… It was TV — it's two completely different worlds. I definitely don't want people to think that being on that show is what got me where I am, because it was a lot more work than just that… I think people have lower expectations from Canadian musicians than we actually deserve… And their thought

that we're going to be just that — Canadian musicians — has actually helped me a lot in pushing myself and wanting to become more than that and show what Canada actually has to offer. Because I feel like people definitely take us for granted, so it's pushed me to become the next Justin Bieber and the next Drake and show what Canada can do. And try to take off that label that they put on us." — Alyssa Reid, Official Biography

PLAUDITS

• Nominated for Pop Video of the Year ("Alone Again") at 2011 MuchMusic Video Awards

• Nominated as Best New Artist at 2012 JUNO Awards (2012)

• Canadian Radio Music Award/Hot AC winner (2012)

• Canadian Radio Music Award FACTOR Breakthrough Artist winner (2012)

• Canadian Radio Music Awards, co-winner of Special Collaboration Award for Artists Against Bullying single, "True Colors" (2013)

9

JOHANNA SILLANPAA

R&B, Soul, Jazz Singer, Songwriter – Solo artist and member of duo, Sillan & Young.

b. Boras, Sweden.

Hometown: Calgary, Alberta.

NOTABLE RECORDINGS

Good Life (2007), *One Wish* (2008), *Under My Feet* (2008 with Sillan & Young), *Make of Me* (2012).

INSIGHTS

"A bluesy Erika Badu meets [Billie Holiday] groove and Johanna's voice is silky, classy, sexy and sophisticated." — Steve Quirk, *Fusion Flavours* (U.K.)

"Johanna's talent and grace are stunning. Take Corinne Bailey Rae, Norah Jones and Joni Mitchell, add some haunting sensuality, brilliant pop influenced songwriting and real jazz players and you've got Sillan and Young." — Cameron Smith, *Smooth Jazz TV*

"I've always enjoyed writing my own songs. My ultimate goal is to be recognized as a songwriter as well as a singer. I admire the careers of artists like Prince and Sting for example. They can write great songs over and over again, year after year, and always maintaining the same amazing writing standard. I figured that the only way to get really good at songwriting is to keep writing and recording, that's why I choose to record my own songs…" — Speaking to writer Eric Boisson

PLAUDITS

- Western Canadian Music Awards Urban Music category nomination (2007)

- Canadian Smooth Jazz Awards nomination as Best Female Vocalist (2010)

- Western Canadian Music Awards Urban Music category nomination (2012)

10

THE WEEKND

Singer, Songwriter, Producer

b. Abel Tesfaye, February 16, 1990, Toronto, Ontario

NOTABLE RECORDINGS AND SONGS

Trilogy (2012), *Kiss Land* (2013), *House of Balloons* (2011), *Thursday* (2011), *Echoes of Silence* (2011), *The Morning* (2011), *The Knowing* (2011),*Crew Love* (2011, Drake featuring The Weeknd), *Rolling Stone* (2012), Remember You" (2012, Wiz Khalifa featuring The Weeknd), *Wicked Games* (2012), *The Zone* (2012, featuring Drake), *Twenty Eight* (2012), *Kiss Land* (2013), *One of Those Nights* (2013, Juicy J featuring The Weeknd)

INSIGHTS

"Abel Tesfaye (a.k.a. The Weeknd) is the most talked-about recording artist in the R&B game (MTV's John Norris called him the 'songbird of his generation' and the 'best musical talent since Michael Jackson'). Since releasing three mixtapes on his website between spring and winter of last year [2011], the Toronto native — and Drake protégé — has cultivated a large following: more than 500,000 on Twitter. After two years of a mostly Internet presence, The Weeknd has finally decided to bare his face to his fans, embarking on his first-ever international tour, which kicked off with Coachella in April [2012]." — The Weeknd places at number 22 in the ELLE magazine feature 30 Under 30: The Essential Names To Know — New Fashion Designers, Artists and Celebrities on the Rise, by Krista Soriano, Michael Solomon and Claire Stern (May 2012).

PLAUDITS

- *Balloons* short-listed for the Polaris Music Prize (2011)

- Named Breaking Woodie at mtvU Music Awards (2012)

- Winner of SiriusXM Indie Award as Solo Artist of the Year (2012)

- On the long list of the annual BBC Sound of... poll of music critics and industry figures in the U.K. (2013)

- Winner of JUNO Awards as Breakthrough Artist of the Year and for R&B/Soul Recording of the Year (2013)

- Nominated in the category of Video of the Year ("Wicked Games") at the MuchMusic Video Awards (2013)

- Nominated as Best New Artist at BET Awards (2013)

...and
The Retrievers

The Retrievers, from Guelph, Ontario, are not in the Top 10 "yet" but my nephew Nick Broster (second from the right) is a member. He reminds me that the aspirations and dreams of songwriters and musicians have not changed so much since I was riding the same bus. They play The Horseshoe, Clinton's and variety of clubs in their hometown; for me it was venues like the Place Pigalle, Chez Monique and various clubs and pavilions in the "cottage country" area of Ontario, north of Toronto. Oh what a feeling it was... what a rush, to take to the stage each night and make music, whether it was your own songs or songs written by another artist that inspired you. May that remain the motivation and inspiration for future generations of Canadian singers, musicians and songwriters.

CREDITS

The images appearing in *Oh What A Feeling* are drawn primarily from two sources: the Martin Melhuish Archives (MMA) and the *Encyclopedia of Canadian Rock, Pop & Folk Music* (ECRPFM). In some cases, the original copyright holder could not be found; in other cases copyright has expired; and in still other cases, publicity photographs and LP/CD covers are considered fair use in illustrating a biographical or critical position.

Page	Description	Courtesy	Photographer	Page	Description	Courtesy	Photographer
COVER	Guitar: Stratocaster	Fender Corporation		52	Percy Faith Publicity	ECRPFM	
Contents	Microphone	MMA		53	Maureen Forrester Stamp	Canada Post	
Foreword	Guitar Header: Les Paul "Log"	Gibson USA		53	Four Lads Sheet Music	MMA	
8	Geist Map	Geist		54	Gisele MacKenzie Publicity	MMA	
9	Chris Taylor with One	Chris Taylor		55	Crew Cuts LP	MMA	
11	Chris Taylor with Drake	Chris Taylor		56	Pricilla Wright LP	ECRPFM	
Introduction	Guitar Header: Patrician	Harmony Guitars USA		56	Elvis and Hank	Unknown	
13	Ritchie Yorke & Ronnie Hawkins	Ritchie Yorke		57	Myrna Lorrie Performance	Uknown	
16	Prime Minister Trudeau	MMA		57	Diamonds Publicity	Uknown	
CHRONICLE				58	Norman Brooks Publicity	Great Entertainer Archives	
Pre-1900	Guitar Header: Les Paul Clunker	Gibson USA		59	CHUM Chart	ECRPFM	
21	Maple Leaf Forever Sheet Music	ECRPFM		60	Little Caesar Photo	Robbie Robertson.com	
22	Huron Carol Stamp	Canada Post		61	The Hawk Advertisement	The Globe and Mail	
23	Scriven Photo	ECRPFM		62	Bonanza Publicity	ECRPFM	
24	Edison Photo	Wiki Commons		1960-1969	Guitar Header: Stratocaster	Fender Corporation	
24	Lady Dufferin Sheet Music	Wiki Commons		63	Ian & Sylvia Publicity	ECRPFM	
25	Edison Doll	ECRPFM		64	Bobby Curtola Publicity	MMA	
25	Edison Gold Cylinders	MMA		64	Robert Goulet Publicity	ECRPFM	
25	Billboard	ECRPFM		65	Oscar Peterson Publicity	MMA	
26	Compo	MMA		66	Richie Knight & The Mid-Knights	Doug Chappell	
26	HMV	MMA		67	CHUM Hit Parade	ECRPFM	
26	Maple Leaf Rag Sheet Music	Wiki Commons		68	Gordon Lightfoot Publicity	MMA	
1900-1909	Guitar Header: Patrician	Harmony Guitars USA		69	Stan Rogers Photo	Canadian Encyclopedia	
27	Mary Pickford Sheet Music	Wiki Commons		70	Tom Nortcott Poster	MMA	
28	Burr Photo	ECRPFM		70	The Guess Who LP	MMA	
28	Fessenden Portrait	ECRPFM		71	Riverboat Advertisement	Bob Hilderley	
29	Phonograph	MMA		72	Tom Connors Stamp	Canada Post	
29	Macdonagh	ECRPFM		72	Dylan & Hawkins Photo	Arthur Usherson	
30	Columbia Advertisement	MMA		73	Zal Yanovsky Publicity	Henry Diltz	
1910-1919	Guitar Header: Patrician	Harmony Guitars USA		73	The Mamas & The Papas Perform	Wiki Commons	
31	Kat-t-t-y Sheet Music	MMA		74	Buffy LP	ECRPFM	
32	O Canada Sheet Music	ECRPFM		75	Tommy Hunter Performance	ECRPFM	
32	Soldier Sheet Music	MMA		75	Buffalo Springfield Publicity	ECRPFM	
33	Recording Studio	MMA		76	The Band LP	ECRPFM	
33	Strutter's Ball Sheet Music	ECRPFM		77	Mandala Publicity	MMA	
34	Wilfrid Pelletier Photo	ECRPFM		78	BS&T Publicity	ECRPFM	
1920-1929	Guitar Header: Country Classic	Gretsch Company		78	Paupers LP	MMA	
35	Lombardo portrait	ECRPFM		79	Steppenwolf LP	ECRPFM	
36	Lombardo Studio	ECRPFM		80	Hair Poster	MMA	
36	CFCF Stamp	MMA		80	John Handy Poster	ECRPFM	
37	CFRB Logo	MMA		81	Clayton-Thomas Performing	ECRPFM	
37	Canadian Wireless	MMA		81	Jesse Winchester Poster	ECRPFM	
38	Squid Jiggin'	LAC		82	Leonard Cohen LP	ECRPFM	
1930-1939	Guitar Header: Nashville Western	Gretsch Company		83	Stampeders Poster	MMA	
39	Tumbling LP	ECRPFM		84	Robert Charlebois LP	MMA	
40	CBC Radio Logo	MMA		84	Chilliwack Publicity	Toronto Star	
41	Jukebox	MMA		85	Joni Mitchell LP	ECRPFM	
41	Wilf Carter LP	ECRPFM		85	Edward Bear Publicity	MMA	
42	Happy Gang Publicity	MMA		86	John Lennon and Ronnie Hawkins	Ronnie Hawkins	
42	Don Messer Publicity	MMA		86	Festival Posters	ECRPFM	
1940-1949	Guitar Header: Telecaster	Fender Corporation		87	Anne Murray Photo	Fraser MacPherson Estate	
43	Hank Snow Portrait	ECRPFM		88	Andy Kim LP	ECRPFM	
44	Ruth Lowe Studio	MMA		88	McGarrigles Publicity	ECRPFM	
44	Lorne Green Radio Station	ECRPFM		1970-1979	Guitar Header: Telecaster	Fender Corporation	
45	Folksongs Book	ECRPFM		89	Anne Murray LP	ECRPFM	
45	Wayne & Shuster Publicity	ECRPFM		90	Irish Rovers LP	ECRPFM	
46	Mart Kenney Publicity	Uknown		90	Full Tilt Poster	ECRPFM	
46	Guy Lombardo Publicity	MMA		91	Crosby ... & Young LP	ECRPFM	
47	Rhythm Pals Publicity	MMA		91	Poppy Family LP	MMA	
48	Dick Todd LP	MMA		92	Lighthouse LP	ECRPFM	
48	45 rpm	MMA		92	Mashmakhan LP	MMA	
49	Admiral FM Publicity	MMA		93	Jimi Hendrix Photo	Unknown	
50	Guy Lombardo Poster	ECRPFM		94	Joni Mitchell LP	ECRPFM	
1950-1959	Guitar Header: Elite Stratocaster	Fender Corporation		96	Procol Harem Photo	Ritchie Yorke	
51	Paul Anka LP	ECRPFM		96	Stampeders Poster	MMA	
52	Moe Koffman Publicity	MMA		97	Dorothy Collins	ECRPFM	

Page	Description	Courtesy	Photographer
98	Heart Publicity	MMA	
99	April Wine Publicity	MMA	
100	Anne Murray	MMA	
100	Randy Bachman Performance	MMA	
101	Gordon Lightfoot Publicity	ECRPFM	
102	BTO LP	ECRPFM	
102	Paul Anka Performance	ECRPFM	
103	Gino Vanelli LP	MMA	
103	Burton Cummings Portrait	MMA	
104	Hagood Hardy LP	ECRPFM	
105	The Last Walz CD	ECRPFM	
106	Valdy Publicity	ECRPFM	
107	Margaret Trudeau Photograph	cbc.ca	
108	Blues Brothers Publicity	Atlantic Records	
108	McLauchlan & Cockburn Photo	MMA	
109	Raffi Publicity	MMA	
110	Sharon, Lois & Bram LP	ECRPFM	
110	David Foster Publicity	MMA	
111	Bryan Adams LP	MMA	
111	Frank Mills Publicity	MMA	
111	Daniel Langois Performance	ECRPFM	
112	Trooper	ECRPFM	
1980-1989	Guitar Header: Stratocaster Elite	Fender Corporation	
115	Long John Baldry Portrait	MMA	
115	Rough Trade Publicity	MMA	
116	Bob & Doug Performance	Wiki Commons	
116	Loverboy Publicity	MMA	
117	Powder Blues Publicity	MMA	
117	Loreena McKennit Publicity	ECRPFM	
118	Sass Jordan Publicity	Sass Jordan	
118	The Nylons Publicity	MMA	
119	Platinum Blonde Publicity	ECRPFM	
119	Ofra Harnoy Publicity	MMA	
120	Triumph LP	ECRPFM	
120	Men without Hats Poster	MMA	
121	Rush Publicity	Martin Melhuish	
122	M+M Publicity	MMA	
122	Lenny Breau Publicity	ECRPFM	
123	Fred Penner Publicity	MMA	
124	Tears Are Not Enough Photo	MMA	
125	Corey Heart LP	ECRPFM	
126	Kim Mitchell Publicity	MMA	
126	k.d. lang Photo	ECRPFM	
127	Michelle Wright LP	ECRPFM	
128	Glass Tiger LP	MMA	
129	Cohen & Warnes Publicity	ECRPFM	
130	Shakin' All Over Poster	John Einarson	
130	Leona Boyd Potrait	Leona Boyd	Ken Williamson
132	Blue Rodeo Publicity	MMA	
133	Rita MacNeil Publicity	ECRPFM	
133	Jeff Healey Publicity	ECRPFM	
134	Cowboy Junkies Publicity	ECRPFM	
135	Tom Cochrane Publicity	ECRPFM	
135	Howard Shore LP	ECRPFM	
136	Dan Hill LP	ECRPFM	
1990-1999	Guitar Header: J-5CT	Gibson USA	
137	Alanis Morissette CD	ECRPFM	
138	Alannah Myles Publicity	ECRPFM	
139	Luc Plamendon Portrait	MMA	
139	Fresh Wes CD	ECRPFM	

Page	Description	Courtesy	Photographer
140	Barenaked Ladies	ECRPFM	
142	Alanis Morissette Publicity	MMA	
143	Ashley Publicity	John Law	
143	Susan Aglukark Publicity	MMA	
144	Roch Voisine Publicity	ECRPFM	
145	Snow CD	ECRPFM	
146	Celine Dion CD	ECRPFM	
147	The Rankin Family Publicity	MMA	
148	Jan Arden Publicity	ECRPFM	
149	Sarah McLachlan Publicity	ECRPFM	
149	Crash Test Dummies CD	ECRPFM	
150	Shania Twain CD	ECRPFM	
151	Beau Dommage CD	Canada Post	
153	Rob McConnell CD	MMA	
154	Econoline Crush CD	ECRPFM	
155	Our Lady Peace Publicity	MMA	
156	Chantal Kreviazuk Publicity	ECRPFM	
2000-2009	Guitar Header: Telecaster	Fender Corporation	
157	Michael Bublé CD	ECRPFM	
158	Diana Krall CD	ECRPFM	
159	Nellie Furtado CD	ECRPFM	
160	Avril Lavigne CD	ECRPFM	
160	Nickelback Publicity	ECRPFM	
161	Leslie Feist Publicity	ECRPFM	
161	Arcade Fire CD	ECRPFM	
162	k-0s Portrait	ECRPFM	
163	Deadmau5 CD	MMA	
163	Michael Bublé Portrait	Uknown	
2010-2013	Guitar Header: Nashville Western	Gretsch Company	
164	Sam Roberts CD	ECRPFM	
165	King Fest Publicity	ECRPFM	
169	Nikki Yanofsky Portrait	ECRPFM	
170	Drake Portrait	ECRPFM	
171	Jian Ghomeshi Publicity	ECRPFM	
172	Deborah Cox Playbill	ECRPFM	
174	Kardinal Offishall CD	ECRPFM	
175	Canadian Musician	Canadian Musician	
177	Justin Bieber Publicity	ECRPFM	
180	Alan Doyle Film Advertisement	ECRPFM	
181	Marianas Trench CD	ECRPFM	
181	deadmau5 Animation	ECRPFM	
183	The Sheepdogs Publicity	ECRPFM	
185	Johnny Reid Publicity	Johnny Reid	
184	Robert Michaels Publicity	Robert Michaels	Manual Munoz Aldana
185	Victoria Levy (Vox lumiere)		
186	Chris Hadfield Portrait	ECRPFM	
CANADIAN HIT SONGS			
188	Guitar Header: Stratocaster	Fender	
188	Sweet Annie Moore Sheet Music	ECRPFM	
189	Billboard	ECRPFM	
193	Just a Baby Sheet Music	ECRPFM	
194	Charmaine! Sheet Music	ECRPFM	
196	Billboard Chart	ECRPFM	
197	RPM Weekly	MMA	
198	CKEY Hit Line	ECRPFM	
199	RPM Weekly	MMA	
201	CHUM Sign	ECRPFM	
202	Billboard Logo	ECRPFM	
203	CHUM CHART	ECRPFM	
206	CHUM Top 100	ECRPFM	
208	FACTOR	ECRPFM	
209	The Record	MMA	

CREDITS